CLICHÉS

CLICHÉS

*Over 1500 Phrases
Explored and
Explained*

BETTY KIRKPATRICK

St. Martin's Press ♋ New York

For Stewart and Trina, the apples of my eye,
the jewels in my crown, my pride and joy,
the salt of the earth and my towers of
strength, otherwise known as my son
and daughter.

Library of Congress Cataloging-in-Publication Data

Kirkpatrick, E. M. (Elizabeth McLaren)
    Clichés : over 1500 phrases explored and explained / Betty
Kirkpatrick.
        p.   cm.
    ISBN 0-312-15494-1
    1. English language—Terms and phrases.   2. Clichés.   I. Title.
PE1689.K48   1997
423'.1—dc21   97-5854
                                                                                CIP

First published in Great Britain by Bloomsbury Publishing

First U.S. Edition: June 1997

10   9   8   7   6   5   4   3   2   1

✵ Introduction ✵

!t has become something of a linguistic cliché to say that it is difficult to define a cliché. Several writers have pointed to the elusive nature of this well-known fracture of our language.

In his Introduction to *A Dictionary of Clichés*, first published in 1940, Eric Partridge observed that it is impossible to get the average person, even 'the averagely well-educated person' to provide an articulate definition of a cliché. According to Partridge, the aforementioned average person when asked to explain the nature of the cliché would say 'Oh, well, you know what a cliché is,' and hesitate and stumble, and become incoherent.

If we took a random sample of 'averagely well-educated persons' today, we would find that, as far as defining a cliché is concerned, things have not changed radically in the half century since Partridge was writing. Most people in this category would know instinctively what a cliché is, but few would commit themselves to an exact definition.

Frank Muir in his Introduction to *The Methuen Dictionary of Clichés*, compiled by Christine Ammer, and published in 1992, comments on the general inadequacies of dictionaries in providing assistance with the task of getting to grips with the cliché. Muir is of the opinion that all they usually do is refer us to 'stereotype' which in turn leads to a description of making cast metal printing plates 'from a mould of wet newspaper into which a frame of moveable type has been pressed and sat upon.'

John Ayto in *The Bloomsbury Dictionary of Word Origins*, published in 1990, explains this allusion further. 'Originally, French *clicher* meant literally "stereotype" – that is "print from a plate made by making a type-metal cast from a mould of a printing surface".' He goes on, 'Hence a word or phrase that was a cliché had literally been repeated time and time again in identical form from a single printing plate.' In non-literal terms a cliché came to describe an expression that was repeated so often that it lost its freshness and became hackneyed.

Frank Muir is perhaps a little unfair to dictionaries as most of them do make the point that clichés are items of language that are overused. *Collins English Dictionary*, for example, defines cliché as 'a word or expression that has lost much of its force through over-exposure'. *The Oxford Advanced Learner's Dictionary* takes up the same theme with 'phrase or idea which is used so often that it has become stale or meaningless'.

H W Fowler in his *Dictionary of Modern Usage*, first published in 1926, makes much the same point in a more literary way. 'Cliché means a stereotype;' he writes, 'in its literary sense it is a word or phrase whose felicity in a particular context when it was first employed has won it such popularity that it is apt to be used indiscriminately.'

In his description of the cliché in *The Oxford Companion to the English Language*, published in 1992, the editor Tom McArthur also emphasizes overuse and consequent loss of freshness and makes the point that cliché is usually a pejorative term. The editors of *The Bloomsbury Guide to Better English*, first published in 1988 as *The Bloomsbury Good Word*

Guide, also dwell on the undesirable aspect of the cliché, indicating that the term 'is almost always used pejoratively'.

Partridge's definition agrees with this judgement. 'A cliché is an outworn commonplace; a phrase, or short sentence, that has become so hackneyed that careful speakers and scrupulous writers shrink from it because they feel that its use is an insult to the intelligence of their audience or public.'

B A Pythian in *A Concise Dictionary of Correct English*, published by Hodder and Stoughton in 1979, testifies to the pejorative nature of the word cliché. His definition, 'an overused expression, so hackneyed as to be both a tired substitute for original thought and an offence to the intelligence of the reader or listener', could hardly be construed as being complimentary.

Perhaps popular feeling against the cliché is best summed up by David Crystal in *English Language*, published by Penguin in 1988. He writes, 'The worst judgement people can pass on an expression is to call it a cliché.'

Thus we have the cliché convincingly established as the bad guy of the English language. Furthermore it is the worst kind of bad guy – the bad guy that used to be a good guy before it suffered a fall from grace or, in the case of the cliché, a fall from freshness. Such a cliché is described in *The Bloomsbury Guide to Better English*, 'Some clichés were quite apt when first used but have become hackneyed over the years.'

Even bad guys have their defendants and McArthur in *The Oxford Companion to the English Language* reminds us that the general dislike of the cliché is founded on a desire for originality of expression and that a desire to strive for linguistic novelty is a fairly modern one. He reminds us that in earlier times some usages and formulas such as stock expressions in literature, proverbs, and quotations from famous writers 'were admired precisely because they were unoriginal, and writers or speakers used them because they were familiar to their audiences'.

With this in mind it is perhaps relevant that the word cliché came into the language as recently as 1890. Before that people seem not to have required an expression with which to express their condemnation of non-originality. They were quite happy to follow their leaders

McArthur is not the only writer to offer a few words in defence of the cliché. Rather surprisingly Fowler does also at a considerably earlier date in *Modern English Usage*. 'What is new is not necessarily better than what is old,' he writes, and goes on to quote J A Spender as saying, 'The hardest worked cliché is better than the phrase that fails.' He even chastises those who are too censorious of clichés, pointing out that 'The enthusiasm of the cliché-hunters is apt to run away with them.'

Frank Muir, writing in *The Methuen Dictionary of Clichés*, also has some words of praise for the cliché, regarding it as vital to those members of the community who are not very literate or to people, namely politicians, who require a means of hiding their real opinions. More importantly he views clichés as being 'an important part of our spoken language, warm and colloquial, a kind of shared, shorthand way of conducting a conversation'.

Thus we have the cliché – a pejorative term for an expression that has lost its first bloom and thus its potency but is nevertheless widespread and sometimes even loved. Partridge refers to the fact that '[their] ubiquity is remarkable and rather frightening,' and muses 'Why are clichés so extensively used?'

He goes on to answer his own question by giving a variety of possible reasons. Haste, mental laziness, convenience, 'a half-education – that snare of the half-baked and the ready-made', and 'a love of display' are all put forward as possible causes.

However much we may learn about clichés, they have a habit of remaining rather shadowy figures in our language. Unlike with, say, the simile, we cannot simply supply a succinct and readily comprehensible definition that will enable everyone instantly to recognise them when they are encountered. They are impossible to pigeonhole. Classifying something as being overused and stale does not immediately call to mind a distinctive linguistic category.

With most linguistic categories there is not much room for individual opinion. A simile is either a simile or not; its classification is not dependent on the personal persuasion of the reader or the user. In less clear-cut cases, such as metaphor, there may be scope for occasional arguments as to category but nothing like the scope for disagreement that exists with regard to the categorization of a cliché.

Partridge refers to the potential for dispute with regard to clichés by citing a conference 'of learned and able men' in November 1939. 'Someone brought up the subject of clichés; everyone's opinion was different: what one included, another excluded; what one excluded, another included. In short, it is **a vexed question** (cliché).' Some might call it **a hornet's nest** (cliché or is it?).

Webster's Dictionary of English Usage, edited by W Ward Gilman and published in 1989, agrees that individual interpretation is central to the categorization of the cliché. It suggests that one realistic way of approaching the subject is 'simply to call a cliché whatever word or expression you have heard or seen often enough to find annoying.'

Given the level of personal interpretation necessary to categorize the cliché, this suggestion has great merit. There is, however, a problem. If the category is as amorphous and unwieldy as this suggestion indicates, how did it ever get to be a category in the first place? We could all have commonplace books of tired linguistic phrases which we find annoying and which we feel warrant the category of cliché but would they ever coincide, even in part, with everyone else's? A slightly more rigid classification seems necessary, although the personal angle has to remain at the forefront of this.

The major problem with the cliché category is that, rather like the English language itself, it is an inveterate borrower. Shamelessly it takes items from other well-documented categories and converts them into clichés. It might be seen as the magpie of the language, taking for its own glittering phrases that properly belong elsewhere but, unlike the magpie, destroying the glitter as it does so.

In order to achieve a sufficient degree of staleness to qualify for the rather dubious title of cliché, it is usual for an expression to have had a first life in some other linguistic category. There are several of these categories and several authorities have written about them. Since it seems to be in the nature of clichés to sow dissension among their observers, it is perhaps inevitable that the categories of the various authorities often do not coincide to any great extent.

Partridge distinguishes four categories of cliché. These are 1. Idioms that have become clichés. 2. Other hackneyed phrases. 3. Stock phrases and familiar quotations from foreign languages. 4. Quotations from literature. Of these he claims that groups 1 and 2 form at least four-fifths of all clichés.

Group 1, which he also calls idiom-clichés, he defines as 'those idioms which have become so indiscriminately used that the original point has been blunted or even removed entirely'. He cites **to leave the sinking ship** and **to take pot luck** as examples of the category. Of course this categorization raises the question of the definition of an idiom which could give further grounds for dispute.

In Partridge's Group 2 he includes what he calls 'non-idiomatic clichés, phrases so hackneyed as to be knock-kneed and spavined', a terrible condemnation indeed. These he subdivides into General, examples cited being **down to the last detail** and **to nip in the bud**; Sociological, Economic, Political, examples cited being **beyond the pale** and **leave the door open**; Journalism, examples cited being such familiar friends as **a reliable source of information** but also including such unusual phrases as **laying heretical hands on our imperishable constitution**; Literary, examples cited being **a sop to Cerberus** and **Pandora's box**, as well as the now rare **the eternal verities**.

I must say I get quite confused in the course of this category and I suspect that Partridge does also. But then I think that some degree of confusion is an inevitable accompaniment of any attempt at categorizing clichés. They are a maze just waiting to trap us.

Partridge seems on slightly firmer ground with his Group 3 and Group 4. Group 3 consists of phrases and quotations from dead and foreign languages, whether these be of the 'tag' variety, that is 'phrases apprehended without reference to an author', including **in flagrante delicto** (in the very act of committing a crime), **terra firma** (dry land), and **je ne sais quoi** (I don't know what) or what he calls 'the full-blooded quotations' variety.

Into this latter category he puts **sic transit gloria mundi** (thus passes the glory of the world), **timeo Danaos et dona ferentes** (I fear the Greeks even when they bring gifts) and **plus ça change plus ça reste la même chose** (the more it changes the more it is the same thing). Several of his examples in this category, and indeed in the 'tag' category, have passed from common use with the general decrease in familiarity with the classical languages and so have forfeited their cliché status.

Partridge's fourth and final category comprises quotations from literature, also dubbed quotation-clichés. From the Bible he cites among others **their name is legion**, many of the others having slipped from cliché status as knowledge of the Bible declined.

His quotations from literature include **there are more things in heaven and earth . . .** (from Shakespeare), **a dim religious light** (from Milton), **a thing of beauty is a joy for ever** (from Keats) and **Barkis is willin'** (from Dickens). He also includes misquotations, and lists as examples **fresh fields and pastures new** based on Milton's 'fresh woods and pastures new' (from *Lycidas*) and **a little knowledge is a dangerous thing** based on 'a little learning is a dangerous thing' from Alexander Pope's *An Essay on Criticism*.

I have dwelt at such length on Partridge's categorization for several reasons. First, it is inherently interesting – or at least I think so; second, it seems only fair that all this early spadework should receive due recognition in any work on clichés, and, third, it serves as a valuable jumping off point for any more modern attempt at definition and categorization.

Fowler's *Modern English Usage* also recognized that there were several divisions within the cliché category. It contends that there is a kind of hard core of clichés 'that always deserve the stigma – those threadbare and facetious ways of saying simple things and those far-fetched and pointless literary echoes'. To illustrate this category, it cites **filthy lucre**, **tender mercies**, and **suffer a sea change**, as well as the now rare **own the soft impeachment**, an accusation of a not very serious fault.

In other cases, however, Fowler declares that whether or not they deserve the stigma of cliché depends on the manner of their use. 'That depends on whether they are used mechanically, taken off the peg as convenient reach-me-downs, or are chosen deliberately as the finest way of saying what needs to be said.' He argues that writers 'would be needlessly handicapped' if they felt unable to use such potential clichés as **Hobson's choice, a white elephant** or **feather one's nest**.

The distinction which Fowler draws between these two suggested categories is not all that easy to comprehend and could easily give rise to dispute. If a writer can use **Hobson's choice** 'as the finest way of saying what needs to be said' rather than as a cliché, why should he/she not be able to use **suffer a sea change** in the same way? Or has time destroyed some subtle distinction between them?

In the course of his article on the actual word cliché, Fowler refers us to several other articles for examples of different kinds of cliché. These include Hackneyed Phrases, Battered Ornaments, Irrelevant Allusions, Siamese Twins and Vogue Words. All of these categories can be clichés.

His article on Hackneyed Phrases in fact seems to be more or less an article on clichés themselves, since he cites a host of them, including **blessing in disguise, conspicuous by his absence**, and **damn with faint praise**. Fowler instructs the writer to beware if hackneyed phrases should spring to mind. 'He should take warning that when they suggest themselves it is because what he is writing is bad or it would not need such help. Let him see to the substance of his cake instead of decorating with sugarplums.' For those feminists who are concerned with the implication here that all writers are men, it should be pointed out that Fowler's *Modern Usage* was first published when the fair sex were still slaving over a hot stove and rocking cradles.

The Battered Ornament category suggests a knick-knack that has not stood up very well to moving homes or changes of ownership. But Fowler uses it to describe what he calls a rubbish heap. In it he includes **alma mater** (a phrase used to describe one's old school or college), **hoi polloi** and **suffer a sea change**.

His Irrelevant Allusion category deals with the fact that certain words always spark off in some people particular allusions, usually of a literary nature, which are not necessarily apposite to the situation. For example, when something relating to method arises, **method in [the] madness** will be mentioned, however inappropriate. Likewise, the concept of rottenness will give rise to a reference to **something rotten in the state of Denmark**, an allusion to Shakespeare's *Hamlet*.

The article on Siamese Twins indicates that this category 'is a fruitful source of clichés'. Fowler writes that the term Siamese Twins is 'a suitable term for the many words, which, linked in pairs by "and" or "or", are used to convey a single meaning'. He makes the point that many general Siamese Twins are purely tautological, a synonym or near-synonym being added simply for emphasis. His list of examples includes **betwixt and between, bits and pieces**, and **leaps and bounds**.

As Fowler points out, some Siamese Twins are indivisible because one of the pair is used in an archaic sense and would not be understood if used alone. These include **kith and kin, hue and cry, might and main, odds and ends**. He further comments that in the case of some Siamese Twins the two words involved may not be actual synonyms but associated ideas. These include **flotsam and jetsam, frills and furbelows**, and **thick and fast**.

He cautions writers against them as he cautioned them against Hackneyed Phrases. He warns that 'such clichés are always lying in wait to fill a vacuum in the brain'.

Fowler also cites Vogue Words as a source of clichés, saying that a Vogue Word 'emerges from obscurity, or even from nothingness or a merely potential and not actual existence, into sudden popularity', and gives as examples **blueprint** and **breakthrough**. He comments that the meaning of such words is by no means immediately comprehensible to the average person 'who has to find out its meaning as best he can'. As a result of this struggle, the Vogue Word frequently undergoes a change of meaning. 'It does not mean quite what it ought to, but to make up for that it means some things that it ought not to, by the time he has done with it.'

Modern commentators on the language will recognize this phenomenon immediately. In the modern world, Vogue Words and expressions are constantly being spawned, and frequently changing their meaning, or even becoming virtually meaningless, as they get handed on from user to user. One has only to think of **the bottom line** with its various meanings to appreciate this point.

A special warning to young people is given in Fowler's article on Vogue Words. They are exhorted 'that their loose use is corrupting the vocabulary, and that, when they are not chosen as significant words but gatecrash as clichés they are repulsive to the old and the well-read'. Nowadays, at least, it would be unfair to single out the young, as the Vogue Word cliché is extensively used by a wide range of people, irrespective of age. The young might bring us some slang terms that we would rather not know about but they really cannot be saddled with the blame for clichés.

Both Partridge's *Dictionary of Clichés* and Fowler's *Modern Usage* dwell quite extensively on the nature, sources and categorization of clichés. Modern usage guides tend to have less space to devote to the task but *The Bloomsbury Guide to Better English* gives some guidance on categorization.

The editors list various categories with examples. One of these consists of 'overworked metaphors and similes' and is illustrated by **leave no stone unturned** and **as good as gold**. Another suggested category is 'overused idioms', examples being **add insult to injury** and **a blessing in disguise**. A category is devoted to the clichés of public speakers, examples of which include **someone who needs no introduction** and **in no uncertain terms**. Quotations, or misquotations, from the Bible and Shakespeare form another category and are illustrated by **pride goes before a fall** and **a poor thing but mine own**. Journalists are singled out as being among the worst offenders in cliché use, being much given to such expressions as **strife-torn countries**, and **categorical denials**. Lastly comes the newly coined phrase that can easily become a cliché overnight, examples being **keep a low profile** and **at this moment in time**.

At the end of this round-up of the views of commentators on clichés, it is quite clear that the cliché, although a major part of our language, is difficult to sum up. The main problem seems to lie in its categorization and in getting people to agree on this. I am prepared to attempt to establish some kind of proposed solution to the first of these problems, although not to the second. The propensity of the cliché to cause dissension seems too deep-rooted. We seemed doomed to disagree about what is a cliché and what is not.

When faced with a problem of supreme difficulty, I am essentially one of those who search diligently for the easy option. Therefore, as my first category, I have selected the Simile Cliché. Most people either know or once knew what a simile is, the signpost 'as' or 'like' being a dead giveaway.

In the Simile Cliché category I have included **cool as a cucumber, deaf as a post, good as gold**, and **as old as the hills**. Also included are **like a breath of fresh air, like a house on fire** and **like two peas in a pod**.

There is not much room for disagreement over my second category. This I have dubbed Foreign Clichés, and the category encompasses those clichés which retain their foreign form although they have been welcomed with open arms into the English language. Most come from French and include **cause célèbre, coup de grâce, de rigueur, je ne sais quoi** and **pièce de résistance**. Latin phrases are also represented but there are fewer of these than would have been common before the decline in popularity of classical languages in our schools. They include **terra firma** and **deus ex machina**.

Many clichés start life as proverbs or sayings, thereby giving rise to the category which I have called Proverb Clichés, although it also includes sayings. Examples are **the early bird catches the worm, forewarned is forearmed, little pitchers have big ears, make hay while the sun shines, many hands make light work** and **one good turn deserves another**.

Several proverbs and sayings appear only in part as clichés. The whole saying might occasionally appear but a truncated form is more common. To this I have assigned the category Allusion Cliché and in it I have included **a bird in the hand**, an allusion to the proverb a bird in the hand is worth two in the bush, **birds of a feather**, an allusion to the proverb birds of a feather flock together, **new broom**, an allusion to the saying a new broom sweeps clean, **the grass is always greener**, an allusion to the saying the grass is always greener on the other side of the fence and **there's many a slip**, an allusion to the saying there's many a slip between cup and lip.

The Allusion Cliché category is not restricted to proverbs and sayings. I have also used it to cover those clichés which are references to quotations, but do not comprise the whole quotation, as **the best-laid schemes** which is a reference to a quotation from a poem by Robert Burns, *To a Mouse*, the whole quotation being 'The best-laid schemes of mice and men gang aft agley'. It also includes references to legends and anecdotes, Bible stories, etc, as **the Midas touch**, a reference to the king in Greek legend who was given the gift of having everything that he touched turn to gold, **kill the fatted calf**, a Biblical reference to the story of the prodigal son in *Luke* 15, **forbidden fruit**, a reference to the Biblical story of Adam and Eve, and **manna from heaven**, also a Biblical reference.

My Quotation Clichés category includes full quotations and misquotation. These include quotations from literature, such as **damn with faint praise** from Alexander Pope's *Epistle to Dr Arbuthnot*, **for this relief much thanks** from Shakespeare's *Hamlet* and **the unkindest cut of all** from Shakespeare's *Julius Caesar*. It also includes ecclesiastical quotations such as **cover a multitude of sins** from *1 Peter 3:8* and **for better or worse** from *The Book of Common Prayer*.

It is common in English for quotations to be misquoted. If such misquotations become common enough, they become clichés and have been included under the Quotation Cliché classification. These include **a little knowledge is a dangerous thing**, a misquotation of 'a little learning is a dangerous thing' from Alexander Pope's *An Essay on Criticism* (1709), **fresh fields and pastures new**, a misquotation of 'fresh woods and pastures new' from Milton's *Lycidas*, and **money is the root of all evil**, a misquotation of the 'love of money is the root of all evil', a Biblical quotation from *1 Timothy* (6:10).

Another category corresponds to Fowler's Siamese twins classification, which I have chosen to call Doublet Clichés. As is the case with Siamese twins, this covers doublets containing synonyms, those containing near-synonyms and those containing associated ideas. Examples include **bag and baggage, bits and pieces, leaps and bounds, odds and ends, over and done with, safe and sound** and **the dim and distant past**.

Another category is Euphemism Clichés. Since many euphemisms are used so frequently, they qualify as clichés on the grounds of over-use. Many people use them automatically without giving thought to using a more down to earth, or even more honest, expression. Examples are **economical with the truth, kick the bucket, powder one's nose**, and **spend more time with one's family**.

For my next category, and one which is extremely extensive, I have decided to adopt Partridge's Idiom Cliché classification. As with his classification, this will include metaphor clichés. The category includes **the light at the end of the tunnel, make waves, on the warpath, paper over the cracks, par for the course, ring the changes** and **take the bull by the horns**.

In common with Euphemisms, many Catchphrases are so commonly used that they become clichés and thus they also represent a category. By their very nature catchphrases, phrases that in some way catch our attention and are repeated frequently, often as a kind of slogan, are usually topical and short-lived. The Catchphrase Cliché is one of the categories most likely to change with fashion, but it often stays on in the language as part of the folk history of a particular time.

Catchphrase Clichés are commonly found in areas such as advertising campaigns, memorable remarks made in films, or quotations from television programmes that gain popular appeal. They include such phrases as **does your mother know you're out?, don't call us, we'll call you, a man's gotta do what a man's gotta do, no names, no pack drill, no show without Punch, tell that to the marines** and **you can't take it with you**.

Vogue expressions, also known as buzz words, can also very quickly become clichés. As with catchphrases, they, as their name suggests, are very much part of the fashion of the day and tend to be ephemeral. Sometimes Vogue Clichés start life in a technical or specialist area of language, where they are perfectly acceptable, only acquiring cliché status when they are transferred to the general language and are subject to overuse. **The bottom line, gameplan, the generation gap** and **the name of the game** are cases in point.

Very many clichés are simply put in to fill up sentences (since the sentences are complete without them). I have designated these Filler Clichés, in view of the fact that they are just filling space. Sometimes the space involved is paper space but more frequently it is air space, Filler Clichés being frequently used in speech.

Clichés in this category are almost the equivalent of a signature tune as far as some people are concerned. We all have friends who insert **the thing is, just between you and me, you know what I mean, believe it or not, needless to say** and so on into practically everything they say.

The use of Filler Clichés is far from restricted to informal speech. You will find it not only in gossip between neighbours but in public speaking, as in the speeches of politicians and in the remarks of after-dinner speakers. Indeed, I would include **unaccustomed as I am to public speaking** in this category and such time-wasters as **at this moment in time**, since many speakers turn to it while they are thinking of something else to say.

As I have pointed out, the cliché does not relish being pigeonholed and there are a great many clichés which do not readily come within the confines of the above categories. To them I have assigned another category and have decided to adopt Fowler's Hackneyed Phrase as its designation. Arguably this could encompass the whole of the cliché linguistic category but I intend to restrict it to those overused phrases which have lost their freshness and which cannot be neatly or justifiably slotted in elsewhere, phrases that have gained widespread popularity over a period of time and sometimes seem to have come out of nowhere.

It is a difficult category to pinpoint exactly and will inevitably involve some degree of cross-over with other categories. It will be helpful to cite a few examples. These include **better late than never, a blazing inferno, by the same token, the blushing bride, a can of worms, common or garden, the end of an era, the envy of the world, a general exodus, the happy couple, in the cold light of day, make an offer that one cannot refuse, the one that got away,** and **pale into insignificance.**

I was tempted to subdivide some of these categories, particularly the last of these, the Hackneyed Phrase, but I resisted the temptation, partly because I felt that once I had started subdividing it would have been difficult to draw the line and avoid over-fragmentation. For example, I was tempted to have separate categories for sport and medicine, but then what about other specialist areas? Since clichés only really become clichés when they are part of the general language and send their tentacles out to affect all of us I decided to stick with the general category. If potential clichés stay within their specialist areas then it would be more accurate to describe them as jargon.

Journalese would seem an obvious separate category. Admittedly sports commentators are guilty of doing to death such eminently forgettable phrases as **game of two halves** and **get a result,** but for the most part the sin of journalists with regard to clichés is simply one of degree. This is perhaps not surprising when they are faced every day of their lives with a blank page to fill for the general public. Given the scope of journalists, most members of the general public would be just as cliché-ridden. You only have to listen to someone being interviewed on radio or television to get evidence of this. Alternatively, listen to the average public speaker, not to mention the average politician who frequently uses clichés to sidestep issues.

Tabloid journalists, however, are another matter, especially when dealing with headlines. Anyone under about three years old is 'a tot', any scientist is 'a top boffin', any fire, however small is 'an inferno', anyone who is trying to prevent a crime is described as 'having a go', and anyone in hospital is 'battling for life'. Sometimes this headlinese affects the rest of us and expressions such as **tug-of-love** come into being as clichés.

Instead of subdividing the broad categories, I compromised by pointing out which clichés are likely to have a particular relevance to a particular field. For example, **as well as can be expected** has distinct medical leanings since it is a favourite piece of information given to a patient's relatives by medical personnel. Likewise **till the fat lady sings** often has sporting associations, and **unavoidable delays** appeared in business and transport contexts.

Since it is difficult to pigeonhole clichés, it is inevitable that there will be some degree of cross-over between the categories. Some, for example can be both Hackneyed Phrases and Filler Clichés.

There are just two other categories that I would like to mention, both more nebulous than the rest and difficult to encapsulate in a dictionary. One is what I shall call the Situational Cliché. This is a kind of verbal Pavlovian response invariably given by someone when encountering a certain situation. It is perhaps best instanced by the neighbour who is progressing down the street, just as you are washing your car, and who almost inevitably comes out with, 'When you've finished that you can come and do mine' or 'It's bound to rain now'. Some situations are just bound to inspire unnecessary comment. Another one is occasioned by one happening to mention that one is going to church. Here the Pavlovian reponse, usually among non-church-goers is 'say one for me'.

The last category is not really one that is likely to make an appearance in a reference book for the general public, since it is the In-group Cliché. All families have them, phrases which have all the people familiar with the background to them having either a quiet smile or a loud guffaw – or occasionally a long sigh – and everyone else looking blank. Examples here are somewhat superfluous since they vary so much from family to family and group to group.

According to my children, I indulged in so many of these when they were growing up that they contemplated collecting and publishing them. Their least favourite and most annoying they claim was 'It comes from within'. This was said in relation to studying and was usually prefaced by 'I'm not going to nag you about studying'. My defence is that it was a successful cliché. They are now both graduates with jobs.

To return to the theme of more general clichés, in this collection I have included some information on the use of clichés and their likely users. This indicates whether they are more likely to be found in informal contexts, whether they are likely to be restricted to any one section of the population, such as older people or younger people, and so on.

As far as clichés are concerned usage is everything. With this in mind I have included examples of usage showing the clichés in action in an attempt to capture the flavour of the individual clichés.

Also included, where appropriate, is information on the derivation of the cliché. This is particularly so in the case of Idiom Clichés.

Information is also given as to the time-scale of clichés. This is not easy to do, given that clichés, by their very nature, exist in a pre-life before they become clichés.

I started this Introduction with a linguistic cliché and so I shall end with another one. No dictionary would be complete without it being pointed out that it is not claiming to be comprehensive, this being impossible in view of the constraints imposed by space. This is an almost de rigueur comment by reference book editors. It is, however, not only a cliché, it is also true, but then there is no suggestion that clichés, although they lack freshness, lack verity.

All that I have attempted to do is to bring you a selection of clichés which indicate the sheer width and diversity of the range. It is this aspect of the cliché that gives it the edge over other linguistic categories. Being an inveterate borrower, the cliché category has succeeded in making itself into either a treasure trove or a rag bag, depending on your point of view.

This book is neither a defence of clichés nor a condemnation of them. It simply contains some reflections on this most controversial of linguistic categories and an attempt to impose some degree of order on what is essentially a lawless part of the English language. At the very least I hope it contains food for thought. Enjoy!

BETTY KIRKPATRICK 1996

CLICHÉS

A

absence makes the heart grow fonder is a proverb cliché indicating that, if two people who love each other are separated, the separation is likely to intensify their love for each other, as *They work in different cities and are together only at weekends. Still absence seems to make the the heart grow fonder.* The sentiment can also be extended to absence from a place or situation, as *I am actually glad to be back at work again. Absence makes the heart grow fonder.* The expression was originally the first line of an anonymous poem published at the beginning of the seventeenth century. It became a cliché towards the end of the nineteenth century and is still used today, although often in an ironic or humorous context, as *I see you have come back to work. Absence must have made the heart grow fonder.*

accident waiting to happen, an is a hackneyed phrase used to describe a potentially dangerous situation that could very easily turn into a disaster, as *The council should board up that old house to stop the children playing there. It's an accident waiting to happen,* and *That rickety bridge is in dire need of repair. It is an accident waiting to happen.* As a cliché it became very popular in the 1980s and 1990s, especially among journalists and other commentators on society.

accidents will happen is a proverb cliché indicating in a philosophical way the inevitability of mishaps, no matter how much care is taken to avert them. It is often used with the intention of soothing the person involved in the mishap, but it frequently serves to annoy said person who is busy coping with the aftermath of the mishap. The expression has been a cliché since the late nineteenth century and is still common today, being used especially by those with a taste for platitudes and by those who feel that every situation requires a comment.

accidents, a chapter of see *chapter of accidents, a.*

Achilles heel is an allusion cliché meaning a weak spot, a flaw that makes one vulnerable, as *He was a brilliant and brave statesman but his Achilles heel, his love of beautiful women, led to his downfall.* The expression has been used figuratively, often in literary contexts, from the eighteenth century, gradually becoming a cliché. It is still used as a cliché today, especially by people of a literary bent. The allusion is to a Greek legend in which the mother of the Greek hero Achilles held him by the heel and dipped him in the River Styx so that he would be invulnerable. Only his heel remained unprotected and he was eventually killed by an arrow which pierced his heel.

acid test is an idiom cliché referring to a test which will either prove or disprove the truth or worth of something, as *The footballer appears to have recovered from his injury but the training session will be the acid test of his fitness.* The expression was first used literally to denote a test for distinguishing gold from other metals.

across the board is a hackneyed phrase meaning applying in all cases or categories, as *The unions insist that the percentage increase apply across the board, to management as well as shopfloor workers.* It became a popular cliché around the 1960s and is still common today, especially in situations involving money or economics, such as wage bargaining. In origin it referred to horse-racing in America where it described a bet placed on a horse to cover all possible winning places, second and third place as well as first place.

act together, get one's see *get one's act together*

actions speak louder than words is a proverb cliché indicating that what people do is more important than what they say, the implication being that it is easy to talk but actions require effort, as *She is always going on about the plight of the homeless but she never gets involved in any of our fundraising for them. She should realize that actions speak louder than words.* The sentiment appeared in an ancient Greek proverb but the actual wording of the present saying dates from the nineteenth century. As a cliché it is still quite common today, often being used critically against those who prefer talk to action.

add fuel to the fire is an idiom cliché meaning to inflame or exacerbate a situation, often one involving hostility or dispute, as *Our disagreement was not serious until the other side added fuel to the fire by accusing us of hiding the truth.* An alternative form of the expression is **add fuel to the flames**, both phrases referring to the fact that added fuel increases the strength of flames. The concept has been around since Roman times and as clichés both expressions are still common today.

add insult to injury is a hackneyed phrase meaning to insult or cause harm to someone whom one has already harmed, as *His car bumped into her when she was on a pedestrian crossing and then he added insult to injury by calling her careless.* The concept is an old one but the cliché dates only from the twentieth century.

after due consideration is a hackneyed phrase often used as a business cliché. It is most commonly found in rather formal written contexts and supposedly indicates that the user has given the matter a great deal of thought before coming to a decision. In fact it is usually virtually meaningless, being simply a polite convention, as *After due consideration we regret to have to tell you that your application for employment has on this occasion been unsuccessful.* It has long been a business cliché but is becoming rather dated as business letters, in common with most aspects of modern life, become less formal.

after one's own heart is an allusion cliché applied to someone or something that holds particular appeal, as *He is a man after her own heart. He loves good food and wine.* The expression has been a cliché since the late nineteenth century and is still common. In origin it is a Biblical allusion to *1 Samuel* (13:14) 'The Lord hath sought Him a man after His own heart, and the Lord hath commanded him to be captain over His people'.

against the grain, go see *go against the grain*

age before beauty is a catchphrase cliché supposedly used when allowing someone older to go before one into a room, etc, although this seems rather arrogant if used seriously. It is often nowadays used humorously or ironically, as *The old man held* the door open for the young women saying with a smile, 'Age before beauty!' As a cliché it dates from the late nineteenth century, its use today being rather dated.

alarums and excursions is an allusion cliché meaning confused activity, commotion or hullabaloo, as *It was a case of alarums and excursions in the Smith household when Mary announced that she was moving in with a married man.* As a cliché it dates from the twentieth century, being used by people of a literary bent, and nowadays used by them in a humorous context. In origin the expression refers to a stage direction in Elizabethan plays, such as Shakespeare's history plays, to indicate a vague representation of the edge of a battle.

alive and kicking is a doublet cliché, both words in the context meaning much the same thing, as *I thought he had died but I met him at a school reunion and he was alive and kicking.* As a cliché it has been popular since the middle of the nineteenth century and is still common today, its use being restricted to informal or slang contexts. In origin it was a term used by fishmongers to emphasize the freshness of their wares. A less colourful form of the expression is **alive and well**.

all and sundry is a hackneyed phrase meaning everyone, both collectively and individually. It is almost a doublet cliché, since sundry, while not quite meaning all, means several. It has been a cliché since the early nineteenth century but as a concept it is much older. Nowadays it is often used in a derogatory way, as *We don't want all and sundry joining this club.*

all chiefs and no Indians is a hackneyed phrase which refers to a situation or organization in which there are too many people issuing instructions and too few people carrying them out, as *With so many*

additional managers this place is all chiefs and no Indians. As a cliché in Britain the expression dates from the middle of the nineteenth century. It originated in America and has the variant form **too many chiefs and not enough Indians**.

all ears, be is an idiom cliché meaning to pay close attention, as *If you want to talk about what's bothering you, I'm all ears.* The idea has been common for a long time and is still popular today in an informal, and often in a humorous, context. The expression may derive from *Comus* (1634) by John Milton: 'I am all ear and took in strains that might create a soul under the ribs of death.'

all Greek to me is an allusion cliché used to refer to something that is completely unintelligible. The allusion is to Shakeapeare's *Julius Caesar* (1:2) where Casca says of Seneca's speech 'For mine own part it was Greek to me'. Seneca actually did speak in Greek so that some people would not understand what he was saying, but the expression began to be used figuratively. It is still used as a modern cliché, mostly by people of a literary bent, and often to describe something technical or specialist in nature, as *They tried to explain the new computing system but it was all Greek to me.*

all in a day's work is a catchphrase cliché indicating, somewhat philosophically or resignedly, that whatever happens has to be taken in one's stride, since it is part of one's job or duty, as *Firefighters' lives are often at risk but they know it is all in a day's work.* As a cliché it dates from the twentieth century. It is still quite common today and is sometimes used in humorous or ironic contexts, as *You always have to clear up after him, but it's all in a day's work.*

all intents and purposes, to is a doublet cliché meaning in practical terms, in all important ways, virtually, as *He occasionally spends a night at home but to all intents and purposes he and his wife are separated*. It has been a cliché since the middle of the nineteenth century and is still common in fairly formal contexts.

all mod cons is a hackneyed phrase which is a shortened form of 'all modern conveniences'. The expression was originally applied to property and meant up-do-date plumbing, such as bathrooms, and was part of estate agents' jargon, as *a desirable rural cottage with all mod cons*. It is still used with this meaning but as up-to-date plumbing has become more or less the norm in modern housing the phrase has come to be used in a wider, although mostly in a humorous or ironic, context as *Her home office has all mod cons – word processor, fax, answering machine*, and *Talk about all mod cons. The office the agency sent me to didn't even have an electric typewriter*.

all over bar the shouting is a catchphrase cliché which refers to a situation where the outcome is certain although it is not yet generally known, and so all that is to come is the official announcement or reaction, such as the applause or retribution. It was originally applied to sports events, as *The team is so far ahead that no other team can win the league now. It's all over bar the shouting*. But then its meaning was extended to cover wider contexts, as *The jury are considering their verdict. It's all over bar the shouting*. The expression has been common since the late nineteenth century and is still widely used today in all but the most formal contexts. An earlier form of the expression was **all over but the shouting**.

all part of life's rich pattern is a catchphrase cliché used in a satirically resigned

or philosophical way as a comment on the trials of life, as *After work I have go to the supermarket, collect the drycleaning and pick up my daughter from her friend's house. Ah well, it's all part of life's rich pattern!* As a cliché it became popular in the second half of the twentieth century. An alternative, and now rarer, form is **all part of life's rich tapestry**.

all part of the service is a catchphrase cliché originally used commercially to customers, as *Certainly we deliver free of charge. All part of the service, sir*. This meaning still exists but the cliché is also used in a non-commercial, humorous or light-hearted way, as *Of course it's no trouble to run you home after dinner. All part of the service!* As a cliché it became popular about the middle of the twentieth century and had its origins in an advertising slogan used by the clothing company, Austin Reed, in the 1930s.

all present and correct is a catchphrase cliché meaning that everything is in order, as *I have checked that everyone is back in the bus. All present and correct!* and *All present and correct. I've checked today's takings*. The expression has a military origin, having been used by sergeant majors on parade when reporting to the officers in charge. As a cliché it was popular around the 1930s. It is still used today but its use tends to be restricted to older men with a military background or by people being deliberately satirical.

all right for some, it's is a hackneyed phrase used to express disgruntlement or mock jealousy of someone else's good fortune, as *Look at all those people sitting in the park sunning themselves while we're working. It's all right for some!* The cliché dates from the twentieth century and is still common in informal contexts.

all right on the night, it'll be is a catch-phrase cliché originally used in consolation after a bad dress rehearsal of a play or show and dating from the later part of the nineteenth century. From about the 1920s it began to be used in wider contexts referring to things that had gone wrong initially but were optimistically thought to be going to turn out all right when the occasion demanded, as *The football team were absolutely hopeless at their last training session before the big match. Still, it'll probably be all right on the night.* As a modern cliché it is used in informal contexts.

all's well that ends well is a proverb cliché putting forward the point of view that as long as something turns out all right one can forget about any troubles that are involved in getting to that point, as *We had a lot of trouble setting this house to rights but it's perfect now. All's well that ends well.* The proverb is one of long standing and the same sentiment is found in proverbs in other languages. As a cliché it is still widely used today.

all singing, all dancing is a hackneyed phrase which was originally applied to a stage show to emphasize the splendid scale of the performance in order to tempt audiences to go and see it, as *You just have to come and see the all-singing, all-dancing show at the Playhouse!* As a cliché it was extended to a wider context in the late twentieth century, particularly to machines or systems of some kind, as *I just want a car that gets me to work. I don't want one of these all-singing, all-dancing expensive models,* and *They bought an all-singing, all-dancing camera for their holiday and then they couldn't work out how to use it.*

all systems go! is a catchphrase cliché used to refer to a state of readiness for imminent action. It had its origins in the launching of American rockets for space exploration, and especially for the moon landings in the 1960s and 1970s which received world-wide television coverage and helped to bring the expression to a wide audience. It then came to be used to refer to any state of readiness, as *Are the children ready to take part in the swimming contest. It's all systems go here!* It was frequently used in a humorous context, as *It's all systems go here! The bride is having hysterics about her taxi being late and her father has lost his speech.* As a cliché the term is not as popular as it was, perhaps because the space programme is not as active or as publicized as it once was.

all things considered is a hackneyed phrase which refers to the ultimate summing up of something when all aspects of it have been taken into account, as *All things considered, I think our play was quite successful.* As a cliché it became popular in the late nineteenth century and it is still widely used today. It is less formal than → **after due consideration**.

all things to all men, to be is an allusion cliché indicating that someone is willing to adapt so as to be liked by, or to please everyone or as many people as possible, as *You cannot count on his support. He keeps changing his mind. He tries to be all things to all men.* This rather dubious way of gaining popularity is usually referred to in negative terms nowadays, as *You will have to decide which side you are going to support. You cannot be all things to all men.* The allusion is to a Biblical passage, to 1 *Corinthians* (9:22) 'I am made all things to all men, that I might by all means save some.'

all-time low is a hackneyed phrase referring to a record low level. It can be used either literally, as *Temperatures have reached an all-time low for the time of year,* or figuratively, as *Morale reached an all-time low in the team as we lost match after match.* The opposite is **an all-time high,** as *House prices have reached an all-time high in the area,* and *Enthusiasm for the sport has reached an all-time high.* As clichés the expressions date from the twentieth century.

all to the good is a hackneyed phrase indicating something ultimately advantageous, although this fact might not at first be obvious, as *It's all to the good that you couldn't get a booking in Greece in August. It would have been far too hot for you.* It has been a cliché since the late nineteenth century. In origin, 'good' as an accounting term referred to profit or worth.

and that's that! is a hackneyed phrase used to emphasize that what one has said is to be regarded as final, and is not to be argued with, as *You are not going out before your homework is finished and that's that!* As a cliché the expression dates from the nineteenth century and is still common, often being used by irate parents when delivering ultimatums. An alternative form of the expression, possibly even more emphatic in its use, is **and that's flat!**

any port in a storm is an idiom cliché indicating that if one is in trouble one is not too particular about the form potential relief takes, as *He didn't want to take the job as nightwatchman but he was unemployed and it was a case of any port in a storm.* The expression dates from the eighteenth century and is still common today. The origin is the obvious one that in extremely stormy weather a ship would go into any port that would provide shelter.

anything that can go wrong will go wrong is a catchphrase cliché which is self-explanatory. It originated in America around 1950, probably in the form of **if anything can go wrong it will.** It is still used as a cliché today but in Britain nowadays it is more usually known as Sod's Law and less commonly as Murphy's Law, as *Sod's Law dictates that if a piece of buttered bread falls it falls buttered side down.*

apple of one's eye, the is an allusion cliché used to refer to someone who is very much loved and cherished, one's favourite, as *She loves all her children but her youngest is the apple of her eye.* The expression has been popular since the eighteenth century and is still common today. The allusion is to a Biblical passage, to *Deuteronomy* 'He kept him as the apple of his eye.' The term refers to the fact that the pupil of the eye was once thought to be a solid apple-shaped body.

apron strings, tied to is an idiom cliché used to refer to someone who is too much under the influence of a woman, especially a mother or wife, as *He never goes out with the people from work. His mother doesn't like them and he's tied to her apron strings.*

cost an arm and a leg, is an idiom cliché used to refer to the high price of something, as *Houses in that area cost an arm and a leg.* The cliché originated in America and has probably been popular in Britain since the 1970s, being used in informal or slang contexts. The same sentiment is contained in the expression **cost the earth**.

armed to the teeth is an idiom cliché meaning fully equipped to the extent of being overequipped. It originally referred to weapons used in battle and the concept of being armed to the teeth dates back to the fourteenth century. It was popularized by Richard Cobden, the English economist and politician, in a speech against what he saw as Britain's excessive expenditure on armaments (1849) and became a cliché around that time. It then became used in more general contexts. Nowadays it is used mostly informally and often in a humorous or satirical way, as *The tourists were armed to the teeth with photographic equipment*, and *Whenever he gets home late he is armed to the teeth with excuses.*

as a matter of fact is a hackneyed phrase sometimes used to preface a piece of additional or explanatory information, as *He certainly has not left town. As a matter of fact, I saw him last night.* It is also frequently meaningless through habitual use.

asking for it is a hackneyed phrase used to suggest that a woman who has been raped, or has otherwise received unwelcome sexual attention, has been acting or has been dressed in a provocative way so as to give the man involved the impression that she wanted to have sexual intercourse with him. It is only fairly recently when more women are bringing accusations of rape to the notice of the courts that this supposed justification for rape has been challenged. The cliché, however, remains very common, and because of the increased number of rape trials currently enjoys a high profile.

ask me another is a catchphrase cliché used in an informal context when one does not know the answer to a question, *Why is he so nasty? Ask me another!* It dates from the late nineteenth century but is now rather dated.

as well as can be expected is a hackneyed phrase most commonly found as a medical cliché. It is used by people involved in the care of the sick when they do not wish to commit themselves to being too optimistic about a patient's condition but equally do not wish to sound too pessimistic. It tends to irritate the relatives of the patient who feel that they are being deprived of information, as *She phoned to ask how her father was after his operation but all she was told was that he was as well as could be expected.* The cliché dates from the late nineteenth century.

at a loose end, see *loose end, at a*

at daggers drawn see *daggers drawn, at*

at long last is a hackneyed phrase meaning finally, after a lengthy wait or delay, as *We waited for ages at the bus stop and at long last the right bus appeared.* In the sixteenth century the expression was **at the long last**. The modern form has been a cliché since the beginning of the twentieth century.

at one fell swoop is an allusion cliché to Shakespeare's *Macbeth* (4:3) 'Oh Hell-kite! All? What, all my pretty chickens and their dam at one fell swoop?' The word 'fell' in this context means 'savage', the kite being a bird of prey. As a cliché the expression dates from the nineteenth century and means at one stroke or operation, as *He lost all his money on the stock market at one fell swoop.*

at this juncture is a hackneyed phrase simply meaning now. It frequently appears in formal reports, such as are issued by the police, politicians, etc and are quoted in the press, as *At this juncture we cannot say whether foul play is involved.* As a cliché it dates from the twentieth century. It predates **at this moment in time** and is not subjected to the satire with which the latter is treated.

at this moment in time is a hackneyed phrase and filler cliché which simply means now. It was a vogue cliché of the 1970s, being much used in the course of the Watergate investigation in the United States. It is still used today, sometimes seriously by people who misguidedly think it sounds impressive or by people who are playing for time while, for example, thinking of a convincing reply in the course of an interview, as *At this moment in time we have not yet finalized our education policy.* Sometimes people use it satirically. An expression which shares its meaning but enjoys slightly more credibility is **at this juncture**.

at your earliest convenience is a hackneyed phrase mostly used in business contexts such as in formal letters, as *We should be grateful if you would reply to our letter at your earliest convenience.* It is frequently a request for payment of a bill and as such is a kind of euphemism cliché since the phrase really indicates that the bill should be paid at once.

avoid like the plague is a simile cliché meaning to avoid contact as much as possible, as *Avoid him like the plague. He is such a bore*, and *I avoid the town centre like the plague on Saturday afternoons*. The cliché is common today in rather informal contexts. The expression is a very old one, having been used by St Jerome (AD 345–420), and originally referred to the need to avoid contact with anyone suffering from an infections or contagious disease.

away from one's desk is a hackneyed phrase which is often also a euphemism cliché in business contexts. It is mostly used by secretaries, assistants, colleagues, etc as a reason or excuse for someone not taking a telephone call. It is frequently used as a euphemism for 'does not wish to speak to you'. It became popular as a cliché in the 1980s. See also **in a meeting**.

axe to grind, an is an idiom cliché meaning a personal or selfish motive, as *He is very much in favour of the proposed carpark but he has an axe to grind. He owns a shop right beside the site.* It has been common as a cliché since the middle of the nineteenth century. Its origin is thought to lie in a story about a boy who was fooled into turning a grindstone while the owner sharpened his axe on it. The story has been attributed to Benjamin Franklin, the American politician (1706–90).

❦ B ❦

baby, left holding the is an idiom cliché meaning left with all the responsibility for something that is really either a shared responsibility or the responsibility of someone else, as *We were supposed to rent the house together but the others backed out leaving me holding the baby*, and *My brother volunteered to do our grandmother's garden and then went to the cinema leaving me holding the baby*. Originally the expression was applied literally to an abandoned mother. It is still a common cliché today, being used in informal contexts.

baby with the bathwater, to throw out see ***throw the baby out with the bathwater***

back number is an idiom cliché used to refer to someone who is no longer popular, effective, etc, as *He was quite a well-known singer in the seventies but is a bit of a back number now*. In origin the expression refers to back issues of newspapers which of course do not carry items of current news. As a cliché the figurative use of the term has been used since the beginning of the twentieth century. As the meaning suggests it is used in a derogatory way.

backroom boys is a hackneyed phrase used to describe the people who work away in the background and hardly ever get the acknowledgement their work deserves, this being reserved for those associated with the same project who are more in the public eye. The term dates from World War 2 and was used originally to refer to the scientists and technicians who contributed so much to warfare but went largely unnoticed as they were not in the front line. The expression is still used today to refer to essential but unobtrusive workers of either sex, as *When the actor won an Oscar for his film appearance he acknowledged the invaluable role played by the backroom boys*. It is more likely to be used by older people who may remember the origin of the phrase and it has rather a dated ring.

backseat driver is an idiom cliché used to describe someone who interferes in some project without having any involvement in it and usually without any knowledge of the subject, as *We would get this meal cooked a whole lot faster if you backseat drivers would stop telling us what to do*. The expression is also used literally to refer to someone in a vehicle, often someone who cannot drive, who offers unwanted advice to the driver. The term dates from the early twentieth century and in origin refers to the passenger in a chauffeur-driven car who gave the driver directions.

back to basics is a hackneyed phrase used to refer to a return to a simple, rudimentary method of doing something. It has been used to refer to educational methods, as *There are some people who believe that more children would learn to read and write if we got back to basics in the classroom*. In the 1990s it became used politically by the British government in their advocacy of a reinstatement of moral values supposedly common in the past.

back to square one is an idiom cliché used to indicate that it is necessary to go back to the beginning again or think something through again from the beginning, since the original attempt has not been successful, as *This timetable isn't going to work. It's back to square one!* and *He's hit a snag in his research project and so it's back to square one.* The expression may have been popularized in the 1930s by reference to the numbered grid, representing a football pitch and printed in the programme guide, which was used by radio sports commentators when giving a commentary on a match. In origin it probably refers to board games, such as snakes and ladders, where a player has to go back to the first square after incurring a certain penalty. Alternatively it may originally have been a reference to hopscotch. It is still a common cliché today, usually being used in rather resigned tones. Some of the same sentiment is conveyed by the expression → **back to the drawing board**.

back to the drawing board is an idiom cliché used to indicate that something has gone wrong with a scheme and one will have to start again and reappraise the situation, as *The rota system for overtime is not working. I suppose it's back to the drawing board.* In origin it refers to an architect or designer redrawing plans. It was popularized during World War 2 by the caption to a cartoon by Peter Arno in *The New Yorker* which depicted an aircraft exploding into the ground while a designer with a roll of blueprints stood by. As a cliché it is still popular today, usually said in rather resigned tones. Some of the same sentiment is conveyed by the expression → **back to square one**.

back to the wall, have one's is an idiom cliché meaning to be in an extremely difficult or dangerous situation, so that one has to make a final defensive stand in order to survive, as *During the recession a lot of small firms had their backs to the wall.* If one has one's back to the wall, no retreat or escape is possible and one has no alternative, if one wishes to remain alive or undefeated, but to stand and fight, with the wall acting as a defence from the rear. The expression dates from the sixteenth century but it was popularized by an order given to British troops by General Haig near the end of World War 1: 'With our backs to the wall and, believing in the justice of our cause, each one of us must fight on to the end.' As a cliché it is still common today and is often used to refer to a difficult financial situation.

bag, in the is an idiom cliché meaning certain, as *The export order's in the bag,* and *The league cup's in the bag. No other team can catch them now.* As a cliché the expression dates from the twentieth century and probably has its origin in a game bag used for holding the hunter's catch. The cliché is still common today, being used in informal or slang contexts.

bag of tricks is an idiom cliché referring to the equipment that someone uses to do a job. In origin the expression refers to the bag of tricks that a travelling magician would carry around to be used in his show. As a figurative expression it usually carries the suggestion that there is some mystique about the equipment as it is used by someone with a specialist skill that others do not share, as *There is something wrong with our central heating. We'd better send for Mr Jack and his bag of tricks,* and *The child had a very sore throat but the doctor arrived with his bag of tricks and gave him an antibiotic.* The expression dates back to the late seventeenth century and became common in the nineteenth century. It is still quite common today. An alternative form is **box of tricks**.

balance, hang in the is an idiom cliché which is used to describe a situation where there is doubt or suspense about the outcome of something, and often where the uncertainty is between two opposite possibilities, as *The condition of the accident victim is hanging in the balance*. *He is in intensive care*, and *His career is hanging in the balance*. *If he is found guilty of drink driving he will lose his job*. Frequently the expression is associated with fate, as *The fate of the workers is hanging in the balance while they are waiting for the outcome of the proposed merger*. The balance referred to is the old weighing device consisting of two pans, in one of which was placed the thing to be weighed and in the other of which was placed weights of known measure, some being added or taken away until the two pans balanced and the weight of the contents of the first pan was established. The expression dates from the fifteenth century and has been used ever since. It is still popular as a modern cliché.

bald as a coot is a simile cliché meaning completely bald, as *He has been bald as a coot since he was quite a young man*. It is the standard description of total baldness. In origin it refers to a water bird with black plumage but which has a white beak extending to its forehead, giving it the appearance of baldness.

ballgame, a different is an idiom cliché which was a vogue cliché of the 1970s and 1980s and is used to indicate a completely different situation, with a different set of considerations to be thought of, as *You can't compare the political situation then and now. It's a totally different ballgame*. The cliché is American in origin, ballgame being much more common in American English than it is in British English, and has never really become naturalized. As a cliché in Britain it is now fading slightly in popularity as is the

way of vogue clichés, having always been regarded as rather jargonistic.

ballpark figure is an idiom cliché which became a vogue cliché in Britain in the 1980s, meaning an approximate estimate, a rough guess. The expression is American in origin, being derived from baseball, **in the ballpark** meaning within certain limits. It has come to be a cliché chiefly in the sphere of finance and business which is, of course, international, and one that frequently uses American English. The cliché has never become widespread in general British English.

ball's in your court, the is an idiom cliché indicating that it is up to the other party in a situation to act. In origin the expression refers to tennis. As a cliché it dates from the middle part of the twentieth century and it is still common today, being used in informal or slang contexts.

banana skin, a is an idiom cliché which refers to something which, figuratively, might make you fall flat on your face and therefore look foolish. The image of someone slipping on a banana skin, usually while everyone else present laughs heartily, is an old one, being a favourite of compilers of comics and cartoonists. It was popular in a political context in 1980s Britain during the Thatcher administration. As a cliché it is one of those that seems to come and go, as though people forget about it for a while and then suddenly remember how appropriate it is. It is a term which appeals to journalists and is often used by them in connection with the world of politics where there is usually no shortage of people indulging in the kind of behaviour that warrants the use of the cliché, as *This latest scandal involving a Cabinet Minister is yet another banana skin for the Government*.

bandwagon, jump on the see *jump on the bandwagon*

bang one's head against a brick wall is an idiom cliché meaning to try assiduously but in vain, or with little hope of success, to achieve an objective. It is often used of someone who is trying to get someone else to understand something or to follow a piece of advice, as *You'll just be banging your head against a brick wall if you try to persuade him to stay on at school*, and *We tried to get her to see a doctor but we were just banging our heads against a brick wall*. The expression is long established and its origin suggests going to a lot of trouble (and pain) and achieving nothing. As a cliché it is still widespread today in all but the most formal contexts.

baptism of fire is an idiom cliché which refers to someone's introduction to, or first encounter with, something that is likely to be an ordeal, as *She has finished her teacher training course and is about to face her baptism of fire in the classroom*. The expression was first used figuratively of soldiers being exposed to gunfire for the first time, and as a cliché with this meaning dates from the nineteenth century, the wider meaning being a later development. It is still common today in a wide range of contexts, sometimes being used humorously.

barking up the wrong tree is an idiom cliché meaning directing one's efforts or energies in the wrong direction, as *The police have taken in him for questioning but they are barking up the wrong tree. I know who the real culprit is*. As a cliché the expression dates from the nineteenth century and is still popular today in rather informal contexts. In origin it refers to the former American practice of raccoon hunting when trained dogs would bark up trees at night to indicate where the raccoons were. Sometimes they made a mistake and quite literally barked up the wrong tree.

bark is worse than his bite, his is an idiom cliché indicating that someone appears and sounds much fiercer and sterner than he or she actually is, as *All the children are scared of the new teacher, but people say that her bark is worse than her bite and that she can be very kind to her pupils*. The expression dates from the middle of the seventeenth century and is a common cliché today. In origin it refers to a dog that might growl and snarl but will not actually bite people. The cliché is sometimes reversed for humorous or satirical purposes, as *Watch out for the new boss. She looks very gentle but her bite is worse than her bark*.

barrel, have someone over is an idiom cliché indicating that one has someone totally in one's power, as *He has the workers over a barrel. He pays them rock-bottom wages because he knows they wouldn't get other jobs*. As a cliché it dates from the twentieth century and is still common today, being used in informal or slang contexts.

batten down the hatches is an idiom cliché meaning to make oneself as secure as possible in expectation of trouble. In modern times it is frequently associated with an economic or financial situation, as *Small firms that cut their expenditure and batten down the hatches will stand the best chance of surviving the recession*. The expression has been used figuratively since the late nineteenth century and is still quite common today. It is nautical in origin, referring to the preparation of a ship for stormy weather by fastening down the battens (strips of wood that were nailed to the masts) and spars, and covering the hatchways of the ship with tarpaulin.

battle royal, a is an idiom cliché which refers to a fierce quarrel or row, often involving several people, as *There was a real battle royal when the landlord of the pub refused to serve one of the customers.* In origin the phrase refers to cockfighting in the seventeenth century, a battle royal being a fight in which more than two birds were involved. The expression was used figuratively from the eighteenth century. As a cliché it is less commonly used today than it once was.

be-all and end-all is a hackneyed phrase meaning the thing that is of most importance, as *Money isn't the be-all and end-all of life, you know,* and *She thinks that getting married is the be-all and end-all of a woman's existence.* As a cliché it has been in common use since the nineteenth century. It is still used today but in rather a restricted range of contexts. Its most famous literary use is in a passage from Shakespeare's *Macbeth* (1:6) when Macbeth in a soliloquy is thinking about murdering Duncan 'that but this blow might be the be-all and end-all here'.

beat about the bush is an idiom cliché meaning to approach something in a roundabout or ultra-cautious manner, to shilly-shally, as *I wish the boss would tell people directly if they're being made redundant. He keeps beating about the bush.* The expression dates from the sixteenth century and became a cliché in the late eighteenth century. Both it and the practice it refers to are very popular today. In origin it refers to beating bushes in order to flush out game birds from their hiding place so that they may be shot.

beat a hasty retreat is a hackneyed phrase meaning to depart or get out of the way as quickly as possible, as *The children beat a hasty retreat when they realized that they had*

broken a window. The expression is military in origin, where it originally referred to the practice of beating a drum as a signal to the troops to retreat. Later in military terms it came to mean simply to retreat and later still came to be used figuratively. It was a cliché from around the middle of the nineteenth century but nowadays usually has 'hasty' in the expression.

beaten track, off the see *off the beaten track*

beats cock-fighting, it is a catchphrase cliché indicating that something is either superior or desirable in some way or that it is remarkable, as *A fortnight in the Bahamas may not be everyone's ideal holiday but it sure beats cock-fighting,* and *He's broken the record for the course again. Doesn't that beat cock-fighting?* As a catchphrase the expression dates from the early nineteenth century. As a cliché it is still found today but it is becoming rather dated.

beats me, it is a hackneyed phrase indicating that one is absolutely baffled by something, as *It beats me why she stays with him. He's always after other women.* The expression has been common in Britain since the 1920s and is still a common cliché today, being used in an informal context.

because it's there is a catchphrase cliché used in defence of taking part in something the motivation for which other people cannot understand, regarding the venture as too dangerous, uncomfortable, boring, etc. The phrase was used by George Leigh Mallory (1886–1924), a famous mountaineer, with reference to his attempt on Mount Everest, an attempt which was unsuccessful and from which he disappeared. It was later popularized by Edmund Hillary, whose attempt to climb the same mountain was successful (1953). As a modern cliché it is still frequently used with reference to mountaineering, as *So many people risk their lives on Scottish peaks in the winter but when you ask them why they do it they say, 'Because it's there'*. It is also used of other sporting activities, as *When we asked him why he wanted to swim the channel all he could come up with was 'Because it's there'*. More recently it has extended its use to cover less obvious areas of interest, mostly in a humorous or ironic way, as *They say they drink such a lot of whisky because it's there*.

bed of roses, a is an idiom cliché used to refer to a very pleasant, comfortable or trouble-free situation, a bed of roses being a very beautiful place to be, if you do not take into consideration the thorns. The expression is mostly found in the negative, as *Life on the dole isn't exactly a bed of roses*, and *Being a single mother is hardly a bed of roses*. As a metaphor it has been in use since the sixteenth century and has been a cliché since the middle of the nineteenth century. The cliché is widespread today, especially in view of the fact that the absence of trouble-free situations grows ever more common.

bee in one's bonnet, a is an idiom cliché meaning to have a fixation or obsession about something, as *I should warn you before you start the job that the boss has a bee in his bonnet about punctuality*. As a cliché the expression dates from the eighteenth century, although the idea is older. It is still very common today. In origin a comparison is being made between a bee buzzing around in a panic-stricken way when caught inside a hat and an idea that goes round and round irrationally in one's head.

beer and skittles is an idiom cliché meaning a life of ease and enjoyment. The expression is often negative in its implications, as *He thinks that the life of a student is all beer and skittles*, and *Being a courier for a holiday company is not all beer and skittles*. The game of skittles is associated with beer, since it is often played in pubs. As a cliché the expression dates from the middle of the nineteenth century and is still in common use today.

bee's knees, the is an idiom cliché meaning the very best, as *She is a very poor singer but she thinks she's the bee's knees*. The expression is American in origin and probably dates from the 1920s. As to derivation it seems likely that the knees of the bees are popular only because the two words happen to rhyme. The cliché is still popular in an informal or slang context.

before you can say Jack Robinson is a catchphrase cliché used to indicate great speed, usually with more optimism than actuality, as *I'll have this room decorated before you can say Jack Robinson*. The identity of Jack Robinson remains obscure, despite much speculation. His earliest recorded written appearance is in Fanny Burney's *Evelina* (1778) 'I'd do it as soon as say Jack Robinson'. A likely explanation seems to be that both elements add up to a very common name, in much the same way that John Smith does. As a cliché the expression probably dates from the nineteenth century and is still in common use today.

beg, borrow or steal is a hackneyed phrase meaning to obtain by any means possible, as *Our car's broken down. We'll have to beg, borrow or steal transport to get to the wedding on time*. The expression dates from the time of Chaucer in the fourteenth century and as a cliché is still popular today, often being used in humorous contexts.

beggars can't be choosers is a proverb cliché referring to the fact that people who are greatly in need of something are not in a position to pick and choose or to be critical of what is offered, as *We are not particularly fond of the house but it was the only one in our price range and beggars can't be choosers*, and *She did not want to work in a factory but she has no qualifications and beggars can't be choosers*. The proverb appeared in John Heywood's collection of proverbs in 1546 and has remained popular as a saying ever since. As a modern cliché it is extremely common, often being used in rather sanctimonious tones of another person's misfortune.

beginning of a new era, the is a hackneyed phrase meaning the start of some completely new stage or development, as *In technological terms the invention of the computer was the beginning of a new era*. The phrase suggests some major new development but in fact the cliché is frequently used to refer to minor changes, or even trivial changes, as *The discarding of the uniform heralded the beginning of a new era for the school*, and *We believe that our current publicity campaign marks the beginning of a new era in marketing*. The cliché dates from the end of the nineteenth century and is widely used today, especially by journalists, politicians and those making public speeches. An alternative form is **the beginning of an era**.

beginning of the end, the is a quotation cliché, being a translation of a remark made by Talleyrand to Napoleon after the battle of Leipzig was lost (1813) *'C'est la commencement de la fin'*, although he may not have originated the phrase. The expression refers to a situation or event that marks the start of ruin, disaster, or some other misfortune, as *They only divorced this year but it was the beginning of the end when he had an affair with his secretary a few years ago*, and *The building of the new supermarket was the beginning of the end for many of our local shops*. It has been a cliché since the middle of the nineteenth century and is still common today, often said in rather lugubrious tones.

be good is a catchphrase cliché used as a parting greeting in informal, humorous expressions, as *I must be off now. Have a good holiday and be good!* The expression often carries sexual connotations and is still sometimes found as **be good and if you can't be good be careful**, although this longer form is now rather dated. The expression dates from the beginning of the twentieth century in America when it was the title of a song 'If you can't be good be careful' written by Harrington and Tate. The same sentiment is found in → **don't do anything I wouldn't do**.

behind the scenes is a hackneyed phrase used to refer to activities that take place away from the public eye. The expression sometimes carries the suggestion that the activity is secret or even underhand, as *The official talks received a lot of media attention but we think most of the negotiations went on behind the scenes*, and *A great deal of lobbying went on behind the scenes before the new leader was elected*. This is not necessarily the case and it can be used with the same sentiment as → **backroom boys**, as *She always take the credit for the organization but most of the work is done by people slaving away behind the scenes*. The expression can also be used adjectivally, as *We think that there was a great deal of behind-the-scenes wheeling and dealing before the merger of the companies took place*. In origin the expression refers to the fact that in the seventeenth and eighteenth century theatre, especially in France, a great deal of the violent action, such as murders, took place literally behind the scenes. The expression has been used figuratively since the late eighteenth century, becoming a cliché around the middle of the nineteenth century. As a cliché it is still in common use today.

believe it or not is a filler cliché used to alert one's listener to the fact that one is about to say something surprising, as *Believe it or not, he was considered the best applicant for the job.* It is sometimes used virtually meaninglessly by people to whom it has become a habit. It has been a cliché since the middle of the nineteenth century, perhaps having been popularized by a London show entitled *Believe It or Not* (1939–40). In America it was popularized by the cartoonist Robert Leroy Ripley who used the expression as the title of a cartoon series first published in 1918. As a cliché it is still widespread today, being used in informal contexts.

believe one's eyes, cannot is a hackneyed phrase used to emphasize the surprising or unusual nature of what is revealed, as *I could not believe my eyes when I saw a well-dressed woman calmly take a dress off the rack and put it in her briefcase,* and *The children couldn't believe their eyes when they saw the huge Christmas tree.* The expression probably dates from the seventeenth century and became a cliché around the late nineteenth century. It is still common today in informal contexts.

be like that is a hackneyed phrase used to someone who will not agree to do as one wishes, as *Be like that! I'll borrow someone else's book,* and *Be like that! We'll go to the cinema without you.* It is found in informal contexts and is frequently used by children who are peeved by the lack of cooperation on the part of their friends.

be mother is a hackneyed phrase used to mean to pour out tea or coffee or generally act as hostess, as *I'll be mother. Do you take milk and sugar?* It is still used nowadays but it is often regarded as being rather 'twee'. People who use it often do so in a deliberately humorous way.

be my guest is a catchphrase cliché used to indicate that one does not mind someone borrowing or taking something, as *Of course you can borrow my magazine. Be my guest!* and *Yes, you can have the last cake. Be my guest!* The expression has been popular since the 1950s and is still a common cliché used in informal contexts. It is often now used ironically to indicate that someone has borrowed or taken something that one thinks properly belongs to one, or has done something rather high-handedly, as *Actually that was my trolley but be my guest!*

belle of the ball is a hackneyed phrase used to refer to the most beautiful or best-dressed woman at a social gathering, not now necessarily a ball or dance, as *You'll be the belle of the ball in that dress.* It is often now used ironically to describe someone who thinks she is the most beautiful or elegant woman present and who puts on airs. *Belle* as a noun in French means beautiful woman, and the word was adopted into English early in the seventeenth century.

bells and whistles is a hackneyed phrase used to refer, usually in a derogatory way, to features that are purely decorative, being neither functional nor necessary. The term is often applied to machines or gadgets, such as computers, as *I just want an efficient basic model. I don't want any bells and whistles,* and *He just wants a car that will get him from A to B. He doesn't want to pay extra for a lot of bells and whistles.*

bend over backwards is an idiom cliché meaning to go to a great deal of trouble, often excessively so, as *We bent over backwards to make her feel at home but she never really settled in*. The expression often carries the implication that the undue exertion is in vain. It originated in America around the 1920s and is much used as a cliché today. In origin it refers to the physical exertion required to bend backwards. An alternative form is **lean over backwards**.

benefit of the doubt, give the is a hackneyed phrase meaning to treat someone as innocent, even though there may be some doubt or some evidence to the contrary, as *We can't prove that he stole the money and so we must give him the benefit of the doubt, but he was the only person with access to it*. It is sometimes used in a humorous or ironic context, as *If you say you were ill yesterday we'll give you the benefit of the doubt but it was a scorching day and you've got a suntan*. In origin the expression refers to the fact that in law a person is presumed innocent until proved guilty beyond doubt. It has been used figuratively since the nineteenth century and has been a cliché since around the turn of the century, being still commonly used today.

be seeing you! is a catchphrase cliché used as a standard informal greeting on parting from someone, as *There's my bus! I must go! Be seeing you!* It has been common since the middle of the 1940s and is still used today, often being shortened to **see you!** Unlike the more modern **see you later!** it does usually mean that the user will see the person so addressed again.

best bib and tucker is a hackneyed phrase used to refer to one's best clothes, as in *If you're going to dinner with her parents you'd better look out your best bib and tucker*. The expression is used in informal or slang contexts and is now rather dated. It dates from the eighteenth century. In origin it refers to parts of clothing worn only to

rather formal events. A bib was a man's formal shirt front or a frill worn on a shirt front, and a tucker was a piece of lace worn on the neck and shoulders by women.

best-laid schemes, the is an allusion cliché used to reflect the fact that the most carefully made plans can go wrong, as *She had the holiday planned down to the very last detail and then there was a ferry strike. Ah, well, the best-laid schemes . . .* The allusion is to a passage from a poem by Robert Burns. In *To a Mouse* (1786) he wrote 'The best laid schemes o' mice and men gang aft agley'. Sometimes the cliché is extended to include the whole quotation as *We had booked a weekend break and then our daughter got chicken pox and we had to stay at home. It's true that the best laid schemes o' (of) mice and men gang aft agley*. The longer version is less common than the shorter one. As a cliché it dates from the late eighteenth century and may have been common before its use by Burns, although he certainly popularized it. The expression, like the concept, is still common today.

best of British, the is a catchphrase cliché, short for **the best of British luck**. It is now used ironically, to indicate that the situation referred to is very difficult or impossible, as *Well, if you think you can get that stain off the carpet, the best of British to you*. The expression is probably military in origin, dating from World War 2, and may have been used ironically from its inception. As a cliché today it is found in informal or slang contexts and is somewhat dated.

best thing since sliced bread, the see *greatest/best thing since slice bread, the*

best things in life are free, the is a catchphrase cliché whose meaning is self-evident. The phrase is the title of a song from the Broadway musical *Good News* (1927) and the title of a film which was released in 1956. Both of these helped to establish the phrase as a common twentieth-century cliché and catchphrase. It is frequently now used ironically, since only people who are comfortably off are in a position to make this claim.

be that as it may is a hackneyed phrase which is also used as a filler cliché. It is equivalent to 'that may be true', as *You say that he is basically honest. Be that as it may, we are almost certain that he took the money.* Sometimes it is used virtually meaninglessly by people to whom it has become a habit. The expression dates from the nineteenth century. It is still common today and although it has rather a formal ring, it is found in informal as well as formal contexts.

better half, one's is a hackneyed phrase used by some men to refer to their wives, as *Thanks for the invitation. I'll have to ask my better half.* The idea of two people being two halves of a whole goes back to Roman days, when Horace used it to refer to friends. The term dates from the sixteenth century. Originally it, too, referred to close friends or lovers, eventually coming to mean a wife. As a jocular cliché it has been common since the middle of the nineteenth century. It is rather dated today when many women would regard it as patronizing although it is ostensibly a compliment.

better late than never is a hackneyed phrase used in an attempt to minimize the inconvenience caused by lack of punctuality. As a sentiment it dates from Roman times. The expression appears in several early collections of English proverbs, sometimes given in the extended form **better late than never, but better never late.** As a modern cliché it is extremely common, a reflection of the fact, no doubt, that lateness is extremely common. The expression is used by people who are late themselves in cheerful disregard of the effects their poor time-keeping may have on others. It is also used by those at the receiving end of the unpunctuality seemingly in cheerful or polite acceptance of the unpunctuality but sometimes said through gritted teeth.

better safe than sorry is a hackneyed phrase advocating the virtues of safety and caution and pointing to the dangers of ignoring these, as *You'd better go back and check that you locked the back door. Better safe than sorry,* and *Have you checked the tyres and oil? Better safe than sorry.* As a cliché it dates from the twentieth century but the idea is considerably older. The cliché has a marked tendency to sound smug as though the person giving the advice knows best, and is frequently a source of annoyance to recipients of the advice.

between a rock and a hard place is an idiom cliché meaning a situation in which one is faced with a choice of two equally unpleasant or unacceptable choices, a rock and a hard place meaning the same in this context, as *I'm between a rock and a hard place. If I stay with my present company I have to move to another branch at the other end of the country. If I leave I'll have to take a job with a firm that doesn't pay so well.* It dates from the early twentieth century in its native America but its appearance in British English is fairly recent and even now it is sometimes used by people who are consciously using it as an Americanism. The phrase conveys the same sentiment as the older idioms **between Scylla and Charybdis** and **between the devil and the deep blue sea.**

between jobs is a euphemism cliché meaning unemployed. It sometimes genuinely means that someone has left one job and is waiting to take up another which has already been negotiated. Frequently, however, it is used to avoid having to admit to being unemployed or redundant, as *My husband is between jobs at the moment and so he is concentrating on the garden.* The cliché dates from around the late 1970s when general unemployment became a serious issue in Britain. It is a more general form of the theatrical euphemism **resting**, used of an actor who is without work for a while.

between you and me is a hackneyed phrase used to impress on someone the need for secrecy. In fact, it is more usually taken as a signal for the revelation of a really juicy piece of gossip which the hearer will then rush to pass on to someone else, as *They're supposed to be married, but between you and me I know for a fact that he is married already.* A later alternative form is **between you, me and the gatepost** which means much the same as the original form and dates from the late nineteenth century. Dating from around the same time is **between you, me and the bedpost** but this is no longer common. It is very common for people to use the phrase ungrammatically, as **between you and I**.

beyond our ken is a hackneyed phrase meaning beyond our understanding or experience. It is often used to refer to the understanding of mortals generally, as *I would never dare dabble in spiritualism. Some things are beyond our ken.* Indeed the expression **beyond the ken of mortal men** also exists, although it is not now commonly used. The expression is also used to refer to the particular rather than the general, as *It is beyond our ken what she sees in him but she is going to marry him,* and is sometimes used in humorous contexts.

As a cliché it dates from the late nineteenth century.

beyond the pale is a hackneyed phrase meaning morally or socially unacceptable, as *Her parents are very broad-minded but the conduct of her fiancé's drunken friends at the party was beyond the pale.* As a cliché the expression dates from the late nineteenth century. It is still common today and is often used in humorous or ironic contexts, as *I'm sure that we won't be invited to the wedding. It's to be a big society event and we are beyond the pale.* In origin the expression refers historically to the Pale in fourteenth-century Ireland which was the part within the bounds of English rule and therefore thought by them to be an area of civilization or superiority, anyone living outside this being deemed vastly inferior. A pale was first a stake of the kind used to build a fence, then its meaning extended to describe an area separated by a fence.

bide one's time, to is a hackneyed phrase meaning to wait for the right opportunity before taking any form of action, as *Now is not a good time to ask your father for a loan. You should bide your time and wait until he's in a better mood.* It often carries some rather sinister connotations, as *The landlord is being too nice. I think he's just biding his time to find a reason to throw us out.* The expression has been a cliché since the later part of the nineteenth century and is still common today. The verb 'to bide' is obsolete in English except in this expression, although it is still common in Scots.

Big Brother is watching you is a quotation cliché warning of the power that the authorities have over us, including that of surveillance, as *I know that surveillance cameras in the city centre might make the place safer but it does savour a bit of Big Brother is watching you.* The quotation is from

George Orwell's *Nineteen Eighty-Four* (1949). As a cliché it has been generally used since about 1960, although it was used by people of a literary bent before then. Before Orwell, 'big brother' was a synonym for kindly protection.

bigger they are, the harder they fall, the is a catchphrase cliché referring to the fact that the downfall of someone important is much more dramatic than the downfall of someone of lesser status. It is usually said with approbation, the user of the phrase being glad of the downfall, as *He is in a position of power just now but after the merger there will be a management shake-up and he will be out. The bigger they are, the harder they fall.* As a catchphrase it dates from the late nineteenth century and is still common as a cliché today. In origin it probably refers to boxers, since someone who is large and heavy falls down harder than a lighter person.

bird in the hand, a is an allusion cliché which refers to some kind of advantage that one already has or that one is sure of being preferable to something that one might acquire, as *You should stay in this job until you get another one. You know what they say about a bird in the hand.* The allusion is to the proverb **a bird in the hand is worth two in the bush**. The full version is also used as a cliché, as *We must find a flat before we give the landlord notice. A bird in the hand is worth two in the bush.* The proverb first appeared in English in the fifteenth century and appeared in Greek and Latin before then. Both the full proverb and the truncated version are commonly used today, particularly by people who like to give cautionary advice to others.

birds of a feather is an allusion cliché used to refer to people who are very similar in character, tastes, attitudes, etc, often in a derogatory way, as *I'm not surprised they go everywhere together. They're birds of a feather,* and *The two older boys are birds of a feather and have both been in prison but the youngest one is honest and hard-working.* As a cliché it has been common since the nineteenth century and is still popular today. It is an allusion to the proverb **birds of a feather flock together** meaning that people of like tastes and character tend to stick together. The proverb has been popular since the seventeenth century but the sentiment is much older, having been used in Greek and Roman times.

bite off more than one can chew is an idiom cliché meaning to undertake more than one is likely to be able to deal with effectively, as *She is trying to save for her holiday but she has bitten off more than she can chew. She cleans offices in the morning, serves in a shop in the afternoon and babysits in the evening,* and *I think the student has bitten off more than he can chew by taking on five subjects in his first year.* As a cliché it dates from the late nineteenth century but cautionary advice against overburdening oneself dates from the Middle Ages.

bite the bullet is an idiom cliché meaning to steel oneself to accept something distressing, unpleasant, etc, as *I know you hate telling people that they are to be redundant but you'll just have to bite the bullet and get on with it,* and *She was dreading going to see the doctor but we finally persuaded her to bite the bullet and make an appointment.* The expression dates from the twentieth century and is still common today, being used in informal or slang contexts. In origin it probably refers to the days before anaesthesia, when soldiers wounded in battle were given a lead bullet to bite on to brace themselves against the pain of surgery.

bite the dust is an idiom cliché meaning to die or come to an end, as *Many of the gangsters bit the dust in the raid,* and *Our plans to go away for the summer have bitten the dust. We've no money.* It became current in America in the late 1930s and later became common in Britain. As a cliché it is still popular today, being used in very informal or slang contexts. In origin the term comes from Western films in which cowboys and Indians were frequently shot and fell off their horses dead into the dust.

blazing inferno, a is a hackneyed phrase used to describe a fire. It is much used by journalists, especially in headlines, as *man leaps from roof in blazing inferno.* It would properly be used to describe a very large and dangerous fire, but is in fact often used to describe anything bigger than a small garden rubbish fire, the tabloid press having a weakness for exaggeration, which sells more copies of newspapers. As a cliché it dates from the late nineteenth century.

blessing in disguise, a is a hackneyed phrase which described a piece of seemingly bad fortune that turns out to be some form of good fortune, as *His gambling losses were a blessing in disguise. He had become addicted and decided to stop.* The phrase appears in a poem by the eighteenth century poet, James Hervey 'E'en crosses from his sovereign are blessings in disguise', 'cross' here meaning 'burden'. The expression has been a cliché since the late nineteenth century and is still widespread today.

blind leading the blind, the is an allusion cliché used to describe a situation in which the people in charge who are meant to be instructing or guiding others know no more than the people that they are in charge of, as *The courier who was meant*

to be showing us around the area kept getting lost. Talk about the blind leading the blind, and *They've put me down to teach geography and I know nothing about it. It's a case of the blind leading the blind.* The allusion is to the Bible, to *Matthew* (15:14): 'Let them alone; they are blind leaders of the blind. And if the blind lead the blind, both shall fall in the ditch.' Much the same sentiment as the latter is contained in a proverb featuring in John Heywood's collection of 1546: 'Where the blind leadeth the blind both fall into the dike.' It is still a widespread cliché today.

blood is thicker than water is a proverb cliché meaning that, however binding the ties of friendship, those of family are stronger, as *My best friend's looking for a place to live, but so is my sister. I've got only one spare room and blood's thicker than water.* The concept dates from the Middle Ages and the term appears in John Ray's collection of proverbs in 1670. As a cliché it is still very common today.

blot on the landscape, a is a hackneyed phrase used to refer to something that is considered a disfigurement on the landscape or environment, as *I'm glad they've demolished those high-rise flats. They were a real blot on the landscape.* As a cliché it dates from the late nineteenth century and is still common today, probably because there are so many blots on the landscape.

blow hot and cold is an idiom cliché meaning to vacillate between being enthusiastic and apathetic about something, as *It's difficult to get a decision out of the planning committee. They seem to be blowing hot and cold on our project.* The expression dates from the sixteenth century and has been a cliché since the eighteenth century. It is still common today. In origin it refers to Aesop's fable in which a centaur assumed that a man must be blowing hot and cold from the same mouth because he blew on his hands to warm them and on his soup to cool it.

blue-rinse brigade, the is a hackneyed phrase used to refer to well-off, middle-aged women with time and money to spare, who as a group tend to play a significant part in the management of local affairs, the running of local branches of political parties, etc. Since they are seen to be interfering as well as formidable, the term is used in a derogatory way, as *Local government around here is full of the blue-rinse brigade*, and *We don't want too many of the blue-rinse brigade on the school board*. The cliché dates from the second part of the twentieth century. In origin the expression refers to the fact that women whose hair is going grey sometimes have a blue-rinse put through it to make it less dingy, although this practice has grown less common as hair colouring techniques have improved.

blushing bride is a hackneyed phrase used to refer to a woman on her wedding day. It is particularly beloved of some journalists, as *The blushing bride was attended by two flower-girls*. As a cliché it dates from the twentieth century and is now rather dated, as indeed is the concept. In origin it refers to the fact that brides were traditionally pure and modest.

bone of contention, a is an idiom cliché meaning a cause of dispute, as *The communal wall has been a bone of contention between the two neighbours for years*. As a cliché the expression dates from the nineteenth century and is still in widespread use today. In origin it refers to a bone which is being fought over by two dogs.

bone to pick, a is an idiom cliché indicating a cause of dispute or complaint that requires discussion, as *I have a bone to pick with you. I gather that you have been going around saying that I'm dishonest*. The expression dates from the sixteenth century and refers to dogs worrying over a bone. In this it bears a resemblance to **a bone of contention**. As a cliché it is still popular in informal contexts. It is often used humorously.

bottom line, the is a vogue cliché with its origins in accountancy, where it refers to the bottom line of a financial statement which indicates the extent of the profit or loss. It is one of several terms that began life in a specialist field and then crossed over to the general language. It began to be used figuratively in the middle of the twentieth century and rapidly became a cliché. In the 1980s it practically reached saturation point, journalists, as always in such a situation, playing a part, but aided and abetted by people in the public eye and people being interviewed on radio and television. With its financial connections it was perhaps the ideal cliché for the 1980s, a decade that seemed obsessed with money, and indeed may be considered to be the linguistic equivalent of the Yuppie. People are often slightly confused as to the exact meaning of specialist expressions that become generalized. The result is that **the bottom line** has a range of meanings, from the final outcome of something (as *The talks went on for days and even then the bottom line was that they agreed to differ*), to the crux or most important point of something (as *The bottom line of the discussion is who is going to provide the money*), to the last straw (as *He always shouted her at her when he came home drunk but the bottom line was when he hit her. She left him*). The popularity of the term perhaps waned in the 1990s but that is mostly because it was difficult for any phrase to sustain the level of coverage which it achieved. It is, however, almost certainly one of those rather annoying clichés that will keep popping up.

box of tricks see *bag of tricks*

breath of fresh air, like a is a simile cliché used to indicate someone or something new and refreshing, as *The young members who have just joined the club have been like a breath of fresh air. It was getting so fuddy-duddy*, and *The ideas which the new members have brought to the committee are like a breath of fresh air.* The term became current in the middle of the nineteenth century and is still widespread today. Earlier forms of the expression were **like a breath of heaven** and **like a breath of spring**.

bright-eyed and bushy-tailed is an idiom cliché meaning lively and alert. The expression is used in informal, and often in humorous, contexts, as *How can you look so bright-eyed and bushy-tailed this morning when we've all got a hangover?* In origin it refers to the alert aspect and bushy tail of the squirrel and probably came to Britain from America, where it dates from the 1930s.

brother's keeper, I am not my see *keeper, I am not . . .*

brownie points is an idiom cliché meaning credit for doing something right or for doing a good deed, as *I'll get brownie points from my mother if I clean my room without being asked.* It is often used humorously or ironically and sometimes carries a suggestion that the person getting the brownie points is something of a self-seeker, as *He gets a lot of brownie points from the boss for doing unpaid overtime.* As a cliché it dates from the later part of the twentieth century. There is some dispute over the origin. The obvious origin would appear to be to the

Brownie guides, who received awards or badges, but more for levels of proficiency in various fields, rather than for the good deeds which they were expected to perform without reward. An alternative suggestion is that the expression refers to a points system for employees operated by American railway companies. Yet another suggestion is that **brownie points** shares an origin with brown-nosing which means sucking up to someone in authority and is synonymous with arse-licking.

buck stops here, the see *pass the buck*

bury the hatchet is an idiom cliché meaning to make peace, to end a quarrel or argument, as *He and his brother quarrelled and hadn't spoken to each other for years, but they buried the hatchet when their mother died.* As a cliché the expression dates from the beginning of the twentieth century and is still popular today in informal contexts. In origin it refers to some North American Indian tribes who buried a hatchet on declaring peace.

business, do the is the hackneyed phrase used to mean to accomplish something. As a cliché the expression dates from the second part of the twentieth century and is still common today in informal or slang contexts. It is particularly common in sporting contexts, being exceptionally popular with football commentators to describe scoring a goal or achieving victory, as *They can still win if their striker can do the business in the second half.*

business is business is a catchphrase cliché indicating that the profit motive takes precedence over all other considerations, as *He says that he would like to rent his cousin one of his holiday cottages free of charge but business is business.* As a cliché it dates from the twentieth century.

Nowadays the motivation of the expression is more common than the expression itself.

buy a pig in a poke is an idiom cliché meaning to buy or accept something without examining its quality with the implication that an apparent bargain may deceive, as *He bought a pig in a poke with that car. It was cheap but it kept breaking down.* As a cliché the term dates from the nineteenth century but the idea is much older. The cliché is still common today. In origin it supposedly refers to an old fairground trick when a trader would sell a piglet in a poke (a bag) so that the purchaser could not see it before paying for it. It shares this origin with **let the cat out of the bag**.

by the same token is a hackneyed phrase, often used simply as a filler cliché. As a hackneyed phrase it means in the same way, for the same, or an associated, reason, as *Conditions are so bad that many of the staff are leaving and by the same token those who remain are demoralized.* This is a phrase to which some people become addicted and they use it without thinking and almost without meaning. As a cliché it dates from the late eighteenth century.

C

call a spade a spade is a hackneyed phrase meaning to be direct and blunt, as *They call it giving me early retirement. I call it sacking me. I prefer to call a spade a spade.* Although there is much to be lauded in straightforward talking as opposed to euphemism, there is no doubt that many people who are fond of this expression pride themselves on being blunt to the extent of rudeness or tactlessness, as *They say he has learning disabilities but I prefer to say that he is mentally handicapped. I call a spade a spade.* The expression has been current in English since the sixteenth century but common enough to be called a cliché only since the nineteenth century. The concept, and possibly the wording, is much older, going back to Greek and Roman times. Those for whom directness is not enough were wont to rephrase the expression as **call a spade a bloody shovel** but this version, if not the thinking behind it, is now not so common.

call it a day is a hackneyed phrase meaning to stop work or to stop doing something either for a time or permanently, as *We've run out of paint and so we might as well call it a day*, and *After forty years as caretaker he has decided to call it a day.* As a cliché it dates from the twentieth century and it is still common, being used in informal or slang contexts. In origin it means that those concerned are treating a particular time as though it were the end of the working day, irrespective of what the time actually is. The end referred to does not in fact have to do with work, the cliché being wider in

its application, as *They have not been getting on well for years, so they've decided to call it a day and get a divorce.*

call me old-fashioned is a hackneyed phrase used as an introduction to a thought or attitude that is no longer fashionable, as *Call me old-fashioned but I don't like the idea of men and women being together in the same hospital ward.* It is often used virtually meaninglessly by those to whom it has become an annoying habit, or in humorous contexts.

calm before the storm, the is an idiom cliché used to describe a period of quiet before the onset of violence, protest, quarrelling, etc. It is usually used by someone predicting, often on the basis of experience, that some form of outburst is about to take place, as *I haven't heard from my mother since I wrote and said I was giving up my job and travelling round the world. This is just the calm before the storm.* The phrase was much used by statesmen in 1938–39 with reference to the period before World War 2 broke out, and was later used in a wider variety of contexts. It has been a cliché since the late nineteenth century. In origin it refers to the period of rather eerie stillness that often precedes a storm.

can of worms, a is an idiom cliché used to refer to a problematic and involved situation that is very difficult to deal with and the full extent of which is hard to estimate, as *I wish that I'd never got involved in this project. It's a real can of worms. All the other* organizers are quarrelling with each other and most of them are related. In origin it refers to a container of wriggling worms to be used as bait for anglers. The worms form a tangle and are practically impossible to separate. The expression often includes the word 'open', as *If you try to sort out the quarrel between your neighbours you'll really be opening a can of worms*. It is American in origin and in Britain dates from the later part of the twentieth century. It is found in informal or slang contexts.

cards on the table, lay one's see *lay one's cards on the table*

carry the can is an idiom cliché meaning to take responsibility or blame where that properly lies with, or should be shared by, someone else, as *He can't complain about having to carry the can for his department's mistake. That's part of the manager's job*, and *The rest of the robbers ran away and left the get-away driver to carry the can*. As a cliché the expression dates from the second part of the twentieth century and is still a popular cliché today, being used in informal and slang contexts. In origin it is probably a military expression which was used to refer to the man selected to carry the beer for a group and to carry the can back when it was empty.

cart before the horse, put the is an idiom cliché meaning to reverse the correct or usual order of things, as *He has painted the walls before the ceiling. Trust him to put the cart before the horse*. It became a cliché in the eighteenth century although the expression is considerably older and the concept even older still, going back to Greek and Roman times. It is still a common cliché today.

castles in the air is a hackneyed phrase used to refer to dreams of future happi-

ness, wealth, etc that are unrealistic and so very unlikely to come true, as *She talks of buying a house in the South of France but it's just castles in the air*. The expression **build castles in the air** has been a semi-proverbial saying for some considerable time and **castles in the air** has been a cliché since the nineteenth century. It is still common today. An expression that conveys the same sentiment is **castles in Spain**, although this is now rare.

cat got your tongue? see *has the cat got your tongue?*

catch one's death is a hackneyed phrase that exaggerated the danger of getting cold or wet, as *Surely you're not going out without a coat in that rain. You'll catch your death*. The expression has been popular since the late nineteenth century. It is still used today, but often by older people, in informal or dialectal contexts.

catch redhanded is an idiom cliché which means to find someone in the very act of committing a crime or misdeed, as *He was taking the money from the till when the boss came in and caught him redhanded*. Originally the crime concerned was murder, the image being of a murderer caught with blood on his or her hands. The expression was later extended to cover other crimes. It has been common since the nineteenth century and is still common today, often being used in humorous contexts, as *Ah, caught you redhanded eating chocolates. I thought you were supposed to be on a diet*.

Catch 22 is an allusion cliché used to describe a situation in which one cannot possibly win, as *It's a Catch 22 situation for young people today. They cannot get jobs without experience but they cannot gain experience without jobs*. It is an allusion to the title of a book by Joseph Heller

Catch 22 (1961). The catch refers to the plight of Captain Yossarian, an American bombardier. He wanted out of taking part in any more bombing missions since he did not wish to be killed. The best way to bring this about was to be declared crazy and so he tried to become so categorized. However he was told that if someone wanted to be grounded out of concern for his life that was clearly the thought of a sane mind and he could not be declared crazy. The phrase became a cliché in Britain in the 1970s and is still popular today.

caught napping is an idiom cliché used to indicate that someone has been caught unawares or offguard, as *The first snow of winter caught the roads department napping. They had not enough grit.* As a cliché it dates from the twentieth century and is still popular today in informal contexts. The sentiment was used by Shakespeare in *The Taming of the Shrew* (4:2) 'Nay, I have Ta'en you napping, gentle love.' In origin it refers to finding someone having a nap or short sleep. It is also found in the active form **catch someone napping**

caught with one's trousers down is an idiom cliché meaning discovered in an embarrassing or compromising position, as *He was really caught with his trousers down. He was sitting in the boss's office with his feet up on his desk and smoking a cigar when the boss walked in.* The expression dates from the twentieth century and is still popular, the American equivalent being **caught with one's pants down**. There are two suggested origins. One is that it refers to a man who is having an illicit love affair and is caught in the act by his lover's husband. The other is that it refers to a man who is encountered relieving himself outside, possibly a soldier encountered by one of the enemy. The expression is also found in the active form **catch with one's trousers down**.

cause célèbre (French for 'famous case') is a foreign cliché used to refer to a legal trial or case that attracts a great deal of attention, as *The trial of Ruth Ellis was a cause célèbre because she was the last woman in Britain to be hanged.* As a cliché it dates from the middle of the nineteenth century. It is not so common today as it once was, although it is still used by journalists, often of cases that are in fact quite minor.

chain reaction is a hackneyed phrase and vogue cliché referring to a situation involving a series of events, in which each event causes another, as *When Jack refused to go to school it started a chain reaction among the children in the district. Jim wouldn't go if Jack wasn't going and Jim's sister wouldn't go if Jim wasn't going.* It is one of several clichés which have their origins in technical language, since a **chain reaction** was originally a term used in chemistry and nuclear physics in the 1930s and referred to a reaction that created energy or products that in turn caused further reactions without further energy input from outside. The expression passed into the general language and became popular in the 1970s. As a modern cliché it is still widespread, its technical connections having been largely forgotten by all but specialists. Very often the idea of a series of changes has also been lost and the phrase is used simply to describe any change, often quite minor.

chalk and cheese see *different as chalk and cheese*

chalk it up to experience is an idiom cliché indicating that there is nothing to be done about some setback or piece of misfortune, as *It's annoying that they promised you the job and then turned you down but there's nothing you can do about it. You might as well chalk it up to experience.* The expression **chalk it up** was used to refer to the practice of keeping a record of who owed what in pubs, etc by chalking it on a slate or blackboard. Later, scores in games were chalked on slates. **Chalk it up to experience** dates from around the nineteenth century and today is being used mainly in informal contexts.

champing at the bit is an idiom cliché meaning showing signs of great impatience, as *I wish my husband would hurry up with the car. The children are champing at the bit to go to the seaside.* It has been in use as a figurative expression since the beginning of the twentieth century. It is a popular cliché today, being used in informal contexts. In origin it refers to a racehorse chewing at its bit at the start of a race while waiting impatiently to be off.

change of scene, a is a hackneyed phrase used to indicate a move from one place or situation to another, often temporary and often regarded as being beneficial in some way, as *She was ill and has gone to spend a few days by the sea for a change of scene,* and *He thinks that he's been in the computing industry too long and he's looking for a change of scene.* As a cliché the expression dates from the late nineteenth century and it is still extremely common in all but the most formal of contexts. In origin it refers to the changing of a scene in the theatre.

chapter of accidents, a is a hackneyed phrase meaning a series of misfortunes, as *Don't mention our holiday. It was a chapter of accidents from beginning to end,* and *The car got a flat tyre, I broke the heel of my shoe and I got caught in a thunderstorm. Talk about a chapter of accidents!*

charmed life, lead a is a hackneyed phrase meaning to be extremely lucky, to be involved in a great many risky or dangerous situations but always to remain unscathed, as *The mountaineer has taken part in many dangerous expeditions but he's never even had a minor injury. He leads a charmed life,* and *He's been involved in a great many shady deals but the police never catch up with him. He seems to lead a charmed life.* The expression was used by Shakespeare in *Macbeth* (5:8) in which Macbeth says 'I bear a charmed life which must not yield to one of woman born.' It has been a cliché since the middle of the nineteenth century and is still common today. It literally means to lead a life that is protected in some way by magic.

cheap and cheerful is a catchphrase cliché used to refer to furniture or clothes with the implication that to have spent more would not have been justified. It is sometimes used in a deliberately deprecatory way, just as one might say 'This old thing!' of a dress, as *Oh do you like it? We just wanted something cheap and cheerful for the children's rooms.* It is also sometimes used as a not very subtle way of criticizing someone else's taste, often in rather a bitchy way, as *That's a nice dress you're wearing – something cheap and cheerful for the summer.* As a cliché it dates from around the 1960s.

cheek by jowl is a doublet cliché, cheek and jowl being more or less synonymous. It is used to mean very close, often excessively, uncomfortably or inappropriately close, as *He is such a snob that he objects to going on buses and standing cheek by jowl with what he calls the rabble,* and *In that part of town historic old buildings stand cheek by jowl with ghastly concrete office blocks.* The expression has been current since the sixteenth century. It has been a cliché since the middle of the eighteenth century and is still widespread today.

cheque is in the post, the is a hackneyed phrase used as a business cliché. It is often, in fact, used as a euphemism for 'It is our intention to put the cheque in the post as soon as we can spare the money but we do not wish to admit that', or even as a downright lie told in the hope that the potential recipient of the cheque will stop harassing the potential payer. To those whose salary is paid into a bank automatically at the end of the month this cliché may sound amusing. To those who work freelance it has an all too familiar and depressing ring. As a cliché it dates from the twentieth century and is rampant today.

chiefs and no Indians, all see **all chiefs and no Indians**

children of all ages is a hackneyed phrase usually used in rather hearty tones when trying to interest people in some form of merchandise or leisure venture, as *This board game is suitable for children of all ages*, and *Children of all ages will enjoy a day out in the theme park*. The implication is that something will appeal not only to actual children but to those who are youthful enough in their attitudes, and fun-loving enough, to enjoy it as adults. As a cliché it dates from the twentieth century and is still found today. It almost always sounds cringe-making.

chip off the old block, a is a hackneyed phrase used to describe someone, often a son, who is very like a parent, often his father, in attitude, talent, character, appearance, etc, as *He is a very talented writer. He's a chip off the old block and no mistake*, and *He is a real chip off the old block. He's just as mean as his father was and never gives a penny to charity*. The expression dates from the seventeenth century, although it originally took the form of a **chip of the old block**. As a cliché it dates from the eighteenth century.

chop and change is a doublet cliché meaning to make constant changes, as *I thought that she had finished writing the novel but she keeps chopping and changing it*. The expression dates from around the middle of the sixteenth century and as a cliché dates from the eighteenth century. It is still a common cliché today. Literally it means to barter and exchange.

circumstances beyond our control is a hackneyed phrase used as an official excuse for things that have gone wrong, whether or not the circumstances were beyond the control of the person making the excuse. It is used, for example, in letters replying to complaints about late orders, as *We are sorry that you have not received the goods which you ordered. This is due to circumstances beyond our control and we have contacted the manufacturer*. It used to be a favourite of people giving reasons for delays or cancellations on public transport, in reality giving no reason or explanation at all. The cliché dates from the twentieth century. It is still used today, but probably less frequently, perhaps because people have become more inventive about composing excuses, perhaps because the public are now less likely to accept a bland excuse, or perhaps because people are less polite and less likely to answer letters or bother giving excuses. When it is used it is found either in fairly formal contexts or in humorous contexts.

clear the air is an idiom cliché meaning to remove any confusion or misunderstanding from the situation, to make an atmosphere less tense, as *There is such an atmosphere in the office since things started going missing. I wish the police would find the culprit and clear the air*, and *She thinks he is trying to get her job. It's time she had it out with him and cleared the air*. The expression became popular in the late nineteenth century and is still popular in all but the most formal contexts. In origin it refers to the sultry atmosphere before a storm that is dispersed when it starts to rain.

clear the decks is an idiom cliché meaning to get ready for action, sometimes carrying the implication that any obstacles or details that are in the way should be removed, as *Right then, let's clear the decks for the party!* and *We'd better clear the decks for the delivery of new stock.* As a figurative expression it dates from the eighteenth century and as a cliché from the late nineteenth century. It is still common in fairly informal contexts today. In origin the phrase refers to the clearing of the decks of ships in preparation for battle.

close shave, a is an idiom cliché meaning a narrow, and often lucky, escape, as *That was a close shave. I nearly bumped into my teacher and I'm supposed to be off sick.* The expression dates from the nineteenth century and in origin it refers to the fact that if someone shaves very closely he may well cut himself badly, especially when shaving with an old open-style razor. As a cliché it is common today in informal contexts. An alternative form of the expression is **a close thing**.

close your eyes and think of England is a catchphrase cliché, possibly originally given as a piece of advice to someone living abroad in circumstances which were either hard or not to their taste, but becoming more popular in a sexual context as a piece of advice to a woman who did not wish to have sexual intercourse with her husband but who thought that she had to put up with it. The catchphrase dates from the late nineteenth century. As a cliché today it is used in humorous or satirical contexts, as *Her new husband is very rich but he is old and ugly. I don't know how she can bear to be with him but I suppose she must just lie back and think of England.*

coals to Newcastle is an idiom cliché meaning something unnecessary or superfluous, as *It's a kind thought but please don't buy a cake for my mother. It'll be coals to Newcastle. She spends half her time baking, and I wouldn't move there to find a job. It would be coals to Newcastle. They have enough unemployed there already.* The extended form of the expression is **carry coals to Newcastle**. It was used figuratively from the seventeenth century and is a common cliché today. Newcastle-upon-Tyne was a centre of the coal-mining industry.

coast is clear, the is an idiom cliché meaning that one can escape or proceed without the likelihood of getting caught because there is no one watching, as *The reporters are waiting to interview her. She has asked us to tell her when they've gone and the coast is clear,* and *He stole the money from the old man's house while his sister kept watch to make sure that the coast was clear.* The expression has been popular since the eighteenth century and is still common today in informal contexts. In origin it may refer to smugglers commenting on the absence of coastguards from the shore.

cold blood, in is a hackneyed phrase used to describe an act carried out with calculation and cruelty, as *She did not kill her husband in a fit of passion. She poisoned him in cold blood.* As a cliché it is very frequently associated with murder and is common today. In origin it refers to an old belief that the blood was very hot when one was excited but very cold when one was calm.

cold feet, get is an idiom cliché meaning to become afraid and decide against taking some form of action that one had hitherto plucked up courage to do, as in *He was going to ask her to marry him but at the last* *minute he got cold feet,* and *She was going to throw in her job and work her way round the world but she got cold feet.* The expression dates from the nineteenth century and is still a widespread cliché today, being really the only phrase that springs to mind to describe the situation. Its origin is uncertain. It has been suggested that it may derive from soldiers retreating from the battle because their feet were frozen.

cold light of day, in the is a hackneyed phrase referring to a time of calm and careful thought, as *It seemed like a good idea to give up our jobs and go to Greece when we had had a few drinks, but next morning in the cold light of day it seemed a mad scheme.* An earlier form of the expression was **in the cold light of reason.** This is still found but it is less common. The expression dates from the nineteenth century and is a common cliché today, aptly describing the effect that reality has on our wilder enthusiasms.

cold shoulder, give the is an idiom cliché meaning to snub or ostracize someone, as *Her fellow workers all gave her the cold shoulder when they discovered that she had beaten her children.* The expression dates from the nineteenth century and appears in the works of Walter Scott. In origin it may refer historically to giving cold shoulder of mutton to guests, instead of a hot meal of a better cut of meat, thereby indicating that they were not welcome and so snubbing them.

cold water on, pour is an idiom cliché meaning to discourage or lessen enthusiasm for, as *The children wanted to sleep in a tent in the garden overnight but their parents poured cold water on the idea.* The concept dates from Roman times, having been used by Plautus. As a cliché it dates from the nineteenth century and is still widespread.

come back, all is forgiven is a catchphrase cliché used humorously or ironically to refer to someone who has left, or been dismissed from, a job, organization, etc, as *None of us can figure out the filing system. Come back Mary, all is forgiven.* The expression probably dates from the end of the nineteenth century and was a popular military catchphrase. As a cliché it dates from the second part of the twentieth century.

come full circle is a hackneyed phrase used to refer to a situation in which events have run their course and things have returned to their original state, as *His greatgrandfather had to sell the manor house in the nineteenth century but he made a fortune in oil and has bought it back again. Things have come full circle.* The idea is that a cycle has been completed. The expression is often extended to **the wheel has come full circle,** an expression that was probably originated by Shakespeare in *King Lear* (5:3) 'The wheel is come full circle.'

come home to roost is an idiom cliché referring to the fact that someone's mistakes, misdeeds, etc have rebounded on him or her, as *He was really horrible to Jim when he was a department manager and Jim was a trainee, but his nastiness has come to roost since Jim was made managing director.* The expression is frequently found in its fuller version **chickens come home to roost,** as *She had been embezzling small amounts of money for years but her chickens only came home to roost when the company was taken over.* The sentiment was referred to by Robert Southey in *The Curse of Kehama* (1809): 'Curses are like young chickens; they always come home to roost.' As a cliché the full expression dates from the middle of the nineteenth century. Both the shortened and full versions are still common today. In origin it refers to chickens returning to their roost at the end of the day, this concept of course predating modern chicken rearing systems in which the birds lack that kind of freedom.

come into the body of the kirk is a hackneyed phrase used to a group of people to encourage them to move closer together, especially to encourage them to sit together in a hall, rather than be spread round it, as *You latecomers needn't sit at the back. Come into the body of the kirk.* In origin it refers to people going to sit in the main part of a church, 'kirk' being the Scots word for church. As a cliché it now tends to sound rather cosy, although it is the kind of expression to which some people, especially now older people, become addicted, often to the annoyance of their listeners.

come out of the closet is an idiom cliché meaning publicly to admit that one indulges in a pastime that others might disapprove of, and that one has hitherto kept secret. It can be used of a wide range of interests and is often used humorously, as *We all thought that she was such an intellectual but she came out of the closet and told us that she reads romantic novels,* and *He is a gourmet chef but he came out of the closet and admits to using tomato ketchup on his own food.* Originally its use was restricted to people revealing that they were homosexual and in this sense it is now usually shortened to **come out.** Closet in American English means a cupboard or wardrobe. **Come out of the closet** in its more general use dates from around the mid 1970s and is still common today in informal contexts.

come to grief is a hackneyed phrase used to mean to end in disaster, to fail, as *Our plans for expansion came to grief when the recession started.* The expression has been popular since around the middle of the nineteenth century. As a cliché it is still common today, being used in all but the most formal contexts. Grief is a rather old-fashioned word for sorrow or unhappiness.

come up and see my etchings is a catchphrase cliché used to ask someone to visit one's flat, ostensibly to admire one's collections of drawings, but really with a view to having a sexual relationship. Although it originally applied only to men inviting women, in these more enlightened days the expression has achieved unisex status. Its early history is uncertain but it is likely that the catchphrase dates from around the beginning of the twentieth century. People who use it today do so in a consciously dated way for humorous effect, as though satirizing an old melodrama. The same kind of sentiment is expressed in **come up some time and see me,** which Mae West uses in the 1933 film *She Done Him Wrong.*

come up to scratch see *up to scratch*

come to the same thing is a hackneyed phrase indicating that one thing or situation is basically much the same as another, that in essence there is no difference between them, as *It comes to the same thing whether you say he was declared redundant or whether you say he was sacked.* A fuller form of the expression is **come to the same thing in the end.** As a cliché it dates from the end of the nineteenth century and is still widespread today.

commanding lead, a is a hackneyed phrase used to indicate the margin by which someone or something is winning. It can apply to a wide range of contexts such as sport, as *Last year's champion has a commanding lead in the marathon event*, and *The favourite had a commanding lead but fell at the last fence*, to elections or political opinion polls, as *In the last published opinion poll the opposition had a commanding lead over the government*. It is a cliché much used by journalists and often the commanding lead referred to is not as substantial as the phrase suggests.

comme il faut (French for 'as it should be') is a foreign cliché used to mean according to etiquette or convention, as *It used not to be comme il faut for a woman to enter a church without wearing a hat*, and *Until fairly recently it was considered comme il faut for men to stand up when a woman came into a room*. The expression was popular in English from the early part of the nineteenth century. It is still found today but its use is often considered rather pompous. It is otherwise used in humorous or ironic contexts.

common or garden is a hackneyed phrase meaning ordinary or common, as *I'm looking for a pair of common or garden sandals. I don't want to spend a fortune on them*, and *We're looking for a common or garden radio for our daughter. We don't want anything hi-tech*. The phrase was originally used of plants that could commonly be found with or in gardens and has been popular since the end of the nineteenth century. It is still a widespread cliché found in a variety of contexts.

conspicuous by his (her or **its) absence** is a hackneyed phrase indicating that the absence of someone or something is noticeable and likely to be remarked upon, as *The politician was conspicuous by his absence from the dinner. The press are saying that he is going to resign*, and *Any mention of tenants' rights is conspicuous by its absence*

from this agreement. The idea goes back to Roman times, having being used by the historian, Tacitus. The English St Lord John Russell used the expression in an election address in 1859 and it became popular shortly after that. As a cliché it is still used today. It can sound rather pompous but it is also used in a humorous or ironic way, as *Isn't it odd that Jack is always conspicuous by his absence whenever there is any work to be done?*

cool as a cucumber is a simile cliché used to indicate the measure of someone's calmness or composure, as *Everyone else was in a panic when the house went on fire but mother was cool as a cucumber*. The popularity of the phrase probably owes as much to alliteration as it does to the fact that the inside of a cucumber is very cold – hence its almost routine presence in salads. The association of coldness and cucumbers was remarked upon by the English dramatists Beaumont and Fletcher in *Cupid's Revenge* (1615) in which 'young maids' were described as being 'as cool as cucumbers'. The expression is a popular cliché today, as is **cool, calm and collected** which is also used to emphasize someone's self-composure.

corridors of power is a hackneyed phrase used to describe the power invested in government ministries and top civil servants. The expression was first used by the English novelist C P Snow in *Homecomings* (1956) and was the title of one of his later novels (1964). As a modern cliché it is used to refer collectively to the people who make the decisions that govern our lives. Such people are often projected as being more concerned with personal power and internal power struggles than the issues for which they are responsible, as *What do those in the corridors of power care about the plight of old age pensioners?* As a modern cliché it is has a special appeal for political journalists.

cost the earth see *arm and a leg, cost an*

coup de grâce (French for 'blow of mercy') is a foreign cliché used to mean a finishing stroke, something that finishes something off, as *The firm had been struggling for several years and the start of the recession delivered the coup de grâce.* The phrase means literally 'a stroke of grace' as though the event or situation in question was on the whole a good thing, as though it were putting someone or something out of his or its misery. This idea that the finishing stroke is advantageous in some way has not necessarily survived in the modern cliché which frequently simply means that the end has come for someone or something. As an English expression it became popular in the nineteenth century. It is still used today, particularly by people of a literary bent.

cover a multitude of sins is a quotation cliché meaning to be applicable to a wide range of things, especially undesirable things, as *He says that he sells antiques but the term antiques can cover a multitude of sins.* In origin the phrase is a deliberately misapplied Biblical quotation, from *1 Peter* (3:8) 'Charity shall cover the multitude of sins'.

crazy like a fox is a simile cliché meaning seemingly very foolish but actually very cunning, as *People say that he was crazy to marry a much older woman but he was crazy like a fox. She is very wealthy and he has expensive tastes.* It was the title of a book by the American humorist S J Perelman (1945), although the phrase probably dates in America from the 1930s. Its popularity was increased by being the title of an American TV series (1984). As a cliché in Britain it is more recent, probably dating from the second part of the 1980s.

Foxes are traditionally associated with cunning and so if they appear to be crazy, the implication is that there must be a hidden reason.

crème de la crème (French for 'cream of the cream') is a foreign cliché used to refer to the very best. It was popular in English by the beginning of the nineteenth century. As a modern cliché it is used either by educated people who could be accused of showing off their knowledge and sounding rather pompous, or by people who are using it in a humorous or ironic way. The term was used by Muriel Spark in her novel *The Prime of Miss Jean Brodie* and the popular film version probably led to a renaissance, although mostly in its humorous use.

cross that bridge when one comes to it is an idiom cliché meaning to delay a decision or action until it becomes necessary and so avoid anticipating trouble, as *We have enough problems organizing the concert without worrying about the artists not turning up. We'll just have to cross that bridge when we come to it.* Its ultimate origins are unknown although the phrase is based on a proverb **don't cross the bridge until you come to it**, referred to as an old proverb by Henry Wadsworth Longfellow in *The Golden Legend* (1851). The cliché is still widespread today, but is anathema to those who like to legislate for every possible contingency.

cross the Rubicon is an idiom cliché meaning to take action from which there is no turning back, as *He has left his job and they won't take him back. The Rubicon is crossed.* A popular expression since the eighteenth century, it refers to the crossing of the River Rubicon, which separated Italy and Cisalpine Gaul, by Julius Caesar in 49 BC. This action was carried out with the aim of invading Italy and was done in defiance of Pompey and the Senate. As a modern cliché it is used mainly in either a serious or humorous context by people of a literary bent.

cross to bear, have a is an allusion cliché indicating that someone has to put up with some form of burden or distress. The allusion is to the Biblical account in which Simon the Cyrene had to carry the cross upon which Christ would be crucified at Calvary. The cross symbolized not only the suffering of Christ but the distress of human beings. As a modern cliché the expression tends to be used in a less serious or ironic way to describe something that is relatively trivial, as *Our neighbours have dogs and we don't like dogs. Still they are pleasant people and all of us have a cross to bear,* and *The new job comes with a company car and an expense allowance. Ah well, all of us have a cross to bear.*

cry all the way to the bank see *laugh all the way to the bank*

cry over spilled milk is a proverb cliché which expresses the folly of spending time regretting something that has been done and cannot be undone, as *you threw your money away when you bought that car but there is to use crying over spilled milk.* The idea dates from the seventeenth century and the expression became a cliché towards the end of the nineteenth century. The cliché is one of those rather bracing expressions that tend to irritate the listener rather than offer comfort or encouragement. All of us like to spend some time wallowing in our own misfortune and this cliché represents an attempt to deprive us that pleasure. The origin is obvious. Once milk is spilled one cannot retrieve it for use.

cry wolf is an idiom cliché meaning to give a false alarm, having done it so often that no one any longer takes it seriously, as *She kept claiming to be ill to attract sympathy. When she collapsed, they thought she was crying wolf and ignored her.* The expression has been a cliché since the nineteenth century and is still popular today. In origin it refers to a story about a shepherd boy watching his sheep on a hillside. Because he was lonely and afraid he used to call 'Wolf!' so that people would come to his aid and he would have company. After people had responded to his call several times and found nothing, they ignored his call when a wolf really did attack his sheep.

cup that cheers, the is an allusion cliché referring to tea, and found in Cowper's *The Task* (1783) 'the cups that cheer but not inebriate'. Originally the expression was used to differentiate between tea and alcoholic drinks. As a modern cliché it is dated and is mostly used humorously. Its use is frequently considered pompous.

cut a long story short is a hackneyed phrase which does not always live up to its promise. Although it is a seeming pledge to abbreviate rather than launch into an involved tale, it is sometimes used meaninglessly by people who go right on to tell the full version. The expression has been a cliché since the late nineteenth century and is still commonly used today, particularly by people to whom it has become a habit.

cut and dried is a hackneyed phrase used to describe something that is settled and definite, as *We had hoped to put the idea to the vote but the plans were all cut and dried before we got to the meeting.* The expression dates from the early eighteenth century and is still a widespread cliché today. In origin it probably refers to timber which is cut and dried before being used.

cut both ways is a hackneyed phrase meaning to have an effect on both sides of a question, to have advantages and disadvantages for both parties involved, as *Having a long term of notice on your contract cuts both ways. It means that if they declare you redundant you will have a lot of time to find another job, but if you are offered something better by another company they might not hold the job open that long.*

cut no ice is an idiom cliché meaning to make no impression on, to have no influence on, as *She usually sweet-talks people into doing what she wants but her flattery cut no ice with the headmaster.* The expression is American in origin and dates from the late nineteenth century. Its origin is uncertain, but it is perhaps derived from an icebreaker that fails to break up ice floes as it should.

cut one's coat according to one's cloth is an idiom cliché used to mean to adapt one's expenditure to one's means, as *He is always going to be in debt until he learns to cut his coat according to his cloth.* The expression has been a cliché since the nineteenth century and is still popular today among the ranks of people who like to offer other people advice. The cliché is usually received with irritation

by those to whom it is directed since it sounds so smug. In origin the phrase refers to tailoring.

cutting edge, at the is an idiom cliché which is also a vogue cliché. As is the case with several vogue clichés, it has its origins in specialist language, since it was originally used in the field of science and technology. It was used to refer to research that was in the forefront of new developments, its use being then extended to the general language to cover a wide range of contexts, as *He is a competent enough modern artist but no-one could say that he was at the cutting edge,* and *As a musician he tends to play traditional pieces. His programme never contains any material at the cutting edge.*

cynosure of all eyes is an allusion cliché used to refer to someone who is certain of attention, as *When she entered the room in that dress she was the cynosure of all eyes.* The expression has been a cliché since the nineteenth century. As a modern cliché it is mostly found in formal contexts. It is an allusion to John Milton's *L'Allegro* (1632) 'the cynosure of neighb'ring eyes.'

D

daddy of them all, the is a hackneyed phrase, found in informal contexts, and meaning the finest, greatest, most extreme, etc example of something, whether pleasant or unpleasant, as *He's caught big fish before, but that's the daddy of them all,* and *They've had rows before but this one's the daddy of them all.*

daggers drawn, at is an idiom cliché. It describes people who are very hostile towards each other, as *It is difficult working in a firm where the two partners are at daggers drawn.* In origin the allusion is to two enemies with unsheathed daggers who are about to fight.

damage, what's the see *what's the damage?*

damned clever, these Chinese is a catchphrase cliché used in 'The Goon Show', a zany BBC comedy radio show, featuring Peter Sellers, Harry Secombe and Spike Milligan, which was first broadcast between 1952 and 1960. It was an extremely popular series which became a cult, and its devotees still use this phrase, as do some younger people who have been attracted to the series from hearing recordings of it. The Chinese were popularly supposed to be clever and wily, in the way that other races are supposed to have other characteristics. The term is used in describing something exceptionally clever or cunning, with or without Chinese connections. Thus a piece of labour-saving electrical or electronic equipment might elicit the remark.

damn with faint praise is a quotation cliché meaning to compliment with so little enthusiasm that the supposed compliment creates the opposite effect, suggesting at best a lukewarm approval or at worst an understated disapproval, as *When the music critic said that her playing was an interesting interpretation of the piece, the pianist felt that she had been damned by faint praise.* This is a long established cliché, being originally a quotation from Alexander Pope's *Epistle to Dr Arbuthnot* (1733) 'Damn with faint praise, assent with civil leer, and, without sneering, teach the rest to sneer.'

damp squib, a is an idiom cliché meaning something which turns out to be a complete failure or flop, especially when it has promised to be very successful, exciting, etc, as *The protest meeting about the new road was a damp squib. Hardly anyone turned up.* The expression is usually found in rather informal contexts. Originally it refers to a small firework which, if damp, would fail to explode.

dance attendance on is a hackneyed phrase meaning to carry out someone's every wish and obey every whim. It has been in the language since the sixteenth century, at first in the sense of waiting for someone in authority, such as a monarch or noble, to grant one an audience. As a modern cliché it is used in a derogatory way, as *Her lazy husband expects her to dance attendance on him all weekend.* The term has its origins in the old custom of a bride having to dance with all the wedding guests at the wedding feast.

dancing in the streets tonight see *there'll be dancing in the streets tonight*

Daniel come to judgement, a is a quotation cliché from Shakespeare's *Merchant of Venice* (4:1), being the phrase with which Shylock first greets Portia in her role as judge. In his opinion she, like Daniel in the Bible, she is displaying wisdom beyond her years. As a cliché, now usually used by people of literary tastes, either in formal or ironical contexts, it is used to refer to someone in a decision-making role whom one considers to be exceptionally effective, largely because his/her judgement coincides with one's own.

Darby and Joan is a quotation cliché which is used to refer to an old couple who have been happily married for a long time, as *All their friends seem to be divorced but Mr and Mrs Jones are a real Darby and Joan*. The phrase was coined by Henry Woodfall, who used it in a ballad he wrote about the long-lasting and loyal relationship of his employer, John Darby, and his wife, Joan. In modern usage it may refer to any elderly couple, whether happy or not, and is sometimes used ironically of young people, as *they've been going out for six months now – a real Darby and Joan*.

darken someone's door is a hackneyed phrase which is always used in the negative, as *The delinquent son was told never to darken his father's door again*, and *'Get out and don't dare darken my door again,' he shouted in fury*. It indicates that someone should go away and not return and is used nowadays in rather literary or formal contexts by older rather than younger people. As a cliché the expression dates from the nineteenth century, while the origin is a reference to someone's doorway being darkened by a visitor's shadow.

dark horse, a is an idiom cliché meaning a person who may have unexpected qualities or abilities but tends to keep them secret, as *The shy new girl turned out to be a bit of a dark horse and was the life and soul of the office party*, and *In training he didn't look very good but he proved to be rather a dark horse and won the race*. As a cliché the term dates from the nineteenth century and has it origins in horse-racing, referring to a horse about whose previous record little was known. It is still widespread today.

darkest hour is just before the dawn, the is a hackneyed phrase dating as a cliché from the twentieth century and used as an annoying platitude to encourage someone to believe that things are about to improve, as *I know that things are going badly for you but the darkest hour is just before the dawn*.

dawn on is a hackneyed phrase dating from the nineteenth century and indicating that a person has suddenly begun to understand something, as *It suddenly dawned on him that he had been made a fool of*. The origin is a metaphorical reference to the coming of dawn and so light. This is such a common cliché that many will simply regard it as part of the language.

day in, day out is a hackneyed phrase meaning constantly, with the sense of unrelieved, relentless monotony, as *It rained day in, day out, throughout the whole holiday*, and *Day in, day out, we had to listen to her complaints*.

day of reckoning is a hackneyed phrase meaning the time at which one will be called upon to justify one's actions and when the consequences of said actions will have to be faced, as *The student had a good time going to many parties but he knew the* *day of reckoning would come in exam week.* The term is Biblical in origin referring to the Day of Judgement, when God will pass judgement on all people.

days are numbered used mostly in informal contexts, is a hackneyed phrase indicating that the life, career, usefulness, etc. of someone or something is over, the implication being that that is going to be so short that it can be counted in days. It appears in such contexts, as *We better all look for other jobs. The company's days are numbered,* and *This machine's days are numbered. It's too expensive to run.* The cliché dates from the nineteenth century.

D-day is a hackneyed phrase referring to a day when something important is scheduled to take place, as *The children have been preparing for the exams all term. Tomorrow is D-day.* Historically D-day refers to June 6 1944, the day on which the Allies began their landings in Northern France to stop the advance of the German forces during World War 2. 'D' means day and is simply a military convention used for emphasis, although it is often popularly but wrongly taken to mean 'designated'. As a cliché, D-day now tends to be used by older people who lived through the war.

dead and gone is a doublet cliché which simply emphasizes the fact that someone or something has died or perished, as *They did not appreciate his genius until he was dead and gone,* and *Most of the old village customs are dead and gone.*

dead as a dodo is a simile cliché which simply emphasizes that something is extinct or no longer fashionable or popular. It is used of customs, ideas, attitudes, plans, etc, but not usually of people, as *The tennis club has no active members anymore. It's dead as a dodo,* and *All the old country*

traditions are dead as a dodo in the villages near the city. The dodo was a flightless bird discovered on the island of Mauritius in the early seventeenth century and was extinct by 1700 because it was very easy to catch. The dodo has long been gone but the cliché is still generally popular.

dead body, over my see *over my dead body*

dead but won't lie down is a catchphrase cliché meaning that someone or something has no chance of success but will not recognize the fact and give up, as *He's standing again for president of the club, although he's failed three times already. He's dead but he won't lie down.*

dead duck, a is an idiom cliché, used mostly in informal contexts, meaning someone or something with no hope of success or survival, as *His plan to expand the restaurant is a dead duck without planning permission,* and *If the farmer catches the girl trespassing, she's a dead duck.*

dead from the neck up is an idiom cliché, used in informal or slang contexts to indicate that someone is extremely stupid, as though he/she had no brain, as *Don't expect him to come up with any ideas. He's dead from the neck up.*

dead horse, flog a see *flog a dead horse*

dead in the water is an idiom cliché which is used to describe something which has no hope of success, as *During the recession any plans for expansion are dead in the water.* It is frequently used in business jargon to refer to a company that is ripe for takeover since it is simply drifting rather than making any progress. The cliché dates from the twentieth century and in origin the allusion is to dead fish.

dead loss, a is a hackneyed phrase used in informal contexts to mean someone or something completely useless, ineffective, etc, as *She's very clever but she's a dead loss as a teacher*, and *This holiday resort was a dead loss for young people. There was nothing to do.*

dead men's shoes is an idiom cliché referring to the job or position of someone who has either died or has left under unfortunate circumstances, as *There are few opportunities for promotion in the firm. It's a case of waiting for dead men's shoes.* The cliché dates from the nineteenth century. The origin is a reference to someone waiting for someone to die so that he/she can inherit his/her shoes or other goods.

dead of night is a hackneyed phrase meaning the middle of the night. The expression is most commonly found in rather literary or formal contexts, as *The children were found wandering at dead of night in the forest.* In origin the phrase compares the most silent, darkest part of the night to the silence and darkness of death.

dead to the world is a hackneyed phrase meaning very deeply asleep, so as to be completely oblivious of one's surroundings, as if one were dead, as *We tiptoed so as not to wake the children but they were dead to the world.* The cliché dates from the twentieth century.

dead, wouldn't be seen is a hackneyed phrase indicating a complete disinclination or aversion to doing something, as *I wouldn't be seen dead wearing that school uniform*, and *She wouldn't be seen dead going out with him.* It is always used in an informal or slang context.

deaf as a post is a simile cliché meaning extremely deaf. The simile dates from the

sixteenth century but as a modern cliché the expression tends to be used in a derogatory way, for example by someone irritated at not being able to make himself/herself heard, as *There's no point in asking that old man for directions. He's deaf as a post.*

Dear John letter, a is a hackneyed phrase which refers to a letter or message from a wife, girlfriend or partner to indicate to the recipient that the relationship with the sender is at an end, as *The prospective bridegroom received a Dear John letter on the eve of the wedding.* Originally an American expression, it originated during World War 2, when many servicemen received such letters because of the strain of prolonged separation.

dear life, for is a hackneyed phrase meaning to the best of one's ability, as fast, hard, etc as one can, as *We'll have to run for dear life to catch that bus.* The implication of the phrase is that one is going as fast as possible, etc. as though one's life depended on it. It is usually used in an informal context.

death by a thousand cuts is a catchphrase cliché meaning destruction by a series of minor blows rather by one major one, as *The company gradually went bankrupt as many of their small customers failed to reorder. It was death by a thousand cuts.* The expression is an allusion to the English translation of the phrase 'He who is not afraid of death by a thousand cuts dares to unhorse the emperor' which appears in the Chinese Leader Mao Tsetung's *Little Red Book* (1966).

death, catch one's see *catch one's death*

deathless prose is a hackneyed phrase used nowadays ironically to mean not, as literally, unforgettable prose, but very bad, talentless writing or a piece of unimportant writing, as *'Fourth form essays,'* sighed the teacher, *'another lot of deathless prose.'*

death's door, at is an idiom cliché meaning extremely, or terminally, ill, as *The old man has recovered although they thought he was at death's door.* The origin of the phrase lies in the idea that death was a place that departed souls went to. The expression was used in the sixteenth century and has been considered a cliché since the nineteenth century. It is still common today.

death trap, a is a hackneyed phrase used to indicate something that is dangerous, as *They should do something about the fire precautions in these old buildings. They are real death traps.* The expression is apt to be used in an exaggerated way to indicate something that is only mildly unsafe and is frequently used by journalists.

death warmed up, like is a simile cliché always used in a derogatory and informal context, as *Were you out all night? You look like death warmed up!* It dates from the twentieth century.

delicate condition a is a euphemism cliché for pregnancy. Nowadays people tend to be more frank about pregnancy and the expression tends now to be used by older women, not used to this frankness, as *You should not carry heavy bags in your delicate condition.* It is sometimes used satirically by younger women.

deliver an ultimatum is a hackneyed phrase popular among journalists as well as others to indicate that someone has given someone else a final warning of some kind, as *The terrorists delivered an ultimatum that they would shoot the hostages if their demands were not met immediately.* As is common in journalism, the expression is sometimes considerably more dramatic than the event referred to requires.

de rigueur (French for 'of strictness') a cliché meaning required by etiquette, rules, fashion etc, as *School uniform is absolutely de rigueur on official outings.* It is used in English rather formally, often pompously.

desert a sinking ship is an idiom cliché referring to the fact that people show a distinct tendency to abandon organizations or people that are showing signs that they are about to fail, become bankrupt, etc, as *Most of the firm's employees are looking for new jobs. They are like rats deserting a sinking ship.* The origin of the phrase lies in the fact that rats were said to desert a ship when it was about to founder or run aground.

des res is a hackneyed phrase with its origins in the jargon of twentieth century estate agents. Short for 'desirable residence', it is often used mockingly or ironically, as in *Now that they are married they have moved into a des res on the new estate.*

deus ex machina (Latin for 'god out of a machine') is a foreign cliché only used nowadays in literary or formal and rather pompous contexts. It refers to a person or event that offers unexpected and fortuitous assistance in a difficult or dangerous situation, as *The theatre company thought that they would have to disperse but salvation came in the form of a deus ex machina, John Richards, a wealthy industrialist, who wanted to invest money in the arts.* The origin of the expression lies in ancient Greek theatre where a god appeared on the stage from a machine or mechanical contrivance to resolve some aspect of the plot.

dice with death is an idiom cliché meaning to do something very risky or dangerous, as *That young man is dicing with death driving at that speed.* Its origin refers to playing a game of chance in which dice are thrown.

didn't he do well? a catchphrase cliché having its origins in a remark always made by Bruce Forsyth, the presenter of a late twentieth-century television game show, called 'The Generation Game', at the end of the final game, which involved the winning competitor memorizing as many objects as possible which have passed on a conveyor belt. The cliché is sometimes used ironically to indicate that someone has done badly, as *She just lost us the match. Didn't she do well?*

die in harness is an idiom cliché meaning to die while one is still actively engaged in work, as *The old man was forced to retire although he wanted to die in harness.* The expression is a reference to working horses which died working and so in harness. The expression is still common today although the concept of early retirement has made the practice less common.

die is cast, the is an idiom cliché indicating that a step has been taken from which there is no turning back, as *The die is cast. I've sold the house and now I'll have to move.* It is a translation of the Latin *alea jacta est,* traditionally said to be the comment made by Julius Caesar on crossing the River Rubicon into Italy with his army in 49 BC, thus effectively declaring war on the Roman administration. It is a very common cliché and although it sounds very dramatic it is used in quite ordinary situations. See also **cross the Rubicon.**

die the death is a hackneyed phrase meaning to be completely unsuccessful or in-

effective. It is often used of theatrical productions or players, as *The new comedy act died the death in the local club,* but is also widely used more generally, for example by journalists, as *The politician's speech on education died the death in a hall full of teachers.*

different as chalk and cheese is a simile cliché meaning totally unlike. Obviously chalk and cheese are completely different both in appearance and taste. The cliché is most usually applied to people who are utterly dissimilar, as *You wouldn't believe that they're twins. They're like chalk and cheese.*

different ballgame see **ballgame, a different**

dig one's own grave is an idiom cliché meaning that someone is in the process of bringing about his/her own downfall, as *The employees dug their own grave when they conspired to get rid of their manager. The new manager sacked them all.* A more modern, and more informal, form is **dig a hole for oneself.**

dim and distant past, the is a hackneyed phrase which is also a doublet cliché, dim and distant being near synonyms in this case. Although the phrase originally referred to the distant past, as a cliché it is usually used humorously to refer to the fairly recent past, as *I knew him in the dim and distant past when I was at school.* The cliché dates from the late nineteenth century. An alternative, more informal, form is **the dim and distant.**

dinners, more – than you've etc had hot see **more – than you've etc had hot dinners**

dirty old man, a is a hackneyed phrase used to describe a middle-aged or elderly lecherous man, usually one showing a sexual interest in young women or girls or in pornographic material, as *There were a lot of dirty old men watching a blue move.* The expression is sometimes abbreviated to **DOM**. Dirty old men are typically depicted as wearing raincoats.

dirty tricks campaign, a is a hackneyed phrase used to describe a sustained and underhand attempt to discredit someone or something. Originally the term was used mainly in connection with politics, as *The articles on MPs' private lives were thought to be a dirty tricks campaign to bring down the government*, but it has now become more generally used. The expression is one that frequently appeals to journalists.

dirty work at the crossroads is an idiom cliché meaning dishonest or underhand activity, as in *Some valuable documents have disappeared. We suspect there's been some dirty work at the crossroads.* There is doubt over the origin of the expression although it has been suggested that it derives from the historical practice of burying at crossroads the bodies of people not entitled to a Christian burial in a churchyard.

do someone proud is a hackneyed phrase meaning to treat someone exceptionally well. The expression is frequently used of hospitality, as *The bride's parents certainly did us proud at the wedding reception.*

does your mother know you're out? is a catchphrase cliché used derogatorily to indicate that the user thinks that the person addressed is very naive, inexperienced or is younger than he/she is trying to make out, as *When the young man asked her to dance she said, 'Does your mother know you're out?'* It is always used to convey scorn.

dog eat dog is an idiom cliché meaning extremely ruthless competition, as *The young candidates are all good friends but when it comes to getting a job these days it's a case of dog eat dog.* In origin the expression refers to the fact that if it is the only method of survival then a dog will eat another dog, as indeed humans have been known to eat humans in a similar situation. The expression is widely used. Although it is subject to overuse it remains quite a useful phrase since it captures a situation in very few words.

dog in the manger is an idiom cliché referring to someone who keeps something that is wanted by someone else simply out of selfishness or spite, not because he/she has any wish to have it, as *The child has outgrown all those toys but he's too much of a dog in the manger to lend them to his young cousin.* Its origin lies in a fable about a dog who prevented other animals from going near the hay to eat it although the dog did not want it himself. The expression has been a cliché since the middle of the nineteenth century.

dog's life, a is an idiom cliché meaning a miserable way of life, as *He leads a dog's life with that nagging wife of his*, the wretchedness of a dog's life having been recognized since the sixteenth century. However, given the fact that dogs in Britain at least usually lead a very comfortable existence, the term is now frequently used ironically, as in *'Ah, it's a dog's life,' he said, smoking a cigar and putting his feet up on the coffee table.* The expression dates from the sixteenth century and has been a cliché since the middle of the nineteenth century.

dolce vita, la (Italian for 'the sweet life') is a foreign cliché meaning a life of luxury or indulgence, as *The tired mother sometimes envied the dolce vita of her highly paid single friends.*

donkey's years is an idiom cliché which means a very long time, but in fact it is mostly used as an exaggeration, as *I haven't seen him in donkey's years*. This probably refers to the week before last. Its origin is uncertain but it is possible that the term refers to the fact that the donkey is a comparatively long-lived animal. Alternatively it is a pun on a donkey's ears which are very long. An alternative and common form is **donkey's ages**. The expression dates from the late nineteenth century and is still common today in informal contexts.

don't call us, we'll call you is a catchphrase cliché with its origins in the twentieth-century American entertainment industry. Traditionally, it is said to aspiring actors to whom it is not intended to award park for which they have auditioned. As a cliché it is more generally used as an indication of likely rejection, as *I got an interview for the job but I think it's a case of 'Don't call us, we'll call you,'* and *He said he would phone her but I think he meant 'Don't call us, we'll call you.'*

don't count your chickens before they're hatched is a proverb cliché, still very commonly used as a warning to people not to put faith in things which they don't yet have, as *You'd better not leave your job until you receive an official offer for the other one. Don't count your chickens before they're hatched.* The expression appears in various negative forms, as *It would be unwise to count your chickens before they are hatched.*

don't do anything I wouldn't do! is a twentieth-century catchphrase cliché used to someone going to some social occasion, on holiday, etc. It frequently carries sexual overtones, as *Enjoy the date with your new girlfriend and don't do anything I wouldn't do.* See also **be good!**

don't just stand there is a hackneyed phrase used to incite someone to action, as *Don't just stand there! We have to finish this work today.* It is sometimes lengthened to **don't just stand there, do something** or facetiously to **don't just stand there growing in the carpet.**

don't tell anyone, but . . . is a filler cliché used supposedly to exhort the listener to treat the following statement with confidentiality, but actually as a signpost to indicate that what is to come is a juicy piece of gossip that is too good to keep to oneself. A typical example is *Don't tell anyone but I saw our neighbour with another woman last night.*

do one's own thing is a hackneyed phrase with its origins in the 1960s when such an attitude was part of the Hippie culture. It suggests that individuals should do what they want to, regardless of circumstances. Much of the slang of this era has become dated but this expression has survived as a cliché, as *I don't like joining clubs. I like to do my own thing.* However, it is now frequently used satirically.

do the honours is a hackneyed phrase used when inviting someone to act as host or hostess in some way, such as pouring tea, cutting a cake, opening wine or carving poultry. The expression is still common in certain circles, especially among older and better-off people. Younger people would consider it rather pompous, unless it was being used facetiously. See also **be mother.**

dot, on the see *on the dot*

dot the i's and cross the t's is an idiom cliché meaning to put the finishing touches to something or to take great care over the details of something, as *I have more or less* *finished the proposal but I want to dot the i's and cross the t's before presenting it to the committee.* People who use this expression are often themselves very meticulous and tend to be ridiculed by more slapdash people. In origin the expression refers to the fact that careful writers will take time to dot the i's and cross the t's, a feature of handwriting that can easily be omitted when one is writing quickly or carelessly.

doubting Thomas is an allusion cliché referring to Thomas, one of Christ's apostles, who refused to believe that He had risen from the dead. It has become the standard expression for someone who displays incredulity, as *It is possible that your friend is a changed character. Don't be such a doubting Thomas.*

down-and-out is a twentieth century hackneyed phrase meaning destitute, utterly poverty-stricken. It is used as an adjective, as *down-and-out people without homes* and as a noun, as *the part of the city where the down-and-outs hang out.* The expression, which is frequently, but by no means always, used derogatorily has its origins in boxing, referring to a boxer who gets knocked down and stays down for long enough to be counted out.

down the hatch is a hackneyed phrase used as a toast. The cliché dates from the twentieth century but it is now rather dated. It refers to a hatch or opening in a ship's deck through which cargo and people pass below, the implication being that this resembles the human throat

do you come here often? is a twentieth-century catchphrase cliché traditionally used as a conversation starter at public dances. Now that such dances are no longer a major part of the social scene, apart from discos, the cliché is more com-

monly used facetiously. It might, for example, be said to someone met regularly at the job centre.

draw a blank is an idiom cliché meaning to be unsuccessful, to make no progress, as *The police thought they had a new lead in the murder hunt but they drew a blank.* In origin the expression refers to drawing a blank ticket in a lottery or raffle.

draw in one's horns is an idiom cliché meaning to spend less money, as *Now that I am working only part time I have to draw in my horns.* Although common before that, the phrase became something of a vogue phrase in the recession of the late 1980s and the 1990s. The origin is an allusion to the fact that a snail can withdraw the soft projecting parts of its body, which resemble horns, inside its shell if it feels itself to be in danger. The expression has been considered a cliché since the nineteenth century although it entered the language around the fourteenth century. It is still common today

draw the line at is an idiom cliché meaning to set a limit in one's behaviour, etc that stops short of something, as *The tradesman is not completely honest but he draws the line at breaking the law.* The cliché dates from the nineteenth century and is still common today. In origin it refers to the drawing of lines to indicate boundaries, as in some kinds of games.

dressed to kill is a hackneyed phrase meaning dressed in one's best and most eye-catching clothes, as *The two girls were dressed to kill as they left for the party.* The expression is American in origin and dates from the nineteenth century. It may be an allusion to warriors getting painted up before going to meet the enemy and making a conquest.

dribs and drabs is a doublet cliché meaning very small quantities, as *They expected crowds of people at the opening of the store but the customers came in dribs and drabs.* It is used in informal contexts.

drink like a fish is a simile cliché. Although not particularly apt as a simile it is the standard cliché to describe the act of one who regularly consumes too much alcoholic drink, as *You'll find him in the pub every night. He drinks like a fish.* Fish are open-mouthed most of the time, supposedly giving the appearance of constantly drinking. The expression dates from the seventeenth century.

drive a hard bargain is a hackneyed phrase meaning to make sure that one gets the best deal possible from a transaction, as *We sold the house but the buyers drove a hard bargain and we got less than we hoped.* The association of drive and bargain is a long established one, being used by the English poet, Sir Philip Sidney, who wrote 'there never was bargain better driven' in *My True Love Hath My Heart* (1583).

drop dead is a vogue cliché of the 1990s meaning exceptionally. It is colloquial and most likely to be used by the young and trendy. It is invariably used with a term that flatters, as *Did you see her new boyfriend? He's drop dead gorgeous.*

drop in the bucket, a is an idiom cliché meaning a very small proportion of the actual amount required for something, as *Dad's lending me some money but it's a drop in the bucket compared with what I need for a deposit on the house.* A more formal version of this cliché is **a drop in the ocean**. A very early, slightly different form of the expression is found in *Isaiah* (40:15) in the Bible: 'behold the nations are like a drop of a bucket and are counted as the small dust of the balance.'

drop of a hat, at the is a hackneyed phrase meaning at once, without delay, without much encouragement or excuse, as *His ex-wife made him very unhappy but he would have her back at the drop of a hat.* The cliché dates from the twentieth century and in origin refers to the fact that historically a hat was often dropped as the signal to start a race.

drown one's sorrows is an idiom cliché dating from the twentieth century and meaning to take a great deal of alcoholic drink so that one becomes oblivious of one's troubles. A typical example is *When his marriage was in difficulties he used to go to the pub every night to drown his sorrows.*

dry as a bone is a simile cliché used to indicate extreme dryness, usually of the soil, as *No wonder these plants are dying. The garden is as dry as a bone.* It refers to the dry bones of dead creatures.

dry as dust is a simile cliché meaning extremely dull or boring, as *We stopped going to the lectures because they were dry as dust.* As a cliché it dates from the eighteenth century and is still popular today.

ducking and diving is a hackneyed phrase, almost a doublet cliché since the words are closely related, used to descibe someone who is being evasive, as *You'll never get him to give a straight answer. He's one of those politicians who's always ducking and diving.* As a cliché the expression dates from the later part of the twentieth century. It is very popular today in informal contexts. In origin it refers to someone who is always trying to avoid being seen by ducking or diving out of sight.

Dutch courage is a hackneyed phrase used to refer to courage induced by alcohol in situations in which one might otherwise be afraid to act, as *We'd better go to the pub. We'll need a bit of Dutch courage if we're going to ask the boss for a rise.* The expression has its origins either in the fact that the Dutch historically had a reputation for heavy drinking or to the fact that gin was introduced into England in the seventeenth century by the followers of the Dutch-born William III.

dyed-in-the-wool is a hackneyed phrase used in a derogatory way to describe someone who is of very firmly fixed opinions, as *It was the usual contest between dyed-in-the-wool Tories and dyed-in-the-wool Socialists.* The origin of this twentieth-century cliché lies in the fact that dyed-in-the-wool was once a technical description of yarn which was dyed before it was spun, the implication being that dyed-in-the-wool opinions and attitudes are acquired when one is very young.

E

each and everyone of us is a filler cliché, dating from the nineteenth century, which is used rather pompously simply to mean all of us, as *Each and everyone of us must contribute to this worthy cause.* At best it is used for emphasis but it is frequently simply meaninglessly repetitive.

eager beaver is a hackneyed phrase which is an allusion to the simile **work like a beaver**, the beaver being traditionally famed for its industriousness. The cliché **eager beaver** is used to refer to a person who is particularly enthusiastic or industrious. It is frequently used as a term of disapproval, as *He always wants to go on working when we are ready to go home. He's such an eager beaver!* As a cliché it dates from the twentieth century.

eager for the fray is a quotation cliché, taken from Colley Cibber's version of Shakespeare's *Richard 111* (5:3) 'My soul's in arms and eager for the fray.' It means that one is ready for battle, and as a cliché indicates that one is anxious to get on with whatever challenge awaits one, as *At the start of every new term one of their teaching colleagues always says, 'Well, are you eager for the fray?'* The cliché dates from the nineteenth century and is still used today but often in a satirical context. An alternative, and now slightly more common form, is **ready for the fray**.

eagle eye is a hackneyed phrase which is a metaphorical reference to the fact that the eagle, in common with other birds of prey

is very sharp-eyed. The cliché, which dates from the middle of the nineteenth century can either be a reference to someone's sharp eyesight, as *The pupil smuggled her friend a note but she was spotted by the eagle eye of the headmistress* or to someone's general vigilance, as *The crime rate is quite low here. The area is under the eagle eye of Chief Superintendent Robinson.*

ear to the ground, an is an idiom cliché indicating an ability to keep well-informed. Dating from the late nineteenth century, the expression mostly appears in such phrases as **keep one's ear to the ground**, to make sure that one is well-informed about what is going on around one, as *I hear that there are going to be some changes in the company. Keep your ear to the ground.* The origin is said to lie in the reputed American Indian technique of putting an ear to the ground to hear sounds, such as that of horses, far away.

early bird catches the worm, the is a proverb cliché which is used to recommend or justify an early arrival at an event, etc, as *Get there when the jumble sale opens if you want the best bargains. The early bird catches the worm.* Frequently only part of the proverb is used as an allusion, as *I thought I would be first to arrive. You are an early bird.* The proverb dates from the early seventeenth century.

early days, it's is a hackneyed phrase dating from the twentieth century and indicating that it is too soon in any project, etc to be able to have any results or draw any conclusions, as *The patient doesn't seem to be responding to treatment but it's early days*. The expression is frequently used as an excuse for lack of progress.

early to bed and early to rise (makes a man healthy, wealthy and wise) is a proverb cliché, although only the first part is usually quoted and this usually in the form of allusion as *I want to be in bed before midnight. You know what they say about early to bed, early to rise*. The cliché is mostly used rather pompously or facetiously.

earnest consideration is a hackneyed phrase, often a business cliché, dating from the late nineteenth century and now used mainly in formal contexts, as *We are in receipt of your complaint and will give the matter our earnest consideration*. This is rather a meaningless phrase since the consideration given is likely to be no less perfunctory than any other, only holding out the promise of this as a placatory gesture.

earnest desire is a hackneyed phrase used to suggest that someone is exceptionally anxious to do something. Frequently, however, it is used as an exaggeration of the degree of desire to do something good, or even as a cover-up for a non-desire to do something, simply because it is in the interests of the person supposedly expressing the desire so to do. A typical example would be *The barrister said that his client expressed an earnest desire to lead an honest life in the future*.

earth moved, the is a twentieth century catchphrase cliché usually found in the form of a question **did the earth move for you?** The cliche indicates intensity of sexual satisfaction and is often used humorously in comedy sketches. A form 'Did

thee feel the earth move?' was used by the American novelist Ernest Hemingway in *For Whom the Bell Tolls* (1940).

easier said than done is a hackneyed phrase pointing out the obvious fact that it is easier to talk about doing something than actually to accomplish it. The expression is common in contexts such as *'If you aren't happy in your job', she said, 'you should look for another one.' 'Given the high rate of unemployment, that's easier said than done', he replied*. The expression dates from the fifteenth century and is still a common cliché today.

easy come, easy go is a hackneyed phrase indicating something, usually money, that is acquired without effort and which therefore can be spent or dispensed with in a casual manner without causing any concern, as *He won £300 on a horse and lost it at cards. Easy come, easy go.* and *She has had three husbands in the course of seven years. Easy come, easy go.* The concept is a very old one but the cliché in its current wording dates from the nineteenth century. It is found in informal contexts

easy, easy is rather an unusual cliché in that it is a slogan that has become a hackneyed phrase uttered in hopeful anticipation of victory. As a kind of slogan, it is most usually heard as a chant shouted by football supporters. As a cliché, it has extended its area of influence and is to be found in other areas of competition such as politics, as *We've got the best candidate. It will be easy, easy*. Unfortunately neither the slogan chant nor the cliché, both dating from the twentieth century, always live up to their expectations and they are often simply examples of bravado.

eat, drink and be merry, for tomorrow we die is an allusion cliché, being a Biblical reference to *Isaiah* (22:13) 'Let us eat, drink and be merry, for tomorrow we die'. Brewer in his *Dictionary of Phrase and Fable* comments that this was a traditional saying of the Egyptians who often exhibited a skeleton at their banquet to remind guests of the shortness of life. As a modern cliché it is usually used as an interjection on happy occasions which occur just before the impending arrival of some stressful or unwanted event, as *Last night out before the final exams, lads! Eat drink and be merry, for tomorrow we die!*

eat humble pie is an idiom cliché dating from the late nineteenth century and meaning to acknowledge in a humiliating way that one has been completely wrong, as *She was so adamant that she was right and then she had to eat humble pie in front of everyone when she was proved wrong.* The origin lies in the fact that humble pie is a corruption of 'umble pie', a dish made from the umble or offal of deer and therefore eaten by the servants while the lord and his guests ate the better cuts of meat.

eat like a horse is a simile cliché dating from the eighteenth century and used of someone who consumes large amounts of food, as *He must be ill, eating so little. He usually eats like a horse.* The cliché is usually used in a derogatory way suggesting over-consumption of food. The opposite of this is **eat like a bird** which dates from the twentieth century.

eat one's hat is a hackneyed phrase used to indicate that the speaker is convinced that something is unlikely to be true, etc, as *I'll eat my hat if he gets here in time.* It first appeared in print in *Pickwick Papers* by Charles Dickens (1836) 'Well if I knew as little of life as that, I'd eat my hat and swallow the buckle whole.'

eat out of house and home is a hackneyed phrase meaning that a person eats so much that the host or provider of the food cannot afford the food bills, as *Her children always ask their friends home for meals and they are eating her out of house and home.* The expression is found in Shakespeare's *Henry IV*, Part 2 (2:1) when Falstaff is said by Mistress Quickly to have 'eaten me out of house and home'. The cliché is often used in a humorous context.

eat your heart out! is a catchphrase cliché used nowadays to refer to someone who has cause to be jealous of one, especially when this was not always the case, as *Now that he has a beautiful girlfriend of his own he can say 'Eat your heart out!' to all those Romeos who used to tease him for being womanless.* The cliché used to be a catchphrase popular in show business directed by someone who had just done something particularly well at someone who was famous for this skill, such as an unknown singer saying, *Frank Sinatra, eat your heart out!* As an idiom, **eat one's heart out** means to worry excessively or to pine for something or someone, as if consuming one's heart in grief, as *Ever since her fiancé went to war she's been eating her heart out for him.*

economical with the truth is a euphemism cliché meaning lying or being less than totally truthful, as *He hesitated to be absolutely forthright and call his boss a liar, but he certainly suggested that she was being economical with the truth.* The cliché became popular in the mid 1980s when Sir Robert Armstrong, the British Cabinet Secretary, used the phrase when representing the British government in its attempt to prevent publication of Peter Wright's book *Spycatcher* in the Supreme Court of New South Wales. It became regarded as a kind of symbol of the civil servant's and politician's reluctance to be open, but in fact the expression was not originated by Armstrong or by the civil service. Mark Twain is quoted as having said, 'Truth is a valuable commodity, we need to be economical with it.' And Edmund Burke is said to have commented, 'We practise economy of truth, that we may live to tell it longer.'

egg on one's face, have/be left with is an idiom cliché popular in Britain in the late twentieth century. It means to be left looking a complete fool, as *Our neighbour is always telling us about how efficient and organized she is, but she was left with egg on her face when her car ran out of petrol just after she left home.* It has two possible origins. One is the obvious one, that one has forgotten to wipe the remains of an egg which one has eaten from one's face. The other suggestion is that the egg on one's face is a reference to raw eggs with which a hostile audience might pelt a performer or speaker.

elbow grease is a hackneyed phrase meaning hard physical effort, as *You don't need an expensive polish to bring a shine to that table. You just need elbow grease.* This cliché is based on an old phrase which goes back to the seventeenth century and is still popular today.

elementary, my dear Watson is a catchphrase cliché which refers to Dr Watson, who was the friend and helper of Sherlock Holmes in the Arthur Conan Doyle detective stories, and indicates that something is very simple and obvious. This is not strictly a quotation cliché, since Conan Doyle himself did not actually use the expression, although his son, Adrian, in conjunction with John Dickson, used the phrase in some of the follow-up stories, and adaptors of the stories for films and television also

used it. It is used usually humorously, in such contexts as *Of course I found out the name of her new boyfriend. It was elementary, my dear Watson.*

elephant never forgets, the is a proverb cliché indicating that someone has a good memory and is unlikely to forget something, as *Don't expect the headmistress to forget about your punishment exercise. The elephant never forgets.* The expression is usually used in a light-hearted or humorous context. As to origin it is obviously difficult to assess the extent of an elephant's memory but it has a reputation for having a good memory because it supposedly long remembers trainers or people who worked with it or were kind to it.

eleventh hour, the is a hackneyed phrase meaning the last possible moment, only just in time, as *When the band called off we thought that we would have to cancel the dance, but we found a replacement at the eleventh hour.* It has been suggested that in origin the expression is an allusion to the Biblical parable of the labourers in *Matthew* (20:9) 'And when they came that were hired about the eleventh hour they received every man a denarius.' – a reference to the fact that workers taken on at the eleventh hour of a twelve-hour day received as much pay as those who started work at the beginning of the period. If this is taken as the origin, then the cliché would be categorized as an allusion cliché, but Partridge rejects this as the source and certainly there is no obvious connection apart from the actual wording of the phrase.

embarras de richesses (French for 'embarrassment of riches') is a foreign cliché meaning an overabundance of something. It is used in formal contexts, as *It was felt by the people that for the king to have ten palaces* *was an embarras de richesses* or by someone rather pompous who is showing off his/her knowledge or education. As is the case with many formal or pompous phrases the expression is sometimes used facetiously, as *We knew they wanted children but six seems to be an embarras de richesses.* The phrase is sometimes used in its English translation as *I do not mind the odd visitor but five is an embarrassment of riches.*

empty nest is a twentieth century hackneyed phrase meaning a household from which all the children have left, leaving either the mother or parents lonely. It is frequently found in the expression **the empty nest syndrome,** as *She should get a job to get her out of the house. She's depressed because she's suffering from the empty nest syndrome.* In origin the expression refers to a bird's nest from which all the fledglings have flown.

end of an era, the is a hackneyed phrase meaning the end of some aspect or stage of something. The phrase suggests that it refers to the end of something important, as *When the last steam train was taken out of regular service it was the end of an era.* In fact the cliché is often used to refer to something fairly trivial, as *It was the end of an era when they left the street.* The expression dates from the late nineteenth century and is much used today, especially by journalists, politicians and those making public speeches.

end of one's tether, the is an idiom cliché meaning the limit of what one can endure, the very limit of one's resources, as *I am worried that she may have a nervous breakdown. She is at the end of her tether looking after the children and her elderly parents.* As a cliché the expression dates from the nineteenth century while its origin lies in the tether or rope that ties up an animal

to allow it to move or graze only as far as the length of the tether allows. The cliché, in common with the state it describes, is common today.

end of the road, the is an idiom cliché used to refer to the end of something, such as a business, career, life, etc, as *The recession was the end of the road for a lot of small businesses.* The origin is the obvious one of the end of a stretch of roadway or the end of a journey.

ends of the earth, the is an allusion cliché meaning the remotest parts of the world. The Biblical allusion is to *Psalms* (98:3) 'All the ends of the earth have seen the salvation of our God.' When the earth was thought to be flat, it could be said to have 'ends'. As a cliché the expression dates from the late nineteenth century and nowadays is often used in an exaggerated way for emphasis, as *He would go to the ends of the earth to find something that would make her happy.*

enfant terrible (French for 'terrible child') is a foreign cliché meaning a person, often a young person, with new and unconventional or startling ideas, who embarrasses older or more conventional people by his/her behaviour, remarks or attitude, as *The managing director is now captain of the golf club and an elder of the church but I remember him when he was the enfant terrible of the firm and shocked all the older employees.* It is difficult to find an appropriate English translation of this phrase which is one of the reasons why it is so commonly used.

English as she is spoke is a deliberately ungrammatical hackneyed phrase used to mimic the English of someone who is either not very fluent or is speaking ungrammatically. It is sometimes applied to uneducated native speakers and sometimes to speakers of English as a foreign language. Despite the fact that the British are notoriously bad at foreign languages, this does not stop them ridiculing foreigners trying to speak English, as *Oxford Street is full of tourists. Talk about English as she is spoke.*

English disease, the is a catchphrase cliché used to describe industrial strikes, a common phenomenon in the 1960s and early 1970s in Britain, when the trade unions were very powerful. The phrase has also been used to describe other social ills, such as class conflict and economic stagnation. It has even referred to some physical diseases, such as bronchitis or syphilis and also to sexual activity, such as whipping, which involves physical punishment. As a modern cliché, however, it commonly refers to industrial disputes, although the expression has lost prominence with the decrease in the incidence of the phenomenon it describes.

enjoy! is a vogue cliché of the twentieth century which first invited people to sample and enjoy food, as *Mum has cooked us one of her special casseroles. Enjoy!* and was then extended to other commodities such as books. The expression is Yiddish in origin and has come to Britain from America.

enough is enough is a hackneyed phrase used to indicate that it is time something was brought to an end, as *'All right children,' said the teacher, 'enough is enough. You've all had a good laugh and now it's time to get back to work'.* It frequently takes the form of quite a stern warning that no more will be tolerated. The expression appears as a proverb in John Heywood's 1546 collection of proverbs.

enough said is a hackneyed phrase indicating that no more need be said on a particular subject. The implication is that the rest is obvious or could be readily deduced at least by people in the know, as *I saw him coming out of her flat this morning. Enough said!* Gertrude Stein wrote a poem entitled *Enough Said* (1935) which consists solely of the expression repeated five times. The cliché also exists in a shortened humorous form, **nuff said**, which is found, for example, in comics and cartoons.

envy of the world, the is a hackneyed phrase used to describe an aspect of life in a country that is thought to be of an exceptionally high standard. It is frequently used to describe aspects of life in Britain, although the statement so used is often at least debatable and is frequently just wishful thinking, as *I can safely say that our education system is the envy of the world.* As a cliché it dates from the twentieth century. It is used today chiefly by journalists and old-fashioned optimists.

'er indoors is a catchphrase cliché meaning wife, the implication being although supposedly indoors a lot and so not often visible, wives nevertheless have a great deal of influence. The catchphrase was popularized by the television series *Minder*, first screened in 1979, in which the chief character, Arthur Daley, played by George Cole, referred to his wife in this way. This is one of several clichés used to refer to a wife. See also **better half**.

err on the side of is a hackneyed phrase meaning to indulge in what might be seen as a fault, in order to avoid the opposite, and even greater, fault, as *They decided to err on the side of caution and not buy a house when the market was so uncertain.*

esprit de corps (French for 'team spirit') is a foreign cliché used to describe a sense of unity or common purpose within a group.

53

It is mostly found in literary or formal contexts where it is thought to sound better than 'team spirit', as *In his retirement speech the chairman spoke of the esprit de corps that had always existed among his board members.* It has been used by English speakers for some considerable time. Jane Austen used it in *Mansfield Park* (1814), although she misspelled it as *esprit du corps*.

eternal triangle, the is an idiom cliché referring to three people who are involved in some kind of romantic intrigue. It can consist of two men and one woman with both men having love affairs with the woman. Alternatively, it can consist of two women and one man with the two women both having love affairs with the man. Sometimes the members of the triangle are all aware of the situation which they are in, and sometimes only one of them is. The expression is frequently used by someone when he/she finds out that a married, or otherwise attached, friend is having an affair. *Ah, a case of the eternal triangle,* he/she might well say, probably either pompously or ironically. The phrase was coined by a book reviewer in the *London Daily Chronicle* in 1907 and is still very common today.

et tu Brute (Latin for 'and you Brutus') is a quotation cliché from Shakespeare's *Julius Caesar* and are the words with which Caesar recognizes the fact that his friend, Brutus, is one of the conspirators in his murder. As a cliché it is used to a friend who has let one down, perhaps because he/she has taken some form of action against one. For example, if all the cabinet ministers passed a vote of no confidence in a prime minister he/she might say to a colleague who was thought to be exceptionally loyal, 'Et tu Brute!' Nowadays the expression is sometimes used in humorous contexts also.

eureka! (Greek for 'I have found it') is a quotation cliché used to announce one's delight at having made a discovery or at having found something, as *Eureka! I've just discovered how to work the video machine.* The expression is often now used in a humorous context. The exclamation was first made by Archimedes in his bath when he discovered that a body displaces its own bulk in water when immersed.

even his/her etc best friends won't tell him/her etc. is a catchphrase cliché originally indicating that someone has a problem relating to personal hygiene, such as an unpleasant body odour or bad breath. It is sometimes now also used to indicate a fault or habit in someone that people might be aware of but not comment on. The catchphrase probably originated in an advertising campaign relating to personal hygiene.

every cloud has a silver lining is an idiom cliché indicating that there is some redeeming quality in even the worst situation, as *At least now you don't have a job you'll have more time to spend with your family. Every cloud has a silver lining.* People to whom such a remark is addressed can find it very annoying, feeling that the users of it are being platitudinous. As a cliché it dates from the early twentieth century. In the 1930s Noel Coward reversed the concept to form **every silver lining has a cloud** in one of his songs.

every dog has/will have his day is a proverb cliché meaning that everyone will have a period of success, happiness in life at some stage. As a cliché it is usually used as a consoling phrase when times are bad or as a remark to inspire optimism, as *It's* *too bad you didn't get that job, but I'm sure you'll get one soon. Every dog has his day.* The cliché is sometimes contracted simply as an allusion to the whole phrase, as *He's going through a bad patch just now, but you know what they say about every dog.* Frequently people who are at the receiving end of the cliché find it annoying and even patronizing.

every effort is being made is a twentieth century hackneyed phrase usually used to reassure people who fear that very little is being done or who feel that very few results of any effort are in evidence. It appears in such official statements as *A police spokesman said that every effort is being made to trace anyone who may have witnessed the attack.*

every inch a/the is a hackneyed phrase used to indicate that someone is the perfect example or epitome of something, as *She would not swear. She is every inch a lady.* It is usually found in complimentary expressions and is mostly used by older, rather conventional people who value the attributes with which it usually comes accompanied. Sometimes the expression is altered slightly to **every other inch a**, indicating either that someone is not quite the perfect example of something or that someone is not in any way a good example of something. The title of the autobiography of the actress Beatrice Lillie is *Every Other Inch a Lady* (1973).

every little helps is a proverb cliché indicating that every contribution to a collection, cause, task, etc, no matter how small, is valuable since a whole is frequently made up of many parts. It is a cliché much used by people who are collecting for charity, indicating that ever the smallest contribution is welcome. In common with other such stock responses, the expression can

be very irritating in its predictability. The saying is said to be based on the old proverb, 'Everything helps', quoth the wren, when she pissed in the sea.

every man jack is a hackneyed phrase meaning absolutely everyone, as *I shall see to it that the boys are punished, every man jack of them.* It was used by Charles Dickens in *Barnaby Rudge* (1841) and has been a cliché since the late nineteenth century.

everything but the kitchen sink is a hackneyed phrase used to refer to a great deal of luggage, etc, as *When we go on motoring holidays we seem to take everything but the kitchen sink.* Its use implies that much of the luggage taken is unnecessary or inappropriate. The expression became popular in World War 2 although it was in use earlier in the twentieth century.

everything in the garden's lovely is a catchphrase cliché indicating that everything is going well and that things could not be better, as *Their marriage hit a bad patch last year but now everything in the garden's lovely.* The expression comes from the title of a song popularized by Marie Lloyd, a music hall singer who died in 1922. It is sometimes used to suggest that there is something rather smug and unexciting about someone's way of life, that it resembles a well-kept suburban garden.

everything you always wanted to know about (something) but were afraid to ask is a quotation cliché which has become a catchphrase. The expression refers to the title of a book, *Everything You Always Wanted To Know About Sex But Were Afraid To Ask*, written by David Reuben and published in 1970. It owes its popularity to the fact that Woody Allen used it as a film title in 1972. Several books have been published bearing similar titles but the expression is also frequently used in conversation to indicate a very large quantity of material or information, as in *There you are! A whole section on photography. All you ever wanted to know about cameras but were afraid to ask!* The expression is sometimes used in the negative for humorous effect to suggest too much information often of a boring nature, as *I thought the speaker would never shut up. Her talk was everything you never wanted to know about feminism and were afraid to ask.*

explore every avenue is a hackneyed phrase used to indicate that a subject will be looked into extremely carefully and thoroughly with a view to finding the best means of doing something, etc. It is usually regarded as a pompous and roundabout way of saying that very little will in fact be done, although it will be made to appear that this is not the case. It is apt to appear in such contexts as a formal reply to a letter of complaint or in a promise from a politician or civil servant, as *You may be assured that we shall explore every avenue to find a plan for the town centre that is acceptable to everyone.*

express our appreciation is a hackneyed phrase used to mean either to applaud a speaker or performer by clapping one's hands or to make a financial contribution towards a gift for someone in acknowledgement of services rendered. It is a formal and often rather pompous expression, often lengthened to **express our appreciation in the usual way**, as in *Now ladies and gentlemen, after that excellent talk, I am sure that you will wish to express your appreciation in the usual way by putting your hands together.*

✷ F ✷

face that launched a thousand ships, the is an allusion cliché referring to Helen of Troy whose beauty was a contributory factor in the launching of the Greek fleet which sailed for Troy to avenge Menelaus, husband of Helen, who had gone off with Paris, the son of the king of Troy, and started the siege of Troy. The actual phrase is a quotation from Marlowe's play *Faustus* (Circa 1588) As a modern cliché it is often used not to refer to great beauty but to great ugliness, as *He's very handsome but have you seen his wife? Talk about the face that launched a thousand ships!*

face the facts is a hackneyed phrase meaning to force oneself to accept and deal with the actual reality of a situation instead of ignoring it, putting it to the back of one's mind or taking a romantic or unrealistic view of it, as *I know you think that a baby won't change your lifestyle, but you have to face the facts. Someone will have to look after it.* The expression is an analogy with **face the music.**

face the music is an idiom cliché meaning either to confront a difficult situation boldly or bravely, or to meet the consequences of one's behaviour boldly, as *The boys played truant yesterday and had fun at the seaside. Now they'll have to face the music in the headmaster's study.* There is some dispute about the origin of this expression. At least three possible explanations have been put forward. One suggests that it comes from the fact that a singer faces the orchestra when he/she sings in opera or a musical show, while another suggests that it refers to a theatre performer having to face the members of the orchestra in the orchestra pit as well as the audience. The idea of facing a punishment is perhaps best accounted for by the suggestion that the expression refers to the military practice of playing drums when a soldier was dismissed from the service as a punishment or that it refers to a military band playing The Rogue's March at a similar event.

fact of the matter, the is a filler cliché which is simply an unnecessarily long way of saying fact or truth, as *I am sorry to pull out of the trip at the last minute, but the fact of the matter is that I simply can't afford the fare.*

factor is a vogue cliché which became popular in Britain in the 1980s to indicate something that has an effect on an issue, event, etc, as in Falklands factor, that is the effect that the Falklands War had on the standing of the government of the day. It is used in a variety of situations and is particularly popular with journalists. A recent example, is **the feel-good factor.**

fair and square is a doublet cliché since square here means the same as fair. The expression has been recorded since the early seventeenth century and still appears in a wide variety of contexts, as *I am sorry that I lost the election but I was beaten fair and square by an excellent candidate.*

fair game is an idiom cliché indicating that someone or something is a legitimate or fair target for attack, criticism, mockery, etc, as *The film star objects to intrusions into her private life, but journalists regard everybody famous as being fair game in their investigations.*

fair sex, the is a hackneyed phrase used to describe women. It is rather dated but is still used, especially by older men. Women tend to object to its use on the grounds that it is patronizing, suggesting that all that matters in a woman is her looks. It is used in such contexts as *the fair sex, bless them. Where would we be without them?*

fairweather friend is a hackneyed phrase used to describe someone who is a friend and companion while things are going well, but who disappears when things start to go wrong, as *Jane always seemed very popular but when she was dismissed very few of her colleagues stood by her. They were just fair-weather friends.*

fait accompli (French for 'accomplished fact') is a foreign cliché meaning something that has already been accomplished or carried out, as *They would have tried to stop their daughter's marriage but it was a fait accompli by the time they found out about it.* It is widely used, although mostly in fairly formal contexts, there being no common native English phrase used in the same context.

fall between two stools is an idiom cliché meaning to be unsuccessful with regard to two courses of action, categories, etc because of being unable to decide which to opt for or because of trying to achieve both, when these are not compatible, as *He tried to make the same product fit the domestic and the export market but it fell between two stools and didn't do well in either.* The cliché is the standard way of describing something that does not suc-

cessfully and convincingly fit into a category. The origin of the expression is a reference to someone who cannot decide which of two stools to sit on and falls between them while hesitating.

fall by the wayside is an allusion cliché referring to the Biblical parable about the sower of seeds, some of which fell by the wayside and were devoured by fowls and did not grow (*Luke* 8:5). In the parable, the seed was the word of God and the seeds that fell by the wayside represented people who heard the word but were led astray by the Devil. As far as the cliché is concerned, it means to fail to continue to the end, to fail to see something through, as *A large number of runners started the marathon but several fell by the wayside,* and *She keeps beginning new diets but she always falls by the wayside.* Although the expression has rather a literary sound, the cliché is still fairly widely used.

fall on deaf ears is a hackneyed phrase meaning to be totally ignored or disregarded. As a cliché it implies the person concerned does not wish to hear what is being said, as *Her parents tried to warn her that he was a rogue but their warnings fell on deaf ears.* The phrase dates from the fifteenth century and has been a cliché since the nineteenth century.

fall (or land) on one's feet is a hackneyed phrase meaning to come out well from a situation that could have proved disastrous. It is particularly applied to someone who has a habit of doing this, as *People thought that Jack had made a terrible mistake buying that old house, but he sold it to a developer at a profit. He always falls on his feet.* The origin lies in the fact that the cat has the unusual ability to land on its paws, when it jumps, falls or is thrown from a height.

famous last words is a hackneyed phrase used as a remark to someone who has just said something that is likely to be disproved or is likely to prove inappropriate, as 'At least I got rid of him easily,' said Mary as she closed the door on the double-glazing salesman. 'Famous last words,' said Joan. 'He's just coming up the path again. He must have been at his car collecting leaflets'. It is thought to have become popular in World War 2.

In origin it is a reference to the dying words of famous people, which are often noted for posterity.

far and away is a doublet cliché used to indicate the degree to which something or someone exceeds others, as She is far and away the best candidate for the post and This car is far and away the most reliable we've had. It is usually found in a complimentary context but is also found in critical or condemnatory contexts, as This is far and away the worst food I've ever eaten. It has been a cliché since the nineteenth century.

far and wide is a doublet cliché meaning extensively. It is used for emphasis to describe how far-reaching, thorough, etc something has been, as We searched far and wide before we found a cottage we liked. It has been a stock phrase in the language from earliest times.

far be it from me is a hackneyed phrase which suggests that the speaker is too modest or discreet to, but is going to anyway, as Far be it from me to tell you how to run your life, but I really don't think that you should marry him. The expression dates from the late fourteenth century and has been common since the late eighteenth century. It is still commonly used today by people who like to interfere and also by people who use it meaninglessly as a linguistic habit.

far cry, a is a hackneyed phrase used to indicate a great difference, as Her present lifestyle is a far cry from the one she used to enjoy. The expression used to be used literally as well as figuratively but as a current cliché it is used only in figurative contexts. In origin it is thought to refer to the measuring of one's distance from one's enemy by the estimation of the shouting distance.

far from the madding crowd is a quotation cliché from Elegy Written in a Country Churchyard (1751) by Thomas Gray. It is also the title of a novel by Thomas Hardy (1874). The expression is used to refer to noisy hordes of people and is always found in contexts suggesting a desire to get away from these, as They love walking in the hills, far from the madding crowd. Madding is obsolete except in this phrase.

fast and furious is a doublet cliché meaning hectic. It is usually applied to fun or some form of game or sport, as The fun was fast and furious at the children's Christmas party. Nowadays it is not commonly used in informal English but would still be commonly found, for example, in reports of social events in local newspapers. Its association with fun has its origins in Robert Burns' poem, Tam o' Shanter (1793) 'The mirth and fun grew fast and furious.'

fast lane, the is a vogue cliché which became popular in Britain in the 1970s meaning a high-pressure, swift-moving career or lifestyle. It is found in such statements as He couldn't take life in the fast lane any more. He's left the city and gone to the country to write books. and She loves being in the fast lane. She got bored looking after the children. In origin the expression refers to the outside lane of a motorway which people use to overtake others.

fat chance is a hackneyed phrase said by someone to stress the unlikelihood of something, as *You want tickets for tonight's performance? Fat chance. They've been sold out for weeks.* The cliché originated in America but is now widely used in informal contexts in Britain.

fate is sealed, his/her is a hackneyed phrase indicating that it is quite inevitable that something, usually something bad, is going to happen to someone, as *We don't know the result of Peter's trial yet but his fate is sealed. The jury have just returned to their seats.* It is more usually found nowadays in a jocular or facetious context, as *Ah well, John's fate is sealed. Anne has started going out with him and she's looking for a husband.* The origin of the expression is an allusion to the fact that the edict of a monarch directing someone to be hanged, etc would bear the royal seal.

fate worse than death, a is a hackneyed phrase meaning rape or seduction and refers to the days when the loss of virginity was a great disgrace to a young woman and would seriously affect her chances of marrying. As a modern cliché it may be used in a humorous context of a sexual encounter that is quite welcome, as *He's asked you to stay the night at last. Oh, a fate worse than death.* It is also used facetiously or ironically, as *to have to listen to her talking all day would be a fate worse than death.*

feather in one's cap, a is an idiom cliché indicating a special achievement or honour that one has reason to be proud of, as *Getting a representative into the national team is a real feather in the cap of our local athletics club* and *It's a feather in her cap to get such a famous writer to speak to the women's group.* The term was a cliché by

the eighteenth century and is still common nowadays.

The origin of the phrase lies in the fact that it was the custom among North American Indians to place a feather in a warrior's headdress or cap for every member of the enemy he killed.

feather one's nest is an idiom cliché meaning to provide for oneself or make a profit for oneself while engaged in some activity where one was not meant to be doing this, as *The local organizer has been accused of feathering her own nest at the expense of the charity and has been dismissed* and *The sales manager has been feathering his own nest for years by over-claiming on his expenses.* The expression is still common and has its origin in the habit of birds of making their nests soft and comfortable to hatch their eggs in. It has been a cliché since the eighteenth century.

feel a different person is a hackneyed phrase meaning to feel much better in terms of health or general wellbeing, as *Since he started taking those pills he has felt a different person* and *She feels a different person since she's been able to get out a bit more.* The expression is most likely to be used in informal contents.

the feel-good factor is a vogue cliché which became popular in the 1980s and 1990s to indicate an effect caused by people feeling pleased with their lot. It is particularly used of the influence of perceived affluence on people, on how they vote in opinion polls and elections and on their spending patterns, as *The government hopes that the fall in interest rates will create a feel-good factor among the electorate* and *The department stores think that their increase in sales is due to a feel-good factor in the country.*

feel it in one's bones is an idiom cliché meaning to feel intuitively that something is the case, to have a premonition about something. The something in question can be either good or bad, as *I feel it in my bones that he is going to get the job* and *I feel it in my bones that there is something not right with the firm*. The origin probably lies in the fact that people with rheumatism or arthritis sometimes claim to be able to predict when it's going to rain because of the ache in their bones or joints.

feel one's age is a hackneyed phrase indicating that one is becoming aware of the effects of advancing age, as *Old Jack is still working at the age of 70 but he's talking of retiring. He says he's feeling his age.* It is sometimes used facetiously as *I was going to do so many things when the twins started school but I don't have the energy. I think I'm feeling my age!* The expression has been a cliché since the late nineteenth century.

feet of clay, have is an allusion cliché. It indicates that a person who is held in high regard has an unexpected fault or failing, as *She used to regard her father as some kind of god but she realized that he had feet of clay when she discovered that he mistreated his employees,* and *After her death he discovered that his adored wife had feet of clay. She had been having an affair with a neighbour for years.* The Biblical allusion is to the *Book of Daniel* (2:33) in which an idol is described as being made of gold, silver and bronze with legs of iron, and with feet of iron and clay. The cliché is currently found in quite informal contexts as well as more literary ones.

festive occasion is a hackneyed phrase used to describe a celebratory or special social occasion, as *We like to dress up at Christmas and on other festive occasions.* The expression which is still widely used, partly

because it is difficult to think of an alternative, has been a cliché since the late nineteenth century.

few and far between is a doublet cliché which simply reinforces the idea of seldomness. The things that are described as being seldom or widely spaced-out may be pleasant or unpleasant, as *Since the baby was born our nights out have been few and far between,* and *Fortunately his asthmatic attacks are few and far between now.* The expression is used by the poet, Thomas Campbell in *The Pleasures of Hope* (1799) 'What though my winged hours have been, like angel-visits, few and far between.'

fiddle while Rome burns is an allusion cliché indicating that someone is occupying himself/herself with trivialities or minor pursuits while something important required urgent attention, as *When the men walked out on strike in the middle of a rush export order, the production manager went out to lunch. Is that not fiddling while Rome burns?* The allusion is to the legend that Nero, Emperor of Rome, played his lyre and watched the flames from a tower when Rome was on fire (AD64). It has been a cliché since the nineteenth century and is still common.

field day, a is an idiom cliché meaning great activity or great success, as *The press will have a field day when they find out that the politician has left his wife for a young girl.* The expression has its origin in a special day that was set aside for military manoeuvres and exercises. It was later transferred to civilian occasions, such as school outings or other enjoyable events. Nowadays, however, the activity is usually centred on someone else's misfortune, as in *The local gossips had a field day when the bailiffs arrived at his house.*

fighting chance, a is a hackneyed phrase used to indicate that there is a possibility of success if every effort is made, as *He didn't run very well today but he still has a fighting chance of getting into the team if he trains hard.* This an extremely common expression in a variety of contexts and is frequently used to describe someone who is very ill but who has a chance of survival. The origin is an allusion to a physical fight or battle· that one might win if one tries one's very hardest.

fighting fit is a hackneyed phrase meaning very well or healthy, in good physical condition, as *Her father was very ill for a while but he is fighting fit now.* The origin is an allusion to a boxer being in good enough condition to fight.

fight tooth and nail is a hackneyed phrase meaning to struggle with all one's strength and resources, as *They fought tooth and nail to stop the new road being built but they lost.* The origin lies in the fact that animals and people will use all the physical means at their disposal, such as teeth and nails, in order to win a fight if there is a lot at stake. As a phrase it has been in the language since the sixteenth century and it is thought to have been a cliché since the mid nineteenth century. It is still commonly used, often as a declaration of intent, as *'We shall fight tooth and nail to prevent the closure of the school,' . . . declared the chairman of the protest group.*

figment of one's imagination, a is a hackneyed phrase meaning something which one has imagined and which has no reality, as *She said that she saw a man in the garden but I'm sure that it was just a figment of her imagination.* The word 'figment' on its own refers to something that is a fantastic notion or fabrication, and so there is a tautological element in the

expression. The phrase appears in *Jane Eyre* (1847) by Charlotte Brontë 'The long dishevelled hair, the swelled black face, the exaggerated stature, were figments of imagination.'

filthy lucre is an allusion cliché meaning money, as *I detest the man but I wish I had his filthy lucre.* It is found in an informal or slang context and is frequently used in a critical or condemnatory sense, as *All she cares about is filthy lucre.* The expression originally meant money acquired by dishonourable means and before that base profit. It is a Biblical allusion to 1 Timothy (3:3) 'Not given to wine, not greedy of filthy lucre, but patient, not a brawler, not covetous.'

fill the bill is an idiom cliché meaning to be exactly what is required, to be suitable, as *I couldn't decide what to wear to the wedding but this dress will fill the bill.* Although American in origin, it is now commonly used in British English, though not in formal contexts. In origin it refers to the practice of first listing the leading performers on a theatre advertising bill and then filling it up by adding the back-up, lesser known and minor performers.

find one's feet is a hackneyed phrase meaning to become able to cope with a new situation, as if finding out where to place one's feet. It is used in rather informal contexts, as *It's too soon to tell how good the new receptionist is. She's still finding her feet.*

fine tooth comb see **go through with a fine tooth comb**.

finger in every pie, a is an idiom cliché meaning involved in many activities at once, as *I don't know how he keeps track of his business interests. He has a finger in every pie,* and *If you want to know anything* *about village life, ask the vicar's wife. She's got a finger in every pie.* The implication is not a flattering one, since the phrase usually suggests either that something vaguely dishonest is involved or that someone is interfering. The origin is an allusion to someone in a kitchen tasting several pies.

finishing touches is a hackneyed phrase meaning the last details that make something complete or perfect. It is found in a variety of contexts, as *I have iced the birthday cake. It just needs a few finishing touches.* and *My brother is just putting the finishing touches to the speech he is giving to tomorrow's conference.* The origin of the expression lies in the the last strokes that an artist marked in a painting.

fire away! is an idiom cliché used as an informal interjection telling someone to go ahead and say what he or she wants to say, as *OK, I've found a pen, fire away and I'll try to get all the message down,* and *I don't mind answering the questions on your questionnaire. Fire away!* In origin the expression refers to an instruction to begin firing a gun.

firing on all cylinders is an idiom cliché referring to an internal combustion engine, as in a car, which is working effectively at full strength. As a cliché it is commonly used in the negative to indicate that something or someone is not working at full strength or with maximum effort, as *You'll have to excuse me. I have a cold and I'm just not firing on all cylinders today.* The expression is, however, not always used in the negative and is found in such contexts as *The factory will have to be firing on all cylinders to get these orders out on time*

first and foremost is a doublet cliché, first and foremost in this context being more or less synonymous, meaning most impor-

tantly, as *We need many things for the new house, but first and foremost we need a new bed. He had many good qualities but first and foremost he was a good friend.* It is found in a variety of contexts and has been used as a cliché since the mid nineteenth century.

first come, first served is a hackneyed phrase indicating that if something is limited, those who come first will obtain it at the expense of those who follow. *You can't book tickets. They are on sale on the night of the performance and it will be a case of first come, first served.* It is a widespread cliché being used in all but the most formal contexts, *As a saying it has been in the language since the middle of the sixteenth century.*

first see (the) light of day is an idiom cliché meaning to be born, be first invented, have its first performance, be first in evidence, etc, as *The team have spent years researching a new drug but I don't think it will ever see the light of day,* and *His new opera first saw the light of day in Milan.* The cliché dates from the mid nineteenth century. It is now more frequently used of things than of people.

first thing is a hackneyed phrase meaning early in the day, as *The teacher says that she wants all the essays on her desk first thing,* and *She can never eat anything first thing.* So successful is the phrase as a cliché that it is difficult to think of a suitable alternative. To some extent it is an imprecise term since its timing depends on how early one starts one's day.

first things first is a hackneyed phrase stressing that the most important things should be dealt with first. It seems to state the obvious, as *The homeless family have a lot of problems, but first things first. We must find them somewhere to live,* and can be a very irritating cliché. Sometimes it is used facetiously or ironically, as *We have a lot to get through at the meeting this morning but first things first. Let's have a cup of tea.* The expression dates from the nineteenth century.

first water, of the is an idiom cliché now usually meaning out-and-out, of the very worst kind as *He is a villain of the first water* and *She is married to a bastard of the first water.* The term was originally used in a more complimentary way as *He is an artist of the first water,* but this use is now considerably less common than its condemnatory equivalent. In origin the expression alludes to a system of grading diamonds by which they were classified into three waters, according to their colour or lustre, the latter being likened to the clarity and shininess of water.

the first ... years are the worst is a hackneyed phrase suggesting that the initial period of anything is the worst and if you can tolerate that, you can tolerate the rest that is to come. The number of years cited varies from a relatively small number, such as 5, to an exaggerated total, such as 100, as *So you're just married. Never mind, the first ten years are the worst,* and *Welcome to the workforce. You'll find the first hundred years are the worst.* The cliché is always used in a humorous or ironical context and probably has its origin in a military catchphrase from about the time of World War 2 – 'Cheer up, the first seven years are the worst', seven years referring to a regular soldier's length of service.

fish out of water, a is an idiom cliché referring to someone who is completely out of his/her element or feels uncomfortable or ill-suited to a particular environment or situation, as *The young man is very shy and is a fish out of water at parties.* It can also be used as a simile cliché as **like a fish out of water** as in *As an older woman she feels like a fish out of water in an office full of young people.* It is found in a wide variety of contexts. The origin is the obvious one that a fish cannot survive long out of water. The expression has been a cliché since the mid nineteenth century but as a phrase has been in the language much longer.

fit as a fiddle is a simile cliché indicating extremely heathy, in very good physical condition, as *My mother has been ill but she is fit as a fiddle after her holiday.* The origin is uncertain, there being no obvious reason why a fiddle should be a model of fitness.

fit for a king is a hackneyed phrase meaning of exceptionally high quality, as *That was a meal fit for a king.* The origin is obvious, that only the best was good enough for a royal personage. It has been a cliché since the eighteenth century but in modern times the expression is usually associated with food.

fits and starts, by is a doublet cliché since fits and starts are virtually synonymous in this context. The expression means at irregular intervals, spasmodically, as *The students are meant to be working hard for their exams but they tend to work by fits and starts.* The phrase has been in the English language since the early seventeenth century and is such a well-established cliché that any synonym for it sounds less appropriate.

fit to hold a candle to, not is an idiom cliché meaning not able to be compared with, utterly inferior to, as *Not only is he less qualified than his predecessor but he is not fit to hold a candle to him.* The expression is also found in the form **cannot/can't hold a candle to** which has the same meaning but tends to be used in less formal contexts, as in *Most of the modern pop stars couldn't hold a candle to Elvis*. In origin the expression refers to the menial task of holding a candle for someone so that he/she might see to do something. The phrase has been in the language since the middle of the seventeenth century and has been a cliché since the nineteenth century. Lord Byron used a version of it in *On the Feud between Handel and Bononcini* 'Others aver that he to Handel is scarcely fit to hold the candle.' The cliché is always used in the negative.

flash in the pan, a is an idiom cliché which refers to a brief and unexpected success which is not sustained, as *The student did brilliantly in his first exam, but it proved to be a flash in the pan*. The origin of the expression refers to a seventeenth century flintlock musket. In this a spark from the flint ignited a pinch of gunpowder in the priming pan, from which the flash travelled to the main charge in the barrel. If the charge failed to go off there was only a flash in the pan. The idiom originally meant an abortive effort but has had its present meaning since the 1920s.

flash through one's mind is a hackneyed phrase meaning to occur to one suddenly and possibly briefly, as *It flashed through my mind that he was lying*. The origin of the expression is an allusion to lightning flashing and it has been a cliché since the late nineteenth century.

flat as a pancake is a simile cliché meaning completely flat, as *When he got to his car one of the tyres was flat as a pancake*. As a simile the expression has been in the language since the sixteenth century but its status as a cliché is considerably more recent. Nowadays its use tends to be restricted to tyres or terrain, as *He misses the hills. The land around here is flat as a pancake*. It is also

sometimes used to describe the bust of a woman when it is less than generous, but in this sense it is usually a derogatory term.

flat denial is a hackneyed phrase used to indicate a complete and unconditional denial, as *The politician has issued a flat denial that he has in any way been involved in the fraud*. This cliché is usually found in journalists' reports. It frequently has an effect opposite to the one intended, in that people often take a flat denial to be an admission of guilt. The expression has been in the language since the early eighteenth century.

flat out is a hackneyed phrase meaning as hard, fast, energetically, etc as possible, as *The staff are working flat out to get the orders out on time*. and *I can't go any faster. The car's going flat out as it is*.

flattery will get you nowhere is a hackneyed phrase originating in the middle of the twentieth century and indicating that there is no point in saying good or admiring things about someone or something just to get one's own way as this will be unsuccessful. It occurs in such contexts as *You can stop paying me compliments. Flattery will get you nowhere and I'm still not going out with you*. The expression is sometimes turned around to mean the opposite, as **flattery will get you everywhere**. This is used in humorous contexts, as *Well I could try and get you a ticket for tonight's performance. Flattery will get you everywhere*.

flavour of the month is an idiom cliché referring to someone or something that is very popular for a very short period of time, as *You're flavour of the month. Why don't you ask the boss if we can leave early?* and *This week the headmaster is backing more freedom for the pupils, but that's just the flavour of the month. By the end of the month he'll be back* to expelling everyone for the least thing. The cliché originates in the latter part of the twentieth century and is derived from attempts by ice cream shops in America to get their customers to try a different flavour each month.

flesh and blood has two cliché meanings. One refers to family and relatives, as *My brother hardly ever visits us. He seems to prefer his friends to his own flesh and blood.* This has been a cliché since the nineteenth century but appeared in the language much earlier. For example it occurs in Shakespeare's *Merchant of Venice* (2:2) 'If thou be Launcelot, thou art mine own flesh and blood.' Nowadays the expression is often used in rather sentimental contexts. The second cliché means more or less human nature, usually with an emphasis on the frailty of human nature, especially when sexual matters are involved, as in *He said that seeing his wife in another man's arms was more than flesh and blood could stand,* and *You can't blame young people for wanting to live together. They're only flesh and blood.*

flog a dead horse is an idiom cliché meaning to pursue a futile aim, especially to go on trying to arouse interest in a subject which has already been fully discussed, but which is no longer interesting, relevant or topical, or which has already proved a failure, as in *He's flogging a dead horse trying to get money for his new business. He's already tried all the banks.* It was used in the 1860s to describe Lord John Russell's attempt to bring a new reform bill into Parliament, when the members were totally apathetic towards the issue. The most obvious origin of the expression is an allusion to someone fruitlessly whipping a dead horse to get it to work or run a race.

flotsam and jetsam is a doublet cliché meaning odds and ends or articles of little worth, as *It's not really an antique shop. It's full of flotsam and jetsam.* Sometimes it is used in a derogatory way of people meaning the down-and-outs, as *It's the area of town where the flotsam and jetsam hang out.* Although flotsam and jetsam are connected, they were not originally synonyms. Both were connected with wreckage found on the sea. Flotsam technically referred to articles found floating in the sea, formed from Old French *floter*, to float. Jetsam technically referred to articles thrown overboard to lighten a ship when it was in trouble and is a shortened form of 'jettison'. The expression has been a cliché since the nineteenth century.

fly in the face of danger is an idiom cliché meaning to oppose or defy something dangerous in a seemingly foolhardy way, as *We advised him not to compete in the race when he was unused to the car, but he insisted on flying in the face of danger,* and *She wanted to tell the headmaster that he had made a mistake but she decided not to fly in the face of danger.* In origin the expression is thought to allude to a frightened or angry hen flying in the face of a threatened enemy, such as a dog. The expression is not restricted to danger. **Fly in the face of providence** is common, as *I told him to check his fuel supply but he would fly in the face of providence and ignored my advice.* The cliché is also found in such expressions as **fly in the face of public opinion**, as *The government might have been re-elected but it flew in the face of public opinion and did nothing about unemployment.* It is a general, widespread cliché used in both written and spoken English.

flying colours, with is an idiom cliché meaning very successfully, as *She thought she might have failed the exam but she passed* *with flying colours.* This cliché is found in a variety of contexts and has its origin in the fact that sailing ships which were victorious in battle sailed with their flags, or colours, hoisted high.

fly in the ointment, the is an allusion cliché from the Bible. It refers to *Ecclesiastes* (10:1) 'Dead flies cause the ointment of the apothecary to send forth a stinking savour; so doth a little folly him that is in reputation for wisdom and honour.' As a cliché the expression is used to refer to something that detracts from the pleasing, enjoyable or attractive nature of something, as *It's a wonderful holiday spot. The fly in the ointment is the time it takes to get there.* It is a widely used cliché in all but the most formal contexts.

fly off the handle is an idiom cliché meaning to lose one's temper. Originally American, the expression has its origin in an axe or hammer, the handle of which becomes loosened and flies off after it has struck a blow. It is widely used, but only in more informal contexts, as *I tried to tell her that I didn't break the window but she flew off the handle before I could explain.*

follow in the footsteps of is an idiom cliché meaning either to be someone's successor, as *The professor is looking for a young man of talent to follow in his footsteps,* or, more commonly, to do the same kind of work as, or lead the same kind of life as, someone, as *I think he's going to follow in his father's footsteps and be a doctor,* and *We're worried that he may be a good-for-nothing and follow in his father's footsteps.* The origin alludes to someone following the footsteps or footprints of a guide.

follow suit is an idiom cliché with its origin in card games, such as whist or bridge. It literally means to play a card of the same suit as the previous player. As a

cliché it means to do as someone else has just done, as *When the shop steward walked out of the meeting the rest of the workers followed suit.* It is widely used but tends to be commoner in more formal contexts. The expression has been used in a non-literal sense since the middle of the nineteenth century.

follow that cab /taxi/car is a catchphrase cliché used humorously, for example, when a party has to split up into two or more taxis or private cars, as *Follow that car. We don't know where the restaurant is.* In origin the phrase refers to a line popular among film scriptwriters and used in the course of an exciting chase. There is no specific source.

food for thought is a hackneyed cliché meaning something worth thinking about, as *That was an interesting speech. I am sure that it has given us all food for thought.* The expression dates from the early nineteenth century and is a popular cliché today.

fool's paradise a is a hackneyed phrase meaning great happiness that is based on an illusion, as *She's so much in love with him that she's living in a fool's paradise. He's married and still living with his wife.* The expression has been a cliché since the nineteenth century but it has been part of the language since the fifteenth century.

fools rush in is an allusion cliché to the proverb **fools rush in where angels fear to tread** which is itself used as a cliché. Both the shorter and longer versions are used to describe impetuous or insensitive people who do not stop to consider the effects of their actions or words, as *Trust Mary to ask Jane where her engagement ring is. Talk about fools rushing in. Jim and Mary have just split up.* The expression has been popular since the nineteenth century. As a cliché it is still common today as indeed are the fools so described.

foot in it, put one's see *put one's foot in it*

footloose and fancy free is a hackneyed phrase meaning without any commitments or ties. It is frequently used of someone who is not involved in any romantic attachment of a binding nature, as *There's nothing to stop you working abroad. You're footloose and fancy free,* and *She would like to marry some day but just now she's footloose and fancy free.* The word footloose suggests that one is free to go anywhere that one chooses. Fancy free in the sense of not romantically involved occurs in Shakespeare's *A Midsummer Night's Dream* (2:1) 'The imperial votaress passed on, in maiden meditation, fancy-free.'

for better or worse is a quotation cliché, being a slight misquotation from the marriage service in *The Book of Common Prayer,* in which the bride and groom exchange vows 'for better, for worse, for richer, for poorer, in sickness or in health.' It is now used more generally meaning in whatever circumstance, good or bad as *Well, I made the decision to emigrate and I'll have to go through with it, for better or worse.*

forbidden fruit is an allusion cliché to the Bible. It refers to the story of Eve in *Genesis* in which she eats the forbidden fruit from the tree of knowledge and is consequently expelled by God with Adam from the Garden of Eden. It is now used to refer to any illicit pleasure, as *They're under age but they try to get into the nightclub because it's forbidden fruit,* and *He knows she's engaged but he's asked her out. You know what he's like with forbidden fruit.*

foregone conclusion, a is a quotation cliché from Shakespeare's *Othello* (3:3) 'But this denoted a foregone conclusion.' As a cliché it means a result that is either known already or is entirely predictable and so can be taken for granted, as *There's*

very little point in their bothering to play the match. Peter's so much the stronger player that it's a foregone conclusion.* As a modern cliché it is used in a variety of contexts.

forewarned is forearmed is a proverb cliché indicating that prior knowledge of an impending event enables one to be prepared for it. It occurs in a variety of contexts, as *I'm glad you told me that she is going to ask me for a loan. Forewarned is forearmed,'* and *Thanks for telling me that they're planning a surprise visit. That gives me time to get ready. Forewarned is forearmed.* In origin the expression is a translation of a Latin proverb *praemonitus, praemunitus.*

forlorn hope, a is a hackneyed phrase meaning an enterprise that has little chance of success, as *They've applied for time to pay back the loan but it's a forlorn hope.* It also means a very faint hope, as *We are praying that they're still alive but it's a forlorn hope. The coastguards have found an empty boat.* In origin it is a mistranslation of the Dutch *verloren hoop,* meaning a lost troop of soldiers, *hoop* having been taken wrongly to mean hope.

for this relief much thanks is a quotation cliché from Shakespeare's *Hamlet* (1:1). It originally referred to military relief, but as a cliché it is used humorously, as *You've come to take over the babysitting? For this relief much thanks!* It tends to be used by people of rather literary tastes.

forty winks is a hackneyed phrase meaning a short sleep, as *Father always has forty winks after lunch.* It is widely used in informal contexts but its origin is uncertain. The expression has been used since the early part of the nineteenth century.

free, gratis and for nothing is a hackneyed phrase simply meaning free, without charge. It is used for emphasis, free, gratis and for nothing all being synonyms, in informal, often humorous, contexts as *You don't need a ticket for the match. You'll get it free, gratis and for nothing.*

-free zone is a hackneyed phrase used to indicate that a place or situation is free from the thing specified, as *Please put your cigarette out. This is smoke-free zone.* It is often used humorously or satirically, as *Thank goodness this department is still a woman-free zone.* As a cliché the expression dates from the twentieth century and is probably based originally on **war-free zone**. It is extremely common today.

fresh fields and pastures is a quotation cliché which is in fact a misquotation from Milton's *Lycidas*, the correct quotation being 'fresh woods, and pastures new'. Despite its literary connections it is a widely used cliché in both informal and formal contexts, as *I've been in this job for several years. I think it's time for fresh fields and pastures new.*

from the cradle to the grave is a hackneyed phrase meaning all one's life, at all stages in one's life, as *They expect the state to provide for them from the cradle to the grave.* It has been in the language for some considerable time, having been used by the essayist Richard Steele in 1706 'From the cradle to the grave he never had a day's illness.' It has been a cliché since the nineteenth century. Churchill used it in a radio broadcast in 1943 'National compulsory insurance for all classes for all purposes from the cradle to the grave.'

from the sublime to the ridiculous is a hackneyed phrase indicating that there has been a drastic reduction in the scale, importance, quality, etc of the subjects being discussed, as *We've really gone from the sublime to the ridiculous. A minute ago we were talking about the reduction in the*

defence budget. Now we're talking about cake recipes. Napoleon is said to have used it, in French, to describe the retreat of his army from Moscow, but the idea is thought to have come from Tom Paine's *The Age of Reason* (1794) 'One step above the sublime makes the ridiculous, and one step above the ridiculous makes the sublime again.'

from the word go is a hackneyed phrase meaning right from the very beginning. It is mainly used in informal contexts, as *That pupil has been nothing but trouble from the word go,* and *The holiday was a disaster from the word go.* In origin it refers to the call at the beginning of a race, etc.

from time immemorial is a hackneyed phrase meaning from earliest times, beyond anyone's recall, as *There has been a standing stone there since time immemorial.* The cliché is sometimes used in humorous, informal contexts to mean quite a long time, as *Those curtains have been up in her front room since time immemorial.* The term may derive from English law where it meant beyond legal memory, i.e. before the reign of Richard I (1189–1199).

fullness of time, in the is an allusion cliché referring to the Bible, *Galatians* (4:4) 'But when the fullness of time was come, God sent forth His son.' As a cliché it is used in formal contexts, frequently rather pompously. It is often used when conveying a reproach to someone who is considered to be impatient, as *We shall consider your request in the fullness of time, but we have a large number of applications to deal with.*

full steam ahead is an idiom cliché meaning as fast as possible, as *Now that have the go-ahead for the order it will be full steam ahead to get it done on time.* In origin the expression refers to a steam engine as used in trains and steam ships, 'full steam' indicating that a boiler had developed maximum pressure and so was able to go at maximum speed. In its figurative context the expression became popular in the late nineteenth century.

funny ha ha is a hackneyed phrase meaning funny in the sense of amusing. It is found in informal contexts, as *When she said that her father was funny I thought she meant funny ha ha.* The expression is often used in conjunction with its converse, funny peculiar, as *His stories are funny peculiar, rather than funny ha ha.*

F-word, the is a hackneyed phrase which could also be regarded as a euphemism cliché used as a substitute for 'fuck', a word which is supposedly still taboo but which is widely used in ordinary speech and in modern novels and plays, although not yet officially in newspapers or radio or television. **The F-word** is used in situations where fuck is supposedly taboo but is in many ways less acceptable than the word for which it is substituted, since it sounds so ridiculous. Because of this latter fact it is often used satirically and people often send it up by coining other words in analogy with it where there is no suggestion of anything taboo, as the M-word for money or the S-word for sex. The analogy is also extended to other words that are taboo, as the C-word for 'cunt'.

⁂ G ⁂

gainful employment is a hackneyed phrase meaning paid employment, a job. It is used nowadays in formal or rather pompous contexts, as *The judge asked if the accused was in gainful employment,* although it is also used in humorous or ironic contexts.

game is not worth the candle, the is a proverb cliché indicating that the project, etc involved is too troublesome, difficult, etc for the advantages it would bring, as *I gave up having a weekend job. I was paying so much tax that the game wasn't worth the candle.* It is a translation of the French *le jeu n'en vaut la chandelle* which meant literally that the card game being played was not worth the cost of the candles required to provide light for it, the amount of money at stake being so low. The English version appeared in John Ray's collection proverbs of 1678 and it is still popular today.

game of two halves, a is a hackneyed phrase much used by sports commentators or those involved in a sport to remind people of the obvious fact that football matches, etc are divided into two halves. It is usually used to indicate that there could be a complete turnaround of fortunes in the second half, especially if tactics are changed. Frequently it is used almost meaninglessly, it being the fate of sports commentators to have to make comments when there is nothing meaningful to say.

gameplan is a vogue cliché popular from the 1980s and referring to a series of tactics by which it is hoped to attain an objective, as *She says that taking a shorthand and typing course is just part of her gameplan to become a journalist.* Basically it means simply plan but it is used in an attempt to make a statement sound grander. The term originates in American football.

gather ye rosebuds while ye may is a quotation cliché used as a recommendation to make the most of a good opportunity or a good period of one's life while one can, as it probably will not last, as *Gather ye rosebuds while ye may. You're not getting any younger,* and *I have a feeling that the future for the industry's not too good. Gather ye rosebuds while ye may.* As a cliché it tends to be used by people who have rather literary tastes. The expression is a quotation from the English poet Robert Herrick's *To the Virgins, to Make Much of Time* (1648).

a gay Lothario, is an allusion cliché, being a reference to *The Fair Penitent* (1703) by Nicholas Rowe, in which it is used of a character 'Is that haughty, gallant, gay Lothario?' The expression is used to refer to a man who is a habitual womanizer, as *He's always chatting up the women in the hotel bar. He's a real gay Lothario.* As a modern cliché it tends to be used mainly by older people or people with literary tastes. Nowadays, when gay most frequently means homosexual, rather than merry, the term might be misinterpreted. In any case the word gay is frequently omitted, as *He's quite a Lothario.*

general exodus, a is a hackneyed phrase meaning a general movement of people from a room, building, area, etc, as *At lunchtime there is a general exodus of office workers from the tower block,* and *There is a general exodus of the inhabitants from the city during August.* The expression has been a cliché since the late nineteenth century.

generation gap, the is a vogue cliché referring to the differences in attitudes, social values, lifestyle, etc that exist between one generation and another, especially those between parents and their adolescent children, as *Their plans for Christmas night say it all about the generation gap. The parents want a quiet family night in playing Scrabble. The teenage children want to go to an all-night disco.* Although this phenomenon existed before the later part of the twentieth century it was then that young people sought to assert their identity and acquired more freedom. Thus the differences between the generations became more marked and were given a name.

gentleman's agreement, a is a hackneyed phrase used to refer to a non-written agreement, such as might be sealed by the handshake of two gentleman, as *We had a gentleman's agreement about the division of our relative's property but my brother broke his word.* Nowadays it is a unisex term, women as well as men being able to strike such agreements. In these times of hard-nosed business deals, people tend to view a gentleman's agreement with cynicism, agreeing with A J P Taylor in *English History 1914–45* (1965) 'much used hereafter for an agreement with anyone who was obviously not a gentleman and who would obviously not keep his agreement.'

get a life! is a hackneyed phrase used as general term of abuse, as *Of course I'm going to get there on time. Get a life!* It dates from the later part of the twentieth century and is much used by young people, having overtaken most other forms of abuse. The expression suggests that the person to whom the remark is directed is rather a sad case who has no life worth speaking of.

get a result is a hackneyed phrase used by sports commentators and those involved in sport. It is a curious phrase since by the very nature of things a result will be achieved, whatever its nature. As a cliché the expression dates from the later part of the twentieth century and is used to refer to the fact that it is important for a particular team to win or score a goal in a football match.

get away from it all is a hackneyed phrase dating from the second part of the twentieth century and meaning to get away from one's usual daily routine, usually by taking a holiday. It is much used by holiday firms and travel journalists, as *So if you fancy getting away from it all on a winter break, this could be the place for you.*

get down to brass tacks is an idiom cliché meaning to begin to deal with basic principles or issues, as *We shall allow some time for initial pleasantries and then get down to brass tacks,* and *During the meeting on the economy it was almost impossible to get the politician to get down to brass tacks and stop talking about theories.* It is a late nineteenth century expression which is thought to have its origin in the brass tacks marked at one-yard intervals on a shop counter, for measuring cloth, etc. Thus, getting down to brass tacks literally meant measuring precisely. As a modem cliché it is used in all but the most formal contexts.

get in on the act is an idiom cliché meaning to get involved in an undertaking, usually when one is unwanted, as *We had enough people on the committee but Mrs Jones just had to get in on the act.* In origin the expression is an allusion to an act in the theatre, the implication being that someone has succeeded in getting involved in someone else's act and so will get some of the applause. The likelihood is that the cliché originates from the days of music hall. The American comedian, Jimmy Durante, popularized it in the 1930s. As a modern cliché it is used mainly in informal contexts.

get into trouble is a euphemism cliché meaning to get pregnant while one is unmarried, as *In those days girls who got into trouble were automatically expelled from school.* It is no longer generally considered a social disgrace to be pregnant and unmarried and so the cliché is rather inapt nowadays. However the expression is still widely used by some older people whose attitudes may not accord with modern thinking.

get more than one bargained for is a hackneyed phrase meaning to be confronted with a greater problem, etc than one had expected, as *The boxer thought that he would defeat the local champion easily but he got more than he bargained for.* The expression has been a cliché since the late nineteenth century.

get off one's chest is a hackneyed phrase commonly used in fairly informal contexts and meaning to disclose something that has been worrying, upsetting, annoying, etc one, as *If I've said something to annoy you I wish you'd get it off your chest.* It is as though one has removed a burden from one's bosom or heart. The *London Daily Chronicle* of 1902 described the expression as 'a horrid vulgar phrase'.

get one's act together is a hackneyed phrase dating from the second half of the twentieth century and meaning to get oneself organized, as *If you don't get your act together and start applying for university places you'll be too late.* It is used in informal or slang contexts.

get one's money's worth is a hackneyed phrase used mainly in fairly informal contexts indicating that one has obtained full value, as *We certainly got our money's worth at the concert. There were three encores.* The term 'money's worth' appears in Shakespeare's *Love's Labour's Lost* (2:1) 'One part of Aquitaine is bound to us, Although not valued to the money's worth.' The current expression dates only from the nineteenth century.

get one's teeth into is an idiom cliché meaning to begin to tackle something in a determined manner, as *He's bored. He needs a job that he can get his teeth into.* The origin is an allusion to teeth sinking into something substantial. The expression has been a cliché since the early twentieth century and is still common in fairly informal contexts.

get out of bed on the wrong side is an idiom cliché meaning to get up in the morning in a bad temper, as *What a mood the boss is in this morning! He certainly must have got out of bed on the wrong side.* The expression is an allusion to the legendary superstition that it was bad luck to put the left foot down first. If someone had a day of exceptional ill luck it was put down to rising from the wrong side of the bed. By the nineteenth century the concept of ill-luck had changed to bad temper. As a modern cliché it is found mainly in informal contexts.

get out while the going's good is a hackneyed phrase meaning to leave at an opportune time before things take a turn for the worse, as *Mother hasn't found out about your school report yet. I would get out while the going is good.* The cliché dates from the early part of the twentieth century and is used mainly in informal, often humorous, contexts. In origin the expression may be a reference to the 'going' or state of the ground in horse racing.

get the message is a hackneyed phrase meaning to understand, especially to understand the significance of something that had previously escaped one, as *It wasn't until she put in ear plugs that he got the message and realized how loudly he was snoring.* The cliché is used only in informal or slang contexts.

getting on is a hackneyed phrase meaning growing old or elderly, as *No wonder her memory's getting bad. She's getting on you know.* Frequently the expression is modified to **getting on a bit**. The expression **getting on** is also used to mean getting quite late, as *I think we'd better start dinner without him. It's getting on.* In both meanings the expression is used in fairly informal contexts.

gift of the gab, the is a hackneyed phrase meaning the ability to talk fluently and eloquently, as *He should get a job as a salesman. He's really got the gift of the gab.* 'Gab' here means mouth, being related to the slang word 'gob'. The expression is usually said with light criticism or grudging admiration and is found in informal contexts. It became popular in the eighteenth century.

gild the lily is an allusion cliché, being a reference, although not an exact one, to Shakespeare's *King John* (4:2) 'To gild refined gold, to paint the lily, To throw a perfume on the violet . . . Is wasteful and ridiculous excess.' It means to add unnecessary ornament or decoration, as *I don't know why she wears so much make-up. She's so pretty that it's gilding the lily.* It can also mean to exaggerate, as *He won't have told her the truth about his holiday cottage. He'll have gilded the lily a bit.*

gird up one's loins is an allusion cliché meaning to prepare for action, as *We have guests coming for dinner. We'd better gird up our loins and start cooking.* It an allusion to several passages in the Bible, as in *1 Kings* (18:46). 'He girded up his loins, and ran.' In Biblical times the Jews wore loose clothing and tied it up with a girdle only when they were going to work or be active. The apostle Peter used the expression figuratively 'gird up the loins of your mind' (*Peter* 1:13) and it has been a cliché since the nineteenth century. Nowadays it is usually mostly found in a humorous or ironical context.

girl Friday is a hackneyed phrase indicating a female personal assistant, as *The boss has advertised for a girl Friday to do his secretarial work.* The term is analogous with **man Friday**, a general assistant, but is considered sexist.

give a dog a bad name is an allusion cliché to an old proverb **give a dog an ill name and hang him**. It means to damage the reputation of someone by speaking ill of him/her, as *It just takes a few dissatisfied customers to affect business. Give a dog a bad name, as they say.* The expression has been a cliché since the early nineteenth century.

give and take is a hackneyed phrase meaning mutual concessions, a willingness to grant or allow a person something in return for being granted something oneself, as *In marriage there has to be some give and take,* and *If there is going to be a new wages agreement there will have to be* some give and take between the management and the union. The expression can also be used as a verb, as *It's difficult to fit into a new school. You have to learn to give and take.* The phrase has been in the language since the eighteenth century and it has been a cliché since the middle of the nineteenth century.

give an inch is an idiom cliché, an abbreviated version of **give someone an inch and he/she will take a mile.** It indicates that it is inadvisable to make any concession at all to a person because he/she will take advantage of the concession to try to obtain even more, as *If you let her start work late one morning she'll try to do it every morning. Give her an inch and she'll take a mile.* An earlier version of the expression was **give him an inch and he will take an ell.** This appeared in John Heywood's collection of proverbs in 1546.

give a wide berth to is an idiom cliché meaning to avoid, as *If I were you I'd give your father a wide berth. He's furious with you for damaging the car.* Literally the expression meant to give a ship plenty of space to manoeuvre safely. The phrase has been a cliché since the second part of the nineteenth century.

give it a miss is a hackneyed phrase used in informal and slang contexts and meaning not to go to something, as *We usually go to the village fête every year but this year we'll be away and so we'll have to give it a miss.* The expression is used in informal contexts.

give one's back teeth is an idiom cliché meaning to do absolutely anything to obtain something that one wants very badly, as *I would give my back teeth to live in a house like that.* The expression was previously **give one's eye teeth**, eye teeth being the upper canine teeth so called since they are

situated under the eyes. Originally the expression was **to give one's eyes,** as in *Barchester Towers 1857* by Anthony Trollope 'Bertie would give his eyes to go with you.' The modern cliché is used in informal or slang contexts.

give the old heave-ho to is a hackneyed phrase meaning to get rid of someone, to ask someone to leave, as *She was so inefficient that the boss gave her the old heave-ho after a week.* The cliché is used only in informal or slang contexts.

give up the ghost is a hackneyed phrase originally meaning to die, being found in the Bible in the *Book of Job 14:10* 'Man dieth, and wasteth away: yea man giveth up the ghost.' The 'ghost' referred to is the soul which is thought to be separated from the body on death. As a modern cliché it means to give up, to stop trying, as *He has been turned down for so many jobs that he's given up the ghost.* It is also applied to machinery, etc which breaks down, as *This car won't get us any farther. It's given up the ghost.* As a modern cliché the expression is used in informal contexts.

glutton for punishment, a is a hackneyed phrase referring to someone who seems to seek out or actively enjoy unpleasant or burdensome tasks, as *The new teacher has actually volunteered to take his third year class on a weekend trip. He must be a glutton for punishment.* The cliché is usually used in humorous or ironic contexts. An earlier form of the expression was a **glutton for work** which dates from the latter part of the nineteenth century.

go against the grain is an idiom cliché meaning to be contrary to a person's principles, feelings, wishes, etc, as *It goes against the grain for her to have to ask her father for money. She's so independent.* In origin the expression is a reference to the grain of wood. It is easier to cut or plane wood with the grain rather than across or against it.

go by the board is an idiom cliché meaning to be abandoned, as *Her resolution to diet went by the board when she was given a box of chocolates.* The board referred to is the side of a ship and the expression originally meant to fall overboard and so be lost. The modern cliché is used in informal contexts and was common by the late nineteenth century.

God's gift is a hackneyed phrase which is used to indicate someone marvellous, very handsome or beautiful, indispensable, etc as though he/she had been heaven-sent. The phrase is always now used ironically of someone who has an over-rated opinion of himself/herself, as *He thinks he's God's gift to women but all the girls in the office laugh at him.*

goes without saying, it/that is a filler cliché used to indicate that something need not be said since it is so generally well known or accepted, as *It goes without saying that pupils are expected to arrive on time.* The expression is often followed by the very statement that supposedly need not be said and is frequently virtually meaningless. Sometimes, indeed, what follows is not at all obvious or generally accepted and may not even be true, as *It goes without saying that we have the best education system in the world.* Some authorities state that the cliché is a translation of the French *cela va sans dire* and dates from the late nineteenth century.

go from strength to strength is an allusion cliché, being a Biblical allusion to *Psalms 84:7* 'They go from strength to strength, everyone of them in Zion appeareth before

God.' The expression means to improve markedly and progressively and is found in such contexts as *Setting up the business took a long time but it's going from strength to strength now.* It has been a cliché since the middle of the nineteenth century.

go haywire is a hackneyed phrase meaning to go hopelessly wrong, to start behaving or working totally erratically, as *Our computing system has gone completely haywire.* Originating in America, the actual origin of the expression is uncertain. It is probably an allusion to the fact that the coils of wire used for tying bundles of hay easily became entangled.

go in one ear and out the other is a hackneyed phrase meaning to make no impression on a hearer or listener, as *His mother kept telling him to clean his teeth after meals but her advice went in one ear and out the other.* The expression is commonly used in informal or humorous situations.

golden boy/girl is a hackneyed phrase meaning a young man or woman of great talent, popularity, etc, as *She is the golden girl of British athletics.* The expression is much used by journalists, particularly in a sporting context.

golden opportunity, a is a hackneyed phrase meaning an exceptionally good or favourable chance, as *Being invited to give a talk at the conference is a golden opportunity to get your name known in the profession.* The expression has been a common cliché since the middle of the nineteenth century.

golden rule, the is a hackneyed phrase meaning the rule or principle which is the most important in a particular situation, as *When dealing with customers the golden rule* is *always to be polite*. It is often used in rather a dogmatic or patronizing way. Originally the term indicated the principle that one should always do to others as one would wish them to do to oneself.

gone for a burton/Burton is a hackneyed phrase meaning lost, ruined, dead, etc. The expression is found in informal or slang contexts, as *I thought I might get my stolen car back but it seems to have gone for a burton*. In origin the phrase was an RAF expression during World War 2 meaning missing, presumed dead or drowned. The origin of this is uncertain but it has been suggested that Burton was short for Burton ale, several ales being produced at Burton-on-Trent, and that to go for a burton was to go for a drink, i.e. to be in the drink, 'drink' being slang for sea.

good as gold is a simile cliché meaning extremely good when referring to behaviour, particularly that of children, as *The baby was good as gold when her parents were out*. The cliché dates from the nineteenth century.

good clean fun is a hackneyed phrase meaning harmless or innocent entertainment or activities, as *The school party may usually be just good clean fun but the staff are worried about drink and drugs being brought in*. As a cliché the expression dates from the 1930s and now tends to be used either by older people or in an ironical context.

good in parts is an allusion cliché indicating that there are some good points or aspects about something, but generally conveying a critical rather than a complimentary opinion, as *The play was good in parts but it needs a lot of rewriting*. The expression refers to a saying 'good in parts, like the curate's egg' which first appeared in the illustrated satirical magazine *Punch 1895*. An illustration showed a young curate being asked by his bishop if his breakfast egg was to his liking. Too nervous to say that it was not, the young man replied that 'Parts of it are excellent!' As a cliché the phrase dates from the twentieth century and now tends mostly to be used by older or rather literary people.

good old days, the is a hackneyed phrase meaning the past, especially when looked upon with nostalgia by someone who remembers it, as *In the good old days we could have got there by train but they closed the line*. As a cliché the expression dates from the twentieth century and is sometimes used ironically. The sentiment goes back to ancient times.

goods and chattels is a hackneyed phrase meaning all one's belongings, as *She left her husband and appeared on our doorstep with all her goods and chattels*. As a cliché the expression is commonly used in a humorous or ironical context. In origin the phrase was a legal term referring to all a person's movable property. The expression dates from the sixteenth century and has been a cliché since the eighteenth century.

go off at half-cock is an idiom cliché meaning to act or start prematurely or without sufficient preparation and so be unsuccessful, as *The council's new traffic scheme has gone off at half-cock. It needed more research*. In origin the expression refers to the firing mechanism of a matchlock gun. This could be set, supposedly securely, half-way between the firing and the retracted positions. However, if the mechanism slipped, the gun went off unexpectedly and the shot was obviously wasted. The cliché is frequently used by journalists among others.

go overboard is an idiom cliché meaning to display a great deal of enthusiasm, often excessive enthusiasm, for something or someone, as *She's certainly gone overboard for that shade of green. She wears it all the time.* The expression which is found in informal contexts, has its origins in going to the extreme act of jumping off a ship. As a cliché it has been popular since the first half of the twentieth century.

go round in circles is an idiom cliché meaning to make no progress although frequently putting in a lot of effort, as *We've discussed ways to deal with the company's financial problems all day and we're just going round in circles.* In origin the expression refers to a person who is lost going round in circles without ever reaching his/her destination. An alternative form is **run round in circles**.

gory details the, is a hackneyed phrase meaning the unpleasant details of something. It derives from the word 'gore', meaning blood which has been shed and has clotted. As a cliché it sometimes retains its connections with blood, as *I'm sorry you had to have an operation but I don't want to know the gory details.* But frequently is more generally applied, as *She's bound to tell me about her marriage break-up, I hope she spares me the gory details.* As a cliché it dates from the twentieth century and is still common in rather informal contexts

go the extra mile is a vogue cliché of the late twentieth century meaning to put in the extra effort, money, etc required to do or achieve something, as *Management and unions are very close now but neither of them will go the extra mile to achieve an agreement.* It is particularly popular among politicians and journalists. In its Biblical origin the phrase refers to *Matthew* (5:41) 'And whosoever compel thee to go a mile go with him two.'

go the whole hog is a hackneyed phrase meaning to do something completely and wholeheartedly, especially with regard to spending money or effort, as *I was going to buy a new dress but I decided to go the whole hog and buy shoes and a bag as well.* The expression, which is used in informal contexts, is American in origin and has been a cliché since the nineteenth century. The ultimate origin of the expression is uncertain but it may be an allusion to the fact that hog was once a slang word for 'shilling'.

go through with a fine tooth comb is an idiom cliché meaning to search or study something very closely and carefully, as *You should always go through legal documents with a fine tooth comb.* The phrase is popular with journalists, for example when describing police searches. Its origin refers to the kind of comb commonly used to find and remove lice from hair.

go to rack and ruin is a doublet cliché since rack is an old variant of wreck and therefore meant much the same as ruin. It means to get into a state of neglect, decay, disorganization etc, as *He says he's emigrating because this country's going to rack and ruin.* It has been a cliché since the late eighteenth century although it has been in the language since the end of the sixteenth century.

go to the dogs is a hackneyed phrase meaning to be ruined. The expression can be used either of institutions, etc, as *That used to be a very good restaurant but recently it's gone to the dogs,* or of people, as *After he got into university he went to the dogs and failed all his exams.* When used of people, the ruination is often of a moral nature and is usually self-induced. The expression has been a cliché since the late nineteenth century although it has been in the language for longer than that. As a cliché it is used mainly in informal contexts. Its origins lie in the fact that dogs were generally considered to be inferior creatures.

go to the other extreme is a hackneyed phrase meaning to adopt a course of action, thought or attitude that is completely the opposite from the one which one has previously held, as *When the child was scolded for being late she went to the other extreme and now arrives at school half-an-hour early.* As a cliché it dates from the late nineteenth century.

go to town is a hackneyed phrase meaning to do something with great thoroughness, enthusiasm or expense, as *She's really gone to town on redecorating the house. She's practically rebuilding it.* It is used mainly in informal contexts. American in origin, the expression dates from the nineteenth century and refers to the fact that country people tended to go to town on special or important occasions.

grand old man, the is a hackneyed phrase used to refer to someone who is eminent and long-serving in a particular field, as *Nelson Mandela is now regarded by many as the grand old man of South African politics.* Prime Minister William Gladstone was referred to as 'the grand old man of British politics'. It does not appear to be one of those terms that have been reformed by feminism, as 'grand old woman' is not much in evidence. The expression dates from the late nineteenth century.

grasp the nettle is an idiom cliché meaning to tackle a problem boldly and firmly, as *If you think that she stole the brooch you must grasp the nettle and accuse her.* The cliché, which dates from the late nineteenth century, is commonly and frequently used by people who like giving others advice. Nettles are popularly held to sting less if one grasps them firmly.

grass grow under one's feet, not to let the see *not to let the grass grow under one's feet.*

grass is always greener, the is an allusion cliché based on the proverb **the grass is always greener on the other side of the fence,** which itself is used as a cliché. Both expressions are used to indicate that someone else's lot in life, or some other situation, often seems preferable to one's own, whether or not this is actually the case, as *I think you would be better staying in your present job. You know nothing about the other firm. You know what they say about the grass being always greener.* As a cliché it dates from the nineteenth century and, in common with the condition it describes, is very common today.

. **greatest/best thing since sliced bread, the** is a hackneyed phrase meaning someone or something marvellous or wonderful, as *To her the new car's the best thing since sliced bread.* It is commonly used ironically of people, as *You'd better not disagree with the new manager. He thinks he's the best thing since sliced bread.* The cliché is always used in informal contexts, often in an ironical or derogatory way. In origin the expression, which dates from the middle of the twentieth century, refers to the fact that sliced bread was regarded as a great labour-saving convenience when it was first introduced.

great unwashed, the is a hackneyed phrase meaning the common people. As a cliché it was popular from the middle of the nineteenth century and is now rather dated. However, it is still used by snobbish people, both old and young, who regard themselves as superior to others, as *I don't think I'll go to the hunt ball this year. They've started letting in the great unwashed.* It is also often used ironically, as *You won't find her at university dances. She's scared of mixing with the great unwashed.*

Greek, all see *all Greek to me*

green-eyed monster, the is an allusion cliché meaning jealousy. It is a reference to Shakespeare's *Othello* (3:3) 'Oh, beware my lord of jealousy, It is the green-eyed monster which doth mock the meat it feed on,' says Iago to Othello. As a cliché it dates from the nineteenth century and is still very commonly used in a wide variety of contexts, as *Bob thinks he fancies his brother's new girlfriend but it's just a case of the green-eyed monster.* The cliché is also used to indicate envy or covetousness as well as jealousy, as *She's just being nasty to you because she wants a car like yours. It's the green-eyed monster.*

green light, the is an idiom cliché meaning permission to proceed, as *As soon as we get the green light from the planning department, we'll start on the extension.* It is frequently used by journalists and headline writers. As a cliché it dates from about the mid nineteenth century and owes its origin to traffic lights where green means go and which were first used on railways.

grim death, like is a hackneyed phrase meaning very firmly and determinedly, as *The child was so scared of traffic that she clung to my hand like grim death.* The cliché dates from the middle of the nineteenth century and in origin refers to the unbreakable grip that death has on people.

grim reaper, the is an idiom cliché meaning death. It refers to the representation of death as an old man with a scythe. As a

modern cliché its use tends to be restricted to people of rather a literary bent, who often use it in ironical or humorous contexts, as *I think I'll retire soon. I want to do some travelling before the grim reaper catches up with me.*

grin and bear it is a hackneyed phrase meaning to put up with something unpleasant without complaining, as *I know you don't like studying when your friends are out playing, but your exam's tomorrow. You'll just have to grin and bear it.* As a cliché the expression dates from the late nineteenth century.

grind to a halt is an idiom cliché meaning slowly to come to a standstill, as *Work on our new house has always been slow but now it has ground to a halt completely.* The cliché, which in origin refers to an engine that gradually ceases to function, is widespread and is frequently used by journalists and headline writers. It dates from the twentieth century.

grin like a Cheshire cat is a hackneyed phrase meaning to smile broadly, as *He stood there grinning like a Cheshire cat while we tried to push the car.* It is often used in a derogatory way, the user being annoyed by the smile which is often of a triumphant, smug, etc nature. The ultimate origin of the expression is unknown, but it has been suggested that Cheshire cheese was once sold moulded like the face of a smiling cat. Although the expression was popularized by Lewis Carroll in *Alice's Adventures in Wonderland* (1865), it has been in use since the eighteenth century.

grist to the mill is an idiom cliché meaning something which brings profit or advantage, as *Collect as much stuff as possible for the church jumble sale. All is grist to the mill.* The expression has been a cliché since the nineteenth century although it has been used figuratively since the sixteenth century. Grist was corn for grinding which thus kept the mill operating profitably.

guiding light is a hackneyed phrase referring to a person or thing that has helped to shape one's life or career, as *The headmaster of his primary school was the famous scientist's guiding light,* and *Her mother's stand against sexism was the guiding light of the girl's early life.* As a cliché the expression dates from the mid nineteenth century and has its origin in a light from a lantern, etc which shows people the way in the dark.

❧ H ❧

hair of the dog, a is a hackneyed phrase used to refer to an alcoholic drink taken as a supposed cure for a hangover, although it is just as likely to prolong said hangover. It is a common cliché today, as *How about a hair of dog? You look absolutely terrible*, and has been so for a considerable time. It appeared in John Heywood's collection of proverbs (1546) and has its origin in an old remedy for a dogbite which consisted of burning the hair of a dog and placing it on the bite.

halcyon days is an idiom cliché referring to times that are remembered with nostalgia as being happy or perfect, as *The old women were looking at old photographs and talking about the halcyon days of their childhood.* The expression dates from the late sixteenth century and has been a cliché since the middle of the nineteenth century. In origin it refers to the old belief that the kingfisher, whose Greek name is *halcyon*, laid its eggs on the sea during a fourteen-day period of calm and good weather.

half a loaf is better than none is a proverb cliché which urges the advisability of being satisfied with what you have rather than spending time looking for or wishing for more. It is an old proverb, having appeared in John Heywood's collection (1546) and is still a common cliché today, as *Don't be too disappointed about not passing all of your exams. You passed quite a few and half a loaf is better than none.* The cliché conveys rather a smug, self-righteous sentiment and tends to irritate the person to whom it is directed.

hale and hearty is a doublet cliché, hale being an archaic form of healthy, and hearty meaning much the same in this context. The cliché is used to emphasize how healthy or fit someone is, as *The old man is well over eighty but he is remarkably hale and hearty.* The expression has been a cliché since the middle of the nineteenth century and is still popular today.

half the battle is a hackneyed phrase used to refer to a very successful beginning which will make the rest of an enterprise easier, as *It is going to be difficult getting funding for the new project, but if we get a government grant, that will be half the battle.* The expression became a cliché in the second half of the nineteenth century and is still common. It is a shortened form of the saying **the first blow is half the battle**, an expression dating from the eighteenth century.

hand in glove with is an idiom cliché referring to close association or intimate terms. It often carries a suggestion of dishonesty, as *He was not involved in the corruption investigation, but people think he was in hand in glove with the people who were found guilty of bribery.* The expression has been a cliché since the late nineteenth century and is still common. It is derived from an older expression **hand and glove** which appeared in John Ray's collection of proverbs (1678), and refers to the fact that a glove is very close to the hand.

handle with kid gloves is an idiom cliché meaning to treat extremely carefully or sensitively, as *You had better handle that customer with kid gloves. He has good grounds for complaint and he is absolutely furious,* and *The situation between the two countries is at a very delicate point and must be handled with kid gloves.* It has been a cliché since the late nineteenth century. In origin it refers to the fact that kid gloves are very fine and delicate.

hand over fist is an idiom cliché meaning very quickly or in large amounts, usually with reference to making money, as *They have been making money hand over fist with their food delivery service.* It has been a cliché since the nineteenth century. The expression was originally **hand over hand** and was a nautical term referring to the way sailors climbed a rope.

hands are tied, one's etc is an idiom cliché indicating one's powerlessness to act. It is a favourite let-out of bureaucrats, who use it as an excuse for not taking action. Their argument is that they are so restricted by rules and regulations that they are not free to take the action that someone wishes them to take, as *If it were left to me I would give you permission to have a street collection for your charity but my hands are tied.* The figurative form of the expression has been in existence since the seventeenth century. It is related to **bound hand and foot** or **tied hand and foot** which carry the same connotations. This was a cliché in the earlier part of the twentieth century but is no longer common.

hands down, win see *win hands down*

handwriting is on the wall see *writing is on the wall, the*

hang in the balance see *balance, hang in the*

hanged for a sheep as a lamb, might as well be is a proverb cliché indicating that one might as well commit a major crime, misdeed, etc rather than a minor one if the extent of the punishment is going to be the same, or that one should not indulge in half-measures. The proverb has been in existence since the seventeenth century and has survived to this day as a widespread cliché. It is now often used in a humorous context, as *I've broken my diet and had an ice cream and so I might as well be hanged for a sheep as a lamb and have a box of chocolates.* In origin the proverb refers to the days when the theft either of a sheep or a lamb was punishable by death.

happily ever after, live is a hackneyed phrase used to refer to a happy future existence, often in relation to a couple who have just married. The expression has been a cliché since the eighteenth century and is the classic ending of many fairy stories, as *The frog was turned back into a handsome prince. He then married the beautiful princess and they lived happily ever after.* The expression is still common today, but given the rate of marriage break-up, it is often used in ironic or humorous contexts, as *Mary and Jim got married five years ago and lived happily ever after until last year when they got divorced.* In ironic or humorous contexts the cliché is also applied to situations not involving marriage, as *What have the kids to look forward to? They leave school and live happily ever after on the dole.*

happy couple, the is a hackneyed phrase used to refer to a couple who are being married, who are just about to be married, or who have just been married. The cliché has been popular since the middle of the nineteenth century and is still common today, being much used by journalists, as *The happy couple posed for the cameras after the ceremony.* Nowadays it is frequently used in a humorous context. The term is also sometimes extended to include other than bridal couples, as *Here is a picture of the happy couple celebrating their golden wedding.* An alternative form of the expression is **the happy pair.**

happy event, a is a euphemism cliché used to refer to Childbirth. It is still used, even though people are now much more open about referring to pregnancy without euphemism. The users are mainly older people, especially women who have not yet been affected by the new frankness, as *I hear that your granddaughter is looking forward to a happy event.* It is also used humorously by journalists or by younger people.

happy hunting ground is a hackneyed phrase indicating a place where one often goes, especially in order to obtain a great many things that one wants, as *The local market used to be a happy hunting ground for antique dealers but nowadays it just sells rubbish.* As a cliché it dates from the twentieth century and is still in common use today. In origin it refers to the fact that American Indians believed that after death they would go to a kind of heaven which would be very well stocked with game.

happy pair, the see *happy couple, the*

hard act to follow, a is a hackneyed phrase used to describe someone or something that is outstanding that will be difficult to emulate, as *Our chairman has unfortunately retired and we shall have to replace him. It's a pity; he's a hard act to follow,* and *Last year's village fête was such a success that it will be a hard act to follow.* The expression is American in origin and takes its derivation from vaudeville. It expresses the difficulty of following a successful act which has found favour

with the audience in case one cannot achieve a similarly high standard. In Britain the cliché dates from the second part of the twentieth century and is used in informal contexts. An alternative form is **a tough act to follow.**

hard and fast rule is a hackneyed phrase used to refer to rules that cannot be altered or dispensed with whatever the circumstances, as *The pupils can choose whether or not to wear school uniform. There are no hard and fast rules on the subject.* The original form was **hard and fast line** which was first used in political contexts in the late nineteenth century. As a cliché **hard and fast rule** dates from the twentieth century. In origin the expression refers to a nautical term, 'hard and fast' referring to a ship that has run aground.

hard facts is a hackneyed phrase simply meaning facts, 'hard' being used for emphasis to indicate that the facts cannot be denied, as *I am sorry that they are having to leave the flat but the hard facts are that they cannot afford the rent.* It is sometimes simply used meaninglessly by people who hardly ever use simple words without some form of qualification. The expression has been a cliché since the middle of the nineteenth century.

has the cat got your tongue? is a catchphrase cliché used to someone who has given no reply or comment when one might be expected. It is most often used to children who understandably have nothing to say to the other clichés frequently directed at them by adults, as *What are you going to do when you grow up? Has the cat got your tongue?* The origins of the phrase are obscure, but it has been common since the middle of the nineteenth century, although recently it has become rather dated. Children continue to suffer from it but it is usually directed at them by older people.

have . . . will travel is a catchphrase cliché. The original catchphrase dating from the early part of the twentieth century was **have gun will travel**, supposedly popularized by a personal advertisement in *The Times*. It was further popularized in the 1960s by the Western television series bearing the title and was then used humorously of items other than guns, as *I'm looking for a job anywhere. It's a case of have typewriter, will travel*, and *The lease on my flat is up. Have bed, will travel.*

have a bone to pick see *bone to pick, a*

have a finger in every pie see *finger in every pie, have a*

have a lot on one's plate is an idiom cliché meaning to have many matters which require one's attention. It is used very commonly in informal contexts, many of them involving business, as *I'm sorry that I didn't return your call but I've got a lot on my plate just now*. In origin it refers to a plate of food that is somewhat overfull and so will take a long time to eat.

have a nice day is a catchphrase cliché used as a standard greeting. It is still considerably less common in Britain than it is in America, where it was popularized by truck-drivers on their CB radios, but is sufficiently common to be annoying. It tends to be used by sales assistants and others who really do not care whether you have a nice day or not, but is sometimes used ironically to someone who has been particularly rude to one or who has done one a particularly bad turn, *Oh, you've given me a parking ticket? Have a nice day!* **Have a nice one** is an even more annoying alternative form of the expression.

have I got news for you? is a hackneyed phrase used to try to impress one's listener with what one is about to say, the implication being that the information is either startling or unwelcome to the receiver, *You thought he was the best candidate for the job? Well, have I got news for you? We've discovered that his qualifications are phoney!* and *Were you planning a weekend away? Well, have I got news for you? The boss says that we have to work overtime this weekend to finish the order*. The expression is American in origin and has been popular in Britain from the second part of the twentieth century. Its use tends to be restricted to the kind of person who likes to bring bad news.

have it in for is a hackneyed phrase meaning to have a grudge against someone or to feel spiteful towards someone, as *He's had it in for his neighbour ever since she complained about his dog*. It has been a popular cliché since the first half of the twentieth century and is still widespread today.

have one's hands full is an idiom cliché meaning that one has a great many things to do, as *With two young children to look after she has her hands full*. The expression dates from the fifteenth century and is still very popular today.

have something up one's sleeve see *up one's sleeve*

have the other half is a hackneyed phrase meaning to have another drink. It originally referred to having another half pint of beer, to follow a half pint already drunk. It was then extended to other drinks, as *You've finished your whisky? Will you have the other half?*

have what it takes is a hackneyed phrase indicating that someone is sufficiently talented, hard-working, etc to achieve what he or she is aiming at, as *She wants to be a professional singer but the competition is so great and she really doesn't have what it takes.* The cliché dates from the twentieth century and is still very common today. It is rather a patronizing cliché since the user is sitting in judgement on someone's else's capabilities

have you heard the latest? is a catchphrase cliché used by someone who cannot wait to impart the latest piece of juicy gossip, as *Have you heard the latest? Mary and Jim have split up!* It is a twentieth century cliché and is still popular today.

head and shoulders above is an idiom cliché used to refer to someone who is immeasurably superior to others, as *She is bound to do well in the exams. She is head and shoulders above the other pupils.* It has been a cliché since the middle of the nineteenth century and is still widespread. In origin it refers to someone who is so tall that his head and shoulders are literally above the smaller people in a group.

head over heels is a hackneyed phrase meaning utterly and completely. The cliché in its modern form and in its association with love dates from the nineteenth century and is still popular nowadays, as *He has fallen head over heels in love with his best friend's fiancée.* The implication of the phrase is that one is so much in love that one is turning upside down. It does not seem particularly appropriate and it was originally found in the more appropriate form of **heels over head**, which dates from the fourteenth century.

heads will roll is a catchphrase cliché which carries the threat that someone is going to be in trouble or be punished in some way, as, *If the boss finds out that the office door was left unlocked overnight, heads will roll!* The expression became popular about the middle of the twentieth century and is still quite common. In origin it refers to heads rolling after they were cut off by the guillotine, used in France for executions.

heart in mouth, with is an idiom cliché used to emphasize the extent of one's fear or alarm, as *With heart in mouth I watched the child balancing on the parapet of the bridge.* The expression dates from the sixteenth century and has been a cliché since the eighteenth century. It also exists in the form **my heart was in my mouth**, as *Our hearts were in our mouths as we watched the police trying to get the man down from the roof.* In origin the expression refers to the choking feeling that is caused by sudden fear or panic, as though one's heart had jumped into one's mouth.

heart in the right place, have one's is an idiom cliché meaning to be well meaning, to have good intentions. The expression has been a cliché since the later part of the nineteenth century. It is still popular today, often carrying the suggestion that the virtue referred to compensates for some other fault, as *He did the wrong thing by taking the child in, but his heart was in the right place,* and *The headmistress seems very stern but her heart is in the right place. She is very understanding if the children have real problems.* In origin it refers to the old belief that the heart was the seat of the emotions.

heart-to-heart is a hackneyed phrase meaning a confidential and intimate conversation, as though people's hearts were close together. It is an abbreviated form of **heart-to-heart talk** which has been a cliché since the beginning of the twentieth century. **Heart-to-heart** is still a popular cliché today and usually carries the suggestion that people are opening up to one another and not hiding their feelings.

helping hand, a is a hackneyed phrase which is rather a tautological way of saying simply help or assistance. The expression dates from the fifteenth century and has been a cliché since the eighteenth century. It is still common today in rather informal contexts, as *We are moving house tomorrow. Could you give us a helping hand?*

helping the police with their inquiries is a hackneyed phrase which is sometimes a euphemism cliché referring to someone who is making a statement to the police, and sometimes is being held by them, in connection with some form of crime, as *A local man is helping police with their inquiries into the disappearance of the child.* It is an expression much used by journalists, probably because they are quoting the guarded statements of the police, who have to be careful what they say for fear of prejudicing the outcome of any future trial. The phrase has become particularly widespread because of the popularity of crime fiction and crime series on television.

here we go! is a twentieth century cliché used to imply repetition, usually the repetition of something which one has already found tedious, as *Here we go! She's going to tell us about her struggle to get to the top again.* The expression is also used in the more obvious sense of 'we are about to start'. When trebled, **here we go!, here we go!, here we go!**, the expression becomes a well-known football supporters' chant.

hide one's light under a bushel is a quotation cliché meaning to be so modest and retiring that one conceals one's talents, as *I didn't know you could sing like that. You must have been hiding your light under a bushel,* and *She is actually a very accomplished pianist but she rarely plays in public. She prefers to hide her light under a bushel.* The expression is a quotation from a Biblical passage, in *Matthew* (5:15) 'Neither do men light a candle, and put it under a bushel, but on a candlestick . . . let your light so shine before men that they may see your good works.' Bushel refers to the container in which was measured the unit of weight also called a bushel. It has been a cliché since the middle of the nineteenth century.

high and dry is an idiom cliché meaning abandoned in a very difficult situation, as *We thought that he was giving us a lift back to town. We were left high and dry when he drove off without us.* The expression has been a cliché since the late nineteenth century and is still common, usually in an informal context. It is nautical in origin, referring to a ship that has run aground.

hit it off is a catchphrase cliché meaning to get along very well, as *I wasn't looking forward to meeting her since we have very little in common, but in fact we hit it off very well.* The expression dates from the late eighteenth century and is still a common cliché, being used in all but the most formal contexts

hit or miss is a hackneyed phrase meaning haphazard or random, as *I've made something for the child to eat but I don't know what she likes and so it's a bit hit or miss.* As a cliché the expression dates from the twentieth century although the concept is much older, dating from the sixteenth century. In origin it refers to the hitting or missing of a target.

hit the nail on the head is an idiom cliché meaning to be absolutely accurate, to say or do exactly the right thing, as *I think you hit the nail on the head when you said that she was naive,* and *You hit the nail on the head when you diagnosed that the child had measles.* The analogy dates from the early sixteenth century and it has been a cliché since the nineteenth century. In origin it refers to hitting a nail right in the middle of its head with a hammer.

hive of industry, a is an idiom cliché used to refer to a place where there is a great deal of activity going on, as *All the children were busy writing a story. The classroom was a real hive of activity,* and *We were all sewing like mad to get her wedding dress finished in time. The room was a hive of industry.* The expression has been a cliché since the late nineteenth century and is still popular today. In origin it refers to the fact that insects which live in hives always seem to be engaged in frantic activity.

hold one's own is a hackneyed phrase meaning to succeed in maintaining one's position against competition or attack, as *She was much the less experienced tennis player but she held her own against the defending champion.* The expression has been in use since the sixteenth century and was a cliché by the nineteenth century. The expression is also used as a medical cliché. In describing a patient's condition, it means that he or she is not getting any worse and is putting up a fight for survival, as *He was very badly injured in the accident but at the moment he is holding his own.*

hold the fort is an idiom cliché, often a business cliché, meaning to look after something while someone is away or until someone arrives, as *I have to go to the dentist this morning. Do you think you could*

hold the fort to save me closing the shop for the morning? The phrase is American in origin, dating from the American Civil War, and as a cliché dates from the twentieth century, being still popular today.

hold your horses is an idiom cliché, often found in the imperative, used to urge someone not to move or act so quickly or hastily, as *Hold your horses! You can't book the holiday yet. We haven't all agreed on where we're going.*

holding the baby see *baby, left holding the*

home James! is a catchphrase cliché used to tell the driver of a car or bus to drive off, as *Right! Everyone is back in the bus. Home James!* and *The children are settled in the back seat. Home James!* It is a shortened form of **home James and don't spare the horses!** The expression dates from the late nineteenth century and is still used today in a humorous way, although it is rather dated. In origin it refers to a person telling his coachman to take him home as rapidly as possibly.

honest truth, the is a hackneyed phrase used to emphasize the truth of something, as *I had nothing to do with it and that's the honest truth.* It dates from the late nineteenth century and is still a common cliché. Not infrequently it is used to try to hide the fact that the user is in fact lying.

hope against hope is an allusion cliché meaning to go on hoping or wishing for something when there is little probability of the hope or wish being realized, as *The children were hoping against hope that it would snow on Christmas Day, although they were having a very mild spell of weather.* It has been a cliché from the late nineteenth century and is still common today. The expression is a Biblical allusion to *Romans* (4:18) 'Who against hope believed in hope that he might become the father of many nations.'

horns of the dilemma, on the is an idiom cliché meaning faced with two equally undesirable potential courses of action, as *She was on the horns of a dilemma. She could not decide whether to accept a lift home from him and be bored out of her mind or to wait for the bus and get soaking wet.* In medieval rhetoric a 'dilemma' was a way of arguing which consisted of proving that one of two statements must be true, both being damaging to one's opponent's case. It was likened to a two-horned animal. In choosing which of the two statements he preferred to admit as truth, the opponent was pictured as having to throw himself on to one or other of the 'horns'. As a modern cliché the expression tends to be used by people of a literary bent or by people who use rather formal English.

horses for courses is a catchphrase cliché meaning what is suitable or appropriate for someone or something is not necessarily so for others, as *We like to try to provide a wide range of hobbies for our members to choose from. We know there are horses for courses,* and *This drug worked for your mother but it might not work for you. There are horses for courses in the medical world.* As a general cliché the expression has been popular since the later part of the twentieth century. In origin it refers to horse racing in which some courses suit some horses better than others.

hot dinners, more – than you've etc had see *more – than you've etc had hot dinners*

how long is a piece of string? is a catchphrase given as a reply to a question when one has no idea of even an approximate answer, as *How long will it take to finish this? How long is a piece of string?* The question need not be in any way related to length, as *How much would it cost to renovate that old house? How long is a piece of string?* It started out as a kind of trick question from about the 1920s and developed into its present use later.

how time flies is an idiom cliché used to emphasize how quickly time seems to pass, as *Is it midnight already? How time flies!* The connection between time and flying is an old one, the Romans having had the proverb, *tempus fugit,* meaning time flies, or flees. The modern cliché dates from the twentieth century. It is still common today, sometimes being used ironically, especially when it is extended to **How time flies when you're having fun,** as *This lecture seems to have been going on for hours. How time flies when you're having fun!*

how to win friends and influence people is a catchphrase cliché mostly used nowadays in an ironic way, as *You have just upset the whole office with your tactless remark. How to win friends and influence people!* and *He really knows how to win friends and influence people. He just poured a glass of red wine down the boss's wife's dress.* The expression originated in America and became popular as the title of a book by Dale Carnegie (1936). In its straight version it has been a cliché in Britain since the late 1940s.

how was it for you? is a hackneyed phrase of the second part of the twentieth century used as a stock phrase to inquire after a partner's level of sexual satisfaction during intercourse. It is so hackneyed that is now mostly found in humorous or satirical contexts, such as comedy shows.

hue and cry is a hackneyed phrase used to indicate an uproar or public protest, as in *There was a real hue and cry when they threatened to close our local post office*. It has been a cliché since the middle of the nineteenth century. In origin it refers to an Anglo-Norman legal term, *hu et cri*, for the summons issued to members of the public to join the hunt for someone who had committed a crime. They were required by law to shout and make other noise.

if the cap fits, wear it is a proverb cliché meaning if the situation applies to you, you should admit and accept the fact, as *I don't know if she's right when she calls you a womanizer but if the cap fits, wear it.* Sometimes the cliché is shortened to **if the cap fits**, with the second part being understood, as *No one has accused him of getting the job dishonestly, but if the cap fits.* The cap may refer to the cap traditionally worn by the court fool.

if the mountain will not come to Mohammed, Mohammed must go to the mountain is a proverb cliché indicating that if the person or thing that one wishes to see is unwilling or unable to come to one, then one must go to that person or thing. The second part of the saying is often omitted, as *I asked my sister to come and discuss our father's birthday party, but she cannot leave the children. Ah well, if the mountain cannot come to Mohammed.* The cliché is often extended to mean that if one. cannot get one's own way then one should accept the fact and adopt an appropriate course of action. The origin of the expression refers to a story in which Mohammed, asked to give proof of his miraculous powers, ordered Mount Sofa to come to him. When this failed to happen, he accepted that he would have to go to it. The cliché is used in a variety of contexts but tends to be restricted to people of a literary or academic bent.

if the worst comes to the worst is a hackneyed phrase meaning if the most disadvantageous circumstances should occur, and is usually followed by some fairly radical expedient, as *If the worst comes to the worst, we can always sell the house and buy a small flat.* The expression dates from the late sixteenth century and has been a widespread cliché since the late nineteenth century.

if you can't beat 'em/them join 'em/them is a catchphrase cliché of American origin dating from the early 1940s, as *If the students upstairs are insisting on having a party you might as well go to it. If you can't beat 'em, join 'em.* The cliché is mostly used in informal contexts.

if you can't stand the heat get/keep/stay out of the kitchen is a catchphrase cliché indicating that a person should not undertake a difficult job unless he/she is prepared and able to cope with the stress and strain of it, as *The young woman burst into tears on her first day as a teacher and was told by a colleague, 'If you can't stand the heat, stay out of the kitchen.'* The cliché is American in origin, dating from the mid 1950s, and is associated with President Truman particularly with reference to the American presidency.

if you've got it flaunt it is a catchphrase cliché dating from the second part of the twentieth century and meaning you should make the most of what you have. It is frequently associated with physical assets and is used in informal contexts, as *Why shouldn't she wear a low-cut dress. She's got the figure for it. If you've got it flaunt it!*

ignorance is bliss is an allusion cliché, being a reference to the closing lines of *Ode on a Distant Prospect of Eton College* (1742) by Thomas Gray. 'Where ignorance is bliss 'tis folly to be wise.' The expression means that sometimes it is better not to know the true facts of a situation for the sake of one's peace of mind, as *She thinks her husband is faithful and don't tell her otherwise. Ignorance is bliss, as they say.* As a cliché the expression dates from the nineteenth century.

I hate to mention it but . . . is a hackneyed phrase used to introduce something that the hearer is not going to want to know. Often it introduces something that the speaker will actually enjoy saying, rather than hating it, as *I hate to mention it but you now owe me over £200.* It is mostly found in informal contexts and dates from the late nineteenth century.

I hope we will always be friends is a hackneyed phrase commonly used when announcing the break-up of a relationship to a girlfriend/boyfriend/partner/spouse, as *I'm moving out because I don't love you anymore and I've found someone else. But I hope we will always be friends.* The statement, originating in the second part of the twentieth century, usually does little to alleviate the situation as the other half of the partnership is not usually in the mood to be disposed to friendship.

I'll be in touch is a hackneyed phrase, dating from the second part of the twentieth century, frequently used informally simply to bring a conversation or informal meeting to an end, with the user often having no serious intention of getting in touch, and sometimes having the definite intention not to do so, as *I'm sorry I can't come to the party with you but I'll be in touch.* An alternative to this expression is

I'll give you a ring or **I'll give you a call**, yet another being **I'll get back to you**.

ill-gotten gains is a hackneyed phrase meaning money or profit obtained in an illegal or bad way, as *He's in prison but his wife and family are living off his ill-gotten gains.* It is often nowadays used ironically or humorously, as *Well, it's pay day. What are you going to do with your ill-gotten gains?* As a cliché it dates from the nineteenth century.

I'm a stranger here myself is a hackneyed phrase, dating from the second part of the twentieth century, and said by someone who is asked for directions in a place which is unfamiliar to him/her, as *I'm sorry I don't know where the post office is. I'm a stranger here myself.* It is the kind of cliché that one often criticizes others for using and then finds oneself automatically using it when faced with the appropriate situation.

in a certain/interesting condition is a euphemism cliché meaning pregnant, as *At one time women were expected to leave work if they were in a certain condition.* Established as a cliché since the mid nineteenth century, it is rather dated now that people are less inhibited about referring to pregnancy frankly and is mostly used by older people in rather formal contexts, or by others in an ironical or humorous way. See also *delicate condition.*

in all conscience is a hackneyed phrase meaning by any reasonable standard, to be fair, as *I cannot in all conscience recommend him as a good worker.* It has become a habit with some people and is often used virtually meaninglessly as a filler cliché. It has been commonly used since the eighteenth century.

in all honesty is a filler cliché which is seemingly used to underline the truth of something but is usually used meaninglessly as a conversation filler and is often used just as a habit, as *In all honesty, I think we should finish work for today.*

in a meeting is a hackneyed phrase used as a business cliché, dating from the second part of the twentieth century, which is often a euphemism cliché for not wishing to be contacted or communicated with, as *I am sorry Mr Jones cannot listen to your complaint in person. He is in a meeting.* It is usually used by a receptionist, secretary, assistant or other member of staff to protect a colleague from an unwanted intrusion, whether he/she is in a meeting or not.

in a nutshell is a hackneyed phrase meaning very briefly, as *In a nutshell they lied.* It is an extremely widespread expression. As a cliché it dates from the mid nineteenth century and refers to the fact that a nutshell holds very little. Pliny, the Roman writer, in his *Natural History* wrote that Homer's epic poem, the *Iliad*, was copied in such tiny writing that the entire text might have been enclosed in a nutshell. It is by no means uncommon for the cliché to be used to introduce a fairly lengthy statement and so to give the hearer false hope of brevity.

in a tick/in two ticks is a hackneyed phrase for a very short time, although this can turn out to be a longer time than the user promises, and is often used simply to give false hope of speediness, as *If you have a seat the doctor will be with you in a tick.* In origin the expression refers to the ticking of a clock. It is more colloquial than **in a minute** and is the kind of cliché that becomes a habit with some people.

in cold blood see *cold blood, in*

inferno, blazing see *blazing inferno.*

in flagrante delicto is a foreign cliché. The English cliché means in the very act of committing an offence, as *She thought her adultery would go unsuspected but her husband came home and found her and her lover in flagrante delicto.* Despite the literal meaning, A P Herbert in *Unholy Matrimony* suggested 'in flagrant delight' as an alternative. As a cliché in English it has been common since the nineteenth century, although nowadays it tends to be used either in formal contexts or by people of an academic or literary bent.

in high dudgeon is a hackneyed phrase meaning resentfully, huffily, as *She went off in high dudgeon when we refused to do what she wanted.* 'Dudgeon' is an archaic word for anger. The expression has been a cliché since the mid nineteenth century.

in less than no time is a hackneyed phrase meaning very quickly. It is used in informal contexts often to try to placate someone who is impatient, as *Don't cry. Your mummy will be here in less than no time.*

inner man, the is a hackneyed phrase meaning one's stomach, as *I'm almost ready to go but the inner man is in need of some sustenance.* Originally the expression applied to the soul but it has had its present meaning since the late eighteenth century. Nowadays it is usually used humorously or pompously.

in no uncertain terms/manner is a hackneyed phrase meaning clearly and frankly, as *I told her in no uncertain terms exactly what I thought of her behaviour.* As a cliché it dates from the twentieth century.

ins and outs, the is a hackneyed phrase meaning all the aspects and details of something, as *I'm not agreeing to the plan until I've had a chance to consider all the ins* *and outs.* In origin the expression refers to the various windings and turnings of a path and thus to the intricacies of a situation. As a cliché it dates from the late nineteenth century and is now used mostly in informal contexts.

in one ear and out the other see *go in one ear and out the other*

in point of fact is a filler cliché meaning the same as **in fact** which is itself often a filler cliché. Both are often used meaninglessly and so unnecessarily, as *In point of fact I haven't seen him for weeks.* **In point of fact** dates from the early eighteenth century but it is still very much used today.

interesting condition see *in a certain condition*

in the bag see *bag, in the*

in the balance, to hang see *balance, hang in the*

in the cold light of day see *cold light of day*

in the dark is an idiom cliché meaning having no or little knowledge about something, ignorant of something, as *The workers are completely in the dark about what's happening to the firm.* The expression has quite a modern ring to it but in fact the equating of darkness with lack of knowledge goes back to Roman times. It is still widespread today in informal contexts.

in the dim and distant (past) is a hackneyed phrase usually used humorously to indicate the near, or the relatively near, past, as *I used to wear shoes like that in the dim and distant when I was a teenager.* As a cliché, the expression dates from the twentieth century.

in the family way is a euphemism cliché meaning pregnant, as *She's taking time off work because she's in the family way.* This is a considerably less formal cliché than **in a certain condition** and has survived the modern, open use of the word "pregnant".

in the final analysis is a hackneyed phrase simply meaning in the end, as *You can make as many suggestions as you like but in the final analysis she will do just as she pleases.* It is a pretentious alternative to **after all is said and done** and is a cliché that some people easily become addicted to.

in the land of Nod is a hackneyed phrase meaning asleep, as *The children were all safely in the land of Nod when we left.* Nod was the name of the land to which Cain was exiled after killing his brother, Abel (*Genesis* 4:16) but the expression more probably has its origin in the association between feeling sleepy and the act of nodding. Jonathan Swift (1667–1745) wrote in *A Complete Collection of Genteel and Ingenious Conversation* that he was 'going into the land of Nod' meaning that he was going to sleep. The cliché is usually used in a rather humorous context nowadays.

in the land of the living meaning alive, in existence, is an allusion cliché, being a Biblical allusion to *Jeremiah* (11:19) 'Let us cut him off from the land of the living, that his name may be no more remembered.' As a modern cliché the expression is often used humorously or in informal contexts, as *I'm lucky to be still in the land of the living after that heavy branch fell on me.*

in the pipeline is a hackneyed phrase which was a vogue expression in the 1960s and 1970s. It means under way, awaiting processing, as *The present figures do not take account of wage increases that are in the pipeline.* Pipeline literally refers to a long pipe for conveying oil, water, etc. If the commodity is still in the pipeline it has not yet come through.

in this day and age is a filler cliché which simply means now, as *Fancy having such dreadful toilet facilities in this day and age.* It is an extremely widespread cliché used in all but the most formal contexts.

iron hand in the velvet glove, the is an idiom cliché indicating severity or mercilessness which is hidden under the guise of kindness or leniency, as *The children thought that they would have an easy time with the smiling young teacher, but they soon discovered that it was a case of the iron hand in the velvet glove.* In *Latter-Day Pamphlets* (1850) Thomas Carlyle ascribes the phrase to Napoleon Bonaparte.

it fell off the back of a lorry is a hackneyed phrase, dating from the mid twentieth century and used informally to describe something that has been acquired cheaply and fortuitously, often by questionable means, as *You won't get a mountain bike as cheaply as Jim's. I'm sure his fell off the back of a lorry.* The expression frequently refers to stolen, or possibly stolen, goods, the implication being that the item in question was taken from the back of a lorry rather than falling off.

it goes without saying see *goes without saying, it/that*

it happens is a hackneyed phrase indicating a philosophical acceptance of some unpleasant event, as *It's sad that they've divorced but it happens.* An alternative form is **these things happen**. Both clichés can be very annoying or upsetting to someone to whom something unpleasant has just happened and is not yet at the philosophical stage.

I think I can safely say is a filler cliché which is a meaningless and rather pretentious introduction to a statement. It is a cliché often adopted by public speakers, as *I think I can safely say that educational standards have never been higher.*

it never rains but it pours is a proverb cliché indicating that when something bad happens it is either very bad or is accompanied by several other bad things, as *The fridge has broken down and now the car won't start. It never rains but it pours.*

it's a far, far, better thing that I do now is an allusion cliché being a reference to a speech by Sydney Carton in *A Tale of Two Cities* (1859) by Charles Dickens 'It is a far, far better thing that I do than I have ever done.' People using the cliché usually wrongly add 'now' to the original speech. As a cliché it is now usually used by people of literary tastes in a humorous or ironical context, suggesting in an exaggerated way that something quite minor is an act of great self sacrifice, as *My sister couldn't get a ticket for the concert and so I gave her mine. It's a far, far, better thing that I do now.*

it's always darkest before the dawn is an idiom cliché used to cheer up people who are in some kind of trouble by people who are not, as *I know you're feeling hurt by your wife's rejection but things will improve. It's always darkest before the dawn.* Nothing brings out clichés in some people like other people's misfortunes. Instead of keeping silent, which would be preferable, they feel obliged to come out with platitudes, which at best is annoying. An alternative form is **the darkest hour is just before the dawn**.

it's a small world is a hackneyed phrase used, for example, when one encounters someone one knows in somewhere unexpected, as *We were climbing in the Himalayas and met our next-door neighbours*. *It certainly is a small world*. The cliché dates from the twentieth century.

it's for your own good is a hackneyed phrase used when something unpleasant has happened to or been said to someone, often by way of some kind of punishment, and often to a young person, as *We did not want to cut off your allowance but it's for your own good*. *You must learn the value of money*.

it's not for me to say is a hackneyed phrase which is virtually meaningless since the user goes on to say what he/she thinks, despite the disclaimer, as *It's not for me to say, but he is quite obviously making the biggest mistake of his life*. This is the kind of cliché that easily becomes habit-forming.

it's not the end of the world is a hackneyed phrase indicating that, however bad a situation is, things could be worse. It is used to refer to a wide variety of situations, from the relatively minor, as *I know you have missed the bus but it's not the end of the world*, to the major, as *I've just been declared redundant but I suppose it's not the end of the world*.

it stands to reason is a filler cliché that simply serves as an introduction to something that someone is going to say. Often what is said is not particularly reasonable or obvious. Indeed often the reverse is the case, as *It stands to reason that the staff will do anything to keep their jobs*. The expression has been current since the sixteenth century, becoming a cliché about the nineteenth century.

it takes all sorts (to make a world) is a hackneyed phrase indicating that humankind is made up of many different sorts of people. It is usually used in reply to someone who is complaining about someone else, as *You might think he's got peculiar tastes, but it takes all sorts*. Sometimes the phrase is extended, as *She's not exactly my favourite person but it takes all sorts to make a world*. In its longer version the expression has been current since the seventeenth century and in its shorter version since the late nineteenth century, becoming a cliché in the twentieth century.

it takes one to know one is a catchphrase cliché used informally to indicate that someone who is swift to identify and criticize a wrongdoer of some kind is often guilty of a similar offence, in the way that a thief would be swift to spot the signs that someone had stolen something, as *Mary's husband says that Jim is being unfaithful to his wife*. *Well, you what they say*. *It takes one to know one*. The cliché dates from the twentieth century.

it takes two to tango is a catchphrase cliché indicating that some activities involve two people and so both must accept some responsibility for them. The expression, which has been popular since the 1930s, often has sexual connotations, as *You can't put all the blame on your husband's girlfriend*. *It takes two to tango* and is used in informal contexts. The tango is a dance of Latin American origin for couples.

it will all out come out in the wash is an idiom cliché meaning that everything will work out satisfactorily in the end, as *Try not to worry about your sister's marriage problems*. *It will all come out in the wash*. The expression dates from the nineteenth century and in origin refers to the removal of dirt and stains from clothes by washing.

I've got a headache is a hackneyed phrase popularly supposed to be used by a woman as an excuse for not having sex, as *Not tonight darling. I've got a headache*. It is now often used in a humorous or ironical context. As a cliché it dates from the twentieth century.

J

jack of all trades, a is a hackneyed phrase used to refer to someone who can turn his or her hand to a wide range of tasks, as *There is no need to get a whole team of tradesmen to do your repairs. The man who lives next door to us is a real jack of all trades.* The expression has been in existence since the early seventeenth century. As a cliché it is becoming rather dated and is frequently used disparagingly. It is sometimes accompanied by the suggestion that someone who tries his or her hand at a wide range of jobs is unlikely to be really skilled at any of them as in the expression **a jack of all trades and master of none**.

jam tomorrow is a hackneyed phrase indicating that prosperity or happiness will come in the future, usually with the suggestion that one will have to put up with a certain amount of hardship, misery, etc until the rosy future arrives. It was exceptionally commonly used in Britain when Margaret Thatcher was Prime Minister in the 1980s, as *There is little point in promising people jam tomorrow when they are losing their jobs because of the recession.* It is still popular as a cliché, being usually used in relation to the economy. In origin the expression is an allusion to *Through the Looking Glass* (1872) by Lewis Carroll, in which the Red Queen offers Alice a job with 'twopence a week, and jam every other day . . . jam tomorrow, jam yesterday, but never jam today.'

jaundiced eye, a is a hackneyed phrase used to mean from a cynical viewpoint as though looking only for the bad points or disadvantages of something, as *Our neighbours look on anything young people do with a jaundiced eye.* The expression became a cliché in the nineteenth century and is still common today. In origin it refers to the old belief that to someone who was suffering from jaundice, a condition in which the skin and the whites of the eyes turn yellow, everything which he or she looked at seemed to be coloured yellow. The playwright, John Webster, refers to this belief in *The White Devil* (1:2) (1612) 'They that have the yellow jaundice think all objects they look on to be yellow.'

je ne sais quoi French for 'I do not know' is a foreign cliché used to refer to something that one cannot define exactly, as *She was by no means beautiful but she had a certain je ne sais quoi.* As a cliché it was popular from about 1890 but is now dated. It is still used but only by pretentious people who are trying, usually unsuccessfully, to impress others, or by people who are using it in a consciously humorous or ironic way.

jet set, the is a hackneyed phrase used to refer to wealthy and fashionable people who have a great deal of leisure time and travel from one fashionable resort to another, as *It was the time of year in Cannes when the jet set arrived.* The term was originated in the 1950s and rapidly became a cliché. As a cliché it is still used today but it is becoming rather dated as foreign travel becomes more and more common in the lives of ordinary people and is no longer the province only of the rich. It is in fact now used of people who are very wealthy and fashionable, whether or not they engage in continuous travel, although in origin the expression refers to travel by jet-propelled aircraft which began in the 1950s and was very expensive.

jewel in the crown, the is an idiom cliché and also a vogue cliché used to refer to the best part of anything, as *The visitors were attracted by the Highland scenery which is the jewel in the crown of the Scottish tourist industry*, and *Lack of money has forced her to sell the painting which was the jewel in the crown of her private collection*. The popularity of the cliché in recent years is a result of the televising of *The Raj Quartet* by Paul Scott. The first book of the series was entitled *The Jewel in the Crown*, the 'jewel' being India, and the crown being that of Queen Victoria. The origin of the phrase may lie in the title of a painting *The Jewel in Her Crown*, mentioned in the first volume of Scott's quartet and depicting the Queen receiving a large jewel (representing India) from an Indian prince. The application of the expression **jewel in the crown** was commonly used to describe the British colonies in the first part of the twentieth century. It is now frequently subject to overuse in a more general context.

Job's comforter is an allusion cliché used to describe someone who, although pretending to comfort or sympathize with someone who is undergoing some form of misfortune or distress, is in fact exacerbating the distress, as *His friends visited him in hospital to cheer him up but they turned out to be real Job's comforters by telling him how ill he looked and how they knew of someone with his condition who had never walked again*. It has been a cliché since the middle

of the eighteenth century and is still widespread today. The expression is Biblical in origin, being an allusion to *Job* (16:2) where Job refers to his friends as 'miserable comforters.'

jobs for the boys is a catchphrase cliché used to suggest that people are getting jobs or posts because they know someone with influence in the relevant area, as *The foreman on the building site would only take on tradesmen if they knew one of his friends or family. It was an obvious case of jobs for the boys but he got away with it*. The expression became popular in the 1930s and is still popular, as indeed the practice is. It is often used in connection with politics, as *The government were accused of jobs for the boys when it came to selecting members of the various committees*.

jockey for position is an idiom cliché meaning to try to manoeuvre one's way into a position of power, wealth, etc, as *Now they have heard that the managing director is retiring, all the other executives are jockeying for position*. In origin the expression is an allusion to racing where it refers to a jockey trying to manoeuvre his horse into a winning position. It was in existence in its racing meaning in the early part of the twentieth century and began to be used figuratively in the 1950s. It is mostly used in a business context today and usually in a derogatory way.

join the club! is a catchphrase cliché used to express sympathy or solidarity to someone who is experiencing an unfortunate situation which other people present have already experienced, as *Has she stopped speaking to you? Join the club! She has completely ignored us since she met her new smart friends*. The expression began to be popular in the late 1940s and is still used widely today in an informal context.

jolly hockey sticks is a catchphrase cliché used to describe a hearty, robust, games-playing girl, woman, school, club, etc, as *We have decided not to send our daughter to the local girls school. It is too jolly hockey sticks for words and she is very artistic.* The expression, which is used in a derisory way by people who are not themselves the open-air, games-loving types, was used in the BBC radio show, *Educating Archie* by Monica, Archie's girlfriend, the show being broadcast in the late 1940s and the early 1950s. It is thought to have been coined by the actress, Beryl Reid.

jump down someone's throat is an idiom cliché meaning to reply to someone in a very sharp or angry way. It is used in informal contexts and is often considered unnecessarily sharp by the receiver of the remark, as *There is no need to jump down my throat just because I am a few minutes late.* The expression has been in existence since the late nineteenth century, Anthony Trollope having made use of it in *Cousin Henry* (1879) 'Was she to jump down your throat when you asked her?'

jump on the bandwagon is an idiom cliché meaning to associate with something because it is fashionable or because it is going to be advantageous to oneself, as *When the property market was booming in the 1980s many people jumped on the bandwagon and set up as estate agents.* As a cliché the expression is still popular today and has its origin in the fact that in the southern states of America it was common for a band to play on a wagon being driven through the streets to advertise some forthcoming event, political meeting, etc. At election times people would jump on the wagon to show their support for the relevant candidate.

jump the gun is an idiom cliché meaning to act prematurely or impetuously, as *They*

jumped the gun by starting to build the new house before they had planning permission. The expression has been popular since the middle of the twentieth century and is still widespread today in an informal context. In origin it refers to competitors who start out before the sounding of the starter's gun that marks the beginning of a race.

just deserts is a hackneyed phrase meaning a deserved reward or punishment, as *Let us hope that the person who committed this horrible crime gets his just deserts.* Nowadays it is used in a formal context. Historically the word 'desert' in this context means what is deserved, commonly used until the middle of the eighteenth century but obsolete since then except for its use in this cliché.

just doing my job is a twentieth century catchphrase cliché usually used by over-zealous people in some form of relatively minor authority to indicate that they are not being deliberately obstructive or obstreperous but are simply obeying the procedure as set down by the rules of their jobs. It is a cliché guaranteed to arouse wrath in those to whom it is addressed and has associations with the ultimate in military disclaimers of all responsibility 'We were just obeying orders', which gives the user licence to do just about anything in the name of authority. The sentiment behind **just doing my job** is timeless and so the cliché is still alive and well in many bureaucratic areas of society.

just for the record is a filler cliché used to emphasize that note should be taken of what is being said. It does not suggest that someone write down, or in any way officially record, the remarks that follow the statement but simply that the speaker wishes to make his or her position clear, as *Just for the record, it was not my suggestion* *that we go to France on holiday.* It became popular from the 1950s and is still extremely common, being used mainly in an informal context. In origin the expression refers to the keeping of official records.

just one of those things, it's is a catchphrase cliché expressing a philosophical view that certain situations or events happen inexplicably and that there is nothing one can do about them, as *There is no point in worrying about the plant dying while you were taking care of the house. It was just one of those things.* It has been popular since the middle of the 1930s, being popularized by a Cole Porter song having the expression as its title.

just the job is a catchphrase cliché indicating that whatever is being referred to is

exactly right or what is required or is particularly pleasant, as *Ah, a cold beer after a hard day's work. Just the job!* In origin the expression was military slang and as such has been in use since about 1935. It gradually became more general and was in general civilian use from the 1950s. As a cliché it is still common in an informal or slang context.

just what the doctor ordered is a twentieth century catchphrase cliché indicating that whatever is being referred to is exactly what is required, suitable or relevant, or is particularly pleasant, as *A holiday in the sun with no work worries. Just what the doctor ordered!* In origin the expression refers to a doctor's prescription or recommended treatment for curing an illness.

❦ K ❧

keep a low profile is a hackneyed phrase meaning to remain as unnoticeable as possible, to keep out of the limelight, as *After the scandal involving the politician died down he kept a low profile for the rest of his career.* As a cliché it has been common since the early 1970s and is still widespread, often used by journalists in connection with political or other public figures.

keep a stiff upper lip is an idiom cliché meaning to keep one's true emotions, such as fear, sadness or despair hidden, and to remain stoical, as *I know that you are miserable because your girlfriend has left you but you really must try to keep a stiff upper lip.* Although the term is American in origin, where it first appeared in the early 1880s, it is frequently regarded as a typically English characteristic, the English tending not to show their emotions in the way that, for example, the Latin races do. The expression came to Britain shortly after its appearance in America and has been a cliché since around 1880. It is still popular today with people who regard the practice as being a virtue but it is often used by others in a humorous or ironic context. The origin of the phrase seems rather odd. It presumably refers to the trembling of the lips as an indication of emotion, as though one were about to cry, but in fact it is usually the lower lip that trembles in such a situation, as any parent who has watched the wobbling of a child's lip before the inevitable ensuing flood of tears will testify.

keep a straight face is an idiom cliché meaning not to laugh or smile but to maintain an expression of gravity. It began to be popular in the 1950s and is still in widespread use, as *I could scarcely keep a straight face when he was taken in by the hoax.* In origin it refers to keeping one's facial muscles tight in order to avoid smiling.

keep at arm's length is an idiom cliché meaning to avoid becoming too familiar or friendly with someone, as *Our neighbours are very pleasant but we try to keep them at arm's length. Otherwise they would always be popping in at all hours uninvited.* Originally the expression was **at arm's end** but by the middle of the seventeenth century it had taken its present form, becoming a cliché about the middle of the nineteenth century. It is still widespread today. In origin the phrase refers to the physical act of preventing someone from getting too close to one by extending one's arm to push him or her away.

keep a weather eye on is an idiom cliché meaning to watch closely, as *Keep a weather eye on the new boy's work. He is totally inexperienced.* The phrase sounds rather literary but it is in widespread use, often with the suggestion that one does not altogether trust the person to whom the weather eye should be directed. It is nautical in origin, a reference to a sailor on a sailing ship watching carefully for signs of a change in the weather that might affect the vessel.

keep body and soul together is an idiom cliché meaning to succeed in surviving physically but only just, to live at semi-starvation level, as *It is difficult to keep body and soul together on such a low income.* The expression came into existence in the eighteenth century, becoming a cliché in the nineteenth century. It is still used today but often in a humorous or ironic context. In origin it refers to the belief that the soul leaves the body on death.

keep it dark is a hackneyed phrase used to urge someone to keep something secret, as *Keep it dark but I've heard a rumour that we are getting a pay rise.* It is often now used in a humorous or ironic context. In origin it was underworld slang and has been in existence since about 1830. The expression means the same as → **keep it under your hat**.

keep it under your hat is an idiom cliché used to urge someone to keep something secret, as *Keep it under your hat but I've applied for another job.* The expression dates from the late nineteenth century and is still common today, being used in an informal or slang context. In origin it refers to someone hiding something under his or her headgear.

keep one's ear to the ground see *ear to the ground, an*

keep oneself to oneself is a hackneyed phrase meaning to avoid contact with other people as much as possible, as *We have not yet got to know our new neighbours as they keep themselves to themselves.* An alternative form is **keep to oneself**, as *I have often seen her at meetings but she seems to keep to herself.* It has been a common cliché since the beginning of the twentieth century.

keep one's end up is a twentieth century idiom cliché meaning to maintain equality

with others in a venture, to perform one's part in something as well as others involved as *All the others in the quiz game were very well informed but we managed to keep our end up.* It is mainly used in informal contexts and in origin is a cricketing term, meaning not to lose one's wicket. Alternatively it is a reference to people carrying a heavy weight, such as a piece of furniture, where it is important that both people keep the ends off the ground.

keep one's fingers crossed is an idiom cliché dating from the twentieth century and meaning to hope and wish for success, as *We are keeping our fingers crossed that we get a fine day for the children's picnic.* In origin it refers to the making of the sign of the cross to avert bad luck or danger.

keep one's head above water is an idiom cliché meaning to remain financially solvent, as *It was difficult to keep the firm going during the recession but we were just able to keep our heads above water.* The expression dates from the early eighteenth century, becoming a cliché in the nineteenth century. It is still very common and is sometimes used of non-financial situations, meaning to keep up with excessive demands or commitments, as *I have so much work on hand that it is difficult to keep my head above water.* It alludes to the need to keep one's head above water to avoid drowning.

keep one's mouth shut is an idiom cliché meaning to keep silent. It is used in very informal or slang contexts, as *If you have any sense you will keep your mouth shut about witnessing the attack. They are very dangerous people.* The expression has been a cliché since the nineteenth century.

keep one's nose clean is an idiom cliché meaning to keep out of trouble. It is used in very informal or slang contexts, as *The boy has already been in trouble with the police and so he'd better keep his nose clean if he doesn't want to end up in prison.* The expression has been existence since the late nineteenth century and has been a common cliché since the 1940s. In origin it probably refers to keeping one's nose out of something and so not getting it dirty, and may first have been popular among criminals.

keep one's nose to the grindstone is an idiom cliché meaning to keep working very hard, as *I shall have to keep my nose to the grindstone if I am going to finish this work by the end of the week.* The expression is often used of rather monotonous work and in origin refers to a grindstone on which knives are sharpened as it revolves. It has been a cliché since the middle of the eighteenth century. The phrase is not only used reflexively as it is possible to keep the noses of other people to the grindstone, as *His parents try to keep his nose to the grindstone as his exams are coming up soon.*

keep one's powder dry is an idiom cliché meaning to be in a state of readiness for possible action, but not yet to take the action, as *I don't think their campaign will damage our business but we should keep our powder dry in case it does.* The phrase was used by Oliver Cromwell to his men before the battle of Edgehill in 1642 'Put your trust in God, but keep your powder dry.' This was a reference to the importance of keeping gunpowder dry because if it got wet it was ineffective. The expression has been used figuratively since the nineteenth century.

keep the ball rolling is an idiom cliché meaning to maintain an activity without a halt, as *She launched the campaign against the closure of the hospital but she needs a lot of supporters to keep the ball rolling.* The expression has been a cliché since the late nineteenth century. Its origin may refer to the importance of keeping the ball in play in ball games.

keep the home fires burning is an idiom cliché meaning to keep things running smoothly in the home, as *Most of her friends go out to work but she prefers to stay at home with the children and keep the home fires burning.* The expression, which was popularized by a song at the time of World War 1, is now dated. When it is used it is often in a humorous or ironic context.

keep the wolf from the door is an idiom cliché meaning to succeed in making enough money to provide food or to keep one solvent. The expression dates from the sixteenth century and has been a cliché since the beginning of the nineteenth century. It is still used nowadays but usually in a humorous or ironic context, as *The job is not particularly well paid but I just about manage to keep the wolf from the door.* In origin the phrase refers to the common belief that wolves are always hungry and eager to eat people.

keep up appearances is a hackneyed phrase meaning to maintain an appearance of respectability, relative wealth, etc irrespective of the true situation or how poor one is, as *He lost his job but he thought it was important to keep up appearances so that his neighbours would not find out and he left the house every morning at the same time as he used to leave for work.* It shares the same twentieth-century sentiment as **keep up with the Joneses**. The expression has been a cliché since the second part of the twentieth century, and is mostly used in a derogatory way.

keep up with the Joneses is a hackneyed phrase meaning to attempt to maintain the style of living and level of spending and acquisition of consumer goods of one's neighbours or acquaintances, as *They do not earn nearly as much as their friends and got into very severe debt by trying to keep up with the Joneses.* The expression is used in a derogatory way, and it is always other people who indulge in this materialistic practice. It has been a cliché since the middle of the twentieth century and has its origins in the title of a comic strip by Arthur R Momand published in the *New York Globe* from 1913. Jones was chosen since it is a common name. Momand is said to have rejected the even more common name Smith because it was the name of his own neighbours and he did not wish to give offence.

keep your chin up is an idiom cliché used, usually in the imperative form, to urge someone not to lose heart or courage, as *I know that the person you have to play is very good but keep your chin up and do your best.* The expression has been a cliché since the 1940s, having replaced the older **keep your pecker up** which had the same meaning but was used in more informal or slang contexts.

keeper, I am not my brother's is an allusion cliché, being a Biblical reference to *Genesis* (4:9), when Cain, after murdering his brother, Abel, and being asked where he was, says to God, 'I know not: am I my brother's keeper?' As a cliché it is often found in the form of a statement rather than a question, and indicates that the person concerned is disclaiming responsibility for another person, not necessarily either a brother or a close relative, as *I have no idea why Jack's late. I am not my brother's keeper.* The cliché is most commonly used by people of an academic or literary bent.

kickstart, give a is an idiom cliché which became a vogue cliché in the 1980s, often

used with reference to the British economy, as *The government is looking for ways to kickstart the economy in order to put an end to the recession.* In origin the expression refers to kick-starting an engine. The cliché means to take affirmative action to make something happen.

kick the bucket is a euphemism cliché meaning to die. The expression dates from the eighteenth century and is commonly used as a modern cliché in a very informal or slang context. The origin of the expression is uncertain. One suggested explanation is that the bucket referred to was an East Anglian term for a wooden frame on which pigs were slaughtered and which was kicked by them as they died. Another suggestion is that people who kill themselves by hanging may stand on an up-turned bucket or something similar in order to tie the rope, the bucket then being kicked away.

kick upstairs is an idiom cliché meaning to promote someone to a position that is higher in rank but carries considerably less responsibility. The practice is carried out in order to get rid of someone whom it would be very difficult, expensive or impolitic to sack. The expression was in use in the early nineteenth century. It is still a common cliché today in informal contexts, although modern business methods which are frequently aimed at reducing budgets, and so staff numbers, seem to be more in favour of redundancy than of kicking people upstairs. It has been used to describe the elevation of a member of the British House of Commons to the House of Lords.

kill the fatted calf is an allusion cliché meaning to prepare a splendid homecoming or reception. In origin it is an allusion to the parable of the prodigal son in the Bible (*Luke* 15), in which the father of the son who had returned home after having squandered his inheritance, instead of punishing him, arranges a splendid feast, for which a 'fatted calf' is to be killed. The expression has been a cliché since the nineteenth century. Nowadays it is often used in a humorous or ironic way for a lavish celebration of some kind, as *Given the size of our salary rise I don't think we will be killing any fatted calves.*

kill the goose that lays the golden eggs is a proverb cliché meaning to put an end to a source of wealth or other form of profit or advantage through greed, thoughtlessness or stupidity. The expression has been widely used since the beginning of the nineteenth century and is still in widespread use today, as *They killed the goose that lays the golden eggs when they began to steal from their old aunt. She found out and cut them out of her will,* and *She killed the goose that lays the golden eggs when she kept forgetting to return books. Her friend, who has a huge collection, refused to lend her any more.* In origin the expression refers to one of Aesop's fables, in which a man, who discovers that his goose has begun to lay golden eggs, kills the goose because he thinks that he will get a great many eggs at once by this means and by doing so deprives himself of the source of the golden eggs.

kill two birds with one stone is a proverb cliché meaning to succeed in achieving two goals by means of one action or effort, as *I killed two birds with one stone while I was at the library. I changed my books and I photocopied some documents on their copier.* The expression dates from the beginning of the seventeenth century and comes originally from Latin. It has been a cliché since the nineteenth century. As to the derivation of the phrase it does not seem very likely that two birds

would ever obligingly stay so close together when being attacked that the attacker could hit both of them at once.

kill with kindness is an idiom cliché meaning to spoil someone, to do someone a disservice by treating him or her with too much indulgence or generosity, as *Giving children a lot of sweets as a reward is just killing them with kindness. Think of the damage to their teeth.* The original saying was '**to kill with kindness as fond apes do their young**', a reference to the fact that apes sometimes hug their offspring in affection so tightly that they kill them. **Kill with kindness** was common in the middle of the sixteenth century and has been a cliché since the early nineteenth century. It is still common today. Thomas Heywood wrote a play called *A Woman Killed With Kindness* in 1607.

kindred spirit, is a hackneyed phrase indicating a person who is very like another in temperament, interests, etc, as *When I introduced my friends to each other it was obvious that they were kindred spirits and they have been close friends ever since.* The expression has been in use since the middle of the nineteenth century and has been a cliché since late that century. It is still widespread today.

kiss and tell is a hackneyed phrase and a modern vogue cliché meaning to reveal an intimate secret. The term has been in existence since the late seventeenth century but enjoyed a new lease of life in the 1980s when it became common for people to have illicit affairs with public figures, such as politicians, and then to tell their stories to the tabloid press for widespread publication, as *The politician has resigned his post in the government after the kiss-and-tell revelations by his ex-mistress.* Since the person who does the telling in such a situation is usually well paid by the press for so doing, a variation has arisen on the theme, **kiss and sell.**

kiss of death, is an idiom cliché meaning a destructive effect, as *Losing his licence because of drink-driving was the kiss of death to his career.* In origin the expression refers to the kiss with which Judas Iscariot betrayed Jesus Christ at the Last Supper, Judas having indicated to the enemies of Jesus that he would identify him to them by kissing him (*Matthew* 26: 47–49). As a cliché the phrase is not related to treachery and dates from about the middle of the twentieth century. It is current still.

knotty question, a is an idiom cliché indicating a difficult problem that is hard to solve. The expression has been a cliché since the nineteenth century. In origin it refers to a knot in a piece of wool, etc which is difficult to undo.

know all the answers is a hackneyed phrase used to describe someone who is, or thinks he or she is, very well-informed or knowledgeable. American in origin, the expression has been popular since the 1930s. As a modern cliché it is usually used in a derogatory way, as *There is no point in trying to give him any advice about driving a car. He knows all the answers.*

know a thing or two is a hackneyed phrase used to indicate that one has a good deal of information about something, or that one has a good deal of experience in connection with something, as *The old man knows a thing or two about engines.* The expression often carries the suggestion that it is not given to many to have this kind of knowledge, as *'I know a thing or two about women,' he leered.* As a cliché it dates from the second half of the twentieth century and is still widespread today, especially among

people who like to impress others with their superiority.

know chalk from cheese, not to see *different as chalk and cheese*

know for a fact is a hackneyed phrase sometimes used to emphasize how certain someone is about something, as *I know for a fact that she leaves those children on their own without a babysitter.* It is often used simply as a filler cliché by people who use it out of habit, almost without realizing that they are using it. In such situations 'know' alone would suffice. As a cliché the expression dates from the twentieth century.

know from Adam see *not know from Adam*

know one's onions is an idiom cliché which, like **know the ropes,** means to have a thorough knowledge of one's subject, although in origin it is rural rather than nautical. As a cliché it is still in current use, as *I enjoyed the talk on local history. The speaker certainly knew her onions,* but it is rather dated.

know the ropes is an idiom cliché meaning to be well-informed about or skilled in something, as *We are not looking for a trainee computer operator. We need someone who knows the ropes.* The expression came into figurative use and then became a cliché in the late nineteenth century. It is still widespread today, being used in all but the most formal contexts. The term derives from the days of sailing ships when it was necessary for sailors to know all about the ropes in order to be able to help sail the boat effectively.

know what's what is a hackneyed phrase meaning to be fully informed about what is going on, as *Vague promises are not enough. We want to know exactly what's what.* The expression was used by Samuel Butler in *Hudibras* (1663) 'He knew what's what, and that's as high as metaphysic wit can fly.' It is possible that he coined the term. As modern cliché it is often used by rather precise people who like everything to be straightforward.

know where one stands is a hackneyed phrase meaning to understand exactly the nature of one's position or circumstances, as *There have been rumours about redundancies and the workers would like to know where they stand.* The expression has been a cliché since the late nineteenth century and is still widespread today.

know which side one's bread is buttered is an idiom cliché meaning to have a clear idea of where one's best interests lie, of what situation or course of action will be to one's advantage, as *The young people know which side their bread is buttered. They would never dream of leaving home and moving into a flat.* The expression is quite old, having appeared in John Heywood's collection of proverbs in 1546. It has been a cliché since the nineteenth century and is still common nowadays.

❧ L ❧

labour of love, a is a hackneyed phrase indicating a task done, not for money or other reward, but out of affection or regard for the person for whom one is doing it or because of the pleasure or satisfaction which one derives from doing it, as *She hates housework and so it is a real labour of love when she cleans her grandmother's house*, and *Turning that waste site into a rose garden is a real labour of love but they are both keen gardeners*. In origin the expression may be Biblical, being a reference to *1 Thessalonians* (1:3) 'Remembering without ceasing your work of faith, and labour of love, and patience of hope in our Lord Jesus Christ, in the sight of God and our Father', and to *Hebrews* (6:10) 'For God is not unrighteous to forget your work and labour of love, which we have shown towards His name, in that ye have ministered to the saints, and do minister.' Both passages refer to people who do God's work as a labour of love.

lady of the house, the is a hackneyed phrase meaning the woman who is in charge of a house and usually refers to the wife of the owner of a house. It is now dated on two counts. The word 'lady' is now usually disliked by modern women, who prefer 'woman', and most women now have jobs outside the house as well as running the home. The expression, in common with **the woman of the house**, is now considered patronizing. As a cliché it became popular in the nineteenth century and continued to be so until the rise of feminism. It is still used by some

people, such as certain salesmen, who have not caught up with the times, and appear on doorsteps saying *Is the lady of the house at home?*

land of milk and honey is an allusion cliché meaning a place providing comfort or luxury. The expression became a cliché in the nineteenth century, and although it is still used today, it is now rather dated, tending to be used by people of a literary bent, as *Some immigrants are disappointed when they arrive in Britain since they are expecting a land of milk and honey and the reality is very different*. The expression is an allusion to a passage in the Bible, to *Exodus* (3:8) in which God tells Moses 'And I am come down to deliver them out of the land of the Egyptians and to bring them out of that land unto a large and good land flowing with milk and honey.' Sometimes the expression appears in a variant form which is closer to the original, **a land flowing with milk and honey**, as *They expected a land flowing with milk and honey, not a land of poverty and unemployment*.

land of the living, in the see *in the land of the living*

land on one's feet see *fall on one's feet*

lap of luxury, the is a hackneyed phrase meaning great ease or affluent circumstances, as *They used to be very poor but since he won the football pools they have been able to live in the lap of luxury*. The expression dates from the late eighteenth century and has been a cliché since the middle of the nineteenth century. It is still in wide-spread use today.

large as life, as is a simile cliché meaning in person or actually, as *We heard that he had died but he turned up at the reunion dinner large as life*. The expression dates from the late eighteenth century and is still a common cliché today.

larger than life is a hackneyed phrase meaning on a grand scale, as *He was a very insignificant person although his father and grandfather were both larger than life figures*, and sometimes has the extended meaning of dramatically exaggerated. The expression is a development of **(as) large as life**.

last but not least is a hackneyed phrase meaning last in terms of sequence but not in terms of importance. It is frequently used in situations where names or items have to be listed but where there is no obvious order of merit, as *We have a number of people to thank for their contribution to the organization of the reception – Jack Jones, Mary Smith, Fred Brown, Jane Green and last, but not least, John White*. Sometimes the impression is even created that the person or thing mentioned last is not the least in importance but possibly the greatest. The expression dates from the sixteenth century, being used by John Lyly in *Euphues and his England* (1580). It has been a cliché since the nineteenth century and is still extremely common.

last legs, be on one's is an idiom cliché meaning to be near to the end or collapse, as *The firm was on its last legs when it was bought by one of its competitors*. It can also be used to mean close to utter exhaustion, as *She rode the poor horse until it was on its last legs*. As a cliché the expression dates

from the twentieth century and is still very common today.

last of the Mohicans, the is a catchphrase cliché referring to the one remaining in a group, series, etc when all the rest have gone. In origin it refers to a novel by James Fenimore Cooper, *The Last of the Mohicans* (1836). The expression probably became a cliché around the turn of the century. It was formerly more commonly used over a wider set of contexts. For example it was once used of the last cigarette in a packet. Nowadays it tends to be used of a survivor of a group that is dying out, as *All the rest of the women go into the village pub but she is the last of the Mohicans and thinks a pub is no place for a woman*.

last straw, the is an idiom cliché having its derivation in the proverb **it is the last straw that breaks the camel's back**. It refers to an event, fact, etc which, when added to all other events or facts that have gone before, makes a situation finally impossible to bear, as *We had to work late every night that week but it was the last straw when we also had to work on Sunday*. Originally, as the derivation indicates, the suggestion was that the final event or act was rather trivial, it being simply the cumulative effect that proved disastrous, but this is no longer the case. The expression has been a cliché since the nineteenth century and is still wide-spread. An alternative form of the same theme, **the last feather that breaks the horse's back**, existed in the seventeenth and eighteenth centuries but this is now obsolete.

late in the day is a hackneyed phrase meaning late or overdue, often with the suggestion of being too late, as *It is a bit late in the day to decide to go to university but if you ring around you might just get a place,* and *It is a bit late to start studying for the exam. It begins in an hour.* As a cliché it dates from the twentieth century and is still widespread.

laugh all the way to the bank is a hackneyed phrase referring to someone's joy at having made a substantial profit, as *People said that he was mad to invest in that scheme but he went ahead and he is now laughing all the way to the bank,* and *I knew him when he lived in miserable poverty but now he is laughing all the way to the bank.* It is a variant of **cry all the way to the bank,** an ironic expression which means much the same, except that the latter places more emphasis on the fact that the investment which led to the profit was in some way wrong, ill-advised, or disapproved of, as *The environmentalists tried to stop him building a factory there but he defied their objections and is now crying all the way to the bank.* The expression originated in America in the 1960s and later spread to Britain where **laugh all the way to the bank** is the commoner expression.

laugh: not to know whether to laugh or cry see *not to know whether to laugh or cry.*

laugh on the other side of one's face is an idiom cliché meaning to feel disappointed, miserable, depressed, etc after having felt happy, successful, triumphant, etc, the implication being that one deserved the change in one's fortunes and might even have brought these on oneself, as *He was boasting about having given so little money to the old lady for the car, but he was laughing on the other side of his face when the car would not start.* The expression sometimes takes the form of **laugh on the wrong side of one's face.** As a cliché the expression dates from the eighteenth century, although the concept is older. It is still common today.

laugh out of court is an idiom cliché meaning to treat someone or something with derision, refusing to take the matter seriously, as *Our request for a pay rise of 15% will be laughed out of court.* As a cliché it dates from the late nineteenth century and is still common, although used in rather formal contexts or by people who have rather a formal manner of speaking and writing. In origin it refers to a court of law. The idea of a case being treated derisively is mentioned in Horace's *Satires* (35BC).

laugh up one's sleeve is an idiom cliché meaning to be secretly amused, often at the expense of someone else, as *She pretended to sympathize with his predicament but all the time she was laughing up her sleeve at him.* As a cliché the expression dates from the late eighteenth century and is still widespread today. Historically the expression originally took the form of **laugh in one's sleeve** and had its origin in the fact that people could hide a smile by hiding their faces behind the wide sleeves of earlier fashions. This expression dates from the early sixteenth century, being included in John Heywood's collection of proverbs.

law and order is a hackneyed phrase, indeed almost a doublet cliché, since the two words in this context are virtually interchangeable, used to refer to the enforcement of a country's laws, as *Both political parties are now putting law and order near the top of their agendas.* The expression has been common since the nineteenth century and is still a common cliché today. Since it is very frequently a political issue it tends to enjoy periodic spells of exceptional popularity. Traditionally it is a cliché beloved of the political right wing which advocates tougher laws and penalties and disliked by those on the left who fear that it is associated with a harsh, insensitive regime.

law unto oneself, a is a hackneyed phrase used to refer to someone who always does things his or her way, taking little note of conventions or rules, and tending to be unpredictable, as *I have no idea whether Mary will agree to the plan or not. She is a law unto herself.* The expression has been a cliché since the late nineteenth century. It is still quite common but usually in the slightly less formal form of **a law to oneself.**

lay it on with a trowel is an idiom cliché meaning to exaggerate one's flattery or complimenting of someone, often in order to achieve something of advantage to oneself, as *It is one thing to compliment a girl on her appearance but he lays it on with a trowel*, and *They wanted her to babysit and so they laid it on with a trowel about how much the children loved her.* The expression refers to the kind of trowel that is used to apply plaster and was used by Shakespeare in *As You Like It* (1:2) 'Well said, that was laid on with a trowel.' It has been a cliché since the middle of the nineteenth century and is still popular today. A modern alternative form is **lay it on thick.**

lay one's cards on the table is an idiom cliché meaning to be absolutely truthful about one's role in a situation, to state openly what one is going to do, as *He should lay his cards on the table and give details of his financial interest in the project*, and *They have laid their cards on the table and said that they will sell the property to the highest bidder, irrespective of who that might be.* The cliché dates from the twentieth century and is still common today, although it is often used as a kind of smokescreen by people who are not really being completely honest about their activities or intentions, but who are using the phrase to deceive other people into thinking that they are honest. In origin the phrase refers to card-playing. An alternative form of the expression is **put one's cards on the table.**

leading light is an idiom cliché referring to someone who is prominent in an organization, as *She is one of the leading lights in the local operatic society.* It has been common since the late nineteenth century, being frequently used by journalists on local papers reporting local events. Nowadays it is sometimes used ironically to describe someone in an organization who thinks too much of himself or herself. In origin the expression is a nautical term for a light used with other marks as a guide to the entrance of a harbour, channel, etc.

lead on, Macduff is an allusion cliché, being a misquotation from Shakespeare's *Macbeth* (5:10). The misquotation dates from the late nineteenth century and is now a common cliché used to urge someone to get going, as *All the people taking part in the search are here now. Lead on, Macduff!* The actual quotation is 'Lay on, Macduff, and damned be him that first cries, "Hold, enough!"' Another expression that is closer to this is **lay on, Macduff.** This was a cliché from the early nineteenth century and was used to incite someone to vigorous action.

lean over backwards see **bend over backwards**

learn something to one's advantage is a hackneyed phrase meaning to hear about something that will result in something advantageous, usually some form of financial profit, for oneself. It originated in the standard legal formula for informing someone about an inheritance, as *If you call at the offices of White, White, White and White, you will learn something to your* *advantage*, and has been a cliché since the late nineteenth century. Nowadays the expression in the general language, as opposed to the language of the law, is usually used in a humorous or ironic context, as *Mary left a message on my answering machine saying that if I called her back I would learn something to my advantage.*

leave in the lurch is an idiom cliché meaning to abandon someone and leave him or her in a difficult situation, as *He promised to lend us his car for our journey but just as we were about to start out he left us in the lurch by saying that he needed it for himself after all.* It is a very old term, dating from the sixteenth century, and has been a cliché since the late eighteenth century. It is still very common today, although it is usually restricted to informal contexts. In origin 'lurch' refers in games such as cribbage to a position in which one player loses by a large margin.

leave no stone unturned is an idiom cliché testifying to the thoroughness of some activity. It is common among journalists and others, such as police officers or politicians, who are anxious to impress on the public that everything that can be done is being done, as *The local police have said that they will leave no stone unturned until the missing child is found.* The expression has been a cliché since the eighteenth century but actually dates back to a Greek legend by Euripides. In it the Theban Polycrates, unsuccessfully looking for the treasure which Mardonius had left in his tent before the battle of Plataea, sought the help of the Delphic oracle who advised him to move every stone. This was later translated as 'turn over every stone'.

leave well alone see *let well alone*

left to one's own devices is a hackneyed phrase meaning left alone to do as one

pleases, as *There are some organized trips during the holiday but we'll be left to our own devices most of the time*, and *The child gets home before the rest of the family and she is left to her own devices until they get back.* The expression has been a cliché since the late nineteenth century. The archaic word 'devices', meaning a plan or scheme, appears in the *Book of Common Prayer* 'We have followed too much the devices and desires of our own hearts '

leg to stand on, not to have a see *not to have a leg to stand on*.

let bygones be bygones is a hackneyed phrase urging someone to forget about the past and the unfortunate things that may be associated with it, such as a quarrel, as *I know your family and his haven't spoken for years, but you should try to let bygones be bygones and write to him.* The word 'bygone' means past or former, as 'in a bygone age' and is archaic. The expression dates from the seventeenth century and is still widespread today. More or less the same sentiment is found in the expression **forgive and forget**.

let me just say is a filler cliché used virtually meaninglessly as there is usually no question of the speaker being prevented from saying what he or she wishes, as *Let me just say how much I admire your work.* It is the kind of phrase that some people use out of sheer habit without realizing it and which is a source of irritation to their regular listeners. It is found in both spoken and written English and is sometimes used for emphasis.

let me tell you is a filler cliché frequently used virtually meaninglessly by people to whom its use has become a habit. Sometimes it is used for emphasis, as *Let me tell you that you will live to regret it.* Unlike → **let me just say** it is usually restricted to spoken English.

113

let's face it is a hackneyed phrase urging someone to accept the reality of a situation, as *Let's face it. He's gone and he's not coming back.* It is also used as a filler cliché virtually meaninglessly by people to whom its use has become a habit. As a cliché it has been common since the middle of the twentieth century. It is found in informal contexts, usually in spoken English.

let's get this show on the road is an idiom cliché urging someone to stop delaying and get started doing something, as *Well, we've had a long enough coffee break. Let's get this show on the road.* As a cliché it dates from the middle of the twentieth century, having its origins in mobile forms of entertainment, such as circuses or fairs.

let sleeping dogs lie is a proverb cliché advising someone not deliberately to look for trouble, not to interfere in a situation with which there is nothing wrong. The expression dates back to the thirteenth century and is still a widespread cliché today, as *I wouldn't mention holidays to the boss. Let sleeping dogs lie; he seems to have forgotten the time you pretended to be off sick.* In origin it refers to a watchdog that has fallen asleep.

let the cat out of the bag is an idiom cliché meaning to reveal a secret, usually carelessly or thoughtlessly, as *Please don't mention the surprise party to Jane. She is bound to let the cat out of the bag.* As a cliché the expression dates from the nineteenth century and is still very common today, particularly in informal contexts. In origin it refers allegedly to a fairground trick by which traders sold unwary buyers a cat in a bag, assuring them that it was a pig. The buyers did not realize their mistake until they let the cat out of the bag by which time it was too late.

let the grass grow under one's feet, not to, see *not to let the grass grow under one's feet*

let well alone is a hackneyed phrase advising someone not to interfere with something if it is all right, in case he or she makes the matter worse, as *I know the picture on her television isn't very good but you should let well alone. She won't thank you if you break it.* The expression has the alternative form **leave well alone**. It was popularized by the eighteenth century prime minister, Sir Robert Walpole, who made it his motto, although the actual expression is considerably older than that. The same idea is found in → **let sleeping dogs lie** and in the modern slang expression of American origin **if it ain't broke don't fix it.**

lick and a promise, a is a hackneyed phrase meaning a superficial wash or clean, as *The boys would never think of washing their necks. They just give their faces a lick and a promise.* The expression dates from the nineteenth century and is still common today in an informal context. In origin it may refer to a cat quickly licking itself clean.

lick into shape is an idiom cliché meaning to get someone or something into a more acceptable form or into the required condition, as *The young runner has great potential but he is not very fit. Never mind, we'll soon get him licked into shape,* and *The house which they've bought is in a terrible state. It'll take a lot of money to get it licked into shape.* The expression dates from the seventeenth century and has been a cliché since the nineteenth century. It is usually used in an informal context. In origin it refers to an old belief that bear cubs are born shapeless and literally have to be licked into shape by their mothers.

lie back and think of England is an alternative form of close your eyes and think of England

life and soul of the party, the is an idiom cliché used to describe someone who is very lively and sociable and who helps to make a party or other gathering a success. The expression has been popular since the late nineteenth century and is still common today. It is sometimes used critically by those who do not like vivacious people.

life in the raw is a hackneyed phrase indicating a rough, uncivilized way of life, as *She says that she sees life in the raw being a social worker in a deprived inner city area.* The expression has been a cliché since early in the twentieth century and is still common today.

life is just a bowl of cherries is a catchphrase cliché meaning that life is absolutely splendid. It is mostly now used ironically, as *I'm late for work, the car won't start, I've got oil on my shirt. Isn't life just a bowl of cherries?* It originated in America, being popularized by a song sung by Ethel Merman in *Scandals* (1931).

life is not worth living is a hackneyed phrase indicating the depression that someone feels, often as a result of someone else going away, as *She felt that life was not worth living after her fiancé broke their engagement.* The expression has been popular since the late nineteenth century and is still common today.

light at the end of the tunnel, the is an idiom cliché used to refer to a time of happiness after a period of misfortune or to a solution to a problem that has long remained unsolved, as *She has been in a state of black depression but she has at last begun to see the light at the end of the tunnel,* and *The firm has been in financial difficulties but there is now light at the end of the tunnel.* The expression was popularized by American President, John F Kennedy who used it in a press conference about the war in Vietnam (1962). It is still common today.

light fantastic, is an allusion cliché meaning dancing. It is now used in a humorous context, as *Do you fancy a bit of the light fantastic?* It is a short version of trip the light fantastic which means to dance and is also now used humorously, as *He fell down drunk when tripping the light fantastic at the wedding reception.* As a cliché the expression dates from the late nineteenth century. It is an allusion to a passage from *L'Allegro* (1632) by John Milton 'Come and trip as you go, On the light fantastic toe.'

light of day, first see (the) see *first see (the) light of day*

like a house on fire is a simile cliché meaning very well and usually used to describe people who get on very well together, often just after first meeting, as *I was worried that my daughter would be a bit shy at the party but she got on like a house on fire with the other children.* The expression can also mean very quickly, as *Because he is going to a party later he is getting through his homework like a house on fire.* The expression dates from the nineteenth century and is still very popular today. In origin it refers to the fact that houses made of wood or thatch burn extremely quickly.

like clockwork is a simile cliché which is the standard cliché used to indicate the efficient running of something or to indicate regularity, as *The office runs like clockwork when she's in charge,* and *The public transport there runs like clockwork.* In origin of course the expression refers to the mechanism of a clock.

like death warmed up is a simile cliché meaning very pale or ill, as *How is your hangover? You look like death warmed up.* The expression dates from the early part of the twentieth century and may have first been military slang. It is still common today in an informal, and often humorous, context.

like grim death see *grim death, like*

like I need a hole in the head see *need like a hole in the head*

like it was going out of fashion is a simile cliché and also a catchphrase cliché, meaning very quickly or in great quantities. It is most commonly used in connection with spending money, as *Whenever she goes near a dress shop she spends money like it was going out of fashion*, although it is found in other contexts, as *He smokes cigarettes like they were going out of fashion.* The expression dates from around 1930 and is still common today in informal or slang contexts. An alternative form of the expression is **as though it was going out of fashion**. The same sentiment is expressed in → **like there was no tomorrow**.

like something the cat brought in is a simile cliché dating from the early part of the twentieth century. The phrase is used as an informal comment on the untidy, bedraggled or generally unacceptable appearance of someone, as *You can't go to the party like that. You look like something the cat's brought it.* In origin the cliché refers to some kind of prey, such as a half-eaten mouse or bird, that a cat might bring into the house.

like there was no tomorrow is a catchphrase cliché which, in common with → **like it was going out of fashion**, means

very quickly or in great quantities and is usually used to refer to the spending of money, as *In the January sales everyone seemed to be spending money like there was no tomorrow.* The expression has been popular since the middle of the 1970s and is still common today in informal or slang contexts.

like two peas in a pod is a simile cliché, being a standard cliché to express close physical resemblance, as *The twins are like two peas in a pod.* The expression has been in existence since the sixteenth century and is still widespread today. An alternative form of the expression is **like peas in a pod**.

lion's share, the is an idiom cliché meaning the largest portion of something, as *All his children were left some money by the old man but the eldest son got the lion's share.* It has been a cliché since the middle of the nineteenth century and is still common today. In origin the expression refers to one of Aesop's fables, in which the lion got either the largest share of, or indeed all of, any prey killed in hunting since the other animals were afraid of him.

lips are sealed, my is an idiom cliché used to indicate that someone will not reveal what he or she has been told. Although the actual concept is an old one, the expression became current in the early part of the twentieth century, being popularized by Stanley Baldwin, British prime minister, who used it (1937) in reply to questions about whether the then King Edward VIII was going to abdicate. It is still common today and is often used humorously.

lip service, pay is a hackneyed phrase meaning to pretend to approve of or support something while not really doing so, as *The teachers pay lip service to the new* *education policy but they go on using the old methods.* The expression **lip service** has been in existence since the seventeenth century and is a common cliché today. The sentiment, although not the wording, is Biblical. It is referred to in *Matthew* (15:8). 'This people draweth unto me with their mouth and honoureth me with their lips, but their heart is far from me.'

little bird told me, a is a hackneyed phrase indicating that one has heard something but does not wish to reveal the source. A version of the saying appeared in John Heywood's collection of proverbs in 1546, and the actual expression has been common since the nineteenth century. It is still common today but sounds rather coy if used seriously, as *A little bird has told me that wedding bells are in the air*, and is often used humorously.

little black book is a hackneyed phrase used to indicate a notebook in which someone carries details of current and past partners and consults it when he or she is partnerless, as *His girlfriend's just walked out on him and so he's going through the phone numbers in his little black book.* Of course the book need neither be black nor little, it being the concept that is important. As a cliché the expression dates from the second part of the twentieth century.

little grey cells is a hackneyed phrase, dating from the second part of the twentieth century, meaning brains or intelligence. It is used humorously or ironically in informal contexts, as *For goodness sake use your little grey cells and think of a way to get us there on time.* The expression came into being because part of the brain is composed of a greyish tissue which contains the nerve endings.

little knowledge is a dangerous thing, a is a quotation cliché being a misquotation of a

passage from *An Essay on Criticism* (1711) by Alexander Pope 'A little learning is a dangerous thing.' The expression is used as a warning that a small amount of knowledge about a subject can be more dangerous than knowing nothing at all because the knowledge can be applied wrongly, and because one can think that one knows more than one actually does. Nowadays the misquotation is more common than the actual quotation, as *I should call in an experienced tradesman to do your electrical repairs and not get your DIY friend to do them. A little knowledge is a dangerous thing.*

little pitchers have big ears is a proverb cliché meaning that children may overhear things they should not, since people have a tendency to overlook the presence of children, as *Could we discuss this later. Little pitchers have big ears, you know.* The likening of the largeness of children's ears to the handle of a pitcher or jug dates from the sixteenth century and the expression was a cliché from the late part of the nineteenth century.

little woman is a hackneyed phrase sometimes used by sexist men to refer to someone's wife, as *And what are you going to give the little woman for Christmas?* It is now dated, since women have had more status in the community since the rise of feminism, and tends to be used by older men whose attitudes have not changed with the times.

live and let live is a proverb cliché advising people to get on with their own lives and show tolerance for the way in which other people choose to live theirs, as *You should learn to live and let live. It is no business of yours whether they are married or just living together.*

lock, stock and barrel is a hackneyed phrase meaning absolutely everything, as

The landlord said that he wanted the tenants to leave, lock, stock and barrel. The term has been popular since the early part of the eighteenth century and is still commonly used today for emphasis. In origin the phrase refers to the three parts of a gun – the lock or firing mechanism, the stock or handle, and the barrel.

lone wolf, a is a hackneyed phrase which refers to someone who prefers to spend a great deal of time by himself or herself rather than with other people, as *We asked Jim to come on holiday with us but he refused. He's a bit of a lone wolf.* The expression is American in origin and refers to the fact that wolves usually hunt in packs. It dates from the twentieth century.

long arm of the law, the is a hackneyed phrase used to refer to the police force and the legal process generally, the implication being that its influence is extremely far-reaching. It has been popular since the late nineteenth century and is still used today, although it is dated and is usually used in humorous or ironic contexts, as *You can try to hide but the long arm of the law will get you!*

long in the tooth is an idiom cliché meaning old or ageing, as *He's getting a bit long in the tooth to be playing professional football.* The expression has been popular since the nineteenth century and is still common today in informal, and often humorous contexts. In origin it refers to the fact that the gums of horses recede as they grow old which makes it seem as if their teeth get longer. A horse's age is gauged by examining its teeth.

long shot, a is an idiom cliché meaning a guess or attempt that is unlikely to succeed but that is worth trying, as *It is a bit of a long shot but you could try contacting him at his parents' old address.* In origin the expression refers to the fact that early firearms had to be fired from a position near the target in order to be accurate. A long shot was fired from a distance and so would be likely to miss the target. The expression has been used figuratively since the later part of the nineteenth century and is still a common cliché today.

long time no see is a hackneyed phrase used as an informal greeting to someone whom one has not met for some time, as *Long time no see! Have you been away?* The expression is deliberately ungrammatical and has its origins in pidgin English used by the Chinese in the late nineteenth century and is a translation of a Chinese greeting.

loose end, at a is a hackneyed phrase indicating that one has nothing very much to do and has spare time, as *I don't mind doing your shift this afternoon. I am at a loose end anyhow.* The concept was referred to in John Heywood's collection of proverbs in 1546 and the phrase is still a common cliché today, being used in an informal context. In origin the expression refers to a length of rope that has become unfastened leaving an end dangling and not in use.

love is blind is a hackneyed phrase meaning that people who are in love are often blind to each other's faults. It is an old concept, having been referred to by Plato and the phrase was used by Shakespeare in several of his plays, such as *Romeo and Juliet* (2:1). Both the concept and the phrase are still common today, with the phrase often being used in a humorous or ironic context, as *I cannot imagine what she sees in him. No wonder they say love is blind.*

✻ M ✻

make a clean breast of is an idiom cliché meaning to make a full confession of something, as *When one of the other pupils was accused of the theft he decided to own up and make a clean breast of it*, and *She was afraid that her husband would find out that she had had an affair and decided to make a clean breast of it to him.* The expression has been a cliché since the late nineteenth century and is still widespread today. In origin it refers to the fact that the breast or heart was considered to be the seat of the emotions where one's innermost thoughts were kept.

make a mountain out of a molehill is an idiom cliché meaning to exaggerate the importance or difficulty of something, as *He was just a few minutes late but she got very angry and refused to go out with him. She's always making mountains out of molehills* and *They're causing a scene because their neighbour told off their children. They're just making a mountain out of a molehill.* The expression has been current since the middle of the sixteenth century and has been a cliché since the late eighteenth century. Both the cliché and the practice which it denotes are popular today. It is one of those expressions that are mostly always applied to other people, one's own problems always being viewed with a sense of proportion.

make an honest woman of is a hackneyed phrase meaning to marry someone, as *I'm glad you've finally decided to make an honest woman of Jane. You've been going out with her long enough.* As a cliché it dates from the nineteenth century and is still used today, but in a humorous or ironic way. Originally the term was restricted to a woman who had previously been seduced by the man in question and the sexual connotations sometimes survive to this day, as *They've been living together for years but he's now going to make an honest woman of her*, although this is not necessarily the case. In these days of sexual equality the inverse of the phrase is sometimes found, **make an honest man of.**

make an offer one cannot refuse is a hackneyed phrase meaning to offer such advantageous terms that the person who is offered them would be a complete fool to turn them down. The expression is usually associated with the world of commerce or employment, as *We hadn't really thought of selling the cottage but a young couple made us an offer we couldn't refuse*, and *I was perfectly happy with my previous firm but one of their competitors made me an offer that I couldn't refuse.* It often carries the suggestion that there might have been an ethical reason for turning down the offer, but that the size of the amount was enough to still any qualms about this, as *We felt bad about selling the land to the developers but they made us an offer that we couldn't refuse.*

make ends meet is a hackneyed phrase meaning to live within the limits of one's income, the implication usually being that to do so is something of a struggle, as *They are finding it very difficult to make ends meet since the baby was born.* It has been a cliché

119

since the nineteenth century, although the expression itself is much older. In origin it is thought to refer to the beginning and end of one's financial year, as is suggested by the French form *joindre deux bouts de l'annee*, to join the two ends of the year. Another suggestion is that it simply refers to the opening and closing lines of a statement of income and expenditure. The cliché is still widespread today, as is the struggle with which it is frequently associated.

make hay while the sun shines is a proverb cliché meaning to take advantage of any good opportunity that occurs, as *The skiing season there does not last very long and so the local hoteliers have to make hay while the sun shines*. The saying dates from the early sixteenth century and in origin refers to the necessity for farmers to get as much hay-making as possible done in dry weather. It is often abbreviated into an allusion cliché **make hay**, as *We might as well make hay while there is plenty of work around. It usually tails off towards the end of the year.*

make no bones about it is an idiom cliché meaning to be absolutely open and frank about something, often something that one might expect someone to be reticent about, as *She made no bones about it. She told us she was marrying him for his money*. The expression has been popular since the eighteenth century and is still very commonly used today. The origin is uncertain. The most widely held theory is that it refers to bones in a soup or stew, although it has been suggested that its derivation relates to dice-throwing. The idea is that because dice were originally made of bones **make no bones about it** meant literally to throw the dice without any unnecessary delay or preparation.

make no mistake is a hackneyed phrase used for emphasis, as *Make no mistake, he*

will live to regret this*, and *He has a terrible life with her, make no mistake*. It is sometimes extended to **make no mistake about it**. Both expressions are often used by people to whom they have simply become a habit and who are often not aware of it. They are frequently a source of irritation to their listeners. The phrases date from the end of the nineteenth century.

make one's day is a hackneyed phrase meaning to make one very happy, as *Granny's been ill. It will really make her day if you go and see her*. The expression has been popular since around the 1940s and is still common today, being used in informal contexts. Nowadays it is often used ironically, as *The boss has just made my day. He's told me to work late and I have tickets for a show.*

make or break is a hackneyed phrase used to refer to a crucial situation which will end in either complete success or failure, as *He's taking a bit of a gamble. This new job will either make or break his career*, and *This year it'll be make or break for the firm*. The expression has been popular since the middle of the nineteenth century, although it has a very modern ring to it. An earlier form of the expression was **make or mar**.

make short work of is a hackneyed phrase meaning to dispose of something very rapidly, as *The champion made short work of her competitor in the final*. It is often used humorously, as *The children made short work of the jelly and ice cream at the party*. The expression dates back to the sixteenth century and is still popular today, being used in informal contexts.

make the best of a bad job is a hackneyed phrase used to mean to get along as well as one can in unfortunate or adverse circumstances, as *We don't have enough volunteers* to help in the campaign but we'll just have to make the best of a bad job, and There was too little food for the number of people who turned up but we made the best of a bad job. As a cliché it dates from the middle of the nineteenth century, although the sentiment goes back to the seventeenth century. It is still popular today. An earlier form of the expression was **make the best of a bad bargain**.

make the supreme sacrifice is a hackneyed phrase originally meaning to give up one's life either for one's country or to save someone else's life, as Having made the supreme sacrifice for his fellow officer he was buried with full military honours. In this sense it was common from the late nineteenth century on, being particularly popular during World Wars 1 and 2. The expression is still used today, although it is considerably rarer than it once was, and is frequently used humorously or ironically in a variety of contexts indicating some form of minor sacrifice, as He stayed a bachelor until he was forty and then he made the supreme sacrifice, and I know you want to watch the football but could you make the supreme sacrifice and help me with the supermarket shopping? An alternative form is **make the ultimate sacrifice**.

make waves is an idiom cliché meaning to cause trouble, as The committee used to agree on most things until a new member was elected and started making waves. The expression became a cliché in the second part of the twentieth century and has a nautical origin, referring to a ship causing waves in still water by passing through it.

makes you think, it is a hackneyed phrase that has become a catchphrase cliché. The expression dates from around the late nineteenth century, becoming popular around the 1930s. It is still popular in informal contexts today, as It makes you think. Unemployment can happen to any of us. The expression is often extended to **it makes you think, doesn't it?**, as She was so young to die. It makes you think, doesn't it? Both phrases are sometimes used simply as filler clichés by people to whom they have become a habit.

making tracks, be is a hackneyed phrase meaning to take one's departure, often rather rapidly, as Heavens, is that the time? I'd better be making tracks. The expression **make tracks** is American in origin and dates from the nineteenth century. As a British cliché **be making tracks** is found in informal contexts. In origin it refers to leaving tracks or footsteps in the ground as one leaves.

man and boy is a hackneyed phrase meaning all of someone's life or all of someone's working life, as He's worked for that firm man and boy and he still earns a pittance. It is still a popular cliché and it has retained its masculine status, since its female equivalent is not commonly found.

man Friday is a hackneyed phrase meaning assistant, often with the sense of invaluable assistant, as The manager's always saying he doesn't know what he would do without his man Friday, but he gave his personal assistant a very poor pay rise. It is still found as a modern cliché although it has declined in popularity, perhaps because it sounds rather patronizing. In the middle of the twentieth century, its female counterpart → **girl Friday** became popular particularly in relation to office jobs. In origin the expression refers to Daniel Defoe's novel Robinson Crusoe (1719) in which the hero found a young native man on the desert island on which he was stranded. The young man, called Friday because Crusoe met him on a Friday, became his faithful servant.

man in the street, the is a hackneyed phrase meaning the ordinary person, as *The politicians are always pretending to be interested in the views of the man in the street*. The term dates from the early part of the nineteenth century and became a cliché later in the same century. It is still popular today, frequently being used by journalists or by people in public life whose fate depends on said man in the street. Sometimes it is used in a derogatory way by people who think that they are above the social level of the man in the street, as *The man in the street is only interested in his beer and cigarettes*. 'Man' in this context is usually now used to cover both sexes. It is objected to by some feminists and efforts have been made to popularize **person in the street** but with far from widespread success. An alternative form of the expression is **the man on the Clapham omnibus**, but this is now much rarer.

manna from heaven is an allusion cliché used to refer to sudden and unexpected assistance or advantage, as *The car broke down in the middle of nowhere and it was like manna from heaven when a tractor came along and gave us a tow*. The expression is now often used in humorous contexts, this humorous association dating from the early eighteenth century. The allusion is Biblical, 'manna' being used in *Exodus* (16:15) to refer to the food that God miraculously sent to the Israelites on their journey into the wilderness from Egypt.

man of the house, the is a hackneyed phrase used to refer to the man in charge of a household. The phrase is not confined to the role of husband or father but is extended to the oldest male in a household, as *Now that your father's dead, you'll have to be the man of the house and look after your mother and sisters*. Despite the fact that women now run many households with-out a man, the phrase is still found. Salesmen have a habit of using it without ascertaining whether or not there is a man of the house, as *Could I come and demonstrate our double-glazing system when the man of the house is at home?* See also **lady of the house**.

man of the world, a is a hackneyed phrase meaning a man with experience of the world, a sophisticated man as, *I'm sure your story won't shock John. He's a man of the world after all*. The expression in this sense probably dates from the nineteenth century but originally it referred to a man who was married. As a cliché it is still common today and has its counterpart in **a woman of the world**, as *I thought that she was far too much of a woman of the world to get pregnant accidentally*.

man's gotta do what a man's gotta do, a is a catchphrase cliché indicating that there are some things which simply have to be done, whatever one feels about doing them, as *I don't really want to get rid of my assistant but I can't afford her. A man's gotta do what a man's gotta do*. It is usually now used in humorous or ironic contexts, as *I'll have to force myself to go on holiday next week. A man's gotta do what a man's gotta do*. The expression, whose popularity dates from the 1940s, is American in origin. Although its ultimate source is uncertain, it is thought to have been popularized by Western films.

man the pumps is an idiom cliché meaning to lend a hand in an emergency of some sort, as *If we are going to get this export order finished on time everyone will have to man the pumps*. Its popularity dates from the twentieth century and as a cliché is still found today, although it is perhaps rather dated. The expression is nautical in origin.

man to man is a hackneyed phrase meaning frankly. The sentiment contained in the expression dates from the days when there were many areas of interest from which women were excluded and when they were considered too delicate or sensitive to cope with forthrightness. Despite the change in the status and perception of women the phrase still persists today, as *She was very embarrassed when her father said that he wanted to talk man to man with her fiancé.* The expression is often used adjectivally, as *'Well, son, now that you are fifteen it's time that you and I had a man-to-man talk.'* As a cliché it dates from the late nineteenth century. Its female counterpart **woman to woman** is occasionally found, although this implies intimacy.

man who has everything, the is a hackneyed phrase used to refer to someone who is so wealthy that he already has all the consumer goods he could possibly want. It is commonly found in the promotion of luxury goods in the context of gift-giving, as *This diamond pen-holder is the perfect gift for the man who has everything.* The expression is American in origin and probably dates from the early part of the twentieth century. As a modern cliché it is often used of people who are not necessarily wealthy but who have everything that they want. Many women would include most older men in this category. *What do you give the man who has everything for Christmas? I always end up giving my father socks.* The phrase is not restricted to the male of the species, **the woman who has everything** also being found, although perhaps more rarely both linguistically and actually.

many are called but few are chosen is a quotation cliché, being a Biblical reference to *Matthew* (22:14) 'For many are called but few are chosen.' As a cliché the expression dates from the middle of the nineteenth century. It

is found today in humorous or ironic contexts, as *I've been turned down for promotion again. Ah well, many are called but few are chosen,* being mostly used by people of rather a literary bent.

many hands make light work is a proverb cliché usually used to encourage those who do not really wish to be involved in a project, as *If you give me a hand with these dishes we'll get them done in no time. Many hands make light work.* A proverb of long standing, it is still a popular cliché today, often being used by parents or grandparents in an attempt to get younger members of the family to help out with chores.

marines, tell that to the see *tell that to the marines*

marking time is a hackneyed phrase meaning allowing time to pass without making any progress or taking any definite action. As a cliché it dates from the late nineteenth century and is still popular nowadays, as *He is in rather a dead-end job but he is just marking time until he goes to university.* In origin it is a military term, referring to soldiers retaining a marching rhythm by moving the feet up and down as if marching but without actually moving from the spot.

mark my words is a hackneyed phrase used either for emphasis or as a filler cliché, as an introduction to a remark, as *Mark my words, that boy will end up in jail,* and *Mark my words, it will rain today.* As a cliché it dates from the middle of the nineteenth century. Nowadays it is often quite meaningless, being used by people to whom it has become a habit. It is often prefaced by 'you'. See also *you mark my words.*

matter of fact, as a see *as a matter of fact*

123

matter of life and death, a is a hackneyed phrase used to refer to something that is of vital importance, as *Please could you give us a lift to the hospital. It's a matter of life and death.* Frequently the urgency is exaggerated, as *I've got to get this letter in the post tonight. It's a matter of life and death.* As a cliché it dates from the middle of the nineteenth century. It is sometimes used in the form **a matter of life or death** which is more logical but less common.

may all your troubles be little ones is a hackneyed phrase used as a toast to a bride and groom. It is also a euphemism cliché since it is simply a *double entendre* indicating a wish that the couple will have children. It is used only by people who are given to finding this phrase amusing. To others it is at best trite and usually cringe-making, especially to the unfortunate couple on the receiving end of it.

May and December is an idiom cliché used to refer to a relationship or marriage between two people, one of whom is much older than the other, as *It's a real case of May and December. Her husband is old enough to be her father.* The expression is often used adjectivally, as *People say these May and December affairs never last but they've been married for ten years now.* Formally the relationships tended to involve an older man and a younger woman, but it is now quite common for women to be involved with younger men. The idea of comparing relationships is an old one. Chaucer in his *Merchant's Tale* refers to May and January, but May and December has existed since the early seventeenth century.

meaningful relationship, a is a vogue cliché that became popular in the 1970s and reached its peak in the 1980s. Supposedly it refers to a particularly special and deep relationship, as *She thought that she had a really meaningful relationship with Jim but he suddenly went off with someone else.* However, the 'meaningful' part is often practically meaningless, simply being added for the sake of pretentiousness. Its popularity has waned rather in the 1990s but just as one thinks it has gone, it pops up again.

meanwhile back at the ranch is a catchphrase cliché used, usually in the course of rather an involved conversation or story, to indicate that one has returned to the main thrust of the conversation or story or to the main location. In origin it refers to the old silent Western films, where it was a familiar caption indicating that the action had switched to the ranch from the scene of the fight, etc. It probably dates from the early 1920s and is still used today in humorous contexts, as *Mary and Jim were in Greece, Paul and Jane were in Spain, and meanwhile back at the ranch we were looking after all their children.*

meet one's match is a hackneyed phrase meaning to come up against someone who is as good as one is at something, as *She was used to beating the other members of the tennis club easily but she met her match when she played Mary.* The expression was originally to **find one's match** and this dates from the fourteenth century. By the late sixteenth century **meet one's match** was in existence and is a common cliché today.

meet one's Waterloo is an idiom cliché meaning to experience a major defeat or disaster, as *He was boasting that no one could beat him at chess but he met his Waterloo when he played against the defending champion.* In origin it refers to the defeat of the French under Napoleon by the English under Wellington at the Battle of Waterloo in 1815, a defeat that marked the end of Napoleon's power in Europe. The figurative expression probably dates from around the middle of the nineteenth century and is still common today.

message received is a catchphrase cliché indicating that one has understood what has been said or implied, as *Message received. We shall have nothing more to do with him.* In origin the expression dates from radio communications in World War 2, becoming more generally used later in the 1940s and still found as a cliché today. In radio communication the expression was usually **message received loud and clear** and this is also found as a cliché, as is **message received and understood**.

method in one's madness is an allusion cliché referring to the fact that, although someone's action seems strange or foolish there is an underlying purpose to it, as *The teacher lets the children do as they please for a while, but there is method in her madness. They soon tire of it.* The allusion is to Shakespeare's *Hamlet* (2:2) 'Though this be madness, yet there is method in it,' although the idea predates this. It has been a cliché since the early part of the nineteenth century.

Midas touch, the is an allusion cliché meaning the ability to make an undertaking successful or profitable, as *He seems to have the Midas touch. All his companies are doing very well even in the middle of the recession.* The allusion is to a Greek legend in which Midas, a king of Phrygia, asked the gods to turn into gold everything that he touched. The god Dionysus granted his request but Midas regretted it when even the food which he tried to eat turned to gold, and he asked for things to return to normal. By the seventeenth century the idea

was being used figuratively and it is still common today.

mid-life crisis is a vogue cliché used to describe a stage in someone's middle age, often around the age of forty, when he or she assesses his or her life, finds it lacking and often does something out of character, like going off on a completely different course, as *I think he had some kind of mid-life crisis. He suddenly left his wife and children and went to live by himself on a remote island.* The expression became popular in the 1970s and by the early 1980s practically everyone of the appropriate age, particularly if male, was having such a crisis. Its popularity was spread by the many journalists who wrote about it. The cliché is still common today, although probably less so than formerly.

millstone round one's neck, a is an allusion cliché used to refer to a heavy burden or responsibility. The allusion is a Biblical one, referring to *Matthew* (18:6) 'But whosoever shall offend one of these little ones who believe in me, it were better for him that a millstone were hanged about his neck and that he were drowned in the depth of the sea.' A millstone was one of a pair of heavy circular stones used to grind grain. The expression began to be used figuratively around the sixteenth century. As a cliché it is still common today, as *We thought buying this old house was a good idea but it is so expensive to renovate that it's just a millstone round our necks.*

mind boggles, the is a hackneyed phrase used to indicate extreme surprise − to boggle means to baffle − as *The mind boggles at what he might do when he finds out.* The expression has been in existence since the 1950s but became particularly popular from the 1970s. As a cliché it is still common today.

mind how you go! is a hackneyed phrase used as a greeting when parting from someone, as *You'd better get off now if you want to get home tonight. Mind how you go!* It urges people to be careful, meaning the same as → **take care** and has been common since the 1940s. As a modern cliché it is still popular in informal contexts.

mind one's p's and q's is a hackneyed phrase meaning to be very careful about what one does or says, as *You'd better watch your p's and q's when you visit my grandparents. They're very strict and old-fashioned.* The expression dates from the seventeenth century, becoming a cliché in the nineteenth century. It is still used today, being found in informal, and sometimes humorous, contexts. The origin of the expression is obscure. There are various theories. One is that the derivation points to the similarity of the letters p and q to children when they are learning to write. Another is that the two letters are respectively short for pints and quarts as they appeared in the accounts of the owners of taverns.

mind you is a hackneyed phrase either used to emphasize what one is about to say, as *He says that he's telling the truth. Mind you, I don't believe him*, or is used as a filler cliché by people to whom it has become a habit and who are unaware of the fact.

miss the boat is an idiom cliché meaning to be too late to take advantage of an opportunity, as *We were going to put in an offer for the house on the corner but we've missed the boat. It's already been sold*, and *She heard there was a job going in the factory but she applied too late and missed the boat.* The expression dates from around the beginning of the twentieth century and

is a popular cliché today, being used in informal contexts. An expression expressing the same idea is **miss the bus**.

moment of truth, the is a hackneyed phrase meaning a crucial point, the point at which something will be proved to have been successful, etc or otherwise, as *Jim says that he has mended the television set but the moment of truth will be when he switches it on*, and *I followed the instructions for making the cake faithfully but the moment of truth will come when I open the oven door.* In origin the expression is a translation from Spanish of *el momento de la verdad* which refers to the point in a bullfight at which the matador is about to kill the bull. This was described by Ernest Hemingway (1932) in *Death in the Afternoon.* The English expression then transferred to the general language and is a popular cliché today. It is often used of situations that are relatively minor and is frequently found in humorous or ironic contexts.

money is the root of all evil is a quotation cliché, being a misquotation of a Biblical passage. The actual quotation is 'The love of money is the root of all evil' (*1 Timothy* 6:10). The misquotation is commonly used today to indicate that much evil and wrongdoing comes about because of money and materialism, as *There was a big family quarrel over the will when their father died and they have never spoken to each other since. It's true what they say about money being the root of all evil.* Today it is sometimes used in satirical contexts.

month of Sundays, a is a hackneyed phrase meaning a very long time, as *I haven't seen him in a month of Sundays.* The expression dates from the nineteenth century and was probably a cliché by the early part of the twentieth century. The cliché is still popular today, being used in informal contexts. **A month of Sundays** could take some thirty-one weeks.

moot point, a is a hackneyed phrase meaning a debatable or doubtful point, as *It is a moot point whether or not she is a more talented pianist than her sister.* In origin the term meant a case to be discussed by a meeting or 'moot' of law students. It began to be used more generally from the eighteenth century and is a common cliché today, although it is sometimes used wrongly.

more haste, less speed is a proverb cliché used to advocate care and caution against too great a hurry, as *You'll just make mistakes if you rush at that. More haste less speed.* It can be a very annoying cliché to have directed at one, especially if one has no choice but to do something in a hurry. Sometimes the cliché is used to apply to one's own actions, as *Damn! I've laddered my tights. More haste less speed!* The proverb is of long standing and the cliché is still widespread today.

more . . . than you've etc. had hot dinners, I've etc. had is a catchphrase cliché used to emphasize one's wide experience of something, as *I've been involved in more business deals than you've had hot dinners,* and *She's been on more trips abroad than you've had hot dinners.* The expression is used in informal or slang contexts and dates from the twentieth century. Originally the phrase had sexual associations, being used by men to boast of their sexual conquests, as *I've had more women than you've had hot dinners.*

more the merrier, the is a proverb cliché indicating that the more people there are participating in something the more successful it will be, as *Why don't you and your friend come to the cinema with us? The more the merrier,* and *Yes we could do with some*

more volunteers. The more the merrier. It has been a cliché since the nineteenth century, although as a proverb it dates from around the sixteenth century. It has been suggested that James 1 of Scotland may have been the first to use the expression (circa 1423).

more to it than meets the eye is a hackneyed phrase indicating that the speaker feels that a situation, problem, etc is more involved, more significant, etc than at first appears to be the case, as *He seemed to be the obvious thief but the police thought that there was more to it than met the eye,* and *It looked as though the child had fallen off the wall but the doctor thought that there was more to his bruises than met the eye.*

morning after, the is a hackneyed phrase traditionally used to describe the hangover that often follows a night of celebration, as *I wouldn't ask Jack to do too much today. He is suffering from the morning after.* The expression dates from the late nineteenth century and both it and the condition it describes are still extremely common today. Occasionally the expression is extended to mean the unpleasant effects of something other than a drinking bout. The phrase is a shortening of **the morning after the night before** and the full expression is still used.

move heaven and earth is an idiom cliché meaning to make every effort, to go to a great deal of trouble, as *They will move heaven and earth to keep their son out of prison,* and *The villagers will have to move heaven and earth to get the council to keep the local school open.* The expression dates from the eighteenth century and became a cliché towards the end of the nineteenth century. As a cliché it is still used today, although the expression is often a gross exaggeration of the effort put into something.

move the goalposts is a vogue cliché which became extremely popular in the 1980s to describe a situation in which the rules or conditions are changed after the action is underway, as *When we agreed to merge our firm with his we were quite pleased with the arrangements but he keeps moving the goalposts.* Its origin lies in ballgames, such as football.

much of a muchness is a hackneyed phrase used to refer to things or situations which are very similar, as *It doesn't really matter which of the candidates we choose for the job. They're all much of a muchness.* The expression dates from the eighteenth century and has been popular since the middle of the nineteenth century. It is still common today.

multitude of sins see *cover a multitude of sins*

mum's the word is a hackneyed phrase used to urge someone to keep quite about something, as *We're organizing a surprise birthday party for Mary, so mum's the word.* The actual expression probably dates from the early eighteenth century but the association of the word 'mum' and silence is much older, perhaps dating from the fourteenth century. Mum is imitative of the sound made when one's lips are closed. The cliché is still used today in informal contexts.

Murphy's law see *anything that can go wrong will go wrong*

mutton dressed as lamb is a hackneyed phrase used to describe in a derogatory way someone, usually a woman, who is dressed in the style of a much younger person, as *Did you see what she was wearing to the wedding? Talk about mutton dressed as lamb!* The expression dates from the late nineteenth century and is still common today. In origin it refers to a butcher trying to make mutton (meet from an older sheep) look like lamb.

my brother's keeper, I am not see *keeper, I am not . . .*

my heart bleeds for you is an idiom cliché used ironically to indicate that one does not feel a bit sympathetic towards someone, as *She says that she can only afford to buy one new dress a month. Poor soul! My heart bleeds for her.* Presumably the expression was once used in a sincere way, but it has been used in its present sense probably since the late eighteenth century and has been a cliché since the 1940s. It is still common today.

my, how you've grown is a hackneyed cliché much used by people to children whom they might not have seen for some time. It is a cliché which most children dread because there is nothing much that can be said in reply and because it embarrasses them. Adults should note that this particular piece of patronization is best avoided.

my lips are sealed see *lips are sealed, my*

my wife doesn't understand me is a catchphrase cliché used by a man to obtain the sympathy of another woman, usually with a view to having an extramarital sexual relationship with her, as *You mustn't worry about the fact that I am married. My marriage is virtually over. My wife doesn't understand me.* The truth of the matter is that the wife usually understands him all too well and it is the misfortune of the other woman that she might not understand him. Nowadays the cliché is usually used in a consciously humorous way.

❧ N ❧

nail in someone's coffin, a is an idiom cliché meaning something that will harm or destroy someone, as *Having a row with the boss was another nail in his coffin. He's in trouble already for unpunctuality.* The expression dates from the late eighteenth century and is a common cliché today. In origin the phrase refers to the fact that a coffin was nailed down after the corpse was put in it but before it was put in the grave.

nail on the head, hit the see *hit the nail on the head*

name is mud, his/her is a hackneyed phrase meaning that someone has been discredited in some way, as *Her name is mud in the office since she reported her colleague to the boss.* The term dates from the early part of the nineteenth century when it was used in the British Parliament to describe an MP who had brought disgrace on himself in some way. As a modern cliché it is used in informal contexts and is often used humorously, as *My name will be mud if I forget to send my mother a birthday card.* The origin of the expression is uncertain. It may be derived from the fact that 'mud' was an eighteenth century slang term for a fool, or it may simply be that mud is a dirty, slimy substance.

name names, to is a hackneyed phrase meaning to specify the people involved in something, as *The teacher knows who committed the crime but she has not yet named names.* The expression is often used

by people who are proud of the fact that they know something that others do not and want to sow seeds of suspicion, as *I won't name names but one of the bosses is having an affair with his secretary.*

name of the game, the is a vogue cliché that became popular in Britain in the 1970s. It is one of those clichés which is used rather vaguely or even meaninglessly but it usually refers to the thing that is important or central in something, as *In business the name of the game is profit.* The cliché is not so popular today as it was in the 1970s and early 1980s, although it is still fairly common, usually in rather informal contexts. The expression originated in America in the early 1960s.

name to conjure with, a is a hackneyed phrase used to refer to someone who is well-known or famous in a particular field, as *That's a name to conjure with. He was one of the best cricketers of his generation.* The expression became popular in the late nineteenth century and as a cliché is still used today, usually by people who have a fairly formal way of speaking and writing. In origin it derives from words used by conjurors or magicians when performing their tricks, the name in question being a name that could work wonders.

napping, caught see *caught napping*

nearest and dearest is a hackneyed phrase used to refer to someone's relatives and sometimes also to close friends. As a modern cliché it is usually used ironically, as *Her nearest and dearest never go to see the old lady.* The expression dates from the sixteenth century and it has been used ironically as well as literally from its inception.

neat as a new pin is a simile cliché used as the stock phrase to describe something that is exceptionally neat and tidy, as *The whole lived family in one room but it was always as neat as a new pin.* The expression dates from the late eighteenth century and is still widespread.

necessity is the mother of invention is a proverb cliché referring to the fact that people who are in dire need or trouble tend to be inventive and resourceful about finding ways to solve their problems. The expression dates from the late seventeenth century when it was used by playwright William Wycherley in *Love in a Wood* (1671), although the sentiment goes back to the ancient Greeks. As a modern cliché it is frequently used by people who like to be platitudinous about other people's misfortunes, as *If you can't afford to have the roof repaired you should have a go at it yourself. Necessity is the mother of invention.*

neck and neck is an idiom cliché used to refer to the closeness of some form of competition, as *The two teams at the top of the league are neck and neck at the moment,* and *Just before the general election the two parties were neck and neck.* In origin the expression refers to horse-racing where two runners who were close together were literally neck to neck. It began to be used more generally in the early nineteenth century. As a cliché it dates from the twentieth century and is widespread today.

neck of the woods is a hackneyed phrase meaning area or neighbourhood, as *He's*

certainly the best doctor in this neck of the woods. The expression is American in origin, originally referring to an area that was a forest settlement, and dates from the middle of the nineteenth century. It later transferred to Britain where it is still a popular cliché in informal or slang contexts.

needle in a haystack, a is an allusion cliché used to describe something that is very difficult to find, as *Empty country cottages are like needles in haystacks round here these days.* The allusion is to the proverb **to look for a needle in a haystack** which derives from medieval Latin and has its equivalent in several other languages. The aptness of the metaphor has meant that it has retained its popularity through the centuries.

needless to say is a filler cliché used by some to indicate that something need not be said since it is so obviously the case, although in fact the thing that need not be said follows the cliché, as *Needless to say, he never returned the money.* It is frequently used meaninglessly by people to whom it has become a habit. The expression dates from the sixteenth century and is still a popular cliché today. See also **goes without saying, it.**

need like a hole in the head is a simile cliché used to indicate how unwanted or undesirable something is, as *I needed another guest like I needed a hole in the head, but I really couldn't refuse to put them up.* The expression is American in origin, dating there from the 1940s. It spread to Britain where it is still a popular cliché in very informal or slang contexts.

needs no introduction is a filler cliché beloved of public speakers and used to indicate that the person in question is so well-known that he or she does not require to be formally introduced to an audience. The expression is completely unnecessary since it is invariably followed by an introduction, often one of some length, as *I am happy to announce the presence with us today of James White who needs no introduction to an audience of booklovers. He is . . .* The cliché dates from the late nineteenth century and is still heard in halls all over the country.

neither here nor there is a hackneyed phrase used to indicate that something is of no consequence or relevance, as *The fact that I didn't vote is neither here nor there. He lost by a huge margin.* The expression dates from the sixteenth century and has been a cliché since the late nineteenth century. It is still widespread today.

never the twain shall meet is an allusion cliché used to indicate the difference or disparity between two people, as *There's no point in trying to get those two together. He is a devout Tory, she is a devout Socialist and never the twain shall meet.* It is an allusion to a quotation from Rudyard Kipling's *The Ballad of East and West* 'East is East and West is West and never the twain shall meet.' The cliché dates from the twentieth century and is still fairly popular today, mostly in humorous contexts

new broom is an allusion cliché used to refer to someone who has just taken up some kind of new post and who is making changes often of a radical nature, as *The whole filing system has been changed. The new office manager is a bit of a new broom.* It is an allusion cliché to the proverb **a new broom sweeps clean.** As a cliché it dates from the middle of the nineteenth century and is still much used today.

new lease of life, a is a hackneyed phrase meaning renewed or refreshed vigour,

enthusiasm, etc, as *Her hip replacement has given her a new lease of life.* As a cliché it dates from the middle of the nineteenth century and owes its origin to the renewing of property leases.

nice work if you can get it is a hackneyed phrase used to congratulate someone on his or her good fortune and usually said in rather envious tones. It does not necessarily relate to a work situation, as *I hear Frank's gone to France for three months. Nice work if you can get it!* The cliché dates from the twentieth century and is still popular today.

nick of time, in the is a hackneyed phrase meaning just in time, as *I found my ticket in the nick of time. The train was about to leave.* As a cliché it dates from the early part of the nineteenth century. The expression was originally in the nick, 'nick' having the obsolete sense of critical point.

nine-days' wonder is a hackneyed phrase for something that gives rise to much interest and gossip but for a short time only, as *The whole village is talking about her son going to prison but it will be a nine-days' wonder.* As a cliché it dates from the nineteenth century and it is still widespread today. The idea goes back to a saying popular in Chaucer's time.

nip in the bud is an idiom cliché meaning to put an end to something potentially harmful or dangerous before it can develop very far, as *The teachers tried to nip the pupils' protest in the bud before it affected the rest of the school.* The expression dates from the sixteenth century and became a cliché about the middle of the eighteenth century. In origin it may refer to a gardener's method of preventing a plant from flowering, or from an early frost that kills off flower buds.

nitty gritty, the is a hackneyed phrase that was a vogue cliché in the late 1960s and 1970s. Although it has declined somewhat in popularity it is still common today in all but the most formal contexts meaning the basic points or issues of a situation, as *We've discussed the theoretical advantages of the project. Now let's get down to the nitty gritty.* It is held to be Black English in origin, perhaps referring to the grit-like nits that are difficult to remove from the scalp.

no accounting for tastes, there's is a hackneyed phrase used to refer to the seeming inexplicability of other people's tastes and preferences, as *I can't believe they actually chose that wallpaper. Still, I suppose there's no accounting for tastes.* An earlier form of the expression was **there is no disputing about tastes** but the present form was in existence by the early nineteenth century. This wonder at the taste of others remains popular today.

no better than she should be is a hackneyed phrase used to refer to a woman who is felt to be lacking in moral standards, as *His parents are concerned about him marrying her because she's had so many other boyfriends. They think she's no better than she she should be.* Since the cliché dates from the times, which may still be with us, when there was one moral standard for men and another for women, there is no male equivalent of this cliché.

no can do is a catchphrase cliche used to indicate that one cannot do something, that something is impossible, as *You want me to paint your house by next week. No can do!* The phrase is pidgin English in origin and became popular in general English around the beginning of the twentieth century. It is still popular today in very informal or slang contexts.

no comment is a hackneyed phrase used to indicate that someone would prefer to say nothing in response to questions. These questions, sometimes of a personal nature, are frequently set by members of the media to someone who for some reason is newsworthy, as *When asked about the possibility of a divorce, the film actor said, 'No comment.'* It is a response that is given not only by individuals but also by the police and other official bodies.

no expense spared is a hackneyed phrase used to indicate that a lavish amount has been spent on something, as *They had a huge society wedding, no expense spared.* It is often now used ironically, as *We thought we had been invited to dinner but all we got was sherry and peanuts. No expense spared!*

no laughing matter is a hackneyed phrase meaning a serious or grave issue. It is often used in situations in which there is no question of humour, as *You should report her disappearance to the police. It is no laughing matter.* The expression dates from the sixteenth century and is a popular cliché today.

no names, no pack drill is a catchphrase cliché meaning that one is unwilling to give a name to anyone, such as someone who is guilty of something, as *It wasn't Jim who stole the money. I know who it was, but no names, no pack drill.* The expression is military in origin, probably dating from the late nineteenth century and was originally used by soldiers who did not wish to mention any colleague's name in relation to any deed or offence in case he was punished. Pack drill was a form of punishment by which soldiers had to march up and down with all their equipment on their backs. It is now rather dated.

no news is good news is a proverb cliché used to indicate that to hear nothing suggests that all is well since if there has been any form of accident or other disaster notification would have been given by the police, etc. The expression dates from the seventeenth century.

no problem is a hackneyed phrase used as a conventional reply meaning literally that there is no difficulty about a situation. It used to mean much the same as **don't mention it** or as a term of general acquiescence, as *Certainly, I will give you a lift. No problem!* The expression originated in America in the middle of the twentieth century, becoming popular in Britain in the 1970s and now sometimes reaching epidemic proportions. **No sweat** is a more informal version of it. An Australian equivalent which is being popularized in Britain by the Australian soaps shown on British television is **no worries.**

no rest (or peace) for the wicked is a catchphrase cliché used in rather resigned tones simply to indicate that one is very busy, as *I've just got home from work and I have to go to the supermarket and cook the evening meal. Ah well, no rest for the wicked!* The reference to wicked is purely facetious. In origin it may be an allusion to a Biblical passage in *Isaiah* (48:22) 'There is no peace, saith the Lord, unto the wicked.' The phrase was being used by the early nineteenth century and was a cliché by the late nineteenth century.

nose out of joint, put someone's see *put someone's nose out of joint*

no show without Punch is a catchphrase cliché used to refer to a person who seems to have the knack of always turning up at events, usually events that are interesting, exciting, controversial, etc in some way, as *I*

might have known it. There's Mary over there with the protest group. No show without Punch! It became popular around the late nineteenth century and is common today in informal contexts. In origin the expression refers to the traditional Punch and Judy Puppet show, in which Punch is a leading character.

no skin off my nose, it's is a catchphrase cliché meaning it does not matter to me or affect me in any way. It has been popular since the early part of the nineteenth century and is common today in very informal or slang contexts, as *You can move out of the flat if you like. It's no skin off my nose!* In origin it probably refers to boxing or to an exchange of blows.

nose to the grindstone see *keep one's nose to the grindstone*

no smoke without fire, there's is a proverb cliché meaning that every rumour has some foundation or some element of truth in it, as *He's promised her faithfully that he's not seeing another woman but she's heard about it from various people and there's no smoke without fire.* It is an extremely popular cliché, especially among people who love to gossip and cause trouble. An alternative form of the saying is **where there's smoke there's fire.** The sentiment appeared in John Heywood's collection of 1546 having the wording **there is no fire without smoke.**

no spring chicken is an idiom cliché used in a derogatory way to indicate that a woman is no longer young. It often carries the connotations that said woman tries to appear or act younger than she actually is, as *She goes to discos every night but she's no spring chicken. She was at school with my mother's elder brother.* An alternative form is **no chicken.** The expression became a cliché in the nineteenth century, although **no chicken** was used in the early part of the eighteenth century. It is still common today in an informal context but has not yet been affected by unisex considerations in that men seem immune from the term.

not fit to hold a candle to see *fit to hold a candle to, not*

not for all the tea in China is a hackneyed phrase indicating that nothing would induce someone to do something, as *I wouldn't live in that part of town for all the tea in China*. The expression originated in the late nineteenth century and spread to Britain. It is still a popular cliché today in informal contexts.

nothing to write home about is a catchphrase cliché used to indicate that something is very ordinary or mediocre, as *We went to see the new play that got rave reviews but it was nothing to write home about*. The expression dates from the late nineteenth century and in origin may refer to soldiers writing letters when stationed away from home. It is still popular today in informal contexts.

nothing ventured, nothing gained is a proverb cliché meaning that nothing is achieved unless one is prepared to take risks, as *I hesitated about putting money into his new business but then I thought, 'nothing ventured, nothing gained'*. An alternative form of the proverb is **nothing venture, nothing gain**. An older form was **nothing venture, nothing have** which was in use in the time of Chaucer.

not in my back yard is a hackneyed phrase which was something of a vogue cliché in the 1980s. It is frequently abbreviated to **nimby** and sums up the attitude of one who has no objection to something being

built as long as it is not built anywhere near where one lives and so long as it does not inconvenience one. The attitude can be applied to things that are obviously objectionable, such as nuclear waste dumps, but can also be applied to things that are necessary and worthy, such as hostels for the homeless.

not just a pretty face is a catchphrase cliché used to highlight one's skill or intelligence, as *I told you I could fix the TV set. I'm not just a pretty face!* Originally it was used by a woman to a man to remind him that women have intelligence as well as good looks. It became popular around the middle of the twentieth century and is still popular today, although it is now often used ironically or humorously and sometimes by men. A standard facetious response is **you're not even a pretty face**.

not know from Adam is a hackneyed phrase meaning not to know someone at all, to be totally unacquainted with someone so that one would not recognize him or her, as *This man at the party greeted me like a long lost friend but I didn't know him from Adam*. The expression dates from the middle of the nineteenth century and the cliché is still common today, being used of women as well as men. The Adam in question is presumably Adam referred to in the Bible but the origin is otherwise unclear.

not out of the woods is an idiom cliché meaning that someone or something is not out of danger or trouble, as *The patient is very much better but she is not out of the woods yet*, and *The firm has improved a bit financially but it's not out of the woods yet*. An alternative form is **not out of the wood**. In origin it may refer to an old proverb **do not shout until you are out of the wood**. The idea of woods and forests being associated with danger goes back to Roman times. As a cliché it is still popular today being often used as an informal medical cliché.

not to be sneezed at is a hackneyed phrase used to indicate that something, such as an offer or opportunity, should not be dismissed lightly but should be taken seriously, as *Their offer for your house may not be as high as you wanted but it's not to be sneezed at*. The expression was in use by the early nineteenth century and is still popular today in informal contexts.

not to have a leg to stand on is an idiom cliché meaning to have no plausible defence or excuse to offer for one's behaviour, etc., as *He's bound to be found guilty of murder. The defence does not have a leg to stand on*. The expression dates from the sixteenth century and is still common today. Its origin is the obvious one of having no means of support.

not to know whether to laugh or cry is a hackneyed phrase indicating conflicting emotions, as *She didn't know whether to laugh or cry when the last of her children left home. She was glad to have more time to herself but she knew that she would miss them*.

The expression has been a cliché since the nineteenth century although the idea is much older. It is still in common use today.

not to let the grass grow under one's feet is an idiom cliché which is also a proverb cliché meaning not to delay or be inactive, as *If you see a suitable job advertised you should apply for it right away. Do not let the grass grow under your feet*. The expression dates from the sixteenth century and is still popular today in various forms, but always with negative connotations, as *If you want to change jobs you might as well do it now. There is no point in letting the grass grow under your feet*. In origin the expression refers to the supposed fact that if you stand in one place long enough the grass will start growing under your feet.

nudge, nudge is a hackneyed phrase used to indicate some sexual reference, often one that is illicit, as *He says that he needs to take his secretary to the conference. Nudge, nudge!* It is a shortened version of **nudge, nudge, wink, wink** which has the same connotations. The latter originated in the early 1970s in the TV series *Monty Python's Flying Circus* and was probably a cliché by the late 1970s. It is still popular today.

O

odds and ends is a hackneyed phrase used to refer to a miscellaneous collection of articles, as *The drawer of the kitchen table is full of odds and ends*. The expression dates from the eighteenth century and has been a cliché from around the middle of the nineteenth century. It is still widespread today. The original of the term may have been 'odd ends' meaning leftovers from rolls of cloth.

off the beaten track is a hackneyed phrase meaning in rather a remote place, as *The holiday cottage is a bit off the beaten track*. It is also used figuratively meaning unusual or original, as *His ideas on child-rearing are rather off the beaten track*. The cliché dates from the late nineteenth century and is still common today.

off the cuff is an idiom cliché meaning extemporaneously, without preparation, as *The speaker hadn't turned up. We'll have to get someone to speak off the cuff*. The expression originated in America in the early part of the nineteenth century and spread to Britain. In origin the phrase is said to refer to the fact that some speakers, such as after-dinner speakers, write some informal notes on their shirt cuffs as a memory aid rather than prepare a speech completely beforehand. It is still common today in informal contexts and is also used adjectivally, as *He made a few off-the-cuff remarks when introducing the speaker*.

of the first magnitude is a hackneyed phrase derived from the grading of the brightness of a star, the brightest being the first. When used figuratively the phrase originally meant of the highest quality, as *The college produces students of the highest magnitude*. It is also used ironically meaning greatest, as *He is a fool of the first magnitude*. The expression dates from around the seventeenth century and has been a cliché since the middle of the nineteenth century.

of which more anon is a hackneyed phrase used to indicate that one is going to say more about the subject later, as *There was the most terrible disaster at the wedding, of which more anon. I must rush now*. The cliché dates from the nineteenth century. Although it sounds archaic ('anon' meant soon) it is still used now, although usually humorously.

oil and water is an idiom cliché used to refer people or things which are completely incompatible, as *I'm not surprised they've separated. I'm surprised they ever got together in the first place. They're oil and water*. The expression has been a cliché since the nineteenth century. In origin it refers to the fact that oil and water do not mix.

old as the hills, as is a simile cliché meaning extremely old. The expression dates from around the beginning of the nineteenth century and is still common today, as *Some of the local traditions are as old as the hills*. It is also used facetiously of people, as *Children often think that their* *parents are as old as the hills.* It has its origin in geology.

old boy network is a hackneyed phrase used to describe a group of people, usually upper-class people, who have social connections with each other and who help each other in careers, etc, as *James was one of the few students who got a job and that was due to the old-boy network. His father was at school with the chairman of the firm.* The cliché dates from around the middle of the twentieth century and, in common with the phenomenon which it describes, it is still common today. It is mostly used of men, although women are also now beginning to network.

old enough to be her father is a hackneyed phrase used of someone who is in a relationship or marriage with someone much older than herself. The expression is used in a derogatory and disapproving way, as *She must be marrying him for his money. He is old enough to be her father.* Previously a relationship with a marked disparity in ages usually applied to an older man and a younger woman, but now older women often enter relationships or marriage with younger men. Disapproval is shown to them with **old enough to be his mother**.

old enough to know better is a hackneyed phrase meaning that someone is old enough to show maturity and good judgement, as *You children are old enough to know better than to play in the street.* The expression dates from the nineteenth century and is still common today. It is very often directed at children.

old hat is an idiom cliché meaning old-fashioned, unoriginal and uninteresting, as *I'm not going to hear his lecture on psychology. His ideas are old hat.* In origin it probably refers to the fact that hats go out of fashion before they actually wear out. The expression dates from the late nineteenth century and is a widespread cliché today in all but the most formal contexts.

once and for all is a hackneyed phrase meaning finally. As a cliché the expression dates from the twentieth century and is still common today, as *She was told once and for all that she must get to work on time or she would be sacked.* It is often used by people who are delivering ultimatums. The previous form of the expression was 'once for all' which dates from around the middle of the fifteenth century.

once bitten, twice shy is a proverb cliché indicating that if one has been harmed, exploited, etc once by someone or in a particular situation, one will be extremely cautious in future dealings so as to avoid being harmed, exploited, etc again, as *He was very unhappily married once and I don't think he'll marry again. I think it is a case of once bitten, twice shy.* The saying dates from the middle of the nineteenth century.

once in a blue moon is an idiom cliché meaning extremely rarely, as *She goes to see her parents once in a blue moon, although they're now very old.* It is often used as a gross exaggeration. The expression dates from the nineteenth century, although references to a blue moon go back to the early sixteenth century. It is still very common today in informal contexts.

one foot in the grave is an idiom cliché indicating that someone is either very ill or very old. The idea goes back to the sixteenth century. As a modern cliché it is often used in humorous contexts, as *Their teacher is only about 35 but the children think she's got one foot in the grave.*

one for the road is a hackneyed phrase used to describe one last drink before people set off, as *It's nearly closing time. Let's have one for the road*. It probably applies to drivers who were having one last drink before driving home, the expression and the idea both predating modern drink-driving laws. As a cliché it dates from the twentieth century.

one good turn deserves another is a proverb cliché indicating that if one person does another a favour the other person should return it. It is usually said by someone who is in the act of returning a favour, as *You lent me your lawn-mower and so please feel free to borrow my electric hedge-clipper. One good turn deserves another*. The proverb appears in John Heywood's collection of 1546 but it goes back to the fourteenth century. It is still a common cliché today.

one in a million is a hackneyed phrase used to praise someone's good qualities, as *Her father was one in a million. He would have helped anyone*. In origin it refers to statistics and points to the rarity of such a good person. It dates from the twentieth century and is a common cliché today, being used in informal contexts.

one of those days is a hackneyed phrase used to indicate that the user has had a dreadful day when everything has gone wrong, as *Oh, I'm glad to be home. It's been one of those days!* The expression became popular in the 1920s and, like the experience which it describes, it is still widespread today.

one of those things, just see *just one of those things, it's*

one over the eight is a hackneyed phrase meaning one alcoholic drink too many,

that is a drink that makes one drunk, as *He always gets aggressive when he's had one over the eight*. As a cliché it dates from the twentieth century. It is still used today in informal contexts, although it is rather dated.

one that got away, the is a hackneyed phrase originally used by anglers to describe a fish of exceptional size which was nearly caught but got away at the last minute, as *Keep away from old Fred at the bar. He's been fishing and he's just dying to tell someone about the one that got away. In this sense it dates from the early part of the twentieth century but around the middle of the 1940s it came to be applied to a person who escaped from danger*. It is often used facetiously in this sense, as *That's the one she married and that's the one that got away*. As a cliché today the first sense is still common but the second is rather dated.

only time will tell is a hackneyed phrase used to indicate that the outcome of something is not likely to be known for some time, as *They think they have caught her illness but only time will tell*. It is a cliché used by people who can think of no other ending to what they have said or written, whether or not there is any suggestion that the long-term outcome is uncertain.

only too pleased is a hackneyed phrase used to indicate that someone is very pleased to do something, such as help in some way, as *I'll be only too pleased to lend you the book after I've finished it*. It is often used simply for the sake of politeness, the user of the phrase being anything but pleased, but being too polite to say so, as *Why of course, I'll be only too pleased to look after all the animals while you're on holiday*. The cliché dates from the early 1920s and is still common as a polite convention today.

on the ball is an idiom cliché meaning quick and alert. It carries connotations of being extremely well-informed and up-to-date, as *If you're going to take up a job in the money market you'll really have to be on the ball.* In origin it refers to someone taking part in a ballgame who watches the ball closely so as to be ready if it comes to him/ her. The cliché is American in origin and dates from the twentieth century. It is still popular today, being used in informal or slang contexts.

on the dot is a hackneyed phrase used in relation to time and meaning exactly, as *The bus will leave at 6 o'clock on the dot.* The expression is used for emphasis. It dates from around the beginning of the twentieth century and is still widespread in informal contexts today.

on the side of the angels is a hackneyed phrase indicating what is perceived to be the right or moral side of a situation, according to the circumstances, as *She thought for one minute that he was one of the planners but then she realized that he was on the side of the angels and was one of the protesters against building on the green belt.* Exactly who the angels are depends on your point of view. It sounds rather formal although it is in fact quite a common cliché today. The cliché dates from the late nineteenth century. In origin it refers to a speech given by Disraeli at the Oxford Diocesan Conference in 1864. 'The question is this; Is man an ape or an angel? I, my lord, am on the side of the angels.' The original meaning of the expression was to be on the side of those taking a spiritual view.

on the spur of the moment is a hackneyed phrase meaning suddenly, impetuously, as *He was passing the travel agents when on the spur of the moment he went in and booked a holiday to Greece.* As a cliché it dates from the late nineteenth century, although the expression has been in existence since the late eighteenth century. It is still widespread today. The 'spur' in the phrase refers to something that goads a horse to action.

on the tip of one's tongue is an idiom cliché indicating that someone was just about to say something, as *His name is on the tip of my tongue but I just can't think of it.* The expression has been a cliché since the middle of the nineteenth century and it is still widespread today.

on the wagon is an idiom cliché meaning abstaining from taking alcoholic drink, as *He used to drink like a fish but he has been on the wagon since he was up on a drink-driving charge.* The expression is American in origin and dates from the early part of the twentieth century. It then crossed the Atlantic and became a cliché in Britain and it is still popular today in informal and slang contexts. The expression was originally **on the water wagon** and in origin refers to the horse-drawn water wagon which was used to spray dirt roads to keep the dust down.

on the warpath is an idiom cliché meaning in a very angry mood, often seeking revenge, as *I should keep out of your mother's way. She's on the warpath since she discovered you'd damaged the car.* In origin it means engaged in battle and refers to American Indians. The figurative expression originated in America in the late nineteenth century and then spread to Britain. It is still a common cliché in informal contexts.

on this auspicious occasion is a filler cliché used by public speakers on supposedly important occasions, as *We are* *delighted to welcome the mayor to the school on this most auspicious occasion.* Since 'auspicious' means fortunate or favourable, the occasion in question is usually a celebratory or social one, such as the opening of a new building. The cliché dates from the late nineteenth century. Nowadays it is frequently used satirically or by people who are consciously sending the phrase up. As a straight cliché it is rather dated.

on with the motley is a catchphrase cliché meaning it is time to get on with things, whatever has happened. It is usually used in rather a humorous or ironic way, as *I got in very late last night and I don't really feel like going to work. Still, I suppose it's on with the motley.* The cliché dates from the twentieth century and was originally used to indicate that it was time for a show or some form of entertainment to begin, whatever had happened. It carries much the same sentiment as **the show must go on.** In origin it derives from the cry of the clown, *'vesti la giubba'*, in Leoncavallo's opera *I Pagliacci* (1892) which is the traditional story of the clown who has to make others laugh when his heart is breaking. 'Motley' is an obsolete term for jester and also refers to his costume.

on your bike! is a hackneyed phrase used informally and rudely to tell someone to go away, as *No I don't want to buy any double-glazing. On your bike!* The expression has bee popular since the 1960s. Interest in it was revived by advice given to the unemployed by **Margaret Thatcher's** government in the early 1980s that they should get on their bikes and go out of their own area to find work. Norman Tebbit in his address as Employment Secretary to the Conservative Park Conference in 1981 spoke of how his father had 'got on his bike' to look for work in the depression of the 1930s.

open a can of worms see *can of worms, a*

opening gambit is a hackneyed phrase used to refer to someone's opening point in a discussion or to someone's initial course of action or stratagem, often a cunning one, as *Her opening gambit was that her child was not to blame,* and *I think that their opening gambit will be to try to discredit the opposition.* The phrase is tautological, the word 'opening' being unnecessary, since 'gambit' on its own suggests openings. Gambit is an opening move in chess, being the sacrifice, or the offer of such a sacrifice, of a piece in order to acquire some advantage. **Opening gambit** is still widely used today.

open secret is a hackneyed phrase which seems like a contradiction in terms. It is used to refer to something which is supposed to be highly secret or confidential but in fact is extremely well-known, because it has been leaked to so many people, as *It is an open secret that they are planning to marry,* and *They are trying to suppress rumours about the merger but it is already an open secret.* It became popular in the nineteenth century and, since gossip is always a favourite pursuit of us all, it is still common today. In origin it is thought to refer to the title of a play, *Il Pubblico Secreto* translated in 1769 by Carlo Gozzi from *El Secreto a Voces* (The Noisy Secret), a Spanish play by Calderon.

open sesame is a hackneyed phrase used to refer to an event, situation, etc that leads to success of some kind, as *That first audition in the town hall was the open sesame for a glittering career in the theatre.* In origin the expression refers to the story of *Ali Baba and the Forty Thieves,* one of the stories in *The Arabian Nights' Entertainments* (circa 1375). In the story 'open sesame' is the secret password that opens the door to the robbers' treasure cave. By the nineteenth century **open se-same** was becoming a synonym for a password, particularly a password to success. It is a common cliché today.

open the floodgates is a hackneyed phrase meaning to remove some form of restriction or control and so release a great, often overwhelming, amount or number of something, as *When the restraints on wage increases were lifted it opened the floodgates to claims from all the other Unions.* In origin it refers to the opening of gates at a lock or reservoir that hold back a great volume of water. As a cliché it dates from the twentieth century and is common today. As is the case with such clichés it is often used as a gross exaggeration. It is also often used as an excuse for not going ahead with the removal of some form of restriction, as *If we give permission for one of the pupils to go on holiday during term time it will open the floodgates and we'll get a rush of demands from other parents.*

or words to that effect is a hackneyed phrase sometimes used as a filler cliché indicating that something is more or less what was said, as *Her employer said that he was sorry to lose her but that he had no choice, or words to that effect.* It is used to indicate that what one has said is a reasonably close approximation, but it is also used meaninglessly by people to whom the cliché has become simply a habit. The cliché dates from the twentieth century and is still in common use.

OTT is an abbreviation of → **over the top** which itself is used as a cliché in informal or slang contexts, as *He deserved to be punished but it was a bit OTT to expel him.*

out of the blue is an idiom cliché meaning suddenly and unexpectedly, as *I wasn't thinking of changing jobs but this offer came out of the blue.* In origin the phrase refers to

something dropping unexpectedly from the sky. As a cliché the expression dates from the twentieth century and is still widespread today.

out of the mouths of babes and sucklings is an allusion cliché indicating that young and inexperienced people often show unexpected cleverness or judgement, as *Our young daughter asked us why they were digging up nice trees to build a new road. Out of the mouths of babes and sucklings.* Sometimes the expression is shortened to **out of the mouths of babes**. A cliché since the nineteenth century it is now used mostly by people of a literary bent. It is an allusion to the Bible, to *Matthew* (21:16). 'Out of the mouths of babes and sucklings thou hast perfected praise,' and to *Psalms* (8:2) 'Out of the mouths of babes and sucklings hast thou ordained strength.'

out on a limb is an idiom cliché meaning to have opinions that are completely different from the rest of a group, etc, as *She's out on a limb by wanting to diversify their range. The rest of the company want to stick to what they know.* An alternative meaning is in a dangerous or disadvantageous position. In origin the expression refers to an animal being at the end of a branch of a tree and so far from the main tree and safety.

over a barrel, have someone see *barrel, have someone over a*

over and done with is a doublet cliché used to emphasize the fact that something has come to an end, as *There was a feud between the families for many years but that is over and done with now.* The cliché dates from the twentieth century and is still common today.

over my dead body is a hackneyed phrase indicating one's strong opposition to something, as *They'll pull down that tree over my dead body*, and *She'll be invited to the party over my dead body*. The expression is American in origin and dates from the early nineteenth century. As a cliché it is still much used today in all but the most formal contexts by people wishing to emphasize the extent of their opposition.

over the hill is an idiom cliche meaning past one's prime or too old for something, as *He was a magnificent singer in his youth but he is a bit over the hill now*. In origin the phrase refers to a climber who has reached the top of a hill or mountain and is descending the other side. The cliché dates from the second part of the twentieth century and is still common in informal, derogatory contexts today. As the age at which people are supposed to be effective and employable diminishes, so the number of people liable to have the cliché applied to them is increasing.

over the moon is an idiom cliché meaning extremely happy or pleased, as *She was over the moon when she discovered she was pregnant*. As a cliché the phrase dates from the twentieth century and around the 1970s became particularly associated with the reactions of the manager or players of a winning football team when being interviewed after a match. In origin it may be connected with the old nursery rhyme in which 'the cat jumped over the moon.'

over the top is a hackneyed phrase meaning indicating that something is too much, too great, exaggerated, over-dramatic, etc, as *The leading man was good in the play but the leading lady was over the top*, and *It was a bit over the top to sack him just for saying what he thought*. As a cliché the expression dates from the 1980s and is extremely common today. In World War 1 **go over the top** meant to leave the comparative safety of the trench and go over the top or parapet to launch an attack on the enemy.

own goal, an is an idiom cliché used to refer to some misfortune that is the result of some action of one's own, as *The politician tried to start a smear campaign against one of the other election candidates but it turned out to be an own goal when she got a huge sympathy vote*. The popularity of the cliché dates from the second part of the twentieth century and has its origin in football where to score an own goal means to put the ball into one's own net and so give a point to the other side.

own worst enemy, to be one's is a hackneyed phrase meaning to cause oneself more harm or misfortune than anyone else does, as *He's his own worst enemy. Every time he gets a job he loses his temper and walks out*. As a cliché the expression dates from the twentieth century and is still widespread. The idea goes back to Greek and Roman times.

P

paddle one's own canoe is an idiom cliché meaning to be independent, to be self-reliant, as *Now that both her parents are dead she has no choice but to paddle her own canoe*. The expression is American in origin and dates from around the beginning of the nineteenth century. It then crossed the Atlantic and became popular in Britain. As a cliché it is still common today in informal contexts.

paint the town red is an idiom cliché meaning to go out celebrating, especially by going to bars, clubs, etc as *As soon as we heard that we had all passed the exams we started painting the town red*. The expression originated in America in the late nineteenth century, becoming popular in Britain in the twentieth century. It is still common today in informal contexts. Apart from the fact that its origins are American the derivation of the phrase is uncertain. It may simply refer to the fact that red is a cheerful, gaudy, passionate colour.

pale into insignificance is a hackneyed phrase used to mean that in comparison with something else something seems minor or trivial, as *She was feeling very sorry for herself at being on her own with a child, but her troubles paled into insignificance when she met a woman who was a widow with four children under five*. As a cliché the expression dates from the late nineteenth century. Despite the fact that it has rather a formal ring, it is still quite common today.

panic stations! is a catchphrase cliché used to indicate some form of emergency. As a

modern cliché it is used humorously, as *Panic stations! My mother's coming round. We'd better do some clearing up fast*. In origin the phrase refers to a naval expression **be at panic station** meaning to be prepared for the worst. **Panic stations** in a humorous context dates from around the 1940s and as such is still common today.

paper over the cracks is an idiom cliché meaning to pretend that everything is fine and try to cover up any mistakes, disagreements, etc, as *Although they quarrelled all the time, they decided to try to paper over the cracks in their marriage for the sake of the children, and I know that you have major disagreements on the board but you will have to paper over the cracks if you want to sell the company*. In origin it refers to the practice of putting wallpaper on walls to hide the cracks. The expression was said to have been used by Otto von Bismarck in 1865 to describe the outcome of the Convention of Gastein by which it was agreed that Austria would administer the Danish province of Holstein and Prussia would govern Denmark. Its translation into English in 1910 is thought to have popularized the phrase in English. As a cliché and as a concept it is still popular today.

par for the course is an idiom cliché meaning what might be expected, usually something bad, as *I don't know why you were surprised that he let you down. It's par for the course as far as he's concerned*. The expression originates on the golf course where 'par' is used to describe the number of strokes regarded as standard for a particular hole. The expression began to be used figuratively in the general language from the early 1920s and as a cliché is common today, in informal, often derogatory contexts.

part and parcel is a doublet cliché used to refer to something that is an essential part of something, as *Taking the children to school is part and parcel of her job*. The expression was originally a legal term dating from the sixteenth century. It began to be used more generally from the early nineteenth century and is a common cliché today.

parting shot, a is a hackneyed phrase used to refer to an apt or effective remark that one makes as one is leaving, as *As he packed his clothes to leave her, her parting shot was that she had never loved him anyway*. As a cliché the expression dates from the late nineteenth century and is still common. In origin it is a variation of 'Parthian shot' which refers to the habit of the Parthians, famous archers and horsemen of the first century BC, of discharging arrows at their enemy as they rode away.

party line, the is a hackneyed phrase used to refer to the official policy of a political party, government, organization, etc, as *If he follows his conscience he will have to go against the party line and vote against the proposal*. The expression with regard to political parties originated in America in the nineteenth century but it came to be applied more generally in the middle of the twentieth century. It is still a common cliché today, often being found in the phrase **toe the party line**. See also *toe the line*.

party's over, the is an idiom cliché indicating that something, usually something pleasant, successful, etc, has come to an end, as *We're used to long summer holidays from school. Now we're starting work and the party's over. From now on we'll get only two weeks*. The expression has been popular since around the middle of the twentieth century and is still a common cliché today in informal contexts.

pass muster is an idiom cliché meaning to meet a required standard, as *This essay would just about pass muster in the exam but it is not up to your usual standard*. The expression is military in origin and means to pass a review without fault being found. As a cliché it probably dates from around the nineteenth century and is still popular today in rather informal contexts.

pass the buck is an idiom cliché meaning to try to avoid responsibility for something by passing it to someone else, as *It was the school bully who broke the school window but he tried to pass the buck by blaming the younger boys*. The expression originated in America in the nineteenth century, and was originally a term used in poker to refer to a piece of buckshot or other object that was passed to a player to remind him that he was the next dealer. In its figurative version the expression spread to Britain where it became a cliché in the twentieth century. It is still common today in informal or slang contexts. **The buck stops here** is a development of the expression. It means that the ultimate responsibility lies with the person referred to, as *The teacher in charge at the time will not be asked to take responsibility for the behaviour of the pupils. I am the headmaster and the buck stops here*. It was used by Harry S Truman, President of the United States, around 1949 and later became a cliché in both America and Britain, being used in informal and slang contexts.

pass one's sell-by date is an idiom cliché indicating that someone or something is no longer considered useful or effective, as *They're declaring people of my age redundant in the firm and taking on younger people. They think we're past our sell-by date.* As a cliché it dates from the later part of the twentieth century, being used in informal and often humorous or ironic contexts. In origin it refers to the date stamped on perishable goods, such as foodstuffs.

patience of Job is an idiom cliché meaning extraordinary patience or forbearing, as *She must have the patience of Job to look after all those young children and never lose her temper.* As a cliché it dates from the nineteenth century although Job's patience was recognized in print long before that. Job was a character in the Old Testament who bore all his trials with extreme patience although the actual expression, **patience of Job**, does not appear in the *Book of Job* in the Bible.

patter of tiny feet is a hackneyed phrase meaning children, being particularly applied to someone who is expecting, or is likely to be expecting, a baby, as *Jim and Mary have just got married and I wouldn't be surprised if we hear the patter of tiny feet before long.* The expression dates from the late nineteenth century. As a cliché today it is often used humorously or satirically. When used straight it sounds rather coy or twee.

pave the way is an idiom cliché meaning to prepare the way for something or to lead up to something, as *His early research paved the way for the discovery of the new drug,* and *It is hoped the informal discussions will pave the way for formal peace talks.* The expression dates from the sixteenth century and became popular in the nineteenth century. As a cliché it is much used today in a variety of

contexts. In origin it refers to the paving of a road which will make progress along it easier.

pay through the nose is an idiom cliché meaning to pay a great deal of money for something, as *They really paid through the nose for that house and now property prices have slumped and they can't sell it.* The expression dates from around the seventeenth century. Although the origin of the phrase is uncertain, it has been suggested that it is a reference to the 'nose tax' imposed in Ireland in the ninth century, by the Danes, those who did not pay it having to face the punishment of having their noses slit. As a cliché it is widespread today in informal contexts.

pays your money and you takes your choice, you is a hackneyed phrase used to mean that the choices before one are very similar in some way and so one might as well trust to luck when deciding, as *All of the essay questions seem equally difficult. It is a case of you pays your money and you takes your choice,* and *I haven't heard of any of these films that are on at the cinema. It will be a case of you pays your money and you takes your choice.* The expression dates from the nineteenth century and appeared in a nineteenth-century rhyme 'Whatever you please my little dears, You pays your money and you takes your choice.' As a cliché it probably dates from the late nineteenth century. It is still used today in informal and humorous contexts.

pearls before swine is an allusion cliché used to refer to something that someone is not capable of appreciating, as *You should never have suggested taking her to the opera. That's a case of pearls before swine if ever I heard one.* The expression refers to a Biblical passage, to *Matthew* (7:6) 'Neither cast ye pearls before swine.' As a cliché it dates from the nineteenth century. It is often used by rather snobbish people who look down on those who do not share their acquired tastes.

pecking order is an idiom cliché referring to the order of importance or rank in a group of people, as *We can't just sit at any table at the dinner. There is a very strict pecking order. All the senior executives sit at the tables near the top.* The popularity of the expression dates from the twentieth century. The phrase is based on the fact that scientists observed a social system in domestic hens by which each hen in a group is allowed to peck the hen below except for the hen at the end of the row who has to submit to being pecked but cannot do any pecking. This system mirrors similar strict chains of rank.

penny dropped, the is an idiom cliché used to indicate that one has just, and usually somewhat belatedly, understood the significance of a remark, act or situation, as *I couldn't understand why Mary kept shaking her head at me while I was telling Frank about Jim's affair with Jenny. The penny dropped when I realized that Frank is now going out with Jenny,* and *I didn't get the point of John's joke until I was going home in the bus and then the penny suddenly dropped.* In origin it refers to the dropping of a coin in a slot machine which works a piece of machinery. The expression dates from the early twentieth century and is still a popular cliché today.

penny for them, a is a hackneyed phrase used to ask someone what he or she is thinking about, as *You haven't heard a word I've said. A penny for them.* The expression is a shortened version of **a penny for your thoughts**, a saying which goes back to the sixteenth century, having appeared in John Heywood's proverb collection of 1546.

Both expressions are clichés today but the shorter form is the more common.

pick up the threads is an idiom cliché meaning to resume something from where one left off some time before, as *She took time off from her career to look after her children and she's now trying to pick up the threads again,* and *He lost touch with his old school friends when he went away to university but he picked up the threads during the summer holidays.* In origin it refers to beginning to use thread again in sewing. The expression became popular in the twentieth century and is still common today.

picture of health, the is an idiom cliché indicating that someone is looking extremely well. The expression dates from the late eighteenth century and has been a cliché since the late nineteenth century. It is still popular today being used as a compliment to someone's air of well-being, as *She has been ill but she's just returned from holiday and she is looking the picture of health.*

pièce de résistance is a foreign cliché, used to refer to the best example of something or the best part of something, as *He has painted many fine portraits but the one of his sister is the pièce de résistance.* It was originally used in France around the late eighteenth century to refer to the main or finest course of a meal. The expression was adopted into English and was applied in more general contexts. It is still popular today, there being no phrase in English which is quite so apt.

piece of cake is an idiom cliché used to refer to something that is extremely easy or simple, as *He said he thought the exam was a piece of cake but he failed it.* The expression was used by the armed forces in World

War 2 to describe an easy mission. Its ultimate origin is uncertain but it may be connected with 'cakewalk', originally a contest, popular among black Americans in the middle of the nineteenth century, in which couples had to devise innovative and intricate steps while promenading, the winners receiving a cake as a prize. As a cliché it dates from the twentieth century and is still popular today in informal contexts.

pie in the sky is an allusion cliché used to refer to the promise of some form of success or advantage that will never materialize, as *He says that he is planning to get a job abroad but it's all pie in the sky*. The expression is an allusion to a song sung by the International Workers of the World in the early part of the twentieth century. 'You will eat, bye and bye, in the glorious land above the sky! Work and pray, live on hay, you'll get pie in the sky when you die.' It became a cliché in America later in the century and crossed the Atlantic to Britain where it is still popular today in informal or slang contexts.

pig in a poke, buy see *buy a pig in a poke*

pin one's hopes on is a hackneyed phrase meaning to rely on something or someone to bring about the realization of one's hopes or dreams, as *They can't afford the price of the house but they're pinning their hopes on his aunt lending them some money* and *Their team are lying second at the moment and they're pinning all their hopes on their relay team winning the competition for them*. The expression dates from the nineteenth century, an earlier form having been **pin one's faith on**. It may have its origin in the badges which were once worn by troops to show who their leader was.

plain sailing is an idiom cliché used to refer to trouble-free progress, as *We had*

expected to have trouble getting planning permission for our new house but in fact it was all plain sailing. The expression which dates from the nineteenth century is derived from the nautical phrase 'plane sailing' in which navigational calculations were made by plotting them on a flat plane rather than on the surface of a globe. As a cliché it is in widespread use today.

platform on which to build is a hackneyed phrase used to indicate a basis from which other things can be developed, as *These are not our final plans for nursery education but they are a platform on which to build*. As a cliché the expression dates from the second part of the twentieth century, being much used today by politicians and people in public life.

play ball is an idiom cliché meaning to cooperate, as *I thought we could form a car pool to take the kids to school but the other parents wouldn't play ball*. As a cliché the expression dates from the twentieth century and is common today in informal or slang contexts. In origin it refers to the cooperation required in order for two or more people to play a game with a ball.

play one's cards right is an idiom cliché meaning to use one's opportunities cleverly so as to gain maximum advantage, as *They are obviously interested in the project. If you play your cards right I think they might invest some money in it*. When used literally the expression obviously refers to card games. As a figurative expression the phrase dates from the eighteenth century, probably becoming a cliché in the nineteenth century. An earlier form of the cliché was **play one's cards well**.

play with fire is an idiom cliché meaning to do something very risky or dangerous, as *He knew that he was playing with fire having* *an affair with his best friend's wife*, and *Someone should warn Jim that he's playing with fire by teasing Jack*. The figurative use of playing with fire is a very old one. It became popular in the late nineteenth century and is a common cliché today.

pleased as Punch is a simile cliché meaning delighted, as *She is as pleased as Punch at winning the competition, although the prize is a small one*. The phrase refers to Punch of the traditional Punch and Judy Puppet show, in which Punch is portrayed as being very pleased with himself. The expression became popular in the middle of the nineteenth century and is a common cliché today.

plot thickens, the is a catchphrase cliché used to indicate that the situation is getting involved and dramatic. It originally referred to the plot of a play getting very involved. The expression was used by playwright George Villiers in his comedy *The Rehearsal* (1672) 'Ay, now the plot thickens very much upon us.' The phrase was used seriously in some Victorian and Edwardian melodramas and mystery stories. As a modern cliché it is usually used humorously or satirically, often being applied to situations that are not at all involved and certainly not dramatic, as *Mary received some flowers at work and we all thought Jim had sent them, but Jim said he hadn't. The plot thickens*.

pocket, in one's is an idiom cliché meaning influenced or controlled by someone, as *Many people think that some of the council members are in the pocket of the local builder*. The influence or control is often based on dishonesty and often involves bribes. As a cliché it dates from the twentieth century and in origin the phrase refers to the fact that people keep money in their pockets.

point of no return is a hackneyed phrase indicating a critical point in a project or situation which marks the stage after which there is no possibility of turning round or stopping, as *Setting up the new business was so expensive that we thought of giving up but we had reached the point of no return. If we had given up we would have lost all our money*. The term originated in aviation where it referred to the stage in a flight beyond which there would not be enough fuel to return to one's destination. It was used by airmen during World War 2, becoming a cliché in the second part of the twentieth century.

poor are always with us, the is a quotation cliché which is a slight misquotation from Biblical passages, such as *Matthew* (26:11) 'For ye have the poor always with you but me ye have not always', a statement made by Jesus to his disciples. As a cliché the expression dates from the twentieth century. It is used today mostly in humorous or ironical contexts, as *She says her parents-in-law are like the poor, always with them. They are constantly popping in uninvited*.

poor thing but mine own, a is a quotation cliché being a misquotation from Shakespeare's *As You Like It* (5:4) in which Touchstone says of Audrey 'an ill-favoured thing, sir, but mine own.' It is used as a deprecatory way of referring to a possession, although often one is quite proud of the possession so referred to, as *Do you like my new car? It's a poor thing but mine own*. As a cliché it dates from the middle of the nineteenth century. It is still used today but often by people of a literary bent.

pop the question is a hackneyed phrase meaning to propose marriage, as *Did he go down on bended knee when he popped the question?* The expression dates from the eighteenth century and is commonly used today in informal, and often humorous or satirical contexts, although some people would regard it as rather coy. In origin it refers to the person who is proposing marriage being so nervous or embarrassed that he blurts out the proposal as though it were exploding from him. In these enlightened times, of course, the popper of the question can be female.

pound of flesh is an allusion cliché meaning what is due or owed to one, as *I'm sure that our landlord will charge us for the broken chair. He is always one to exact his pound of flesh.* In origin it refers to Shakespeare's *The Merchant of Venice* (4:1) in which the moneylender, Shylock, demands the pound of flesh that was promised him when he lent Antonio money. As a cliché the expression dates from around the later part of the nineteenth century. It is still a widespread cliché today.

pour oil on troubled waters is an idiom cliché meaning to bring calm to an angry or troubled situation, as *Her brother and sister are always quarrelling and it is left to her to pour oil on troubled waters and restore family peace.* As a cliché the expression dates from the middle of the nineteenth century and is still common today. In origin it refers to an ancient practice of pouring oil on rough seas to try and create a calm surface.

powder one's nose is a euphemism cliché sometimes used by women to indicate that they are going to the toilet, as *I must just powder my nose before dinner.* Despite the fact that we live in a society where things are now discussed or mentioned that would once have been considered taboo or not polite, this cliché is still used today, although sometimes in humorous contexts. In origin the expression refers to the fact that women often freshen up their

make-up in a toilet or bathroom as well as attending to more basic bodily functions.

powers that be, the is an allusion cliché being a reference to a Biblical passage, to *Romans* (13:1) 'The powers that be are ordained of God.' It refers to those in authority. As a cliché the expression dates from the late nineteenth century. It is still used today, sometimes in humorous or satirical contexts, as *The powers that be have decided that our school summer holiday will be shorter this year,* and *The powers that be have sent a memo round saying we can work flexitime from now on.*

practice makes perfect is a proverb cliché indicating that the more one does something the better one gets at it. The proverb dates from the fifteenth century and has an equivalent in several other languages. As a cliché it is still popular today, often being used by parents to encourage their children in a pursuit that the parents favour but on which the children may resent spending time, as *You should spend more time at the piano. Practice makes perfect and you might get to play at the school concert.* It is sometimes used humorously or ironically, as *Why don't you try getting to work on time? You may find that practice makes perfect.*

prey on one's mind is an idiom cliché meaning to cause distress or anxiety to, as *Memories of the accident preyed on her mind for years,* and *It preyed on his mind that he might have been able to save the child's life if he had acted more promptly.* In origin it refers to an animal preying on another for food. As a cliché it dates from the later part of the nineteenth century but the expression is older than that.

prick up one's ears is an idiom cliché meaning to start listening attentively, as *The child pricked up his ears when he heard* his *mother mention the word picnic*. As a cliché it dates from the nineteenth century and is still popular today, mostly in informal contexts. The expression itself dates from the sixteenth century and in origin refers to a horse or other animal pricking up its ears at a sudden noise.

pride and joy is a hackneyed phrase used to refer to someone or something of which one is very proud, as *Their grandson is their pride and joy*, and *Those roses were your father's pride and joy and the dog has just dug them up*. The expression comes from a poem, *Rokeby* (1813) written by Walter Scott in which it was used to describe children. As a cliché it is still common today.

pride of place is a hackneyed phrase used to describe the prominent position given to something, as *Pride of place on their mantelpiece goes to the graduation photograph of their grandson*. As a cliché the expression dates from the middle of the nineteenth century and is still common today.

prime mover is a hackneyed phrase used to indicate the person or thing that has been the cause of something or that has been most effective in getting something started, as *The local headmistress was the prime mover in the campaign to keep the school open*, and *The murder of the child was the prime mover in the reform of the law*. As a cliché it dates from the twentieth century and is still popular today in a wide of contexts.

prime of life is a hackneyed phrase used to refer to the most vigorous period of one's life or to the time at which one's talents are at their peak, as *Her father died recently although he was in the prime of life*, and *Many people thought that the actress was in*

the *prime of life when she decided to retire*. As a cliché the expression dates from the middle of the nineteenth century although the idea of a period of life that is particularly vigorous goes back to ancient times and was defined by Plato in *The Republic* as a period of about thirty years in a man's life. Women came off a good deal worse with a period of only twenty years. A related expression is **in one's prime**, popularized by the character of Jean Brodie in Muriel Spark's novel *The Prime of Miss Jean Brodie* which was made into a film (1969). Both expressions are still common today, sometimes being used in humorous or ironic contexts.

proof of the pudding is an allusion cliché referring to a proverb **the proof of the pudding is in the eating**. Both the shorter version and the full proverb are still in common use today. The proverb indicates that it is possible to judge whether something is successful or not only when it has been put to the test and when one has found out whether it does what it was intended to do, etc, as *John is confident that he can mend the car himself but the proof of the pudding will be in the eating*, and *The education authorities think that the new exam system will be more effective but some of the teachers have doubts. The proof of the pudding will be in the eating*. The proverb dates from around the early part of the seventeenth century and in origin refers to the fact that one does not know whether a pudding mixture has been successful until it has been cooked and eaten.

proud parents is a hackneyed phrase often used by journalists, for examples as a caption to a picture, as *The proud parents congratulate the champion*, and *The proud parents leave the hospital with their baby son*. As a cliché the expression dates from the nineteenth century and is still popular today.

public enemy number one is a catchphrase cliché used to describe a person who is undesirable in some way to a particular group or person. The expression was originally applied to a notorious American Midwest outlaw, John Dillinger, by the then Attorney General, Homer Cummings, in the early 1930s. The expression spread to Britain and became popular after World War 2. It is a common cliché today, often being used in humorous or ironic contexts, as *He has been public enemy number one with Mary since he bought the car that she had her eye on,* and *I'm public enemy number one since I told the children they would have to finish their homework instead of going to the cinema.* In America the FBI keeps a list of the ten most wanted criminals but they are not individually ranked.

pull one's finger out is a hackneyed phrase often used as a vulgar instruction to someone to start working faster or more effectively, as *For goodness' sake pull your finger out or we won't get these orders out today.* It is not always used in the form of an actual instruction, as *If you don't pull your finger out we'll all have to work overtime tonight.* As a cliché it dates from the twentieth century, having its origins in RAF slang of the 1930s and is common today in less polite circles of society. An alternative form of the expression is **get one's finger out**.

pull one's socks up is an idiom cliché used to mean to make an effort to do better. It is often children who are at the receiving end of this cliché, as *If you don't pull your socks up you will find yourself repeating the year,* although its use is not confined to them. In origin it refers to smartening oneself up by pulling socks up that have slipped round one's ankles, a common problem for schoolboys wearing short trousers. As a cliché it dates from the twentieth century

and is a common exhortation today, much loved by people in authority.

pull out all the stops is an idiom cliché meaning to do one's utmost, as *If we pull out all the stops we may just get this work finished tonight* and *They pulled out all the stops to find a hospital bed for the sick child.* In origin the expression refers to organ playing. An organ's stops are used to change its sounds and by pulling them all out and bringing into play all the ranks of pipes, an organist can achieve the loudest possible sound. The term began to be used figuratively in the second part of the nineteenth century and is a widespread cliché today in all but the most formal contexts.

pull someone's leg is an idiom cliché meaning to tease or fool someone, as *I don't believe we're getting another week's holiday. You're pulling my leg!* The expression dates from the nineteenth century and was probably a cliché by the end of the twentieth century. It is still common today as an expression of incredulity in informal contexts. In origin it refers to tripping someone up by catching one of his or her legs on something such as a stick.

pull strings is an idiom cliché meaning to use one's influence or power to help bring something about, often secretly, as *At first he was turned down for the job but his father's an executive with the firm and he pulled a few strings.* As a cliché it dates from the twentieth century and is still common today in informal contexts. It is related to **pull the strings** which means to be the person who really, though not apparently, controls affairs or controls the actions of others, as *Mr Brown is the managing director but it's his deputy who pulls the strings.* The expression dates from around the late nineteenth century, being originally used in political contexts and then becoming more general. Both **pull strings** and **pull the strings** refer to puppetry where the puppet master operates the puppets by pulling strings.

pull the other one is a catchphrase cliché used to express one's disbelief at something someone has said, as *You say the car is worth £12,000. Pull the other one!* The expression is a shorter version of **pull the other one, it's got bells on**. The latter may be a reference to the bells that were associated with the traditional court jester or fool. The expression is thought to date from the early 1920s and is a popular cliché today in very informal or slang contexts, the shorter version being the more common. See also **pull someone's leg**.

pull the wool over someone's eyes is an idiom cliché meaning to deceive or hoodwink someone, as *She was out with her boyfriend but she tried to pull the wool over her parents' eyes by saying she was at the library studying.* In origin it refers to someone pulling a wig, once generally worn, over someone's eyes so as to prevent him or her seeing clearly. The expression dates from the early nineteenth century. Like the practice it defines, the expression is still common today.

pull yourself together is a hackneyed phrase used to someone who is very upset about something and is showing emotion in some way. It is a typically British piece of advice given by people who believe one should **keep a stiff upper lip** and is often wrong advice since it is sometimes important to give rein to one's emotions, as in the case of grieving for a loved one. The expression dates from the twentieth century and is still commonly used today. In origin it refers to someone having fallen apart.

put in the picture is an idiom cliché meaning to give someone up-to-date information about something, as *Could you put me in the picture about what's been going on while I've been away?* The cliché dates from the twentieth century and is still common today in informal or slang contexts.

put one's best foot forward is an idiom cliché meaning to make the best attempt possible to succeed, as *The first year of the business is going to be difficult but we'll just have to put our best foot forward.* The expression dates from the sixteenth century and became a cliché around the middle of the nineteenth century. It is still popular today. The origin of the expression is obscure.

put one's foot in it is an idiom cliché meaning to do or say something tactless or clumsy, as *You certainly put your foot in it when you criticized Jane in front of John. She is his fiancée.* The expression has been in use since the eighteenth century and is still commonly used today in all but the most formal contexts.

put one's shoulder to the wheel see *shoulder to the wheel, put one's*

put on one's thinking cap is an idiom cliché meaning to devote some time to thinking or reflection, as *We have to find ways of raising money for the youth club. We'd better all put on our thinking caps.* The expression dates from the late nineteenth century, becoming a cliché in the twentieth century. The origin is uncertain. It has been suggested that it was a cap worn by judges when considering the appropriate sentence for a wrongdoer. An earlier form of the expression was **put on one's considering cap** but this is now obsolete.

put someone's nose out of joint is an idiom cliché meaning to hurt someone or make someone jealous by making him or her feel supplanted or displaced, as *His nose has been put out of joint since his parents brought home the new baby, although everyone is treating him very affectionately.* The expression dates from the sixteenth century and is still very common today. In origin it probably refers to someone getting a blow in the face which breaks his nose, although the nose does not actually have a joint.

put the cart before the horse see *cart before the horse, put the*

put two and two together is an idiom cliché meaning to work out or realize something on the basis of the information that one has, as *I don't know why she didn't put two and two together when he said he was working late at the office so much. Everyone else knew he was having an affair.* The implication is often that there is something suspicious about the situation that the information relates to. The expression dates from the nineteenth century and is a common cliché today. In origin it refers to simple arithmetic. An extension of the expression, and with the same meaning, is **put two and two together and make four**. A related expression is **put two and two together and make five** which means wrongly to deduce something from the facts.

Q

quality of life is a vogue cliché used to describe the non-materialistic side of life, as *If we move right into the country we shall take a huge cut in income and facilities but the quality of life for the children will be greatly enhanced. They will have lots of fresh air and plenty of room to play.* As a cliche it began to become popular in the 1970s and has stayed popular, with the increase in awareness of the importance of leisure and the environment.

quality time is a vogue cliché used to describe the time that a person devotes solely to a child, partner, etc, being too busy at work to spend any more time, as *We pick our daughter up from nursery at 6 o'clock and then we have an hour's quality time before she goes to bed.* The expression originated in America and has been a cliché in Britain since the mid 1980s. It is often the outward expression of an inward guilt complex about not spending more time with one's family.

quantum leap is a vogue cliché meaning a significant advance, a sudden breakthrough, as *The patient's recovery took a quantum leap when they treated her with the new drug.* The term comes from nuclear physics, a quantum leap being a sudden transition from one energy state to another within the submicroscopic atom. In physics the term dates from around 1950 and it began to be used figuratively a few years later, becoming a vogue cliché in Britain in the 1970s. It is one of several clichés that have scientific or specialist origins.

queer the pitch is an idiom cliché meaning to spoil things for someone, to make it impossible for someone to do something effectively, as *He had just persuaded her to go out with him when his sister told her that he was married and queered the pitch.* In origin a pitch was the place where a stall was set up and so if someone queered it, he or she prevented the trader from being able to sell things from it. The expression has been a common cliché since the late nineteenth century

quick as a flash is a simile cliché used to emphasize the speed of someone or something, as *The police were just about to arrest the burglar when, quick as a flash, he leaped over a fence and disappeared,* and *I told her to keep my news a secret but, quick as a flash, it was all round the village.* In origin the phrase refers to a flash of lightning, the expression **quick as lightning** also being common but not as common. The expression probably dates from the eighteenth century.

quick one, a twentieth century hackneyed phrase for a quick alcoholic drink. It is usually used in an informal context, as *Have you time for a quick one after work?*

quid pro quo (Latin for 'this for that') is a foreign cliché meaning tit for tat, the same in return. The expression has been in existence in English since the time of Shakespeare who used it in *Henry VI, Part 1* (5:3) 'I cry you mercy, 'tis but quid pro quo.' As a cliché it is still used today, as *It was a case of quid pro* *quo; they withdrew their ambassador and we withdrew ours,* but not in informal contexts. It tends to be used by people of a literary or academic bent but it is also used somewhat pompously by others who are trying to impress and who might well not know exactly what the expression means. The phrase is used in legal circles.

quiet as a mouse is a simile cliché used to emphasize the silence of someone or something, as *The child was told to be quiet as a mouse while she watched the robin feeding her young,* and *The whole house was quiet as a mouse when the burglar crept in.* The expression has been in existence since the sixteenth century and is an extremely widespread cliché. In origin it refers to the necessity of a mouse to keep absolutely silent in the presence of an enemy, such as a cat, although mice can be extremely noisy if they are scampering around behind woodwork.

quite frankly is a filler cliché usually used virtually meaninglessly, as *Quite frankly, I am strongly opposed to the scheme.* Some people use it extremely frequently without being aware of their somewhat annoying habit.

quite the reverse is a hackneyed phrase meaning the opposite of what has just been stated, as *She is not as naive as she appears; quite the reverse.* As a cliché it dates from the twentieth century. It is still quite common but it tends to be used by people who use rather a formal style of *speech.*

QT, on the is an abbreviation cliché meaning secretly or clandestinely, as *He has just got engaged to Mary but he is still going out with another girl on the QT.* The expression, which is short for **on the quiet**, is still used as a cliché by some people but it is rather dated nowadays.

❧ R ❧

race against time, a is a hackneyed phrase used to refer to an extremely urgent situation, as *I wish the ambulance would come. It's going to be a race against time to get her to hospital on time before the baby is born.* The cliché dates from the twentieth century and is still the standard phrase used today to express urgency. In common with many such phrases the level of urgency is frequently exaggerated. In origin the expression refers to the fact that time is often represented as being swift-moving, as in phrases such as **how time flies**.

rags to riches is a hackneyed phrase meaning from extreme poverty to wealth, usually as a result of one's own efforts, as *His story is one of rags to riches. He was a labourer's son who became a wealthy factory-owner.* It is often used in a business context. The expression became popular in the second half of the twentieth century and is still popular today. Stories of people who go from poverty to riches are the stuff of which dreams and fiction are made. The fairy tale *Cinderella* is a well-known example. A development of the theme is **rags to rags** which is used satirically to describe a person, family or firm who has gone from poverty to wealth and back to poverty again. It is used, for example, of a family firm which was started by someone very go-ahead and talented and then run down by successive family members of a singularly less talented nature.

rain cats and dogs is a hackneyed phrase meaning to rain very heavily, as *We had to*

cancel the picnic because it was raining cats and dogs, and It looks as though it's going to rain cats and dogs. The expression probably dates from the eighteenth century and has been a cliché since the middle of the nineteenth century. It is still widespread today, in informal contexts, as befits a climate where the phenomenon is extremely common. The origin of the expression is uncertain. One suggestion is that in the days before there was efficient street drainage, cats and dogs could drown in the gutters during a heavy downpour.

rain or shine is a hackneyed phrase meaning come what may, as *Don't worry I'll be there, rain or shine.* As a cliché it dates from the twentieth century and is still popular today. In origin it refers to uncertain weather conditions which can often affect the holding of events or people's attendance at them.

rainy day, a is an idiom cliché used to refer to a time when one might be in financial difficulties. It is mostly used in the phrase **keep** or **save something for a rainy day** meaning to save some money while one has it against the day when one might not, as *He's getting a lot of overtime just now but he's spending the money as he earns it. He should be saving some of it for a rainy day.* The concept dates from the sixteenth century. As a cliché the expression dates from the late nineteenth century. In origin it refers to wet days when agricultural workers could not work and so would not earn any money.

rarin' to go is a hackneyed phrase meaning eager to get started on something, as *The child didn't want to start school at first but now she's rarin to go*. In origin it refers to a horse 'rearing' because it is anxious to be off. As a cliché it dates from the twentieth century and is still popular today in informal contexts. It is sometimes used ironically, as *Monday morning and everybody's rarin' to go to work.*

rat race, the is an idiom cliché used to refer to the relentless competitive struggle to stay ahead of one's competitors at work, in commerce, etc. It is often used just to describe the average work situation or modern life generally, as *He was a senior executive in the company but he got tired of the rat race and went to run a croft on a remote island*. The expression originated in America and became a cliché in Britain around the second half of the 1970s. As the struggle to get ahead gets ever fiercer the expression has got ever more popular.

rats deserting a sinking ship see *desert a sinking ship*

read my lips is a hackneyed phrase used to emphasize the truth of what one has just said. The phrase was popularized by US President George Bush in his speech accepting the Republican nomination for president in 1988 when he made a promise not to raise taxes, no matter how much Congress tried to persuade him 'I'll say no, and they'll push, and I'll say no, and they'll push again, and I'll say to them "Read my lips, no new taxes".' The phrase in fact predates this and is thought to have its roots in 1970s rock music. As a cliché today it is often found to emphasize a negative statement, as *Read my lips! I will not give you money to go to the cinema.*

ready for the fray see *eager for the fray*

red-carpet treatment is a hackneyed phrase used to indicate special treatment, usually when applied to that given to important guests, as *Of course the mayor didn't realize how bad the hospital food is. She got the red-carpet treatment and had a gourmet menu*. In origin it refers to a strip of red carpet traditionally laid out for a royal person or other VIP to walk on when making an official visit. The expression dates from the early twentieth century. It is still common today although it is often found in contexts that are critical of the practice.

red-letter day is an idiom cliché used to indicate a special or memorable day of some kind, as *Tuesday is a red-letter day for the children because they are appearing in the school play*. It is often a day which gives rise to a celebration but this is not always the case, as *It was a red-letter day for the whole family when the youngest daughter left home*. As a cliché it dates from the nineteenth century, although it goes back at least until the eighteenth century, and is widespread. In origin it refers to the practice, common from the fifteenth century on, of printing saints' days and feast days on calendars and almanacs in red.

red rag to a bull, like a is a simile cliché used to indicate that someone or something is a source of anger or fury to someone else, as *Don't mention his name to my mother. It's like a red rag to a bull. He once did her out of a lot of money*. As a cliché it dates from the late nineteenth century and is still widespread today. In origin it refers to the erroneous idea that bulls are infuriated by the sight of a piece of red cloth being waved in front of them, hence the red lining of the matador's cape in bull-fighting. In fact, bulls are colour blind and it is the movement, not the colour of the cape, that infuriates them.

red tape is an idiom cliché used to refer to unnecessary bureaucracy and the delays that this often leads to, as *She thought she would get permission to do her research work here fairly rapidly but she had reckoned without the red tape*. The expression is thought to have become popular in the nineteenth century and, in keeping with the fact that the phenomenon plays such a major role in our lives, it is still widespread today, always being used in a derogatory way. In origin it refers to the reddish ribbons that lawyers and bureaucrats use to tie their documents.

reinvent the wheel is an idiom cliché meaning to start from the beginning when there is no need to do so, to fail to take advantage of previous developments or experience in a situation, as *The new managing director has no knowledge of the business and refuses to ask other people for advice. He keeps trying to reinvent the wheel.* The expression dates from the second part of the twentieth century and is still popular today, especially in business contexts.

reliable source, a is a hackneyed phrase used to testify to the authoritative and dependable nature of one's sources for a story or for a piece of gossip, as *I have it from a most reliable source that he is planning to leave her*. It is frequently used by journalists who do not wish to reveal the identity of the source of a story. Frequently the sources are far from reliable, particularly when a piece of gossip is being handed on, it usually being the bush telegraph, rather than a reliable source, that has given rise to the information. As a cliché it dates from the twentieth century and it is as common today as the sources are unreliable.

rest is history, the is a hackneyed phrase used to indicate that no more need be said because it is already well-known, as *She married him when she was very young, She went off with someone else, He killed her lover and the rest is history*, and *He was born of very poor parents, got a scholarship to university, graduated in science and the rest is history*, As a cliché it dates from the twentieth century and may be based on the rather dated cliché **the rest is silence** from Shakespeare's *Hamlet* (5:2).

ride off into the sunset is a hackneyed phrase used to indicate the departure of someone or the ending of something in more or less happy circumstances, as *I didn't think those two would ever get together but they did and they've ridden off into the sunset*. The origin of the expression is not linguistic but visual since it refers to the classic ending of a Western film, popular from the 1930s on, in which the victorious hero literally rides off into the sunset having accomplished what he set out to do.

right as rain is a simile cliché meaning fine, all right, as *She's been ill but she's as right as rain now*. The expression dates from the late nineteenth century and is widespread today. The origin is uncertain but it may refer to the original meaning of 'right' as straight.

ring a bell is an idiom cliché meaning to call something to mind, to remind someone of someone or something, as *His name rings a bell but I cannot quite place him*. The expression dates from the early twentieth century and is still popular today, being used in all but the most formal contexts. In origin it refers either to the memory being alerted in the way that a doorbell or telephone bell alerts a person to make a response, or to the bell that rings on a machine that acts as a trial of strength in a fairground and rings a bell if the competitor is successful.

ring the changes is an idiom cliché meaning to vary one's choice of things, actions, etc, within a possible, and often limited, range, as *She doesn't have many clothes but she manages to ring the changes by wearing different skirts with different sweaters each day.* In origin the expression refers to the ancient art of bell-ringing in churches in which a series of church bells are rung in as many different sequences as possible. The expression took on a figurative meaning around the early seventeenth century. As a cliché it is still popular today, often being used with reference to clothes.

ring true is an idiom cliché meaning to seem likely to be true, as *Everyone else seemed to find her story convincing but it didn't ring true to me.* The expression dates from around the early twentieth century and is still a popular cliché today, having the alternative form **have the ring of truth**. In origin it refers to the practice of judging the genuineness of coins, in the days when they were made of precious metals, by striking them against a counter or something similar to see if they produced the right sound. If made of counterfeit metal they did not.

rising tide is an idiom cliché meaning an increasing amount or trend, as *There has been a rising tide of opposition to the scheme.* The expression began to be popular in the nineteenth century and is still common today, particularly among journalists. It has the obvious origin of the incoming sea tide.

risk life and limb is a hackneyed phrase, meaning to risk death or serious injury, whose alliteration has probably done much to popularize it. The idea has been current since the seventeenth century and the expression has been a cliché since the middle of the nineteenth century, as *Volunteers risk life and limb to rescue climbers who get into difficulties on the mountain.* As a modern cliché it is used either in rather formal contexts or in humorous contexts where the degree of danger is deliberately exaggerated, as *Do you expect me to risk life and limb to get your kite down from that tree?* It is also use by journalists to heighten the danger in their accounts of rescues.

rock the boat is an idiom cliché meaning to disturb the stability of a situation, to cause trouble, as *The firm is just about financially stable again so don't rock the boat by asking for a huge salary increase,* and *We had all just agreed to forget about our difference of opinion when along came Jack who started rocking the boat.* The expression dates from the 1920s and was popularized by the title of a song 'Sit Down, You're Rockin' The Boat' in the musical *Guys and Dolls* (1950). It is still a common cliché today and has its origin in someone risking a small boat capsizing by moving around carelessly in it.

roger! is a catchphrase cliché which was originally used as a codeword of acknowledgement in the RAF and then in the general armed forces in World War 2. The letter R became Roger in the phonetic alphabet introduced in 1941. It had originally been Robert and stood for received (and understood). After the war the catchphrase spread to civilian life. It is still used today to indicate that something has been understood and agreed, but it tends to be used by older people with a military background or by people who are using it in a consciously humorous or ironic way.

rolling stone is an allusion cliché meaning someone who keeps moving around and never acquires much in the way of money or possessions, as *She hopes that he's going to get a job in the local factory and marry her but he's always been a rolling stone and doesn't want to settle down.* The phrase alludes to the proverb

a rolling stone gathers no moss which simply emphasizes the meaning of the shortened version. The proverb dates from the sixteenth century and is still popular today, despite the fact that in modern times moving on from job to job is often thought to be a good thing from the point of view of promotion.

roll on! is a hackneyed phrase used to indicate that one is awaiting the arrival of something with impatience, as *Roll on pay day! I'm absolutely broke!* and *Roll on summer! This weather is getting me down!* The cliché dates from the twentieth century and derives from military catch-phrases of World War 1. These were **roll on the big ship** which expressed the wish that the war would end and a ship would come to take the troops home, and **roll on duration** which also expressed the wish that the war would come to an end, duration being a reference to the fact that volunteers in 1914 had joined up for the duration of the war. The cliché is still commonly used today in a variety of contexts.

Rome was not built in a day is a proverb cliché used to encourage someone to have patience by reminding him or her that aims can take a long time to achieve, as *I know your leg seems to be taking a long time to heal, but try to be patient. Rome wasn't built in a day, you know.* As a proverb it dates from the twelfth century and appeared in John Heywood's proverb collection of 1546. As a cliché it is still popular today. It is beloved of people who like to

make platitudinous remarks about other people's lives and it is resented by enthusiastic people who do not regard patience as a virtue.

rose between two thorns, a is an idiom cliché used of someone or something very attractive and placed between two people or things that are not attractive, as *It's a beautiful house but you should see the buildings on either side of it. Talk about a rose between two thorns!.* It has been a cliché since the nineteenth century and is now mostly used facetiously and ironically, as *Old Fred insisted on sitting between the twins at their eighteenth birthday party. He called himself the rose between two thorns.*

rose by any other name, a is an allusion cliché indicating that it is the basic qualities of people or things that count, not what they are called. As a cliché it probably dates from the nineteenth century. It is still popular today, especially with people of rather a literary bent and it is often used ironically, as *I used to be called his secretary. I'm now his personal assistant but I don't get any more money. A rose by any other name,* and *The ad is for cleansing operatives but they're looking for street cleaners. A rose by any other name.* The allusion is to a quotation from Shakespeare's *Romeo and Juliet* (2:2) and the quotation itself a **rose by any other name will smell as sweet** is also found as a cliché.

roses, roses all the way is an allusion cliché used to refer to a life of ease and comfort. As a modern cliché it is usually used in negative, often ironic contexts, as *He's been in and out of prison all his life. If she marries him it's not exactly going to be roses, roses all the way.* As a cliché the expression is often shortened to **roses all the way**, as *We now have a successful business but I can tell you that it has been far* *from roses all the way.* The phrase is an allusion to *The Patriot* by Robert Browning (1812–89). The cliché dates from the twentieth century and it is still common today, mostly being use by people of rather a literary bent.

rough diamond, a is an idiom cliché used to describe someone who is unsophisticated and rather uncouth in his or her manners and appearance, but who is usually an extremely worthwhile or kind person, as *He's a bit of a rough diamond but he's a very good worker,* and *She's a rough diamond but she was the only neighbour who offered to look after the children when their mother was in hospital.* In origin it refers to the fact that an uncut, unpolished diamond does not look attractive or valuable but may be extremely attractive and valuable after it is cut and polished.

rule the roost is an idiom cliché meaning to be in charge, to be dominant, as *There's no question of any discussions about anything in their house. Their father rules the roost and what he says goes,* and *The deputy manager loves ruling the roost when the boss is away.* As a cliché it dates from the twentieth century and is still popular today. It is found in all but the most formal contexts and is usually used in a derogatory way. In origin it may refer to a cockerel being in charge of hens and choosing which hen should roost near him but an alternative suggestion is that it is a variation of **rule the roast**, a term that originated in the fifteenth century with the same meaning as the present **rule the roost**. It probably referred to the fact that the person who was in charge of the roast (meat) was in charge of the household.

rule with a rod of iron is an idiom cliché used of someone in charge and meaning to be very strict or tyrannical, as *No one misbehaves in that class. The teacher rules them with a rod of iron.* In origin it may be a Biblical reference to

Revelations (2:27) 'Thou shalt break them with a rod of iron.' As a cliché it probably dates from the late nineteenth century and is still widespread today.

rumour hath it is a hackneyed phrase indicating that there is a rumour circulating about something, as *Rumour hath it that there is a new woman in his life.* As a cliché it dates from the late nineteenth century. Although it sounds rather archaic it is still used today, often by people of a literary bent and frequently in a humorous way.

run around like headless chickens is a simile cliché meaning to act in a totally disorganized, often panic-stricken, way, as *The managing director knew everything about the firm. Since he's resigned, the board are running around like headless chickens trying to find a suitable replacement,* and *The opposition accused the government of running around like headless chickens in the face of their economic difficulties.* In origin it refers to the fact that chickens continue to move convulsively for a time after having their heads removed. As a cliché it dates from the late part of the twentieth century.

run it up the flagpole is an idiom cliché, often used as a business cliché, meaning to give something a trial in order to gauge reactions to it, as *We can't decide on a cover for this book. Let's get a trial one done and give it to the salesmen to run it up the flagpole,* and *They have some doubts about the new product. They're going to run it up the flagpole and do a limited production run.* It is American in origin and dates from around the middle of the twentieth century, being a shortened form of **run it up the flagpole and see who salutes**. The longer expression points to the origin. As a cliché in Britain it is more recent, having become popular from the late 1970s. It is still common today, particularly in business circles.

run rings round is an idiom cliché meaning to defeat or surpass someone utterly, as *When it comes to marketing our firm can run rings round theirs,* and *You shouldn't worry about the tennis final. You will run rings round your opponent.* The term dates from the late nineteenth century and is still popular today in informal contexts. It is, for example, favoured by journalists when referring to a sporting rout. In origin it refers to the fact that a runner is so much better than the other competitors that he or she can move along the course while running in circles, rather than in a straight line, and still win.

run round in circles see *go round in circles*

Russian roulette, play is an idiom cliché used to mean to take part in a very risky undertaking the outcome of which is potentially ruinous or fatal, as *Jim's playing Russian roulette going out with Frank's wife while he's abroad. He'll kill him if he finds out,* and *Despite all the warnings about unsafe sex she still goes in for one-night stands. She certainly believes in playing Russian roulette.* In origin it refers to a game played by Russian officers at the court of the Czar in which each player, using a revolver that contained one bullet, spun the cylinder of the gun and aimed it at his head. Since the cylinder contained six chambers there was one chance in six that he would kill himself. As a cliché it dates from the first part of the twentieth century and is still widespread today.

S

safe and sound is a doublet cliché used to emphasize that someone is free from danger and unharmed. The expression, probably because of its alliteration, is a very old one, dating from around the beginning of the fourteenth century and remaining in use through the centuries. It is a popular cliché today, being much used by journalists among others, as *The missing child has been found safe and sound.*

sail close to the wind is an idiom cliché meaning to come very close to breaking the law or rules, as *The police have their eye on the market trader. He has never been prosecuted for receiving stolen goods but he sails very close to the wind.* In origin the expression refers to a ship or boat sailing so close to the wind that it is dangerous. The figurative expression dates from the nineteenth century and became a cliché towards the end of the century. Like the practice which it describes, the cliché is still common today, being found in all but the most formal contexts. An older form of the expression is **sail near to the wind**.

salt of the earth, the is an allusion cliché, to a Biblical passage (*Matthew,* 5:13) in which Jesus told those who were persecuted for him and his beliefs 'Ye are the salt of the earth.' The metaphor refers to the fact that salt was a very valuable commodity since it was used not only to give flavour to food but also to preserve it. As a cliché it dates from the middle of the nineteenth century and refers to people who are really worth-while, having all the sterling qualities, such as kindness, loyalty, etc, as *We really miss our next door neighbour. She was the salt of the earth.*

sauce for the goose is sauce for the gander, what is is a proverb cliché basically indicating that people should be treated equally whatever their gender. The proverb appeared in John Ray's collection of 1678. It could be said to be the forerunner of equality for women although it took a long time for actuality to catch up with the proverb. As a cliché it is still popular today, as *Why shouldn't she have an affair? Her husband's had a mistress for years. What is sauce for the goose is sauce for the gander.* It is often now shortened to **what is sauce for the goose**, the rest of the proverb being understood, as *If he thinks that he can go out on Saturday afternoons without the children, why shouldn't she? After all, what's sauce for the goose.*

saved by the bell is an idiom cliché used to indicate that because of the chance intervention of someone or something, one has been saved from some form of difficult or dangerous situation, as *My mother has just asked me how I had done in my college exams when the first of her guests arrived for the party. Saved by the bell!* In origin it refers to the bell rung at the end of a round of boxing. As a cliché it dates from the second part of the twentieth century and is still popular today.

save for a rainy day see *rainy day, a*

163

saving grace, one's is a hackneyed phrase used to refer to someone's redeeming feature which compensates for his or her negative qualities, as *She was an absolutely dreadful boss. Her saving grace was her sense of humour.* As a cliché it dates from the late nineteenth century and is common today. In origin it refers to the theological concept of grace which delivers people from eternal damnation.

say the least, to is a hackneyed phrase used to indicate that one is stating the case as mildly as possible, as *It will be, to say the least, a difficult journey,* and *The repairs, to say the least, will be rather expensive.* It is sometimes used more or less meaninglessly by people to whom it has simply become a habit. As a cliché it dates from the middle of the nineteenth century and is still in current use.

school of hard knocks, the is a hackneyed phrase used to refer to experience of life. It is often used to contrast that with further education, often in rather a rancorous way, as *They've started employing young graduates at management level. That doesn't give much of a chance to those of us who were educated at the school of hard knocks.* The expression dates from the nineteenth century and is still common in some contexts today. It is particularly favoured by those who have made a lot of money without benefit of formal education.

sea change, suffer a see *suffer a sea change*

seamy side of life, the is an idiom cliché used to describe the unpleasant, dirty, etc side of life, perhaps the realistic aspect, as *She wants to be a social worker but she'll never cope with the seamy side of life. She has very wealthy parents and has led a very sheltered life.* In origin it refers to the side of a garment which has the seams of the cloth on it. Shakespeare used the idea in *Othello* (4:2) 'He turned your wit the seamy side without', and it has been a popular concept ever since. As a cliché it dates from the later part of the nineteenth century.

second to none is a hackneyed phrase used to indicate that someone or something is outstanding, as *He is second to none in English cricket at the present time.* It is often used as a gross exaggeration, as *I am not surprised the village fête was a success. As an organizer she is second to none.* The idea probably goes back to Chaucer's day but the expression itself first appeared in Shakespeare's *The Comedy of Errors* (5:1) 'Of credit infinite, highly beloved, Second to none that lives here.' It became a cliché around the middle of the nineteenth century and is still common today.

search me is a catchphrase cliché used to indicate that one has no knowledge or information on the subject at issue, as *Search me! I've no idea where he gets his money from.* The expression is American in origin and dates from the early part of the twentieth century. It is a common cliché today being used as an exclamation in informal contexts. In origin it refers to someone being searched to see if he or she had any information.

see a man about a dog is a catchphrase cliché used in humorous contexts to indicate that one does not wish to reveal one's destination when one leaves a room, as *Well it's time I went. I have to see a man about a dog.* It is sometimes a euphemism cliché for going to the toilet (see also powder one's nose) and is mostly used by men. The expression has been popular since the late nineteenth century and is still current.

see eye to eye is an allusion cliché meaning to agree but usually used negatively, as *I wouldn't ask them both to be on the committee. They do not see eye to eye on anything. There is no point in continuing the discussion. We will never see eye to eye.* The cliché is a reference to a Biblical passage in *Isaiah* (52:8) 'Thy watchmen shall lift up the voice; with the voice together shall they sing; for they shall see eye to eye, when the Lord shall bring again Zion.' As a cliché it dates from the later part of the nineteenth century and is still common today.

see how the land lies is an idiom cliché meaning to check out and consider the circumstances of a situation before taking action, as *I am not sure how long we will stay with our friends. It depends how many of their family are at home. We shall just have to see how the land lies.* As a cliché it dates from the middle of the nineteenth century and is still popular. It is originally a nautical idiom meaning to get one's bearings.

see the wood for the trees, cannot is an idiom cliché used to indicate that someone is unable to obtain a general or comprehensive view of a situation because of paying too much attention to detail, as *There is no point in asking Mary to review our staffing levels. We'll get such a detailed report that we won't have time to read it. She just can't see the wood for the trees.* The expression is always used in the negative although the negative takes various forms, as *Peter is taking weeks to work out population trends in the area. He never could see the wood for the trees.* The expression dates from the sixteenth century, probably becoming a cliché around the beginning of the twentieth century. It is a common way today of describing someone who is over-meticulous. In origin it suggests that someone is so intent on looking at the individual trees that he or she misses the general view of the wood.

see with one's own eyes is a hackneyed phrase meaning to witness something for oneself or have personal proof of something, as *I would not have believed that she would hit a child if I had not seen her do it with my own eyes.* The expression dates from around the beginning of the eighteenth century, becoming a cliché later in the century and being still current today.

see you later! is a hackneyed phrase used as a greeting to someone on parting from him or her, as a substitute for goodbye or cheerio. The expression is used whether or not the two people concerned are likely to meet again. For example a hairdresser might use it to a chance customer. The expression became popular in the 1980s and is still extremely popular today.

sell down the river is an idiom cliché meaning to act treacherously towards someone, as *They thought he was a trusted employee but he sold the company down the river by telling their competitors their trade secrets.* In origin the expression refers to the practice in America of slave-owners in the upper Mississippi selling slaves down river to the much harsher life on the cotton and sugar plantations of Louisiana. The expression began to be used figuratively in the late nineteenth century and is still common today.

sell like hot cakes is a simile cliché meaning to be sold very quickly, to be a great commercial success, as *His new novel is selling like hot cakes.* The expression is American in origin and refers to the rapid sale of hot cakes, such as pancakes, at fairs, etc. As a general expression in America it dates from the middle of the nineteenth century. It became a cliché in Britain in the twentieth century and is still common today in all but the most formal contexts.

165

separate the sheep from the goats is an allusion cliché which refers to a Biblical passage *Mattlew* (25:32) 'And before him shall be gathered all the nations; and he shall separate them one from the other, as a shepherd divideth his sheep from the goats. And he shall set the sheep on his right hand but the goats on the left.' The expression means to separate the good from the bad, the clever from the stupid, the competent from the incompetent, etc, as *I think this exam will separate the sheep from the goats*. As a cliché the expression probably dates from the nineteenth century and is still common. There are two other clichés which also refer to the good and bad, the superior and the inferior, etc being divided into their categories by some form of test. They are **separate the grain from the chaff** which as a cliché dates from the nineteenth century and **separate the men from the boys** which dates from the twentieth century.

serious money is a vogue cliché of the 1980s, a decade in which money was considered even more important than it usually is. It has survived into the present decade and means money in considerable quantities, as *You would get a stake in that company only if you had serious money to invest*, and *there is serious money to be made in the antiques trade*.

set the Thames on fire is an idiom cliché meaning to be very successful or famous. It is always used in negative, or implied negative, contexts, as *He was a hard-working pupil but we knew he would never set the Thames on fire*, and *Mark will make her a good enough husband but he's not the kind you can imagine setting the Thames on fire, is he?* The expression dates from the eighteenth century and has been a cliché since the middle of the nineteenth century. The expression has been used of other rivers in other languages.

seventh heaven, in is an idiom cliché meaning to be extremely happy, as *She was in seventh heaven when she discovered that she was going to have a baby*. In origin it refers to the fact that both Moslems and the ancient Jews recognized seven heavens in their faiths, the seven heavens corresponding to the seven planets. The seventh and highest of these was the abode of God and the angels. The expression began to be used without any religious significance in the nineteenth century and as a cliché dates from the middle of the nineteenth century. It is still a standard expression of happiness today.

sex rears its ugly head is a catchphrase cliché used to indicate that sex has become involved in a situation, as *We thought that Frank and Jenny were just friends but sex seems to have reared* its ugly head, and *You never get very far in a modern novel before sex rears its ugly head*. The expression became popular in the 1930s. It is still current today in humorous or satirical contexts. The origin is uncertain. It may refer to the rising of a penis or it may refer to the rearing of a serpent's head, perhaps an allusion to the serpent in the Garden of Eden. Other things can be substituted for 'sex' in the expression as **money rears its ugly head**.

shadow of one's former self a is an idiom cliché used to indicate that someone has become much thinner and weaker than before, as *This was the first time I had seen him since he had been ill. I was shocked to see that he is a shadow of his former self*. The expression is also used to indicate a diminution in power or fame, as *It is amazing to think he was one of the world's major political leaders. He is now a shadow of his former self and living in obscurity*. As a metaphor for emaciation the phrase has been in use since the sixteenth century. As a cliché the expression dates from the middle of the nineteenth century and is still common.

shape of things to come, the is a quotation cliché, the expression having been popularized by the title of H G Wells' novel, *The Shape of Things to Come* (1933), although the idea was referred to by Shakespeare in *Troilus and Cressida* (1:3) 'giant mass of things to come.' The phrase became a cliché not long after its use by Wells and is still common, as *We should have known when the first few people lost their jobs because of computerization that this was the shape of things to come.*

shape or form, in any is a doublet cliché meaning of any kind whatsoever. As a cliché it dates from the later part of the nineteenth century and is still a common form of emphasis, as *She will not eat meat in any shape or form.*

share and share alike is a hackneyed phrase meaning to divide something equally. The expression dates from the sixteenth century and has been a cliché since the later part of the nineteenth century. As a modern cliché it is frequently used to children in an effort to get them to share with their friends or siblings, as *It is selfish to keep all your chocolate to yourself. You should offer some to your friends. Share and share alike.*

shed light on is an idiom cliché meaning to explain or clarify something, as *No one can shed any light on the mystery of how the burglar got into the house.* The expression was used literally from the fourteenth century. The figurative expression became a cliché in the later part of the nineteenth century and is still common.

shipshape and Bristol fashion is an idiom cliché meaning tidy and orderly, as *We'd better leave the place shipshape and Bristol fashion for the next tenant coming in.* The expression is nautical – Bristol was a famous English port – in origin and has been a general cliché since the middle of the nineteenth century. It is still found today but it is rather dated and is mostly used by older people.

ships that pass in the night is an allusion cliché used to describe people who meet briefly and then go their separate ways, as *People who meet at conferences are often ships that pass in the night. Very few of them keep in touch with each other.* It is a reference to a passage in a poem by Henry Wadsworth Longfellow. The poem was published in 1873 in *Tales of a Wayside Inn* as 'The Theologian's Second Tale'. The reference is 'Ships that pass in the night and speak to each other in passing.' As a cliché it dates from the later part of the nineteenth century. It is often used today with reference to brief relationships, sometimes of a sexual nature, as *He didn't know that she had had a child by him. He thought he and she were just ships that passed in the night.*

shoot oneself in the foot is an idiom cliché meaning to harm oneself or do oneself a disservice, often while trying to cause harm to someone else, as *The politician was trying to cause embarrassment to the government but he ended up by shooting himself in the foot.* The expression originated in America, the derivation being the obvious one of having an accident with a gun while getting ready to shoot someone, although it sometimes implied that the 'accident' was deliberate to escape military service. As a cliché in Britain it dates from the later part of the twentieth century. Like the practice it describes, it is common today, being used in informal or slang contexts.

short and sweet is a hackneyed phrase used to indicate that something, although brief, is pleasant, lively, satisfactory, etc, as *If you are asked to write a report on a meeting it is best to keep it short and sweet.* The saying dates from the the sixteenth century and has been a cliché since the late nineteenth century. It is often now used ironically, as *He didn't spend much time telling us we were redundant. It was short and sweet.*

shot one's bolt is an idiom cliché meaning to have done all that one is able to do, to have exhausted one's resources, as *They came up with a series of threats to try to make us do as they asked, but we went on refusing and it became obvious that they had shot their bolt,* and *The champion started the marathon race at a very fast pace but halfway through it was obvious that he had shot his bolt and had to retire from the race.* The expression comes from an old proverb **a fool's bolt is soon shot** which probably dates from the thirteenth century. In origin it refers to medieval archery in which the bolt was a short, heavy, blunt-headed arrow fired from a crossbow. An archer who had shot all his bolts was in a perilous position. The expression to **have shot one's bolt** has been a cliché since the middle of the nineteenth century and is still common.

shoulder to the wheel, put one's is an idiom cliché meaning to begin to make a vigorous effort or to work hard, as *The workforce is really going to have to put its shoulder to the wheel if this order is going to be ready in time.* The expression has been popular since the eighteenth century and is still a common cliché today, usually being used to exhort people to maximum effort. It is often used in humorous contexts, as *As usual the headmaster will be telling us to put our shoulders to the wheel and our noses to the grindstone if we want to get through the exams.* In origin it refers to someone pushing a cart that had got stuck in mud.

show must go on, the is a catchphrase cliché meaning that everything must go on as normal, no matter what happens, as *Half the sales assistants are off with flu but the show must go on. The customers are queueing to get in.* The expression was originally a theatrical one, literally meaning that the show had to go, irrespective of what had happened, and in this context dates from the nineteenth century. It became a more general cliché in the twentieth century and is still common today.

sick and tired is a hackneyed phrase meaning completely tired, bored or annoyed at something, as *I am sick and tired of listening to her complaining,* and *We are sick and tired of having to ask our neighbour's son to turn his CD player down.* As a cliché it dates from the twentieth century and is still common today.

sick as a dog is a simile cliché meaning to be very sick, to vomit violently, as *We were both sick as a dog after we ate the mussels. They must have been off.* The expression dates from the sixteenth century and is still common today in informal contexts. There is no obvious reason for believing that dogs are more likely to be sick than any other animals.

sick as a parrot is a simile cliché meaning very unhappy or depressed, often at one's own failure and another's success. As a cliché it dates from the second part of the twentieth century, as *She was sick as a parrot when her friend bought the house that she had wanted,* and is still common today in informal contexts. In the late 1970s it became associated with the reaction of those connected with a losing football team, as *When asked by the commentator how he felt at the end of the match, the manager said that he was sick as a parrot.* The origin of the phrase is unclear. It may be connected with psittacosis, a disease of parrots and other birds that can spread to humans. It may also be connected with an older expression **melancholy as a parrot**.

sight for sore eyes, a is an idiom cliché used to refer to someone or something that is a pleasure to see, as *How nice to see you! You're a sight for sore eyes*, and *The little country cottage was a sight for sore eyes. It was so pretty.* As a cliché it dates from the late nineteenth century and is still common, being used in informal contexts. The implication of the phrase is that the person, etc is such a welcome sight that he or she will bring pleasure to, and so cure, sore eyes.

signed, sealed and delivered is a hackneyed phrase used to indicate that something has been brought to a satisfactory conclusion. Originally it referred to legal documents, such as property deeds, but it came to be used in more general contexts, becoming a cliché in the twentieth century, as *Here are our holiday tickets. Signed, sealed and delivered.*

sign of the times, a is an allusion cliché used to indicate that something is typical of the times we live in, as *It's terrible seeing all these people sleeping rough. Still, I suppose it's a sign of the times. There is so much poverty around.* The expression is a reference to a Biblical passage. According to *Matthew* (16:3), Jesus, when asked by the Pharisees to show them a sign from heaven said, 'O ye hypocrites, ye can discern the face of the sky; but can ye not discern the signs of the times?' As a cliché it dates from the twentieth century and is still common.

silent majority, the is a hackneyed phrase used to describe the bulk of the population who attract less attention than their more vocal counterparts, it being the assumption that they are quite happy with their lot and with how things are going, as *The politician says that the silent majority are in favour of more roads, and that there are just a few protesters who go from site to site.* It is often used in political contexts, being much favoured by politicians and others in public life and by journalists. The expression probably dates from the 1920s and was popularized by Richard Nixon, President of the United States, in a speech on the Vietnam War made in 1969.

sixes and sevens, at is a hackneyed phrase meaning in a state of confusion or disorder, as *There are so many people sick that we have been at sixes and sevens all morning.* The expression has its origin in a game of dice, although which game is not clear. As a cliché the expression probably dates from the twentieth century and is common today in informal contexts.

six of one and half-a-dozen of the other is a hackneyed phrase indicating that there is little or no difference between two things or people, as *It doesn't matter which of the trains you take. It's six of one and half-a-dozen of the other. They go by different routes but get in at about the same time*, and *Either of the candidates would be suitable for the job. It's six of one and half-a-dozen of the other.* As a cliché it dates from the later part of the nineteenth century and is common today in informal contexts.

sixty four thousand dollar question, the is a hackneyed phrase used to describe a question which is very difficult or impossible to answer, as *When do we expect to finish painting the house? That's the sixty four thousand dollar question.* American in origin, the expression dates from the 1950s before becoming a cliché in Britain in the late 1960s. In origin it refers to the title of an American television quiz show on which

$64,000 was the top prize. An earlier expression was **the sixty-four dollar question** which was derived from a CBS radio quiz show 'Take it or Leave It', in which the top prize was $64 dollars and which was broadcast in the 1940s.

skeleton in the cupboard, a is an idiom cliché used to refer to a shameful secret, as *Every family has the odd skeleton in the cupboard,* and *The press are snooping around to see what skeletons in the cupboard they can find in the politician's family.* In origin it refers to a murder victim being hidden away in a cupboard until he or she became a skeleton. As a cliché it dates from around the middle of the nineteenth century. The cliché is still popular today and the skeletons still common.

slave over a hot stove is a hackneyed phrase used to refer to cooking or loosely to refer to housework generally. As a cliche it dates from the twentieth century and is still common today, often being used in humorous or satirical contexts, as *I've been slaving away all day over a hot stove and now they've phoned to say they can't come to dinner,* and *She says that she rushes home from work to slave over a hot stove but in fact she has a housekeeper.*

slight technical hitch, a is a hackneyed phrase used as an excuse for the breakdown of a machine or the delay or non-running of a service. It was common with regard to transport until very recently, as *We apologize for the delay to the 15.30 Edinburgh train. This is due to a slight technical hitch,* and *We apologize to passengers travelling on the 16.00 flight to Milan. The plane has been delayed owing to a slight technical hitch.* Recently those not providing the promised transport service have tended to offer seemingly more specific, but no more enlightening,

reasons, as *We apologize to the delay to the 17.00 service to Aberdeen. This is due to trouble with the overhead lines at Berwick.* This supposed increase in information may well have occurred as passengers grew suspicious and intolerant of 'slight technical hitches'.

slip on a banana skin see *banana skin, a*

slowly but surely is a hackneyed phrase meaning steadily, as *At first the favourite was away out in front. Then slowly but surely the other horse gained on him.* As a cliché the expression dates from the middle of the nineteenth century. In origin it refers to Aesop's fable about the hare and the tortoise in which the steady progress of the tortoise made him a victor in his race against the apparently faster hare.

smell a rat is an idiom cliché meaning to suspect that something is not quite right, as *We smelled a rat when the supposed council workman couldn't find his identification card,* and *The neighbours smelled a rat when they saw the open window. They phoned the police who caught the burglar.* The expression has been in use since the sixteenth century and has been a cliché since the middle of the eighteenth century. In origin it refers to a dog or cat sniffing out a rat.

social whirl, the is a hackneyed phrase used to describe a full social life or social life generally. As a cliché it dates from the late nineteenth century. It is still used today but often in humorous or ironic contexts, as *I left work, picked up the children, went to the supermarket then cooked the evening meal. Just the usual social whirl.*

Sod's law see *anything that can go wrong will go wrong*

so far so good is a hackneyed phrase indicating that progress up till now has been good, with the implication that one cannot rely on this favourable state of affairs continuing, as *It's very tricky driving along this narrow track but so far so good.* As a cliché the expression dates from the middle of the nineteenth century and it is still popular today.

some of my best friends are . . . is a catchphrase cliché which is often used as an excuse for prejudice or bigotry, as *I have absolutely nothing against homosexuals. Some of my best friends are gay.* The expression dates from the 1940s or earlier and was originally used of people of Jewish descent, as *I am not anti-semitic. Why some of my best friends are Jewish.* It is still common today but often in humorous or satirical contexts, as *I don't think we should get rid of the male sex. Some of my best friends are men,* and *I support animal rights but I care about human rights too. After all, some of my best friends are humans.*

some other time is a hackneyed phrase often used as a delaying technique or as an attempt to postpone something indefinitely, as *I would love to have lunch with you some time, but I am very busy just now. Some other time, perhaps.* Frequently it is effectively a euphemism cliché for never. It is an expression with which children become familiar at an early age, as *No, I'm sorry we can't go to the beach today, but some other time when mummy and daddy are not so busy.* As a cliché it dates from the twentieth century.

son and heir is a hackneyed phrase used to refer to the eldest son of a family and frequently to the first, and possibly only, son born to a family, irrespective of whether or not there is anything much to be heir to. It reflects an inheritance law which favours the first born male child. As a cliché the expression probably dates from the late nineteenth century, but it goes back to Shakesperian times. Nowadays it is frequently used by journalists, as *Pictured right are Mr and Mrs Brown with their son and heir leaving his christening ceremony,* or in humorous contexts.

so near and yet so far is a hackneyed phrase used to indicate that something is close but still not attainable, sometimes with the implication that it will never be attainable, as *He very nearly broke the record for the course, but he fell just before the finishing line. So near and yet so far.* As a cliché the expression dates from the later part of the nineteenth century, although the idea goes back to Roman times. Nowadays it is frequently used in humorous contexts, as *Although he had drunk so much, he almost made it home before he was sick. So near and yet so far!*

sour grapes is an idiom cliché used to describe the attitude of someone who disparages something which he or she would like to have but, for some reason, cannot have, as *Don't worry about what Mary says about your new car. It's just sour grapes. She can't afford one.* In origin the expression refers to Aesop's fable about the fox and the grapes in which the fox says that the grapes are sour when he cannot reach them. As a cliché the expression dates from the nineteenth century

speak the same language is an idiom cliché used of people who understand each other very well, often sharing the same attitudes, views, etc, as *They don't mix socially but when it comes to business they speak the same language.* As a figurative expression it dates from the nineteenth century, becoming a cliché in the twentieth century and being still popular today.

spend a penny is a euphemism cliché for going to the toilet. Even in these enlightened days, euphemisms for attending to basic human functions are thought to be necessary and there is the problem of the half-remembered conventions about whether toilet is acceptable, whether one should call it lavatory, or whether one should play safe but informal and just go to the loo. In origin the expression refers to the penny that one had to put in the slot of a cubicle in a public toilet before gaining admittance. See also **powder one's nose** and **see a man about a dog**.

spend more time with one's family is a euphemism cliché used instead of admitting that one has had to leave one's job for some reason, either because one has been sacked or because one has resigned for some rather personal or complex reason. The expression became popular in the 1980s being an excuse given by some politicians in ministerial positions for resigning. It is now frequently used in humorous or satirical contexts.

spick and span is a hackneyed phrase meaning neat and clean, as *My mother says we can do some baking as long as we leave the kitchen spick and span*. The expression is made up of two obsolete words. 'Spick' means a spike or nail and 'span' means a wood chip. The expression refers to the time of sailing ships when a ship that was spick and span was one in which all the spicks and spans were new. As a figurative expression, it has been popular since the the later part of the nineteenth century and is still common.

spill the beans is an idiom cliché meaning to reveal something that was meant to be kept secret, as *We wanted to know what had happened at the confidential meeting, so we persuaded Jim who was taking the notes to*

spill the beans. The expression is American in origin and has been a cliché since the first part of the twentieth century.

spilled milk see **cry over spilled milk**

spirit is willing, the is an allusion cliché to a Biblical passage. It is a reference to *Matthew* (26:41) where Jesus gives advice to his disciples at the last supper 'Watch and pray, that ye enter not into temptation; the spirit indeed is willing, but the flesh is weak.' As a cliché it dates from the late nineteenth century. As a modern cliché it often means simply that, though one would very much like to do something, one simply does not feel up to it, as *I'd love to come to the cinema but I've just got home from working late and I'm exhausted. The spirit is willing but the flesh is weak*. It is often used in humorous contexts.

square peg in a round hole, a is an idiom cliché used to describe someone who is not at all suited to his or her current position, or who is not at all comfortable with it, as *His father was a doctor and persuaded him to study medicine, but he is a square peg in a round hole and hates it*. As a cliché it dates from the later part of the nineteenth century and is still widespread today.

stalking horse is an idiom cliché used to describe some form of pretext, or someone who takes part in some form of pretext. In origin it refers to the practice of some hunters, when stalking deer or other game, of dismounting and hiding behind their horses until they are within shooting range of their prey. In the 1980s and 1990s it has become particularly associated with political candidacy where someone who is not a serious contender for a position, such as the leadership of a party, pretends to be so in order to make it easier for someone else to put himself or herself forward. The figurative use of the expression has been in use since the sixteenth century, Shakespeare having used it in *As You Like It* (5:4) 'He uses his folly like a stalking-horse and under the presentation of that he shoots his wit.'

stand up and be counted is an idiom cliché meaning to show publicly or otherwise obviously one's opinion, attitude, loyalty, etc, especially if this is held only by a minority of people or if it is unpopular, as *We feel that there is a great deal of opposition to the new motorway but sometimes those who are opposed to it are reluctant to stand up and be counted.* The expression is American in origin and refers to standing up so that one's vote can be counted in some form of poll. As a cliché it dates from the twentieth century and is still popular today.

stem the tide is an idiom cliché meaning to halt the course of something, as *The government is trying to stem the tide of opposition to their economic policies.* As a cliché the expression dates from the late nineteenth century and is still popular today. In origin it refers to the holding back of the ocean tides.

storm in a teacup, a is an idiom cliché meaning a fuss over nothing, as *The two families won't speak to each other but it was all a storm in a teacup over two children fighting.* As a cliché it dates from the later part of the nineteenth century and is still popular today as indeed are fusses over nothing.

straight and narrow, the is a hackneyed phrase which is probably an allusion cliché to a Biblical passage 'Strait is the gate, and narrow is the way, which leadeth unto life.' (*Matthew* 7:14). The expression, which means virtue or a virtuous way of life, became popular in the nineteenth century, becoming a cliché in the middle of the century. It is often used today in humorous or ironic contexts, as *I'll have to stick to the straight and narrow for a few weeks. I'm studying for my final exams.*

straight from the shoulder is an idiom cliché meaning in a frank or outspoken manner, as *I hate it when doctors try to hide things. I wish they would just give it to me straight from the shoulder.* The expression has its origin in boxing where someone is given a full-force blow. As a figurative expression it dates from the late nineteenth century, becoming a cliché in the twentieth century. It is often used by people who pride themselves on their bluntness, which is often in fact rudeness.

straw in the wind, a is an idiom cliché used to refer to something that is an indication of how things might develop, as *The reaction of the health unions to their small pay increase is a straw in the wind. There will be general industrial unrest.* As a cliché the expression dates from the twentieth century, although the idea is much older, and is still common today. In origin it refers to using a straw to indicate which way the wind is blowing.

strike while the iron is hot is a proverb cliché meaning to take advantage of an opportunity or favourable circumstances when they present themselves, as *If you want to borrow some money from your father now would be a good time to ask. He has just won some money on the lottery, so you can strike while the iron is hot.* The proverbial saying dates from the fourteenth century and has been a cliché since the nineteenth century, being still common today. In origin it refers to the work of a blacksmith in his forge – iron has to be very hot before it can be hammered into shape.

suffer a sea change is an allusion cliché meaning to undergo a marked change, often for the good, as *This area's certainly suffered a sea change since I last visited it. It used to be a derelict site.* The expression refers to a passage in Shakespeare's *The Tempest* (1:2) 'Nothing of him that doth fade, but doth suffer a sea change into something rich and strange.' As a cliché it dates from the middle of the nineteenth century. It is still used today, particularly by people of a literary bent, and frequently in humorous or ironic contexts. The expression is sometimes shortened simply to **sea change**.

suffer fools gladly, not to is an allusion cliché, being a reference to a Biblical passage 'For ye suffer fools gladly, seeing ye yourselves are wise.' (*2 Corinthians* 11:19) In the passage Paul is pointing out to the Corinthians that those who tolerate fools are themselves fools. As a cliché it dates from the nineteenth century and is still common today, often being used of someone who is intolerant of people generally.

survival of the fittest, the is a hackneyed phrase used to indicate that in the long run it is the strongest who will succeed, as *There is no point in going in for the marathon race if you are unfit. It'll certainly be a case of the survival of the fittest,* and *This firm is so full of office politics that people come and go very quickly. It's a case of the survival of the fittest.* The expression was originated by Herbert Spence in *Principles of Biology*

(1864) when describing Charles Darwin's theory of natural selection. As a cliché it dates from the twentieth century and is still common, sometimes being used in humorous or ironic contexts.

sweetness and light is an allusion cliché being a reference to a passage in Jonathan Swift's *The Battle of the Books* (1697). The expression was popularized by Matthew Arnold in *Culture and Anarchy* (1869). It became a cliché in the late nineteenth century and is common today but mostly in ironic contexts, as *He treats his wife and children appallingly badly, but to the rest of the world he is all sweetness and light,* and *Mary has a hangover this morning and so she is not exactly sweetness and light.*

swings and roundabouts is a proverb cliché being a shortened version of the saying **what you win/gain on the swings you lose on the roundabouts**. Both expressions indicate that the advantages that one achieves in some things are often offset by disadvantages suffered in other things, as *His venture into the stock market was a case of swings and roundabouts,* and *I just got a salary increase when I had to pay a huge car repair bill. What you win on the swings you lose on the roundabouts.* A more optimistic version of the longer expression is **what you lose on the swings you win/gain on the roundabouts**. As clichés the expressions date from the twentieth century and are still used to demonstrate a philosophical acceptance of fate.

T

take a leaf out of someone's book is an idiom cliché meaning to follow someone's example. This mostly refers to a good example, as *I wish you would take a leaf out of your sister's book and keep your room tidy*, but not always, as *I think I'll take a leaf out of Fred's book and start doing as little as possible*. As a cliché the expression dates from the late nineteenth century and it is still popular today. In origin it refers to taking a page out of one's exercise book to copy.

take care is a hackneyed phrase used when taking one's leave of someone. It is used in informal contexts to someone whom one knows fairly well. Literally it urges the other person to take good care of himself/herself but it is frequently used meaninglessly in the way that → **see you later** is used. As a cliché it dates from the later part of the twentieth century.

take it from me is a hackneyed phrase used as a filler cliché. It is either used to emphasize the truth of what is about to be said, as *Take it from me. He is up to no good* or is simply used meaninglessly by someone to whom it has become a habit. The expression has a modern colloquial ring, but it was in use in the seventeenth century. As a cliché it is still popular today, sometimes taking the form **you can take it from me**.

take one's life in one's hands is a hackneyed phrase meaning to do something very risky, as *You take your life in your hands when you cross this road. The traffic goes very fast*. It originally referred to physical risk but it now refers to other forms of risk and is often use in humorous or ironic contexts, as *You'll be taking your life in your hands if you disagree with our next-door neighbour about animal rights*. As a cliché it dates from the middle of the nineteenth century and is still popular today.

take pot luck is a hackneyed phrase meaning to accept an invitation to a meal which is made up of just what the host or hostess was going to have anyway, rather than one which has been specially prepared for a guest, as *You are welcome to have dinner with us as long as you don't mind taking pot luck*. The expression has been popular since the late eighteenth century. It is still a common cliché today, being found in all but the most formal contexts. It refers literally to whatever happens to be in the cooking pot.

take the bull by the horns is an idiom cliché meaning to meet any danger or difficulty with boldness or courage, as *I don't like upsetting her but I'm going to have to take the bull by the horns and ask her to leave. There's just not enough room here*. The expression has been popular since the late nineteenth century and is a common cliché today.

take the law into one's own hands is a hackneyed phrase meaning to take it upon oneself to see that what one perceives as justice is done, as *When the man who attacked his daughter got off with just a fine, he took the law into his own hands* and went out and beat him up. The expression was in existence by the early seventeenth century and is still common today.

take the rough with the smooth is an idiom cliché meaning to be prepared to accept the bad or disadvantageous side of something as well as the good or advantageous side, as *If you go and live in the country you'll have to take the rough with the smooth. It's lovely in the summer but the roads are often blocked in the winter and supplies can't get through.* As a saying the expression dates from the fifteenth century and as a cliché from the twentieth century, being still generally popular today.

take the words out of someone's mouth is an idiom cliché indicating that someone has just said something that one was about to say oneself, as *I was just about to suggest going to the cinema. You took the words out of my mouth.* The expression goes back to the sixteenth century and has been a cliché since the nineteenth century. It is still common today in fairly informal contexts.

take to the cleaners is an idiom cliché meaning to take a great deal of money from someone. It is frequently used in relation to divorce settlements, as *He says that his ex-wife took him to the cleaners but in fact she got very little.* The expression is American in origin and dates from the second part of the twentieth century. As a cliché it is common today in informal or slang contexts. It is related to the idea of being cleaned out, in the sense of having no money left.

talk of the devil is a hackneyed phrase used as a comment on the fact that the person about whom one has just been talking has appeared on the scene, as *Well, talk of the devil! Here's Frank and we were just saying that we hadn't seen him*

for ages. In origin the cliché refers to the saying **speak of the devil and he's sure to appear**. The cliché probably dates from the nineteenth century and is still common today in informal contexts.

tall, dark and handsome is a hackneyed phrase used to refer to the appearance of a supposedly ideal man. The expression is American in origin and dates from the early 1920s. It was probably popularized by being the title of a film (1941) in which Cesar Romero played the lead. Although tastes as to what constitutes an ideal man come and go as frequently as they do in relation to an ideal woman, the expression is still a popular cliché today, often being used in humorous or satirical contexts, as *I wouldn't exactly call him tall, dark and handsome, more small, fat and balding.*

tarred with the same brush is an idiom cliché indicating that someone has the same faults or bad qualities as someone else, as *He is tarred with the same brush as his cousin. They are both conmen.* The expression became popular in the middle of the nineteenth century and is still common in fairly informal contexts today. In origin the phrase probably refers to the former practice of shepherds of applying tar to a sheep's sores with a brush.

teach one's grandmother to suck eggs is a proverb cliché meaning to try to show someone, usually someone more experienced than oneself, how to do something that he or she can do perfectly well, usually better than one can oneself, as *I know perfectly well how to operate the stove. Don't teach your grandmother to suck eggs.* As a cliché the expression dates from the middle of the twentieth century and, although it sounds rather archaic, it is popular today, often among older people who feel that they are being patronized by younger people.

teething troubles is a hackneyed phrase used to refer to the difficult early stages of something, as *We've had a few teething troubles with our new catering business but everything's going smoothly now.* As a cliché it dates from the twentieth century and is still common today in all but the most formal contexts. In origin it refers to the pain that babies experience when their teeth are coming through.

tell me about it is a hackneyed phrase used to emphasize one's agreement with what has just been said, as *'What a pity you didn't get the job,' said Mike. 'Tell me about it!' said Jane.* As a cliché it dates from the later part of the twentieth century. A slightly older phrase which expresses the same sentiment is **you're telling me**.

tell that to the marines is a catchphrase cliché used to indicate that one does not believe something and that only a fool would do so, as *You expect me to believe that he would take a cut in salary. Tell that to the marines!* The expression dates from the early nineteenth century and in origin it refers to the fact that sailors thought marines inferior to them, a marine being a soldier who serves at sea. As a cliché it is rather dated today.

tender loving care is a hackneyed phrase whose meaning is self-evident, as *The child comes from a very unhappy home and is desperately in need of some tender loving care,* and *After her operation she'll need lots of tender loving care.* The expression became popular in the second part of the twentieth century, although Shakespeare makes an early reference to it in *Henry VI* (3:2) 'Go, Salisbury, and tell them from me, I thank them for their tender loving care.' It

was well established as a cliché by the 1980s and is still popular today, often being abbreviated to **TLC** (or **tlc**) which is used mostly in informal contexts.

tender mercies, leave to someone's is a hackneyed phrase meaning to leave someone or something in the care of someone who is inefficient, imcompetent, unsympathetic, etc, as *I'm a bit worried. I've had to leave the dog to Jane's tender mercies. She's so vague she'll probably lose him,* and *We're going on holiday and leaving the house to the tender mercies of our son. Do you think you could keep an eye on things?* As a cliché used ironically the expression dates from the twentieth century. It is still popular today, always being used ironically.

terra firma (Latin for 'firm ground') is a foreign cliché meaning dry land, as opposed to the sea. As an English cliché it dates from the middle of the nineteenth century. It is still used today, as *The sea was so rough that I was glad to get off the ferry and back onto terra firma.* It is rather dated.

thankful for small mercies is a hackneyed phrase indicating that one should appreciate benefits or advantages, however small, as *We've waited ages for a bus and it's so cold. Still, we should be thankful for small mercies. At least it isn't raining.* As a cliché it dates from the late nineteenth century and it is still common today, sometimes being used in humorous or ironic contexts.

thanks but no thanks is a hackneyed phrase which is used to convey an emphatic rejection, *'We're reducing the budget and we've had to make you redundant but we can re-employ you on a short-term contract'. 'Thanks but no thanks'.* It is often rather an impolite rejection, a fact which is made clear only by the tone when spoken. The popularity of the expression dates from the later part of the twentieth century.

that'll be the day is a catchphrase cliché used to indicate the unlikelihood of something, as *You seriously think he would lend us some money? That'll be the day!* The catchphrase dates from the early part of the twentieth century and is still a common cliché today.

that's a good question is a catchphrase cliché which is often used as a filler cliché while someone thinks how best to answer a question, as *How would we solve the present economic problems? That's a good question.* The catchphrase dates from around the middle of the twentieth century and is a popular time-wasting cliché today.

that's all I need is hackneyed phrase indicating much the same idea as the last straw, as *That's all I need. My husband has asked his boss to dinner and I've already got a mountain of things to do.* The expression dates from around the middle of the twentieth century and, as befits an expression of exasperation, it is a common cliché today. An alternative form is **that's all I needed**.

that's for me to know and for you to find out is a catchphrase cliché used as an evasive way of dealing with a question. The cliché dates from the twentieth century and was originally used to answer children in the rather high-handed attitude that adults adopt to children, as *What age am I? That's for me to know and for you to find out.* As a cliché it is now rather dated and is mostly used in humorous contexts.

that's life is a hackneyed phrase used to indicate a resigned attitude towards the misfortunes of life, as *Our team were beaten in the closing minutes of the game. Still, I suppose that's life!* As a cliché it dates from the second part of the twentieth century and is still common today among those who are less than optimistic.

that's the way the cookie crumbles is a hackneyed phrase indicating a resigned attitude to fate meaning that is how things are and there is nothing we can do about it, as *I wish that I hadn't lost my job just before my holiday but I suppose that's the way the cookie crumbles.* The expression is American in origin, as is 'cookie' meaning biscuit, and has been current since the middle of the twentieth century. Although it is American English in form, the phrase is still a common cliché in Britain today.

that would be telling is a hackneyed phrase used to indicate that one knows the answer to a question but that one has no intention of revealing what one knows, as *What did we do last night? That would be telling.* The expression in its present form probably became popular in the twentieth century, although **that's telling** is an earlier form, dating from the early part of the eighteenth century

there are thousands worse off than you is a hackneyed phrase used to console people who have suffered some form of misfortune and are inclined to grieve or complain about it. It is a bracing phrase meant to make people aware of the triviality of their misfortune in a world context. In fact it usually simply makes matters worse, as the person suffering from the misfortune is not in the mood for worrying about the rest of the world, and the person making the comment usually sounds rather smug since he or she has not suffered misfortune. The cliché dates from the twentieth century and is still common.

there are ways and means is a hackneyed phrase used to indicate the fact that if something absolutely has to be done, a way can be found to do it. The suggestion conveyed by the cliché is that this way is not always honest or even legal, as *The bank has refused to lend him money for his new business but I'm sure he will get it from somewhere. There are ways and means.* As a cliché the expression dates from the twentieth century.

there but for the grace of God go I is a catchphrase cliché used to indicate that one might well have been in the same unfortunate position that someone else now is, as *Jim was booked for speeding on the road into town last night. There but for the grace of God go I – and most of the other drivers on that road!* It is frequently used in humorous or satirical contexts, as *I hear Jane is getting married to Frank today. There but for the grace of God go I! I went out with her for a while until I realized what she was like.* As a cliché the expression dates from the nineteenth century and it is still common today. In origin the phrase is said to quote John Bradford who made the remark on seeing some criminals being taken to their execution around 1553. In fact his words, if he uttered them, proved prophetic for he himself was burned at the stake in 1555 for his religious beliefs. The words have also been ascribed to John Wesley and John Bunyan.

thereby hangs a tale is a hackneyed phrase indicating that there is a story, or a bit of juicy gossip, attached to something that has just been said or written, as *I hear that he has decided to take early retirement and thereby hangs a tale*, the implication being that the user of the phrase is about to tell the story. The expression has probably been a cliché since the nineteenth century. It was used by Shakespeare in several of his plays, including *As You Like It* (2:7) although he did not originate it. In origin it is a pun on a tail hanging from an animal.

there'll be dancing in the streets tonight is a catchphrase cliché indicating that an event has taken place that will give rise to general celebration. It is frequently used as a cliché by sports commentators to refer to the celebration that will greet a team's victory in their home town, as *There'll be dancing in the streets of Glasgow tonight.* Sometimes it indicates that the victory was unexpected. The cliché dates from the twentieth century and has the alternative form **they'll be dancing in the streets tonight**.

there's a lot of it about is a hackneyed phrase often used as a medical cliché, as *If you have a sore throat you should go home and take an aspirin and go to bed. There's a lot of it about.* It is often used humorously or satirically in non-medical context, as *Mark's wife has just gone off with Jane's husband. There's a lot of it about.* The cliché dates from the twentieth century.

there's many a slip is an allusion cliché reminding one of the fact that many things can go wrong between a plan or project being conceived and it actually being carried out or achieved, as *I know you're excited that the bank are going to discuss your business plan with you, but don't forget there's many a slip.* As a cliché it dates from the twentieth century and is an allusion to the proverb **there's many a slip between cup and lip**, which is itself sometimes used as a cliché. In origin the proverb refers to the fact that accidents can happen between one first raising a cup and it actually coming into contact with one's lips.

there's no fool like an old fool is a proverb cliché meaning that people who are old enough and experienced enough to know better are just as liable, or even more liable, to behave or speak foolishly as young people are, as *He's nearly sixty and he seriously believes that his eighteen-year old girlfriend loves him for himself alone and not for his money. There's no fool like an old fool.* The saying is an old one and appeared in John Heywood's collection of proverbs of 1546. As a cliché it is still common today, sometimes being shortened to **there's no fool**, the rest of the expression being understood.

there's no such thing as a free lunch is a catchphrase cliché used to indicate that one rarely gets anything for nothing. As a cliché it dates from the later part of the twentieth century and has its origins in the world of PR and business. It refers to the fact that anyone, whom one does not know well, is unlikely to invite one to a business lunch unless he or she is planning to get something out of it, such as promotion for a product.

there's one born every minute is a catchphrase cliché used when someone has been duped or conned, as *Jane lent her camera to a child on the beach and he ran off with it. There's one born every minute.* and *They gave the workman the money in advance to pay for materials and they never saw him again. There's one born every minute.* This comment on the universality of folly dates from the twentieth century and is a common cliché today in informal contexts.

these things happen is a hackneyed phrase usually directed at someone who has suffered some form of misfortune in a supposed attempt to get him or her to see the misfortune in a world context and understand that their misfortune is not unique. It is a meaningless phrase, and in common with other phrases used in such a context, is rather fatuous, its only

advantage being that it sometimes so irritates the unfortunate person that he or she forgets temporarily the cause of the misfortune. As a cliché it dates from the twentieth century.

thorn in one's side, a is an allusion cliché being a reference to several Biblical passages, one of which is in *Judges* (2:3) 'They shall be as thorns in your sides.' The cliché means a source of constant irritation, as *That customer is a real thorn in the manager's side. She is always complaining about the service,* and has the alternative form **a thorn in one's flesh**. As a cliché it dates from the middle of the nineteenth century and is still current.

through thick and thin is an idiom cliché meaning whatever the difficulties or dangers, as *The politician has received a great deal of adverse publicity but his constituency party members have stood by him through thick and thin.* As a cliché it dates from the nineteenth century and is still common today. In origin it refers to terrain with both thick and sparse vegetation or woods. The analogy goes back to the days of Chaucer.

throw in the towel is an idiom cliché meaning to give up or to acknowledge defeat, as *The protesters have spent months trying to prevent the authorities closing the village school but they've decided to throw in the towel.* As a cliché the expression dates from the later part of the nineteenth century and is still popular today in informal and slang contexts. An alternative form of the expression is **throw in the sponge**. Both expressions derive from boxing, from the fact that the sponge (later a towel) used by a boxer was thrown into the ring as a sign that he was conceding defeat.

throw the baby out with the bathwater is an idiom cliché to get rid of something useful while disposing of something useless or unwanted, as *The committee threw out the whole proposal for change although there were some good points in it. They simply threw the baby out with the bathwater.* In origin it may be a translation of the German proverb 'Das Kind mit dem Bade ausschütten', to pour the baby out with the bath. The idea has been common in English since the second part of the nineteenth century, sometimes in the earlier form **empty the baby out with the bath**, which was used by George Bernard Shaw in 'Parents and Children' (1914). **Throw the baby out with the bathwater** is still common today in all but the most formal contexts.

throw the book at is an idiom cliché meaning to rebuke or punish someone very severely, as *The headmaster will throw the book at you if you're caught playing truant again.* The metaphor was originally used in a legal context, meaning to sentence someone to the maximum penalty allowed for the crime. It later became more generally used by journalists, among others. In its general use it sometimes applies to situations involving the law, as *If the police stop you in that car they'll throw the book at you. It's got no brake lights, the front number plate is missing and the tyres are bald.*

tickled pink is a hackneyed phrase meaning extremely delighted, as *She was tickled pink by the birthday card which her grandchildren made for her.* In origin it refers to the fact that someone who is being tickled is laughing so much that he or she turns pink. An alternative, and slightly older, form is **tickled to death** which is still current. As a cliché **tickled pink** probably dates from the twentieth century and is still common today, being used in informal contexts.

tie the knot is an idiom cliché meaning to get married, as *I hear that Frank and Jill have at last decided to tie the knot.* The expression may be a reference to a saying that dates from the sixteenth century. 'To tie a knot with one's tongue that one cannot untie with one's teeth.' As a cliché **tie the knot** dates from around the late nineteenth century and is still current today, being used in informal, and often humorous, contexts.

tighten one's belt is an idiom cliché meaning to reduce one's expenditure, to be more frugal. As a cliché the expression dates from the twentieth century, becoming particularly popular during the recessions in the 1980s and 1990s, it is particularly popular among journalists and other commentators on the financial situation, as *Small firms stand a good chance of surviving the recession if they are willing to tighten their belts.* In origin the phrase refers to a person tightening a belt round his waist having lost weight from eating less, having spent less money on food.

till death do us part see *until death do us part*

till the fat lady sings, it's not over is an idiom cliché which is a vogue cliché of the 1990s. It is used to indicate that one should wait until the end of something before expressing one's reaction, making a decision, etc. The expression is used by sports commentators to urge people to wait until the final whistle before commenting, since last-minute goals have been known to happen. In origin it refers to an operatic production, female opera stars traditionally being somewhat large.

time flies see *how time flies*

time heals everything is a hackneyed phrase used by well-meaning people to try to console someone who has just experienced grief or great misfortune. In fact it is of little value because, although time does diminish most emotional pain, the person being so consoled is not in a condition to appreciate the fact. As a cliché the expression dates from the twentieth century.

tip of the iceberg, the is an idiom cliché used to indicate that some misfortune or bad situation is only a minor manifestation of a much worse situation, as *The school admits that about ten percent of pupils regularly play truant but we think that's just the tip of the iceberg.* As a cliché the expression dates from the second part of the twentieth century. In origin it refers to the fact that the bulk of the mass of an iceberg is below the surface of the water and so not visible.

tired and emotional is a euphemism cliché meaning tipsy or drunk, as *I think you should call a taxi for your sister. She's been at the party for hours and has got a bit tired and emotional.* As a cliché it dates from the later part of the twentieth century and is usually used in humorous contexts. In origin it refers to the fact that alcohol can make people tired and maudlin.

to all intents and purposes see *all intents and purposes, to*

to coin a phrase is a hackneyed phrase used by some people not to introduce a phrase which they have just invented but to introduce a well-worn cliché, as *To coin a phrase, the police will throw the book at him.* The expression is American in origin and became popular in Britain in the middle of the twentieth century. It is still widespread today, sometimes, but by no means always, being used humorously or ironically.

toe the line is an idiom cliché meaning to behave strictly according to the rules or standards set down, as *He'll hate staying with his grandmother. He always complains about having to help with the chores but she'll make him toe the line,* and *Their previous teacher was a bit lax about homework being handed in on time, but this one will make them toe the line.* As a cliché the expression dates from the later part of the nineteenth century and is still commonly used today, particularly by people who like the idea of other people being subjected to discipline. An earlier form of the expression was **toe the mark**. In origin the phrase refers to runners lining up at the start of a race.

tomorrow is another day is a hackneyed phrase used to indicate that anything that has not been done or finished today can be done tomorrow, as *It's well after midnight. Could you not finish that essay another time? Tomorrow is another day.* It is a particularly annoying expression if the person to whom it is directed knows perfectly well that tomorrow is another day but knows equally well that the work being done must be done today, or preferably yesterday. The expression is also used as a term of consolation to someone who has just failed at something, as *I know you failed your driving test but you'll get it next time. Tomorrow is another day.* As a cliché the expression probably dates from the beginning of the twentieth century and it is still commonly used today, particularly by the optimists among us. The popularity of the phrase may have been enhanced by its use as the closing line of the film *Gone with the Wind.*

too good to be true is a hackneyed phrase referring to the fact that something seems so wonderful that there must be a snag attached to it, as *I can't believe that holiday is so cheap. It seems too good to be true.* The expression dates from the sixteenth century and was already a cliché when George Bernard Shaw used it as the title of one of his plays in 1932.

too little too late is a hackneyed phrase used to indicate that action taken to rectify a problem or alleviate a situation is inadequate and too late to be any use, as *The refugees are dying in their thousands. Foreign governments are now sending aid but it is too little too late.* The expression was used by American historian Allan Nevins in an article in *Current History* (May 1935) 'The former allies have blundered in the past by offering Germany too little, and offering even that too late, until finally Nazi Germany has become a menace to all mankind.' The expression became a cliché in the later part of the twentieth century and is extremely common today, being a particular favourite of journalists. It is frequently used in the field of politics or international relations.

too many cooks spoil the broth is a proverb cliché meaning that if there are too many people involved in a project, the quality of the project is likely to suffer, as *I think the organizing committee for the charity ball is too large. Too many cooks spoil the broth.* The proverb has been in existence since the sixteenth century and has been a cliché probably since the nineteenth century. The expression is still popular today.

too numerous to mention is a hackneyed phrase supposedly used to indicate that there are too many people or things involved in something to mention them by name. It is, however, frequently used as a filler cliché to introduce a list of the very names that are too numerous to mention, as *The volunteers who helped with the fête are too numerous to mention. They include . . .* As a cliché it dates from the late nineteenth

century and is still in evidence today in the remarks of public speakers.

touch and go is a hackneyed phrase used to refer to a situation which is extremely precarious or uncertain, as *It'll be touch and go whether the plane lands in time for us to catch our connecting flight*, and *He's had the operation but it'll be touch and go whether he recovers.* As a cliché the expression dates from the middle of the nineteenth century and is still common today. In origin it refers to a vehicle that barely escapes colliding with something.

tough act to follow, a see *hard act to follow, a*

tower of strength is an idiom cliché used to refer to someone who is reliable, supportive and resourceful and so the perfect person to have by one's side in an emergency, as *Their neighbour was a tower of strength to the children when both their parents had to go hospital.* The expression was popularized in 1852 by Tennyson in his poem *Ode to the Duke of Wellington* 'O fall'n at length that tower of strength.' It became a cliché shortly after that and is still popular today.

trials and tribulations is a doublet cliché, trials and tribulations in this context being virtually synonymous, meaning troubles and difficulties, as *The trials and tribulations of being a widow with young children had prematurely aged her.* As a cliché it dates from the late nineteenth century. It is still common today, being often found in humorous or ironic contexts, as *He's just gone out to another business lunch. Oh, the trials and tribulations of being a top executive.*

tried and true is a hackneyed phrase used to refer to something that has been tested in some way and found to be effective or sound, as *She dislike doctors and prefers some of the old tried and true herbal remedies*, and *It was suggested that we overhaul our book-keeping procedures but we decided to stick to our old method that was tried and true.* As a cliché it dates from the twentieth century and is still popular today.

trip the light fantastic see *light fantastic*

true blue is a hackneyed phrase meaning extremely loyal, unwavering. In origin the expression refers to an old proverb, **true blue will never stain**, which dates from the sixteenth century and is now obsolete. The proverb referred to a blue dye that was fast and never ran. The expression **true blue** dates from the eighteenth century and in the late nineteenth century became associated with politics. Nowadays it is very frequently associated with members of the British Conservative party, the colour blue being identified with the party, as *His wife votes Labour but he is a true blue Tory.*

truth will out is a hackneyed phrase used to indicate that sooner or later the true facts will emerge, as *Mary has just found out that Harry's married and she's been going out with him for a year. Truth will out.* The expression dates from the eighteenth century. It is still common today, being often used of some form of scandal.

tug-of-love is a hackneyed phrase much used by journalists, particularly in headlines, to describe a situation in which two divorced or separated parents are fighting over custody of a child, as *Tug-of-love child abducted to Spain*, and *The child at the heart of the tug-of-love row is currently staying with her grandparents.* As a cliché it dates from the second part of the twentieth century. In origin it is an analogy with a tug-of-war, the child acting as the rope.

turn a blind eye to is an idiom cliché meaning deliberately to overlook or ignore something, often something that is either against the rules or something that would not normally be condoned, as *Some of the teachers knew that the senior pupils smoked in the playground but they turned a blind eye to it.* The expression became popular in the nineteenth century. In origin it is said to refer to the behaviour of Lord Nelson at the Battle of Copenhagen (1801). He was second-in-command and he ignored the signals given for the fleet to withdraw by putting his telescope to his blind eye. He then proceeded to attack and the French were defeated and forced to surrender. As a cliché the expression dates from the nineteenth century and is popular today in all but the most formal contexts.

turn a deaf ear is an idiom cliché meaning deliberately to ignore or take no notice of something, as *The children pleaded for mercy for their father but the tyrant turned a deaf ear to their pleas.* The idea goes back to the fifteenth century and a version appeared in John Heywood's proverb collection of 1546. As a cliché the expression dates from the nineteenth century and is still popular in all but the most formal contexts.

turn over a new leaf is an idiom cliché meaning to begin a new and better way of behaving, working, thinking, etc, as *He has been in and out of prison but when his son was born he said that he was going to turn over a new leaf.* The expression dates from the sixteenth century and is a common cliché today, being frequently given as piece of gratuitous advice, as *If you want to pass your exams you'll have to turn over a new leaf and start studying.* In origin it refers to turning the page of a book.

turn the clock back is an idiom cliché meaning to return to the conditions or way of life of an earlier time, as *We are afraid that the present prison legislation will turn the clock back fifty years*. It is often associated with nostalgia or regret for the past, as *She wished she could turn the clock back to the happier times of her youth*, and *Old people often wish they could turn the clock back but they forget how bad social conditions were in the past*. The expression dates from the nineteenth century and is current today. In origin it refers to turning the hands of a clock back.

turn the corner is an idiom cliché meaning to begin to recover. It is frequently used of financial or economic situations, as *The government is trying to convince the electorate that the economy has turned the corner.*, having been used in this sense by Charles Dickens. In this context it is frequently used by journalists. The expression is also used as an informal medical cliché, as *The patient is not completely out of danger yet but I think she has turned the corner*. As a cliché the expression dates from the nineteenth century and is widely used today. In origin it refers to turning a corner and going in a new direction.

turn the other cheek is an allusion cliché being a reference to a Biblical passage where Jesus tells his followers that if someone hit them on one cheek they should offer their attacker the other cheek also 'Unto him that smiteth thee on the one cheek offer also the other.' (*Luke* 6:29). The expression **turn the other cheek** means to accept meekly insults, acts of provocation, attacks, etc, as *It is difficult to ignore their taunts but if you turn the other cheek they'll tire of it and start on somebody else*. As a cliché the phrase dates from the nineteenth century. It is more popular today in these aggressive times than the actual practice it describes.

'twas ever thus is a hackneyed phrase used to reflect on the fact that things do not change, as *The men earn more than the women in the office. 'Twas ever thus!* and *The last bus goes before the end of the concert. 'Twas ever thus*. It is usually said in resigned tones in acceptance of something inconvenient, annoying, etc. As a cliché the expression probably dates from the early twentieth century.

twist my arm! is a catchphrase cliché used in response to a suggested offer, as *I shouldn't really stay and have another drink but twist my arm*, and *Twist my arm! I'd love to stop studying for a while and go to the cinema*. The phrase is from the idiom **twist someone's arm** which means to force someone to do something. The cliché indicates that someone does not really need to be forced but is only too willing to accept the offer. As a cliché the expression dates from the twentieth century and is common today in informal contexts.

two a penny is a hackneyed phrase used to indicate that something is very common, as *Employment conditions are very bad because prospective workers are two a penny*, and *Houses in that area used to be impossible to come by but since the collapse of the property boom they're two a penny*. In origin it refers to things being extremely cheap. As a cliché the expression dates from the twentieth century and is common today, often being used in a derogatory way.

two heads are better than one is a proverb cliché indicating that a problem is likely to be solved more effectively if more than one mind is applied to it, as *Would you like to help me map out our route for tomorrow? Two heads are better than one*, and *I've asked Frank to help me draw up a business plan for the new business. Two heads are better than one and he has a lot of experience of that* *kind of thing*. The proverb is an old one, appearing in John Heywood's collection of proverbs of 1546. As a cliché the expression dates from the twentieth century. It is still widespread today, although not everyone agrees with the sentiment, believing that → **too many cooks spoil the broth**.

two of a kind is a hackneyed phrase used to indicate in a derogatory way that two people are very alike, as *I wouldn't waste sympathy on Jenny for marrying Jim. I know he's violent but in fact they're two of a kind*. As a cliché the expression dates from the nineteenth century. A previous form of the expression was **two of a trade** but this is now obsolete.

two's company, three's a crowd is a proverb cliché indicating that lovers like to be alone, as *I wouldn't accept their invitation to the cinema. They're just being polite. Two's company, three's a crowd*. The saying is an old one and appeared in John Heywood's proverb collection of 1546. Like love itself, the cliché is common today.

U

ugly duckling, an is an idiom cliché used to describe an unattractive or untalented child who grows into an attractive or talented adult, as *Their youngest daughter is now a famous model but she was a real ugly duckling as a teenager.* In origin the expression refers to a story by Hans Christian Andersen in which a cygnet is adopted by a mother duck and is scorned by her and her ducklings because it is so ugly and clumsy until it grows into a beautiful, graceful swan.

unacceptable face of, is a hackneyed phrase used to indicate the less advantageous, popular, pleasant, etc. aspect of something which is otherwise acceptable as *Bomb attacks involving innocent people were the unacceptable face of the protest movement.* The expression is derived originally from **the unacceptable face of capitalism**, a quotation cliché alluding to a statement made to the House of Commons in 1973 by Edward Heath, the Prime Minister of Britain in reference to a financial scandal in which a former Tory Cabinet minister, Duncan Sandys, accepted a large sum of money from the Lonrho Company in return for giving up his consultancy with the firm, the money to be paid, quite legally, into a tax-free account in the Cayman Islands and the situation taking place when the government was promoting a counter-inflation policy.

unaccustomed as I am to public speaking is a hackneyed phrase used by public speakers, such as after-dinner speakers, irrespective of how experienced they are in the art. Since the middle of the twentieth century the expression has mostly been used in a humorous, ironic or quasi-apologetic way, as *This is, the third fête that I have opened this week and so, unaccustomed as I am to public speaking, I shall tell you the advantages of this one.* By the time Winston Churchill used the expression in 1897 in his first political speech in Bath the non-humorous version was already obviously considered to be a cliché. Nowadays the cliché is sometimes shortened to **unaccustomed as I am** . . . since everyone will know what comes next.

unavoidable delays is a hackneyed phrase usually used in a business or transport context as a non-specific excuse for something not being on time or up to schedule, as *We are sorry that you have not yet received the goods which you ordered but owing to unavoidable delays in production we have been unable to process the orders*, or *Owing to unavoidable delays the train is running half an hour late.* The expression has been popular since the late nineteenth century and is often replaced by seemingly more specific but still vague excuses, as *The plane has been delayed owing to a* **slight technical hitch**.

uncrowned king of, the is a hackneyed phrase originally from around the beginning of the twentieth century, indicating that someone is the virtual ruler of somewhere, although not the official ruler. The expression then came to be used figuratively to refer to people who are generally acknowledged to be exceptionally talented and the best in their fields, although they may not be officially recognized as such, as *At that time he was the uncrowned king of rock 'n' roll.*

under a cloud is an idiom cliché meaning in disgrace or under suspicion of some kind, the image being that the rest of the sky is blue but that there is a cloud over one individual. The figurative expression has been in use since the fifteenth century and has been established as a cliché since the middle of the eighteenth century. It is still widely used nowadays, as *The teacher had had a fine academic career but left the school under a cloud after a relationship with a pupil,* and *Money has gone missing from the classroom and the whole of the class feel that they are all under a cloud until the culprit owns up to the theft.*

under that rough exterior is a hackneyed phrase popular since the late nineteenth century and usually accompanied by the ending **there beats a heart of gold**. The expression is still current but is usually used in a humorous or ironic context. Frequently an ironic ending is added instead of the original, as *Under that rough exterior of his there beats a heart of stone.*

under the sun is a hackneyed phrase usually used for example in some phrases relating to space, as *There is nowhere under the sun that one can be absolutely safe from terrorism,* and *The island has the most pleasant climate under the sun.* The expression has been in use since the fourteenth century and has been common enough to be regarded as a cliché since the seventeenth century. It is still in widespread use today.

under the weather is a hackneyed phrase meaning not very well, slightly ill, as *She left work early as she was feeling a .bit under the weather.* The origin of the expression is uncertain but it may refer to the feeling of tiredness and lethargy that some types of weather, such as hot, humid weather, induce.

university of life, the is a hackneyed phrase used to contrast experience with academic instruction. It is most commonly used by people, especially older people, who did not themselves attend university, to young people who are currently in further education and perceived to be having an easy time, as *It was different in my day. I couldn't afford to spend time reading books. I was educated in the university of life.* An expression which conveys the same sentiment is → **the school of hard knocks**. Both expressions became common in the early part of the twentieth century.

unkindest cut of all, the is a quotation cliché meaning the most unkind or treacherous thing that someone could do. It is in fact a slight misquotation of a passage in Shakespeare's *Julius Caesar* (3:2), the full quotation being 'This was the most unkindest cut of all.' The adjustment was presumably made because the original seems ungrammatical in modern English. The quotation is uttered as Caesar is stabbed by his friends, particularly Brutus. The expression has been common enough to be regarded as a cliché since the latter part of the nineteenth century and is still used, particularly by people of a literary bent.

unsung heroes is a hackneyed phrase which refers to people who have done something extremely brave or noteworthy but who have not received official recognition or acknowledgement. These were heroes whose feats were not sung or written about in the long classical epics by people such as Homer. In his *The Lay of the Last Minstrel* (1805) Sir Walter Scott wrote 'unwept, unhonour'd and unsung.' The expression is still commonly used today, as *They were the unsung heroes of the war effort.*

until death do us part is a quotation cliché used to emphasize the extent of the commitment to a relationship of some kind. In origin it is a quotation from the *Book of Common Prayer* and has been commonly enough used to be considered a cliché since the late nineteenth century. *The Book of Common Prayer* refers to marriage but as a cliché the expression can be used of other associations, as *As schoolgirls we promised to be friends until death did us part.* The expression also exists in the form **till death do us part.**

until one is blue in the face is a hackneyed phrase used to indicate supreme but vain effort, as *You can tell him until you are blue in the face that the system does not work but he will not listen.* In origin the expression refers to the fact that one sometimes goes blue in the face if one makes some kind of hard physical effort.

untimely end, an is a hackneyed phrase indicating a premature death or end, as *She worried in case her sons came to an untimely end when climbing in bad weather conditions,* and *They had high hopes of making a success of the new business venture but it came to an untimely end at the start of the recession.* The phrase has been common enough to be considered a cliché since the middle of the nineteenth century. It is still used today although usually in rather a formal context or by people of a literary bent

untold wealth is a hackneyed phrase meaning vast wealth, as *Some merchants amassed* untold wealth by importing goods from the East. It has been common as a cliché since the late nineteenth century.

up and doing is a hackneyed phrase meaning actively busy, especially after a period of illness or inactivity, as *She has been confined to bed since she was injured in the accident and she can't wait to be up and doing.* The expression is used in informal contexts and has been common as a cliché since the late nineteenth century and is still widespread.

up for grabs is a hackneyed phrase used to indicate that something is available to be taken, bought, etc, as *I've heard that there's a job up for grabs in the local computing firm,* and *She is selling the contents of the house and there might be one or two nice antique pieces up for grabs.* The expression is found only in informal or slang contexts. It is American in origin and has been common in Britain since the early 1970s.

up in arms is an idiom cliché meaning very angry at, or opposed to, something, as *The villagers were up in arms when the local school was threatened with closure.* The expression has been in use since the eighteenth century and has been common as a cliché since the nineteenth century. In origin it refers to people literally taking up arms or weapons against an enemy.

up one's sleeve, have something is an idiom meaning to keep something secret for possible use at a later time, as *I thought that management agreed to our request for money too easily. I think that they have something up their sleeve.* In origin the expression refers to the practice among card-sharps in the nineteenth century of keeping a card, often an ace, up their sleeves, for use at an appropriate moment in the game.

upset the applecart is an idiom cliché meaning to spoil a plan or arrangement, as *We spent ages planning the family holiday and then our daughter upset the applecart by getting mumps*. In origin the expression refers to turning over a cart that is selling fruit in a market, although Grose's *Dictionary of the Vulgar Tongue* (1796) suggests that 'applecart' means the human body. It has been in existence in its present form since the late eighteenth century and has been common as a cliché since the middle of the nineteenth century. An earlier form of the expression was **upset the cart.**

up the creek is an idiom cliché meaning in serious trouble or difficulties, as *If he insists on taking his money out of the firm we'll really be up the creek*. The expression is used in informal or slang contexts, the phrase being sometimes extended to **up the creek without a paddle.** American in origin, it began to become common about the time of World War 2. The ultimate origin of the phrase is uncertain.

up to one's ears is an idiom cliché meaning very busy, as though one were almost completely immersed in something as *I would love to come and have lunch but I am up to my ears in work*. It has been common as a cliché since the late nineteenth century although the expression is much older. The same concept is demonstrated by the expressions **up to one's eyes** and **up to one's eyebrows**.

up to scratch is an idiom cliché meaning having met the required standard, as *If your work does not come up to scratch soon we cannot enter you for the exam*. It has been

common as a cliché since the middle of the nineteenth century and is still widespread today. In origin the expression refers to a line once drawn on the floor in the middle of a boxing ring to which boxers had to go after being knocked down to demonstrate that they were fit to go on fighting.

up to the hilt is an idiom cliché meaning to the utmost, completely. In origin it refers to the hilt or handle of a sword or dagger. If the weapon is pushed very hard into someone or something only the hilt shows. It has been common as a cliché since the middle of the nineteenth century and is still much used today, often with reference to debt or guilt, as *He has a title but no money. His estate is mortgaged up to the hilt*, and *I am sure that he was involved in the robbery up to the hilt*.

up with the lark is a hackneyed phrase meaning rising very early in the morning, as *I don't know how she does it. She never goes to bed before midnight but she is always up with the lark*. The expression has been a cliché since the nineteenth century and is still common today. In origin it refers to the fact that the lark, in common with other birds, starts singing very early in the morning.

U-turn, do a is an idiom meaning to reverse one's actions, opinions, etc totally, as *He used to be in favour of closer ties with Europe but he has now done a U-turn and keeps talking of the importance of sovereignty*. As a cliché the expression became common in the 1980s and has its origin in motoring, where to do a U-turn is to turn round and go back the way one has just come.

V

vanish into thin air is a hackneyed phrase meaning to disappear completely and often suddenly, as *One minute the child was playing in the garden; the next minute she had disappeared into thin air.* Air gets thinner the higher one goes because of a reduction in oxygen, but the origin of the expression probably lies in the supposed sudden disappearance of ghosts. It has been in popular use since the middle of the nineteenth century and is still widespread. Indeed hardly anyone or anything ever vanishes without doing so into thin air.

variety is the spice of life is a quotation cliché meaning that life is much more interesting if there is diversity in it, as *I did not really want to have to change jobs just yet, but I suppose variety is the spice of life.* It is a quotation from a poem, *The Talk* by William Cowper (1785), 'Variety is the very spice of life, That gives it all its flavour', the implication being that diversity adds interest to life as spice does to food. It is still in popular general use today.

ve haf vays of making you talk is a catchphrase cliché popular from the middle of the twentieth century indicating in a humorous way that the speaker can easily get the information which he or she requires from the person asked. It is said in a mock sinister German accent, being a send-up of members of the Gestapo as portrayed in British war films. It is still used today but mainly by people of an older generation who remember the war films.

vested interest is a hackneyed phrase of legal origin indicating that someone has a personal interest in something, as *I am not surprised that she is organizing a petition against the new supermarket. She has a vested interest in getting planning permission for it turned down. She owns several of the small shops in the area.* John Stuart Mill wrote in *On Liberty* (1859) 'The doctrine ascribes to all mankind a vested interest in each other's moral, intellectual, and even physical perfection,' and the expression is still much used today. Sometimes the interest is financial, sometimes not.

vexed question, a is a hackneyed phrase indicating a difficult problem that is often discussed without being solved, as *The whole community is in favour of a new sports centre but how we are going to fund it is a vexed question.* In origin the expression is a translation of the Latin *quaestio vexata.* As a cliché it dates from the middle of the nineteenth century and it is still widespread today.

vicious circle, a is a hackneyed phrase indicating a chain of events in which the solution of one problem creates another problem, or else exacerbates the original problem, as *Employment among the young seems to be a vicious circle. They cannot find a job unless they have the relevant experience and they cannot get the relevant experience unless they are already in a job.* The expression has been popular since the middle of the nineteenth century and is still widespread today. In origin it derives from logic, and refers to proving one statement by another that itself rests on the first for proof.

vino veritas, in (Latin for 'truth in wine') is a foreign cliché indicating that when people have drunk too much they frequently become loose-tongued and divulge information that they would otherwise keep secret, as *Well, we were all surprised when he said that he was having an affair with his secretary but you know what they say – in vino veritas..* As a modern cliché it is usually restricted to people who have a background in classical languages or a literary background. To those not having experience of these it can appear pompous.

❧ W ❦

wages of sin, the is a quotation cliché, being a Biblical reference to *Romans* (6:23). It occurs in a letter from Paul to the Romans 'The wages of sin is death' and means the consequences of wickedness. The expression has been considered a cliché since the nineteenth century but is nowadays usually used by older people of a literary bent and even then it is more usually used ironically, as *You should think twice about pretending to be ill when you take a day off to go to the football match. The boss might find out and the wages of sin is death.*

wait and see is a hackneyed phrase which was much used by Henry Asquith when he was Prime Minister of Britain at the beginning of the twentieth century. It is a very widespread cliché used to try and suppress impatience in the person with whom one is dealing, or more especially to postpone having to discuss a matter or make a decision. It is particularly commonly used by parents to children, as *I don't know whether we'll be going on holiday this year. We'll just have to wait and see*, in order to postpone having to say no. Children find it a very tiresome stock response and usually recognize its negative implications immediately.

wait hand and foot on is a hackneyed phrase meaning to attend to the every need of, to look after very assiduously, as *Her husband expects her to wait upon him hand and foot.* The expression is usually used in a derogatory way, suggesting that the person doing the waiting is a self-

inflicted martyr in the opinion of the speaker. The expression is very old and has been very common since the late nineteenth century.

walk on air is an idiom cliché meaning to be extremely happy or elated. It has been common since the late nineteenth century and is still widespread, as *She has been walking on air since she discovered that she is pregnant.* The association of supreme happiness and air is also found in *on cloud nine* and → **in seventh heaven**.

walls have ears is an idiom cliché used to caution that someone may be eavesdropping on a conversation, although no one is doing so in an obvious way. The expression is reputedly derived from a story about Dionysius, a tyrant of Syracuse (430–367BC), in which he was so anxious to overhear what his prisoners were saying that he cut an ear-shaped cave into a rock which connected palace rooms and enabled him to eavesdrop. It is a long-standing cliché and is still popular and widespread, as *Watch what you're saying until we're out of the restaurant. I know it's not busy but walls have ears.*

want to know the reason why is a hackneyed phrase used as a kind of threat, usually by people in authority, such as parents and teachers. The expression is rather dictatorial in tone being used as an ultimatum, as *You will clean your room this morning or I shall want to know the* *reason why.* As a cliché it dates from the twentieth century.

warts and all is an allusion cliché to the instructions given by Oliver Cromwell to Sir Peter Lely when he was painting his portrait that the artist should make him appear as he really was, including any imperfections, such as warts 'I desire you would use all your skill to paint my picture truly like me and not flatter me at all; but remark all these roughnesses, pimples, warts, and everything as you see me, otherwise I will not pay a farthing for it.' The expression, which is widespread in modern times, means despite any shortcomings or drawbacks, as *I hope she is going to marry him warts and all and not try to change him.*

wash one's dirty linen in public is an idiom cliché which has its origin in a French proverb. The expression means to make public one's private affairs, particularly when these are of a scandalous or unsavoury nature, as *We all know that she was involved in a messy divorce case but we wish she'd stop washing her dirty linen in public.* It has been common since the middle of the nineteenth century.

wash one's hands of is an idiom cliché meaning to refuse to have anything more do with or to take any responsibility for, as *A local businessman was going to contribute some of the funding for the new club but there has been so much quarrelling among the organizers that he has decided to wash his hands of the whole project.* The expression has been common since the middle of the nineteenth century and is Biblical in origin. It is an allusion to the behaviour of Pontius Pilate, the Roman governor at the time of the trial of Jesus Christ. In *Matthew* (27:24) he is said to have *'washed his hands before the multitude, saying I am innocent of the blood of this just person.'*

was it something I said? is a modern catchphrase cliché used when someone seems to be avoiding one or not behaving in a friendly or usual way towards one, as *Everyone seemed to leave as I arrived at the party. Was it something I said?* The expression is usually used humorously. As a cliché it dates from the later part of the twentieth century.

waste not, want not is a proverb cliché used to warn someone of the dangers of thriftlessness. It became common in the nineteenth century and is still used nowadays, particularly by older people who were made extremely aware of the virtues of making maximum use of something during World War 2, as *Don't throw out those leftovers – you can make a pie with them. Waste not, want not.* The expression is becoming less common in modern society with its love of the disposable.

watched pot never boils, the is a proverb cliché used to caution someone against being impatient or over-anxious, as this in no way speeds matters up. The implication of the saying is that if you go away and forget about a saucepan of water that you have put on to boil, it seems to boil more quickly than it does if you stand and watch it. The expression dates from the middle of the nineteenth century and is still widespread today, as *The jelly won't set any faster if you keep looking at it. The watched pot never boils.*

water under the bridge is an idiom cliché used to refer to something that is over and gone and so not worth thinking any more about. It dates from the twentieth century and is still widespread, as *She used to go out with the boy next door but that's all water under the bridge. She married someone else long ago.*

water, water everywhere is a quotation cliché usually used when there has been a flood or when it is raining very hard, as *When we were on holiday it was a case of water, water everywhere although the local people said it was usually very dry there at that time of year.* The quotation is from *The Rime of the Ancient Mariner* (1798) by Samuel Coleridge. The cliché is sometimes extended to **water, water, everywhere, and not a drop to drink**, which is a misquotation from the same source of 'water, water, everywhere, nor any drop to drink.'

ways and means, there are see *there are ways and means*

we are not amused is a quotation cliché, being an allusion to a remark attributed to Queen Victoria, as *He is bound to come up with an inventive excuse for being late but we shall make it clear that we are not amused.* Nowadays it is usually used in a humorous or light-hearted context.

wear the trousers is an idiom cliché used to refer to a situation in which the female partner in a marriage or relationship is the more dominant person, as *He owns his own business and makes all the decisions at work but at home his wife wears the trousers.* The expression has been common since the eighteenth century and is still current although the set of social circumstances to which it referred no longer necessarily obtains, in that it is now quite common for women literally to wear trousers and for women to hold positions of responsibility in their own right.

wear a hat is an idiom cliché indicating that one is currently assuming one of two or more positions or roles that one holds, as *He is a teacher at the school but he was wearing his parent's hat when he complained about the education cuts.* In origin the expression refers to the hats associated with different uniforms. It dates from the middle of the nineteenth century.

weather the storm is an idiom cliché meaning to survive some kind of difficulty or crisis, as *During the recession the firm had some financial difficulties but they succeeded in weathering the storm and are now very profitable.* The expression has been common since the middle of the nineteenth century, although it has been in use since the seventeenth century, and is still very widespread, being much used by journalists in particular. It derives from the idea of a ship surviving a heavy storm.

wedded bliss is a hackneyed phrase which refers to the happiness that marriage can bring, as *The old couple have been living in wedded bliss for fifty years.* The expression became popular in the late nineteenth century but nowadays when the phenomenon itself is becoming less common as a result of declining marriage rates and increasing divorce rates, the expression is used less commonly except in humorous or ironic situations, as *Mary and Jim had a real row in the pub last night. That's wedded bliss for you!*

weighed in the balance and found wanting is a quotation cliché meaning tested and found to be deficient in some way. It comes from the Bible and is a slight misquotation of part of the interpretation that Daniel gave to King Belshazzar of the handwriting on the wall 'Thou art weighed in the balances, and art found wanting.' (*Daniel* 5:27) The expression has been popular since the nineteenth century and is still in current use, especially in rather formal contexts, as *Several young men have asked for her hand in marriage but they have all been weighed in the balance and found wanting.*

welcome aboard is a hackneyed phrase used when someone new joins a firm, club, community, etc as *'Welcome aboard!' said the manager. 'I hope you will enjoy working here.'* As a cliché the expression dates from the first half of the twentieth century and is still used today, although mainly by older people and often in rather a pompous way. In origin the expression is probably naval although its use as a standard greeting welcoming passengers aboard aircraft has probably helped to popularize it.

welcome with open arms is a hackneyed phrase meaning to receive someone or something with great enthusiasm and warmth, as *The couple welcomed their new daughter-in-law with open arms*, and *The improvements to the shop have been welcomed by the customers with open arms*. It has been a cliché since the late eighteenth century and is still in widespread use. Indeed people hardly seem to welcome anyone or anything at all unless they do so with open arms.

well and truly is a doublet cliché used for emphasis, as *Our team was well and truly beaten in the first round*. It is extremely widespread, being particularly common in such situations as the opening of new shops, exhibitions, etc., as *I declare this new supermarket well and truly open*. As a cliché it dates from the late nineteenth century.

well-earned rest is a hackneyed phrase meaning a period of leisure or relaxation that is well-deserved following a period of activity, as *Just as she thought she was going to have a well-earned rest from child-rearing she was given her granddaughter to look after*. The expression has been common since the late nineteenth century and often refers to a period of rest at the end of one's career. In modern times it is often used as a euphemism relating to a situation in which someone has been forced to retire or leave a post, as *We are glad that several of our employees are taking advantage of our early retirement scheme and are going off to enjoy a well-earned rest*.

we'll let you know is a catchphrase cliché used to indicate that the speaker does not think very highly of whatever the person addressed is doing, particularly when that person is doing something that requires a degree of artistic talent such as singing, as *Whenever Mary plays the piano her brother annoys her by saying, 'We'll let you know.'* Like → **don't call us, we'll call you**, it has its origins in the entertainment industry, being a stock response to people auditioning for parts unsuccessfully. Although it seemed to offer a modicum of hope it was usually a euphemism for a direct rejection. It is often used in this way nowadays in a business context to reject applications for a job.

we'll see is a hackneyed phrase meaning much the same as → **wait and see** and is used in much the same way.

we must have lunch sometime is a modern hackneyed phrase used as a parting remark to a friend or acquaintance either in person or by telephone. It is often simply a stock response, sometimes even just a way to bring a lengthy or unwelcome conversation to as speedy an end as possible, rather than a serious promise of a future engagement, as *Well I'm running late and I'll really have to go. We must have lunch some time*.

wend one's way is a hackneyed phrase meaning to go or make one's way, the word 'wend' originally in this context meaning to turn. The expression was used originally in the fourteenth century but died out around the sixteenth century. It was later revived and became popular in the early nineteenth century and is now usually used either in a formal, literary or humorous context, as *If we are going to catch that train it is time we were wending our way to the station*.

we're just good friends is a hackneyed phrase used to indicate that there is no romantic or sexual element in a relationship. It usually takes the form of a public denial and is very frequently not the truth, as *'We're just good friends,' the politician told the reporter but he left his wife for his secretary the following week.* The expression dates from the twentieth century when mass communications led to an increased interest in the private lives of people in the public eye.

we shall keep your name on file is a hackneyed phrase which is more or less a euphemism, usually being simply a polite way of rejecting someone's application for a job, as *We are sorry that you have not been successful in your application for the present post but we shall keep your name on file in the event of future vacancies.* Given the number of applications that employers receive for every vacancy, it is extremely unlikely that they are going to store the name of applicants for future use. As a cliché it dates from the recession and consequent joblessness of the 1980s and 1990s.

we wiz/wuz robbed is a twentieth century catchphrase cliché, being an ungrammatical or dialectal form of 'we were robbed'. Originally a sports cliché, it is used to indicate that the users think that they have been treated unfairly in some way usually by the referee or umpire. It was used by boxers and then by football supporters. The expression has gradually begun to be used more widely in humorous contexts by people who would not normally use ungrammatical or dialectal speech, and who are consciously aping the sporting cliché, as *After the latest round of redundancies we all have to work so late that we asked management to pay us overtime but they refused. We wiz robbed!*

what are you going to do when you grow up? is a hackneyed phrase used by adults to children from an early age, usually in a patronizing way and often because the adult in question cannot think of anything else to say, as *What are you going to do when you grow up? I hope that you are going to study hard and get a good job.* It is often the first cliché to which people are exposed and is still used by some older people today despite the fact that the reduction in the number of jobs available in modern society has made the remark exceptionally inappropriate

what did your last slave die of? is a catchphrase cliché used ironically to someone who has asked one to do something that he or she could easily do without help, as *No, I'm not going upstairs to get your handbag. What did your last slave die of?* The expression has been popular since the early twentieth century and is still widespread.

whatever turns you on is a catchphrase cliché used in response to a statement by someone that he or she is going to do something of which one disapproves or feels disinclined to join in, as *No, I don't fancy camping in the rain but whatever turns you on.* The expression dates from the 1960s, 'turn on' being part of 1960s drug slang meaning to excite or stimulate.

what's your poison? is a hackneyed phrase used when asking someone what he or she would like to drink, as in *It's my turn to buy a round. What's your poison?* It dates from the 1920s and is now dated, being used mainly by older people. The reference to poison may be an allusion to the slogan of the Temperance Movement, 'Alcohol is poison'. An alternative form of the expression is **name your poison.**

what's the damage? is a hackneyed phrase used when asking the cost of something, as *That's all I need just now. What's the damage?* The expression has been common since the nineteenth century, having originated in America. It is found in informal contexts and is becoming rather dated.

what with one thing and another is a hackneyed phrase used to suggest a kind of semi-apology because someone is very busy or because there are several complications arising in a situation, as *What with one thing and another I just haven't had time to think about holidays.* The expression dates from the middle of the nineteenth century and is still widespread today

what you see is what you get is a modern catchphrase cliché indicating that someone or something is completely straightforward and above board, as *Some of the members of the committee may well try to deceive you but he is completely honest. With him what you see is what you get.* The cliché is often abbreviated to **wysiwyg** in the field of computers.

wheels within wheels is an idiom cliché indicating something extremely involved and complicated, and sometimes implying something dishonest, as *We tried to find out the cause of the firm's failure but there were wheels within wheels.* It has been a cliché since the nineteenth century and is still widespread. In origin the expression is probably Biblical 'Their appearance and their work was as it were a wheel in the middle of a wheel.' (*Ezekiel* 1:16)

when all is said and done is a filler cliché meaning in the end or often meaning virtually nothing, as *When all is said and done, we all have to die some time.* The expression dates from the sixteenth cen-

tury and has been a cliché since the late nineteenth century. It is still widespread.

when in Rome . . . is a hackneyed phrase advocating the advisability of conforming to the customs, conventions, etc of the environment in which one finds oneself, as *Women do not go out alone there. When in Rome . . .* The expression is a shortened form of **when in Rome do as the Romans do** which is also common. In origin it supposedly comes from the translation of the answer given by St Ambrose to St Augustine and his mother, St Monica, when they asked whether they should fast on Saturdays according to the custom practised in Rome, or whether they should adopt the Milanese custom and not fast. St Ambrose is said to have replied that when he was in Milan he did not fast on Saturday but when he was in Rome he did so.

when I was your age is a hackneyed phrase used by some older people when about to regale a member of a younger generation with tales of how much better, more moral, harder, etc things were in their youth than they are at the time of speaking, and how immeasurably better, more moral, thoughtful, hard-working, poorer, etc they were than the young person being addressed.

when one door closes another opens is a hackneyed phrase used to inspire optimism in someone who has just experienced some form of misfortune. It is often shortened to **when one door closes**, as *I know you've lost your job but you'll probably find a better one. When one door closes . . .* A more pessimistic and humorous form of the cliché is **when one door closes another one slams in your face**.

when one's ship comes in is an idiom cliché meaning when one has made one's fortune, when more affluent times arrive, as *They plan to buy a house of their own when their ship comes in.* The expression derives from the days when merchants used to await the arrival of their sailing ships from foreign parts hoping that they would arrive laden with goods that would make their fortune, there obviously being a degree of uncertainty involved. It has been common since the middle of the nineteenth century and is still widespread today.

when the cat's away the mice will play is an idiom cliché indicating that when a person in authority or control is not present those under his or her authority take advantage and break the rules, do no work, etc. As a cliché the expression is usually shortened to **when the cat's away . . .**, the rest of the saying being assumed to be understood, as *We cannot leave the children in the room without a teacher. When the cat's away . . .* The proverb has been in existence in English since the seventeenth century and the concept exists in other languages also.

when the going gets tough is a catchphrase cliché meaning when a situation becomes very difficult, as *There was no shortage of volunteers at the beginning of the protest campaign, but when the going got tough there was only a handful of us left.* The cliché is a shortened form of the catchphrase **when the going gets tough, the tough get going** which is also a cliché. The expression originated in America, probably in political circles. It has been attributed to Joseph Kennedy (1888–1969), father of President John F Kennedy. A joke form, **when the going gets tough, the tough go shopping**, became popular in the 1980s and since then various people have attached their own joke endings to the catchphrase.

when you gotta go, you gotta go is a twentieth century catchphrase cliché used in informal contexts when someone wants to go to the toilet, as *I was sorry to have to leave the hall and disturb the speaker but you know how it is. When you gotta go, you gotta go!* The expression at the time of the London Blitz in World War 2 indicated an acceptance that one might be killed and that there was nothing that one could do about it, the lavatorial association being a more recent development.

where have you been all my life? is a catchphrase cliché used to flatter and express an exaggerated interest in a member of the opposite sex, usually by a man to a woman, as *I have never met such a beautiful woman. Where have you been all my life?* It originated in America in the early 1920s and became established in Britain around the early 1940s. The expression is still used but it is most frequently used humorously or ironically.

whisper it not is rather a literary hackneyed phrase which is a shortened version of **whisper it not in Gath** and is no longer common. This in turn is a misquotation of a Biblical passage 'How are the mighty fallen! Tell it not in Gath, publish it not in the streets of Askelon.' (*2 Samuel,* I 19–20) As a cliché the expression became popular in the nineteenth century. Nowadays the shortened version is still used but usually only by people of a literary bent and often in humorous or ironic contexts, as *Whisper it not, but he is thinking of taking a bath.*

whiter than white is a twentieth century hackneyed phrase meaning extremely pure, often unbelievably so, as *She is always criticizing the morals of others but from what I hear she is not exactly whiter than white herself.* It refers to an advertising slogan describing the cleaning properties of soap powder.

who/which shall remain nameless is a hackneyed phrase indicating one's reluctance to mention by name the person or thing that one is talking about, as *Someone who shall remain nameless has been stealing money from the till.* The expression has been popular since the late nineteenth century. Nowadays it is found either in formal contexts or in humorous or ironic contexts, as *Someone who shall remain nameless has forgotten my birthday.*

whys and wherefores is a hackneyed phrase meaning all the reasons for something, the details of the background to a situation, as *I just know that they have divorced. I don't know the whys and wherefores.* The expression has been a cliché since around the middle of the nineteenth century and is still widespread today. **Whys and wherefores** could now be considered a doublet cliché, although originally why and wherefore were not synonymous, 'why' meaning the reason for something, and 'wherefore' meaning how something came to be.

wild horses would not drag me is a hackneyed phrase indicating that nothing whatsoever would persuade someone to do something, as *Wild horses would not drag me to a film with so much violence in it.* A related expression is **wild horses would not drag it from me** which means nothing would make me divulge it, which is a later form of **wild horses would not draw it from me** with its origin in medieval torture to make people confess. The expression has been popular since the middle of the nineteenth century.

win hands down is a hackneyed phrase meaning to win very easily or by a significant margin, as *We thought that it was going to be a close match, but our team won*

hands down. The expression has been popular from around the beginning of the twentieth century and is still widespread. In origin it derives from racing, being a reference to the fact that jockeys tend to relax their hold on the reins, and so ride with their hands down, when they feel that they are going to win.

wish you were here is a twentieth century catchphrase cliché popular from having been a stock message on holiday postcards, communications which are extremely difficult to be inventive on. It is often now used humorously or ironically, as *The weather is very wet and the food terrible. Wish you were here!*

witching hour, the is a hackneyed phrase referring to midnight, supposedly the time when witches come out. It has been used as a cliché since the middle of the nineteenth century and is still used although its use now would be considered rather literary or pretentious, as *Come, it is time for us to go home. It will soon be the witching hour.* In origin it is probably an allusion to a passage from Shakespeare's *Hamlet* (3:2) 'The very witching time of night, when graveyards yawn.'

with bated breath is a hackneyed phrase meaning holding one's breath in anticipation, excitement, fear, etc, as *We waited with bated breath as they announced the results of the competition.* The verb 'bate' is an archaic verb meaning to restrain. This phrase has been a cliché since the late nineteenth century although it has been in the language much longer than that, having been used by Shakespeare in *The Merchant of Venice* (1:3) 'Shall I bend low, and in a bondsman key, with bated breath, and whispering humbleness.' Nowadays the cliché is often used humorously or ironically, as *I'm sure the villagers are all* *waiting with bated breath for the result of the elections. Only about thirty percent of them bothered to vote.*

without more ado is a hackneyed phrase meaning right away, as *I think that everything is ready, and so without more ado I shall declare the exhibition open.* It has been a cliché in this sense since the beginning of the twentieth century and is still current today, although usually in fairly formal contexts. 'Ado' means fuss.

wolf in sheep's clothing, a is an idiom cliché meaning a dangerous person who has in some way a deceptively kind or mild exterior, as *He was so charming to everyone outside his home that no one realized that he was a wolf in sheep's clothing and beat his wife and children.* The expression comes from Aesop's fable in which a wolf dresses up as a sheep, or in some versions as a shepherd, in order to get among the flock of sheep to seize one. There is also a Biblical reference in *Matthew* (7:15), where Jesus talks of 'false prophets which come to you in sheep's clothing but inwardly they are ravening wolves.' The figurative expression is an old one, going back to the fifteenth century and became popular enough to be considered a cliché in the middle of the eighteenth century. It is still widespread today.

wonders will never cease! is a hackneyed phrase indicating the speaker's great surprise at something. The expression dates from the late eighteenth century and is often now used in a humorous or ironically context, as *Wonders will never cease! Jim has arrived for work on time.*

word in your ear, a is a hackneyed phrase used to seek someone's attention, usually with a view to saying something relatively confidential, as *A word in your ear. The boss has been complaining about people spending*

too long on their coffee breaks. It dates from the late nineteenth century and is still popular.

words fail me! is a hackneyed phrase used as an exclamation when something is so surprising, dreadful, etc that it is difficult to find words to describe it. The expression has been common since the middle of the nineteenth century and is still current today. Although it sounds rather formal, it is common in everyday situations, as *When I think of the noise our neighbours make, words fail me!*

word to the wise, a is a hackneyed phrase indicating that the speaker is about to give the listener some good advice and that he or she is considered sensible enough to take note of it, as *A word to the wise, now would be a good time to buy property in that area of the city.* The concept of the expression is an old one, several of the classical Roman writers having used it. As an English expression it was used by the playwright Ben Jonson in his play *The Case is Altered* (circa 1600) 'Go to, a word to the wise.' It is still used nowadays especially by people of a literary bent and often in a humorous or ironic way.

working late at the office is a twentieth century hackneyed phrase used as a classic excuse to suggest that someone who is doing something that he or she should not be doing, especially having an illicit love affair, is in fact simply working overtime. It is often now used humorously or ironically, as *Jim never joins his colleagues for a drink after work. He is too busy working late at the office with his secretary.*

work one's fingers to the bone is an idiom cliché meaning to work extremely hard as though one were doing physical work for so long that the skin and flesh came off one's fingers, as *She was left a widow at an*

201

early age and had to work her fingers to the bone to look after her seven children. The expression dates from the nineteenth century and is still commonly used today. In origin it possibly refers to seamstresses sewing until the flesh came off their hands.

world's your oyster, the is an idiom cliché used to try to inspire optimism in someone with the number of possible opportunities that offer themselves. It is usually used to console someone who has experienced some form of misfortune, such as a young person who has just been rejected for a job, and the optimism is often somewhat misplaced, especially in modern society where the number of opportunities is not large and seems to be ever-decreasing, as *If you stay on at school and take your exams the world will be your oyster.* It falls into that class of clichés which are used to console the unfortunate because they are the first thing that occurs to the speaker, rather than because it is likely that they are going to be in any way comforting or reassuring. As a cliché it has been popular since the nineteenth century and is still widely used. In origin the expression may derive from Shakespeare's *The Merry Wives of Windsor* (2:2) 'Why then, the world's mine oyster, which I with sword will open.' The implication is that the world is a place from which success and profit can easily be extracted just as a pearl can be extracted from an oyster.

world of good, do a see *do a world of good*

would you believe it? is a hackneyed phrase used as an exclamation expressing not so much surprise or disbelief, as exasperation, as *Would you believe it? The paper boy has delivered the wrong paper yet again.*

writing is on the wall, the is an allusion cliché used to indicate a prediction of impending disaster or misfortune, a suggestion that a certain event will lead to disaster, as *The writing was on the wall for the small shops when the hypermarket opened in the area.* It is an allusion to a Biblical passage, *Daniel* (5:5-31), in which in the course of a feast given by King Belshazzar a hand appears and writes some words on the wall. When Belshazzar asks Daniel to interpret the writing he tells him that it indicates his coming downfall and Belshazzar is killed later that night. The words concerned were *mene, mene, tekel, upharsin.* The expression has been widely used as a cliché since the nineteenth century and is still popular today. It is also found in the form **the handwriting is on the wall.**

wrong end of the stick, the is an idiom cliché meaning a mistaken impression, as in *Although we explained the situation in great detail he still managed to get the wrong end of the stick.* It has been popular since the nineteenth century and still much used today. In origin it refers to holding a walking stick by the wrong end.

X

X marks the spot is a catchphrase cliché indicating that a cross marks the place where something took place, is situated, etc, as *On the sketch of the area X marks the spot where the corpse was found*. The expression became popular in the 1920s and is still used today, although often in a humorous or light-hearted context, as *This is a postcard of our holiday hotel. X marks the spot where our room is*, or in connection with games or puzzles, such as 'spot the ball' competitions in newspapers in which competitors have to place a cross to indicate where they consider the ball to be in an action photograph of a football match, the actual ball having been blanked out. In origin the expression refers to treasure maps in stories about pirates, a cross being used to mark the supposed location of the treasure.

❧ Y ❧

year in, year out is a hackneyed phrase used to emphasize the relentless continuity, and usually monotony, of something, as *Year in, year out, she had to endure the pain which arose from the injuries she sustained in the accident.* The expression has been popular since the middle of the nineteenth century and is still widespread today.

you can lead/take a horse to water but you can't make it drink is an idiom cliché indicating that it is perfectly possible to establish a set of circumstances which will make it likely that someone will agree to do something, but you cannot force him or her actually to go ahead with it if he or she does not want to do so, as *You can certainly try to persuade all the villagers that moving to the new housing estate is a good idea, but just remember that you can lead a horse to water but you can't make it drink.* The figurative expression appeared in John Heywood's collection of proverbs in 1546 and was probably already in use long before then. It is still a popular expression today.

you can't make a silk purse out of a sow's ear is an idiom cliché meaning that it is not possible to turn something that is worthless into something of value, as *You cannot expect all your piano pupils to become professional musicians. After all, you cannot make a silk purse out of a sow's ear.* As a proverb the expression dates from the sixteenth century and as a cliché it is still widespread today.

you can't take it with you is a catchphrase cliché used to indicate that when you die you cannot take money or any material possessions with you, the implication being that you should enjoy the fruits of these while you are alive. The expression probably dates from around the middle of the nineteenth century and was popularized when it was used as the title of a hit comedy by George Kaufman and Moss Hart that opened on Broadway in 1936. The expression is still widely used today, as *Why don't you use some of your savings to visit your daughter in Australia? You can't take it with you, you know.* It may ultimately be a reference to a Biblical passage. 'For we brought nothing into this world and it is certain we can carry nothing out.' (*1 Timothy* 6:7)

you can't teach an old dog new tricks is a proverb cliché meaning that it is very difficult for older people or people with a great deal of experience in a certain area to be persuaded to adopt new ways, methods, attitudes, etc. The proverb dates from the sixteenth century, having appeared in John Heywood's collection (1546). As a cliché it is still widespread today, as *It is difficult for the older office workers to get used to the new technology. You can't teach an old dog new tricks.*

you can't win 'em all is a catchphrase cliché used to indicate a philosophic acceptance of failure or defeat, as *It's a pity that my application for the course was rejected but never mind – you can't win 'em all.*

The expression originated in America around 1940, becoming popular in Britain at the beginning of the 1960s. It is still widely used today.

you could have knocked me down with a feather is an idiom cliché used to express one's extreme suprise, as *You could have knocked me down with a feather when I walked into the room and saw all my friends. The children had arranged a surprise party for my birthday.* As a cliché it dates from the late nineteenth century.

you know what I mean is usually a filler cliché used virtually meaninglessly by people to whom it has become a habit, as *I am really in need of a holiday. You know what I mean.* Frequently they are not aware of the habit although people who regularly converse with them can find it very annoying. Of course, just occasionally, the phrase is used literally indicating that one assumes that someone understands what someone is getting at. As a cliché it has been established since the late nineteenth century and is still common.

you know what I think? is a filler cliché used in much the same way as **you know what I mean**. The listener is given no say in the matter, although the cliché is framed in the form of a question, since the speaker goes right on to say what he or she was going to say without waiting for a response. As a cliché it has been established since the late nineteenth century and is still common.

you'll look back on this and laugh is a hackneyed phrase of the second half of the twentieth century, used by well-meaning but thoughtless people in an effort to cheer up someone who has suffered some kind of misfortune. In common with other similar platitudes, it rarely has the desired effect,

since the person to whom the remark is addressed feels that he or she will never laugh again. Moreover the situations involved are often of the kind that no one would ever look back on with amusement, as *It does seem hard that your husband has walked out on you and the children and cleaned out your joint bank account. Never mind, one day you'll look back on this and laugh.*

you'll thank me one day is a hackneyed phrase used to try to make some course of action seem more acceptable to the person who is at the receiving end of it. It is often used by older people in authority to young people, as *I know you don't like being made to stay in on a sunny evening to do your homework but you'll thank me one day.* Far from alleviating the situation, the remark usually simply makes the young person more annoyed and rebellious since it sounds so smug. As a cliché if dates from the twentieth century.

you mark my words is a hackneyed phrase which sometimes takes the form of a filler cliché. It is used to impress on a listener the importance and truth of what one is going to say or what one has just said, indicating that one will be proved right, as *You mark my words. He has no intention of marrying her.* As a cliché the expression dates from the middle of the nineteenth century.

you must be joking is a catchphrase cliché used to indicate that the user thinks that the speaker cannot possibly be serious about a remark just made. Frequently the speaker is being quite serious and is not trying in any way to be funny. It is used to express the user's disagreement with or displeasure at what has just been said. As a cliché it has been established since the middle of the twentieth century although it had been used in literary contexts from the nineteenth century. It is still very common today in all but the most formal contexts, as *You are advertising for an experienced chef at £3 an hour? You must be joking!* A slightly sharper form of the expression is **you're joking, of course**, while a more informal variant is **you must be kidding**.

young of all ages, the is a hackneyed phrase popular since the beginning of the twentieth century and used to emphasize the youthfulness in all but actual years of some members of a group. The expression is often used in semi-formal contexts, as in a speech opening a fair, exhibition, etc, as *The fête includes a funfair and we are sure that the young of all ages will enjoy it.* It has a tendency nowadays to sound rather pompous or patronizing.

your chariot awaits is a hackneyed phrase used to indicate that transport is standing by for someone, as *My son is going to drive you home and your chariot awaits.* It nowadays tends to be used by older people, being rather dated, and in a humorous way.

you're only young once is a twentieth century catchphrase cliché advocating that people should enjoy themselves and make the most of their lives while they are young, the implication being that this carefree period is all too transient, as *You should go out a bit more instead of spending all your spare time studying. After all, you're only young once.* It tends to be used by older people who know only too well the truth of the statement.

You're telling me see *tell me about it.*

your guess is as good as mine is a catchphrase cliché used to emphasize the lack of information or knowledge available about the situation in question, as *They may or may not attend the meeting. Your guess is as good as mine.* It dates from the early part of the twentieth century and originated in America. It is still widespread today, being used in all but the most formal contexts.

yours truly is a hackneyed phrase used in facetious informal contexts to mean I or me, as *Whenever the dog needs a walk it always seems to be yours truly who has to take it.* In this use the expression has has been current since the middle of the nineteenth century, although its use as a standard closing formula in letters is older.

❧ Z ❧

zero hour is a hackneyed phrase used to indicate the exact time at which something is due to begin, as *Are all the children ready for the prize-giving ceremony? Zero hour is 2 o'clock.* The expression is military in origin, being first used in World War 1. It gradually began to be used in situations that had no military connections and is still much used today in a wide range of contexts.

THE WHOLE STORY OF
CLIMATE

WHAT SCIENCE REVEALS ABOUT
THE NATURE OF ENDLESS CHANGE

E. KIRSTEN PETERS

Prometheus Books

59 John Glenn Drive
Amherst, New York 14228–2119

Published 2012 by Prometheus Books

Cover image copyright © 2012 Media Bakery
Cover design by Grace M. Conti-Zilsberger

Inquiries should be addressed to
Prometheus Books
59 John Glenn Drive
Amherst, New York 14228–2119
VOICE: 716–691–0133
FAX: 716–691–0137
WWW.PROMETHEUSBOOKS.COM

16 15 14   5 4 3 2

Library of Congress Cataloging-in-Publication Data

Peters, E. Kirsten.
    The whole story of climate : what science reveals about the nature of endless change
/ by Dr. E. Kirsten Peters.
        p. cm.
    Includes bibliographical references and index.
    ISBN 978-1-61614-672-6 (cloth : alk. paper)
    ISBN 978-1-61614-673-3 (ebook)
    1. Climatic changes. 2. Paleoclimatology. I. Title.

QC884.2.C5P48 2012
551.5—dc23

                                                                        2012023389

Printed in the United States of America on acid-free paper

For my friends at St. James,
in particular those who visit me at St. Joe's

CONTENTS

1

FACING OUR CLIMATE ADVERSARY SQUARELY

Geologic evidence plainly teaches that Earth's climate has changed through staggering extremes of balmy warmth to bitter cold. And that's not just a description of ancient history, when dinosaurs roamed the world. Instead, it's the clear record of climate change during recent times, when fully modern *Homo sapiens* left Africa, spread around the world, and ultimately founded our varied cultures and civilizations.

What's even more alarming than the recent dates and staggering scale of climate upheavals is how quickly they have swept over the Earth. Many of these have not been gradual events, unfolding over dozens of centuries or millennia. Indeed, as we now know, most major climate changes in geologically recent times have occurred in a mere twenty or thirty years. In other words, in the span of a single human lifetime, Earth's climate has crashed from warm times much like the present to Ice Age conditions— or rocketed back again to warmth. In between these catastrophic changes there have been numerous smaller, but still substantial, climate shifts. Even these lesser events have been more than sufficient to quickly alter entire ecosystems, and most of them have been devastatingly fast.

The more scientists learn about the natural climate revolutions woven into the fabric of the planet, the greater our awe about how supremely fickle is climate on Earth. And climate upheavals have rearranged more than just entire temperature charts. Wind, precipitation, and other elements of weather have been as varied as temperature change. For example, what is now the driest part of the Sahara Desert was only four thousand years ago a lush and verdant landscape with lakes, fish, crocodiles, turtles, and people. But when climate turned yet another corner in Earth's long history, the rains shifted far to the south and the green splendor vanished, along with the people. Today, in the same spot, there is nothing but sand.

No full climate crash has occurred in the span of written history. That may be chance, or it may be that if there had been a fully global and rapid climate revolution, early civilizations would not have survived, so we would not be here. But, in any event, the simple fact that we don't have *written records* of natural and extreme global climate revolutions accounts for a large measure of the ignorance of even the educated public about the behavior of climate on Earth. But geologists can read the *physical record* of the enormous changes that swept over the globe before civilization was established and our written history commenced. The signs are plain once you learn to see them: Earth's global climate reverses, staggers, and stumbles, again and again, sometimes with changes that occur within the span of a single human life. What's worse, the Earth looks like she may be overdue for another, fully natural, climate revolution, as well as for more moderate and ongoing climate shifts.

The public has heard a great deal in recent years from the ranks of climate science, a discipline that's partially distinct from geology. There's much to be valued in the complex computer models that climate scientists use. But climate science is quite a recent branch of research, and climate scientists are not the only ones with professional opinions about the Earth. For almost two hundred years geologists have studied the basic evidence of how climate has changed on our planet. We don't generally traffic in computer models so much as direct physical evidence left in the muck and rocks of our planet. From those kinds of grubby facts, which this book will explain at a level any interested citizen can follow, we know a great deal about how climate has actually changed. As geologists, we also have evidence from many millennia and even millions of years under our belts, from periods of complete cycles of bitter cold to balmy warmth and back again to deep-freeze conditions.

Regardless of American energy policies and our greenhouse gas emissions, changes in climate—including both massive and moderate upheavals in temperature and precipitation—are going to be a part of Earth's future, just as they have been the bedrock of the past. That's why the public and American policymakers need to understand what geologists know of past climate changes. Failing to discuss the evidence of both massive and moderate natural climate change is like speeding downhill on a bicycle at fifty miles per hour while wearing a blindfold. We can, if we wish, spend the next minute tightening the strap on our helmet. But ripping off the blindfold seems a wiser first step toward giving us a chance of survival. And the only way to start to see around us clearly is to look at the record of what climate has done in Earth's past. Some of the facts we can draw out from the Earth's records are encouraging, while many are quite challenging. But it's surely better to be informed about how climate on Earth behaves than to willfully wear a blindfold at this critical crossroads of our history.

Please understand, geologists are not Luddites who say we should have no concern about our production of greenhouse gases, nor do we argue that what you've heard in the popular press about global warming is hogwash. But some of us believe you've been told only one isolated part of a much longer and richer climate story. To understand what might come next for climate—no matter our carbon policies or lack thereof—you need to understand what geologists know about Earth's past climates.

Here's a simple analogy: if you were facing a crippling medical condition, you might be well advised to seek the opinion of differently trained medical professionals—perhaps surgeons, internists, and pharmacists. In the same way, you are well advised to listen to what geologists—as well as climate and environmental scientists—have to say about Earth's recent temperature and precipitation changes. The framework of geological knowledge is different than that of many climate and environmental scientists, and the advice we offer may differ from that of our colleagues in these younger disciplines. It's not that any one group has a monopoly on everything that's valuable, any more than cardiologists are always right and internists are always useless. Rather, before you make decisions about a route to follow, it's to your advantage to be informed about the lay of the land around you.

At the end of the day, many geologists feel strongly that the best guide we have to the future is the evidence of the past. The Earth's past is the part of the picture that's most clear, providing the data that are least in dispute. The past is also the realm in which geologists excel; it's the part of the puzzle to which we've been devoted for many generations.

As it happens, many geologic principles can be quickly learned by amateurs. In just a few pages, this book will show you how geologists can literally see Earth's recent climates when we look out the window. You, too, can master this skill set, and you'll be able to understand the basic outline of climate, as Nature herself can show it to you around your house or during your summer vacation in the Rockies, New England, or around the Great Lakes. And I'll teach you what you need to know not through a list of facts, but by explaining the *story* of how geologists learned the basic principles that guide our science. In other words, this isn't a textbook, but a narrative, the story of what real-life geologists—complete with human limitations and foibles—learned as they examined the parts of the natural world influenced by climate change. It's an interesting detective story in its own right, but it will also give you the basic tools to see the climate evidence that, indeed, lies all around you.

Here's a warning: you may have to unlearn a couple of things you think you know. For example, many educated Americans live with the assumption that Earth's climate is quite static under natural conditions. The weather of our childhood, after all, felt like it was right and proper, the way the Earth was meant to be—and remain. But thinking of climate as a constant is grossly misguided. The weather of our childhood, in fact, was different from the weather endured by the passengers on the *Mayflower* and also different from that in which Viking raiders harassed the people of Europe a thousand years ago. The weather we knew when we were children—perfect and proper though it seemed—was but a single snapshot of the ceaseless and unfolding process of ongoing climate change.

The notion that climate should remain the same over time is at the core of much of the recent discussion in the public square. Change—including fully natural climate revolutions and more frequent and moderate climate shifts—is understandably frightening. We naturally shy away from it. That's why it's actually comforting to believe the message of extreme environmentalists in recent years. Their argument is that we humans are

in the process of destroying the world as we know it through our production of greenhouse gases, that we are the sole cause of current climate
change. From that premise it follows that if we slash emissions of carbon
dioxide greatly enough, climate will stop changing. That's actually *reassuring* compared to the view offered to us by the Earth herself. The fact
is, if human beings had remained hunter-gatherers throughout our entire
history, never producing a single molecule of greenhouse gases through
agriculture or industry, climate today would still be changing. It would be
lurching toward higher temperatures, crashing toward vastly colder temperatures, or at least swinging toward something different from what has
been. That's just the nature of Earth's climate. It's not to our liking, and
it's not to say we should do nothing about curtailing greenhouse gas emissions, but surely we must look the basic facts of natural change in the face
if we are to have useful policy debates in the public square.

Fortunately, most Americans have another and more useful childhood
touchstone for memories when it comes to climate. Many of us recall the
gist of books about the Ice Age that we read in grade-school libraries.
Those books were decorated with images of saber-toothed tigers, giant
ground sloths, and wooly mammoths. Behind a mammoth or two, in the
distance, there was likely to be a sketch of a great glacier, perhaps with fissures lacing its edges. The world, it was clear in the books, had once been
quite different, in terms of both climate and species.

Although such library treasures gave us some significant information
about climate, it's also true that there's much more that's now known to
science than the mere outline of the deep freeze you saw in grade school.
In the past twenty years, scientists have found a richly detailed record of
climate change in materials as humble as lakebed mud in North America
and as pristine as glacial ice in Greenland and Antarctica. That physical
record has shown us that major climate crashes are interspersed with
the history of milder fluctuations. But "milder" is a comment based on
the Earth's standards, not ours, because even milder changes have led to
famines.

Here's just one example: a dose of natural climate change once hit the
mightiest empire of the Bronze Age, the Egyptian kingdom of the River

Nile and its broad delta. Some 4,300 years ago (2300 BCE), Egyptian civilization was flourishing, built on agriculture enriched by organized irrigation, rather than just the scratch-in-the-dirt approach to farming. Egypt's agriculture had led to population growth, big cities with educated elites, and well-trained and equipped armies. But, quite out of the blue, natural climate change hit the Egyptian empire, and it hit hard.

It wasn't that temperatures changed much in North Africa but that precipitation patterns were altered. We have basic written accounts of this "small" change in climate—small by the Earth's standards. As one written account makes plain, the famine and cultural collapse triggered by this relatively mild climate shift was so great that wealthy families in Egypt ate their own children. Thus, rapid climate change quickly brought the superpower of the day to the point that parents resorted to cannibalism—just so the adults could survive a few more weeks.

While Egyptians were eating their offspring, climate change was affecting other parts of the Earth, too. In general, the higher latitudes of the planet are likely to experience more temperature changes during dynamic times. It is possible that global temperature changes—and their related precipitation changes in Egypt—were one part of what reshaped ecosystems in and around the arctic of that day. It was around that same point that the last, isolated bands of woolly mammoths disappeared from Wrangel Island, off the Siberian coast. The mammoths, that great symbol of the Ice Age in your childhood, had clung on for several thousand years after the enormous climate upheaval that occurred ten thousand years ago, but they didn't make it through the blip that hit them in the Bronze Age.

For animals and for people, Earth's climate is an adversary the like of which many policymakers and environmentalists have not yet dreamed. Natural climate change is the elephant in the room within our public discussion of climate. In our rush to start thinking about limiting our production of greenhouse gases—a goal we will surely undertake to some degree—we've unfortunately left behind the reality of the history of Earth's climate. Natural climate change is fearsome to contemplate, to be sure. But the time has come to acknowledge the geologic elephant that's standing so near us. While we cannot tame or control the beast, we owe it to ourselves to recognize the facts of what Earth's climate is like. Planning for and adapting to climate change is as worthy a goal as limiting greenhouse gases, once we acknowledge how frequent and profound natural climate change is. No matter our political commitments, we can all surely come to better policy judgments about energy and climate by acknowledging the facts regarding how climate behaves. Doing so would certainly be better than prolonging our collective denial of what we are up against.

Here's a first, preliminary sketch of what climate on Earth has been like in the period so crucial to us. Consider it an overview to the facts of life when it comes to climate on Earth, and rest assured this book will explain how this sketch is known to geologists from the same basic physical evidence you will learn to see for yourself in your own backyard.

In recent geologic history, climate has been characterized by long periods of bitter cold during which enormous glaciers covered half of North America. Huge volumes of glacial ice formed during these frigid times. Ice sheets buried almost all of Canada, reaching down into the American Great Plains. The northern parts of the Midwest, the northern strip of the Pacific Northwest, and most of New England were engulfed in ice for tens of thousands of years at a time. As far south as California, glaciers in Yosemite National Park slowly formed at high elevations and flowed downhill, creating the majestic landscape that tourists appreciate today. Even sea level was different during these times of bitter cold. Ocean levels were much lower because so much water was "locked up" on land in the glacial ice. One important effect of the low seas was that people, and animals like the brown bear, were able to walk to North America from the Siberian end of Asia—changing whole ecosystems as they did so.

The public knows of the events just sketched as the Ice Age. Geologists don't use the term *Ice Age* because the interval actually encompassed both ice-cold periods and some vastly warmer times. To geologists, then, *Ice Age* is misleading, so we call the period the Pleistocene (pronounced Plystow-seen) Epoch.[1]

Geologists have been studying the evidence of the Pleistocene's climate for upward of two hundred years. The subject is relatively easy for us to learn about because the glacial evidence lies at the surface of the Earth. Geologists have cataloged hundreds of thousands of pieces of evidence about the timing, movement, and extent of glaciers from around the world. The glaciers, obviously, tell us about precipitation and vastly colder temperatures. From basic evidence, geologists have constructed a detailed nomenclature that describes the many different times within the Pleistocene during which glaciers retreated, advanced again, and then melted away to nothing at all. In short, we have a clear and detailed picture of the worldwide extent of Pleistocene glaciation and various intermittent warm spells that occurred along the way. And, finally, we have a whole library of facts about how very different most of the Pleistocene's climate was compared to the time during which the whole history of human civilization unfolds.

Let's start at the beginning. The worldwide glaciers of the Pleistocene Epoch were born in severe cold about 1.8 million years ago. That date presents an immediate problem for communicating effectively with many people. While geologists are used to considering great expanses of time, it can be a challenge for others to think about ancient dates measured in millions of years. A simple analogy might help. Imagine an empty, one-hundred-yard football field. The length of the football field will give us a way of visualizing the time during which extreme climate change has played out. Now add to the image a single referee standing in the end zone. The end zone with the referee will mark the present day for our analogy. The Pleistocene Epoch begins at the opposite end of the football field, away from the referee. That's one hundred yards down the field, at the point representing approximately 1.8 million years ago in time.

Most of the whole football field corresponds to times of bitter cold—with enormous ice sheets covering Canada, New England, the upper Great Plains, and so forth. But the Pleistocene was not a time of only monotonous cold. In fact, it alternated between long periods of cold—lasting roughly 100,000 years—and short periods of considerably warmer times—lasting about 10,000 years. To visualize this, imagine starting at the distant end zone of the football field, at the start of the Pleistocene. We can count out 5.5 yards in the direction of the present day and the referee. That's the distance that corresponds to about 100,000 years. Those 5.5 yards represent times of cold and worldwide glaciers. But the next half of a yard—just 1.5 *feet*—is a warm time, with glaciers melting away to nothing. That thin, warm slice of time is similar to present-day Earth. Again, the warm period lasts for only half a yard, compared to the preceding 5.5 yards of bitter cold, and the warm times are followed by a return to a long period of cold.

The alternation of cold and warm periods repeats down the entire length of the football field. The cycle is always a *long* period of cold followed by a much *shorter* period of warmth. The exact time intervals are not the same with each cycle, but the basic pattern remains as we move toward the present day, where our referee stands.

The final few yards of the football field are particularly important to us. About 6.5 yards away from our end zone is the next-to-last warm time on the field. Glaciers melted back to nothing during this time. Conditions were a bit warmer than the present day. One geologic name for this time is the Eemian. (Geological science is full of difficult names, and often even has multiple names for what is essentially the same period of time. The Eemian has some other names, too, but they are even more challenging to read or say, so we will stick with the simplest option and call that time by one name, the Eemian.)

If we were transported back to the Eemian, we would feel pretty much at home as far as temperature and climate. If anything, the Eemian would feel one full notch warmer than what we are used to in the present—an example, if you will, of natural global warming. In addition to the warmer global conditions, however, what would likely strike us as most odd would be many enormous herbivores and carnivores, much larger than anything we know today. The Eemian, if you will, is much like what you learned as a child about the Ice Age in terms of many species of flora and fauna, but minus the ice and the cold temperatures.

The warm Eemian time lasts for about half a yard, as usual, after which the Earth returned to bitter cold, with glaciers advancing over continents. The cold continues for several yards on the football field. Then, just 1.5 feet from the end zone where the referee waits, we reach another enormous climate change. Temperatures warm and glaciers retreat radically.

It is in this balmy time, the last half yard on the football field, that something special happens. We don't know exactly why, but it is at this time that we humans change our way of living. Instead of just being hunter-gatherers, we start to deliberately plant and tend crops. We domesticate animals. Soon after those major milestones appear along the roadway of our common history, people make pots, weave cloth, and then record their thoughts with abstract symbols. After that, as you know, we are off to the races as civilized peoples all around the world.

Because of our accomplishments during this last, warm interval, scientists long ago gave this narrow slice of time at the end of the football field a special name: the Holocene Epoch (pronounced Hole-oh-seen).[2]

From the Earth's point of view, the Holocene is *no different at all* from other brief, warm intervals in the Pleistocene, like the first one we mentioned, all the way back near the far end zone of the field, or the Eemian, which is only 6.5 yards from the referee. So, calling the current warm times by a different epoch name is a clear mistake! It simply makes no sense as far as the Earth is concerned. Nevertheless, we gave these last few inches of the football field an exalted status and a new label because we are so enamored with civilization. And because the present warm time is known the world around as the Holocene Epoch, we will use the term in this book.

We've just sketched a whole football field's worth of massive climate changes that occur in a roughly cyclic pattern. But there are also smaller but still staggering climate shifts that occur *within* the long times of bitter cold or the brief times of warmth. That's an important point, because those changes are more numerous and more frequent than the megatrends we've just spread out onto the football field. And frequent changes, of course, are not a good thing for us people. Beyond all that, some of the changes are rapid—so fast we sometimes call them rapid climate change events or RCCEs (pronounced "Rickies"). If we asked our referee to mark RCCEs on the football field by putting down a flag for each one, we'd have to provide him with scores of marker flags—real work for him, and not a comfortable picture for us.

Another disturbing point you may have noted is that the Holocene has already run for about ten thousand years. That means the Holocene is already a bit longer than a good many of the warm times on the football field. Thus, if the Earth continues to behave as she has for the past two million years, we must expect a return to bitter cold at some point, with ice sheets that reach as far south as Nebraska once again. And, as scientists have recently learned, the change to that bitterly cold climate regime is likely to be fast, happening over the course of a generation or two.

That, as they say, is the bad news.

But facts are facts, and they are worth facing squarely rather than trying to ignore in the confusion of bad faith. And, as you know, modern civilization may be changing Earth's climate history by putting such a quantity of greenhouse gases in the air that we are altering climate. In that case, we ourselves may break the cycle represented by the football-field analogy of time. Our own activities may inadvertently help us to avoid a return to crushing cold. That, on the whole, would be a good thing, as cold would end agriculture in most of the world's breadbasket regions, resulting in the deaths of potentially billions of people.

But it's important to note that if we do change climate through our airborne effluents, such a result would be simply chance. We surely didn't produce industrial carbon dioxide with climate modification in mind. And if we raise Earth's temperature substantially, we shall have to adjust to what Earth's climate was like *before* the Pleistocene Epoch, when there were no glaciers at all, anywhere on the globe. Much of Earth history, in fact, has unfolded in exactly such a hot climate, so it would not be a "new day" from the point of view of the Earth. But our civilization would surely be severely challenged to adapt to pre-Pleistocene levels of warmth, just as it would be hard-pressed to adapt to a return to the Pleistocene's bitter cold.

The last possibility we must note for the future is that the sudden change in greenhouse gas concentrations we humans have produced could "push" the inherently fragile climate system too far, causing it to snap. An analogy sometimes used to illustrate this point goes like this: A profoundly drunk man is pretty likely to fall down as he walks home from the bars. We can wait for such an event, watching the drunk as he staggers and careens down the sidewalk, or we can increase the chance of his falling sooner rather than later by giving him a shove. In the terms of this analogy, climate careens around chaotically on its own. We humans were not responsible for the many times it has "fallen" into dramatic changes in the past. But by increasing greenhouse gas concentrations rapidly in a short period of time, we have "pushed the drunk." Climate may become a lot warmer in response to the spike in greenhouse gases we have created. But, as we shall see in this book, Earth's climate has many different elements that are always in play, influencing one another. Because of that, our emissions could actually make the climate stagger and fall in one of several different directions.

But while it makes sense to feel real concern about pushing the drunk, there is a framework to aid your thinking that geology can give you but that climate science simply lacks. Just for example, there is one special plea about carbon-dioxide production that geologists know well, a call to action we have long been making. We'll explore the idea more fully toward the end of this book, but here is the gist of it: we would readily eliminate a significant amount of carbon-dioxide production if we could put together an international effort to extinguish the almost-biblical plague of unwanted coal fires in mining districts around the world. Particularly in Asia, raging and smoldering coal fires both above and below the ground are a curse the world's poor endure each day. Most people don't even know these fires exist, but geologists do—we live and work in the mines with miners—and from Pennsylvania to Alaska in the United States, as well as in mining districts abroad, these smoldering fires are common.

Just as Americans put out the petroleum-well fires of Kuwait at the end of the First Gulf War, we could extinguish many or most of the world's unwanted coal fires, doing both local residents and Earth's climate a major favor. Such work would be vastly cheaper than decreasing carbon-dioxide emissions by putting solar panels on roof tops or sequestering carbon underground next to coal-fired electrical plants. You must allow a geologist a direct appeal that we immediately address the coal-fire problem, for we could benefit the globe at a tiny fraction of the cost of other ways of limiting greenhouse gas production. That's the kind of practical thinking you can get from geologists, and it's one of the reasons you need to hear from us, not just from climate scientists making computer models.

One truth above all stands out in geology. *If we think of climate change as our enemy, we will always be defeated.* That's because climate will always evolve, lurching to new warmer states or crashing into much colder ones. To geologists, it's death, taxes, and climate change that are the true constants of life on Earth. Our goal should not be to hold climate static, but to understand its fully natural but menacing and manic moods. Above all, we must adapt to climate. Included in that adaptation, of course, should be limiting human activities that provoke climate—like pouring greenhouse gases into the skies. But it's also true that we must be honest with ourselves, knowing that the climate of Earth will always change for fully natural reasons regardless of our energy choices. That kind of honesty should allow us to temper at least some of our climate and energy policies in light of their great costs to our economy. It behooves us, therefore, to keep our economy running as best we can so that we can afford to make the transition to a necessarily uncertain future.

And there is much climate science the public has not heard about. One recent hypothesis from an eminent climate scientist deserves special mention because it has not received nearly the attention in the media that the Intergovernmental Panel on Climate Change reports have—but it's actually much more fundamental and significant to our situation. There is plausible evidence that man-made climate change may not be new at all. The hypothesis now being vetted in the climate-science community is that human activities throughout thousands of years of the Holocene have changed climate—essentially fending off a return to giant glaciers here in North America. The argument is that human agriculture—even early farming done with slash-and-burn techniques and hand tools—was enough to increase the two principal greenhouse gases so that we crossed just over a critical climate threshold. Due to these agriculture effects over thousands of years, the argument goes, we've stayed just warm enough that glacial ice masses have not been able to re-form in Canada. We'll address that argument in a special chapter of this book, both because it's so significant in itself and because it's a good example of how science—at its best— unfolds through evidence and argumentation.

Through it all, this book will make clear to you the major assumptions that lie behind all climate predictions—the beliefs about what will happen next that may collapse when the Earth turns yet another small corner in the geologic history of climate. The past is our best guide to the future, and the past is the realm of geology. Personally, I can see the evidence of bitter cold winds of the Pleistocene just outside my house's windows in rural Washington State, and by the time you finish reading this book, you'll understand a great deal about the evidence of geologically recent and dramatic climate change, too; the evidence is available for your inspection from New England to New York and across the Midwest, from the plains of Nebraska to Colorado and Wyoming, and also in such places as the Sierra Nevada of California. If evidence matters to your view of the world, let me show you abundant and clear evidence of natural climate change, all of which is part of the framework needed for understanding recent climate shifts.

We humans can successfully move forward in the face of both natural and man-made climate change. But to do so intelligently and effectively, we must understand and acknowledge the dynamic nature of climate. Let us begin, then, with the story of how geologists learned about the Ice Age that came before the balmier times in which we now live.

2

THE ICE TIME

L ouis Agassiz stands at one of the great transitions in intellectual history, the time in the early 1800s when men called "naturalists" could still comment on a wide range of questions in areas we think of today as biology, geology, chemistry—and even theology. After Agassiz's era came the "scientists," professionals much more neatly divided into groups by discipline and specialization, fully separated from each other and much more divorced from religion. But in Agassiz's day, a wide range of different types of evidence and reasoning could still be pursued by a single individual, an approach that initially helped Agassiz's understanding of major climate change even as it ultimately crippled parts of his thinking.

It was a chance holiday that led Agassiz to recognize evidence of the Ice Age. But chance only favors the fertile mind, and Agassiz was most certainly blessed with the right intellect to make great strides in understanding the natural world when the opportunity arose. Agassiz's normal daily toil in his native Switzerland was demanding work examining fossils in dim rooms that taxed his mind and eroded his poor eyesight. He knew he needed a holiday each year from such labor, and so he chose to spend a few weeks outside in the summer of 1836, walking in the high meadows of the Swiss mountains. But summer holidays don't always proceed as planned, and what Agassiz saw high in the mountains changed the trajectory of his professional life because it taught him about thoroughly radical and quite recent global climate change.

Even prior to that significant summer, Agassiz was well on his way to becoming an early Stephen Hawking of science. Though young, he was already known to all the naturalists of his era because of his work on the fossil record of life on Earth. Agassiz and other naturalists around Europe were just learning to deduce the grand story of life, the history that leads from simple organisms in the sea to complex fish and then amphibians crawling forth on the land. After that, in quicker succession, come reptiles, dinosaurs, birds, and the eventual stunning successes of our own group, the mammals. Agassiz had the deep joy of discovering the story of life not from lines written in books, but from exquisitely preserved fossils that directly recorded the exotic and intriguing species of the past.

One pivotal group in the early history of life is the fish, and the thousands of species of ancient fish were the subject on which Agassiz was focused in the 1830s. Fish were the world's first highly successful group of vertebrates, and fish led in life's story to amphibians, the first large animals to live on land. Agassiz had set himself the task of finding whole fossil fish in stones from a variety of points in the geologic past. Part of his work was to correctly intuit where and how the fish fossils lay inside the stone that had preserved them for ages. He then broke the fragile fossils free of the surrounding rock and caught the first glimpse of ancient life, preserved for eons as if for Agassiz himself.

The work with hammer and chisel wasn't a simple exercise, nor did the newly exposed fossils speak to a linear history. Instead, naturalists like Agassiz learned of many odd and highly varied fish, like the jawless fish that had first arisen in the ancient seas and the fierce-looking armored fish that came later and were built more like tanks than like a familiar trout.

Agassiz was entirely devoted to his work with fossils. Once, quite famously, he faced a particularly difficult fossil, entombed within a stone. He could see just a small amount of the animal at one end of the broken rock. The question was where and how the rest of it lay within the stone. If he guessed wrong, Agassiz would destroy the fossil with the hammer blow meant to liberate it.

Agassiz's intuition of how that ancient fish lay within the stone was literally the best guess of anyone in the world at the time. But, from the small parts of the fish he could see, he knew it was an unusual fossil, and Agassiz hesitated before the block of rock. For days, the fish was on his mind, but he dared not take a chisel to the stone. Then, he dreamed of the fossil fish and sketched the specimen as soon as he woke, so vivid was the picture in his mind. Guided by his drawing, he successfully brought the fossil out of the enclosing rock, showing the world a specimen that fully matched the one his unconscious mind had generated for him in the sketch.

Agassiz was part of the first wave of naturalists to seriously study fossils, and he found the labor fruitful and gratifying. With the passing of each dark winter month in Switzerland, Agassiz made significant progress in a field that combines the best of the geological and the biological sciences. His fame grew across Europe as he published his findings in major tomes. When his books became known in the New World as well as the Old, the name Agassiz became synonymous with the study of nature literally around the world.

But spending year after year studying, cataloging, and drawing fossil fish is enough to wear down even the most dedicated and ambitious young professional. So when the chance arose in 1836 for Agassiz to take a summer walking tour in the Swiss countryside, he wisely took the opportunity afforded him. The intense work of explaining in detail the history of life on Earth could wait, after all, for the next long and dark Swiss winter.

If there is one supreme reason to visit Switzerland at the height of summer, it's to walk on the roof of Europe and see the glaciers that decorate the tops of Swiss mountains. On a warm July day, walking on the glaciers themselves is a diverting excursion. Crevasses and scattered boulders are hazards on the course, but blue glacial ice underfoot and stunningly deep valleys thousands of feet below combine to make the spirits soar. Agassiz, who was trained to carefully study the world around him, found much to intrigue him regarding the glaciers. Like other naturalists, he hadn't thought a great deal about the history of Earth's climate up to that point. But the full significance of global temperature change hit him before his summer walking tour was done.

Prior to the 1830s, most naturalists had paid no more attention to high-alpine glaciers than a farmer might pay to an annoying snow bank that lingers in the spring on the north slope of a field. Pretty much all that was known about glaciers was that they were icy and that, in some years, a particular glacier might come a bit farther down a mountain slope than in other years. Glaciers in July looked to most people like cold, static bits of nature of no more interest than a lump of slush along the gutter of a city street in January. Agassiz shared the common view of glaciers before his holiday in the mountains. Fortunately, however, he didn't have a common mind.

As a native of the area, Agassiz was well familiar with the geography around him that summer. He had fished in the long, narrow lakes that occupy the region's deep valleys. An outdoor enthusiast since his earliest boyhood, he knew the basic geology of the rocks of the Alps and the Jura Mountains—the latter being the source of fossils that gave its name to the Jurassic Period of geologic history. Agassiz also knew—and had summarily rejected—the notion that his friend Jean de Charpentier advanced: that Switzerland had once been engulfed in thick, glacial ice during an epoch of endless winter. Indeed, it was in part to refute his friend's heretical idea that Agassiz had agreed to the summer walking tour in 1836. What could be better for an ambitious young man than having a break from fossils, taking in the beauties of the high elevations, and correcting the errors of a fellow naturalist, all at the same time?

De Charpentier's hypothesis about an ice-engulfed world was easy to scorn because it called for a radically colder climate on Earth in the geologic past. Agassiz—like virtually all the rest of humanity—thought that idea was simply impossible. There could be no real reason, he was sure, for considering the Earth's climate to be so capricious and once so very cold. He wanted to see his friend's reputed evidence, simply to find another way of explaining the rocks and meadows of the high elevations.

But as Agassiz discovered that summer, once you seriously start to look at a glacier and its surroundings, your eyes adjust to seeing a fully different Earth. The alternative world before you is built on a grander scale than you're used to, so seeing the bigger picture is a breathtaking transformation of perspective in itself. Beyond that—in a flash—the visual evidence requires that you accept the reality of staggering climate change. If you aren't used to manic highs, there's nothing like fieldwork in the geologic sciences to get you to a state very near them, and Agassiz quickly found his way to this new and quite different perspective.

The flash to the bigger picture is still the reason why college students taking a freshman geology class today sometimes fall into the thrall of their instructors—at least while pictures of beautiful glaciers and landscapes are shown on the screen at the front of the lecture room. And as certain hikers in the Rockies or visitors to northern national parks know at a visceral level, the Ice Age wasn't long ago at all, and it can literally be seen all around us. Epiphanies exist in science as surely as in emotional life, and glacial landscapes lead many people to wonderful visions of the wide sweep in space and time of major geologic processes. And at the core of both high-alpine beauty and ranger lectures in national parks is the simple idea that climate has been radically different, and quite recently so.

Agassiz's first step toward his new perspective was learning to actually see a glacier for what it is: a body of ice that's on the move. De Charpentier showed Agassiz clear evidence of glacial flow by taking him to a large boulder at rest on the ice. It was a massive stone, partly submerged in the glacier, and its elevation on the mountain in previous years had been noted. The boulder in the summer of 1836 was hundreds of feet farther down the valley than where it had been. On another glacier was an old hut built years before at a particular elevation. It, too, had moved hundreds of feet down the valley from where it had rather recently been. Thus it was that Agassiz understood the first point of evidence: glaciers are icy rivers that flow more slowly than a stream, but that flow downhill just as surely. And glaciers also carry quite a bit of material with them as they move.

In later summers Agassiz was the first person to ever measure exactly how glaciers flow. He drove a series of stakes directly across a Swiss glacier, from one side of a valley to the other, across the glacial ice in between. As the years went by, the stakes near the center of the glacier moved farthest down valley. Those at the edge of the glacier moved hardly at all. Those in between filled in an arc, bowed on the downhill side, showing that the ice in the center of the glacier moved downhill more quickly than the ice nearer the valley walls.

We moderns say that the lower and middle portions of the glacier flow *plastically*. They deform and flow like Silly Putty®, moving slowly but flowing as surely as a stream. But if a glacier is flowing down a Swiss valley, why doesn't the river of ice reach the plains below? Agassiz wrestled with that question in the several years to come after his first foray into the mountains. He studied the *termini* of glaciers—the places where glaciers end at their lowest elevation.

A glacier's terminus is marked by two things: a jumble of rocks melting out of the disappearing ice, and, at least in the summer, a rushing stream of meltwater. Sometimes, as Agassiz found, the terminus is marked by quite a high mound of rock rubble. Such mounds, he realized, are an indication the ice has been melting in the same basic location for several years, with the imbedded stones transported every year to the very end of the glacier and left at the terminus in the mounds of ever-increasing size. In other places in the high Swiss valleys, Agassiz learned to recognize the signs of recent glacial advances that had bulldozed through the old terminus and started the process of establishing a new one at lower elevations. And, on the other hand, some terminal mounds had been left stranded in a valley, a hundred feet or more lower than the modern glacier's terminus as the ice retreated up valley, year by year.

Agassiz came to understand that the terminus of a glacier marks the spot where the rate of ice melt catches up with the rate of ice flow coming down from higher elevations in the valley. The glacier, we could say in industrial terms, is a bit like an icy conveyer belt, carrying stones downhill. The stones are left where the belt system ends because the ice simply melts away in the summer sun.

One lesson that was clear to Agassiz about the terminal end of glaciers is worth bearing in mind today when images of melting glaciers are flashed across television or movie screens. The great melt off at a glacier terminus is impressive, especially in July, with meltwater streams gushing forth from the blue ice. Even more dramatically, glacial ice that reaches the sea "calves" off into icebergs at its terminus. But *such processes are fully natural* and have been going on throughout the whole life of the glacier. When glacial ice reaches the terminus, it stops flowing and melts away or calves off. That's the natural end of all glaciers, but it's one that can be exploited for significant visual effect for those with a bent to do so, which is something to bear in mind.

Agassiz rapidly came to understand that the individual stones that had been embedded in Swiss glaciers—the materials in the rubble that made up the terminus—were not like stones in streams in the plains below. The glacial stones were generally angular in shape rather than round, and they bore characteristic scratches on their faces. Modern backpackers and mountaineers immediately recognize both the angular shape and the grooved scratches on such rocks as characteristic of what is underfoot at high elevations everywhere around the world, from the Alps to the Andes. It is such scratched, angular rocks that make up the material in a glacier's terminus. The mound or heap of such material is known as a terminal *moraine* of the glacier. And, as Agassiz could plainly see, there are other types of moraines, too. Along the sides of many glaciers are long ridges or mounds extending down valley, parallel to glacial ice. They are made up of similar material as the terminal moraine, namely angular stones adorned with many scratches. These ridges are known as *lateral* moraines, suggesting their origin along the sides of glaciers. The stones in such moraines happened to be pushed to the edge of the glacier, where they have accumulated. They remain high on the valley walls until a time when the glacier grows substantially and engulfs them, moving them in the ice once more downhill toward the terminus.

Once Agassiz understood glaciers as rivers of ice with their own rules for moving and amassing stones, the lessons of geology came thick and fast. The scratches in the stones were evidence that the rocks in the glacial ice sometimes ground against bedrock below. The scratches on the individual stones were in random and varied orientation because the rocks had rotated many times as they were carried down the valley in the river of ice. The scratches in underlying bedrock, however, were all lined up, parallel to the axis of the valley, recording the direction of the glacial ice moving downhill. The glacier might flow like Silly Putty, but this was plastic flow that had serious teeth in it—teeth made up of stones ranging from the size of a grain of sand to the size of a small house.

Next Agassiz noted that some outcrops of bedrock had the parallel scratches but were also, on a greater scale, polished quite smooth. In other words, if you look closely at rocks in glacial landscapes you are impressed with their small grooves and scratches. But if you stand back, you see that for many feet in all directions, the bedrock has an undulating, smooth surface. Sometimes, at the right angle and in the summer sun, the surface is actually shiny like a mirror. It's as if the natural bedrock is like the polished marble blocks found in a bank building. On that polished surface, there can be some small scratches, but they don't negate the fact that, on a larger scale, the rock is smooth.

Looking at the glacial ice around him, Agassiz saw that a great deal of the rocky material in a glacier is quite small, nothing more than fine sand and silt particles. This, he reasoned, was the type of material that could smooth bedrock into a polished surface as a glacier moves over the rock below. Large particles in the ice might also scratch the same surface at some point. In other words, the glaciers represented a natural system that was sanding down the mountains of Switzerland, both polishing and scratching them. So substantial was the total erosional force of the glaciers that they had, over time, carved the stunningly deep valleys of Agassiz's home, all of which he saw with new eyes that fine summer of 1836.

A further point about the landscape also became clear. Switzerland's famous mountain peaks are composed of several distinct rock types. Agassiz could quickly see that isolated boulders in the lowlands looked like they were made of the same type of rock of certain distant peaks. The boulders range in size from those about the size of a cow to a few that are the size of a house. The rocks are called *erratic boulders*, and Agassiz saw that no simple stream could have washed the boulders to the lowlands where they rested. Streams don't move boulders the size of buildings, but rivers of ice can carry large boulders in them, as Agassiz had seen at higher elevations. It was quite evident to the naturalist that ancient rivers of ice had once carried the great rocks miles away from their places of origin high in the Swiss peaks.

Another point about the landscape that was suddenly explicable to Agassiz was a particular joy to him. He had grown up as a youthful angler in the many lakes of his homeland—an activity that later led to his interest in fossil, as well as modern, fish. The deep valleys of Switzerland host many long and narrow lakes, and Agassiz realized that what was holding many of the lakes in place were dams made up of old terminal moraines. Such moraines, cutting across valleys, are natural dams. After the retreat of the local glacier, with water flowing down valley in streams, long and narrow lakes can naturally form. Thus it was that ancient rivers of ice and modern streams and lakes began to be twined together in Agassiz's fertile mind.

Another delight is that the lake water itself in glacial landscapes holds evidence of the erosion of the mountains around them. High, glacial lakes are an opaque, turquoise-blue color in the summer—a favorite of modern photographers and the makers of postcards and inspirational wall posters. Because opaque water is not terribly appealing for drinking, however, hikers the world around learn a trick to clear the water. When making a camp at high elevations next to a glacial lake, experienced backpackers immediately scoop up a pot of lake water and let it sit undisturbed. In a few hours, the water's opaque quality diminishes as tiny rock particles— known to hikers and geologists alike as "rock flour"—settle out of the still water in the pan and form a layer on the bottom. The rock flour is suspended while it's in the lake because wind and waves keep the water stirred. It is the suspended tiny fragments of rock that interact with sunlight to produce the unique turquoise color of high glacial lakes. The rock-flour is direct evidence of the pulverizing, erosional force of glaciers. The rock-flour layer in the bottom of a hiker's pan is a tiny volume of what had once been the bedrock of the mountain, material turned to tiny grains by glacial ice grinding over the Earth through great stretches of geologic time.

Once Agassiz truly saw the picture of how the glaciers moved, what moraines and erratics signified, and what the scratches on the polished bedrock meant, he understood glaciers as a prime agent of erosion on Earth. That, in itself, was a great advance for geological science. But Agassiz's most significant insight was yet to come. Quite quickly, he began to look in the Swiss valleys much, much lower than in the neighborhood of the modern glaciers. It was as if his eyes were newly opened, and what he saw changed his understanding of climate immediately.

Agassiz found the now-familiar parallel scratches in polished bedrock dozens of miles below the glaciers of the peaks. He also found the same grooves on the smoothed bedrock of the walls of the valley, standing many hundreds of feet higher than the valley floor. Both lateral and terminal moraines, in just the same way, were in evidence many miles below the modern glaciers or high on the valley walls, and glacial erratics existed at low elevations. Once his eyes were opened to this simple evidence of past glacial action, Agassiz again and again saw the clear natural record left by ancient glaciers on a much greater scale than those of modern Switzerland.

The inference was as immediate as it was significant: at one time, vastly greater and thicker glaciers had filled high Swiss valleys, extending down to low elevations and spilling out onto plains. That could mean only that summers in some past time were extremely short, perhaps barely warm at all, and certainly fleeting. In those ancient times, glacial ice simply did not melt at any of the elevations where Agassiz saw it melting in his day. In other words, the climate of the past was dominated by long periods of cold more bitter than anything even a wizened resident of the Alps had ever experienced.

The evidence was plain, and Agassiz was fully convinced of it. Soon he was telling his friends about what he had seen. Like all enthusiasts, he made some converts and alienated some other people. But he never looked back in his evangelism. He preached the news of climate change as he understood it and invited a number of colleagues to join him in studying glaciers the following summers. Many naturalists of the day took him up on the offer, and most were converted to his basic viewpoint in short order.

In the coming summers, Agassiz and company built a lean-to shelter on a glacier, using a giant boulder to serve as one wall of the structure, and they all went to work to better understand everything from the slow flow of glacial ice downhill to the patterns of meltwater that emerge from the terminus of a glacier each summer. They poured colored water into crevasses and noted where the color emerged farther down the glacier, and they measured the temperature of the ice at various points in the moving mass. Agassiz himself boldly dropped down on a rope into a great crevasse, exploring firsthand the body of the glacier to a depth of 120 feet. That journey, which most certainly put his life at risk because crevasses can close just as easily as they can open, showed exactly how determined the great naturalist was to learn about the newly discovered agent of erosion that testified so clearly to past climates. In short, Agassiz, who personally led all the summer expeditions to the Swiss glaciers, established himself as Europe's foremost authority on glaciers just as he was the clear authority on fossil fishes.

Oddly, Agassiz did miss one significant feature of glaciers that he literally stepped over time and time again. Glaciers are ice that's created from enormous quantities of compacted snow layers. Many glaciers show these former snow layers as distinct layers in the glacial ice itself. The ice layers are visible in many crevasses, but Agassiz apparently didn't think them significant. Much later in the history of science, as we shall see, the distinct layers of glacial ice gave us a clear annual record of climate change. In Agassiz's day the lessons of glaciers were much more general, simply speaking to the fact that the Earth had once known a vastly colder climate.

Agassiz publicly named the bitter climate of the past the *Eiszeit*, or Ice Age. That evocative name is the same phrase schoolchildren today use to describe the time in which the woolly mammoth and the saber-toothed tiger lived. But acceptance of Agassiz's basic insights did not come immediately, and the great naturalist himself was wrong about many aspects of the Eiszeit.

The notion of an Ice Age ran into stiff opposition from most naturalists of the day in part because it appeared to contradict so much of the fossil record of life. Most fossils—like the giant fern leaves in coal beds in Scandinavia or the great swimming and flying reptiles of the Jurassic period, named for the Jura Mountains—seemed to speak of a warmer, not a colder, climate during Earth's past. For ferns to grow in northern latitudes, or for great cold-blooded animals to ply the seas, clearly required that the world must have been a much warmer place in the past. All educated naturalists—including Agassiz—agreed on the basic idea that Earth's past was mostly much warmer than the present.

It's easy for us moderns to accept the two-part idea that ancient geologic history could have been warmer, while more recent Eiszeit times were bitterly cold. That framework of climate change is taught today to most schoolchildren, who learn about the warmer Earth of the dinosaurs versus that bitter cold of the globe in the era of the woolly mammoths. But such a view makes climate look much more variable than many naturalists of the 1830s could accept. It was one thing to picture the world as gradually, over millions of years, cooling from tropical warmth everywhere to more modern and temperate times. It was quite another to think of Europe as blessed with tropic warmth for ages, then plunged into bitter cold, and then resurrected to moderate warmth.

As Agassiz's fellow naturalists told him in no uncertain terms, the Eiszeit hypothesis raised a host of unanswerable questions. Why should Earth's climate change, and change once more, oscillating through geologic time in unpredictable ways? If one accepted the Eiszeit hypothesis, what would be next—claims for more radical climate shifts in one direction or another every time somebody turned over a rock? Surely, if climate could be stood on its head, then everything else we know about the world could be undermined as well.

Most naturalists in Europe thought that the evidence that Agassiz had recorded in such detail in the mountains showed only that climate *in Switzerland* had once been colder. Perhaps, for some reason connected with wind patterns or weather fronts, the Swiss mountains had for a time been quite a bit colder. But that didn't imply that the rest of Europe had experienced bitter cold, let alone the rest of the world. It was better to explain Swiss evidence as a local phenomenon, not something of global significance at all, argued Agassiz's many critics.

It didn't help matters that, in the hot light of the enthusiasm brought on by his alpine epiphanies, Agassiz made some pretty wild claims about the Ice Age. The Eiszeit, he wrote, was a time in which a vast glacier covered most of Europe, extending all the way from Scandinavia to the Mediterranean Sea. Agassiz had, in fact, never seen the Mediterranean, nor is there any evidence of ancient glaciers around it—no polished bedrock with parallel scratches in it, no moraines, no erratics, no tangible evidence of any kind of glacial activity. Agassiz's blunders, of course, opened all his ideas to blistering criticism.

Significant scorn as well as criticism was heaped on Agassiz's head for a number of years. The idea of radical climate change made many naturalists angry as well as skeptical. Some of Agassiz's counterparts actually interrupted his talk at a professional meeting, shouting out their objections and disrupting his presentation. That's an unusual event in professional life, in particular for science professionals. But Agassiz was sure he was right, and the power of his convictions sustained him through the significant disrespect and even outright scorn of some of his colleagues.

Agassiz's basic idea of the Eiszeit would have been a little easier to swallow if naturalists in the 1830s had had a clear understanding of the Earth's polar regions. One reason that American schoolchildren (and their parents) blithely accept the teachings of library books today about the Ice Age is that in modern times we have some pretty clear analogies for what Agassiz's Eiszeit was like. Indeed, most explanations of the Ice Age in schoolbooks refer to the great ice sheets of Greenland and Antarctica to sketch what much of the world was like millennia ago.

But naturalists of the 1830s had no clear descriptions of Greenland or Antarctica. Although men in Viking long boats and sailors in much later whaling vessels had doubtless glimpsed the coasts of Greenland near its midsection, brief visions of ice through the summer fog didn't equate to scientific observation. And there was simply no mechanism for transferring fragmentary knowledge from the hardy northerners who made brief sightings of Greenland's ice to naturalists living back in the heart of civilization.

In short, Agassiz could accept the notion of a Europe buried under a vast glacier, but his critics could not. They couldn't reason by analogy with Greenland simply because no one had clear knowledge of it, and they continued to tell Agassiz he was mistaking some kind of local climate phenomenon for a much larger one.

Not surprisingly, Louis Agassiz took to the roads of Europe in the 1840s both to look for evidence of the Eiszeit beyond the borders of Switzerland and to convert his international colleagues by personally explaining his arguments to them. Luckily for Agassiz, he went north, rather than south, from his home, and that meant his travels took him to regions that had been well and truly glaciated. His most important European foray, by far, was the one that took him to Great Britain. In Scotland and Wales he immediately found the familiar evidence of glaciers, this time in mountains where no modern glaciers exist. The polished bedrock with parallel grooves in Wales and the moraines flung across Scottish valleys all spoke clearly of the Eiszeit in Agassiz's mind. He recognized that some of the lochs in Scotland came from the same set of circumstances, which explained the narrow lakes that filled Swiss valleys. In short, even without active glaciers in the area, much of the British Isles showed clear evidence of the Eiszeit, just like his homeland.

Agassiz also made great headway in Britain on the human side of science. His observations and arguments won the Eiszeit converts, including the allegiance of the naturalist William Buckland. Buckland taught many budding young scholars at Oxford, and his belief in the Ice Age shaped the following generation of scientists in Britain. And, as a jewel added to the crown of the Agassiz visit, Buckland convinced the most significant naturalist of the day, Charles Lyell, of the reality of the Ice Age, using rocks near Lyell's own home.

As Buckland then wrote to Agassiz, "Lyell has adopted your theory *in toto*!!! On my showing him a beautiful cluster of moraines within two miles of his father's house, he instantly accepted it, as solving a host of difficulties which have all his life embarrassed him."[1]

It was a significant conversion, although not as complete as Buckland thought that day. Lyell waffled a bit for a number of years about the significance of glaciers, but he did understand the importance of the Eiszeit hypothesis from that day onward and ultimately he became thoroughly convinced of it. Lyell's conversion was important because Lyell was the towering giant among British naturalists, the man to whom everyone in Britain's scientific circles looked for intellectual leadership. That point is shown by the fact that a young naturalist named Charles Darwin, when he could take only a few books with him on his round-the-world voyage on the HMS *Beagle*, chose to take the Bible and Lyell's book on geology. Converting Lyell to belief in the Eiszeit marked the turning of the tide that had been running against Agassiz and his hypothesis about radical climate change.

Naturalists, just like the professional scientists who followed in their footsteps, loved to resolve tenacious problems. The Eiszeit hypothesis could do just that, which is why Buckland and ultimately Lyell valued it so highly. As one example of the problem-solving power of the Eiszeit line of thought, we'll consider an ancient natural puzzle in Scotland that Agassiz was able to almost instantly resolve. The matter concerned a set of three perfectly parallel indentations in the walls of a certain valley. The parallel markings had puzzled Lyell, Darwin, and many others for as long as the history of British intellectual life records.

The three parallel markings are on the sides of Glen Roy in Scotland. If you stand at the bottom of the treeless valley (or glen), you are struck by the perfectly level markings on the valley wall above and around you. The indentations extend for as far as the eye can see—and that's a long way in the desolation of rural Scotland. Each of the three markings runs at one distinct elevation, without any ups or downs. The three markings are known as the "parallel roads" of Glen Roy because they look like roads laid out by the strictest of surveyors, each set to run at one—and only one—elevation, each cut into the walls of the glen.

The only agent that can make perfectly level markings on the land is a body of standing water. Both lakes and seas are well-known agents for cutting indentations into land, due to waves that dig into a hillside and mark the even and level shoreline extending at one and only one elevation for miles. And, indeed, the "roads" of Glen Roy are sandy, fitting with the notion that they were once the shoreline of some body of water. So far, so good. Evidently, the water responsible for the temporary beaches was at three different elevations over time, with each water level existing for long enough to allow waves to cut into the land and form a sandy stringer.

The valley or glen of the parallel markings opens onto another valley. That is, Glen Roy with its parallel and level hillside beaches leads to another and larger glen. The great puzzle that had stood unanswered for centuries was why the parallel shorelines of Glen Roy end abruptly near the mouth of that smaller glen. They simply stop, as if the body of water that once stood there had existed in some odd kind of half form, unlike a lake or sea that naturally has a shoreline running all the way around it.

One way to phrase the question behind the puzzle of Glen Roy is this: What could have created a deep lake in the valley, and done so in quite recent geologic time, and only created shorelines we can see on certain sides of that ancient lake? Let me put the matter in terms that help lead today's freshman geology students to the answer, and that also reflect the same kind of reasoning employed by Agassiz to solve the riddle. Rephrased in this manner, the question becomes: What natural agent could have dammed Glen Roy and some other glens nearby and then later simply vanished into the air? The answer is glacial ice. The Glen Roy markings, Agassiz argued, are a clue to the power of glacial ice to do more than simply wear down mountains, but to also create deep lakes held in place by ice dams.

Agassiz reported his solution to the puzzle of Glen Roy as soon as he saw the "parallel roads" and their setting. He did so via a letter to Professor Robert Jameson of Scotland, with whom he'd had contact in his travels in the area. As it happened, an issue of Scotland's most significant scientific publication had just been printed. Wanting to get the news of the solution out to the wider world as soon as he could, Jameson convinced a major newspaper in Scotland to run the story of how Agassiz's Eiszeit so elegantly solved what had been a puzzle for British naturalists that had stood for centuries. Both Lyell and his younger sidekick, Darwin, were convinced of Agassiz's explanation as soon as they heard of it through the press. Once the reality of the Eiszeit is accepted and a person learns to see long-vanished glaciers on the landscape, much that had been inexplicable can indeed be understood.

In short, Agassiz's journey to Great Britain was fully as rewarding to him and his hypothesis of radical climate change as it possibly could have been.

In 1846 Agassiz traveled much father from home, this time to North America. Once again, by chance, he had the good fortune to head into glacial lands. With his characteristic enthusiasm for the Eiszeit, as soon as he arrived by ship at Halifax, he began looking for the Ice Age in the New World.

As he wrote: "I sprang on shore and started at a brisk pace for the heights above the landing. . . . I was met by the familiar signs, the polished surfaces, the furrows and scratches, the line engravings of the glacier."[2]

Next, continuing on to Boston, Agassiz found more of the same. Indeed, all of New England soon revealed itself to Agassiz's eye as one great moraine after another, with erratic boulders and other glacial evidence of all types stretching across the land from Maine south to Manhattan. And, gratifyingly, American naturalists hailed Agassiz's icy vision. So great was the opinion of so many Americans, in fact, that the Swiss naturalist soon became a professor at Harvard. When, a few years later, he made an expedition around Lake Superior, which was then an outpost in the American northwest, he again found evidence of glaciers all around him. Agassiz and his Eiszeit were even more triumphant in the New World than they had been in the Old.

So it was that in a short, twenty-year period, Louis Agassiz had established that glaciers had once buried much of Europe and a good measure of North America. It was a major accomplishment, built on his gift for observation and inference, his ability to hold fast to his vision despite intense attacks from colleagues, and his good fortune in traveling to lands that had, in fact, been extensively glaciated. Just two decades after that first telling summer in Switzerland, glacial ice was widely understood by many to have once been the dominant feature of the surface of the Earth from the midlatitudes northward. The Eiszeit had been proven real, evident to anyone with the basic training to see it, and it was apparently the result of substantial climate change on a global scale.

In addition to his other gifts, Agassiz had the ability to popularize science. In America he delighted crowds from Boston to the Carolinas with a series of lectures that explained the basics of the fossil record, as it was then known, and also taught people about the Pleistocene Ice Age. Living in an era when natural history museums were starting to flourish in Europe, Agassiz founded the Museum of Comparative Zoology at Harvard, an institution that still delights crowds with fossils from all parts of geologic history, including the time that glacial ice enveloped so much of the Earth.

But Agassiz himself didn't fare well as a research scientist from about the time of his trip to Lake Superior onward. He had key ideological commitments that precluded his scientific usefulness for the rest of the many years he lived in New England. He believed—as a theological matter more than a scientific one—that God was the cause of the Ice Age and that the Lord himself had sent the glaciers over the land to wipe out all traces of life. The woolly mammoth, the saber-toothed tiger, and even humble worms at the equator, from Agassiz's point of view, all perished in what he came to believe was a rapid descent into a deep freeze so profound that nothing at all survived. That hypothesis helped Agassiz make sense of his religious commitments, which we won't summarize here, but it ended his usefulness in investigating the Eiszeit. Thus the torch of research was passed to other men, including Lyell, still in England, and it fell to them to deduce what actually happened in the Ice Age.

Happily, with hardly a hiccup, the basic facts of Earth's climate in the Ice Age soon became integrated with the standard geologic timescale that Lyell had worked out for the Earth. The Ice Age occurred in what Lyell— using the evolving history of fossils as his guide—called the Pleistocene Epoch. The Pleistocene is the next-to-the-last epoch in all Earth history, the one that came immediately before our own, the Holocene.

In the analogy of Earth time as a football field, which we explored in the first chapter, the Pleistocene accounts for almost all the yardage on the field. Despite Louis Agassiz's shortcomings—and they were substantial— it's worth giving him credit for understanding the stupendous cold that dominated most of the time laid out on our field. Prior to Agassiz, naturalists and laymen alike assumed there had been no such bitter episode on the Earth. But after Agassiz had done his work from Switzerland to Glen Roy to Lake Superior, professional scientists and ordinary citizens alike came to appreciate the brutal cold of much of recent geologic time.

If you visit Harvard University, you can pay your respects to the mortal remains of Louis Agassiz in nearby Mount Auburn Cemetery. Agassiz lies buried beneath a twenty-five-hundred-pound boulder brought there, at what must have been considerable expense, from a glacier in Switzerland. We geologists care a lot about our headstones, and the one above Agassiz seems particularly fitting for the man who first recognized the Eiszeit by studying alpine glaciers and their erratic boulders.

Agassiz's accomplishments are remembered in a variety of ways in the geologic community. Perhaps most fittingly, his name is given to a giant, glacial lake that formed in the Pleistocene Epoch in northeastern North Dakota, northern Minnesota, Manitoba, and western Ontario. Glacial Lake Agassiz was the largest such lake in North America, several times larger than modern Lake Superior. Lake Agassiz was an immense body of frigid waters in the basin of the Red River, a stream that today has the distinction of flowing north out of the United States into Canada. The water was dammed up, forming an enormous lake, because the retreating continental ice sheet blocked its flow to the north. The outline of Glacial Lake Agassiz can be followed today across the plains as stringers of sand and gravel, from the long-ago beaches that lay around the southern edges of the vast, icy lake. Just as in Glen Roy, the evidence of a Pleistocene body of water held in place by an ice dam is plain, at least once the scales fall from your eyes and you can visualize massive climate change.

In time, after Agassiz's death, Harvard University decided to honor and remember the founder of its natural science department by creating the Louis Agassiz professorship, which is held by Harvard's most distinguished paleontologist. Several significant scientists have held the position named for the early naturalist. Perhaps most famously, for decades in the late-twentieth century, the Agassiz professorship was held by Stephen Jay Gould, a powerhouse of research, teaching, and the popularization of science through his magazine columns and books.

Agassiz changed the way scientists and laypersons understand and appreciate climate. Every childhood book you read about the Ice Age should have been dedicated to Agassiz, who popularized science just as much as he advanced it. The Pleistocene Epoch, however, was far from a monotonous deep freeze, and the Ice Age did not wipe out most species of plants and animals that graced the Earth, as Agassiz believed. How the great shifts in climate within the Pleistocene Epoch came to be understood is the subject of the next chapters.

3

STAGGERING COMPLEXITIES AND SURPRISING SIDE EFFECTS

By the time the sun was setting on Louis Agassiz, the great Swiss-born naturalist, a new era in American science had gathered a full head of steam. For the first time, men trained specifically as *geologists* were spreading westward across the growing country, first by the scores and then by the hundreds. Some of the geologists were employed at colleges. Others worked for major mining companies. But many other geologists spent highly productive professional lives in the recently formed state geologic surveys and in the national equivalent, known as the US Geological Survey.

Geologists of this era braved the elements to travel by horse up humble gullies and over majestic mountain passes. They paddled canoes along lakeshores and walked up arroyos. It was a romantic era of outdoor work and rapid intellectual progress for geology, a time when newspaper reporters wrote long stories about the staggering discoveries geologists were making about newly found fossils and natural resources.

The first goal of geological exploration in the 1800s was to produce reliable *geologic maps*. The men who dedicated their lives to this work risked their comfort and safety for the sake of being able to sketch in the blank parts of such maps—because they are the crucial tools geologists use to help us understand the Earth. A geologic map fulfills several purposes. At an elementary level, it shows the rocks in a region, telling us what lies immediately beneath our feet. It also points us toward where, still deeper in the Earth, that same rock bed likely trends. That's quite an accomplishment for a map based on what a field geologist can see only at the surface of the Earth.

Geologic maps are not academic matters. If you are a rural resident and are drilling a well for water, you want to hit material that's porous and permeable as well as water rich so that significant volumes of water can flow from the Earth into your well. That's information a geologic map can provide. Drilling wells is tough and expensive work, so any clues about the solid Earth that can minimize effort and maximize success are highly valuable to someone living in the country—or to a town or city government trying to provide drinking water to residents. Geological maps are also highly prized by prospectors and miners. As an example, consider an independent miner following a small silver vein in the mountains of the western United States in the 1800s. The vein could very easily disappear abruptly at a small fault. Given all that would have been invested to discover and follow the vein, the miner would urgently want to know in what direction—up or down, left or right—to tunnel in order to once more find the vein. A geologic map gives exactly that kind of information, making it a guide to the unseen world of the solid and opaque Earth.

Creating a geologic map is an exercise in making good surface observation coupled with reaching wise estimates of what likely happens beneath the Earth's surface. Those estimates rest on a great deal of experience with rocks and a thorough knowledge of how different types of rocks are born in the Earth. It's not trivial to create a good geologic map in complex terrain, but it's a skill that can be learned. Geologists are still taught how to make geologic maps in much the same way as the men of the 1800s learned their trade. That's why, if you tour the Rockies in the summertime, you can still come upon groups of young geologists in the making going through what's called field camp. The young people—college-level students, mostly—will be busy making measurements of rocks, veins, gravel beds, and much more. From their measurements, and using their knowledge of geologic processes, they'll try to deduce what lies beneath their feet in the third dimension of the solid Earth. At the end of their studies in a particular place, the "final report" from the students is their geologic map of the area, a record of their surface observations and a prediction of what lies underground.

In the 1800s, geologists produced hundreds and then thousands of

geologic maps. And all of those maps, taken together, had major consequences. From long-lived water wells for towns to the underground mining
of gold and silver ore, important work was accomplished in part due to
accurate geologic maps that guided people toward what they wanted in the
Earth. Historians think of the 1800s as one of expansion westward as the
United States grew toward the Pacific, but it was also in a very real way
a time of expansion *downward* as people increasingly learned to mine the
Earth's natural resources at greater depths and in more complex geological
terrain. And as American geologists undertook all this mapping work on
which so much of practical life depended, so did their counterparts around
the world. The age thus marked the first time ever that technically trained
men fanned out to map vast portions of the Earth for the discovery of the
natural resources that make modern life possible.

But there's another purpose beyond the practical that a good geologic
map fulfills. The history of the Earth is revealed by the millions of specific rocks, fossils, and surface features spread around the globe. So, while
groundwater and iron ore were definitely emphasized in the mapping effort
that spanned the middle and late 1800s, geologists of the day always took
time to investigate the abundant evidence that climate on our planet has
been very different from what we know today.

Charles Whittlesey was one of the first American geologists to focus
extensive amounts of fieldwork on the evidence of the Ice Age—or the
Pleistocene Epoch, as it had come to be called in Lyell's language. His official portrait photograph shows a fiercely determined man with a narrow,
flint-like face dressed in sturdy field clothes and holding a rock hammer at
the ready in one hand. He looks both able and willing to deal with anything
and anyone standing in his way. That's a fitting image, for his scientific
work challenged the thinking of many geologists, and his work resulted
in quite a few arguments. But Whittlesey's field evidence was both abundant and telling, and in time his colleagues fully converted to his way of
viewing the world.

One of Whittlesey's first successes regarding climate was understanding that there must be a distinct southern limit beyond which
Pleistocene glaciers had never passed. He went to work mapping out part

of this "glacial boundary," or the mother of all terminal moraines, in the Midwest. Today we know that the line of southernmost glaciation drops from western Pennsylvania across southern Ohio, then moves through southernmost Indiana and Illinois. It runs across Missouri near the middle of the state and from there heads into northeastern Kansas.

The ultimate terminal moraine is easy enough to recognize. North of it are glacial gravels and the jumbled and sometimes angular rocks with striations that Agassiz had learned to recognize. South of the glacial boundary is the countryside that has never been invaded by glaciers. In many ways, this type of basic mapping work by Whittlesey put teeth into Agassiz's general theory of the Ice Age. All too often Agassiz had been content to note glacial scratches on bedrock as he passed, but he generally didn't do the slow work of detailed mapping that shows clearly where and how glaciation had shaped the land. Whittlesey made the detailed case for Pleistocene glaciers across the Midwest. He worked like a patient district attorney amassing and explaining evidence to the jury, and in time Whittlesey emphatically won his case.

The facts about which American lands had been glaciated turned up some interesting sidelights. In western New York, and in Ohio, Indiana, Michigan, Wisconsin, and Illinois—land that had been buried by Ice Age glaciers—a few very lucky pioneers and later farmers found single diamonds in the gravels and sands around their homesteads. Most such finds were absolutely isolated occurrences. For example, a single diamond was found in Ohio, near where the state lines of Ohio, Indiana, and Kentucky all come together. No other diamonds were found in the area—and of course a lot of local people looked for them after one had been discovered!

Geologists quickly saw that the diamonds were in glacial debris, materials that had come south on the vast ice sheet of the Pleistocene. Each diamond was isolated because it was so far from its original source in the Earth. It didn't take geologists long to understand that if they wanted to find the source of the occasional diamond in the upper Midwest, they must look to central or northern Canada. And this is what geologists did, but without success for a very long time. Several generations of exploration geologists, in fact, scoured central and northern Canada for the ultimate source of the diamonds. Isolated gems were found occasionally, but not the diamond-rich rocks that had originally given birth to the long-but-thin trails of diamonds the great ice sheet had created.

When I was a college student at Princeton University in the early 1980s, the mystery of the diamond sources in Canada was still unsolved. Two Princeton geology professors thus spent a summer trying to follow the trail of diamonds "up ice" to the north. They returned with good stories and at least one minor insight into the puzzle—but without any diamonds in their pockets and without the discovery of the source of the gems. The honor of finding the special rocks from deep within the Earth that were the original source of the gems fell to other geologists, including those who have made a fortune in the famous Ekati and related diamond mines of the Barren Lands, about two hundred miles northeast of Yellowknife. The Ekati was discovered in the late-twentieth century—and other mines around it were developed shortly thereafter—a long time, indeed, after geologists of Whittlesey's time first realized that there must be diamond-rich rocks in Canada that had sent a few gems thousands of miles to the south courtesy of staggering volumes of ice.

Perhaps Whittlesey's greatest accomplishment is that he contributed evidence that the Pleistocene was more varied and complex than anyone had first thought. The first clear facts in favor of *repeated* climate changes in the Pleistocene came from humble water wells in the Midwest. As farmers and townsmen in those states dug downward into the Earth for water, they first shoveled their way through mixed glacial debris. Water in that layer often wasn't abundant enough to last through long summers, so the wells had to be extended to deeper levels. Whittlesey realized that well records were notable because a number of wells hit a layer under the glacial debris that contained wood. Then, beneath the wood-bearing layer was a still-deeper layer of glacial materials.

Whittlesey didn't speculate about the origin of the wood layer, although he recognized it as important. But another geologist, following immediately in Whittlesey's footsteps, was the first person to see the regional pattern and grasp what it meant. Under the surface glacial gravels there was a layer recording a forested time that implied a completely different climate for the whole region. This balmier time—something like the present day—had lasted long enough *for soils to form and trees to flourish*. But the mild era was only an interruption in the great, bitter cold of the Pleistocene. In short, the Pleistocene was not a monotonous deep freeze. It was, instead, a period dominated by bitter cold but with interruptions of warmth similar to the present day.

It's worth an aside to mention that the evidence—glacial deposits immediately above and below an ancient forest—is of a type that allows geologists to infer what's called "relative geologic time." No one in the 1800s knew exactly when the ancient forest had grown in the Midwest— was it fifty thousand or one hundred thousand years ago? But even without knowing specific dates, they could infer that the era of the forest came between two bitterly cold times marked by thick glacial ice that had buried the Midwest and deposited glacial gravels. Geologists thus could construct a sequence of events in relative order, saying that first there had been glaciers, then there had been a warm time with soils and a forest, then there had been glaciers once more, and finally there came our own warm times. These types of sequences create what geologists call the relative ordering of events in Earth history. Exact dates—fifty thousand versus one hundred thousand years—depend on other types of evidence, like the radioactive decay of elements. But simply working out the relative or sequential ordering of events in climate history teaches us a great deal.

The lesson to which Whittlesey had helped lead geologists was that Earth's climate had seen multiple climate flip-flops. But at first some geologists didn't want to believe it—anymore than an earlier generation in Europe had wanted to accept Agassiz's arguments. It's psychologically natural to question this kind of evidence. Major and repeated climate flip-flops undermine our confidence that the world will be hospitable to us tomorrow, something all of us want to believe. It had been difficult enough for many people to believe Agassiz's evidence that the world had once been engulfed by an Eiszeit. Now, just a couple of decades later, geologists familiar with the Midwest were asking people to accept the idea of repeated and massive climate changes that ran in both directions, back and forth.

But because the evidence of the water wells was both clear and direct, in a few years geologists were persuaded to accept the notion that the Pleistocene had contained at least one warm time very much like our own epoch. At a human level, this was not a comforting lesson, but science tends to compel its loyal practitioners to accept facts as facts, and professional geologists adapted to the new view of climate and moved forward. The critical wood-bearing layer between the glacial gravels became known to geologists as the *forest bed*. Once it—and its significance for climate—was fully accepted, the forest bed was traced into Indiana and other states, where it had originally been overlooked. The ancient wood spoke to what geologists came to call "the interglacial stage," the balmy time between major glaciations, the time so disturbingly like our own that was snuffed out by renewed bitter cold.[1]

A geologist named Thomas Chrowder Chamberlin, born in the era of Charles Whittlesey, noted the evidence of the forest bed. T. C. Chamberlin, as he is known, was to become a giant figure in American geologic circles, someone whose ideas are still taught to young geologists in the classroom and in summer camps devoted to mapping work.

Chamberlin was born—appropriately enough—on a glacial moraine along what was then the American western frontier in Illinois. When he was a toddler, his family moved by "prairie schooner" to Wisconsin, where they established the family farm near Beloit. After a few years in a log cabin, Thomas and his brothers helped build the foundation of a more permanent farmhouse—a foundation made of Ordovician limestone rich in fossils that had been quarried nearby. Thomas noted the fossils well, and his fascination with geology was born.

As a young man, T. C. Chamberlin started out in the world by teaching high school. His pedagogical approach was all but unheard of in his era—he would take his students outside to simply look at things. In a like manner, he himself continued to learn, and in time he became a professor at Beloit College and a member of Wisconsin's state geological survey.

Northern Wisconsin is covered with glacial debris. One distinctive feature of the moraines in the northern part of the state is the "kettle" country. A kettle is a dip in the land, a natural depression in the extensive moraines. Some kettles are small, just a few feet deep, while others are fifty to sixty feet deep and even farther across. Because Wisconsin is a wet place, many kettles are filled with water, forming numerous lakes. Some kettle lakes have outlet streams, but others do not, being isolated from streams that flow nearby but do not connect to the lake or its enclosing kettle basin.

If you travel south of the glacial boundary, you won't find many streams that pass near lakes but don't connect to them. Indeed, in most parts of the globe, streams either empty into lakes or drain water out of them. In Wisconsin's kettle country, however, nearby streams and lakes often seem not to know of each other's existence. That feels incoherent to anyone familiar with most of the landscapes of the world, and it's part of the topographic peculiarities that geologists call, rather evocatively, "deranged" terrain.

Chamberlin saw that the hummocky moraines of northern Wisconsin were responsible for the deranged drainage patterns of the area. The whole landscape consists of random piles of debris dotted with depressions tossed around like bits of confetti. Chamberlin had the insight to realize that these deranged features would be temporary on a geologic scale. In time, he reasoned, natural erosion of streams downward would regularize the land so that small streams would lead to larger ones and all lakes would have outlet streams that feed into larger rivers. The fact that this had not yet happened in the northern part of Wisconsin meant that the formation of the kettle country was geologically recent. As he traveled in other parts of the glaciated Midwest, Chamberlin saw that deranged drainage was much less pronounced, and in some places it was simply nonexistent. He deduced that northern Wisconsin had been shaped by a more recent glaciation that had not extended to all the glaciated Midwest. To put the matter another way, not all glacial advances in the Pleistocene were the same, and the most recent one had not penetrated as far south as some of the earlier episodes.

Chamberlin and other geologists of the time added to this understanding of multiple glaciations by mapping bedrock in the Midwest. They noted that some of the solid rock of the ground showed glacial scratches that ran in more than one direction. One clear set of striations might be aligned from due north to due south, but another set of parallel scratches on the same outcrop of bedrock might be at a 20 or 30 degree angle to the first. The implication is plain, and American geologists soon accepted the notion that the vast Canadian ice sheet over time flowed over the same spot in somewhat different directions. That likely meant that climate patterns were different even within one glacial epoch, driving ice in one direction for thousands of years, but then altering the pattern, likely because precipitation patterns changed.

Thus it was that in a matter of one generation, geologists had gathered evidence of Ice Age glaciers advancing and covering what had been temperate forests and flowing in varying directions and to different extents during the cold times. But more evidence of climate complexity was yet to come. A Canadian geologist published evidence from the Lake Ontario region of *three*, rather than two, distinct glacial layers separated by times of warmth like that of the present day. Soon, other geologists published evidence for *four* separate glaciations. Geologists could have naturally started to talk of the various glacial eras as the first, second, third, or fourth ones. This, however, would have led to confusion because not all glacial layers are present everywhere. For example, the "second" glaciation in a particular place in Iowa isn't the second one in northern Wisconsin. To clean up the inevitable miscommunication, geologists started to give proper names to the different glacial times.

Here we must face up to the unpleasant fact that names for *time* in geology are usually given based on a *place* where the evidence for those times is clear or abundant. That can seem like a strange custom, but it's the way the geological profession has gone about its business because it at least helps link events that may have occurred millions of years ago to a tangible place in today's world to which we can relate. So it was that American geologists came eventually to name the oldest or earliest glaciation the *Nebraskan*, the next one the *Kansan*, the penultimate glaciation the *Illinoian*, and the final or most recent glacial era (the one Chamberlin had worked on) the *Wisconsinan*.

While American and Canadian geologists were busy mapping the evidence of past climates in the New World, European geologists were doing parallel work in their homelands. They, too, quickly came to realize that the glaciers that had once buried their countries had been intermittent. They, too, gathered evidence for four major times of glaciations. As the North American and European geologists read each other's publications, geologists everywhere were confronted with the clear fact that climate on a fully global scale is highly fickle, oscillating between bitter cold times of glacial advance and times of much more moderate warmth and glacial retreat.

This book began by comparing recent geologic time to a football field. Most of the field is the Pleistocene Epoch, with all its complexities, and the Holocene Epoch is our current warm era. By the late 1880s, the basic outline of that sketch was becoming clear to geologists around the world. Earth's climate was evidently subject to radical changes, with repeated climate reversals. The total number of temperature flip-flops on the field, and the specific dates at which they occurred, was not yet known, but the basic picture and sequence of events could be seen by anyone.

In short, the natural human tendency to think of global climate as stable had been shown to be fundamentally naive. And our current warm times, given the dignified-sounding name of the Holocene Epoch, had been shown to be just like the short-lived balmy periods embedded in the much longer record of bitter cold and extensive glaciation of the Pleistocene. We are living, from this perspective, on borrowed time, waiting for the glaciers to advance once more and bury us just as they did the forest bed of the Midwest long ago. Science, for the first time in Western intellectual history, was predicting a clear "end to the world," at least an end to our world here at moderate latitudes.

It was a disquieting lesson.

But geologists had ways of comforting themselves—and anyone else in need of reassurance about climate. The stupendous change from balmy warmth to bitter cold, geologists in the late 1800s assumed, must take centuries or even thousands of years to unfold. So although the magnitude of climate change was breathtaking, and it certainly looked like the current warm times couldn't last forever, it was common for geologists in the era of Whittlesey and Chamberlin to assert that Americans had nothing to fear. A return to frigid temperatures like those of the Pleistocene would take dozens of generations to transpire. A thousand years for the great change seemed like a good rough estimate for a climate flip, and most of us can't drum up much concern for our society a millennium down the road.

We'll see in the coming chapters that the assumption of gradual climate change was simply incorrect. It was an assumption, after all, not a hypothesis grounded on evidence. But it took another century for indisputable evidence to arrive on the crucial point of how rapidly climate could flip-flop. Meanwhile, so as not to get ahead of our story, we'll return to the late 1800s because there are a couple more important lessons about climate to be learned from the first wave of geological mapping.

Geologists of T. C. Chamberlin's day came to understand several side-lights of extensive glaciation. One realm into which geologists waded was climate's inevitable impacts on sea level. The first piece of headway made in understanding sea-level fluctuations related to the fact that Scandinavia had long appeared to Europeans to be slowly but steadily *rising* out of the ocean. Visiting Denmark and Sweden, Lyell—the great British naturalist of Agassiz's day—had seen the old beaches or "strands" that stand on dry land in many places above modern sea level. In some areas there are several such beach strands, each higher than the last. The evidence of the old shorelines shows that either sea level is dropping or the land is rising. But which is it?

Naturalists like Lyell knew that sea level, as recorded in the shorelines of southern Europe, didn't show evidence of global sea-level decline. Thus, naturalists had admitted that lands like Scandinavia must be slowly rising. That phenomenon was difficult to explain, to be sure, but the facts of regional uplift seemed clear enough.

In the era of Whittlesey and Chamberlin, North American geologists published field evidence showing that the lands around the Great Lakes and Hudson Bay are also rising compared to sea level. The solid ground around Hudson Bay, for example, is slowly increasing in elevation, as is shown by the old shorelines that can be traced in places for many miles around the bay. The old shorelines stand away from the modern beaches and at elevations higher than modern sea level by dozens and scores of feet. Thus, the basic evidence of regional uplift is the same as in Scandinavia, but another aspect of the matter helped solve the riddle of what could cause regional uplift.

The Hudson Bay area, geologists knew, was near the epicenter of the great ice sheet that had grown in Canada and flowed down into the United States. The bay itself—the ocean water we have named after Hudson—didn't exist in the Pleistocene, when the whole region looked like modern Greenland, engulfed by glacial ice. The evidence from Hudson Bay clearly means that the land has been rising *after* the last glaciers left the area and *after* the sea flowed in to make the shorelines that record that rise. To put this another way, during the millennia of the Holocene Epoch—our current warm times—the whole surface of the Earth in the region has been flexing upward. The cause of the uplift, evidently, was linked to the departure of the glaciers.

Geologists realized that just as a large ship will bob upward as its cargo is unloaded onto a dock, so the Earth's crust flexes upward when staggering loads of glacial ice are removed from it as a result of melting. The Earth responds much more slowly to the change than does a ship, so the "bobbing up" process takes millennia. The land around Hudson Bay is therefore still rising, century by century, in response to the off-loading of glacial ice at the start of our epoch. In a similar fashion, all of Scandinavia is rising due to the lifting of the great weight of the glacial ice that used to engulf northern Europe. The rates of rising are similar, by the way, roughly a foot or two a century.

Ideas about sea level lead us naturally back to the flint-faced American geologist Charles Whittlesey. He hypothesized that global, as well as regional, changes in sea level must be related to climate change. Whittlesey estimated the total volume of glacial ice that had existed during the cold times of the Pleistocene in North America, Europe, and so forth. Water that was in those extensive glaciers, he reasoned, must have decreased the total water available to be in the oceans. So Whittlesey looked at the whole, global consequence to sea level caused by extensive glaciation.

Whittlesey published his estimate that global sea level had stood about three hundred fifty to four hundred feet *lower* during the glacial times of the Pleistocene than it does today. That was a shocking figure to consider in the 1800s, but it's an estimate that compares very favorably with actual subsea measurements of ancient shorelines from recent oceanographic studies. Such work shows that, during the cold parts of the Pleistocene, the Atlantic shoreline of the United States stood more than three hundred feet lower than it does today. New York's Hudson River, during those times, cut a significant and sharp valley—now under the sea—and that valley can be traced beneath today's ocean waves for a distance some sixty miles offshore, southeast of the of New York City. Other parts of the ocean shore of what's now New Jersey, Virginia, and the Carolinas stood one hundred miles to the east of where the sea and land meet today.

In short, natural climate reversals affect sea level in two ways. First, as continental-scale glaciers grow during cold times, more and more of the globe's water is "locked up" in enormous glaciers, causing global sea levels to drop tremendously. Oceanfront property in much of the world grows substantially outward toward the seas during these times as the ocean retreats from the land. Then, when climate reverses and warms once again, sea level on a global basis rises as meltwater from glaciers makes its way back to the ocean. Much oceanfront property shrinks as the seas rise and claim more of the solid land. But this global increase in sea level can be modified on a regional scale by the fact that removing great glaciers from the land compels parts of the solid Earth to flex upward. Thus, regional sea level around Hudson Bay and Scandinavia is dropping today with respect to the local landscape and dropping despite global sea-level rise in the Holocene.

The consequences of dramatic sea-level shifts due to climate change are far from academic. North America was peopled during the waning stages of the Pleistocene because sea level was so low that there was a land bridge between Siberia and Alaska. As archeological and even genetic evidence shows, people spread from Asia to Alaska and south through the rest of North America, taking advantage of low water levels. And people were not unique in this respect—the whole ecosystem of the late Pleistocene and Holocene was shaped by the consequences of sea-level changes. As an example, the Siberian brown bear also walked across the land bridge from Asia, spreading over time from Alaska down the coast of what's now

Canada and the American Pacific Northwest. Evolutionary pressures on the brown bear stock led to the development of the inland grizzly bear. Likewise, in the waning part of the Pleistocene, natural selection led the northern polar bear to emerge from grizzly-brown stock. The tale of these three bears, dancing with climate and its effects, is just one example of the biological world's constant flux.

Whittlesey's pioneering work in estimating how much sea level dropped during times of extensive glaciation also ties into the fact that modern shorelines are not nearly as high as they have been in the geologically recent past. In the first chapter of this book we mentioned that the last interglacial time prior to the modern Holocene warmth—an interval called the Eemian, which occurred around 6.5 yards away from the end zone in our football-field analogy—was actually warmer than anything we know today. An extra-balmy Eemian, of course, must have melted more major glaciers than anything we've experienced in modern times, and that means that Eemian sea level must have been a good measure *higher* than what we know in the present. Indeed, we find clear evidence for exactly that in the southeastern United States, where the Carolina and Georgia old shorelines are about fifty miles inland and about 120 feet higher than modern ones, reflecting the significantly higher sea level of those warmer times. That empirical evidence of the scale of natural global warming and resulting higher seas may be worth noting as a general framework when you evaluate what you hear in the press about modest sea-level changes in modern times, such as the rise of one to two feet we've seen since 1850.

But to return to the 1800s, let us note that by the time of Charles Whittlesey's death, geologists were starting to recognize one more major consequence of the enormous climate changes of the Pleistocene. In what's now the western United States, south of the great ice sheet that dominated the northern half of the continent, geologists came across evidence of major and unexpected catastrophes related to consequences of the Ice Age differences in climate.

If you've been to the Great Basin area of Utah, you have an understanding of what an arid climate is like. But, as geologists quickly realized when they mapped the West, such aridity is only recent, and it relates directly to the climate change that buried the Midwest under glacial ice.

Grove Karl Gilbert was the single most significant research geologist of the late 1800s, the man above all others, who came to understand arid lands and how recent climate revolutions have shaped them. Geologists still genuflect when saying his name because he contributed to the solution of many different problems. He's the American version of what Lyell had been in England, a single geologist who shaped so many ideas of his day that it's difficult to understand how people understood the Earth before his time.

As it happened, G. K. Gilbert was a failed high-school teacher. He was a quiet person who never imposed his will on others. That temperament led him to disaster when he tried to teach teenagers in rural Michigan while he was a young man. But teaching's loss proved to be geology's great gain. Gilbert had a keen mind for understanding physical science and applying that knowledge to what he perceived in the world around him. He saw foundational and crucial evidence where others were mesmerized by details, and he reasoned effectively from physical science to its applications within geology. Gilbert was truly, as his chief modern biographer calls him, "a great engine of research."[2] He also became a leader in the US Geological Survey, where his skills and insights became so highly valued over time that he was twice elected president of the Geological Society of America—an accomplishment that has never been repeated by anyone.

Gilbert cut his teeth as a geologist in the federally funded wave of exploration and mapmaking that helped shape the development of the American West. His life spans the time from when the United States still had a western frontier to the fully modern era of the early-twentieth century. Gilbert's major publication of 1890 recorded just how radically precipitation in North America was altered by geologically recent climate change. His piece focused on the Great Salt Lake and the land around it, and from field evidence he carefully and convincingly deduced important consequences of climate change, including consequences no one in the profession would have guessed before his day.

Today the Great Salt Lake of Utah is a briny and shallow pool in the bottom of a large, natural basin. There is no outlet stream leading away from the Great Salt Lake because it's fully enclosed by higher ground around it. If you walk from the briny shore toward the mountains you see in the distance around the lake, you will come to distinctive, ancient shorelines. Gilbert carefully studied these shorelines, including in places where there are enough of them to make a natural "staircase" on the hillside.

Clearly the lake had once been vastly deeper than what it is in modern times. That simple fact implies heavier precipitation patterns in the Pleistocene. Just as the sea around Greenland's great ice cap today is the site of many fierce storms, so land near the North American ice sheet of the Pleistocene was shaped by storms—and the heavy precipitation they bring.

Geologists call the freshwater lake that existed in Utah in the Pleistocene *Lake Bonneville*. The Bonneville Salt Flats, which you hear about in the news when race cars are tested, are on the flat floor of part of the ancient lake. In the Ice Age, the great lake rose and fell over time as precipitation and evaporation varied. It was these changes that led to the "staircase" steps of old shorelines in the hill slopes around the modern Great Salt Lake. At its height, Lake Bonneville was as large as one of the modern Great Lakes in the Midwest, a body of water that had substantial wave action as Pleistocene winds whipped its surface, leading to significant marks on the land.

Generally, lakes have outlet streams. Such lakes cannot rise significantly above their natural levels because, as the surface of the lake water increases a little, more water spills into the outlet stream, decreasing the lake's waters. Because Lake Bonneville had no outlet stream, however, it rose whenever precipitation exceeded the rate of evaporation from the surface of the lake. Over time, in the wettest stage of the Pleistocene, it rose to very great heights indeed. Its shorelines, as we know from the old beach strands, extended north beyond the borders of Utah into southern Idaho and westward from Utah into Nevada.

But obviously there has to be an edge or lip to a basin. Geologists of the 1800s wondered where the relative low point of the Great Basin's enclosure was, the place where lake waters might have overspilled the basin at some point in the Pleistocene. Gilbert, the excellent field geologist and engine of research, found that low place. In the process, he laid the groundwork for the discovery of a major side effect of climate change, one that geologists continued to bump up against in the West throughout the twentieth century.

The lowest point on the rim of the Salt Lake Basin is Red Rock Pass in southern Idaho. At it happens, highway departments as well as geologists appreciate relatively low ground in the midst of higher topography, so it's no surprise Red Rock Pass now has a highway that runs through it. But, of course, in Gilbert's day the highway didn't exist. He got to the pass in the same way he traveled all around the Great Basin, by horse or mule or on foot.

What Gilbert discovered at Red Rock Pass was what happens when an enormous lake overtops the natural dam that holds it back. In the late Pleistocene, when the lake's surface just reached the lowest part of the pass, the great lake started to overspill its container. At first, the amount of lake water running north across the pass and toward the plains of southern Idaho was small. But when water runs over the top of a natural dam, it has a tendency to erode the dam. And when Lake Bonneville's waters eroded that first inch or two of the Red Rock dam that had been holding back the great lake, a large volume of water started to pour out of the basin.

As it happened, the rocks of Red Rock Pass were fairly soft and uncon-solidated. As that first gush of water from Lake Bonneville flowed over the pass, the water eroded the soft rocks a good bit more. That meant yet more water went over the pass, causing a feedback loop. Soon a catastrophic flood was emptying Lake Bonneville, with the floodwaters racing north across the plains of southern Idaho and into the deep canyon of the Snake River. The flood continued, with the torrent growing larger day by day as the feedback effect grew and grew. The Snake River was soon accepting vastly more water into its bed than it had ever experienced in even the heaviest springtime flood. Those floodwaters raced down the great canyon of the Snake, through the rugged terrain of central Idaho, and westward into what's now Washington State. Ultimately, the floodwaters rushed into the lower Columbia River and from there through the Columbia Gorge into the Pacific Ocean.

Today we have fully traced the erosive powers of the great flood from

Lake Bonneville. There are numerous flood gravels—dozens of feet thick in some places in the Snake River canyon—that were created quickly in the violent event. The flood continued for many weeks, geologists have calculated, basing their work on the geographic dimensions of Lake Bonneville and the size of Red Rock Pass. Ultimately, when the down-cutting lake waters reached a firm rock layer at the pass, the flood slowed and naturally came to an end. Lake Bonneville had been greatly reduced in volume and surface area, never to be the same again.

As Gilbert realized, the catastrophic flood of Lake Bonneville occurred late in the Pleistocene Epoch, just shortly before our present warm era. When climate warmed substantially, the ice cap left the continent and rainfall and snowfall in Utah became much scarcer. The region's climate evolved toward what it is today, with cool winters and hot, dry summers. Gradually, evaporation from the surface of what was left of Lake Bonneville far exceeded the input of fresh water from rain and snow in the basin. The lake shrank each year, becoming more and more salty as it did so, ultimately becoming the shallow brine pool of modern times.

When Gilbert published his findings about the catastrophic release of much of Pleistocene Lake Bonneville's water to the north, his conclusions came as a surprise to geologists. As a profession, geologists had assumed that natural change was gradual, a point of view inherited largely from the writings of Lyell. Geologists would have preferred that climate change and everything related to it had happened gradually, with changes measured over centuries or millennia. But the evidence for the catastrophic flood from Lake Bonneville was clear, and the event was soon accepted as one of the surprising side effects of the wet climate of the region during the Ice Age.

Not long after G. K. Gilbert died in 1918 at the age of seventy-five, a young geologist named J Harlan Bretz began to muse that another catastrophic flood had shaped a much larger part of the northwestern United States. In the summers of the 1920s and 1930s, Bretz—accompanied sometimes by a mule to help carry his gear—hiked up the numerous braided or interlaced "coulees" of central Washington State. Grand Coulee is the largest and most well-known of the stark channels of the area. Bretz mapped it with care, but he also explored the scores of other, smaller coulees that cut across the region in a similar fashion. As the years went by, Bretz mapped most of the area, concentrating on surface features and coming to know them better than any other geologist of his generation.

The coulees of Washington State are just the most obvious feature of the "Channeled Scablands," an area where soil is thin or absent and the land has been stripped to bare-bones bedrock. The region is unique in North America, a curiosity that attracts visitors to this day. Like the Wisconsin terrain mapped in the previous century and explained by T. C. Chamberlin, central Washington shows chaotic stream drainage worthy of the technical term *deranged*. Small streams don't lead to larger ones, at least not for very long distances. In fact, some small streams of the Scablands roughly parallel each other, an odd occurrence in all the "normal" parts of the world, where streams lead into one another. Although the area is fairly arid, there are a few small lakes, most located in significant depressions or pits. Streams that run only in the spring are often unconnected to the small lakes, bypassing them completely. All of those features are part of the deranged topography that led many geologists to assume that the area had been scoured by a tongue of the Canadian ice sheet that had flowed down from British Columbia. The Scablands, from this point of view, must be analogous to Chamberlin's kettle moraines in northern Wisconsin.

But Bretz quickly rejected the glacial hypothesis for the origin of the Scablands. The loose rocks of the region do not show the scratches and striations of glacial action. And although there are many ridges of gravel in the Scablands, Bretz believed they were not moraines. Instead, he interpreted what he saw in the Scablands as the product of catastrophic flooding on a scale much greater even than what Lake Bonneville's waters had unleashed.

J Harlan Bretz was unlike the gentle Gilbert, who couldn't control a high-school class. A forceful character, even at his weakest, Bretz loved to argue—and to go his own way. So, acting alone, and without any support from other geologists of the day, Bretz published a hypothesis of catastrophic flooding to explain the entire Scablands region. But, unlike Gilbert's work, Bretz put forward his idea without describing a *source* of the floodwaters he identified as having shaped the land.

A substantial argument about Bretz's views raged for decades in professional circles. Most geologists assumed Bretz was wrong, siding with colleagues who believed the region's topography could be explained by the gradual action of continental glaciers. The argument started to be resolved only in the early 1940s. At that point a young geologist named J. T. Pardee published air photos of western Montana. Taking photos from the air was a new technology, and the view from a few hundred feet above the Missoula area changed the dynamic of the argument that Bretz had begun.

Geologists had long known that during the Pleistocene a deep lake lay in western Montana. If you stand in Missoula, Montana, looking up at the giant hills around you, you can trace with your eye extensive horizontal markings on the land. The marks are old shorelines, cut into the hillside by wave action, as a closer examination of them above the city will demonstrate. The old shorelines run level but curve around all the mountain valleys of the whole region, providing a dizzying and complex array of evidence that shows one simple fact: a deep lake—more than two thousand feet deep—existed in western Montana in the late Ice Age.

Geologists of the 1800s had named the great Pleistocene lake Glacial Lake Missoula. They had traced the parallel shorelines across whole counties and had also noted that the shorelines simply ended in northern Idaho. Recalling Louis Agassiz's triumph in explaining the parallel shorelines on the sides of Glen Roy in Scotland—the marks that ended abruptly at the mouth of the valley—geologists had accepted the notion that a very large ice dam in Idaho had likely held back Glacial Lake Missoula. Just as in Scotland, the only natural agent that could have dammed the entire drainage of the land—and then wholly disappeared—was glacial ice. And, happily enough, there was abundant evidence of glacial ice in northern Idaho, where the ice dam must have been located. The lower Clark Fork River there intersects the Purcell Trench, a great lowland that leads down from Canada, and was doubtless a conduit of glacial ice, as bedrock scratches make abundantly clear.

Glacial Lake Missoula, like Lake Bonneville in Utah, was an enormous Pleistocene lake. But Lake Missoula's existence was enormously more fragile than Lake Bonneville's, because Lake Missoula was held in place by ice, not rock. Pardee's air photos elegantly showed enormous ripple markings west of Missoula, on what had been the floor of the great lake. The megaripples—on a scale so large they look simply like hills from the ground—showed clearly that Glacial Lake Missoula had not drained quietly, but rather had rushed westward in the late Ice Age. The ripples were created by currents, like the ripples you've felt on your feet when you've waded on sand in rivers—but the scale of the currents (and thus the ripples) was breathtakingly different. When geologists took in the full force of Pardee's off-scale photographic evidence, they realized that at some point all the waters of Glacial Lake Missoula headed west at the speed of a freight train. That could only mean that the Pleistocene ice dam that made the lake possible had collapsed.

Glacial Lake Missoula's catastrophic dam failure was the key that led geologists to accept Bretz's argument that most of central Washington State had been carved out quickly by enormously violent and deep floodwaters. Grand Coulee, and all the dozens of other coulees Bretz described, were formed not over millennia by glacial ice, but very quickly by the erosive powers of the catastrophic flood. The deep torrent of floodwater stripped the land bare of soil and carved the deranged drainage so characteristic of the region. Climate and biblical-scale catastrophe were, once again, closely linked. Indeed, once the eyes of geologists were opened about the source of floodwaters coming from Glacial Lake Missoula, they found evidence of *multiple* Bretz-like floods in the Channeled Scablands. Just as the acceptance of one forest bed helped lead to the discovery of other similar features in the Midwest, the acceptance of Bretz's basic hypothesis helped the next generation of geologists to see that Lake Missoula had formed— and catastrophically drained—multiple times as the ice dam that held it back formed and reformed late in the Pleistocene Epoch.

A question naturally arises about the two megaflood sources of the Pleistocene, Glacial Lake Missoula and Glacial Lake Bonneville. Which flooding events came first in the long sequence of events of the waning Ice Age? That question is of the same type that we saw Charles Whittlesey successfully address about the sequence of climate events shown by the forest bed of the Midwest. Geologists can answer such questions of relative time with the help of any location where two pieces of geologic evidence are in direct physical contact. To address which catastrophic Ice Age floods came first, geologists needed to find a place where the evidence of the two events was brought together in one location.

A simple gravel quarry in Lewiston, Idaho, fills the bill. It contains evidence of both the Bonneville and Missoula floods, and it allows even a casual observer to understand which flood happened before the other. The quarry lies next to the Snake River, where it is worked for gravels for construction projects, laying bare a cliff-like front in the deep, loose rocks. At the base of the quarry face are the rounded gravels set down by the Bonneville flood, rocks that are the same type as found in southern and central Idaho. Immediately above the Bonneville gravels are much finer sediments that flowed *up* the Snake River canyon when the wall of water from Lake Missoula reached the Snake. Like the gutter of a roof temporarily overwhelmed by a big bucket of water poured on the roof above it, the Snake River had run backward for a time, choked with Lake Missoula water and sediments during the flood Bretz had correctly described, if not explained.

The sequence of the two events is clearly shown in the gravels, with the Lake Missoula sediments lying on top of the earlier Bonneville gravels. The humble gravel quarry is thus a famous site in geologic circles, a place where you can directly see not just two catastrophes related to climate but also the simple types of evidence geologists use to deduce the sequences of events over the long reaches of geologic time. Like the forest bed of the Midwest, this kind of evidence is indisputable, compelling the observer to accept the description of a relative history of the Earth, including an appreciation of climate change and catastrophes spawned by climate.

From Whittlesey to Bretz, geologists carefully mapped evidence not just of repeated glaciations and intermittent warm spells, but also of global sea-level shifts, vast inland lakes, and catastrophic flooding. By the middle of the twentieth century it had become clear to geologists everywhere both that climate is key to the physical landscape in which we live and that repeated climate changes have created and then snuffed out ancient forests and sea coasts. Even staggering features like the Grand Coulee owe their existence to relatively modest side effects of the great monster that is global climate change.

There's certainly no going back to the comfortable illusion that we live in a world with a climate that's stable or at least predictable. Anyone familiar with geological research knows full well that repeated and substantial climate change is woven into the fabric of the world in which we live, and that such change has many and varied effects.

But now for some good news. Despite the challenges posed to all living creatures by major climate upheavals, it's also true that plants, animals, and people have survived and sometimes even flourished in the last two geological epochs, the highly variable Pleistocene and the modestly variable Holocene. In the next chapter we'll turn to the fossil record of some of your favorite animals from grade school—woolly mammoths, wolves, moose, and saber-toothed tigers—to see how they dealt with the extremes of climate change.

4

FROM WOOLLY MAMMOTHS
TO SABER-TOOTHED TIGERS

L ouis Agassiz, the first person to clearly recognize the signs of the Ice Age in Europe and North America, was in many ways an intellectual progressive. By accepting the facts that pointed to how fickle climate on Earth had been, he earned his place as a major figure among the founders of modern geology. He also was prescient in seeing the likely connection between climate change and the birth and demise of some wondrous species. In short, extinction and climate were closely linked events for Agassiz, and that connection of ideas has proven a fruitful one from his day down to this one.

As we have seen, Agassiz was not a perfect scientist. Some of his observations were quite fuzzy, and often his manic intensity about the Ice Age was simply too extreme to be useful. Important qualifications and serious refinements were all too often missing in Agassiz's work. And he also, as it happened, used theological arguments to address scientific questions—a recipe likely to lead to disappointing results.

When Agassiz was a boy, science and religion were freely mixed together. It was only in the later decades of his life that science became a profession that stood firmly on its own empirical feet, a matter on which theology could not—in the judgment of most intellectuals—usefully comment. While many naturalists and early scientists fully adjusted to that change of worldview, setting aside their religious convictions when they theorized about the natural world, Agassiz never quit blending science and religion as he had when he was young.

Still, despite the double handicaps of an extreme temperament and unfortunate early training, Agassiz got a number of important pieces right about fundamental geology, climate change, and the history of life. Agassiz's errors were significant, but his virtues were so great that they could have made up for even greater transgressions.

The reader may recall that Agassiz didn't start his career as a naturalist investigating glaciers in Switzerland. His true forte was fossil fish, an area he chose to study in part because the fish are the first vertebrates in the history of the Earth. He was, to put it simply, the finest paleontologist interested in fish anywhere on the planet when he was young. Swiss glaciers were really just a summertime diversion for Agassiz, a change of pace from long winters in dim rooms looking at dark fish fossils. But naturally, since his career was highly successful and spanned many decades, Agassiz over time saw many fossil species other than fish. Among them, appropriately enough, were the exotic and wonderfully large mammals that were such a prominent part of Agassiz's Ice Age.

First in the bestiary of the Ice Age is the woolly mammoth, a member of the elephant clan, whose bones can be found in Pleistocene gravels and peat bogs from Europe across to Siberia, and from Alaska throughout Canada and down through the northern United States. The mammoth is the mascot, if you will, of the Ice Age, its profile known to every modern schoolchild. Our interest in the shaggy beasts is not new: the mammoth was unmistakably sketched by early mankind on cave walls.

In places like Siberia and parts of central Asia, there were so many woolly mammoth bones in the permafrost that for centuries local people had used the biggest rib bones and leg bones as poles for tents. Other bones were used like lumber in the treeless land, a handy building material if whacked in half or lashed to each other. The great, sweeping tusks of the mammoths were also pulled out of the frozen ground more recently to be sold into the international ivory trade.

In recent centuries, some of the native peoples in Siberia thought that woolly mammoths might still be living underground, like giant moles. The woolly corpses were always found under the Earth's surface, after all, and there clearly were a lot of them, so perhaps living members of the group were still under the permafrost.[1] For several reasons, neither local residents nor educated, urban sophisticates of the late 1700s and early 1800s found it easy to accept the idea of extinction. America's own Thomas Jefferson and a number of European naturalists spent a lot of time and energy struggling against the idea of extinction—a fact that demands a moment's attention.

Here's the crux of the problem for Jefferson and those who thought like him: the natural world around us—what we see outside the window today—looks well ordered. Species "fit" with each other, each taking up a niche in the complex ecological webs that cover the Earth. And species range from the simple to the complex, with apparently incremental change from little bits of algae to simple vascular plants and worms to clams and higher animals. (We humans look like the most complex animal of all—a fact that's more than a bit nice for our egos.) In short, the living world looks quite complete and well arranged, an observation that has impressed intellectuals in the European tradition pretty much since the tradition began.

For Jefferson and his contemporaries, the natural world was thoroughly complete and well ordered *because Divine Power had made it so.* And that meant that both radical climate change and the extinction of whole species seemed quite unlikely. Climate flip-flops and extinction would appear, from this point of view, to imply that God's creation was imperfect to start with and that it regularly careened out of control through Earth history. But God's good ordering of creation seemed like a sure bet. Most intellectuals of the late 1700s and early 1800s were not slaves to specific Bible verses in Genesis, but they felt more than uneasy with any consideration that the natural world around us might be both chaotic and fickle. Nature was God's handiwork, after all, and it spoke clearly of God's creative powers and his plan for the entire universe.

Jefferson—like many others of his day—thought extinction wasn't likely because it would be an interruption of what the Creator had intended. And if part of the creation failed, the whole might be threatened. As Jefferson wrote:

> The animal species which has once been put into a train of motion, is probably still moving in that train. For, if one link in nature's chain might

be lost, another and another might be lost, till this whole system of things vanish by piece-meal.[2]

So, Jefferson reasoned, if there had once been woolly mammoths breathing in the world, then there must still be mammoths somewhere fulfilling what God meant mammoths, in their wonderful and woolly essence, to be and to do for the created universe.

Jefferson himself studied the partial fossil remains of a curious beast dug up in western Virginia. It had great claws about eight inches long on its paws, thick bones, and a thick skull. Jefferson prepared for publication a good description of the fossil and speculated that it belonged to the cat family.

Happily, before Jefferson's paper went to press, he got a new idea about the fossil from a scientific publication freshly arrived from Europe. The paper described a similar fossil from South America that had been brought back to Europe and identified not as a cat, but as a great ground sloth. Sloths can and do have large claws, and Jefferson, to his credit, apparently realized his error. He published his paper with an added section about the European view, presumably accepting it as correct. Today the technical name of the species he worked with is *Megalonyx* (great claw) *jeffersonii* in honor of the man who first described this particular Pleistocene ground sloth species and launched the serious study of fossils in the young United States.

Still, and this is the most important point, Jefferson didn't really think his ground sloth was extinct. He wasn't, in that sense, a fully modern naturalist. Indeed, he asked Lewis and Clark to keep an eye out for the sloth and also the woolly mammoth as their exploratory expedition made its way westward to the Pacific.[3] Both animals, Jefferson reasoned, had a place in God's design, and thus were quite possibly somewhere "Out West," living their lives and fulfilling their divine mission in the greater scheme of the created world.

There is, of course, a general connection between the ideas of Jefferson and others of his day and a few religious conservatives in American society today. Those who identify themselves as "Creation Scientists" or followers of "Intelligent Design" have a variety of views on various subjects, but they tend to all adhere to the notion that the world around us—including the species of plants and animals we see abroad on the land today—directly and concretely reflect God's plan. There is an order in the biological world, this viewpoint maintains, not because of the food web or natural selection acting over geologic time on Earth's species, but because of God's own (and recent) creation. A mere two hundred years ago, that fundamental notion was the clear and strong framework in which Jefferson and everyone else was schooled.

Arriving on the scene just a few years after Jefferson, Agassiz fully shared the perspective that all species were directly created by God and spoke to God's plan for the world. But Agassiz also had had the good fortune to be trained in Paris early in his life by the outstanding French paleontologist Baron Georges Léopold Chrétien Frédéric Dagobert Cuvier. Cuvier's imposing name is second only to his important contributions to science; his work marked an enormous step forward for understanding the complexities of the history of life on Earth. Cuvier easily left Jefferson in his wake, at least as regards natural history. And as we shall see, Agassiz benefited from Cuvier's fundamental insights. In so doing, Agassiz was later able to make enormous progress in understanding the connections between climate and extinction.

Early in his career, Cuvier astounded Frenchmen—both intellectuals and ordinary citizens—by digging up the bones of elephant-like animals near Paris itself. And that was only the start. Cuvier brought to light more and more ancient animal remains as his life unfolded. People went to the sites of Cuvier's excavations to watch his team unearth the fossils, and then the public lined up again to see the re-creations of the animals he put together for display in national museums. Cuvier was a wizard, conjuring up fierce animals of the past out of the very dirt, and all of France marveled at his work. The fact that Cuvier, though short, was otherwise physically imposing—red hair on top of an unusually large head—added to his total effect on colleagues and the public alike.[4] Cuvier was the scientific tsunami of his day.

Cuvier's special calling was anatomy. When he was young, he had dissected specimens of most of the living species known in Europe, and he learned volumes about living creatures directly from nature. He understood how each bone or organ in an animal relates to the whole. He could recognize Earth's ancient animals from mere scraps of fossil remains, animals as diverse and varied as the known history of life on Earth had produced.

If Cuvier had only been an anatomist, his contributions to paleontology would have been great. But he combined his knowledge of anatomy with what were then the new sciences of physical geology and stratigraphy, and the result was a period of revolutionary progress in understanding the whole history of life. Approaching his research from this greater perspective, Cuvier did two major things right: first, and like Agassiz, Cuvier happened to live and work where certain geologic lessons are abundantly clear, and second, Cuvier listened and learned from a more practical man who understood a lot about the layers of minerals and sediments in the Earth around Paris.

As it happens, Paris sits on sedimentary rock and loose sedimentary deposits, the kind of materials that naturally record the evidence of ancient life. The different layers are quite distinct, and they include those laid down under the sea. The marine layers contain millions and millions of fossils—shallow ocean floors are good at accumulating shells and other remains of marine life. Above and below such layers are ones dominated by freshwater creatures from when the Paris area was covered by freshwater bodies. There are also a few terrestrial (land-based) layers that contain the occasional land-loving creature—such as the woolly mammoth.

Cuvier thus had, readily at hand, a lot of evidence about our planet's past and the history of life on Earth over time. The evidence included fossils from the sea, from freshwater bodies, and from land. And, as it happened, a man named Alexandre Brongniart, who was a contemporary of Cuvier, had already learned to understand a lot about these same sedimentary layers. He had cataloged many of the features of the distinct layers, and he was able to teach Cuvier about how they were laid out in the Earth from top to bottom and laterally over substantial distances.

Brongniart's interest in the layers was both practical and theoretical. He was a mineralogist who later was in charge of a major porcelain factory that produced fine china. Part of that enterprise included painting on porcelain. Both fine porcelain and porcelain paints and glazes require excellent raw materials, ranging from special clays to pure minerals that can be prepared for the paints. The clays and minerals are sedimentary—hence Brongniart's practical interest in understanding the sedimentary Earth layers in and around Paris. On the theoretical side, Brongniart was a naturalist himself, appointed as a professor of mineralogy at the Museum of Natural History in Paris. Like Cuvier, he wanted to see and understand all he could of Earth's long history, and he recognized that the layers recorded sequences of events in geologic time.

But it was Cuvier's genius to cooperate extensively with Brongniart so he could absorb Brongniart's knowledge of the sedimentary layers of the Paris region and apply that knowledge to a better understanding of fossils. In part because of so doing, Cuvier learned to seriously read the history of life on Earth like the ordered pages of a book. Instead of reading a sentence here and there (in the manner that Jefferson did with his sloth), Cuvier could read page by page *in a sequence* through time. Cuvier was one of the first people on the planet to profoundly understand that life's history would be a long and complex sequence of events, but one that a diligent and clever person could learn to deduce systematically. Nothing less than the full and grand story of life, stretching over whole epochs, eras, and eons, was what Cuvier wanted to discover in his geologic studies, and he went to work to do exactly that.

Commenting on the impact and vision of Cuvier, one writer of the time asked:

> Have you ever been cast forth into the immensity of space and time while reading the geological works of Cuvier? Carried by his genius, have you soared over the limitless abyss of the past, as if supported by the hand of the enchanter?[5]

In pursuit of this great project, for four years Cuvier went with Brongniart once each week to supervise the scientific exploration of the layers of the Earth in and around Paris. The two men and their helpers together discovered what lay below the surface of the Earth, and Cuvier got his hands dirty in the best possible way. Unlike modern young geologists in the United States, who are taught their trade in summertime field camps in places like the northern Rocky Mountains, Cuvier and Brongniart and their contemporaries in England and Germany had to discover not just the basic facts of Earth history but the basic *principles* necessary to read those facts from the Earth's historical record. The rate at which Cuvier made progress in becoming a practicing stratigrapher and putting events in the history of life into a geologic framework is simply astonishing. And, in addition to applying his own genius to the work, Cuvier had the ability to organize many technical staff members to help him. He was, in modern terms, a great laboratory director as well as a scientist of piercing intellect. Thus, the description of Cuvier's discoveries and ideas requires a small library, and his impact on the beginnings of the science of paleontology stands unmatched.

Earlier in this book we met Charles Lyell, the greatest English naturalist of the 1800s, the man whom Agassiz worked hard to convert to an acceptance of the Ice Age. One way of showing the esteem with which Cuvier's contemporaries regarded him is to quote a young Lyell. When Lyell first had the opportunity to visit Cuvier's workspace—or holy of holies—he enthusiastically described it in a letter to his sister:

> In every part, it displays that extraordinary power of methodizing which is the grand secret of the prodigious feats which he performs annually without appearing to give himself the least trouble . . . [his] studio contains no book-shelves. It is a longish room, comfortably furnished, lighted from above, with eleven desks to stand to, and two low tables . . . [this] is for one man, who multiplies himself as author and, admitting no one into this room, moves as he finds necessary or as fancy induces him from one occupation to another.[6]

We have another major reason to think that Cuvier was unusually gifted at human relations when he wanted to be. He was one of the very few public intellectuals of his time to work at a high level under radically opposing French governments, ranging from the Revolutionary regime to the Napoleonic government and onward through the days of several French monarchies. Despite the profound political and cultural changes that swept so many intellectuals to their deaths, Cuvier kept his head—literally—and died in his own bed of natural causes in his sixties, the most significant French scientist of his day.

One of the clear lessons Cuvier drew from fossils is also the most profound. Cuvier presented his colleagues with countless points of evidence showing that many species on Earth had become extinct. He studied numerous fossils in a great deal of detail, compared them to living animals, and saw all the similarities and discrepancies between the two sets of evidence. The ancient remains of ground sloths, cave bears, mammoths, mastodons, and much more showed that life on Earth included the full and complete destruction of species.

Cuvier's work on the idea of extinction started with the Pleistocene mammal he first unearthed around Paris. Woolly mammoths, Cuvier argued on many and detailed grounds of anatomy, were in the same group as elephants, but they were also quite distinct from them. And using the geologic information of where in the ground the woolly mammoth fossils were discovered, Cuvier deduced that they were alive and flourishing until recent times. The woolly beasts died off—every last one of them—due to sudden changes on Earth that Cuvier estimated occurred about five thousand or six thousand years ago.[7]

Cuvier published many other important insights about species and extinctions during his prolific career. He no doubt discussed some of them with the young Agassiz when the latter came to Paris to study. As an example, some other naturalists assigned modern elephants the status of long-lost offspring of the mammoths, seeing them as descendents that had wandered into warmer climes to the south of what had been the woolly range. That couldn't be the case, Cuvier argued, because places like Mexico don't have elephants, even though the climate there would be good for them, and they clearly did have woolly mammoths nearby in the United States. Just as their different anatomy suggests, the woolly mammoth and the elephant are distinct species, and the woolly mammoth is well and truly gone, an animal that flourished for millennia and was wiped out by Mother Nature.

Agassiz readily accepted Cuvier's basic ideas about extinction, adjusting his theology as necessary. In part it was because Agassiz embraced the extinction of many, many species on Earth that he was able to build on that notion as soon as his ideas about climate change took shape. Without a doubt, Agassiz correctly intuited a connection between climate and extinction. As we shall see, he got several matters wrong, but the basic link between extinction and climate that Agassiz promoted has proven its worth on several occasions.

As Agassiz's life progressed, first in Switzerland and then in America, he was confronted with the fact that more and more fossil evidence showed that the bestiary of the Pleistocene was both wonderfully diverse and complex. True, the animals of our own Holocene are also present in the fossil record of the earlier Ice Age, but there are additionally many odd, interesting, and enormous mammals from that earlier time that have no living counterpart today.

The discovery of Ice Age fossils has continued from Agassiz's day down to the twenty-first century. We now know that almost none of the Pleistocene mammals appear in the fossil record right at the start of the Pleistocene; neither do they disappear neatly together at the end. Most appear somewhere within the two million years of the Ice Age, and many disappear well before the end of the epoch. But to get a flavor of the bestiary as a group, here is a partial list of the extinct mammals that lived in some part of the Pleistocene. Although these animals roamed the Earth not long ago, they mostly lived in a radically different and much colder global climate:

- Saber-toothed cat or "tiger": thousands of the massive saber-toothed cats were trapped in the tar pits of Los Angeles, perhaps as they tried to feed on trapped mammoths. We also have some fossils of the tigers from other localities, including Peru. There were three distinct species of saber-toothed tigers. Today the cats are often drawn in children's books, and fossil remains are displayed in many natural history museums, where the cat's fierce-looking saber fangs and large, tank-like bone structure make for lasting impressions.

- Some other interesting large cats: the Ice Age lion of the New World was larger and heavier than the lion we know in Africa today. Pleistocene tiger specimens have been found in China. Ice Age leopards and jaguars are also known from the fossil record. All the great cats were larger in the Pleistocene Epoch than they are today, but scientists consider them so closely related to modern counterparts that they are termed subspecies rather than separate species.

- Giant beaver: the largest Pleistocene rodent of North America was a type of beaver that grew to be as large as the modern black bear. This megabeaver, unlike the little beavers we observe today, likely didn't build dams, though it did live in swampy areas adjoining lakes. Specimens have been found from Alaska to Florida. Like our beaver, it was a superb swimmer and could live by feeding on coarse vegetation, which is to say shrubby and woody material.

- Dire wolf: this Pleistocene wolf of North and South America was bigger and sturdier than the modern gray wolf. Its head was larger and broader and its teeth larger and more powerful than any wolf species of the past or present. In the late Pleistocene it ranged from Alberta to South America. No association with people has been inferred. Extinction occurred just as the Holocene Epoch was starting, perhaps due to competition with the wolf we know today.

- Cave bear: Enormous numbers of cave bear remains have been found in caves in Europe. The discoveries of the bear fossils by humans likely date from time immemorial, but they picked up in pace when paleontology was born and naturalists started to try to understand the heaps of animal bones found in some caves. Naturalists pieced together specimens and identified them as belonging to the group *Ursus*. We have more fossil remains of cave bears than of other *Ursus* species because the bears hibernated in caves rather than earthen dens. Those that died during hibernation in the caves were in an ideal environment to have their bones preserved.

- Elk, deer, and moose: a variety of species we would recognize as similar to—but much larger than—modern elk, deer, and moose inhabited the Earth in the Pleistocene Epoch. Some of the large elk had a bushy forest of antlers, and some of the Pleistocene deer were more on the scale of modern elk. An extinct Ice Age moose was even larger than the modern moose, and it is often displayed in natural history museums simply to awe visitors with its size—and the size of its headgear, which causes hunters to drool on their flannel shirts.

• Woolly rhinoceros: this Ice Age version of a rhino, as its name implies, carried a woolly coat over a fat layer. The animal has been found in the frozen soils of Siberia as well as in surface petroleum deposits in the Carpathian foothills. The rhino's horn may have been used to help scrape away snow from the Earth so the animal could eat underlying grasses. Like the mammoth, it could tolerate the tundra—an amazing difference from the rhino species we know today, which lives in warm climes. One puzzle is why the woolly rhino did not, like so many other arctic species, cross the land bridge from Asia to North America. For whatever reason, its habitat did not stretch beyond Asia.

The list of extinct Ice Age animals goes on and on. But as odd and interesting as the complex Pleistocene bestiary is, it's also crucial to note that many large mammals that are very much still alive and well in the natural world around us today were also present in the Ice Age. That is, many of "our" mammals existed alongside the species that went extinct. The bison is one, big horn sheep another. Tundra musk ox and caribou were alive and well in the Pleistocene, and they still flourish in the related modern climates and ecosystems that have simply shifted north. On the carnivorous side, the Ice Age also had its share of timber wolves and cougars, both species still very much with us today. So it's not that the animal kingdom was created anew for the Holocene—as Agassiz unfortunately thought in his more theological moods—but that some mammal species living in the Ice Age came to dominate the scene when those that had been around them went extinct at or near the end of the Pleistocene.

Putting climate and extinction together as cause and effect was part of Agassiz's genius. Unlike Jefferson and others, Agassiz had easily enough accepted the idea that Ice Age mammals had flourished in their time and then been wiped off the face of the Earth. Agassiz thought that climate change was essentially an agent of God's hand, a direct cause of extinctions sponsored by the Creator. Indeed, Agassiz argued that glaciers must have spread from the North Pole to the equator, killing off all plant and animal species. The entire globe was sterilized, he thought, by global glaciers that spread about as quickly as winter falls on the land at the end of autumn. The massive—fully complete—extinction was necessary in some way so that God could create anew in the following epoch.

While Agassiz's specific notions about the causes of extinctions were not particularly helpful, his ideas about temperature change over geologic time were part of the broadly useful thinking of several early naturalists. Agassiz and other early geologists, quite understandably, looked at large fern leaves preserved as fossils in coal beds in northern Europe and inferred that, ages and ages ago, the Earth must have been very much warmer. And, as Cuvier and Lyell and others showed again and again in limestone rocks, there were tropical-type shells in the bedrock of northern Europe. As the 1800s unfolded and similar evidence was found across Canada and the United States, the lesson seemed unavoidable: Earth had been a vastly warmer planet for most of its history. Added to that was the similar evidence of vertebrate fossils: the enormous reptile fossils of the Paleozoic and the dinosaurs and pterosaurs of the Mesozoic all appeared to indicate the world was once tropical—perhaps even balmier than the modern tropics.

Agassiz argued that Earth has seen a series of temperature revolutions—one at each of the times of mass extinction of species that separate geological periods—with times of relative temperature equilibrium in between. Overall, the temperature of the Earth has declined from the heat-soaked days of giant reptiles and ferns as large as trees. The temperate climate we enjoy today is part of this trend toward generally cooler conditions.

Most of the Pleistocene, Agassiz assumed, was actually warmer than today. He called it the "Ice Age" only because he thought it *ended* in an icy shroud of glaciers that covered the Earth from pole to pole, snuffing out all species. So, for Agassiz, mastodons, the dire wolf, marsupial lions, and all the rest lived in a rather balmy climate—but they died out in the bitter cold that marked the complete extinction of life on Earth at the end of the Pleistocene Epoch. That woolly mammoths and woolly rhinos of the Pleistocene were clearly very woolly, with thick layers of fat below their woolliness, was an observation that Agassiz's hypothesis did not well explain. So it was left to others to come quickly to the idea that most or all of the Pleistocene was bitter cold and that the animals in question were well designed for a cold climate. As we have seen, materials like the forest bed that lay in between glacial gravels spoke to warm times—much like our own—that repeatedly, if briefly, interrupted the bitter cold of the Pleistocene. Most of the epoch was heavily glaciated, but there must have been temperate times as well, and glaciers never reached the equator, nor did they snuff out most life, let alone all of it.

What did all this mean for the odd and interesting Ice Age bestiary? Geologists and paleontologists soon came to accept the view that when the Earth in the Pleistocene went through one of its numerous warm spells, the cold-adapted animals likely migrated north. Essentially, that's what is in evidence today: musk ox and caribou, mammals common in the Ice Age, are found today in more limited populations in the tundra at high latitudes. But for most of the Pleistocene Epoch, when global temperatures were bitter, the odd mammals you knew and loved in grade school were abundant in the middle latitudes. Extinction isn't simple, nor is it black and white. Some Pleistocene species went extinct during times of bitter cold, some in times of warmth, like the present, that occurred a million years ago.

We don't understand the causes of extinction patterns with any clarity, and the details of various conflicting hypotheses would take us too far from modern climate science to consider further in this book. Suffice it to say that the best understanding we have of how climate has affected plant and animal species relies not just on the realm of paleontology, but on physical geology—a field that was better and better understood as the 1800s progressed. Physical geology and paleontology can each make the other stronger, just as Cuvier's insights in and around Paris had done regarding both fossils and the physical layers in which they were found. When American geologists increasingly united physical geology and the study of fossils, they left Agassiz behind as surely as he had surpassed Jefferson.

Grove Karl Gilbert, whom we met earlier because of his work on Glacial Lake Bonneville in Utah, was the type of geologist who understood physical conditions well and used them heavily to infer the geologic context of a fossil. Here's one story to illustrate the power of this type of thinking in our country and how advances in science in America could illuminate specifics concerning the dates and times of Ice Age bestiary.

Early in Gilbert's life, he assisted the unearthing of a mastodon's remains from gravel deposits associated with the Mohawk River in upstate New York. When the geologist in charge fell in the diggings and was hurt, Gilbert was put in charge despite his youth and inexperience. After he had fetched the fossil out of the Earth and delivered it for study elsewhere—meeting Agassiz in his Harvard glory in the process—Gilbert took the unusual step of *returning* to the gravels that had yielded the mastodon. Why go back to the empty hole? He knew he could learn by studying the physical context of the fossil—and he had the dedication and insight to teach himself how to do it.

The Ice Age gravel that yielded the fossil had collected in "potholes," the kind of depression you can see on the beds of rivers in New England and the Midwest to this day. Gilbert deduced that the potholes were formed, as he wrote, by "the grinding of stones moved by water."[8]

These round depressions are a bit like bowls, and sometimes they are quite deep, more like test tubes than cereal bowls. Gilbert counted and mapped the potholes, and he also studied nearby Cohoes Falls, which lay upstream on the Mohawk from the pothole that had contained the mastodon fossil.

Here's the background you need for understanding what came next in Gilbert's work. The waterfalls on any river—like Niagara Falls today—recede slowly *upstream* over time. That's because the river erodes the lip of the falls. As erosion occurs, the exact location of the falls moves a little bit—and it always moves upstream.

Since the mastodon lay in a pothole below Cohoes Falls, the age of the mastodon could not be *older* than the time at which the falls would have been at the place of the pothole in the river. In other words, if Gilbert could deduce how fast the falls had receded up the Mohawk, he could put a *maximum age* on the mammoth fossil—a wonderful advance over earlier science in the 1800s, which would have been able to say only that the fossil was from the Pleistocene Epoch, but without attaching any specific dates.

But how could anything clear about the rates of erosions and dates be seen in the mists of history?

G. K. Gilbert had the brilliance to realize he could estimate how quickly the falls had been retreating in recent centuries and thus calculate how quickly they had retreated in recent millennia. He had, after all, the record of trees growing in the area. Gilbert therefore hung by ropes near the falls and cut down the trees so that he could count the growth rings in the wood. Using that information, he knew how long trees had grown at certain distances from the falls. From that information he was able to estimate that the falls were receding up river at a rate of about one foot per century. Measuring from the modern falls to the pothole that had contained the mastodon fossil, Gilbert could deduce that *the fossil was at most about thirty-five thousand years old.* It was an astounding result, one of the rare times in the 1800s that a geologist was able to give a specific date—albeit just a maximum age—to a Pleistocene fossil. And it was yet another example of a glorious unification of the most powerful deductions from physical geology and the science of paleontology.

But few geological samples lie in such special places as the Ice Age mastodon in the pothole that Gilbert studied. What geologists needed in order to unravel Pleistocene history was a much fuller record of time, one that recorded species and climate over broad areas. And, just as important, geologists needed this record to describe absolute, not merely relative, time. The record needed to have some kind of natural clock embedded in the data so that geologists could determine whether specific climate conditions under observation pertained to the region fifteen thousand rather than five thousand years ago, for example.

To get this kind of clear picture of how quickly climate and ecosystems could change in a region, geologists turned for answers to simple layers of clay and muck. The record of climate change and its biological impact, it turned out, was simply in the dirt beneath our feet.

5

MIRACULOUS MUD

His father was Sweden's prime minister and his older brother later held the same office. Growing up in Sweden after his birth in 1858, it must not have been easy to avoid the long shadow cast by his important male relatives. But Gerhard Jakob de Geer was a success in his own right. And by spending most of his time and talent in the new science of geology, it can certainly be argued he made more difference to the greater world than all the Swedish prime ministers of his age.

As a young man, De Geer studied at Uppsala University and then joined the Swedish Geological Survey, where he cut his professional teeth. Like others at work in the geological sciences in his native country, he had the basic choice of directly useful economic work—perhaps related to Sweden's rich copper and iron ore reserves—or not-so-useful but arguably more profound work—related to the climate revolutions of the Ice Age. Perhaps because his family was so successful in many ways, young De Geer had the emotional luxury of choosing the less practical path. In any event, glacial features and climate change soon became his life's work, and he was devoted to it.

De Geer started his professional life making detailed studies of several "raised beaches" that rim Scandinavia above current sea level. The raised beaches are found on land in Sweden and Denmark (and also, the reader may recall, around Hudson Bay). Given that geologists have come to understand that sea level has been rising due to the great melt off of glaciers during the Holocene, the raised beaches are doubly impressive because their existence shows that the land in Scandinavia has been gaining elevation *even more rapidly* than global sea level has been rising.

It's the strong upward movement of local landscapes that leaves old sea beaches high and dry above current sea level. The reason the land is moving upward, of course, is that for many millennia it was being "held down" by the great weight of glacial ice on top of it. The glaciers have melted and gone, and the land is still buoying gradually upward over time, like an enormous ship adjusting as an almost infinitely large cargo is unloaded from it.

De Geer also studied the local glacial moraines that cover much of Sweden. Just as Louis Agassiz had once scrutinized the moraines in Switzerland, and Charles Wittlesey and T. C. Chamberlain had studied the glacial moraines of the American Midwest, De Geer carefully mapped the Swedish moraines around him. And his exploration of raised beaches and complex moraines were good material for teaching a young geologist about the evidence and importance of climate revolutions.

In Sweden, the history of the Holocene Epoch is the grand story of the retreat of enormous volumes of ice under the radical warming of global climate over thousands of years. As the Holocene progressed, the glacial ice mass that had been centered on Scandinavia—the ice that had flowed south into Europe during the Pleistocene—retreated through Sweden northward over the millennia. The retreat was not absolutely steady—there were faster and slower pulses and some back-and-forth reversals to be sure—but the great retreat due to radical climate change is the backdrop against which the recent geologic history of Scandinavia is measured.

With other Swedish colleagues, De Geer mapped out the great retreat of the ice and how and where it had dumped its final load of rock debris—the rocky detritus that's still visible on the surface in many Swedish fields, slopes, and ridges. But the work mapping the glacial stones pales beside that to which De Geer turned next. In 1882 the young geologist suggested that the many small, horizontal layers of clay-rich material exposed as a result of modern erosion were features that had been originally deposited one year at a time.

Each layer is termed a *varve* (related to "layer" in Swedish). The layers that attracted De Geer's attention are quite different from other layers in the Earth, such as the thick and varied ones in which Cuvier had found big bones around Paris. Varves are often razor sharp and horizontal, and they occur as thin layers, usually no more than a quarter inch or a half inch thick. And, quite importantly, varves alternate in color almost perfectly between dark and light bands, making zebra-like patterns when you view them on edge.

Varves are made mostly of clay, a very fine material. The particles in clay are so tiny that they are smooth to the touch. You can learn the basic size of "dirt" particles by rubbing a bit on your front teeth and then checking the result with your tongue. If it feels smooth, it's clay. (Yes, the author has been doing this basic test for decades—and she still has most of her front teeth.) Other parts of varves are made of silt, the particles of which are just one tiny step larger than clay particles.

Like other geologists of his era, De Geer understood the facts about particle size and the environments in which natural materials move and accumulate. Grasping such basics is useful for our story, so let's turn our attention briefly to a few simple lessons that can help the reader appreciate how unusual the fine clays and silts in varves are—and why they can record so much information about climate change over the millennia.

The first concept to understand is that large chunks of material—like boulders—can be moved and deposited only directly by *glacial ice* or else by *torrents of whitewater*, like a fast-moving mountain river. To put it simply, a quiet stream simply isn't going to move a boulder the size of a stove, let alone one the size of a truck.

Here's a thought experiment: say you are walking in the Rockies this next summer and you come upon several boulders. If the boulders have only been moved by ice throughout their history, they will likely be fairly *angular* in shape and, with luck, they will show the characteristic *scratches* or *striations* Louis Agassiz noted long ago. If they have these features, you will diagnose them as boulders moved by ice alone. But if the boulders are in a steep gully at high elevations, it's possible that the boulders were moved to their place of rest by an earlier, torrential mountain stream or by whitewater gushing out of a retreating glacier. Either way, the bouncing action of the boulders in the fast-moving water will have *rounded* them a bit and potentially erased the scratches. Based on a high degree of rounding and a scratch-free surface, you can diagnose the big rocks as having been moved by torrential water flow for at least part of their history rather than by ice alone.

Smaller particles can also tell us quite a bit about the environment in which they formed. Smaller round particles, like *pebbles*, can be moved by large rivers and laid down in gravel bars. *Sand* is moved and deposited by quieter flow, often in larger rivers downstream of the pebbles. When sand is deposited, it makes sandbars. Really fine material—*mud and silt*—makes it all the way to the lower parts of major rivers (like the lower Hudson River and the lower Mississippi River).

But razor-sharp, neat little layers of clay, stacked on top of each other with alternating dark and light colors, simply doesn't fit with the pictures just sketched. To explain varves, we need to explore the idea that was just emerging in geology when De Geer took it up and made it popular.

De Geer knew that the tiny particles of clay in varves indicate a geologic environment that was dominated by truly still waters, such as those of a *lake*. When he began his work on the thousands of varve layers exposed in many locations in Sweden, he realized he was looking at the physical diary of many enormous lakes that had existed near the retreating glacial ice mass that had moved northward as global climate warmed in the Holocene. It was the zebra-like, light-dark-light-dark pattern of varves that raised them to the greatest level of importance. For anyone interested in the history of the Earth's climate, as De Geer most certainly was, the varves were more valuable than anything ever discovered before. Indeed, varves were and are stupendous for geologists because they are created *each year* by annual processes in lakes.

Almost nothing on Earth leaves an annual record of change. Volcanic eruptions create rock layers—but the rocks may form in a few days and then leave many thousands of years "blank" before the next eruption. Coastal areas record evidence of ancient tsunamis that formed in a few hours—but with centuries or millennia once again bare and empty before the record of the next tsunami. Varves are quite different—and vastly more important—because they record simple but direct evidence of what each and every year has been like for one portion of the Earth.

Swedish varves had formed, De Geer reasoned, on the bottoms of large glacial lakes that existed along the southern margin of the massive Swedish ice sheet. Cold, northern lakes create varves because brief summertime conditions in the lakes are quite different from the long, northern winter. In the summer, streams of meltwater carrying particles feed into the lakes, and the surface of the lake is ice-free. Summer winds carry silt and dust to the lake's surface. Water movement is enough to keep clays suspended in the water—so they don't settle to the bottom. The particles that do settle to the bottom are ever-so-slightly coarser than clay, consisting mostly of material like silt that leaves a slight grittiness on your teeth. That size of silt, as it happens, is light colored.

In the winter, the lake is quite a different body. It freezes over, so there's a solid surface on top of it. No wind can create waves or otherwise disturb the water. Inlet streams are frozen, too, so there isn't material being washed into the lake. The only particles in the water during this time of year are very fine clays, the tiny particles that remained suspended in the water all summer long because they were so small. In time, during the long winter, they too settle out. And, as it happens, very fine Earth material is dark colored, quite different from the light-colored summer layer.

Each *pair* of dark- and light-colored layers make up the single unit called a varve—the pair, together, represents a single year's history in a northern lake, just like the dark and light bands of a tree's growth ring represent one year. Varves, by the way, are still forming in arctic lakes. But the discovery of hundreds and even thousands of varves made visible in one place for inspection garnered De Geer's full attention because he realized how much information about Earth's past he might be able to learn from the neatly colored and paired sets of layers.

De Geer went to work matching the varves he found in various locations in Sweden, showing that there were similar patterns in the varves of the same time in different areas. De Geer and his students matched variations in thickness of varve layers over a 120-mile-long line near Stockholm. They found that there were eight hundred varves in the area, with varves matching the retreating terminal moraine formed by Sweden's great ice sheet. This meant it had taken the last portion of ice some eight hundred years to melt away to nothing. This was revolutionary science because it attached a clear date to events in the Holocene, and it garnered his work great interest. In time, one of De Geer's assistants worked out the field evidence showing that the final inland ice left the area about 6700 BCE—a firm date all the more valuable in the days before carbon-14 and other radioactive dating techniques.

Alas, De Geer was ultimately carried away by his success. He became convinced that he could see matching patterns in the records of varves from Sweden, the Himalayas, North America, and beyond. It was a bit as if one were to cut down trees in Wisconsin, the Yukon, and in Brazil and then testify to the world that one had found the same pattern of thick and thin growth rings corresponding to good and lean years for trees on a global basis. At least one of De Geer's closest colleagues, it seems clear, seriously tried to warn him of his errors. But De Geer reacted with denunciations and arguments rather than with reflection or reconsideration. In short, he plunged on with his global interpretations, ultimately alienating most geologists, who didn't see the worldwide varve patterns at all as he did.

De Geer can be rightly criticized—like Agassiz before him—for letting his ideas carry him beyond good evidence. But, like Agassiz, he contributed a lot to the understanding of climate change, and it's easy to feel at least some sympathy for the enthusiasm of someone who initially discovered such a new vision of the world and rightly deduced so much from it. De Geer gave the intellectual world a remarkable gift: the first year-by-year account of regional climate changes in the late Pleistocene and the Holocene. His pioneering work inspired other geologists—literally around the world—to develop similar histories explaining how climate in their regions had evolved over time. Those are amazing legacies to leave science, and they are enough to allow us to remember De Geer's name with respect despite the shortcomings of part of his work.

But we have not scratched the surface of the importance of mud to modern science. Muck and mire also contain tiny bits of evidence from the whole *ecosystem* around glacial lakes and bogs when the mud formed. And, in the end, it has been the microscopic bits of the biological record that have proven the most important for deducing past climates.

As it happens, the geologist who pioneered much of microscopic biological work came from Sweden, too. Ernst Jakob Lennart von Post arrived on the scene just a few years later than did De Geer. Unlike De Geer, who grew up in a well-off family at the heart of Swedish society, Von Post's early childhood was marked by tragedy. His mother died when he was a year old, and he had no older brothers and sisters to soften that blow. He was raised largely by his father from that point onward. But he must have excelled in school, for when he was seventeen he started his studies at Sweden's premier university, Uppsala. He went on to earn both a bachelor's degree and the equivalent of a master's.

In his master's work, Von Post threw himself into studying peat bogs. And what Von Post found in peat layers gave the scientific world its first detailed information about regional climate change over the millennia and the real impact of climate revolutions on living creatures of former times. Because it's the actual impact of climate on the living world that we care so dearly about, we'll consider the realm of pollen with some detail.

For many Americans of the twenty-first century, voluntarily studying peat bogs may seem an odd professional choice. But Von Post dove into peat in part because geologists take as a sacred responsibility the task of understanding, identifying, and helping to provide energy sources for our societies. For many centuries, peat had been exactly that—a significant source of energy for northern Europe.

Peat is made of old plant remains—the dead wreckage of plant life of the past that accumulates in bogs and mire before it can rot and fully break down. If you dry peat out in the summer—as peasants of northern Europe had done for centuries—it has enough carbon content to be burned for heat in the winter. The smoke that results is extremely sooty and foul, but if peat is all you have to get you through the winter, it's a usable fuel source.

Von Post was one of the first geologists to start looking seriously at peat not just as the common but dirty fuel of last resort, but in terms of what it could tell science about Earth's climate history. Peat is literally the remains of Earth's plants, at least those plants that excel at living in soggy conditions in low areas. If you dig deeply down into a peat bog, you'll find layers in the peat. These are not beautiful annual layers, like varves, they are just the more common layers that denote some variable passage of time. In the various layers you'll likely see small twigs and bits of plant matter from what grew in that spot a few millennia ago.

A good naturalist can sometimes identify and list the plant species that were growing in that particular place just from looking at the twigs and small remains with a simple magnifying glass. And here's the crucial point: if you know the plant species growing in a region a thousand years ago, you know a *great deal* about the climate of that time. As every gardener knows, plants grow only in the climate "zones" they prefer. So if peat's twigs and leaves can lead to the identification of several individual species, they can tell you—sometimes quite specifically, it turns out—the climate conditions of that peat bog in the past.

In the early 1900s scientists started their peat work with exactly this sort of reasoning in mind. They dug down into peat bogs, mapped general layering, and studied bits of plant matter whenever such matter was still big enough to be identifiable. Although their work didn't result in a beautifully precise annual record of the past like the record found in De Geer's annual varves, the peat work had much more meaningful information about climate content embedded within it.

Today a lot of the hard work of hand digging through peat bogs and marsh mire has been replaced by an activity called *coring*. We'll meet coring in a later chapter with respect to glacial ice, so it's worth taking a moment to clearly explain the basic geometry of the activity. It's not a complex task: you yourself did it as a child if you ever pushed a drinking straw through a piece of Jell-O®. When you artfully twisted the straw and removed it from your food, the gelatin stayed inside. If you squeezed the Jell-O out of the straw, you had what Earth scientists would call a "core" of the gelatin.

In the context of both lake beds and peat bogs, here's how coring is done. Scientists (or their younger and stronger helpers) push a metal tube measuring two or three inches in diameter down into the mud. In low-budget work, this is often accomplished by banging on the top of the tube with hammers. For better organized and financed work, it can be most helpful to use a tube that has teeth cut into the bottom. With a motor, the tube can then be spun so that the teeth bite into the muck. When the work is motorized, the activity is called drilling, and the tube with teeth is a special type of drill bit.

Whether a geologist uses hammers or a motorized drilling rig, the goal of the activity is to insert the tube into the Earth and thus isolate a narrow column of mud. When that's accomplished, the tube and its contents are retrieved. The core of muck and mire is then pushed out of the tube, forming a long rod of sample material. This geologic prize is then carefully transported to the laboratory for examination.

Von Post examined many Swedish peat bogs. Then he looked at the muck he brought back to the lab through a microscope, leading him to study the *pollen grains* trapped in the layers. It was the clear evidence of changes in pollen over time that led Von Post and his fellow researchers to a much greater understanding of regional climate change than anything De Geer, or indeed any geologist in the world, had yet been able to offer.

The fundamental reason for the new wave of success was simply the botanical fact that the pollen produced each year with wild abandon by flowering plants is distributed around a region on the slightest breeze. This process can distress people with allergies, since pollen from a wide variety of plants will blow for considerable distances. But the upside, if you will, of the far-flung life of pollen grains is that pollen from a whole district can reach lowland areas like bogs and lakes. To a geologist, these are areas of interest because they record botanical evidence in layers over time. For example, pollen that blows out onto the surface of a glacial lake is likely to hit the water and be trapped within it. In time the pollen will gently rain down through the water to the varve layer forming on the bottom, and there it will accumulate and be buried by later clays. In a similar fashion, even more pollen accumulates in swampy bogs and mires. There are no neat dark-and-light annual layers in such marshes, but there are basic layering structures, with deeper layers clearly corresponding to older conditions. And once pollen falls into a bog, it stays put, awaiting the day when a geologist arrives to core for it.

By fortunate chance, pollen is remarkably sturdy stuff. It can be buried in mud for thousands of years and emerge with its physical structures fully intact, a positively exquisite joy for scientific observers to behold under the microscope. By a second fortunate chance, many plants can be identified simply by the pollen they produce, sometimes at the level of species, sometimes at the broader level of genus. The pollen of cold-tolerant pine trees, for example, can be distinguished from aspen or birch, which love still-colder climes, and such information readily translates into what the ancient climate of the whole region around the peat bog was like thousands of years ago. Pollen from warmth-loving oaks looks quite different again. Oaks indicate warmer times than do pines—and Scandinavian researchers quickly saw that there was a much warmer time in our own epoch, the Holocene, in which oaks had actually flourished in Sweden!

The pollen work got a lot of attention in the European scientific community because it spoke directly to how plant ecosystems had changed in the whole region from the late Pleistocene Epoch down to modern times. Soon other geologists—and botanists—across northern Europe began similar studies, becoming dedicated catalogers of pollen in a wide variety of muddy Earth materials. So, in two or three generations, a vast compendium of knowledge about past climate in many places on Earth was gained from locations rich in ancient pollen.

In the 1940s and 1950s the detailed picture of changing plant communities as recorded by pollen grains was united with what was then the new technique of carbon-14 dating. A particular layer of a peat horizon that contained the remains of a twig, for example, could be dated with carbon-14. The pollen from that layer could be used to deduce plant communities that reflected the regional climate of that specific time—say five thousand years ago.

It's worth reviewing some recent *climate periods* for northern Europe known to us by pollen studies, varve calibration, and carbon-14 dating. As you will readily see from this quick overview of the climate record of northern Europe as revealed principally by pollen, climate change has been ceaseless and varied, even in this geologically short period.

In the late Pleistocene, northern Europe was in a cold and dry climate regime called the *Oldest Dryas* time. *Dryas* is the scientific name of an arctic wildflower that grows in the tundra, and its abundant pollen in the cores of Denmark make it clear that the climate was a bitter one, roughly similar to central or northern Alaska today. The tundra wildflower gives its name to several bitter times, this being the first one. Denmark during the Oldest Dryas time was a plain of tundra permafrost without trees. Southern Sweden was still buried by glacial ice. Sea level stood much lower than at present, and there was a wide land bridge between the British Isles and the rest of Europe—a fact we can deduce in several ways, including from the abundant bones of woolly mammoth found on the floor of what's now the shallow sea that separates the United Kingdom from France and Norway, bones so abundant we have dredged them up and drilled into them on our way to North Sea oil deposits.

The Oldest Dryas climate regime lasted until the region became warmer and wetter, at which point it was replaced by a new regional climate regime called the *Bolling Oscillation.* The Bolling Oscillation is marked by the presence of pollen from scattered small willows and birches in Denmark as well as continued pollen from tundra plants. Glacial ice melted back from southern Sweden at this time. The region was in a phase that puts it on the borderline between tundra and taiga. This warmer and wetter time lasted only about five hundred years, however, before regional climate swung back to what it had been.

The *Older Dryas* comes next. It was a colder and drier tundra time, much like the Oldest Dryas had been. Then, as the pollen record shows, the regional climate again warmed and became wetter during the *Allerod Oscillation.* The Allerod time had at least as much vegetation as the Bolling Oscillation. It also had more abundant birch trees, meaning it likely was a tad warmer than the earlier oscillation. The Allerod lasted for about a thousand years, and the remains of the great ice sheet retreated farther north in Sweden and Norway during this time.

The pollen record shows that the area was next plunged into renewed and bitter cold more extreme than the conditions during the Oldest and Older Dryas. This period of time, called the *Younger Dryas*, saw trees disappearing under fierce temperature declines. In the next chapters, we'll examine in detail the evidence that this shift to renewed bitter cold took place very rapidly, certainly within a single human lifetime. For now, suffice it to say that the speed of this climate change doubtless decimated human and animal populations that had become used to the warmer conditions of the millennium-long Allerod Oscillation. In the new climate regime, only tundra plants could survive in the region, as is shown by the pollen trapped in the peat bogs. Geologic evidence indicates that the remnants of the great ice sheet actually *advanced* during this time, the final bitter hurrah of the latest part of the Pleistocene Epoch.

The bitter climate regime lasted about five hundred years in southern Scandinavia, longer in other places. According to the pollen record, the frigid era ended quickly, again over the span of one human life. The new, milder regional climate regime is called *Pre-Boreal time*. This phase of the pollen record marks the start of the Holocene Epoch, our own times, which, as we saw using our football-field analogy of time, accounts for only the last few feet. For southern Sweden and Denmark, the Pre-Boreal brought warmth sufficient that a birch forest, with some pine, covered much of the landscape, creating abundant birch pollen in the peat layers for the first time. Indeed, some birch stumps are present in layers of bog from this era. The pollen record shows quaking aspen in the mix of trees as well. These were the "good times" for early people of the area, good at least compared to anything they or their ancestors had known. But it must have still been a harsh life, much colder than today.

The next climate shift was toward greater warmth. *Boreal time* represented a longer period that changed the whole ecosystem of the region. The "good times" had become even better for people. Pine pollen becomes abundant in the peat layers of Boreal time in southern Scandinavia. The great ice sheet melted quickly back northward, retreating to higher latitude and higher elevations, never to disturb southern Sweden again. Global sea level started a dramatic rise as water that had been locked up in glaciers for millennia was set free to run to the sea. The land bridge between the British Isles and Ireland was severed, making Ireland an island. For a time, what's now Britain was still connected to continental Europe, but by the end of Boreal time sea level had risen enough that Britain also became an island.

The next climate shift in the region saw even warmer conditions. The change ushered in the *Atlantic time*. Pine and birch trees were joined by oaks and elm. Even Finland supported elm trees. In short, climate had become warmer than the present day. That bears repeating: the pollen record indicates that the climate of northern Europe was *warmer* in the Atlantic period than it is today. Prehistoric people in the region had never had it so good—nor, in fact, would they ever again.

As we shall see later in the book, the warmth of the Atlantic time was not just regional; it was global. The era is defined with somewhat different dates in various parts of the world, but it is clear everywhere in the physical record and is known as the *Holocene Optimum.* The optimum corresponds to the late Neolithic and Bronze ages in human history. People around the world fared better than ever before, with the first organized societies based on extensive and successful agriculture springing up in places like Mesopotamia, Egypt, India, and China. That doesn't mean that the warm climate led to the advance of civilizations—but early agriculture could not flourish, of course, if climate had been variable and bitterly cold.

During the Atlantic time, the remnant of the great Scandinavian ice sheet lay in Lapland, and it was shrinking throughout the balmy period. Global sea level surged upward during Atlantic time as the much larger ice sheet in Canada melted dramatically. Throughout most of the Atlantic time, in fact, global sea level was about ten to twelve feet higher than sea level in the twentieth century. Again, the fact bears repeating: sea level in the optimum times was *higher* than it was when you were born.

The warmest part of the Atlantic was at the end of the optimum. But, as always, regional climate shifted once more. The pollen of the peat bogs in southern Sweden and Denmark makes it clear that regional climate cooled as the Atlantic ended and *Sub-Boreal time* started. The time of the transition was about when the Bronze Age turned into the Iron Age. Although the Sub-Boreal times were not as optimal for people in northern Europe as the Atlantic period had been, archeological evidence makes it clear that human populations of the area persisted and that early agriculture took hold in northern Europe, perhaps because of the revolutions in metal use and other technological advancements.

Finally we reach our own times in the peat bog record, the era in which the pollen in the peat is similar to the pollen being produced around Denmark and Sweden today. Our period is known as the *Sub-Atlantic* time.

It is not as warm as the Atlantic, but it is warmer than the Sub-Boreal. Starting around 500 BCE, a mixture of pine and beech woodland takes over the region, with more grasses than earlier. Civilization during the Sub-Atlantic creeps northward into Europe from more advanced parts of the world to the south. By 1000 CE, pollen makes it clear that Europe starts to enjoy a mild, warm pulse within Sub-Atlantic time. These somewhat balmier times are known to historians as the Medieval Warming. The Medieval Warming comes to an end over the course of just a few years during the 1300s, with the onset of a mildly cooler and wetter climate that runs to the mid-1800s. Historians have called this colder time the "Little Ice Age." The Medieval Warming and the Little Ice Age were not changes in climate on the scale of all the other divisions just mentioned—they were much milder phenomena. But they are noted here because the reader may have heard of them and because they show that the major divisions—like the Sub-Atlantic time—were never uniform or monotonous.

Von Post and his colleagues in Scandinavia used pollen grains in muck and mire to clearly establish nearly a dozen major divisions in climate regime in the Holocene Epoch and the very latest part of the Pleistocene. The various climate periods were of different lengths, and some were more extreme than others. Many of them revolutionized the entire plant ecosystems of southern Scandinavia, and they doubtless hit human populations hard at the same time. In short, following the pioneering work of De Geer and Von Post, geologists had quickly come to a detailed understanding of how amazingly common climate change is—very much including change on a scale that makes the living landscape wholly different from what had come before in broad regions.

The results of pollen studies from Scandinavia inspired similar work all around the world. In the wonderfully named Dismal Swamp of Virginia, for example, pollen in cores of mud reveals a warming climate that by 10,500 years ago had—for the first time—as much oak pollen as pine pollen. Tree, shrub, and herb pollen then varies over the millennia in regular ways that can be plotted and named in the same *manner* as Von Post and others did in southern Sweden, although of course with different *specifics* in Virginia.

In short, from pollen studies all around the world in the 1940s, 1950s, and 1960s, it became abundantly clear to geologists that regional climate changes are always occurring on Earth. We can clearly see that cold times are replaced by mildly warmer ones only to be punctuated yet again by colder ones. Drier times that favor grasses are replaced by wetter ones that evolve toward different conditions once more. The record of tiny grains of pollen in humble muck and mire, as accumulated by the Earth and studied so patiently by generations of geologists and botanists, makes clear the ceaseless nature of regional climate change even within broadly stable climate regimes like the Holocene Epoch.

All climate change is important to the fate of plants and animals. The climate changes we sketched in northern Europe doubtless came at a high cost to living organisms, including people, and we have every reason to believe the same about the area around the Dismal Swamp as well. But, as it happens, northern Europe and Virginia were both late in developing societies with written records. If we look at the lands where full civilizations first flourished, we can get a human measure of the cost of regional climate change.

As an example, consider the time near 2300 BCE. It was an era in which large cities graced the Earth in Egypt, Mesopotamia, and India. Simple, scratch-in-the-dirt farming had been replaced by organized agriculture, including irrigation on a large scale. The wealth that resulted from this revolutionary phase of civilization allowed for a greater division of labor than ever before in the history of humanity. Some people spent their whole lives as scribes, employed just to write ideas and numbers down; these were the world's first intellectuals. We know of this era in part through archeological evidence like pots and gold jewelry, but also from written records etched in clay tablets. From such records we know that trading networks brought goods from central Africa up to Egypt, and from there across the Middle East. Goods were also exchanged to and from India. The pyramids of Giza had already been built, and Egyptians of the time could have been forgiven for thinking that they lived amid an empire so great it could never fail.

We know what happened next from written records. The people living through the Great Transition didn't understand it in modern terms. But a scientist would say that regional climate change, like that recorded by Von Post's pollen, swept across Egypt and the Middle East with catastrophic results for human societies.

Even with the tools of organized agriculture and irrigation in place, rain is the crucial ingredient of all farming. Unfortunately for the people in the civilizations of both Egypt and the lands between the Tigris and Euphrates, the precipitation patterns changed enough across the whole region that crops simply failed. When they failed again and again, year after year, the civilizations of the times collapsed. One governor in southern Egypt explained it succinctly, writing that "all of Upper Egypt was dying of hunger to such a degree that everyone had come to eating their children."[1]

It's important to note it wasn't only the poor who were eating their children. Or the outcasts. Or the slaves. It was "all of Upper Egypt." The picture of human despair and misery that the phrase evokes roars like a lion down the millennia. Regional climate change is ready to pounce on us at any time. Exactly this sort of climate change—enough to change what crops we can grow or what trees grow in the woods where we live—is common, natural, and ongoing on Earth. The geologic record shows us that basic picture in many ways, including in the patterns of varves and especially in the pollen grains locked in lake sediments and bogs.

In the 1800s, geologists showed the world how fierce an adversary natural climate change in the Pleistocene Epoch had been. In the early 1900s, De Geer and Von Post showed us that the Holocene Epoch, our own era, is also subject to a great deal of climate change on a regional level. Evidence of major climate evolution in what's now the southwestern United States would come not from mire and mud, but from ancient timbers and old tree stumps.

6

WOOD REVEALS CLIMATE CLUES

For an unlikely tale of how an astronomer dabbled in archeology and gave the next boost to climate science, we turn to Andrew Ellicott Douglass. Born a day after the Fourth of July in 1867, shortly after the close of the Civil War, Douglass was the fifth of six children of an Episcopalian minister living in Vermont. Baby Andrew was christened in honor of his paternal great-grandfather, Andrew Ellicott, a noted surveyor in the early life of the nation who had assisted Pierre L'Enfant in laying out the streets of Washington, DC. By good fortune, the household of Reverend Douglass had inherited Ellicott's early scientific instruments, including a small telescope. It could be said that young Andrew had chosen his family well, and his interest in science dated from his earliest youth. When an aunt gave the lad a star atlas as he neared his eleventh birthday, Andrew immediately started to explore the night sky with the Ellicott telescope, taking the first step on the long trajectory of his scientific life.

Douglass studied for four years at Trinity College in Connecticut. He did well in college, earning honors in astronomy, physics, and mathematics. He also excelled in botany and zoology classes, and he wrote a paper on aluminum that won Trinity's Chemical Prize. An 1888 photo of Douglass at Trinity shows a serious young man, standing tall in front of a blackboard covered in figures. Douglass was one of the last scientists we'll meet who studied many different things without specializing in just one discipline like most researchers who came after him. Still, his main early interest was astronomy, and astronomy remained his core concern throughout his life.

After Douglass graduated from Trinity, he went to work for the Harvard Observatory. He gained valuable experience there, and his background and interests took him abroad as part of Harvard's Boyden expedition to South America. On that trip the young man helped to establish the university's observatory in Arequipa, Peru. Already an impressive young scientist, and with the good sense to appreciate geology, in his free time Douglass studied fossils he found in Peruvian rocks. Returning to Boston, he met the amateur astronomer Percival Lowell, and it was Douglass's association with Lowell that led him in a roundabout way to his later work related to climate.

Percival Lowell was from the wealthy and influential Lowell family, which had dominated New England history for generations. Percival's brother, Abbott Lawrence Lowell, was president of Harvard for a time. His sister, Amy, was a notable poet of the day. Percival spent some years as a businessman in Asia, but his personal interests led him to become a serious, if amateur, astronomer by the early 1890s. Percival knew of Giovanni Schiaparelli's research, in particular the results of a study of Mars conducted in 1877, during a rare excellent period for viewing the red planet. That work led Schiaparelli to describe a series of linear features or "canals" on Mars. Lowell, like some others of his time, believed the channels were evidence of an advanced civilization intent on bringing water from the Martian poles to the drier, lower latitudes of the planet.

Lowell was not an experienced astronomer in the 1890s, but he had growing interests in the field and, unlike so many intellectuals, he had a personal fortune with which to fund his efforts to seriously study the natural world. He knew the next good period for Mars viewing was due to arrive in late 1894, and Lowell wanted to have a telescope set up in an ideal location by that time so that he could pick up where Schiaparelli had left off.

With that goal in mind, Lowell hired Douglass as his assistant. In 1894 the pair traveled to Arizona, where Douglass canvassed the territory for the best site for a telescope. The young astronomer was looking for clear conditions, of course, and also for what is known as "steady" air. Atmospheric currents obscure observations of the night sky, causing minute but problematic movement in what an astronomer sees through a telescope. Areas that have both clear and steady air are not common, and Douglass had to search the night sky from many different spots while maintaining the ability to move around the territory by day in an era before the automobile or even decent roads. Still, in time the young astronomer determined that a spot outside the small town of Flagstaff, just south of the Grand Canyon, would be favorable for an observatory. At the impressive elevation of seven thousand feet, Douglass supervised the construction of what became the Lowell Observatory.

Lowell, with the assistance of Douglass, set to work studying Mars as soon as possible. Although there were some ups and downs in the saga, the early work went well enough from Lowell's point of view. He believed that he could see canals on Mars and that the canals were more pronounced at some times than at others. He thought the variability of the canals meant that vegetation along them grew when Martians were releasing water through their irrigation networks. Lowell also thought that large, dark patches on the planet—which he took to be vegetation—waxed and waned with the seasons.

To be sure, there were intervals when observing the night sky outside Flagstaff wasn't ideal. Dust and atmospheric currents created problems. Both Lowell and Douglass felt frustration with conditions at times. At one point the astronomical work was uprooted and moved to a site in Mexico. The observatory there was thirty miles from Popocatepetl, Mexico's best-known mountain. Douglass, an avid mountain climber, hiked to the top of the eighteen-thousand-foot peak. Always the scientist, Douglass carried a barometer with him to measure atmospheric pressure so he could infer the altitude of the mountain.[1] But soon enough, because of problems at the Mexican work site, Douglass and the telescope returned to the Flagstaff area, where the Lowell-Douglass partnership had first yielded good observational results.

As the years rolled by, Douglass generated a lot of data that Lowell used in support of his theory about a civilization on Mars. But all was not well between the two men. Douglass came to think that Lowell was ignoring good evidence that ran counter to his views. As time went along, the younger man became more and more concerned both about Lowell's published arguments themselves and the use to which Douglass's work behind the telescope had been put by the senior partner of the pairing. In a letter to a colleague, Douglass confided, "It appears to me that Mr. Lowell has a strong literary instinct and no scientific instinct."[2] Soon enough Douglass wrote again in more adamant and more detailed terms. Lowell, he stated, was guilty of the cardinal sin of "hunting up a few facts in support of some speculation instead of perseveringly hunting innumerable facts and then limiting himself to publishing the unavoidable conclusions, as all scientists of good standing do, in whatever line of work they may be engaged."[3] For one reason or another, the recipient of the letters ultimately showed them to Lowell. Naturally, Lowell did not appreciate the manner in which Douglass had written about him, and he immediately fired Douglass.

While being abruptly fired was quite shocking to Douglass, he rallied soon enough, perhaps because he immediately had to start making a living outside Lowell's observatory. To support himself, the astronomer turned to teaching at the small "normal school" in Flagstaff. He taught geography as well as Spanish history and language. He also ran for, and won, the position of justice of the peace. But Douglass's interests in science ran deep, and he remained a committed astronomer at least in his private thoughts even while he made a living in quite different arenas.

It was at this point that Douglass's life took another turn, one that was to define the rest of his career as a scientist. While working in Flagstaff, Douglass was impressed by the large ponderosa pines being felled in the area by the timber industry. The pine logs, of course, showed annual growth, with the most recent ring just under the bark and the oldest at the center of the log. In a leap of creative imagination, Douglas wondered whether the trees could help him investigate one of his interests in astronomy. It was as a by-product of his idea that Douglass started a new branch of inquiry into climate change, so it's worth following his reasoning about tree rings and what he guessed might have influenced them.

As an astronomer, Douglass knew quite a bit about the sun. Among the sun's interesting features are sunspots—dark blotches that sometimes appear on the face of the sun. The written records of astronomers had long shown that sunspots vary greatly in their numbers over time. Aside this variability, astronomers had documented what seemed to be a pretty clear cycle within the larger variations that occurred. In other words, the number of sunspots seems to go up and down each eleven years as well as change significantly over much longer periods.

Douglass, like others, wondered whether the sunspot cycle might affect climate on Earth. If sunspots were linked to climate, and climate influenced the growth of trees, then changes in tree rings might help him study the eleven-year sunspot cycle. If the investigation proceeded ideally, Douglass could hope to generate data about the sun's cycle from tree rings going back to the time prior to when astronomers began looking at the solar surface and keeping records about the spots.

Douglass's first effort to measure the width of tree rings occurred in the log yard of the Arizona Lumber and Timber Company in January 1904. In some ways it was a peculiar time to launch his research program, since there was snow on the ground and it wasn't easy to make fine measurements of small tree rings in the cold temperatures. But Douglass either liked something he saw in the tree rings that day or was simply determined to do more work before evaluating his data. He persuaded lumber company personnel to cut off the ends of logs and the tops of stumps and send them to him so he could work more carefully indoors. In that way, he soon had twenty-four specimens. By 1906 he had collected twenty-five additional samples of fresh wood from the Flagstaff area. Two of the samples were from trees more than five hundred years old, an interesting and gratifying fact that showed some individual pines might well yield a long record of regional climate effects.

Many tree rings are actually quite narrow, so doing the work of measuring their width was slow work. At first, Douglass and an assistant simply laid a ruler on the cut end of the wood samples. Using a magnifying glass, they measured the width of each ring. It took five years to record the width of ten thousand rings. Studying all the measurements he had obtained, Douglass was hopeful of seeing an eleven-year cycle in the sequence of thick and thin rings. But Douglass was disappointed to discover only a minor effect, with factors other than sunspots controlling most of the pattern of thick and thin growth rings that corresponded with good and bad years for pine growth. To meaningfully search for a clear eleven-year cycle, Douglass realized, he would need more evidence.

The next chapter in the story shows that a good idea in science can lead to applications far removed from what first inspires it. Douglass realized that he did not, after all, have to limit his work to trees that had just been cut down by timber companies. There were two other main sources of wood available to him, each of which went farther back in time than living trees. First, there were the tree stumps and dead remains of older trees, still in their natural habitat, that were in good enough shape for study. And then, because of the particular archeological setting of the area, there was another set of samples, too.

In scattered areas around the Southwest one can find pieces of wood that people used to build dwellings in much earlier centuries. One such type of dwelling is the Navaho hogan. Abandoned hogans are often well preserved in the dry climate of the region that's been home to the Navaho for generations. Additionally, some timbers used for roof beams and other structural supports are embedded in the mud-based structures built by still-earlier peoples in the Southwest. Thus, native societies had inadvertently made old wood samples available for an enterprising researcher.

Douglass had come to know by heart the thick-and-thin patterns of tree rings in fresh-cut ponderosas, those that had recorded growth rates from the earliest 1900s, going back in time, year by year, from there. Indeed, quite early in the initial work he conducted in 1906 with the lumberyard samples, he noted a distinctive pattern of narrow rings that was twenty-one years old, that is twenty-one rings counted inward from the bark of the freshly fallen logs. Douglass next examined a tree stump near Flagstaff. The same pattern of narrow rings was present in the stump, but only eleven years from the outer bark ring. The two observations allowed Douglass to deduce that the stump had been cut ten years prior to the samples in the log yard. Checking with the owner of the land on which the tree stump stood, Douglass obtained confirmation of what he had inferred from the pattern in the rings. Good and bad years for tree growth gave Douglass a sort of "fingerprint" he could recognize, first in one wood sample, then in the next. Finding and using such fingerprints is the simple but powerful procedure known as cross-dating wood.

Essentially, Douglass had started to catalog a couple different effects in the tree-ring widths he was measuring. There were some really good times for trees, years and even decades when a specimen had grown a lot each year due to good conditions. There were also wretched years—although clearly not enough to kill the tree in question if it had continued to grow in the next season and subsequent years. Those great and awful years were what made cross-dating of samples possible; they established the clear fingerprints that were the same from one sample to the next. Then, superimposed on this strong good-versus-bad set of effects was the minor up-and-down cycle that seemed to run for eleven years. But because the major effects were big, it could be hard to see the eleven-year cycle, perhaps especially because tree rings are not necessarily large, and Douglass at first had only magnifying glasses and other very basic technology to help him in his work.

Soon Douglass was looking for tree-ring samples he could cross-date not just in ponderosa trees and stumps, but also in much more ancient wood. When he could, he sampled wood from archeological sources. And, when his time permitted and he could travel, he started to study still-living trees that were much older than the ponderosas of northern Arizona. In 1915, and again in 1918, he traveled to sequoia groves in California. On his second trip, in what's now King's Canyon National Park, he found a truly enormous tree stump. Carefully sampling a section of the stump, he sent the specimen to Arizona. Counting rings, Douglass found that he had acquired a sample from a sequoia tree that had been alive in 1304 BCE, more than three thousand years earlier.[4] Douglass had come to realize the staggering length of the natural record created by trees in the West. However, the question of whether different tree species in different locations would show regional climate effects, let alone an indisputably clear record of the sunspot cycles, remained.

While the climate aspect of tree-ring research was not fully resolved, progress was being made on other fronts. By 1929, at which time Douglas was on the faculty at the University of Arizona in Tucson, he felt he could reliably use cross-dating techniques to establish the exact ages of a small but increasing number of early timber-supported structures in the region.

With that growing list of successes, as well as his work based on logging samples, the science of *dendochronology* gradually became better established. The polysyllabic word *dendochronology* is not as inscrutable as it may seem. *Dendron* is Greek for tree, *chronis* means time, and *logos* means reason or thought. So dendochronology is reasoning about the passage of time from the evidence of trees, a field invented by A. E. Douglass the astronomer.

But tree-ring techniques allowed Douglass, and the archeologists who quickly joined him, to do more than just tell time. Soon researchers were putting two and two together in new ways, hypothesizing that climate changes that led to growth spurts or stunting in trees had also helped shape the story of human history in the Southwest. Some civilizations, researchers began to believe, collapsed not due principally to disease or war, but because climate change had eroded their way of life. In a number of places, the tree rings showed that the soil had been wet for decades and even longer, times during which trees did well and laid down thick growth rings. Presumably, these were good times for native societies in the area. But the tree rings also showed that regions were greatly drier for long periods, intervals that must have caused the decimation of human populations in the challenging climate of the Southwest. Furthermore, even within the wet times there were individual years or decades of drought—times during which native civilizations must have been severely tested.

To say anything specific about the weather in the past, however, to flesh out generalities like "wet" versus "dry," required that the thick or thin rings be *calibrated* to climate information. The only way to approach this task was to take weather records in Arizona and compare them to recent tree-ring widths. In other words, if a ring measuring an eighth of an inch grew in weather conditions that were known in 1903, then Douglass could infer that those were likely the conditions the tree had experienced much earlier, when it had grown a similar amount. Unfortunately, the weather record that scientists had at their disposal in Arizona was painfully short, simply because the history of meteorological measurement wasn't as long as it would have been in a more developed place like London. That, in turn, meant that there weren't many measured meteorological values a person could compare or average together, a fact that decreased the confidence one could put into the exercise of inferring specifics about the weather of the past. Still, the limited modern weather records that did exist linked tree-ring research not only to generalities about climate trends, but also to more specific information concerning the weather long before meteorological records had existed in the region.

But while the principles of the new science of dendochronology were as simple as the thumbnail sketch just described, there were some devils in the details that we need to consider. These points, interesting in themselves, also explain why tree-ring research never yields crystal clear data about past climates. We'll start with some of the most obvious limits that produce "fuzziness" in the tree-ring data, then we'll consider some of the more complex ideas in this area.

First, it's worth noting that the seasonal growth of a particular tree is affected by factors other than the weather. Trees vary, one from another, just like people do. The genetic makeup of each individual tree is unique, so one particular tree may grow a bit more quickly than another. Highly local conditions can also change over time. It's easy enough to see that if part of the soil near a tree has been eroded, this will impact the tree's root system and put a crimp on its growth, at least until the situation stabilizes. Then again, an infestation of insects may affect a tree in one valley more than the same type of tree ten miles away. Or one tree may suddenly start to get a lot more sunlight when an old, big tree in the neighborhood finally falls. These kinds of factors produce significant variations among individual specimens, and that fact means that researchers need to average together samples from many specimens of a single tree species in one region over the same time period. Some dendochronologists think that measuring an average of twenty-five to thirty tree-ring records in a locale is an essential first step in getting around the problem of individual variability. While it may be easy enough to find thirty samples in some locations for particular periods, it obviously becomes less and less likely the more ancient the wood samples are.

Another issue is more general. Trees that are fortunate enough to live on good soil and near local sources of groundwater often grow at steady rates. Such growth translates into trees that are tall and well formed; they also have rings that are wide and quite uniform in thickness. While trees like that might make good specimens to decorate at Christmas, their uniform growth rings makes them entirely useless when it comes to inferring anything about past weather patterns. That's why, instead of looking at superb botanical specimens, dendochronologists focus their work on wood from trees that are living a tough life due to poor soil, steep slopes, the absence of local groundwater, or some other challenge. It's these "tortured" trees that are the most likely to grow very little during years of scarce rains or do poorly after a harsh winter and a late spring. What this means, of course, is that few trees in the woods are likely to be good samples for the scientist. Indeed, it may be quite a small fraction that yields useful ring patterns. Again, this increases the challenge of finding enough good samples to say with much certainty what past conditions were like.

Another factor of dendochronology relates to wood itself. In the spring, a tree grows rapidly, creating new cells on the outside of its trunk and branches, just under the bark. These cells, called *earlywood* or *springwood*, are large and have thin cell walls; both these factors contribute to making the wood relatively light weight for its volume. In the summer, growth slows. Denser latewood is formed, creating the band that's relatively dark when you look at the end of a piece of lumber. But occasionally the sequence of a perfect pair of springwood and latewood doesn't hold up. If conditions—weather or disease—severely test a tree one year, it won't grow over all its surfaces. That may mean that a particular sample of wood taken by the dendochronologist will have a missing ring in it, which will result in the scientist's inferences being off base by a year.

A few trees also try to trip up scientists by revealing a "false ring" made of latewood that's in the middle of springwood. These features, sometimes known as double rings, usually can be distinguished from true rings because the errant dark ring is likely to change gradually rather than more abruptly into the springwood that lies on either side of the false latewood. It's not clear what creates such double rings, although people have speculated that aberrant conditions during the middle of the growing season or even highly local issues might be the cause. In any event, if a dendochronologist doesn't recognize the false ring for what it is, year-by-year counting back in time will end up off by a year.

There are also special issues for tree rings across entire regions. In this regard, Douglass caught an enormously good break. By the simple chance of his location, his work with tree rings started in Arizona. That's important because the state is not exactly a lush garden. Or, as a scientist would put it, there is one dominant environmental factor that limits the growth of almost everything in the region, namely precipitation. In wet years, the plants of Arizona grow a lot. In dry ones, they don't. So, one factor controls the basics of the thick-thin patterns of the tree rings with which Douglass started his studies. As we will later see, precipitation need not be the key variable for inferences about past climates based on tree rings everywhere around the globe. In far northern boreal forests, for example, the dominant environmental factor that controls plant growth is often the temperature of the brief growing season. Dendochronology in such locations can thus give us information about colder versus warmer summers in the distant past.

When we discussed A. E. Douglass's work around Flagstaff and among the sequoias, we were starting with the ideal case, one in which abundant samples from living trees can be collected. Living trees are important because they ground the timeline of the rings firmly in a specific date, namely the present. They provide a starting point for the construction of an absolute chronology for trees in a region, the type of work that yields specific information about which ring corresponds to 1812, for example, or which ring grew in 1776.

Of course, some deadwood in the forest may have a series of rings yet not be related to the known timeline of an area. The deadwood may simply have grown before the oldest dates of the master chronology worked out by the scientist from all samples linked to the present day. In that case, a researcher can measure and record the features of the rings and have a pretty good idea of the experience of a tree during some period in the distant past. But the scientist won't be able to say specifically when those seasons occurred. Such a "floating" tree-ring record contains valuable information, but it's not tied to a specific date. The shorter the master timeline of an area, the more likely it is that a record from a particular piece of deadwood will be floating.

Despite all the limitations of tree-ring research, it's impressive what the patient study of old wood can tell us about dates and conditions in the past. It wasn't too long after Douglass started his work that American researchers with interests in archeology began taking note of the research techniques the astronomer had pioneered. In 1921, Neil Judd of the Smithsonian Institution was given a grant by the National Geographic Society to go to Chaco Canyon, New Mexico, to study spectacular ruins there. He was eager to use Douglass's scientific principles on the ancient wood of the structures. The crown jewel of Chaco Canyon is Pueblo Bonito, a so-called great house that fully lives up to its name. In its prime, Pueblo Bonito was a building of five stories, over one hundred thousand square feet, and at least seven hundred rooms. It was constructed out of stone slabs and tim-bers—a source of wood that obviously made it attractive to an archeologist willing to use the new science of tree-ring research in his work.

Douglass could not come to the site of the great house in the field season of 1921 because he was setting up a new telescope outside Tucson. But near the end of the summer he sent some of his coring tools to Judd. Judd used Douglass's equipment to take samples of some beams. In June 1922 Judd returned to the site and went to work in earnest on wood samples at the ruin, sending the samples to Douglass in Tucson. Finally, in September, Douglass was able to break free of other work and briefly visit Pueblo Bonito. By the end of October, back in Tucson, Douglass had worked out from the evidence of the wood samples that there were two separate periods during which the ancient residents of Chaco Canyon had constructed their buildings. The longer one lasted 250 years, the shorter 160 years. That was valuable information for archeologists, far more spe-cific than what they had previously known. But the records were floating, meaning they were not tied to specific dates.

In recognition of the progress Judd and Douglass were making, the National Geographic Society agreed to support more work in the area. So, in 1923, the Beam Expedition was launched, a project which ran off and on for several years. By August 1927, using evidence from a variety of sites,

Douglass had a timeline of tree rings that had one long sequence tied into the absolute date of the present, but he still had two floating sequences. In other words, he could put the ancient history of the Southwest in a basic timeline, but there were two gaps in the chronology. This meant that he still could not place a specific year on the construction of many of the prehistoric buildings. The first gap, known as "Gap A," was between the floating chronology of Pueblo Bonito and the ruins of what's called the Citadel. The second, "Gap B," was between the time of the Citadel and the record of modern trees.

Douglass was able to close Gap A first. But Gap B remained an unknown interval. Unfortunately, that meant that everything coming before it—much of the prehistoric record of civilizations in the Southwest—was still only a floating chronology. For a time Douglass and his associate Lyndon Hargrave made progress pushing back the absolute record from the present day using timbers from Oraibi, a Hopi village that's the oldest continuously inhabited settlement known in North America. But even the oldest pieces of wood preserved in the Hopi buildings were simply not old enough to resolve the year in which the floating sequence ended. Another approach was needed if Gap B was going to be bridged.

By 1929 the National Geographic Society was tired of funding tree-ring expeditions that had not led to a full chronology of Pueblo Bonito and other ancient ruins of the Southwest. The society gave Douglass $5,000 for the summer field season of 1929, but it looked like that might be the last grant it would be willing to make. Perhaps because of the pressure to finish the grand timeline of the prehistoric civilizations, Douglass made some wise choices in determining how he would direct the work of the upcoming, crucial field season. He hired two assistants and sent them in the spring to a number of ruins to look for pottery fragments thought to have come from the general time period in which Gap B occurred. Ruins associated with cultural objects from the missing era, after all, might well contain beams made of trees cut during that time. The decision to use pottery as a first clue for what to investigate was fortuitous because it turned out that potshards from the time of Gap B were both distinctive and rare. Known as Little Colorado Polychrome, the pottery is orange, and it was present in only four of the twenty ruins the assistants surveyed. One of those four was the Show Low/Whipple Ruin, which looked promising for further dendochronology work in part because it is near a pine forest, meaning the ancient residents likely had access to wood for building and burning.

Douglass's assistants went to work on the ruin, looking for ancient wood within it. As luck would have it, Douglass arrived on a crucial day of their investigations, just shortly after a charcoalized beam fragment seven inches in diameter had been unearthed. The researchers removed the piece of beam, tagged it as sample HH-39, and went to the local village hotel for their supper, taking the sample with them. After the men had eaten—even scientists have their priorities—they adjourned to the living room of the small hotel and examined HH-39 in the flickering light of a gasoline lamp.

The first news was good, as the year 1237 CE near the core of the beam was easily identified. As Douglass later rather colorfully put it, "We learned that this charred old stick began its life as a promising upright pine A.D. 1237, just ten years after the Sixth Crusade moved eastward."[5] That pushed the date of tree rings known from the present farther back in time. Further examination of the ancient beam proved even more gratifying. Douglass and his coworkers quickly saw that a full forty-nine years of the HH-39 record was the same as some of the younger rings from the floating chronology. With one stroke, the previously floating timelines had been tied into the present day. Specific dates could at last be assigned to ancient ruins in many locations around the Southwest.

Douglass was so pleased that he had trouble getting any rest that night.

> Lying awake, I visualized all the individual rings concerned in this agreement and became completely satisfied that the relationship between our prehistoric and historic ring records had been definitely ascertained.[6]

The Cliff Palace at Mesa Verde dated at 1073. The Balcony House was constructed between 1190 and 1206. The Sliding Rock Ruin of the Chinle area dated to between 936 and 957. At Grand Gulch, Utah, people had built structures between 1133 and 1135. And on it went, with specific dates now applied to ruins that had been known only on the long but previously floating chronology Douglass and coworkers had deduced prior to the discovery of the crucial sample HH-39.

The next question focused on what could be deduced about climate and its effects on the history of Pueblo Bonito, the heart of the great culture that had made use of Chaco Canyon. The evidence of tree rings showed tantalizing clues that Chacoan civilization expanded and ultimately disappeared during times with quite different precipitation patterns. Starting in 1050 CE, and for the next thirty-five years, rainfall never fell below the average mark. Times were good for the people of the area, who farmed on a system of simple irrigation. By 1075 Chaco Canyon was undergoing a period of extensive construction, and Pueblo Bonito rose as the heart of a cultural system connecting surrounding villages. From about 1050, and for the next sixty-five years, the Chacoan civilization had enough resources to not only feed itself and expand its buildings, but also to invest labor into the construction of a network of roads connecting villages with the great house of Pueblo Bonito. There were some dry intervals that must have been a test, but in general the world seemed to smile on the people of the area, as tree rings from 1100 to 1130 indicate that both average precipitation and the crucial summertime rains were above normal amounts.

But starting in the year 1130, precipitation crashed to lower values. That's also just around the time the people of the area stopped constructing buildings. In 1133 the people of Chaco Canyon must have been cheered when summer rainfall increased for a season. But that was the end of their good fortune, for both summer and annual precipitation declined for most of the *next fifty years*. Long before the drought ended, the civilization that had boasted Pueblo Bonito at its heart had disappeared. The great house was given up to ghosts and stood empty until it fell into ruins.

To be sure, the tree rings cannot clearly tell us that climate change caused the collapse of the local culture. But they do tell us that precipitation—so crucial to people in an arid land—underwent a downturn just at the time the Chacoan civilization stopped its building program and went into the decline from which it never recovered. And even without the smoking gun of cause and effect between weather and the early civilization, the evidence of tree rings is as clear as crystal in one regard.

Precipitation in the region varied substantially, and changes often occurred quickly. Furthermore, the changes in precipitation were erratic, with long, wet periods punctuated randomly by short droughts and individual wet years or intervals of several years in the middle of long droughts. Like the daily ups and downs of the stock market, the short-term changes were imposed on longer-scale variations. And, most notably of all, conditions could change greatly in a year or two, never returning to normal within the span of a human lifetime. Such are the facts made evident by tree rings, and they suggest conditions that could easily wipe out early agricultural civilizations in an arid region.

The almost-storybook discovery and interpretation of sample HH-39 from Pueblo Bonito, with the final tie-ins to specific dates, was deeply gratifying to Douglass. It's no surprise he soldiered on with his archeologically based tree-ring work. By 1934 he had a full timeline of wood samples from prehistoric ruins going back more than 1,900 years. But it was never the ancient peoples of the Southwest that primarily interested Douglass. He wanted to know the history of climate in the region because he believed knowing past weather cycles could help him understand solar cycles, and that knowledge would ultimately allow for the prediction of climate on Earth in the present day.

Even prior to his research efforts into the archeology of the Southwest, Douglass had done some important work on his deeper concern, linking the sun to tree-ring patterns via regional climate changes through time. Although Douglass didn't know what caused sunspots, he suspected the up-and-down cycles in the number of sunspots through time—a cycle lasting about eleven years—controlled at least some weather variations. As early as 1913, Douglass had invented a clever mechanical device that helped him look for cycles in long series of data. He refined that invention through 1918 and coupled it with a photographic image that showed the presence of cycles as a series of lines. His inventions helped him look through his growing set of tree-ring data for cycles.

In 1919, Douglass's first major volume on tree-ring research was published by the Carnegie Institution of Washington, which had started to finance part of his work. By that time Douglass and his assistants had measured the widths of over seventy-five thousand tree rings. The ponderosa pines of the Flagstaff area, Douglass argued, showed that over the previous 160 years, ten of the fourteen highs and lows in the sunspot cycle were followed, four years later, by highs and lows in tree-ring widths. It was an encouraging result. By the early 1920s, Douglass had more evidence that he believed linked tree rings to sunspots. In both the ponderosa pines of Arizona and the sequoias of California, Douglass thought he could see evidence of the eleven-year sunspot cycle—but he was puzzled by one part of the tree record. The ponderosa and sequoia specimens simply didn't show the cycle from the 1650s to the 1720s. As a good scientist, Douglass reported all he knew in his publications, including the period in which the cycle in the tree rings was absent. But he was frustrated by his inability to explain what had happened to the eleven-year cycle during those decades in the late 1600s and early 1700s. In February 1922 Douglass heard from E. Walter Maunder, a famous British astronomer of the day who was familiar with Douglass's work half a world away. Maunder had amassed data on sunspots using the written records of astronomers in Europe going back to the invention of the telescope. He had found a relatively clear eleven-year cycle in sunspots except for the period from 1645 to 1715, when hardly any sunspots had been seen from Earth at all. This period, which came to be called the Maunder Minimum, corresponds to what historians generally see as the coldest time of Europe's "Little Ice Age."

Douglass, of course, was delighted to hear from Maunder. The written astronomical records of Europe had confirmed that the tree-ring record of the American West was real and regular, that it was evidently influenced by the eleven-year sunspot cycle, and that the period when that cycle had stopped was recorded faithfully by tree growth on Earth. A cosmic connection to weather, and through weather to tree growth, was coming clearly into focus, just as Douglass had hoped.

In 1928 Douglass published a second major volume with the Carnegie Institution. By that time he and his assistants had data from more than 175,000 tree rings. In the tree rings from the Flagstaff area, Douglass felt he had good measurements of ponderosas from the years 1300 through 1925. For most of that record, the tree rings showed an 11.3-year cycle of growth. From 1630 to 1850 the cycle was interrupted, however, and that period appeared to stretch beyond the Maunder Minimum. The ponderosas also showed longer-term cycles than the eleven-year cycle, with ups and downs in growth occurring at fourteen- and twenty-one-year intervals. Most importantly for Southwest history, there was a cycle to the period of droughts, when the ponderosas had grown little and their tree rings were very narrow. The droughts could be divided into two groups. Smaller droughts appeared to occur every forty to fifty years, while a cycle of major droughts stood at the 150-year mark.

Douglass was encouraged by the evidence of the eleven-year cycle of growth because it tied into what was known about solar activity. But he had no explanation for the other, longer cycles, including the periods of drought so important to humans living in the Southwest. He was bewildered. To add to the problem of trying to explain what the tree-ring measurements appeared to show, the cycles were not clearly evident through the whole record of the ponderosas. In other words, the eleven-, fourteen-, and twenty-one-year cycles of growth and the forty-, fifty-, and 150-year cycles of drought were evidently not permanent through time. The cycles came and went, being clear in the data for some intervals and absent or at least less clear for others. Explaining the record of the tree rings looked daunting, indeed.

Still, there was basic encouragement in the massive amount of data. Ponderosas usually reflected an eleven-year cycle that Douglass believed must be linked to the sunspot cycle. That was an important finding. And because Douglass was an astronomer and a scientist of the highest caliber, he wanted to do more than just describe cycles through time. He really wanted to know, among other things, what caused the sun to have increasing and decreasing numbers of sunspots each eleven years. There must be some physical change in the sun at work over the years, and a regular change at that. To Douglass, the change in the sun was vital to understand. As he wrote, "Until we know the physical cause of cycles we can not say how long a mechanical repetition will last, for it may break down at any time."[7]

Although the number of different cycles was mystifying, and although the fundamental cause of the sunspot cycle remained unresolved, Douglass's work was clearly making some progress toward his ultimate goal of being able to predict weather patterns on Earth. In the spring of 1932 Douglass presented his work on tree rings and their cycles to the National Academy of Sciences—a significant honor. His work, however, drew criticism from important scientists. The main weakness of the data, from the point of view of significant scientists of the time, was the intermittent nature of the cycles in the tree rings. In the physical world, cycles don't stop running for intervals and then start up again. For example, the sequence of high and low tides in a bay form a cycle in the strongest sense of the word. The rhythm of the tides is clear and permanent. Tides don't disappear for days or years at a time. The tidal cycle is caused by the moon, the moon is always present near the Earth, and nothing about the picture changes. That's the kind of evidence and explanation that scientists, especially physical scientists, like. Douglass's tree-ring cycles, unlike the tides, were intermittent. They were clear for some types of trees in some regions for a few centuries, then they were weakly present or even absent for a time. That not only made an explanation for them problematic, it made some scientists not directly familiar with all of Douglass's tree-ring measurements unsure of the basic patterns Douglass was so certain he was seeing in the data.

Douglass understood the criticism, although he felt it did not do justice to the evidence of the tree rings. He returned to Arizona, and when his other duties permitted, he continued his work, still hopeful that he had good evidence that would ultimately be vindicated as the best way to predict the weather. But the greatest enemy of all intellectuals—time itself—had been ticking away. By 1937 Douglass was seventy years old. While he was still healthy and vigorous, he also was old—quite old by the standards of the 1930s. Not surprisingly, Douglass retired in 1937 from active duty as a faculty member at the University of Arizona. But, true to his passion, Douglass retained directorship of the Tree-Ring Research Laboratory. The astronomer (turned archeologist turned climate scientist) was finally free to focus on the goal he had set for himself near the turn of the century: predicting climate cycles, at least as they were expressed in the American West (and possibly beyond the region).

In some ways, the period of Douglass's "retirement" was his true Camelot. He had trained a fine staff for the tree-ring laboratory, and they handled all the routine work of generating data from growth rings. Douglass himself was free to work on the big questions of climate, and he dug into the subject with his usual energy. In light of the evidence of the eleven-year cycle in the rings of many trees, data that appeared linked to sunspot cycles, Douglass wanted to explore what could cause the sun to go through changes over time in such a regular fashion. Other astronomers had worked on that issue, as well, because the sun's behavior was an interesting intellectual question, even for those who might doubt the sunspot-weather connection. Attention had focused on whether the movement of the planets around the sun could cause solar variations. Planetary movement, after all, was one feature of the solar system that underwent regular cycles through time.

Douglass thought the planetary angle regarding sunspots well worth investigating, and he was in a good position to do so due to his original work in astronomy. Like others in the field before him, he focused for a time on the movements of the largest planets, Jupiter and Saturn. Even though those planetary giants are distant from the inner parts of the solar system, they have effects here. Unfortunately, from the point of view of trying to explain the sunspot cycle, alignments of Jupiter and Saturn occur on a 9.93-year cycle that, though close to the 11.1-year cycle of sunspots, is still far from an exact fit.

In May 1942, government officials in the Southwest asked Douglass to work on climate predictions for them. Specifically, they wanted to know when they should anticipate particularly wet years that would lead to floods. The request caused Douglass to renew his work into planetary motions and tree-growth patterns. Carefully, Douglass studied other planetary combinations beyond just those of Jupiter and Saturn. He looked at the four largest planets and the potential relationship between their positions and the sunspot cycles. With four planets to consider, the combinations of alignments exploded in complexity, offering many different cycles to consider. Douglass also studied variations in the sunspot cycle itself, which is far from a clockwork phenomenon. One day, when again considering the whole complicated subject, he realized that the alignments of Jupiter and Saturn, called their conjunctions and oppositions, were only about 1 percent different from one aspect of the sunspot cycle variation. He was shocked, but also delighted, to see the correspondence. He immediately set to work demonstrating to himself that in his best tree-ring data, he had a 60 to 70 percent success rate in the correlation of planetary alignments and tree-ring growth patterns for the previous thousand years. While not mathematically perfect, that degree of success fit with his long-held belief that whatever influenced solar variations also determined ups and downs of climate on Earth.

Soon Douglass refined his work. He set out the argument that periods of maximum rainfall, as shown in the tree-ring record, best corresponded to the conjunction and opposition of three major planets. When four major planets were in the right position, the effect on the tree-ring patterns— and hence presumably on ancient sunspot activity—was even stronger. But complexities continued to abound. At times, from what Douglass could determine, it took only the alignment of Jupiter and one other major planet to create a peak in maximum rainfall in the Southwest. Nothing, it seemed, was simple. Still, by late summer 1945, as World War II was winding down, Douglass felt he had identified patterns in planetary motions that matched 16.5 rainfall peaks out of an average of 18 peaks per century. If you accepted the validity of intermittent cycles, as Douglass did, it all looked like progress, but even he had to admit that his demonstration of the pattern lacked mathematical perfection.

In any event, Douglass wondered, just how would planetary motions affect the sun in ways that determine terrestrial weather? About this central intellectual question, Douglass could only speculate. Like others, he assumed that planetary alignments changed the distribution or movement of electrical charges in the sun's dynamic atmosphere. Alterations in electromagnetic patterns were then expressed in changes to the streams of charges coming toward Earth and affecting our planet's magnetism. But even if that general picture were the case, how this translated into different weather patterns remained an enigma. At the end of the day, Douglass's central work had two intellectual weaknesses. First, the patterns that might link tree rings to weather to planetary motions were complex and didn't always seem to hold up through time. Second, there was no strong explanation of the mechanism of causation from the planets to the sun to the rainfall of the American West. It was no minor matter that Douglass had constructed a framework for describing weather patterns on the scale of years and centuries and had gathered a great deal of data that appeared to support the general connection that he had proposed. But, at the same time, and as he himself seemed to know, he couldn't explain all that he had originally hoped to explain. Most importantly, he didn't feel he could predict the weather. So, perhaps for more than one reason, Douglass failed to publish a final volume on the work toward which he had directed his investigations for years.

Today, matters largely stand where they were when Douglass grew too old to make further progress on his quest. While some researchers believe solar variations are crucial to weather patterns on Earth at different timescales, others abhor that emphasis, looking only to processes on our own planet for explanations about climate variations through the centuries. The solar connection to weather is one that ignites fierce debates in science, although the public often doesn't hear about them. Perhaps the next generation will make more progress in this arena, but at this point the matter remains unresolved.

But despite the shortcomings of dendochronological research (when compared to what Douglass had originally been hoping to demonstrate), the field provided meaningful data on what climate in the past has been like on Earth. It's no surprise, then, that by the 1920s and 1930s Douglass had an increasing number of colleagues interested in what they could learn about weather patterns by studying tree rings. As a group, they all caught a lucky break. In several parts of the West, well beyond sequoia groves, there are individual trees that have lived for staggering amounts of time. The Utah and Rocky Mountain types of juniper have life spans up to three thousand years, and bristlecone pines can live for up to five thousand years. In short, the unusually long lives of some of the tree species in the temperate latitudes of the West and the sensitivity of some of them to climate greatly help the science of dendochronology, making it easier to create master chronologies of an area and begin to appreciate weather variations over recent millennia.

Since A. E. Douglass's day, tree-ring measurements have been made from different locations around the globe, and the simple passage of time from when Douglass measured those first rings in the snowy yard of the Arizona Lumber and Timber Company has helped us improve our understanding of what tree rings really tell us about weather. Meteorological records in the Intermountain West didn't go back very far when Douglass began his studies. In other words, Douglass knew that a tree ring from 1898 corresponded to a certain amount of precipitation as recorded in the weather books of Flagstaff, but he didn't have a lot of other, similar years to which he could compare tree-ring and weather data. But today we have more than an additional century's worth of meteorological measurements from all around the West, a huge improvement for our ability to better infer past conditions from tree widths.

In another substantial advance, we now have computerized technology to manipulate large data sets of ring widths. Douglass spent a great many working hours over the years looking for the eleven-year sunspot cycle in his tree-ring measurements, a laborious task in his day. Scientists today record measurements digitally and later manipulate them using a stroke or two on a keyboard. Additionally, many scientists are vastly better educated in statistics than the young Douglass could have imagined. The reader is warned, however, that in a later chapter we will consider a very public case in which climate scientists may not have fully understood the statistics they employed.

On the positive side, as the history of dendochronology expanded in the twentieth century, much more was learned about the wood that was being studied. In addition to just counting rings and measuring their width, scientists found useful information in the *density* of the wood. The density of the latewood, for example, might correlate better with the weather of summer than just the width of a tree ring that included spring growth. Thus, density measurements gave scientists another factor to consider. While in the Southwest the main control on tree rings was precipitation, in

northern boreal and taiga forests the dominant control was often temperature. The qualification "often" turned out to be needed, however, as a warm
summer seemed to lead to a wide tree ring only if precipitation was also
adequate during the brief growing season of such northern lands. In other
words, a wide growth ring in a tree in the Canadian boreal forest from the
year 1776 might correspond to a truly warm year with a modestly useful
precipitation pattern for tree growth, or it might mean the year 1776 had
only a moderately warm summer, but one with good precipitation patterns.

As the twentieth century unfolded, scientists went to work teasing out
all the climate information they could from the record of ancient wood.
Researchers also started to compare the evidence of tree rings with what
was known about past weather and climate from other types of research. In
other words, anything that could be said about climate in earlier times from
the evidence of varves, for example, could be compared to tree-ring information. Ditto for pollen types that recorded what plants lived in a place
in the past. It wasn't that any of this work led to fully precise information about past climate, but researchers at least started to grope their way
toward knowing in general terms how climate had varied in recent centuries and millennia. While the early work of Douglass had been relatively
simple and direct, only specialists in two or three subdisciplines could
fully follow the research efforts that started to spring up in dendochronology in the latter part of the past century. But one pattern remained clear
from the time of Douglass onward: tree rings show that climate is more
variable than stable, with periods of high- and low-temperature swings or
of greater and lesser precipitation on the regional scale. Again and again,
researchers found evidence of climate variation quite apart from the mild
changes perhaps linked to sunspots. Indeed, the main lesson of dendochronology was the omnipresence through all millennia of substantial climate
changes that were more significant and rapid than most people felt comfortable contemplating.

But another quite different and exceedingly useful research tool was
developed in the twentieth century that can be brought to bear on questions
of ancient wood and climate. It depends on the simple fact that trees are
made of carbon. And carbon, it turns out, has a way of telling time that's

built right into some of its atoms. So it's not just by counting tree rings in wood that we can peer backward into history, year by year, but also through measurements of what's called carbon-14. This method has turned out to be important because it gives us a way of approximately dating wood that's from the late Ice Age or Pleistocene Epoch, thus giving us a way of saying something about weather patterns in truly ancient samples.

A scientist named Willard F. Libby was the man who studied carbon in all its glorious atomic details. Coming onto the scene after Douglass's youth, Libby earned his bachelor's degree in chemistry from the University of California, Berkeley, in 1931, during the discouraging times of the Great Depression. Just two years later, in a remarkable intellectual achievement, he earned his doctorate. Like other scientists of his generation with expertise in physical chemistry, he worked for the government during World War II. In 1945, he moved to what's now the Enrico Fermi Institute at the University of Chicago. In the years that followed he studied an unusual type of carbon, part of a lifetime of research that ultimately led to the Nobel Prize in Chemistry in 1960.

What, you might ask, is so special about carbon that it is worthy of the highest award in science? In part, the answer is that carbon on Earth helps scientists tell time, just as much as a calendar on the wall helps you keep track of the passage of days in a month. That statement requires a bit of an explanation, but the basics of the matter are simple enough.

As you likely know, we are essentially made of carbon, with water and some other ingredients thrown in. We are indeed what we eat, so it's no surprise that our food is rich in carbon. The carbon in food comes from plants. (Even if you eat a diet rich in roast beef and cheese, like the unwise author of this book, you are eating carbon from plants because cattle eat vegetation and get their carbon from that source.) Trees, of course, are plants; they get their carbon from trace amounts of carbon dioxide in the air, which they "breathe" in and use to construct their carbon-rich cells.

As it happens, not all carbon atoms are the same. That's where the work of Libby comes in. Most carbon on Earth—the overwhelming majority of the stuff—has a weight of twelve units and is known as carbon-12. We won't bother with the details of what the weight of an atom actually means.

All that matters is that atoms vary in terms of their weight, and most of the carbon in you and in the carbon dioxide of the air is carbon-12. It's also relevant to note that carbon-12 stays exactly the same over time, just as you would expect. Once a carbon-12 atom, always a carbon-12 atom.

But you've doubtless heard of carbon-14. This type of carbon shows up in the news from time to time when it's used to assign a date to artifacts like the Shroud of Turin. More relevant to our concerns, carbon-14 can be used to date old wood, which means it can help us cross-check the chronologies established by tree-ring research. Most delightfully of all, carbon-14 can also assign a date to a tree-ring record that is so old it will always be "floating," not tied to specific years. Indeed, carbon-14 can help us date wood that's tens of thousands of years old.

To understand how researchers can assign ages to organic materials, we need to learn a bit more about the rare type of carbon. Carbon-14 is produced in Earth's atmosphere when cosmic rays from outer space hit nitrogen atoms in the air. Carbon-14 has the special property of being radioactive, meaning its atoms change to another element over time, releasing energy as they do so. So, unlike carbon-12, carbon-14 is not stable. That's why carbon-14 is sometimes known as radiocarbon or "hot" carbon. To put the matter another way, hot carbon is the radioactive form of the element, the kind of carbon that releases energy as it decays to another element. The rate at which carbon-14 is transformed to other matter is most conveniently measured by what's called its half-life, or the time it takes for half of the carbon-14 in a sample to become a different element. In Libby's day, the half-life of carbon-14 was thought to be 5,570 years. Later, more precise measurements have put the half-life closer to 5,730 years. Today we know that value with a high degree of precision.

But, you may ask, how does radiocarbon find its way into plants like trees? When carbon-14 is formed in the atmosphere, the newly made hot-carbon atoms combine with oxygen to form carbon dioxide, a special form of carbon dioxide bearing the radioactive component of matter. The hot carbon dioxide circulates in the atmosphere, and it's absorbed by vegetation and passed from there into herbivorous animals and the rest of the food chain. If the amount of carbon-14 in the air is constant, we'd expect the ratio of carbon-14 to carbon-12 in living creatures to also be constant. In other words, while an atom of carbon-14 in your left pinky just decayed, you'll replace it when you eat lunch tomorrow, a meal that will contain fresh carbon-14. So far, so good.

But no organisms are immortal, not even the bristlecone pine. This means that when plants die, they stop taking in carbon dioxide, and when animals perish, they stop eating the carbon-containing plants. The key point is that the only change that will occur in a deceased organism's remains is the gradual disappearance of carbon-14. In other words, the ratio of carbon-14 to carbon-12 will slowly but predictably decrease. That's the magic that opens the lock of telling time in ancient tree specimens: the *longer* it has been since a piece of wood was alive, the *lower* the amount of carbon-14 that remains in it. So when we compare the carbon-14 to carbon-12 ratio of a piece of old wood to more modern values for that ratio, we can calculate how old the sample is by way of the half-life value.

Willard Libby wrote the book on carbon-14. His insight made possible a whole new way of assigning ages not just to pieces of wood, but to artifacts like cloth and marine organisms like sea shells. Many organic remains that contain carbon and are younger than the age at which carbon-14 is essentially gone from a sample can be assigned a date based on their radio-carbon content. We owe Libby a lot for his lifetime of work on the fundamentals of atoms and how they behave—which is why he was awarded the Nobel Prize.

There are, however, certain wrinkles regarding carbon on Earth. The first concerns an intriguing and impressive fact about our own civilization, and it anticipates an idea we'll consider when we discuss global warming, so it's quite worth noting here. As we all know, we have burned a lot of coal, natural gas, and petroleum since the advent of the industrial revolution. The three fossil fuels are exactly that—truly ancient sources of carbon. Because the fossil fuels we use each day are exceedingly old, they don't contain carbon-14 any longer. The interesting thing about that simple fact is that the carbon dioxide we humans have been producing in our engines and smokestacks for the past three hundred years doesn't contain carbon-14. Instead, it's carbon content is rich in carbon-12. And that means we have changed the ratio of carbon-14 to carbon-12 in the atmosphere by just a bit. A scientist named Hans Suess, whom we'll meet again, calculated that our civilization's activities had diluted the concentration of carbon-14 in the atmosphere by about 2 percent. That's an interesting result, but it's an academic point as regards carbon-14 dating. In other words, industrial dilution of carbon-14 doesn't threaten the utility of using radiocarbon as a dating method, since our real interest lies with samples that are three thousand or thirty-three thousand years old, not those that date from the time in which our smokestacks have changed the ratio of the two types of carbon.

There are other complicating factors related to carbon-14 dating, but they do not undermine the general utility of using radiocarbon to date organic materials. That's why carbon-14 dating has been of great use in subjects as varied as climatology and the study of religious relics. Because wood is made of carbon, carbon-14 can provide dendochronologists with a date for a sample of interest. This is particularly useful when a piece of wood a scientist is studying cannot be related to a master chronology of tree rings in a region. In other words, when a wood sample yields floating ring measurements because the ancient tree predated the master chronology that's known in the area, carbon-14 provides a way to say something about the date of the weather changes recorded in the width and density of the tree rings from the isolated sample.

The utility of carbon-14 for dendochronology is sometimes highly impressive. In a recent study from Chile, for example, ancient wood that had been buried by a volcanic mudflow came to light due to recent erosion. The wood was part of several tree stumps of a species of conifer. The samples of wood recorded a 1,229-year history of tree-ring variations. Because the wood was very old, it could not be directly tied into ring-width changes known in living trees or any other samples. However, carbon-14 dating enabled researchers to establish that the stumps were about fifty thousand years old—a date that fit well with what geologists believe was the time period of the volcanic activity. This meant that the evidence of weather and climate changes spanning the 1,229 years worth of tree rings occurred about fifty thousand years ago, well back in the Pleistocene Epoch. The samples showed evidence that supported conclusions that would have been generally familiar to Douglass: ring width, and therefore presumably the weather of that ancient time, varied greatly, indicating substantial and frequent increases and deceases in temperature and precipitation as well as similar changes on a longer timescale.

The Chilean example is just one of thousands of pieces of tree-ring work that have combined with other specialties to teach us more about the way climate has behaved in the past. But although tree rings can tell us a good bit about the history of a specific local or regional weather variable, it's quite tough to say much about *global* climate from tree-ring data. That's true in part because there are many regions on Earth that don't yield numerous, useful, and old wood samples. Beyond those limitations, because of the number and intellectual priorities of scientists around the world, and because of the smaller landmass and therefore fewer tress in the Southern Hemisphere, dendochronology in the Southern Hemisphere largely lagged behind the development of the science in the northern half of the globe during the twentieth century.

Another issue that limits the global scope of dendochronology is that even in the Northern Hemisphere, where tree-ring science is most helpful, there are only particular regions where it is a useful exercise. The tropics are not such a place because of natural conditions that make for more uniform growth in vegetation and destroy wood shortly after it dies. The far reaches of the northern arctic lack trees from which to draw samples. Even places along the eastern seaboard of the United States have proven quite challenging for tree-ring research. Most of the species of trees native to the region are relatively short-lived, and many were cut down during colonial times and the early national history. In the parts of Europe south of Scandinavia, the situation is broadly similar, with relatively few useful samples. In the Mediterranean region the history of early agriculture is significant: long ago the peoples of the region felled forests in order to till the soil and provide grazing land for livestock.

In the varied regions of Asia, research into tree rings in the twentieth century sometimes had much more to do with human history than specifics about forests. In general, the local societies did not support a significant scientific community doing abstract research like investigations into the history of climate. However, that began to change toward the close of the century, as the technical sophistication of people in those regions evolved. By the turn of the millennium, tree-ring research done by scientists in China started to complement information gleaned from other parts of the world. In one 2003 study about the Tibetan Plateau, the Chinese authors describe a 2,326-year tree-ring record for the Dulan area of central Asia. (The conclusions rest on modern wood samples and specimens from ancient tombs, a turn of events that would doubtless resonate with Douglass.) The scientists conclude that the largest amount of change in locally crucial spring precipitation patterns occurred around 350 to 400 CE. They also think they see evidence of at least a modified Medieval Warm Period in their tree rings running from 929 to 1031 CE. Just as in other studies, the data from the Tibetan Plateau make one thing clear: tree growth has apparently changed substantially in different years owing to significant changes in annual weather patterns—and that means that the peoples of that region doubtless suffered from the upheavals of climate just as much as the people of the ancient civilization of Pueblo Bonito.

As we will see a bit later in this book, in recent years there has been a veritable explosion of scientific effort flowing into the realm of climate research. Tree-ring data have become one sort of evidence that modern climatologists use to try to understand what Earth's past was like. Specifically, tree rings help supply us with information about weather conditions prior to the keeping of written meteorological records. And tree-ring data are valued by scientists because they sketch conditions that were experienced by the trees *each year*. That's the kind of highly detailed weather record that climatologists treasure. The evidence from tree research has been fed into the climate models that attempt to grapple with how temperature has varied in the past and may unfold over the rest of the twenty-first century. It's in connection with this that the reader may have heard something about tree-ring research in the news, and in a later chapter we will consider again the context of recent work by scientists that tries to weave together the evidence of tree rings, varves, pollen deposits, and more to help us understand what may lie ahead for the rest of this century.

While the evidence from tree rings is not as precise as meteorological records, it is at least some indication of what conditions have been like in a given region. Part of what modern climate science does is the art of extracting what it can from the "fuzzy" information of natural samples that were influenced by a host of factors, one of which was local weather. A measure of the ferocious public argument about the validity of the predictions of climate scientists for the future flows from the fact that our evidence of past weather around the world is imperfect, scattered, and variable. We simply don't have the best, clearest evidence from all time periods of the past, and we certainly don't have it from all regions around the world. Still, a pattern seen in growth rings in a tree stump is truly evidence from ancient history, a clear and dramatic step up from having no data on which to proceed as we think about climate change of both the past and the future. In that sense, we are in the debt of Percival Lowell, who fired A. E. Douglass from his position at the Flagstaff Observatory, thus forcing Douglass to think outside the box in analyzing climate variations by looking at the tree rings of ponderosa pines as a clue to ancient weather.

It's also worth noting that Douglass was one of the last of his breed, a scientist who worked largely alone during the most significant and creative phases of his life. In later years, scientists investigating climate have generally collaborated and cooperated with colleagues throughout their careers. The social method of doing science has several advantages, in particular now that large government grants go to groups of researchers spanning institutions, disciplines, and sometimes even national boundaries. But the independence of earlier scientists like Douglass has intellectual merit, too, exactly because it's not subject to the perils of groupthink, let alone any conscious decision to accept orthodoxy for the sake of getting along with a professional team.

Although he was frail and his head was decorated with white hair, Douglass must have felt deep satisfaction in March 1960. He was ninety-three years old when over one hundred people gathered to dedicate Kitt Peak National Observatory in southern Arizona. Many of those assembled greeted Douglass, the well-known astronomer and founder of the Tree-Ring Research Laboratory at the University of Arizona. Younger scientists asked to be introduced to him. Over many decades since he first arrived in

Arizona in 1894, Douglass had investigated patterns on Mars, in the sun, and in the growth rings of trees. When he died in 1962, Douglass had every reason to feel satisfaction with his long record of wide-ranging scientific productivity.

7

THE EVIDENCE OF THE ICE

He was an idealistic young man, pulled into the orbit of a major scientific expedition to Greenland in 1930. Fortunately for Ernst Sorge, he was not only young, but also strong. Alfred Wegener was the expedition's leader, a weather scientist turned geologist famous for his radical theory called "continental drift." But Wegener collapsed and died between camps on the ice sheet of Greenland, leaving the rest of the crew on its own. Sorge spent the long arctic winter in a snow cave with two other men, one of whom was severely ill with frostbitten feet. Nevertheless, despite the all but superhuman challenges the three faced, out of that dark winter came the first clear light shed on how enormous glaciers record changes in climate with amazing detail, allowing us to interpret global, not just regional, climate revolutions.

Sorge's task on the expedition was to investigate the glacial ice itself. He and his companions occupied a camp literally dug into the deep snow of central Greenland. Conditions were even worse at the camp than they would have been along the storm-swept coast because central Greenland enjoys an elevation of almost ten thousand feet. The altitude made temperatures extremely cold, even by the standards of Greenland! Worse, due to the thin air, the men became winded when they exerted themselves. Nevertheless, in a feat of personal and scientific accomplishment, Sorge used much of the winter to hand excavate a stairway down fifty feet into the snow beneath the men's tiny living area. With nothing but a makeshift kerosene lantern to illuminate his work, Sorge's descending stairway led him back in time—and propelled later scientists radically forward to a new understanding of the natural world.

At ten thousand feet, snow falls in central Greenland throughout all

131

seasons, the whole year round. To put it another way, there is normally no melting of snow during the summer in the central parts of Greenland—just summer snowfall piling on top of the previous winter's snow. When snow is buried it becomes denser and eventually crystallizes into material with a consistency of cornmeal that geologists call *firn*. As Sorge excavated beneath the men's crude living quarters, he cut small blocks of firn out of the material through which he was tunneling. Sorge carried the blocks up to the snow cave to measure the size and weight of the firn precisely. This allowed him to calculate the density of the material. In a general way, density of firn increases with depth, since the weight of accumulating snow compacts the firn beneath it. But Sorge also found that changes in density showed annual layers in the firn: each winter layer in central Greenland is a little denser than the nearest summer layers.

Each pair of density fluctuations Sorge recorded corresponded to one year's total snow accumulation. Thus, as he excavated his stairway into the ice cap, Sorge could count back in time, year by year, like a child counting tree rings on a stump or a Swedish geologist counting varve layers. Sorge's measurements, which he published after he returned to civilization, made it clear to scientists that ice sheets had clear layers in them, layers corresponding to annual deposits. As we shall see, the evidence about climate embedded in the layers of snow and ice is much different than the evidence contained in varves. The crystalline annual layers of glacial ice have now become the gold standard for evidence of how Earth's global climate has behaved in the past.

But we are getting a bit ahead of the story. Back in the dark snow cave in central Greenland, Sorge accomplished another scientific task during that long Greenland winter. He set off small explosions at the surface of the snow, and using the expedition's seismograph, he measured how long it took for the seismic waves he created to travel down through the ice sheet, hit bedrock, and return to the camp. From the travel-time measurements, Sorge estimated the depth of the ice sheet to be over two thousand yards, or more than a mile. We now know that the depth of the ice is about two miles, but Sorge's was the best measurement of his time—and even it meant that a stupendous number of annual layers of firn and ice rested under the young man's excavations in the snow cave. Thus, the main results of the Wegener expedition were clear despite the death of its leader: Greenland's ice cap was rich in annual layers, and the total number of layers in the frozen record of the glacial ice was simply enormous.

After Sorge's groundbreaking work there was a lull in glacial research, as virtually all technical effort in Europe was siphoned into the run-up to World War II. But in the late 1950s, and off and on in the decades that followed, scientists and engineers made several efforts to follow up Sorge's pioneering work. The first task was to set aside hand excavation techniques in favor of motorized drills to pierce the ice. The drill bits used were like pipes—hollow in the center—so that material from the ice could be pulled up to the surface in what's termed a "core." In a variety of efforts, several teams drilled into both the Greenland and antarctic ice sheets and retrieved long cores of firn and ice from the drill holes.

Ice behaves oddly under the pressure of thousands of feet of overlying ice. At some depths in a huge glacier, the ice shatters like an eggshell, while at other depths it almost flows like molasses. The fragility and variability of the ice posed great challenges for the drilling teams. But over the decades the roughnecks, engineers, and geologists who labored at the drilling sites made progress. Step by step, teams recovered better and longer cores from the ice sheets. Crews then shipped the ice cores to deep-freeze lockers at scientific facilities where the specimens could be sliced and studied. Ultimately, a laboratory was constructed in the United States to maintain below-freezing temperatures so the samples would not be in danger of melting, even if the scientists who work there run the risk of turning blue from cold.

The modern investigations confirmed Sorge's finding that Greenland's firn and ice contains annual layers. In fact, the annual layers are often plainly visible to the eye under the right light. But it's also true that the layers become thinner the deeper the drills penetrate into the glacial ice mass. This is because glaciers always flow. In the case of central Greenland, the deep ice, just above where Sorge's seismic waves bounced off the bedrock, is flowing toward the sea. The flowage thins the individual layers in the same way that a rubber band becomes thinner as you stretch it. Nonetheless, the annual ice layers, which become thinner with depth, are still detectable in Greenland all the way down to a few feet above the base of the great ice mass.

Perhaps the crucial point about the ice cores is that the glacial ice contains tiny air bubbles—small but precious samples of the air that had been present as the snows fell in millennia past. As snow is buried and becomes firn, some of the trapped air within it can move around in tiny gaps in the frozen structure. But a point is reached, as more and more layers of snow fall and build up, at which the buried ice becomes dense and plastic such that it fully encapsulates and isolates the air within it as small and isolated bubbles. From that time on, the tiny samples of air remain virtually just as they were when they were sealed off in the glacial ice. By counting the winter-summer layers in the drill cores, scientists working on Greenland ice cores can assign a date to the ancient air samples. Back in the laboratory, they then extract the small samples from the ice and analyze them, in the process recording our best evidence of how Earth's atmosphere has changed over millennia.

It's simply chance that the air bubbles are preserved in glacial ice, but it's surely a fortunate fact. For climate studies, it's a bit like the chance fact that pollen happens to be so sturdy that it will survive millennia buried in soggy peat or in lake sediments. No one could have confidently predicted either of these points in the era of T. C. Chamberlin or G. K. Gilbert, but they have helped our studies of climate change in the twentieth century and into the twenty-first. In summary, pollen tells us a lot about regional climate change, while the air bubbles in glacial ice, for their part, give us a clear record of how the composition of Earth's global atmosphere has changed over time. That information is key to any discussion of global warming due to increasing carbon dioxide in the Earth's atmosphere.

Beyond the air bubbles, the ice contains other physical evidence of climate and weather. During the long decades between Sorge's work and the most successful glacial drilling of the 1980s, the overall precision of laboratory work improved tremendously. Today, scientists are able to analyze minute traces of salts, dust, and volcanic ash present in the ice-core layers. And an entirely new laboratory technique also came onto the scene as the drilling teams were making progress on their work. That technique proved to be astoundingly useful in unraveling the glacial ice's clues about climate.

The technique rests on natural differences between oxygen atoms. Ice is made of two hydrogen atoms and one oxygen atom, the familiar H_2O formula of high-school chemistry. But not all oxygen atoms are the same. Some oxygen atoms have a weight of sixteen units. But there are other, heavier oxygen atoms that weigh eighteen units.

Snow forms from water vapor in the air. The vapor has a particular sixteen-to-eighteen ratio of oxygen atoms. What matters for scientists interested in climate is that under arctic and antarctic conditions, the weight ratio in the snow that forms from the water is primarily a function of the *temperature* of the air when the snow formed. This means that by measuring the sixteen-to-eighteen weight ratio in oxygen from samples extracted from the ice, scientists can calculate the *temperatures* of the ancient past.

In some ways, the success in drilling, retrieving, and analyzing the deep ice cores of Greenland and Antarctica is almost miraculous. By sheer good fortune, several important factors about climate can be measured from glacial ice cores that offer glimpses back through the Holocene and well into the Pleistocene. In terms of the football-field analogy of our first chapter, we now have an almost *annual record* of air composition that stretches back in time from our referee in the end zone way out onto the field of Earth history.

Here's a summary of information we can glean from ice cores. From the oxygen weight ratios of the ice we can determine the average or typical annual *temperature* for the region around the ice core. From the tiny air bubbles we can determine the *composition of Earth's atmosphere*; as a bonus, we can often determine the amounts of *dust, volcanic ash*, and the concentration of trace amounts of *salts* locked in the ice as well. Some of those trace constituents give us a record of typical *wind speed*—another important climate variable.

By the late 1980s, drilling teams were pulling deeper ice cores from both the Greenland and antarctic ice sheets. Scientists in several nations were analyzing the cores using the new techniques, and the data of Earth's climate rolled in like the tide. What emerged from the sea of information was a startling new understanding of how climate on Earth varies. The new picture of climate is most readily understood with a specific example, so we'll take a quick look at one crucial period of time in the very late Pleistocene, or just a couple of feet from the referee standing in the end zone of our football-field analogy. We'll explore the story of what happened at that time as it may have seemed to the people of the day, referring back to the ice cores and what they recorded as we do so.

When the most severely cold times of the Wisconsin period of the Pleistocene had passed, the massive ice sheets and mountain glaciers went into retreat the world around. Climate had been warming for centuries— just as we saw from the evidence of the pollen record of northern Europe. Hunter-gatherer clans of people had been taking advantage of the new lands exposed by the melting continental ice sheets around the world. A group of people archeologists call the *Natufians* was prospering in western Asia and the Middle East during this time, making the most of the milder climate. Times were good, at least compared to what they had been like for longer than any humans could possibly recollect.

But the comfortable world of these Natufians ended over just a few years when cold and dry winds swept over the land and climate changed abruptly back to the ice-box conditions that dominate most of our football-field analogy of time. Evidence from the ice cores shows that the *temperature* transition was fast—occurring over about a dozen years. We know that piece of information from the oxygen-weight ratios locked in the glacial ice and the number of layers that span the great transition. In central Greenland, typical temperatures fell in a jaw-dropping plunge. *Strong winds* became the norm at the same time. We know about the winds from the increased dust and salts blown into central Greenland and preserved in the ice. Even the *composition of the air* changed quickly, with a sharp decline in "swamp gas" or methane (natural gas) in the tiny air bubbles of the ice cores. We know that methane is a by-product of decomposition in soggy ground, and scientists think that when there is a worldwide reduction in sogginess—because land freezes over into permafrost—methane in the atmosphere naturally drops.

In short, the world had changed.

The Natufians who lived through the great disaster could only marvel at how the climate of their childhood differed from the climate they experienced as adults. Once the great change had swept over the lands of western Asia, the cold conditions lasted for more than a thousand years. It was simply brutal, and the human cost must have been immense. This was the climate-change event we met in the last chapter under the name the Younger Dryas. We discussed evidence for it found in the pollen record in peat and varves—evidence confirmed in exquisite detail by the measurements that can be made from the layers in glacial ice of that age.

The start and end of the Younger Dryas are wonderful examples of rapid climate change events. We met those climate revolutions in chapter 1, calling them RCCEs ("Rickies"). RCCEs were not what geologists or any other scientists expected to find in the record of the history of climate on Earth. But abundant evidence for RCCEs hems us in, and we are thus bound to accept their existence.

Let's return to our imperiled Natufians, the real people who felt the agony of the arrival of the Younger Dryas. Once the RCCE swept over them, wild game doubtless dwindled, and some wild staples must have simply disappeared. To the north in Scandinavia, glaciers advanced over forests. The ice cores confirm what the pollen record had early told us: bitterly cold and windy conditions prevailed for more than a thousand years. Even to the south of the areas hit by the worst of the cold, wind and drought were characteristic of the Younger Dryas—climate change with a different twist, if you will.

During this difficult time some groups of Natufians migrated and disappeared from the stage of history. Archeological evidence suggests that a few Natufians and their descendents created a new way of life in the Middle East. They became good nurturers of wild plants—a transitional step toward farming. They were, if you will, gardeners of nature, using nature's plants for their purposes as best they could. Over time, and doubtless with real cost, later peoples following in their footsteps learned to plant and cultivate wild grains like a grass called *einkorn*. Farming even primitive grain crops by hand gave people an advantage in gathering relatively predictable calories and therefore surviving the more difficult climate—so they lived from one year to the next and refined their elementary farming techniques. In time, the survivors of climate change created the new plant we call *wheat* and ushered in the full era of agriculture around the Mediterranean.

The Younger Dryas started with breathtaking speed. It ended in about the same way. The record of glacial ice reveals that the Younger Dryas ended very quickly, perhaps over the span of as little as three years. The cold times were simply over, and warmer years began once more.

With the new warmth that came at the end of the Younger Dryas, worldwide glacial ice returned to the business of retreating rather than advancing. The late Pleistocene dissolved into the warmth of the Holocene Epoch—with subsequent upheavals in plant and animal communities that our ancestors must have coped with as best they could. No one alive at the time could have remembered how quickly the world "fell apart" more than a thousand years earlier when the bitter cold times began. Those who lived through the decade that marked the "great warming" must have marveled in their turn at how fundamentally and quickly the world can change.

Let's look at the whole picture of how temperature on Earth has varied as the ice-core record shows it. We'll present what scientists know about the last 420,000 years. That figure will take us back to about the twenty-five-yard line from the end zone in our football-field analogy of time, a range some forty times the length of the entire history of civilization. To get that far back in time, we'll turn to the record of the glacial ice in central Antarctica, which was drilled near a Russian station called Vostok and reported to the scientific community in 1999.

The Vostok ice record of 420,000 years covers four great cycles of climate change on Earth. The record shows transitions from long periods of bitter cold to short times of warmth—like the present day—and then back to bitter cold once more. To put it another way, the record spans four deep-freeze times during which enormous ice sheets covered Canada, the northern United States, Europe, and more. In between those times are four times like the ages during which the forest bed grew in the US Midwest, periods during which most glacial ice was gone from the face of the Earth—very much like the present.

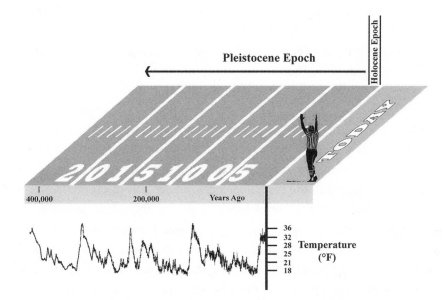

Figure 7.1. Temperature variations over the past four hundred thousand years, as recorded in an ice core. Adapted by permission from Macmillan Publishers Ltd. J. R. Petit et al., "Climate and Atmospheric History of the Past 420,000 Years from the Vostok Ice Core, Antarctica," *Nature* 399, no. 6735 (June 3, 1999): 429–36, copyright 1999.

Figure 7.1 shows how temperature as recorded in the ice's oxygen data has varied in the Vostok core record, imposed on our football-field analogy of time. Earth history unfolds toward the end zone in which our referee is still patiently standing. Looking closely at the figure, we can see several significant features. The four major "warm times," or periods roughly like the present day, are the upward peaks on the graph. They occur in the following places:

- near the present (the heavy black segment of the graph to the far right, the last few inches of the field)
- about 125,000 years ago (the Eemian time mentioned in the first chapter, and also the time of the forest bed, lying near the seven-yard line of our football field)

- about 230,000 years ago (the sharp peak lying near the fifteen-yard line of our football field)
- and about 325,000 years ago (about the twenty-yard line of our football field)

As you can see, the *shape* of the warm peaks varies. Interestingly, of the four warm times shown, it's only the current warm time that has a blunt appearance at its peak. This means that the warm climate of the Holocene Epoch is unusual in how stable the balmy times have been. (But "stability" here is relative. From the last chapter the reader will recall that the pollen record in peat indicated dramatic changes in the whole ecosystem of southern Sweden during these "stable" times.) As archeology and then history teach us, it's only during the Holocene that world civilization developed. It may well be that we owe the existence of our society, in part, to the unusually flat portion of the peak that's superimposed on the last few inches of our field. The success of agriculture, with all that it implies about the possibility of towns and the division of labor that made writing and the rest of our cultural inheritance possible, blossomed in the warmth and *the relative stability* of the Holocene Epoch.

Another point to note about the figure is that in the Earth's previous warm time, the Eemian period about 125,000 years ago, temperatures around the drill site in Antarctica were warmer than at present. In fact, all the warm times in the Antarctic ice-core record were warmer than our stable warm time—the Holocene Epoch.

The graph from the ice core surely shows high peaks and deep valleys in the temperature record. But another clear lesson to draw is that while we can see some broad trends, it's also true that those trends are "interrupted" by spikes throughout the whole time shown by the evidence from the ice core. Climate, clearly, is a complex and chaotic system, one that "jumps around" a lot. We will say more about that point in the chapters to come, but for now the graph speaks eloquently for itself.

Another point is also evident from the ice-core temperature record. In the context of the whole graph, it looks like the Holocene Epoch is due to end. Roughly speaking, if we expect natural climate rhythms to continue as they have, the Earth appears quite ready for a hundred thousand years of deep-freeze cold, with glaciers burying much of the lands many of us inhabit.

Just as the geologists of the 1800s had come to suspect on the basis of glacial moraines and ancient forest beds, we modern geologists agree that our own epoch won't last forever. Renewed bitter cold for the Earth is to be expected, and the ice core makes it look like the bitter cold is imminent on the scale of Earth time. That, as they say, is the bad news—stupendously bad, actually, as RCCEs like the Younger Dryas often descend on the globe so quickly that you and I could experience a dramatic plunge into bitter cold temperatures within the span of our lives. Such a change could easily mean the end of agriculture in the breadbasket regions of the United States, Canada, Eastern Europe, and Russia, thus interrupting global food supplies and leading to the deaths of millions—or even billions—of people and the collapse of whole societies.

But to evaluate whether the Holocene Epoch is in fact in its last breath and a new "ice time" is returning even as you read these words, it helps to understand what we can of the *causes* of the four broad temperature cycles illustrated so clearly by the ice-core record and known in more general terms to geologists of the 1800s. What, after all, creates the pattern of roughly one hundred thousand years of cold followed by ten thousand years of warm and then back to frigid times?

One of the first people to address that topic was James Croll, a fascinating and brilliant Scotsman who was born into humble circumstances and had to leave off his formal education when he was thirteen. He worked at a variety of jobs when he was a teenager and young man. When he landed a job as a custodian at Andersonian College in Glasgow, he used his access to the library to teach himself what was then modern science and math. When he'd educated himself sufficiently on the subjects, he started to write technical papers and submit them to the best British journals, where they were accepted and published because their content was so clearly good. In 1867 he was granted a job with the Geological Survey of Scotland.

Croll, of course, didn't know the fine details of annual climate change as shown by the evidence of the ice-core record. But he knew the broad pattern of change reported in the publications of T. C. Chamberlin, G. K.

Gilbert, and their British counterparts. That was enough to intrigue him about the *causes* of the four glacial ages, the four bitter times on our graph. The hypothesis Croll put forward was based on the insight that Earth's climate is ultimately controlled by the warmth of simple sunlight. That general notion is, in fact, quite correct, as those of us who have been downwind of a volcanic eruption know well. When sunlight is blocked, for example by volcanic ash and debris in the air, temperatures on the ground plummet. Diminished sunlight leads to cooler temperatures on the ground because the vital warmth that feeds weather and climate always comes from the light of the sun.

Croll realized that the only factor that can make the strength of sunlight on Earth vary on the scale of one hundred thousand years is one part of the complex manner in which our planet orbits around the sun. In school you were perhaps taught that the Earth's orbit is elliptical (a tad like an egg in outline) rather than circular. What you likely were not taught, however, is that over long stretches of time, Earth's orbit varies in this regard. Sometimes we are on a more strongly elliptical path (more eggy), sometimes a more strongly circular one. The two different orbit phases create different distances between the Earth and the sun. When we are farther away—even a little bit—the planet gets less sunlight. When we are closer, we get more. Small differences in sunlight can make for big differences in temperature, a point we'll come back to in a moment.

Croll outlined how the Earth's orbit has changed from egginess to circularity over geologic time and published it as the best explanation of the big-scale cold and warm times of the Pleistocene and Holocene. For a while, all seemed to be well in the scientific world because most scientists accepted Croll's explanation without seriously investigating it. Alas, the matter was not so simple. Croll's own work showed that the more circular versus more elliptical phases of Earth's orbit predicted that the last bitter cold times would have ended about eighty thousand years ago. Even without a precise knowledge of varves, carbon-14, and all the rest, geologists were sure the Pleistocene lasted for many tens of thousands of years beyond that mark. As an example, even Gilbert's mastodon in the pothole in New York was roaming the country perhaps about fifty thousand years later than the date for great climate change given by Croll's work. Thus, Croll's idea, which had looked good in some ways, failed to accomplish what was needed.

In intellectual life, just as in business, government, and the military, the larger a problem is, the longer it's likely to be ignored by most people. Thus, Croll's work—and its shortcomings—remained largely unaddressed until the early 1900s, when a Serbian engineer took them up. The Serb, as it happens, has a challenging name for English speakers: Milutin Milankovitch. Milankovitch's main insight was to take Croll's initial idea about the significance of orbital changes and extend that notion in ways that helped it to fit the facts of big-scale changes revealed by the ice-core record and mastodon remains.

As you perhaps recall from childhood lessons, the four seasons—winter, spring, summer, and fall—occur because the Earth's poles are inclined to the plane around which we orbit the sun. The inclination is, in fact, represented on school globes. The north pole on a globe is thus "tipped" about 23 degrees from vertical. On June 21, the north pole is tipped toward the sun, making the days in our hemisphere long (and *warm* because of the increased length of sunlight each day and the fact that the sun is higher in the sky at noon). On December 21, when the Earth has traveled halfway around its orbit about the sun, the north pole is still tipped the *same way in space*, but that means it's tipped away from the sun. So December delivers short days (and *cold* ones because of the decreased length of the days and because the sun is lower on the horizon, even at noon).

But Earth's angle of tilt is not absolutely constant. It changes over time, varying from about 22 degrees to about 24 degrees. To put it another way, a child's globe should have a little adjustment added so that the globe could be tilted a little more toward the vertical or away from it over time. The adjustment would be small, measured as an angle. But in the real world this factor makes a difference to the Earth, creating times of more extreme differences between summer and winter and times of less extreme differences between the seasons. We move from less tilt to more tilt and back again about every forty thousand years.

Another orbital variation of the Earth is related simply to the timing of the seasons. December 21, the first day of winter in our hemisphere, occurs when the Earth is actually closest to the sun in terms of the elliptical (eggy) shape of our orbit. This means that our winter season is moderated a *little* bit by the fact that we are slightly nearer the sun and are therefore picking up a little more sunlight energy through the winter months. In contrast, about 11,500 years ago, December 21 fell at the time that Earth was farthest from the sun on its elliptical path—this accentuated the coldness of those northern winters in the latter part of the Pleistocene Epoch. To put it another way, every twenty-three thousand years the Earth goes through a full cycle in which the seasons occur at different points along the Earth's elliptical path around the sun.

Croll had known these basics. But Milankovitch, the patient Serb with the difficult name, took Croll's idea and added more to it. He calculated the total effect of all three of Earth's orbital variations both for the Earth as a whole and for an acre of land at different degrees of latitude. Because all his calculations had to be done with a slide-rule and a pencil—the most sophisticated "calculators" of his day—this effort actually required years and years of work. He found that because the three types of orbital variations occur on different timescales, their effects sometimes add up more than at other times. This pushes the Earth toward more extreme seasons or more extreme temperatures, a manic-depressive cycle without moderating medication, if you will. At other times, the effects are muted and diminished because different factors cancel each other's impact.

Milankovitch's complex calculations were a vast step up from Croll's hypothesis. Today, no geologist or climate scientist doubts the general effects on climate that Milankovitch calculated. But it's also true that the four broadest peaks and valleys of the graph earlier in this chapter don't match up exactly with where Milankovitch's calculations would place them. They're close to being as predicted—so orbital factors do indeed seem crucial—but there can still be thousands of years of "slippage" in the climate system, during which temperatures remain very low even though it looks like they should have risen, or vice versa.

One reason temperature isn't simply dependent on orbital variations alone is this: the variations determine how much sunlight reaches the *upper atmosphere* of Earth. That's not the same as knowing how "warm" the sun feels here on the surface of the planet. Total impacts on climate from the orbital variations are complex because they are moderated by many factors, including three major factors we should mention now.

First, the average cloudiness of the atmosphere is important. Clouds, as you know, are white, and white materials reflect light, which is why pale concrete stays cooler in the summer than black asphalt. Because clouds are white and high in the atmosphere, they reflect a lot of sunlight back into space, lowering average temperatures. But, as it happens, cloudiness varies greatly over time in response to many factors here on Earth. To put it simply, clouds are huge in determining weather and climate. Unfortunately, even scientists today can predict little about cloud formation—a large drawback in our ability to forecast the weather beyond next week or predict climate beyond the next decade.

Second, the amount of open sea versus land is important in determining temperatures. The open sea (like asphalt) absorbs much of the solar energy that strikes it, while land (like concrete) reflects a larger fraction. But lowered global sea levels due to glaciation can reduce the amount of open sea present on Earth and increase the amount of continental shelf that's above water, thus reflecting more energy. This is a small effect compared to cloudiness, but there are times in Earth's climate history when a small input is the critical "shove" that topples the fragile equilibrium and plunges us into colder or warmer times—and the total area of open sea around the globe can be such a factor.

Third, the amount of snow-and-ice cover is another major player in determining temperature on Earth because white material reflects so much sunlight, lowering temperatures on Earth. The matter of snow and ice brings us to the concept of *feedback*, which is highly important in climate studies. "Positive" feedback is a change that tends to lead to more changes *in the same direction*. An example of positive feedback from the stock market might be that a natural disaster can scare investors into selling stocks. The sell-off can drive down prices, which can scare other investors into also selling, an effect that drives down prices still more. Even though the prices are falling, we speak of the feedback as "positive" because the first change (selling and price decline) leads toward more of the same (selling and price decline). The stock market clearly has other factors at play that prevent complete market runaways from positive feedback, but in the short term such influences are real, as we saw to our sorrow in the fall of 2008 when enormous changes in the Dow were the daily norm.

In the realm of climate, an example of positive feedback is this: during a time in which climate cools, snow covers more land in the winter and snow cover lasts longer in the spring. Snow always reflects sunlight energy, sending much of it back through the Earth's atmosphere and out into space. This means that a *cooling trend* that leads to increasing snow cover can lead to *further cooling*. This could tend toward a runaway effect, at least in theory, in which more ice and snow leads to a cooler climate, which leads to more ice and snow, leading to an even cooler climate, and so on. Luckily for us, the alteration of bitter cold and warmer times in the record of the Pleistocene Epoch makes it clear that other processes than the one just sketched are also at work on Earth.

"Negative" feedback refers to changes that tend to slow or stop the original change. Here's an example from the financial world. Imagine that the price of wheat rises to record highs next fall. In response to that, farmers across North America seed more wheat fields for the coming growing season. As long as the weather cooperates, more wheat will be harvested the following fall. Having a lot of wheat on the market will tend to drive down the price of wheat. That's a "negative" feedback, not because it's bad for farmers, but because the increased production is a change that tends to slow or stop the original change of increased prices.

An example of negative feedback in the realm of climate would be a period of warming on Earth that leads to warmer ocean temperatures, which then lead to higher evaporation rates from the seas and therefore more clouds. Cloud cover reflects a portion of all sunlight energy that strikes it, sending the energy back into space, which leads to decreasing temperatures. That means that the later cooling moderates or lessens the original warming influence.

The key difference between positive and negative feedback is simply that negative feedback doesn't lead to changes that can "get out of hand" even in the short term. From the point of view of human civilization, negative climate feedbacks could be a very good thing because they act to dampen potentially dangerous initial changes. Positive feedback, on the other hand, magnifies the effects of the initial change. But from the point of view of the Earth rather than us, both positive and negative feedbacks contribute to the dominant theme of climate, which is change followed by change followed by yet more change.

You, the patient reader, are now in a position to understand in general terms why the variations in Earth's orbit over time don't translate into temperatures on the ground in a simple way—or why the peaks and valleys of the graphs shown from the ice-core record don't all match up nicely with Milankovitch's calculations. To put it simply, Milankovitch correctly calculated the variations in the sunlight reaching the upper atmosphere of Earth for many different latitudes, but these changes are moderated through a number of positive and negative feedback processes. The orbital variations have indeed led our planet to the major, long-term climate shifts seen in our football-field analogy of time, but not in a simple way that means we can predict temperatures from solar input alone.

Here's the bottom line: climate is always going to be in a state of *adjusting* to many factors—both those here on Earth and those relating to our position with respect to the sun. Climate adjustments, of course, mean change. Climate responds to the three fundamental orbital factors and how they "add up" through time. In the process, climate adjusts to changes created by both positive and negative feedback here on Earth. All of these factors are working on climate at the same time.

Let's go back to a simple notion. As geologists have long known, glacial ice once covered everything from the north pole to Nebraska. This deep freeze was in keeping with the particulars of Earth's orbit around the sun, although there was not any instant cause and effect at work. As climate on Earth headed toward warmer times, the ice sheet retreated from Nebraska, northward into the Dakotas, then Canada, ultimately leaving even Canada as bare ground. As it did so, the amount of sunlight energy striking land (rather than reflective ice) increased, further warming the climate, owing to a positive feedback mechanism. On the other hand, as global climate warmed during this period, the surface layer of the seas increased a little bit in temperature, leading to more evaporation, which in turn led to more clouds, which reflected sunlight in the atmosphere, acting as an overall brake on the warming process. Thus, fundamental changes in Earth's orbit shape climate, but not in a simple one-to-one sort of way in which exact predictions based exclusively on orbital parameters can be made.

In short, Earth's climate system is exceedingly complex, and many factors influence it at any given time. Milankovitch's idea about the importance of changes in the Earth's orbit around the sun has been vindicated in general terms by all later science. But we still cannot predict Earth's future climate by calculating our orbital state. What this means—the important point for you—is that scientists cannot say in any precise way when the Holocene will naturally collapse into a renewed deep freeze. Different thoughts and hypotheses have been put forward in this regard in recent years, but they are all debatable. We simply don't know what we don't know, including the most crucial information of all: our own civilization's future climate.

The basic news is even a good bit worse than that. In addition to the three Milankovitch cycles, there are two other cycles with much faster tempos that help determine climate. The first is a cycle that runs every six thousand or so years, the second a cycle that lasts about fifteen hundred years. It's these shortest of cycles that appear to relate most directly to rapid changes in climate during the latter part of the Pleistocene, events that gave our ancestors the climate terrors of intervals like the Younger Dryas. The quicker cycles don't make for such massive change as the Milankovitch cycles, but they are really more significant factors for climate change of the sort that affects civilizations, simply because they occur much more often. To put it another way, the ice-core graph is frightening not only because it looks like the warmth of the Holocene is due to end, but also because the whole graph is so "spiky," with major ups and downs on a finer scale within every stage of the broader trends.

In order to get our arms fully around what we as humans face regarding natural climate change, let's look the tiger in the eye in the next chapter and examine the faster-tempo cycles that can—and surely will—clobber us at some point in the years to come, just as they have done in the past.

8

EVEN MORE FREQUENT BOOM-BUST CYCLES

S ome glacial ice is pretty filthy stuff. True, there are a few glaciers that are made of clean and beautifully blue ice—the ones that show up pictured in advertisements. But much glacial ice is packed full of silt, sand, pebbles, and even boulders the size of trucks and houses. As summer visitors to alpine glaciers know, when a glacier is melting backward up its valley, the terminus area is made of loose silt, sand, and jumbled rocks of all sizes. When the wind blows, as it does in the mountains quite a bit, such areas are no place to picnic—and no picnic for doing careful scientific measurements or even keeping clothes halfway clean. Silt and sand blow around until a calm afternoon arrives, allowing geologists and hikers alike to amble below the glacier without grit in their teeth—at least for a few hours.

It was the many rocks embedded in Pleistocene glaciers that scoured the solid Earth and created the deep, majestic valleys of Yosemite and the Alps. Because of such abrasion, the rocks in glacial ice end up with the striations Louis Agassiz noted. And it turns out that the same glacial grit gave scientists their first clear evidence of a climate cycle that repeats about every six to seven thousand years.

In the later decades of the twentieth century, many geologists still looked at rocks on land in the old-fashioned way of walking over them, hammer in hand, and bashing off pieces of outcrops. That's how geologists are trained, and some of us never graduate beyond it. But other geologists, increasingly known as *marine geologists*, had also appeared on the scene. They worked in groups from ocean-going research vessels and drilling platforms, funding their expensive science via major grants from national and international institutions.

We cannot fully explain the findings of marine geologists in terms of a single person—like Agassiz or G. K. Gilbert—because their work had to be collaborative, simply due its nature. It takes many hands to do research from a ship. But even in a field dominated by teams and groups, some specific results and some individual researchers stand out. One geologist of this sort had the imposing name of Harmut Heinrich. In the late 1980s, Heinrich was a young professional, just starting out in science. He jump-started his career with a bang by publishing the results of his pioneering work looking at layers of sediments on the seafloor of the North Atlantic.

The floor of the sea, not surprisingly, is covered in fine sediment that has settled down from the water column above it over vast amounts of time. The deeper you core into the seafloor sediments, the older the material. What Heinrich found in the seafloor sediments of the North Atlantic was both clear and quite startling. At regular intervals, the layering of the deep seafloor was littered with small rock debris of many different types and sizes, the kind of material geologists would clearly and immediately recognize as originating in glaciers.

At first blush, it may be difficult to see the relationship between the deep seafloor and glaciers on land. But perhaps if you conjure up in your mind's eye the sinking of the *Titanic*, you'll start to see the connection. Icebergs are made of glacial ice, and icebergs have been floating around the North Atlantic throughout the last two geological epochs. When an iceberg breaks up or melts—as it must in time—it drops the rocks embedded within it into the sea. The rocks may be big or small, but they all sink through the vast depths to the seafloor below. They then rest on the seabed, surrounded by the much finer sediment that normally rains down on the seafloor, until they are covered by later, fine sediment.

Heinrich had discovered layers that were abundantly and especially rich in these glacial rocks, those that fell into the depths as icebergs melted and broke. Each of the special layers showed that huge numbers of icebergs had been—for some reason—launched into the seas at particular times. The large fleets of icebergs were so impressive to Heinrich and other scientists that they began to call them "armadas"—one of the rare times when geology as a discipline has given the broader world a neat turn of phrase that evokes how different past climate has been on Earth. At the times of the icy armadas, only submarines diving deep would have had an easy time crossing the North Atlantic—ships would have been all but doomed.

Here's how to think of these armadas of icebergs and how they formed: The enormous glaciers that buried much of Canada and Scandinavia in the Pleistocene ultimately flowed into the sea. As the glacial ice advanced into the ocean water, it "calved" or broke off, just as glaciers do today in Alaska, where cruise ships ply the waves so tourists can see the dramatic process. The calved chunks of glacial ice, complete with rocks embedded in them, are icebergs. Over time, of course, the icebergs drifted on prevailing currents in the oceans. Ultimately, they broke up and melted, and the glacial rocks embedded in the ice fell to the seafloor.

It wasn't surprising that Heinrich observed some ice-drop rocks in the seafloor sediments. That was to be expected. But researchers were amazed that he found the rocks clustered in layers that occurred in sediments about six to seven thousand years apart. In other words, for some reason, the large armadas of icebergs hit the seas at regular intervals.

Today, in honor of Heinrich's initial work describing the layers, each one is referred to as a *Heinrich event*. And, as is the custom in modern science, the layers are denoted by a simple nomenclature, namely H_0, H_1, H_2, H_3, and so forth, stretching back in time.

What would cause the armadas of icebergs at regular six- to seven-thousand-year intervals? One point of evidence that starts to address that question is the fact that Heinrich events in the seafloor match up quite well with the coldest shifts in climate we see in the ice-core record. In other words, it looks like a drop into especially bitter-cold times led to faster glacier flow into the seas, especially in Canada, or that a growth in glacial or sea ice in Canada affected the climate and led to a drop into colder times in central Greenland. The ice-core record also shows us that these bitter intervals linked to the armadas are followed by substantial changes toward warmer temperatures.

Scientists have increasingly linked these shifts to complex changes in the oceans. Although we land-dwelling organisms don't really appreciate it, it's the oceans and their circulation that are key to the climate around us. Although the weather on land is important to our plans for this coming weekend, it is conditions in the oceans that control what weather will be like over the longer term. And simply because we humans live on the land, scientists still stand at square one in understanding the seas. With respect to our knowledge of the oceans, both geologists and climate scientists are a bit like Louis Agassiz was when he took his first summer holiday to the alpine glaciers of Switzerland. But researchers are at least getting started in the serious study of the seas, and we won't have to wait as long for significant results as we did with early geology because so many more researchers are at work, and they have more sophisticated instruments at their disposal.

While Heinrich events can be alarming from a human point of view, the news of more frequent climate change is actually even worse. Heinrich cycles are actually stately and slow compared to the shortest repeating cycle, which affects climate about every fifteen hundred years. These shorter cycles are more important to civilization because they affect the world more often, hence they are more likely to affect *our* world. These are the cycles, the patient reader may recall, that contributed to what our referee marked with flags on the football-field analogy of time in the first chapter of this book. The resulting forest of flags first convinced us that Mother Nature is far from benign. Today many of the abrupt changes in climate we first marked with those flags are known in technical circles as Dansgaard/Oeschger events, named for the Danish and Swiss researchers who helped scientists recognize and understand them.

As we've seen with pollen studies and ice-core evidence, modern geologists know well that climate does not evolve gradually and smoothly over great periods of time. Evidence makes it clear that Dansgaard/Oeschger warming events affected climate during the later portions of the Pleistocene. Some of these events were much larger than others. To keep matters simple for a moment—and it is a simplification—we can think of Heinrich events as occurring every six thousand years and pushing climate toward frigid temperatures, with Dansgaard/Oeschger cycles giving climate a push in the warmer direction every fifteen hundred years.

Enter stage left an old-fashioned geologist named Gerald Bond, an American who started his scientific career like G. K. Gilbert and so very many others—by looking at rocks on land. One set of rocks was a special favorite of Bond. These rocks came from the Cambrian Period, a time on Earth half a billion years ago that started when simple life-forms in the sea first evolved from worms and jelly-fish-like animals into much more complex creatures with shells, legs, and eyes. The Cambrian rocks that record life's dramatic history were formed by sediments on ancient sea-floors, but these sediments have long since been formed into solid material that requires a rock hammer and plenty of strength to break apart. The Cambrian rocks have also been pushed up on land, where they were first named by British geologists. Over time, geologists discovered other Cambrian rocks from all the world around.

Bond was just one of many "real geologists" who carried a rock hammer, walked around on land, and looked at rocks. But, as fate would have it, he and a colleague wrote a research grant proposal to look more closely at regular cycles that occur in some Cambrian rocks. The cycles in the ancient sediments had long been a puzzle. Using a new optical approach, the idea was to characterize the color of the modern sea-core sediments for comparison—some of which researchers thought might have been formed in response to large-scale orbital cycles.

In the review process for the grant proposal, Bond's idea caught the eye of scientists studying Earth's temperature cycles in the Pleistocene and Holocene Epochs. They believed that Bond's interests might well reflect—of all things—the recently discovered Dansgaard/Oeschger cycles in Earth's most recent history. Bond soon threw in his lot with the marine geologists and climate scientists, and the union proved intellectually fruitful.

Bond and his colleagues looked at the fine sediment of the seafloor—the ooze and muck that accumulates over millennia regardless of whether glacial debris is raining down on the bed of the ocean. They discovered that there are places on the Atlantic seafloor where there is a clear and regular color record of sediment, going back in time. To be sure, the seafloor is not a pristine year-by-year record of conditions, as are varves of lakebeds and the ice-core layers. But the muck and mire of parts of the seabed is laid down in sequence, and it reflects conditions that can be interpreted by scientists. In short, the work of Bond and his colleagues convinced scientists everywhere that the seafloor record could complement the land and ice-core records in terms of its information about climate.

That brings us to the final Pleistocene cycle we'll consider, and we'll keep the image brief. Looking at both ocean and ice records, Bond and colleagues showed that the multiple Dansgaard/Oeschger cycles that occurred between a given pair of Heinrich events were likely to be warmer or colder than Dansgaard/Oeschger cycles between the next pair of Heinrich events. In other words, the ups and downs of temperature of the fifteen-hundred-year cycles tend to be reset to new levels at Heinrich events every six thousand years or so. Each of these distinctive packages of Dansgaard/Oeschger cycles with the Heinrich offsets is called a *Bond cycle*. If the cycles within cycles are not entirely clear to you, don't put too much energy into unraveling it all. The point is that the Heinrich events seem to reset the global climate system to mildly warmer or colder conditions, as usual, with "mildly" being an adjective that makes sense from the Earth's long-term point of view, though not necessarily from our short-term point of view. Faster-tempo ups and downs occur in packages after such shifts.

In the last few pages, we've met climate cycles that run at a quick tempo—certainly quick enough to cause enormous trouble to human societies. The pattern of the cycles is clear and is agreed upon by everyone who has looked at the data. Indeed, even an aging geologist with trifocals, such as myself, can pick out the changes in the data generated from ice cores, seabed coring, and the like. But the *causes* of the three cycles are not so clear to scientists. There are good hypotheses about each, but at this point the ideas are simply hypotheses. And beyond that disquieting fact, there are many ups and downs for climate *within* the three cycles just discussed. We have no clear explanation for those changes, and they are certainly sufficient to affect civilizations in fundamental ways. In short, and as we have said before, Earth's climate is a highly complex system with many variables, a system we cannot predict because we cannot even explain its past changes. Science has forged remarkable advances in our understanding of the natural world in recent decades, but Earth's climate is a system so unique, complex, and unstable that it will defy our attempts at explanation and prediction for at least generations to come.

But one point we do understand is that the basic effect of the three fast-tempo climate-change events—the Heinrich, Dansgaard/Oeschger, and Bond cycles—have been strongly muted in their intensity during the Holocene Epoch. To be sure, there have been significant Holocene climate changes. We saw that in the pollen record of Scandinavia, for example. But the three fast-tempo cycles that are so clear in ice cores and the seabed from the late Pleistocene become much smaller blips as we move into our own Holocene times. In fact, because they are so small, there's a debate in scientific circles about which minor temperature change may relate to which cycle. Some scientists argue that rapid changes in the Holocene occur over a somewhat different time cycle, one lasting between two and three thousand years rather than fifteen hundred years. At this point, no scientist fully understands the change in frequency and size of the events in the Holocene versus the Pleistocene Epochs. This surely isn't just an academic matter; the frequency of the cycles is crucial to predicting when major climate change will next occur. It's understandable that citizens feel science is letting us all down on this crucial matter, but we simply don't know what we don't know—and I think it will take us decades to develop a clearer picture of how natural changes in the Holocene have been unfolding.

The good news is that, no matter how you slice it, our epoch is both warm and *relatively* stable. That doubtless contributed to the fact that early civilizations were able to take root rather than being wiped out by major climate change as soon as they had formed. If early Holocene farming societies had faced more extreme events—like the onset of the Younger Dryas and other climate crashes of the latter part of the Pleistocene—and faced them at frequent intervals, our own civilization might well have never come into existence.

Perhaps looking at the Holocene in a little detail can give us some ideas of what natural changes have been like and what—one way or another—

we have survived. As we noted when we discussed the pollen record, the balmiest part of the Holocene runs from about eight thousand years ago to four thousand years ago, with the exact times of this climate "optimum" varying with location around the globe. But the fact that the Holocene is relatively stable and that the climate was warmer at that time than it has been in more modern history did not protect the people of that age from all climate *variability*.

The ice-core record makes clear that a substantial and rapid change in climate occurred around eight thousand years ago, or about 6000 BCE. In the North Atlantic region, the Greenland ice core suggests that temperature dropped when the event began. As usual, the change hit hard and fast. To the south of Greenland, the temperature fall would have been much less than in the arctic, but it was still significant and abrupt. Although this cooling was not as severe as the Younger Dryas, and although it lasted only decades rather than a millennium, it must have destroyed many of the agricultural communities around the world that had come into existence by that time. After all, even modern farmers in the United States would see crop failures with a sharp drop in temperature. And we are talking here about crop failures lasting for several decades.

To the south of the middle latitudes affected by the cold, there would have been a rearrangement of weather patterns, likely bringing drought to areas that didn't directly feel the staggering drop in temperature. It's a matter of vocabulary whether or not you want to call this event a full rapid climate change event. It's decidedly smaller than the fast-tempo-cycle events of the Pleistocene, yet it's magnitude was beyond anything in written history and it's almost psychologically overwhelming to contemplate. Such an event—if it were to occur today—would likely lead to the deaths of hundreds of millions or more because food production would immediately decrease in the crucial middle latitudes that are the world's breadbasket.

We don't have written records from the climate change event that happened eight thousand years ago because people had not yet learned to record their thoughts in clay tablets, let alone on paper. But if we move forward in time, we reach recorded history, that is, the era in which people started to write down what was happening around them. A milder climate event from the period of written history occurred around 4,300 years ago (2300 BCE). But "milder" is once again a relative term—it was climate change that wrecked the major civilizations of the time.

The Bronze Age was in full swing 4,300 years ago. This was the time during which people farmed not only around the Mediterranean, but also elsewhere, using irrigation canals and complex forms of community labor. In the Middle East, the Akkadian civilization flourished. In India, the Harappan civilization was well established. The Giza pyramids in Egypt had been built by this point, and the Pharaohs of the Old Kingdom might have been forgiven if they took their pivotal place in the world for granted.

But the Old Kingdom, the Akkadians, the Harrappans, and other cultures of the time rapidly collapsed—quite possibly simply due to climate change. As usual, in southern areas like the Mediterranean, it was drought rather than cold that unfolded across the land as climate lurched into a new regime. There's physical evidence of drought that appears as sandy layers in the soil around the Middle East at the time in question. In Egypt, the cataclysm hit hard, with the collapse of the elaborate and sophisticated empire that had depended on annual flooding of the Nile to water its fields. Rulers rapidly came and went in the Old Kingdom of Egypt during a time of what must have been great political instability. The famine that resulted from the drought was so severe that parents in Egypt—according to written records—ate their own children. The human cost of climate change is written into that single image: hunger so great that people cannibalized children to stave off death for a time.

The civilizations of Europe that gave birth to our own have been relatively lucky—we have never seen climate change on the scale of that which occurred earlier in the Holocene, let alone late in the Pleistocene. But it's also true that climate has been far from static as the culture of Europe formed and blossomed. The Roman Empire grew in a period of good weather, a modestly balmy time long known to historians as the Roman Warming. For several centuries, harvests were good as a result of the stable and generous climate that provided warm and dry summers that favored crops. Ancient Romans cultivated wine grapes farther north in Italy as the centuries went by, apparently in response to the climate change. At the end of the Roman Empire, cooler times prevailed. Colder and wetter summers decreased harvests—perhaps hastening the implosion of what was then Europe's great superpower.

The cool period that followed—coinciding with the Dark Ages—is one you likely skipped over in history class. That's principally because civilization was hardly present in Europe, with just a few scattered clerics able to read and write. Most people lived close to the land in conditions that left no time for anything other than trying to survive another day. The later part of this difficult time saw Norse raiders—possibly hard-pressed to feed themselves at home—perfecting the Viking longboat, the stealth weapon of its day. Stealing up coastal waters and rivers, the pagan Norse would arrive to kill Christians, plunder the churches, and take food stores.

The cold and wet centuries of the Dark Ages dissolved in time into a new and balmy era, the Medieval Warming. Many cultural changes happened at the same time that climate evolved toward warmth. For one thing, the Norse slowly converted to Christianity, beat their swords into plowshares, and went to work as farmers, leaving the rest of Europe in peace. But it was the warming climate that contributed to better crops all over Europe. Populations expanded and were more stable, ultimately leading into the high culture of the Middle Ages, when towns and markets flourished and the great cathedrals of Europe were constructed. Those cathedrals included enormous and majestic structures with intricate stained-glass windows—achievements quite unlike anything ever known before in Europe.

Around 1120, a monk named William of Malmesbury traveled through England, admiring the fruits of the land. "Here you may behold . . . publick roads full of Fruit-trees, not planted, but growing naturally," he wrote.[1]

Even more impressive to William were the grapes, which grew well and yielded sweet rather than tart fruit at harvest. The vines were planted out in the open, not sheltered from wind—yet they flourished, year after year. A long growing season—warm springs, summers, and falls—is needed to increase the sugar content of grapes, and that's what the English grapes had in 1120. Malmesbury wrote that "the wine has no unpleasant tartness. . . . [It] is little inferior to the French in sweetness."[2]

As climate first warmed, the Norse colonized Iceland and then Greenland. In Iceland, the Norse populations grew and harvested the queen of grains—wheat—during this period. The Norse built two substantial communities in Greenland and were soon successfully raising cattle and cutting hay there—all of this near the great mass of glacial ice later drilled and analyzed in the service of climate science.

We know about how the Norse lived in Greenland partly from the written records they kept and partly from archeological evidence that has been unearthed in recent years. It's beyond dispute that *thousands* of Norse farmers lived in Greenland—in time they merited their own bishop, sent from Europe by the Catholic Church to oversee them. Some Norse sailed even farther west during these warm and good times, exploring the northeast coast of North America centuries before the voyages of Christopher Columbus. L'Anse aux Meadows, in Newfoundland, is a site of archeological remains that testify to how mobile the Norse were during these temperate times around and after the turn of the first millennium.

The Medieval Warming that had blessed Europeans ended with an onslaught of cold and wet summers in the 1300s that led to crop failures in most of Christendom. In Western Europe the change arrived in 1315 with noticeably different conditions and harvests. Seven weeks after Easter, it started to rain. And the rain came down in sheets, again and again. Fields turned to shallow lakes. In towns, the streets and alleyways were quagmires. Most of the summer was similar. August and September were cold. At what should have been harvest time, oats and hay lay flat on the earth. As historian Brian Fagan writes, "Oxen stood knee deep in thick mud under sheltering trees, their heads turned away from the rain. Dykes were washed away and royal manors inundated."[3] Perhaps most telling of all descriptions, the year of rain was so terrible that even Europe's endless military campaigns and wars were stopped.

In the winter, people endured hunger as best they could and prayed for a change. But in the spring of 1316 the rains were so heavy they prevented the proper planting of oats and barley. Enough rain fell in the growing season that at least one writer of the time likened what was happening to Noah's flood. Historians think that for cereal crops—plants like wheat—

the year 1316 was the worst ever in the Middle Ages. By the late fall of 1316, many parts of Western Europe were in chaos due to the wet conditions and the two failed harvests. Farmland that had been hacked out of the forest in previous generations was abandoned because neither draft animals nor peasants were present to work it. Later, even royalty suffered—in England, King Edward II could not command as much bread for his court as he wanted.

Historians call the result of this mild climate change in Europe— "mild" at least by Earth standards—the Great Famine. It was the start of what's known to historians as the Little Ice Age. (Naturally, geologists would prefer another name for this period because the 1300s were nothing like the Pleistocene Epoch. But geologists cannot control how historians label recent centuries.)

Crop yields at the start of the Little Ice Age were sharply down, and widespread famine unfolded. European population fell as the very young, the old, and the ill simply died off from hunger stress. Even the hale and hearty were imperiled as *years* of hunger took their toll. Whole villages were abandoned as people took to the roads in search of some place that had food. Some historians attribute the social upheaval that followed with the end of the feudal system, which had been marked by laborers who had been tied to land. And some experts think the famine and upheaval contributed to the weakened population that was then decimated by the Black Death when it reached Europe in the 1340s.

There were a few rallies. Off and on, in the 1320s and 1330s, there were some years that were warmer and drier. But such years came in small groups, with a return to colder and wetter growing seasons for other years. King Edward and his good people could not fully grasp it, but the world had changed, and it would not be the same until closer to our own times, around 1900.

In the 1340s, really cold temperatures joined the rain that marked earlier years. We see the signature of the colder times in the Greenland ice-core record as well as in the written records of Europe. In Iceland, the Norse population dropped sharply when the cold summers hit. Crop failures followed one another. Famine took hold of the island, which was increasingly surrounded by icy seas for greater and greater portions of the year. The population dropped markedly and the number of Icelanders never returned to what it had been until modern times.

In Greenland, the story was the same, only more extreme. Greenland (despite its fine name, inspired by Erik the Red's gift for public relations) is a pretty tough environment in the best of times. While thousands of Norse had indeed farmed in Greenland during the Middle Ages, they did so on a knife's edge with respect to climate. They raised hay near an ice sheet—not exactly a recipe for guaranteed success over time. True, they also fished and hunted, as all rural people do. But a good bit of their way of life was based on dairy farming, just as it was back in Scandinavia.

At the time the Greenland ice core shows a clear drop in temperatures, a Norwegian church leader sailed north along Greenland's coast to what had been known for centuries as the Western Settlement. But instead of finding at least a thousand or two Norse, he found no people at all. The church was intact but vacant. There were a few wild sheep and cattle, the descendents of the animals the colonists had tended, but there were no people.

Recent archeological work suggests the Norse of the Western Settlement slowly starved due to the change to a cooler climate. We have evidence of this because the Norse—and I feel free to say this as a Scandinavian—had the habit of living in houses graced with a great deal of filth on the floor. The filth is quite useful for telling us how they lived. Straw, which was swept out only in the spring, covered the floor of Norse housing for most of the year. Bones and trash were often simply dropped on the straw. The farm animals lived in one part of the house, along, of course, with their manure.

One Norse house in Greenland that was well preserved has been seriously studied. Called Nipaatsoq, the evidence within the dwelling tells of the last winter of the Norse family that occupied it—a family that had likely seen much of the community around it wither away.

If you have ever taken a whole chicken apart in your home kitchen you may have realized that your knife makes certain marks on the chicken bones in the process. Butchering larger animals with blunter instruments leads to even clearer markings. Archeologists are expert at seeing and understanding such evidence, which makes clear if an animal was eaten by humans rather than by animals.

The debris on the house floor shows that early in that final winter, the occupants butchered and ate their five dairy cattle. When dairy farmers butcher the last of the herd, you know they feel they have no other choice for survival. Scattered around on the floor are a few bits of arctic hares and other small animals that could be hunted in the winter. Finally, in the topmost layer of floor debris, there are the bones of large hunting dogs. The dogs, it's clear, were the last to go, after they had perhaps been used for one final effort at hunting the small wild animals.

There were no human remains at Nipaatsoq. We must assume the family, having exhausted all of its resources, including prized cows and hunting dogs, made one final attempt to travel some place where other Norse might be faring better. Alternatively, it's possible that some Norse "went native" and joined the Inuit, who could survive in Greenland because they successfully hunted ring seal for food. We don't know. The family simply disappeared from their house, just like the other families of the Western Settlement.

The more southerly Eastern Settlement in Greenland did not succumb so quickly to the frigid years, likely simply due to its location. Indeed, there were at least some Norse there for more than a century. But, in time, Norse culture disappeared from all parts of Greenland, including the Eastern Settlement. The written records of births, marriages, and deaths of the Norse, kept in churches, simply peter out and then stop.

To be fair, we should mention there were certainly factors other than climate at work in the story of the Norse history of Greenland. When Erik the Red first arrived in Greenland with his early colonists from Iceland, they moved into what was then an unoccupied land. For one reason or another, the Inuit were not around the areas of the Norse settlements at that time. That was a stroke of good fortune, like the warming climate.

In Greenland the Norse found trees that had never been logged and pasture that had never been grazed. They went to work at first by burning trees to make more pastureland for their animals. In time, the Norse felled the trees of Greenland for their wood. They used the biggest trees for building, but they also heated their homes with wood, an ongoing demand that guaranteed the cutting of more and more of the forest. And they needed more firewood than one might first imagine. As a people based on dairy farming, they had to deal with the significant and daily demands of cleaning the implements they used for milking their herds and making cheese. So—as the scientist and writer Jared Diamond points out—they had to produce significant amounts of boiled water twice per day to wash out their dairy equipment.[4] Heating water to the boiling point consumes a great deal of energy, so yet more wood was consumed for this task, even during Greenland's brief summer!

And the Norse changed Greenland in other ways. The sheep and cattle of the Norse made good use of the verdant summer pastures, but their hooves damaged the fragile turf of the landscape as the generations rolled by. The destruction of the thin soils increased erosion. Then, because wood had become precious, the Norse began to dig up turf to use as construction material. Finally, the Inuit started to appear around the Norse communities as time progressed, likely putting pressure on the Europeans in several ways.

Still, climate change itself has its clear victims, and the Norse of Greenland were at the wrong place at the wrong time when "mildly" cooler times began. It's quite evident the Norse didn't have enough to eat, and their reliance on farming as they knew it—raising hay in the summers for cattle and sheep to eat in the winters—could not be sustained in the face of the cold snap that hit the North Atlantic and Europe in the 1300s.

From Roman times to the Dark Ages to the Medieval Warming and the Little Ice Age, we can see that very minor climate changes contribute to enormous human suffering. Setting aside greenhouse gases and industrialization for a moment, we'd all like to know if Mother Nature has another such fully natural change in store for the world soon. We don't know the answer to that, but some scientists think of the onset of the Little Ice Age as a muted rapid climate change event. If so, it's doubly interesting compared to other climate changes because we know something about the sun during the later portions of the Little Ice Age that may be relevant to what caused the drop in temperature during the period. The reason is simply that we have written records about human observations of the sun through tele-scopes starting in the early 1600s. Before we consider them, however, it's important to note that scientists on all sides of the sun-climate debate are known for becoming quite agitated regarding hypotheses linking the sun's variations and Earth's climate. Forewarned is perhaps forearmed.

Here are the basic issues: Although the sun is a remarkably reli-able source of energy in our solar system, its activities are not absolutely constant. One part of its variability is represented by *sunspots*, the dark blotches that appear on the face of the sun. Humans have observed and documented sunspots for centuries. Modern scientists can also infer the record of ancient solar activity, at least to some degree, through the isotope record of certain elements on Earth. Sunspots are just one indication of the changes or cycles the sun appears to go through due to its own internal processes. There's a strong solar cycle every eleven years. There are likely other, longer cycles as well, although the data about them is subject to different interpretations. Because we don't understand the sun's internal processes, and we don't have data from telescopes stretching back for mil-lennia, we still have much to learn.

We met sunspots when we were considering the work of A. E. Douglass. They are the darker regions that intermittently appear on the face of the sun. Although the spots are relatively cool, during the height of the solar cycle they are complemented by other zones called *faculae* (Latin for "torches") that emit enough extra energy that times of many sunspots are also times when extra energy leaves the sun.

Here's the important point: sunspot activity dropped and remained quite low during the late 1600s and early 1700s, part of Little Ice Age. This period of few sunspots is known as the Maunder Minimum, after a man who championed its significance. The Medieval Warming, by con-trast, was a time of high sunspot activity, as we infer it from isotopes. Such correlations of highs and lows don't *prove* a climate effect, but they are surely intriguing.

Scientists don't think the drop in sunspots, acting by itself, could account for the magnitude of climate change involved in the Little Ice Age. But one hypothesis in play is that great changes in sunspot frequency may have been an initial cause that was amplified by climate processes here on Earth. Sunspot numbers have certainly soared in recent times, which may be related to why the Little Ice Age ended around 1850 and more recent warming has graced the Earth.

To repeat: in some circles, even mentioning that variations in the sun's output might be driving certain climate cycles on Earth is enough to start quite a heated discussion. Understandably, scientists want to explain all they can about Earth's climate with reference to materials and processes here on Earth—things we can study directly. Once solar cycles are called upon to explain the weather, there's nothing more that can be explained, since we cannot truly sample, measure, or explain the inner workings of the sun. And many serious scientists have looked at the statistical evidence and don't see a connection between the sun's cycles and climate changes. At the same time, those who believe in the solar hypothesis continue to pursue research projects, as well they should if science is to progress even via negative results that confirm there is no connection.

Another general word here about science and the public seems appropriate at this point. The inability of scientists to explain—and thus predict—many of the cycles of climate change on Earth is understandably a frustration for citizens. Just as I'd like my medical doctor to understand the state of my health and give me a prognosis each time I walk through his door, so ordinary citizens think that geologists and climate scientists should be able to understand and predict what comes next in Earth's long history of staggering climate changes, milder ups and downs in temperature and precipitation, and everything in between. Unfortunately, just as my doctor cannot often tell me what my life will be like in the months or years to come, scientists cannot predict even fully natural climate change given the record of past revolutions and evolutions in temperature. Those are the simple facts, ones we must live with as a society.

But let's back up to the 1300s and the onset of the Little Ice Age. As the ice-core record and written history in Europe make clear, the Little Ice Age ran from the early 1300s to about 1850. Although the climate change led to hunger, death, and dislocation for many, particularly at its outset, other Europeans later clearly made cultural progress despite the challenging turn in climate. One element of the story was certainly technological change. The Enlightenment, the scientific revolution, and the strengthening of nation-states changed the face of Europe. By the middle of the Little Ice Age, the Portuguese and Spanish sent ships across the Atlantic in search of new trade routes to the Far East. Soon, the English created the American colonies. Our own society was born in the cool times of the Little Ice Age.

By 1850 climate was changing again—this time in the direction of renewed warmth. Harvests improved, in part because of climate change but also because of the explosion of technological progress that we have come to expect as normal in the modern world. Population in Europe and here in North America increased substantially because of abundant harvests and the total impact of the industrial revolution. The temperatures of the Little Ice Age faded into the past, with milder winters and warm summers sweeping both Europe and North America.

Now we've come to the point in the story at which climate change and human record keeping fully overlap. Around 1850 is the time when modern weather records started to be kept in both Europe and North America. That's because the middle of the 1800s was the first time—not so very long ago—that good, reliable thermometers were widespread and employed to monitor the weather. To put it another way, most American and European weather records start by chance *just as a period of renewed warmth* was unfolding into the Northern Hemisphere.

Even keeping that important fact in mind, it can be disconcerting to see temperature data from the United States that show—sometimes rather starkly—a warming trend throughout the whole historical record. It takes some discipline to remind yourself that *recorded history* is only that—the length of time over which we have reasonably reliable written records of weather. In America, local weather records start in the mid to late 1800s. We should expect those records to be rising in many locations, given the general trend of ice-core measurements through the same time.

Here's a related point about written weather records that merits our attention. Some scientists and members of the media publish graphs from time to time that show what they term "global temperature." One example is shown here in figure 8.1.

Figure 8.1. Global temperature through historic time. Data adapted from National Aeronautics and Space Administration (NASA) information available at http://data.giss.nasa.gov/gistemp/graphs_v3/Fig.A2.gif (accessed July 15, 2011).

Similar figures can be found in a variety of publications, but it's not entirely clear what, exactly, they are meant to depict. The graphs are generated by taking temperature measurements from written records around the world and giving them a weighted factor to account for what area they might be thought to represent. For example, there may be seventy-five weather stations in Iowa that have records dating to the late 1800s but only a few such stations in the Yukon with similar records—so the latter temperature records would be multiplied by some factor to help prevent them from being "drowned out" by the more numerous measurements in Iowa. The sum of everything is then divided to create an average figure for temperature—which is then plotted through time.

But it's not clear what an "average temperature" really means. The average could be exactly the same, year after year, if temperatures in some areas go down and others go up. The poles, for example, might become warmer while the latitudes of Central America become cooler. Clearly, the climate would have changed in both places—but the average "global temperature" could be exactly the same.

Physical scientists usually think that a body has a particular temperature only if it has that temperature *everywhere throughout it*. If the temperature is different depending on location, then the most meaningful way of analyzing temperature is to take all the spatial complexity into account and report it all. Although we can average all the weather data we have from written records, the exercise appears to some scientists to be largely misleading unless qualified with a mountain of specific information.

To put it another way, in the autumn you could average all home and visitor football scores across the country from the scores reported in the sports media on a particular weekend. But what matters to fans is their own team's score—and that of their specific opponents that day—and you'd lose that information if what you reported was the average home and visitor scores for all the games combined.

On that note we'll close our tour of faster-tempo temperature changes on Earth. The Holocene—our own epoch—has been mercifully spared the full impact of great changes like the Younger Dryas in the Pleistocene. Why has the Holocene been so different? We don't know. About all we can say with certainty at this point is that even without major rapid climate change events, there have been changes in temperature substantial enough to affect many civilizations in the Holocene. Bronze Age societies staggered in what seem to be substantial periods of climate change. Much more mild differences are known from Roman times onward in Europe and the North Atlantic, and even they clearly shaped civilization. Cold and wet summers and resulting crop failures ended the golden age of medieval Europe and ultimately may have helped end the feudal system, ushering in the modern structures of European society.

Although we have focused in this chapter on temperature changes, climate is much more than temperature. Total precipitation, average wind speeds, humidity, and more make up the whole fabric of weather and climate. But if temperature has the complexities that have been mentioned, you can perhaps see that adding all these other factors into our discussion would have taken up the rest of the book. Suffice it to say that this has been a one-dimensional discussion of climate change, focused on temperature, and that even this simplistic approach has taken us some time and effort.

9

HAVE HUMANS SHAPED CLIMATE FOR MILLENNIA?

William Ruddiman is a climate scientist who had a long career as a researcher at Columbia University's prestigious Lamont-Doherty Observatory. He then became a professor of environmental science at the University of Virginia. He has published in major climate-science venues, given countless talks at international meetings of scientists, and collaborated with the best scientists on many projects over decades. Now retired, he is still more intellectually active than many scientists at midcareer.

Because of Ruddiman's earlier successes, he could have coasted along in his professional life at any point in the last decade. But that's clearly not in his nature. Instead, he's been engaged in advancing a new idea about the climate of the Holocene Epoch. Using several points of evidence, he argues for the hypothesis that humans have been shaping Earth's climate not just in the past two centuries due to our burning of fossil fuels, but in fact for many *thousands of years* as we have gradually modified the planet's surface and, in the process, inadvertantly helped meet our current needs.

A word here is needed about what a scientist means by the word *hypothesis*. A hypothesis is a possible explanation for data, the "best thought" of a researcher at a given time. But a given hypothesis will not necessarily be accepted by other scientists. It's a good idea—but only that. A scientific *theory* refers to a much stronger idea. A theory often is built on several hypotheses that have stood the test of time. A theory is both wide and deep—scientific knowledge like Newton's theory of gravity or the modern theory of plate tectonics. You can bet against a hypothesis, if you wish, but I'll take your money any day if you bet against a theory.

Ruddiman, then, has an idea—a hypothesis—that's worth our consideration even though it's not an established theory. Using the ice-core record, Ruddiman sees evidence that very early agricultural practices changed the concentration of the two most significant greenhouse gases on Earth, carbon dioxide and methane. Perhaps most interesting of all, he thinks those changes are what have prevented the Holocene from seeing the renewed growth of continent-size glaciers. In short, Ruddiman's work raises the possibility that all the ancestral Farmer Bobs in our family tree happened to make a living in a way that altered the atmosphere just enough to keep the climate of Canada, the northern half of the United States, Europe, and Russia favorable to people.

Ruddiman's original and bold hypothesis has garnered attention in scientific circles—as well it should—although it hasn't been widely disseminated to the public. We'll explore Ruddiman's basic thinking here and, in the process, review some of factors that clearly contribute in major ways to controlling Earth's climate. Our work in the coming pages will nicely set the stage for what is ahead in the next chapters, namely how the burning of fossil fuels since 1700 CE has changed Earth's atmosphere and what that may yet mean for climate. But because thinking about the relationship between humanity and climate is crucial for the policies of the twenty-first century, it's especially vital that citizens understand Ruddiman's hypothesis that we have already been altering climate for millennia. We surely have to come to grips with our past before we can usefully address the discussion of our future and the very recent climate change that dominates discussion in the public square.

We must start this chapter by noting that a hypothesis like Ruddiman's takes time for science, as a discipline, to examine, critique, revise, and reject or accept. That process is underway now in scientific circles. The outcome of the collective work of science cannot be known in advance. It will take years, possibly decades, for Ruddiman's ideas to be fully addressed. They may be shown to be quite incorrect, or they may lead to still other ideas we have not yet envisioned. But one thing is certain: Ruddiman's hypothesis about agriculture and climate, his other scientific ideas published over decades, and his lifetime of professional work are all scholarly and absolutely respectable. There's simply no dispute about any of that in the ranks of science. In other words, people can disagree with Ruddiman's science, but his work is reputable and his hypotheses are respected in the professional realm of empirical inquiry about the Earth.

As we've seen, the exquisitely detailed data that emerged from the ice cores of Greenland and Antarctica in the 1980s and 1990s shook up climate and geological science. Like everyone else, William Ruddiman was understandably fascinated with what had been discovered. But looking at the ice-core evidence about greenhouse gas concentrations and temperatures, he noticed something that bothered him. Ruddiman had, as he describes it, a "Columbo moment,"[1] one of those moments of bafflement that the actor Peter Falk was good at conveying in the long-running police detective series on television some years ago. The ice-core data made a great deal of sense, and it was beautifully regular in many ways. But, as Ruddiman says, there was *just one small thing* that bothered him as he looked at the record of temperature and greenhouse gases in the Holocene Epoch. And, although it has taken him years of patient work, his initial puzzlement over the data has led him to put forward compelling ideas that are now widely discussed in the technical community.

Ruddiman's Columbo moment occurred as he was looking at the ice-core record of natural gas, which the patient reader will recall is called methane by scientists. Methane is a powerful greenhouse gas—more powerful, molecule-by-molecule, than carbon dioxide. As it happens, the methane that wafts into the atmosphere doesn't remain in the Earth's air terribly long. Therefore, if the ice core shows a spike upward in the methane concentration of Earth's atmosphere in a few centuries, scientists think that period of time had an increased rate of methane production. And that means that all the ups and downs of methane as shown by the ice-core record contain quite a bit of information about *how quickly or slowly methane was created on Earth* in the years of the Pleistocene and Holocene Epochs.

As we've noted before in this book, methane is largely produced on our planet in warm swamps and cool northern bogs where vegetation partially breaks down and oxygen is limited in wet conditions. Methane is also made in the guts of ruminant (multistomach) animals, where grasses break down with limited oxygen, and in the interior of termites, our insect friends who can eat wood and break it down internally. Finally, infrequently over time in geologic history, methane has rather spectacularly "burped" upward from the seafloor and joined the atmosphere—events that punctuate the more gradual cycles of change for the gas in Earth's atmosphere.

Although we've seen many times that Earth's climate is complex and subject to variation for a host of reasons—including reasons we are far from understanding—some cause-and-effect relationships are clear and accepted by everyone in science whom I know. The three large variations in Earth's orbit around the sun have cycles of about one hundred thousand years, forty-one thousand years, and twenty-three thousand years. Milutan Milankovitch, the Serb who calculated the combined effects of Earth's orbital variations backward in time for many different latitudes, worked out how climate should vary—at least in general terms—over the millennia. In other words, it's variations in our orbit around the sun that stand as major causes of Earth's temperature and greenhouse gas concentrations.

Here's the connection between Milankovitch cycles and methane—and the matter that gave Ruddiman his first, clear, Columbo moment. Back about eleven thousand years ago, the most significant fact about the Earth's relation to the sun was that total sunlight hitting the Earth was at a high level. Since then it has dropped to what will be its very lowest point in the whole cycle that governs it. The cycle in question drives the intensity of tropical monsoon seasons each summer. This means that today we are at a relative low point for such monsoons and therefore for the wetlands they create.

We know about the cycles of Earth's methane values in exquisite detail because of the air bubbles trapped in the glacial ice of Greenland and Antarctica. The cycles follow a regular pattern, in highs and lows that even a college freshman can pick out of the data. As Ruddiman readily saw, methane in the ice-core bubbles was high about eleven thousand years ago—just as it should have been. As time inched forward from that point, the ice showed methane beginning a jagged but downward trend to around five thousand years ago (3000 BCE). As methane decreased, the Holocene Optimum was passing; temperatures on Earth gradually declined a bit, as expected, although with the usual temperature ups and downs we've seen repeatedly from the pollen and ice-core records.

As he sat looking at the data, if Ruddiman had covered up the numbers running from 3000 BCE forward, he would have been quite confident in his predictions for what should have followed. Earth's climate, Ruddiman would have predicted, would gradually cool as that interval unfolded, and methane (a strong greenhouse gas) would continue to decline to the lowest values of its whole cycle in the ice-core record.

The good news (at least for climate science's record of predictive power) is that Earth's climate indeed cooled from five millennia ago to 1700 CE. So, we scientists can chalk one up for the team! But as Ruddiman looked at the ice-core data, he saw that methane started to *rise* rather than fall, beginning about five thousand years ago. And it *rose in each millennium* from that time onward. Most remarkably of all, methane rose almost to the levels where it had stood eleven thousand years ago—that is, the highest point of its natural cycle—even though today it should be at its lowest point in the cycle controlled by Earth's orbital variations and their effect on tropical monsoons.

Ruddiman was understandably puzzled. As he has written: "[It] just didn't make sense to me. The methane increase in the last 5,000 years was in direct violation of the "rules" that had held up so well over the preceding hundreds of thousands of years. How could a guiding principle that had operated so effectively for so long have suddenly and totally collapsed?"[2]

In response to the puzzle, Ruddiman did what a good scientist should—he looked for known Earth processes that could help him explain the data as a result of some unusual circumstances. Since swamps and wetlands of the tropics are the biggest annual source of methane input into the air on Earth, Ruddiman wondered if they had been—for some reason—growing over the last five millennia rather than shrinking as orbital variations would have predicted. But other scientists pursuing different projects had established the fact that natural wetlands in the tropics have been declining over the last ten thousand years, just as they "should" have done due to the orbital variation's impact on monsoon cycles. So Ruddiman had to conclude that the extra methane wasn't coming from tropical swamps and wetlands.

Next, Ruddiman looked at the peat bogs of the northern boreal and tundra regions of the Northern Hemisphere. These areas, like swamps in warmer climates, create a great deal of methane because vegetation that dies within them uses up the oxygen in the water and doesn't completely break down. The methane from peat bogs then wafts into the atmosphere. But again, Ruddiman was frustrated in his attempt to explain what was plain in the ice-core record. There was good evidence that peat bogs and boreal wetlands were actually producing *less* methane over the most recent five millennia in question, not *more*.

In short, atmospheric methane went up from 3000 BCE to modern times, and it did so even though climate was cooling and all specific evidence from local environments in both the tropics and the boreal said that methane in recent times should be at its *lowest* natural ebb.

So it was that Ruddiman had the idea that perhaps early agriculture had increased methane levels in the atmosphere, working slowly and steadily through much of the Holocene Epoch. He knew that he needed to learn all he could from archeologists and historians about early farming practices and the extent and timing of agricultural expansion around the world. We, too, must therefore brush up a bit about the prehistoric Farmer Bobs who wrested a living from the soil all around the world for thousands of years. With that history under our belts, we can see if agriculture indeed looks like it could alter methane at the right time and in the right degree to explain the anomaly that Ruddiman had identified.

First we should note that, for most of the time represented by our original football-field analogy of time, people lived as hunter-gatherers. They were relatively passive participants in nature, perhaps following herds of wild animals and gathering nuts, seafood, and fruit where they could. People in the Pleistocene were nomads of this sort, moving with the seasons. It was a lifestyle carefully tuned to nature because everything depended on changes in the wild animals and plants around the humans. Sometimes we're inclined to romanticize the hunter-gathering lifestyle, but for most of those early people, life was lived on the edge of hunger for much of their short lives. Outside of a few areas of tropical abundance, humans had to deal with ceaseless movement in search of food, all the exertion of hunting, fishing, gathering, and processing hides, and the difficulties of securing firewood with only the most basic of stone tools.

Perhaps we might have remained hunter-gatherers forever. But it's clear that's not the way the story of human history unfolded. One point to note that helps explain trends toward agriculture is that in many parts of the world, farming yields a more predictable supply of calories than does simple hunting and gathering. Perhaps even more important, agriculture creates food in the form of grain that can easily be stored for the winter. When domestic animals are added to the picture, it's apparent that early farmers had the benefit of grain stores and an animal or two they could slaughter in the late fall to help tide them over through the dark and cold part of the year—the time when hunting and gathering puts people most clearly on the brink.

But how and when did our hunter-gatherer ancestors become farmers? We know when farming began from an accumulation of archeological evidence around the world. Agriculture sprang up around eleven thousand to twelve thousand years ago in the Near East, partly in connection with the history of the Natufians toward the end of the climate upheaval called the Younger Dryas period. Shortly after that time, agriculture appeared in China and in the Americas, and later elsewhere. The type of crops grown in early agricultural communities and the domesticated animals kept in different cultures varied substantially depending on what plants and animals were native to the areas in question. In other words, early agriculture varied in specifics. But all early farming was undertaken in a broadly similar manner wherever it was practiced.

The general theory of how farming arose independently in various places around the world is that hunter-gatherers would naturally note all the details of the plants that gave them the most food. In other words, if your life depends in large measure on what you can gather from certain trees, bushes, and grasses, you'll become a good student of all the plants around you. Our ancestors would have known where the best tubers tended to grow and where the best nut trees stood. It could have been one short step from such knowledge to a slightly more active relationship with nature—namely that of occasionally "gardening" the natural world. If you want tubers to thrive in one spot where they used to do well and are now struggling, you might pull up a few of the other plants that seem to be competing for space among them. Or if a berry bush is being smothered in a plant that's not useful to you, you could hack out the offender in the spring and expose the bush to the blessings of sunlight in the summer, all for your benefit.

Archeologists think that people in early societies around Mesopotamia became "gardeners" of Mother Nature late in the Pleistocene. And, as it happened, there were plant species in Mesopotamia, like wild grasses, that had seeds large enough to be worth gathering by hand. For example, early people gathered the seeds of a type of grass called *einkorn*. Those seeds were much smaller than a present-day grain of wheat, but they still packed enough calories to be worth gathering and storing away against winter hunger. Because these early societies were so fully immersed in nature, day after day, they well understood that what they gathered and ate were seeds—seeds that could grow into another einkorn plant the next year. At some point, it seems clear, early cultures began to plant reserves of their einkorn, planting likely in spots where they knew it tended to do well. The next fall, they had more to harvest—and thus early agriculture was born.

We'll never know in detail how particular transitional societies mastered the basics of agriculture, but the physical archeological evidence we do have fits with the picture just sketched. We can safely surmise that early farmers were eminently practical people who understood both plants and animals, so it's not a surprise that by the time people were starting to seriously cultivate einkorn and other "nearly wild" strains of wheat along the Tigris and the Euphrates, they had also started domesticating animals. Among the first livestock to be brought into the human community were goats and sheep.

We modern people are a bit out of touch with the natural world. But even we know that we can shape the types of animals that dogs and cats become over time by breeding those with favorable characteristics to one another. Over time, selective breeding is an exceedingly powerful force. Over the generations, it seems clear that early societies used selective breeding of domestic animals ranging from goats and sheep to cattle and horses. They produced animals with enhanced characteristics that were more useful to people. In a similar way, early human societies also shaped their crops. By plucking and saving the best seeds and planting them, people determined how einkorn and other early strains of wheat changed over the generations. And change they surely did, getting larger kernels on larger heads first, and ultimately heads of grain that remain intact, clinging to the stalk such that they could be carried to where people could thresh the harvest.

In the Near East the first emphasis in agriculture was on the cereal grains of wheat, barley, and rye, complemented by peas and lentils that greatly supplemented protein needs. As the millennia of the Holocene Epoch unfolded, flax and later the date palm and the olive joined the societies around the Fertile Crescent. Domestic cattle joined our communities early as well. Donkeys were later, camels the latest of all.

East Asia was the world's second agricultural society. The first grain to be farmed there appears to have been millet, supplemented in time by rice. The history of rice farming was particularly interesting to William Ruddiman, the climate scientist who was puzzled by greenhouse gas concentrations in recent millennia. He learned that rice farming grew over several thousand years in China. Wild strains of rice in the highlands had been gathered by people in the earliest Holocene, with the true planting of rice arising over time about six to eight thousand years ago. But rice farming in this era was modest—possibly limited to poking sticks in the wet soil and dropping in rice grains. By five thousand years ago (3000 BCE), however, Chinese farmers were using the diversion of streams and rivers to expand the acreage of wetlands in which they could grow more and more rice. The jump to making these "paddies" expanded rice harvests greatly.

Rice paddies were and are significant to climate.[3] To put the matter simply, every acre of a rice paddy is a fertile, man-made swamp. In most of the world, animal waste is added to rice paddies as fertilizer, increasing its fecundity significantly. Once the Chinese were growing rice with such success, irrigation and rice paddies spread to many parts of Asia around 3000 BCE. Human populations in the same areas—China, Southeast Asia, and India—affected strongly by rice farming, grew in response to a better and more predictable food supply. More rice meant more people, and more people in turn meant more and more rice cultivation, with paddies spreading over more of the Earth. This isn't to say there was a "population explosion" in prehistoric times (in the sense of the rapid exponential growth we've seen in the past few centuries). But, at the same time, it's only fair to realize that human populations have been growing for millennia, and that although the growth rate was low, the total change was significant—simply because we are talking about changes that build on themselves for thousands and thousands of years.

The timing of the growth of rice farming in Asia immediately garnered Ruddiman's attention, and it appeared to match the methane record of the ice-core bubbles. Rice paddies and the increase in methane in Earth's air both appear in the record at 3000 BCE (five thousand years ago). It's difficult to tell, of course, exactly how many acres of rice paddies graced the Earth five thousand years ago. But to get a handle on questions of the quantity of methane preindustrial societies emitted, Ruddiman looked at the year 1700, a time about which we know a great deal. World population is pretty well known for 1700, standing at about 650 million people. Knowing how much methane we produce today with a population of six billion, and setting aside all modern, industrial sources of methane, we can estimate how much nonindustrial methane the activities of people in 1700 emitted. Extrapolating back farther with estimates of early human populations, we can estimate how much methane the activities of people emitted five thousand years ago, the time at which methane concentrations in the air bubbles of the ice cores begin their upward trend. Using these types of calculations, ancient Asian rice production was sufficient in scale to account for what the ice-core record shows about methane increases, Ruddiman decided.

As Asian societies were expanding their early efforts at agriculture in substantial ways, similar stories of farming success were in clear focus around the globe. Here in the Americas, for example, people of the early part of the Holocene had also gone through the transition from a nomadic, hunter-gatherer life to agricultural communities—although their living was necessarily based on a different set of crops and domestic animals from those of Asia or the Fertile Crescent. One important plant was maize (corn). The history of corn is fascinating, and it shows the rewards early societies reaped from the patient, yearly selection of the seeds of the plants they cultivated. The wild form of corn is *teosinte*, a plant that has ears (sets of seeds) that are only one inch long in total. (With cobs that measured one inch, you can imagine how small the corn kernels in teosinte are!) But by selecting the corn from the largest ears to replant in the following spring, Central American farmers steadily changed the maize plant, generation after generation. By the time Europeans arrived in the Americas, native tribes were farming corn all the way to New England, corn that had cobs and kernels smaller than what you see in the grocery store, but still ones that you would easily recognize for what they are.

Ruddiman reviewed all forms of farming, not limiting himself to rice paddies, because all cultivation produces greenhouse gases due to two agricultural side effects. First, all farmers who have seeds they want to plant in the spring need *cleared ground* on which to plant them. Prior to modern times, the principle method early societies used for clearing forested land was girdling trees to kill them before returning in a couple of years to burn them down. The ash from the resulting conflagration contains some mineral nutrients, which settle usefully into the soil. Preparing land for farms via these "slash and burn" techniques is, in fact, exactly how people go about clearing parts of the Amazon jungle today. Burning trees in uncontrolled wildfires obviously produces carbon dioxide, but it also creates methane, hence it was of interest to Ruddiman. No matter what crops early societies tended, in all parts of the world where human populations were growing and agriculture was expanding into forests, methane was being produced at faster and faster rates as ground for planting was cleared.

Here's an image that Ruddiman uses to make his point about the importance of the staggering levels of change on the surface of the planet that early agriculture produced. If we had a time-lapse video of the Earth made from space, we would see dark green forests of the earliest Holocene (ten thousand years ago) gradually replaced by light greens of pastures and dark browns of plowed croplands. We humans have changed the *whole color of our planet* in many places and over great expanses of land, and we did so long before modern times.[4] A second basic factor links agriculture to methane. People who are successfully farming more and more land, creating growing human communities over the centuries, also have an increasing livestock population. That's important because many of our domesticated animals produce significant amounts of methane. In particular, it's often said that livestock like sheep, horses, and cows produce methane "at both ends"—that is to say, both when they belch and when they fart. You can think of that as part of the complex processes such animals must successfully perform to break down grasses into usable energy (something other animals like us cannot come close to doing). The price of the amazing digestive abilities of our livestock is a great deal of belching and farting—as you know if you've spent time around ruminant animals. So it seems reasonable to suppose that as we humans cleared forests and grazed more ruminant animals on the grasses that sprang up on the land, the internal processes of those animals gradually produced more methane that wafted into Earth's atmosphere.

From the evidence about methane, it was a short step for Ruddiman to begin considering the trends in carbon dioxide over the Holocene Epoch. But carbon-dioxide levels in the air around us are a much more complex matter than methane. Carbon dioxide varies due to all three Milankovitch orbital variables, not just principally one. Carbon itself is also packed into pretty much every part of the climate system on Earth, where it can flow back and forth between *reservoirs*, as scientists call them. You can think of this as each carbon atom being worth a penny, and an international banker somewhere shuffling a hundred billion dollars worth of pennies from one bank to another, then from a bank in one nation to some international bank, and also from another bank account into a speculative investment. Now imagine a hundred such bankers with a thousand such banks and accounts to choose from—and that image only starts to conjure up the complexity of the carbon cycle on Earth.

Carbon exists in the air around us, in the vegetation all over Earth, in the soils that are rich in roots and decaying plants, in rocks like marble and limestone, in the oceans as dissolved minerals, and in the tissue of plants and animals that team in the seas. The various "bank accounts" of carbon see atoms naturally shuffled between them, at different rates and partly in response to what other elements in the banking system are doing. Keeping track of major changes in the system is much more complex than understanding the major banks on Wall Street. To sum matters up, the carbon cycle is complicated, and it is also poorly understood, which means that scientists cannot explain how and why carbon reservoirs vary over geologic time. They are crucial to *controlling* climate, and they also vary in *response* to climate, but we just don't understand some of the fundamental variables concerning carbon on Earth at this time. (This whole book could have been devoted to carbon cycles and the great deal we do not know about them. Perhaps we can thank a higher power that we'll only have to trek through a few more paragraphs about carbon before getting back to Professor Ruddiman.)

Looking at the ice-core record, the good news is that the carbon dioxide in recent geological epochs is quite clear and fairly regular. A high level of carbon dioxide in Earth's atmosphere was reached just before the "warm times" of the Holocene, the preceding Eemian (the warm time of 125,000 years ago), and all the preceding warm intervals of the Pleistocene that we met on our football-field analogy of time. Again, at this level, even college freshmen can pick out the regularities. And the Holocene, in this regard, fits Earth's usual pattern, with high carbon-dioxide levels just before the start of the Holocene. After this peak carbon-dioxide level was reached, carbon-dioxide concentrations in the air started to decrease, just as they had in the Eemian and other such balmy intervals in Earth history.

So far, so good. The carbon system was behaving as expected, Ruddiman thought, as he looked over the ice-core data of the Holocene. And after peaking early in the Holocene, carbon-dioxide levels decline through time, just as they had in the Eemian and similar warm intervals.

But at eight thousand years ago (6000 BCE) the whole picture changes. Instead of continuing downward, the carbon-dioxide numbers stop declining and then start to rise. They grow through the next millennium, and grow each millennium from then onward, increasing though modern times. That trend, compared to carbon-dioxide behavior, as it's known from other parts of the ice-core record, didn't look "natural" or expected to Ruddiman.

Ruddiman thought the carbon-dioxide record was interesting. It gave him his second Columbo moment. He studied the systems and relationships that may control carbon dioxide in the air to see if he could find a reason for this change in behavior about eight thousand years ago. But, just as was the case with methane, he couldn't find any natural reason for the falling numbers to stop, turn around, and grow and grow throughout the rest of the Holocene Epoch.

Ruddiman turned his attention to the first step of most agriculture around the world: the clearing of forests to make farmland. Essentially, trees "lock up" carbon and store it in large trunks and branches that last potentially for centuries. Underground roots do the same. But as humans cleared forests all around the globe using fire or axes, land was altered from being natural "carbon banks" (trees) to being plowed fields or pastures that simply don't store as much carbon. To put it another way, when farmers clear land, either by simply burning the forest or by cutting it down, they essentially take the carbon that had been locked up in the wood and soil and put it into the atmosphere. If they continue to prevent forests from returning to their fields—and that's exactly what farmers the world around are very much dedicated to doing—we should expect carbon-dioxide levels in the ice-core record to rise whenever humankind as a whole is *expanding* its agricultural fields. Exactly that, says Ruddiman, is the cause of the general trend we see in carbon dioxide over thousands of years since the early to middle part of the Holocene.

The two greenhouse gases—methane and carbon dioxide—that have been climbing in recent millennia as agriculture has changed the face of the Earth are not some abstract or academic matter. The practical question of importance to all of us is how much early farmers around the world may have altered climate. Ruddiman calculates that the "extra" methane and carbon dioxide that agriculture has produced over the millennia accounts for an *increase in global average temperature of about 1.5 degrees Fahrenheit*. That may sound small, but as we shall see it's a substantial result for global climate. And if Ruddiman is right, then it's the early farmers in our family tree who have prevented massive glaciers from returning to the Earth. In other words, ice sheets like the one that covered Canada and flowed down into New England and the Midwest throughout most of the Pleistocene Epoch would today be oozing south if our ancestors had remained hunter-gatherers.

At this point, all your toil as a reader in earlier chapters, where you learned about glacial evidence, will be richly rewarded. As you well know as a veteran of those pages, since the 1800s geologists have made many maps of glacial features. It's something we do quite well (if we do say so ourselves). The basic results of the work are something scientists all agree on, and we know a lot about climate history from this point of view just by looking at the landscape that glaciers made during the Pleistocene Epoch.

Geologic maps show us that during the long, bitter cold periods of the Pleistocene Epoch, the rough mix of glacial material called *till* was laid down over much of the Earth around 45 degrees latitude and higher. Geologists can deduce when those enormous ice sheets melted off the land by doing varve counting, carbon dating, and similar work on the materials we find associated with the till or the enormous glacial lakes that formed as the ice retreated. This work for North America is summed up in figure 9.1. The map shows the extent of glacial ice over time in North America. The numbers on the map are *age*, measured in thousands of years ago, and they show how the great ice sheet retreated through the millennia.

As you can see, great masses of ice covered parts of the Ohio River Valley and all of New York State and New England, North Dakota, and much of Montana and northern Idaho in the period from twenty-one thousand to seventeen thousand years ago—the last of the long, cold periods of the latter part of the Pleistocene. By the time of the later Pleistocene, about fourteen thousand years ago, the ice sheet had almost entirely retreated from the United States into Canada. The ice sheet was still massive, even measured on a continental scale, and climate near it was partially controlled by its presence each year, but the total glacial ice extent was smaller than what it had been. By eleven thousand years ago, the main ice sheet had retreated to the land all around what we call Hudson Bay. (Of course, as the figure shows, what was to become Hudson Bay was still buried in ice.) As you can see, by seven thousand years ago, around the warmest part of the Holocene (the optimum), the once-massive ice sheet occupied only a small bit of land to the east and north of Hudson Bay.

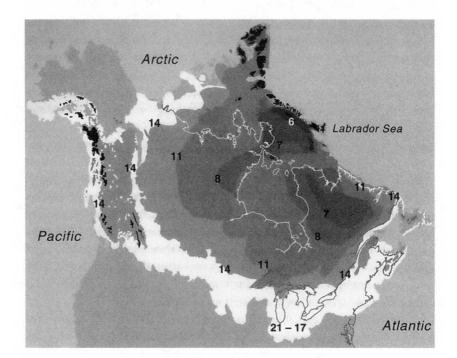

Figure 9.1. The retreat of the most recent ice sheet in North America, from twenty thousand years ago to six thousand years ago. Numbers on the map indicate ice location in thousands of years. From William F. Ruddiman, *Plows, Plagues, and Petroleum: How Humans Took Control of Climate* (Princeton, NJ: Princeton University Press, 2005). © 2005 by Princeton University Press. Reprinted by permission of Princeton University Press.

As you will recall, climate has cooled slightly since the times of the optimum. Knowing that, you'd likely expect the ice sheet and snowfield remnants just east of Hudson Bay to have been static or to have *grown* in the millennia since the optimum. But instead they have shrunk, and that fact is just another way of grasping Ruddiman's puzzlement about what's been happening with climate in recent times.

To be sure, it's highly convenient for humans that the ice sheet continued to shrink after the optimum rather than start to regrow. One of the reasons that's important relates to the concept of *positive feedback* we mentioned earlier. Ice sheets reflect a lot of sunlight, while bare earth absorbs the energy of sunbeams. This means that if glaciers grow and cover the land, they tend to promote a *cooler* climate, which then makes for more glacial growth. The effect can be a runaway cooling, a classic example of positive feedback from the natural realm.

If permanent snowfields or the remnant of the great ice sheet had started to regrow when climate cooled after the optimum, that could have triggered a still-cooler trend in temperatures. Yet more cooling, added to the original cooling trend, would have increased the tendency toward further glacial expanse, and thus climate might have become a *whole lot cooler* after the optimum. If that had occurred, human history might look very different—it's tough to make a living farming if there are frosts in midsummer.

Why didn't we slide into increasingly cooler millennia with an expanding ice sheet in Canada? Ruddiman's ready answer is the increasing proportion of greenhouse gases we humans have created since the optimum. It's our farming history, he argues, that has held at bay a return to Pleistocene glaciers. We've been on the knife's edge of heading back into expanding ice sheets, including right here in continental North America. But the modest increases in carbon dioxide and methane in the atmosphere due to agriculture have been just enough to hold in some of the Earth's warmth and prevent a regrowth of the great glaciers that dominated most of the Pleistocene. So, if Ruddiman's hypothesis is right, we've unwittingly changed climate for many millennia, and we're doing so in a way that's been highly fortunate for us.

Note that Ruddiman is not saying that humanity's very recent greenhouse gas history is just "fine and dandy" with him. The history of changes due to industrialization and the global population explosion of the past two centuries alarm him as much as it does others. He has recently written explicitly on that point. For even if Ruddiman is right that people have been adding to greenhouse gases for millennia—and doing so in ways that have been crucial for climate—it's also true that what we've accomplished in the past two hundred years is a sharp departure from anything we may have done earlier.

But it's also true that Ruddiman's hypothesis gives us quite a different psychological context from which to understand global climate change. Avoiding a return to ice sheets stretching ever farther south in Canada is certainly a *good thing* from a human point of view. Particularly for those of us living in the middle latitudes of North America, avoiding a cooler climate is a blessing. And people all around the world eat many of their meals from crops grown in the "breadbasket" areas of Canada, the United States, eastern Europe, and Russia—all of which lie at high enough latitudes that they would be vastly less productive in a significantly cooler climate. It is really quite possible that we have indeed changed climate—and changed it for the better from the point of view of anyone who values humanity as we know it today, with the needs of people around the world to eat their supper tonight clearly in focus.

Still, it's important to emphasize that Ruddiman's idea about how ancient agriculture shaped climate is only a hypothesis. Some climate scientists subscribe to it, others are indifferent, and many have attacked it. There are several grounds for criticism. One of the most fundamental is simply that modest increases in carbon dioxide and methane since the middle of the Holocene may be related to entirely natural factors we haven't yet plumbed. Just because greenhouse gases go up modestly for unexplained reasons around the time agriculture starts doesn't—*in itself*—mean that agriculture caused the increase. Sadly, we still know so very little about the controls on methane and carbon dioxide; it's impossible to fully say what accounts for their behavior.

In short, the jury is still very much out on the idea that relates the history of agriculture to greenhouse gases and global climate. But the concepts and evidence Ruddiman puts forward demand to be part of the public discussion of climate. Ruddiman could be right. We do ourselves no favors by thinking that *any* change people have made to the Earth is necessarily a bad thing. We humans are part of nature, and it's interesting to note that the changes we've created as we try to meet our needs *may* have been influencing climate for thousands of years. If that's the case, the changes have likely been highly fortunate for us, at least up until recent times.

The agricultural hypothesis for what's happened with Earth's climate since the middle of the Holocene is a good example of how science works. At present, Ruddiman has put forward a serious idea based on evidence, calculations, and careful reasoning. Some scientists are inclined to agree with him. Others disagree and are putting forward evidence and reasoning to support their counterarguments.

Unfortunately, the process of examining a scientific hypothesis takes time to run to a conclusion—time that's likely measured in the range of years or even decades. That simple fact can make for a lot of frustration, particularly from people outside the technical community. But scientists simply cannot know more than we know at a particular time. And scientists disagree with each other for *good* reasons, because we have valuable ideas and insights that demand thorough examination. This means that new discoveries are not made on a timetable that's convenient to others.

An analogy that may be helpful is to think of what it's like when you face a difficult medical problem and you consult several specialists about it. Those of us who have lived for several decades are familiar with the fact that if you consult a medical specialist such as a cardiologist, you may be advised to undertake a particular course of action. If you get a second opinion, however, you may well hear something quite different (which is why second opinions can be quite valuable). If you consult yet a third cardiologist, you may hear something in between or yet again different from anything you've heard up to that point. That's not to say that cardiologists don't know anything about heart problems and how to treat them. (They surely understand hearts better than I ever will.) But even cardiologists live out their professional lives with only a partial understanding of a person's condition, what has contributed to it, and what could potentially improve heart function in an individual. And the whole profession of cardiology is changing at the same time, so old ideas are rejected as new and better ones come into view. Significant change in our understanding of climate, from this point of view, is to be expected, and indeed welcomed. Climate science is still in its infancy, as is shown by the fact that it's only in this decade that it's occurred to climate scientists that humanity may have started shaping climate before written history began.

In the final analysis, the most impressive point about Ruddiman's hypothesis isn't the idea that we may have been changing Earth's climate for millennia. What is most arresting, many people might observe, is how little attention it has garnered in the public square. Every day the media run stories on the link between industrialization and climate change. How is it, we can surely ask, that agriculture's plausible effect on climate is so routinely ignored?

In recent years the public, including the intelligencia and public servants, have been hammered by the connection between industrialization, climate, and public policy, the "great trifecta" of debate now dominating the public square. Industrialization, to be sure, has greatly changed the concentration of greenhouse gases in the atmosphere. Values of both carbon dioxide and methane, as we shall see, have shot up in recent decades, a fact that should push the Earth to conserve heat energy that otherwise would radiate back into space. And wholly human-made greenhouse gases, such as CFCs (chlorofluorocarbons), do the same thing. In short, we do indeed have reasons for grave concern about how rapidly the atmosphere is changing and what this may portend for climate.

But the great trifecta of public consciousness—industrialization, climate, public policy—is based on only a fragment of greater knowledge scientists have been explaining to all who would listen from the 1830s onward. As you have seen up to this point, scientists know from a variety of evidence that Earth's climate changes *naturally, rapidly, repeatedly, and disastrously.* We know those facts of nature—and you now know how it is that scientists understand the evidence that makes those lessons plain.

The unfortunate fact is that if we think the "right" carbon policy will produce a stable climate, we will always be defeated. Nothing about Earth's climate is static, and we cannot make it so. We would be well advised to go into the future with our eyes open, not shut, to the climates of the past. That is the plain teaching of the Scandinavian pollen and varves, the glacial tills of the Midwest, Glacial Lake Agassiz in Canada, and the ice cores of Greenland and Antarctica.

But first, before we reach the concerns being aired in the public square about greenhouse gases caused by industrialization, we must look at what scientists were researching in the years just prior to the rise of the trifecta framework.

10

FROM EFFORTS TO MODIFY CLIMATE TO FEARS OF GLOBAL COOLING

Carroll Livingston Riker was an American engineer, inventor, and sometimes politician. He lived in the glorious time when engineers were widely respected—like rock stars are today. Riker worked on the Panama Canal—the greatest engineering success of his age—and he held more than twenty patents at the time of his death at seventy-eight in 1931. Among Riker's smaller accomplishments was fitting the first ships with refrigeration devices for the shipment of perishable goods across the Atlantic. The larger feathers in Riker's cap came in two kinds: technical engineering contributions and helping to inspire bills before Congress for major civil-engineering projects.

Riker's first and lasting love was the water of Earth: the ways, the powers, and the meanderings of the ocean and river currents of the world over time. In that sense, he was close to being a proto-oceanographer— a field not yet fully invented in his day. That also made him the watery equivalent of a geologist, a field that happened to have started to develop a good bit earlier simply because we humans live on land rather than under the sea.

Born on Staten Island, Riker spent a portion of his youth being educated by private tutors—and he had the good fortune to teach himself about currents and waves from firsthand study. While still a teenager, he designed the hull of a steamboat. His adult career then included major civil-engineering projects in Panama and on the Potomac River. In the latter project, he created the first powerful pumping dredge to fill the Potomac flats. Most notably, he did so for less than half the cost the federal government had first estimated the work would cost, a feat perhaps not repeated in the history of major governmental projects since that time.

Riker was not just a hypomanic professional and politician active on a variety of fronts, he was also a man who naturally sketched out the very largest of ideas. Applying the lessons he knew of ocean currents and the engineering prowess he had seen America pull together in Panama, he came to the conclusion that civil-engineering projects could favorably influence regional climates. In 1912 Riker published an argument for diverting the Gulf Stream as a means of changing climate in eastern Canada. He argued that for $190 million, less than the cost of building the Panama Canal, Americans could build a two-hundred-mile-long jetty running east from Newfoundland across the relatively shallow Great Banks. This would turn the cold Northern Labrador current that flows southward along the margin of Canada, making the cold waters then flow toward the east. (Technically, the structure Riker planned would be a "groin," not a "jetty," but in common usage most Americans think of groins as jetties.)

Riker's plan hinged on diverting the warm Gulf Stream. The natural path of the great current pushes warm water from the Gulf of Mexico northeast on a slanting trajectory across the Atlantic, contributing to the moderation of the climate of Britain and northwest Europe. But if even part of the Gulf Stream could be turned to run straight northward up the western side of Greenland, it would warm both eastern Canada and western Greenland. The change in regional weather would be dramatic. Those in favor of the plan believed that much could be gained from a balmier climate in Canada and—after the Greenland ice cap melted—that great expanse of land could become useful.

Turning such a great force as a major ocean current isn't something to be done by brute force. But that is where Riker's knowledge of the sea came to the fore. When water currents are forced into sharp turns, such as his plan proposed with the jetty, they slow down. As their speed is retarded, the sand they've been moving is deposited. Because the Labrador current carries a lot of sand, Riker calculated it would soon stabilize the narrow jetty he envisioned, making it into a wide feature with a backbone of jetty material but a broad northern slope of sand. (This is the same, well-known phenomenon you can see at work on jetties all along the eastern seaboard of the United States today, where sand "piles up" on the up-current side. It's also something Riker would have observed from his childhood onward throughout life—and it's a fact still taught in introductory geology and oceanography classes in colleges throughout the land.)

The important net result of Riker's jetty would be that the cold Labrador current would encounter the warmth of the Gulf Stream in much deeper waters than it does now, and the depth would mean that the cold water could sink below the warm current—rather than clashing with it and pushing it east. Riker's jetty would thus produce a sinking cold current, disappearing into the vast depths of the Atlantic, and a warm Gulf Stream at the surface headed northward between western Greenland and eastern Canada—with enormous regional climate changes as a result. Riker maintained his plan would create a mild climate for eastern Canada, end the endless winter fogs off the Newfoundland and Labrador coasts, and eliminate iceberg hazards to shipping in the North Atlantic. Bringing the benefits of warmth to Greenland, Canada, and the heart of the polar ice pack all the way to the North Pole looked like the next great achievement to come after uniting the Pacific and Atlantic Oceans in Central America via the Panama Canal.

Had Riker's jetty been constructed, and had it worked as intended, it would have helped Canada more than perhaps any other nation. This certainly suggested that Canada should have undertaken to pay for the project. But Canada, then as now, was a small nation compared to the United States. Just as Canada had not reached out and claimed land in Panama to build a canal there, it didn't seem likely that Canadians would put the needed $190 million and thousands of working men and engineers into the jetty project. There were other problems with Riker's plan. The *New York Times* editorial board argued against it, pointing out that if the Gulf Stream were diverted, Great Britain (and the rest of Europe) would suffer horrible climate change, being suddenly thrust into a major cooling trend. That argument was significant to many Americans, both those with relatives in

Europe and those with business dealings there. Thus, for a combination of political, moral, and technical reasons, the Riker plan failed to gain a critical aggregate of support. When World War I started in 1914, Riker's idea dropped off the collective agenda, and the engineer put his energies into other projects. Today, many citizens don't know Riker's name, let alone the history of his plans and calculations for deliberately changing climate.

In later decades other engineers pursued some of the same general goals that Riker had embraced, but in quite different ways or with other intentions. Amid the Cold War, for example, various efforts to change the weather were not only planned, but also executed. Blending military matters with climate and environmental concerns was sometimes known by the ugly acronym "EnMod," the deliberate modification of the environment either as a weapon of war or in response to natural climate change. Programs like POP EYE, Project Skywater, and Project Cirrus were just a few of the efforts that resulted from the general understanding that climate and weather are crucial for both our civilian lives and our military activities.

Southeast Asia was the US military's laboratory for testing the principles of environmental and weather modification. Between 1967 and 1972 the Pentagon spent millions of dollars each year to seed rain clouds in that region, in particular near the roads and trails over which resistors brought supplies into South Vietnam. The plan was to bog down the enemy in mud. At the time, military planners and a number of weather and climate scientists believed strongly in the efficacy of seeding clouds to create rain. But, with hindsight, it's highly likely the whole effort had only marginal impact on precipitation.

The cloud-seeding program was undertaken to lessen the bloodbath toward which our efforts in Vietnam were sliding, saving both American and Vietnamese lives. But the program and its supposed results were kept a secret from the American public until Dr. Daniel Ellsberg released a classified internal history of the war known as the Pentagon Papers and Senator Claiborne Pell held hearings about EnMod in Southeast Asia. Partly as a result of that secrecy, and also due to the influence of the growing environmental movement here at home, waging war through weather modification quickly acquired an odious repute.

Efforts to *improve* weather in the United States were another matter. Many people, scientist and laypersons alike, believed in such projects or hoped for their success.

Then, as now, people living along warm-water coasts fear hurricanes for much of each year, so it was natural for them to ask if anything could be done to modify, break up, or divert the massive and destructive storms. Project Cirrus and Project Stormfury seeded rain clouds to try to break up hurricanes' vast energy patterns. The storms were not clearly diminished, however, and sometimes the hurricanes changed course in unexpected ways after seeding. Naturally, national leaders feared hurricanes could be made more likely to reach land due to the interference of humans. Of course, hurricane paths always change, and sometimes markedly so. But the very real political dangers of messing with Mother Nature became clear to Congress—and the efforts were eventually dropped.

In the upper Great Plains, however, federal- and even state-based programs of cloud seeding were generally much better received. They were undertaken during the growing season to increase rains for crops. Farmers in the Dakotas, in particular, were glad for the efforts, crediting the seeding with at least some raindrops. But again, in hindsight, it's not clear that any of these programs changed the weather to a significant degree. If they did affect natural precipitation, they did so only in small proportions, and few would argue that the scattered raindrops they created were worth the millions of dollars spent to generate them.

The effort invested in American weather and environmental modification programs at home and abroad in the 1960s and early 1970s is testimony to the desire Americans had in that era to bring weather and climate *under human control*. As with Riker in 1912, that spirit was clearly quite different from our own, twenty-first-century perspective. It's worth noting that, in matters of climate, and as late as the 1960s, Americans didn't view nature as necessarily benign or beneficial. Instead, many people thought our task as humans was to harness nature for our own interests, to shape it in accord to human values. For myself, I hold no opinion about which view is right or wrong. I am simply trying to point out that we Americans held quiet different views of climate and nature just fifty years ago—not terribly far back in our deep, dark past.

If you had asked scientists, around the time that the Vietnam War was winding down, what naturally lay ahead for regional weather and global climate patterns, most of them would have voiced general concern about two issues. One concern, based on evidence from Earth's past, was that our current warm times, the Holocene Epoch, would likely be coming to a close, and sooner rather than later. Whether the end would come in the twenty-first century, or not until many centuries later, wasn't clear. But the passing of the Holocene—with a return to Ice Age bitter cold and mile-thick glaciers covering Canada, the northern United States, and Scandinavia—was definitely on the horizon somewhere.

At the same time, there was another factor to consider. Scientists knew that by burning fossil fuels our societies were adding lots of carbon dioxide and other greenhouse gases to the atmosphere—and we were doing so at an increasing rate. Greenhouse gases, of course, would tend to warm the whole Earth. A few technical people saw such warming as potentially very fortunate, an event that could help delay the onset of the next Ice Age. Some others, however, were deeply concerned that the warming would become pronounced and be more of a problem than anyone fully realized. We will devote the next chapter to greenhouse warming, where we can give it the space and time it deserves. That chapter, indeed, will be a long and detailed one, in some ways the most demanding of this book. But, for now, we will set aside warming concerns. Here, our main attention will be focused on global cooling, about which some serious scientists of the 1960s and 1970s were truly concerned—for good, empirical reasons.

It was in the context of a fear of global cooling, as well as warming, that the National Academy of Sciences—the nation's most prestigious groups of scientists from all disciplines—published its volume *Understanding Climatic Change: A Program for Action* in 1975.[1] The "action" in question was expanding study of climate and funding for climate research. If regional and global temperature and precipitation determined the course of so much human history, and if science stood on the brink of understanding climate more thoroughly, then this—the prestigious National Academy of Sciences argued—was the time for society to pony up and fund major climate research as had never been done in the past.

Possible global warming and global cooling in the twenty-first century are both mentioned in the book. It is global cooling that gets some telling attention with respect to the natural end of the Holocene Epoch and a return of the Earth to Pleistocene levels of bitter cold. And the report points out that not all the cooling the Earth seemed to be experiencing in the 1970s was natural. Human-made particulate pollution in the atmosphere, the scientists warned, would tend toward cooling the planet by decreasing the effective amount of sunlight received at the surface of the Earth. At the same time, however, human-made carbon-dioxide contributions to the atmosphere would push the planet toward warming. At the time the report was written, the authors judged the carbon-dioxide factor to be more significant. But if both carbon dioxide and particulate pollution were to grow at equal rates, the authors warned that the effect of particulates would grow compared to that of carbon dioxide, an eventuality that would push the planet in the colder direction.

As one might expect, some scientists in the then Soviet Union were even more deeply alarmed about cooling than their American counterparts. Most of the Soviet Union lay at extreme northern latitudes and far from the climate-moderating effects of warm-water oceans. If some American scientists were concerned about the post–World War II cooling trend, it's easy to guess what Soviet scientists thought might well be in the cards for their nation. Borrowing the goal of the old Riker jetty-building project, if not the specific methods, the Soviets developed plans to melt the ice of the polar sea by spreading black coal dust over the ice in the summer to make it absorb, rather than reflect, the sun's heat. The plans were perhaps partially based on an old, peasant tradition in Russia, that of sprinkling ashes and dirt on snowdrifts in the spring. The dark material helped the snow and ice melt faster, freeing valuable spaces like garden plots from the last effects of each winter.

Sadly, the basic reason there was real fear of global cooling in the 1970s wasn't that government officials clearly remembered the lessons of geology you have mastered in this book. Instead, the visceral concern was based on the weather pattern of three decades, from the early 1940s to the early 1970s. In that period, weather stations all over the land's surface showed that the Northern Hemisphere—where most of humanity lived and most crops were grown—cooled significantly. In particular, here in the United States, where we had many good weather stations with highly automated and reliable measurements, temperatures clearly and sharply declined. There was simply no way to dispute the trend, and it was disturbing.

Temperature changes on Earth tend to be greatest at high latitudes (near the poles) and much less at lower latitudes. In keeping with that fact, the cooling effect of the 1940s through the1970s was the strongest in the arctic, where some stations saw an average temperature drop of about 3.6 degrees Fahrenheit *each decade* or about 10.8 degrees Fahrenheit in total. That's a staggering drop into the frozen abyss. In Iceland, the drop was a bit less than 4 degrees Fahrenheit over the thirty years. Lower latitudes saw more modest cooling, but the trend was clear.

Colder and longer winters and cooler summers have very real effects on people. Cold kills. Far, far more people die on cold winter nights than on hot summer days. The thirty-year cooling trend acted on the world as if the land itself had been moved northward, pushing heating bills up and threatening people with the simple but very real physical stress of cold. The impact on agriculture was significant and even more fearful to many. Measurements showed that the growing season in Great Britain had been reduced by at least two weeks during the thirty years of cooling—a horticultural impact that every gardener can relate to.

For its part, the news media reported a blizzard of cold weather events, some so odd they made even the general public take notice and seriously consider the prospect of a coming Ice Age. Among the reports were:

- frost and even snow in Brazil that destroyed most of that nation's coffee crop, sending prices sky high
- an "armada" of ships bringing supplies to the oilfield near Prudhoe Bay, which was trapped in arctic ice
- the winter of 1975–76 for the lower forty-eight states was dominated by what the National Weather Service called "record cold"; San Francisco experienced its heaviest snowfall in eighty-nine years

- most ominously for worldwide food productivity, the globe seemed to slide into a period of major changes in precipitation patterns, with major to massive droughts in India, Central America, the Caribbean, South Africa, and Northern Australia

It's no wonder that popular magazines famously put the Ice Age threat on their covers. It was only a short—if rather hysterical—jump from data about the weather to fear of global climate change and a return to the Pleistocene. And while it's now easy enough to criticize the people of the 1970s for what they thought, fear of a slide into a frigid world was founded on the hard facts of the daily news, on decades-long weather patterns, and on the lessons of geologic history. It looked objective and significant to a good many souls.

It's also true that many wise people realized that losing part of the American wheat and corn crop due to cold springs and cool summers, or losing so much of the Brazilian coffee crop to frost, didn't equate to never being able to grow those crops in their accustomed places again. Similarly, they were aware that the thirty-year cold snap in North America might not continue to worsen. After all, there had been a significant cooling in our hemisphere in the late 1700s and early 1800s. The winter that George Washington and his troops endured at Valley Forge was famously bitter. During several of the winters of the Revolutionary War, cannon could be dragged across the waters from Brooklyn to Staten Island, so substantial was the ice on top of the salt water. That cruel period of cold had come to an end. The renewed cold of the twentieth century, some reasoned, could do so, too.

Or not.

Because there's no way to predict complex systems with many feedback influences we don't understand, there is simply no way to know with certainty what global climate will be like in twenty-five, fifty, or seventy-five years. That's the crux of the climate problem—a problem science cannot solve for a society that grapples with its fears about temperature threats. But the main fear for many in the 1970s—in particular laypersons, but also some scientists—was continued cooling, an event that would indeed be disastrous for the United States and Canada, for Europe, and for what was then the Soviet Union.

Since global tensions between the superpowers were already so high, it was inevitable that the cooling trend would be analyzed by our military and governmental leaders with an eye toward defending our ability to procure enough food and energy for American citizens in a climate that might well descend into greater cold. The United States and Canada started the decade of the 1970s in a strong position regarding food. Combined, the two countries produced most of the wheat traded on the global market. But the American psyche, used to abundance, with unrestricted agricultural and industrial inputs, was in for a major jolt when the Organization of Petroleum Exporting Countries (OPEC) embargoed crude oil—a crucial input for transportation, industry, and modern agriculture. With climate fears as a background, and the pain of OPEC's embargo in the foreground, voices were raised asking Americans to realize we had to change our way of understanding the world.

For most of the twentieth century, the basic American farm problem had been too much grain harvested each fall, with resulting poor prices and economic pressures on farmers. We as a nation therefore put programs in place to encourage farmers to produce *less* from their land. That was our custom. But in the 1970s, poor weather contributed to a real decline in our grain output. In 1974, food production in the Midwest fell by 16 percent. To be sure, economic and political factors had an impact on production, too, as they always will, but weather matters in farming, and the weather of the period wasn't good. Outside the United States, the partial or total loss of specific crops in the early and mid-1970s could also be traced to changing weather. In this context, the fear of a cooling climate and food shortages was understandable, even if it seems too strong as viewed from our modern vantage point.

One thing is certain: wherever fear lurks in the human mind, there is also the opportunity for aggression.

"Food is a weapon and [Americans] should use it,"[2] said Daniel P. Moynihan, who was then the ambassador to India—a nation to which we had sometimes *given* food in the past.

As always in the public square, politics, economics, ideology, and more were mixed with ideas about climate change. But using food as a weapon in an overcrowded world—and one that now looked like it was cooling and becoming hungrier—was fully in keeping with the spirit of the times.

Like the general public, scientists read the news reports about cold winters and wondered what they might mean. For some scientists, perhaps the most interesting question in the 1970s was this: How close was North America to potentially sliding into the conditions needed to start regrowing continental ice sheets? Two studies published during that period addressed the basic question and gave scientists reasons for pause. The first suggested that the recent centuries of the "Little Ice Age" had been close to starting a full-blown inception of continental glaciers in Canada. The second was perhaps even more ominous, as it examined snow-cover data from the early 1970s that showed increasing snow on the ground compared to 1967. If that trend continued (due to the positive feedback loop of snow reflecting the sun's energy), it was reasonable to fear that northern North America could be headed rapidly back into the danger zone of year-round snow and ice accumulation.

The first of the two studies was the sort geologists and botanists perhaps do best, resting on simple outdoor evidence—a bit like Von Post's pollen evidence from the varve layers of Scandinavian lakes. The study hinges in part on lichens, the little "splotches" of color that cling to rocks. As everyone knows from looking at rock surfaces or even concrete in an urban environment—places like the foundations of old churches—lichens will grow pretty much anywhere from the Northwest Territories to New York. If you scrape a lichen off a rock with your thumbnail, perhaps while idly daydreaming as you sit to rest on a boulder in a national park, you will be erasing the result of decades or even centuries of work on the part of the sturdy but slow-growing lichen.

Lichens make a living using nothing more than their rock, the occasional drop of rain, and the blessings of sunlight. The rock provides them with a place to stand and a few mineral salts, but it's light that gives them the energy for metabolism and growth. If cut off from sunlight for extensive periods, lichens simply die. And that fact gave scientists in the 1970s a significant clue about just how close we have recently been to re-entering a period of new and expanding glaciation in eastern Canada.

Geologists of the day knew that Baffin Island, off the northeast coast of Canada, was one of the sites where the massive ice sheets of the Pleistocene originated. In 1975, at the height of our fears of the coming cold, the prestigious journal *Science* reported that there was ample evidence that lichens in Baffin Island died off in quite recent times—during the last few centuries of the historic Little Ice Age.[3] They did so, presumably, because they were covered by permanent snowfields, that is, a blanket of snow that lasts all summer, cutting them off from the sun. With permanent snowfields, and snow added each winter, layers will accumulate, ultimately creating the pressure at depth that can turn the snow to coarse firn and then to ice. Ice will, over time, build up and begin to flow, creating a new glacier. But *when* was it that permanent snow covered and killed the lichens, threatening the start of this chain reaction? Are we talking ancient history or something closer to the present day?

There are two ways to tell how old lichens—living or dead—actually may be. One is to use carbon-14 dating techniques in a laboratory. But the other way of dating lichens essentially depends on their size, and it gives useful information about such issues as when lichens again started to grow on Baffin Island, which is when the year-round snowfields finally left.

The basic idea involved is simple enough. If you look at a freshly broken surface of rock—or even new concrete in a city—it is clean and free of lichens. But if you look at the south side of an old stone bridge, built at a time we know from recorded history, you'll find it covered with lichens of different types. You can measure the size of the lichens and start to determine from your numbers how quickly (or slowly!) the lichens grew. Do that again for the north side of the bridge, and for bridges of different latitudes, and you are on your way to understanding the whole wide world of lichen growth. Because there are many different types of lichens and local habitat conditions to consider, it takes time and experience to do the work well—but scientists have constructed the kind of database needed to predict how quickly lichens will grow in a given locale. This type of work makes it possible for scientists to determine the age of the *oldest currently living lichen* in the area of Baffin Island. That time identifies when the snowfields retreated and lichen growth returned to the land. More complicated reasoning and evidence, as well as modern data-gathering techniques such as the use of satellite imagery, can contribute to our understanding of when the enormous snowfield first formed and grew. In fact, the researchers used satellite imagery as they deliniated lichen-free areas in the north-central parts of Baffin Island.

Here's the result of the work: the gap in lichen life on Baffin Island is from about 1600 CE to around 1900, roughly the coldest parts of the Little Ice Age. According to the researchers, the snow cover during that time snuffed out the little lichens, which were cut off by snow from their energy source for much too long for them to survive. The report was more important than just an account of the perils of being a lichen in northern Canada; it also sketched a picture of what may be a major climate tipping point. The hypothesized snow blanket in northeastern Canada and other such snow blankets on the ground, we think, can initiate a "positive feedback loop" for cooling climate. Year-round snow reflects away sunlight's energy in all seasons, leading to a time of greater and greater cooling in the region—and ultimately globally. That can lead to more snowfields, leading to more cooling, and so on.

The snowfield–sunlight reflection feedback loop was in the minds of scientists concerned with global cooling in the 1970s. And instead of thinking about centuries worth of evidence, as with lichen growth, some scientists started to publish data about *annual increases* in snow and ice cover in the Northern Hemisphere that were happening at the time. Based on satellite data acquired between 1971 and 1973, a 1974 article in *Science* reported evidence of increasing snow and pack-ice cover in the Northern Hemisphere.[4] The authors argued that the increasing snow and pack-ice cover could be sufficient to create the potential for alterations to the hemispheric heat balance. The horrendous weather of 1972 and 1973, the authors speculated, could have been influenced by the simple variable of snow and pack ice because it's the most important of the seasonal variations that affect the globe's heat balance. If a similar uptick in the growth of snowfields and ice packs occurred seven more times, the authors warned, then North America could well be back in conditions in which glaciation could start.

Clearly, in the 1970s, respected scientists and groups within the National Academy of Sciences feared global cooling and a return to Pleistocene levels of bitter cold. Other scientists feared global warming more than cooling—the subject of the next chapter. It may at first be hard to accept that both fears were fully reasonable, but I think the record is clear on that.

In recent years, as the debate about climate change has become both fully politicized and amazingly shrill, it's become the custom of some groups to debunk or attack some of the groups of researchers or their publications from the 1970s, in particular those that were based on cooling fears. But it's a simple fact that some scientists of that time felt they had scientific evidence portending at least an imminent return to a Little Ice Age and, perhaps, a dreaded return to Pleistocene levels of cold. Others, as we shall see, were gravely concerned about increases in greenhouse gases even though temperatures were mostly dropping at the time.

Let's turn now to fears of a warming Earth and the evidence on which those fears are based.

11

GLOBAL WARMING DISCOVERED

Progress in science sometimes occurs suddenly and dramatically as new ideas are launched largely by individuals. More often, headway is slower, and many different people over decades or generations contribute key ideas that gradually become crucial to a broader theory. The global-warming hypothesis—the idea that human-made carbon dioxide, methane, and other greenhouse gases will lead to a warmer world that will be disadvantageous—is a result of this latter sort of scientific research.

In this chapter we'll skate quickly through the earliest discovery of fundamental global-warming ideas and evidence, then we'll slow down a bit as we get to the modern era of the thick-and-fast discoveries that came in the last parts of the twentieth century. Although the story we'll present has some complexity, this is the final installment of the case for global climate change, and in particular change triggered by industrialization around the world. In other words, the reader can take heart from the fact that we are nearing the end of our core efforts. The most important goal is now in sight.

We'll start with a physical chemist named John Tyndall who lived and worked in the 1800s. In Tyndall's day, scientists were investigating the behavior of heat and light. It was part of the greater story of working out the background of the basic science of energy. Some scientists of that time began to study infrared heat, the kind of energy that's picked up today in "night vision" goggles. Most people in Tyndall's era expected gases to be "transparent" to infrared radiation, just as air is transparent to visible light.

Tyndall discovered that the matter was more complex. He was the first person to clearly note in a laboratory that some gases absorb a great deal of infrared radiation while others absorb nearly none. He showed that nitrogen and oxygen—the most common components of air—do not absorb infrared energy. That was in keeping with general expectation. But Tyndall had other gases at hand in his laboratory, and so he checked them as well.

It can seem odd to modern readers, but in the middle to late 1800s, homes and buildings in urban areas in Europe were illuminated at night by "coal gas," a combustible gas made by heating coal while restricting its access to oxygen. Coal gas was dirty and nasty stuff, mostly composed of methane (natural gas), but some of it contained considerable quantities of carbon monoxide and other gases. It had to be manufactured in cities in chemical plants, then piped from those plants to street lamps, houses, and more.

Coal gas was piped to Tyndall's laboratory. When he used his equipment to measure the infrared heat adsorption of coal gas, he found that it was a strong absorber of infrared energy. He also discovered that carbon dioxide and water vapor are strong infrared absorbers. In 1859 Tyndall published his findings. His work is worth highlighting because it's the cornerstone of greenhouse theory. That's because heat in the infrared part of the spectrum is the sort of energy the Earth could easily either *lose* in larger quantities to space, resulting in vastly colder equilibrium temperatures for the planet, or *retain* above current levels, potentially resulting in a warmer world.

Now we can skip forward and move from Great Britain to Sweden. Near the turn of the twentieth century there was a physical chemist named Svante Arrhenius who was working on a number of chemical problems along with some issues in geology. Arrhenius took an interest in infrared adsorption and what was then the new idea about a greenhouse effect. Like other scientists of his day, Arrhenius's interest in the matter was linked to efforts to answer the question of what had ended the Ice Age. Like some others, Arrhenius thought of the greenhouse effect as a good thing, one that had brought much-needed warmth to the Earth and likely still moderated climate for our benefit in the Holocene Epoch. But in his usual bold manner, Arrhenius broke new ground when he sketched an equation relating the concentration of carbon dioxide in the air to temperature change for the planet. Further, Arrhenius and his colleague Arvid Högbom put two and two together and saw how people were, at least in principle, influencing climate. After all, because industrialized society burned fossil fuels and created carbon dioxide, Western civilization was clearly contributing to greenhouse gas concentrations in the air. Tyndall had not noted that connection—although it was obvious in retrospect. To be sure, however, Arrhenius and others saw the potential of industrialization to change climate as a *good thing*, something that could prevent the return of the Ice Age deep freeze.

Although it seemed clear that people were contributing carbon dioxide to the air by burning fossil fuels, there were those who thought that the Earth would compensate for that input. More vegetation might take up carbon dioxide, for example. And since the gas is soluble to some degree in water, the vast oceans of the Earth might simply absorb the relatively small amount of carbon dioxide humans produced. But in 1938 Guy Callendar took the next step forward for our story by arguing that carbon-dioxide concentrations in the air had risen significantly since the 1800s. His paper suffered strongly from the fact that there simply were not good and reliable ways of measuring trace amounts of carbon dioxide—his data about the past seemed more like estimates than firm observations. But his argument served to renew interest in the matter.

Other scientists soon contributed to greenhouse ideas after Callendar. Gilbert Plass was a significant researcher in the field, and other names could be mentioned. But no one was more significant than an oceanographer named Roger Revelle. Revelle earned his doctorate in the 1930s and was, during World War II, in the Navy. In 1957 Revelle coauthored a paper with a colleague named Hans Suess, whom we briefly met before in our discussion of carbon-14. The pair argued that the world's oceans would absorb carbon dioxide from industrialization at a *slower rate* than believed earlier. That meant, of course, that carbon dioxide would build up in the air at a *faster rate* than earlier conceived. The point implied that a greenhouse effect due to human emissions of carbon dioxide would be more significant than previously believed. And Revelle and Suess realized that additional carbon dioxide might make the Earth much warmer than we would like—an unpleasant greenhouse rather than simply a blessed one that rescues us from a return to the Ice Age. Still, in 1957 the scientists thought the changes they envisioned would take a century or more to unfold, and that didn't seem like an alarming prospect. Part of the reason for their complacency was that they didn't clearly anticipate exponential growth in global population and global industrialization. But Revelle's interest in the whole matter had been ignited by his 1957 work, and he would continue to do a great deal of pioneering global-warming science and public outreach work throughout the remaining decades of his life.

One piece of public outreach had particularly big impact. In the mid-1960s Revelle gave a talk about the greenhouse effect at Harvard University. An undergraduate named Al Gore Jr. was in the audience. The young Gore—a senator's son—was impressed by Revelle's idea that humans could be doing damage not just to the local environment, but also to Earth's whole atmosphere and thus to global climate. As the story goes, Revelle showed the audience what then existed of precise and meaningful measurements of carbon-dioxide concentration in the air over time. Those measurements, made by Charles David Keeling, are shown in their entirety to modern times in figure 11.1.

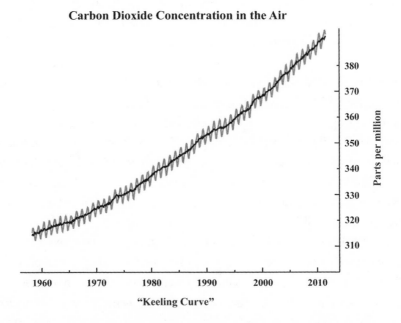

Carbon Dioxide Concentration in the Air

"Keeling Curve"

Figure 11.1. Recent values of carbon dioxide in Earth's atmosphere. Note that the rate of increase in carbon dioxide is itself increasing. Data adapted from National Oceanic and Aerospace Administration (NOAA) information available at http://www.esrl.noaa.gov/gmd/ccgg/trends/ (accessed July 15, 2011).

The Keeling data, known as the Keeling "curve" in the lingo of science, vary a little by season, summer versus winter, as plant growth surges and drops to near nil, especially at more extreme latitudes of the Northern Hemisphere. That's why there are numerous smaller-scale "squiggles" on the graph. But averaging out those little ups and downs creates the broad sweep upward in carbon dioxide that's clear on the figure and important to climate concerns. Importantly, the figure shows that carbon-dioxide concentrations in the air are increasing, *and they are doing so at an increasing rate*. That is to say, the curve in the more recent years shows a steeper slope than previously. The clear rise of carbon dioxide over time, and the increase in the rate of that growth, is the kind of evidence that alarmed Revelle—and has alarmed all scientists I know who have examined it since.

Revelle remained a major voice arguing for the significance of anthropogenic (human-made) climate changes through the 1980s. By that time, climate science had grown from an obscure backwater of research to a well-funded branch of inquiry. It's therefore appropriate to slow the pace of our tale so that we can look in more detail at a couple of representative people and their recent work.

The first person we'll discuss is Paul Mayewski, who had many things on his mind in 1988. Along with other American researchers, he had asked the National Science Foundation for the tidy sum of $25 million for a study of Earth's climate. The work would allow scientists to drill down into the center of the Greenland ice cap through all the glacial ice that had accumulated there to the very bedrock itself. The project was to be called the Greenland Ice Sheet Project Two (GISP2).

Mayewski is the kind of scientist who does a lot both at his desk and away from it. He founded the University of New Hampshire's Climate Change Research Center, and he has been codirector of the Institute for Quaternary and Climate Studies at the University of Maine, Orono. And unlike most more sedentary geologists and climate scientists, he is a fellow of the Explorers Club. Still, any professional gets rattled by some things, and in the book *The Ice Chronicles* Mayewski explains that he was no exception to that rule. In 1986, two years prior to requesting funding for GISP2, his colleagues had elected him chairman of the working group, with overall responsibility for preparations for the ice-core project. At times, considering the logistical and scientific headaches involved, Mayewski wondered whether he'd been caught up in a case of "be careful what you wish for."

The working group had made what turned out to be a very fruitful choice of tactics. A team of European scientists was also going to work in central Greenland, and the two groups would drill and interpret two separate cores just a few miles apart at the crest of the Greenland ice cap. The reason that strategy was to be crucial to deducing a great deal about climate change—and particularly episodes of rapid climate change—was that the two cores would yield unambiguous records of ice layers and their significance. If both showed a rapid cessation of the Younger Dryas period that ended the Ice Age and began our own epoch, then the similar layers on the vast ice sheet would clinch the argument.

The site of GISP2 was at an elevation of more than ten thousand feet. The European drilling site (called GRIP) was stationed about nineteen miles to the east of GISP2. The severe conditions at high elevation in central Greenland mean that temperatures are well below freezing even in the summer. As our earlier German hero, Ernst Sorge, knew well, it is a challenging place to survive, let alone do science.

To get the job done, the researchers dug a long trench in the snow for processing the ice cores as they were brought to the surface by the drilling teams. The Core Processing Line (CPL) was housed in this covered trench. It afforded the teams of workers a methodical way of doing the same things to each section of core. The last step of the CPL was core packing for storage and then shipment under refrigeration back to the United States. But even in the relatively simply equipped CPL, the scientists discovered substantial changes in the layers that reflected major climate change.

One method scientists could use to deduce changes in the ice core was testing the conductivity of the core. A station in the CPL passed an electrical current through the ice. Ice is a poor conductor, but it allows a bit more current to flow through it when it's impure. (This may make sense when we recall that, for example, salt water or battery acid allow current to flow through them while distilled water allows almost no electricity to move through it at all.) The natural acidity of summer versus winter snow-fall varies, a fact that helped scientists note annual layers in the ice core.

But subtle visual clues also exist in the Greenland ice. One of the sci-entists charged with the task of visually counting the layers and looking critically at the details within them on a light table was Richard Alley. Alley has become a famous climate scientist in the years since GISP2. He—and other colleagues—worked eight- to twelve-hour days in the CPL because their eyes were the best at seeing the details of not just the layers, but also how the ice in each layer might differ from that above or below it. The layers, of course, are not all pristine or perfect. Some were thicker, some thinner. Alley has become a premier climate scientist in more recent years, but his time spent simply counting and recounting layers at GISP2 was absolutely crucial to science because each layer measured out one year's passage of time. In the end, it was the basic counting of layers back through time, coupled with more sophisticated measurements, that con-vinced the world that rapid climate change events (RCCEs) were indeed as radical and rapid as had been earlier suggested.

The first double check of dates was the year 1783, which was when a volcano in Iceland named Laki erupted catastrophically, sending volcanic ash and sulfuric acid across Greenland. Alley counted his layers down from the surface of the snows where the core began, double-checking his counts against a tally each evening. When the Laki layer was reached, Alley's count was off by one to two years, an acceptable level of error in natural materials recording two centuries' passage of time. RCCEs, like the onset of the Younger Dryas, were used as additional double checks. When Alley and his colleagues compared counts with those of the Europeans working on the GRIP core, acceptable agreement was evident.

The ice in the layers themselves came into play at this point. As dis-cussed earlier in this book, the ice can be analyzed for isotopic informa-tion that leads to an understanding of the temperature at the time the layers of snow originally formed. This gave researchers part of the prize they sought: a highly detailed record of how climate in the Greenland area had changed over thousands of years. Finally, the tiny air bubbles trapped in the ice told scientists how greenhouse gas concentrations had changed in tandem with temperature. The total achievement was breathtaking, even for the usually cautious and skeptical scientific community. The ice-core work was a smashing success and the information it provided quickly became the foundation for modern climate science.

In many ways, it's easy to romanticize projects like GISP2, which took place in harsh terrain far from the everyday lives almost of us lead. But it should not be forgotten that Alley, Mayewski, and scores of their colleagues spent much time on the total effort represented by the ice-core work, including years of grant writing and preparation for their fieldwork. There were also the academic years full of as much laboratory and administrative work as could be crammed into busy teaching lives. Finally, the scientists' work was challenging on a physical level. The scientists, men and women, older and younger, worked in temperatures ranging from –22 to –4 degrees Fahrenheit. But, of course, the reward was that when the GISP2 drilling team hit the bedrock of Greenland—ten thousand feet beneath the researchers' feet—the scientists were able to broadcast a message to the world. The longest and oldest ice core, spanning over one hundred thousand years, lay in their hands, and they had good reason to be proud of the accomplishment.

By the early 1990s, the laboratory work on the GISP2 and GRIP cores quickly established several things. Both drill cores showed rapid changes in the climate of Greenland going back many thousands of years into the Holocene and Pleistocene Epochs. The staggering and ceaseless seesaw of temperature from the data in the Greenland ice core—and later the antarctic cores—is impressive, as figure 7.1 clearly shows. The ice-core data make it clear as crystal that temperature on Earth is never static, that change is the rule, not the exception. The cores also demonstrated that the broad ups and downs in temperature correlate in a general way to major changes in concentrations of greenhouse gases—information shown here in figure 11.2.

Furthermore, the abundantly clear and frighteningly numerous RCCEs we have discussed before in this book accounted for one unambiguous scientific result of the mammoth ice-core projects. RCCEs show plainly that temperatures and climate can plummet to new levels of frigid cold or skyrocket to warmth in a decade. For years climate scientists had held out the hope that although the Ice Age may have seen some radical and fast changes in climate—likely due to feedback loops when so much of the planet was covered in ice—our own epoch was a quieter and gentler time. But the ice-core record quickly showed that milder RCCEs have occurred even in our own warm epoch. One hypothesis about what would cause sharp changes—even radical ones—and do so abruptly on a fast timescale involves ocean circulation, particularly ocean movements in the North Atlantic.

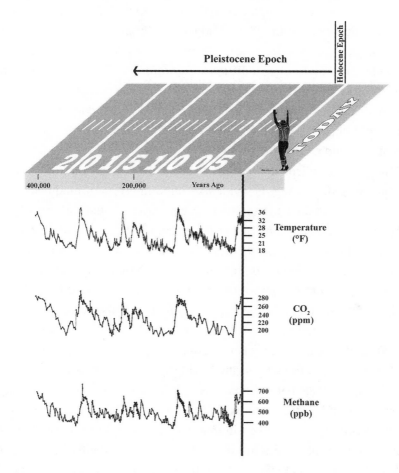

Figure 11.2. Temperature, atmospheric carbon dioxide, and atmospheric methane, as revealed by ice-core research. Adapted by permission from Macmillan Publishers Ltd.: J. R. Petit et al., "Climate and Atmospheric History of the Past 420,000 Years from the Vostok Ice Core, Antarctica," *Nature* 399, no. 6735 (June 3, 1999): 429–36, copyright 1999.

As the engineer Carroll Livingston Riker had known, the movement of ocean water carries more heat than movement of air. (We can demonstrate that easily by measuring how much heat it takes to warm a pot of pasta water—it's a lot—versus how much heat is required to warm the same volume of air—comparatively, a tiny amount.) This fact has important consequences for the "heat budget" all around the Earth. Cool and dense ocean water near the coast of Greenland sinks into the ocean depths. The water then flows at great depths southward. The Earth has several such patterns of surface ocean currents that move to where they cool and sink, with much deeper masses of water flowing in ways that compensate for the surface currents. These are responsible for enormous distribution systems of heat and cold around the planet.

Happily for scientists, ancient ocean currents and their characteristics can be studied using the evidence found in layers of mud and marine creatures deposited on the seafloor. Oceanographers have a host of ways of studying sea conditions of the past, ranging from looking for glacial gravels—which end up on the seafloor when icebergs impregnated with gravels are carried to sea and break up—to much more sophisticated chemical techniques. Different currents in the world's seas have different chemical and isotopic characteristics. By studying the shells of sea creatures that long ago fell to the seafloor, scientists can infer patterns of ancient ocean currents and how they have changed over time.

One challenge in using seabed evidence about past ocean conditions and climate is that marine creatures burrow into the muck and ooze of the seafloor and disturb its layers. But some regions of the ocean's bed are not significantly disturbed in that way, and Gerald Bond of Columbia University went about finding them. In the North Atlantic he took good, undisturbed cores and studied their layers going back through time. He inferred past temperatures by recording the ratios of the remains of small, cold-tolerant versus warm-tolerant creatures in the layers. Bond discovered that his work on the seafloor reproduced the basic patterns of the Greenland ice core.

This was crucial evidence that what affected weather above Greenland also affected ocean conditions, and vice versa. In other words, the seas and the skies were connected, and both changed behavior at very near the same times. Similar evidence has been generated by oceanographers all over the world. If we had any hope left that massive climate change affected only the pollen of Scandinavian lakes or the ice of Greenland, we've long since set it aside. Global climate change is exactly that—global—and it affects the world even at the middle latitudes.

But let's focus one more time on the North Atlantic, for there was another lesson to be learned from that region. From oceanographic lines of evidence scientists had come to believe that when the North Atlantic conveyor belt of ocean flow shuts down, the world changes dramatically. In the words of modern climate science, the conditions of the North Atlantic can "flip." Such flips are behind some of the RCCEs we have discussed in earlier chapters. The evidence of flips has led climate scientists to decrease the earlier attention we paid to *warming* versus *cooling* trends in climate. Many scientists more simply and directly address times that appear to be more *predictable and stable* versus those that are *chaotic and unpredictable* because "flips" are likely to occur within them.[1] An analogy is sometimes made with light switches. There are two kinds of light switches: dimmers and standard switches. Dimmers allow for incremental change but standard light switches are either on or off. Standard switches flip between two states, just like climate does in the case of RCCEs, as the evidence provided by the Greenland ice and the oceans show. By the mid-1990s scientists had good reason to think that global climate has repeatedly operated like standard light switches, flipping from one climate state to another in ways that affected much of the globe at or nearly at the same time.

Many other details of climate change were added to our store of knowledge by GISP2 and GRIP and other work coming out of antarctic ice cores. The details were inescapable: carbon-dioxide and methane concentrations in the ancient atmosphere varied substantially, and they did so in sympathy with variations in global temperatures. In other words, when temperature goes up, so do the greenhouse gases. When the greenhouse gases decline in concentration, so does temperature.

But which is causing the other? As we mentioned in an earlier chapter, there is reason to think that higher temperature could cause higher greenhouse gas concentrations. Methane, for example, is likely to increase in concentration because permafrost melts under a warmer climate regime. And warmer oceans would release some of the carbon dioxide dissolved in them. So which is it—does rising temperature create more greenhouse gases or does an increase in greenhouse gases create temperature increase? The chicken-and-egg question has not been fully resolved. But here are some important thoughts about the matter.

Most Americans who have seen Al Gore Jr.'s documentary *An Inconvenient Truth* or who have followed public global-warming arguments are sure of one thing: they believe *the ice-core record shows* that carbon-dioxide and methane increases create warmer temperatures on Earth. But the significant news is that the facts actually run in the reverse direction. On long timescales, increases in temperature, controlled by the Earth's orbit around the sun, create more methane and carbon dioxide. That's right: from what most scientists can tell, greenhouse gases are not the primary driver of long-term climate change on Earth—Milankovitch's orbital variations are. Still, everything about climate is complex, and it's quite possible that greenhouse gases can help trigger changes at particular times, or they can help exaggerate feedback processes already underway on Earth. But it's the orbital variations of the Earth around the sun—the three major interacting Milankovitch cycles—that give the general form to the ups and downs on the temperature plot in figure 11.2. Greenhouse gases and many other variables on Earth simply follow those ups and downs in temperature.

Here's the double-barreled argument about the primacy of temperature, as ably presented a few years ago by Richard A. Muller, a physics professor at the University of California at Berkeley.[2] (We'll have more to say about Muller's recent thoughts about climate change toward the end of this chapter, but we'll deal first with his earlier ideas.)

Study figure 11.2 again. It shows that, through geologic time, both carbon dioxide and temperature vary a lot in the ice cores, and they do so in roughly similar ways. The chicken-and-egg question cannot be well answered from the Greenland and Antarctica ice cores alone. Changes in temperature and carbon dioxide occur so closely together in time that we cannot with certainty say which comes first. The ice-core record is a very good one, but even it's not perfect. Carbon dioxide is a gas, and, as such, it moves around for a while in the layers of snow before becoming trapped in bubbles within glacial ice. There's always therefore a "fuzziness" to the time horizon of carbon dioxide in the ice-core records—they don't exactly match up with the layer of ice they are in, and we cannot generally say to which specific, nearby layer they belong.

In 2003 this fuzziness factor was addressed for one major climate-change event in an antarctic ice core. This transition had attributes that made a close analysis of timing possible—unlike many ice cores harvested around the world. A team of researchers published the results of their work on the unusually useful core in the journal *Science*, arguing that, at a major climate transition, temperature changed *first*. Carbon dioxide increased six hundred to one thousand years later. (That figure fits with the notion that carbon dioxide from the deep ocean takes about eight hundred years to circulate upward to the surface, where it can be warmed and released into the atmosphere.)

Still, as we have discussed earlier in this book, there can be complex feedback processes in global climate change, both positive and negative ones. So the evidence and argument of the 2003 research does not mean that greenhouse gases don't affect climate. They do. But they don't look like a primary driver, at least not in the quantities we've seen on Earth in the Pleistocene and Holocene Epochs.

Let's take a critical look at figure 11.3, which amplifies figure 11.2 to include information on very recent carbon-dioxide changes.

Note the vertical distance on the graph from the place where industrialization begins to the dot showing today's value of carbon dioxide in the air, essentially shown by the lower half of the dotted line. According to the best science, that increase in carbon dioxide to current levels should create a temperature increase of about 1 degree Fahrenheit. Now, note carefully that the vertical increase in carbon dioxide you just studied is about equal in size to previous carbon-dioxide changes at the end of natural climate-change cycles. But when those earlier, natural changes occurred in carbon-dioxide concentrations, temperature rose by 10 to 15 degrees Fahrenheit, for example when the Ice Age ended and our balmier times began. This again suggests, as Muller argues, that greenhouse gases are not the primary "driver" of major temperature change on Earth. If they were, we would be living in a world a whopping 10 to 15 degrees warmer than when significant industrialization began. The takeaway message is that climate is more complex than sound bites and even documentary films present it to be.

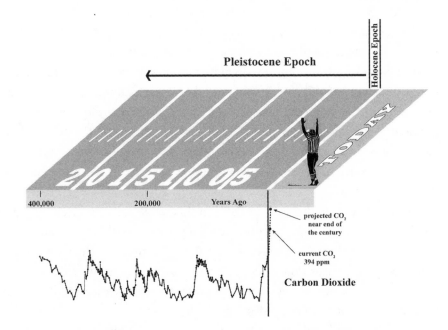

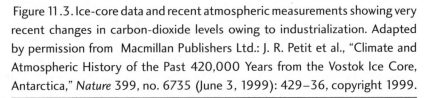

Figure 11.3. Ice-core data and recent atmospheric measurements showing very recent changes in carbon-dioxide levels owing to industrialization. Adapted by permission from Macmillan Publishers Ltd.: J. R. Petit et al., "Climate and Atmospheric History of the Past 420,000 Years from the Vostok Ice Core, Antarctica," *Nature* 399, no. 6735 (June 3, 1999): 429–36, copyright 1999.

But we humans are not off the hook with respect to recent climate change. To confound us all, the facts do not—I repeat, do not—mean that on the *short* timescale of industrialization we are not increasing temperatures through our production of greenhouse gases. As just mentioned, the increase in carbon dioxide since industrialization began is calculated to have brought about a temperature increase of at least 1 degree Fahrenheit. Add other greenhouse gases to the picture, plus the fact that we are producing all of them at increasing rates, and the situation is one that understandably concerns both scientists and laypersons alike.

Now we must tackle quite another problem. For it's a simple fact that *describing* climate change satisfies no one. The question that arises is this: Can climate change be *explained* so that we know what creates the many variations in the ice cores and the ooze of the seabeds? A description of what has happened is a necessary first step toward understanding climate, to be sure, but it's only that—a first step. The several more-interesting questions concern why climate has flipped, time and time again; why great glacial advances have waned entirely; and why in recorded history the warmth of the medieval period gave way to the cold, wet times of the Little Ice Age. If we want to ever predict what will come next, after all, it would help to be able to explain what has occurred up to this point, including, it's to be hoped, such extreme events as the Younger Dryas.

Before launching into what can be said about possible explanations of climate change, let alone what the future holds, a word here is in order about broader intellectual discussion. This chapter is in part the story of ongoing scientific work and what it appears to tell us about what lies ahead. But we run into an immediate problem, for up to this point this book has been a history of Earth's climate and a history of how scientists learned about climate.

History is the study of events far enough in the past that we can consider them with at least a tincture of dispassion. The decisions made during the Vietnam War, for example, are a fit subject for modern historians—but the war America is fighting in Afghanistan today is not a subject that historians will study dispassionately until that conflict has fallen well into our wake. Journalism, on the other hand, is the arena where current events can be considered. The exact line between journalism and history may be fuzzy at times—when will historians start writing about the campaigns of Mitt Romney and Barack Obama in the fall of 2012?—but the idea that there is a distinction between history and journalism is clear.

There is a field of science writing that is, essentially, journalism. It reports on discoveries as they are announced. The main drawback with this science-based journalism, just as with journalism more broadly conceived, is that it is subject to the winds of the pubic square. And in the last two decades, those winds have been blowing very strongly with regard to climate science. Scientists, citizens, and politicians have all been buffeted by them at some point, with denunciations of "deniers" or "warmers" going back and forth like Ping-Pong® balls. Nevertheless, we need to discuss the blossoming science that's been recently done, including in the young field of climate modeling and prediction. We must say something about the Intergovernmental Panel on Climate Change (IPCC), the umbrella organization designed to organize work in climate science and bring scientific reports to the world public. All of this is fraught with some hazard, but the task cannot be ignored.

We will start by returning to scientific history, from which we can at least approach parts of the present cautiously. From the 1960s forward, but particularly in the 1980s and more recently, a group of climate scientists were working on the project of *explaining* the evidence brought back from the seafloor, from ice cores, from peat bogs, and from glacial gravels all around the world. These scientists were "modelers," or those who built mathematical models to try to mimic the trends in the data that those who go to the field and bring back samples have produced via laboratory work. The modelers and the fieldworkers each need one another for any complete understanding of climate. The modelers can hardly function without data from the real world and, in general, the field and laboratory scientists don't have the time and expertise to place their work into enormously complex global models.

During the last three decades, of course, the modelers have been helped in their work not just by new ice-core and oceanographic data, but also by the revolution in computing technology that has made it cheaper and faster, year by year, to do more and more calculations. Today desktop machines do more computing than what, in the old days, a "mainframe" computer shared by many people could accomplish.

Enter onto the stage at this point a colleague of Paul Mayewski, a mathematician named David Meeker. The two close friends, using different gifts, each contributed to what we know of climate change. Meeker's task, roughly speaking, was to study all the factors that looked like they were significant controls to the record of climate change in the GISP2 ice core. Meeker—and many other researchers—have found significant regularities in the ice-core data. In some ways, statistically speaking, most of the GISP2 record is quite regular. That doesn't mean we know how all the controls are producing the patterns, but rather that, mathematically speaking, we see regularity in the data. Still, this descriptive statistical work is a huge step forward; some of the fog of complexity about climate on Earth has been penetrated.

But regularities don't mean we can predict the future well, at least not in a way that helps our society. The basic mathematical patterns in the GISP2 core are long term. The statistical behavior Meeker and others have presented is regular only on timescales of more than five hundred years. Clearly, however, if our climate lurched into a different regime for sixty years, for example, whole nations would be impacted (and people might be quite angry with climate scientists for not predicting the change). Additionally, all researchers I know note that there is a chaotic element to climate on Earth and thus to climate change. From this point of view, it's impressive that there is as much regularity in the GISP2 data as there is, because there's also an untamed beast in climate, something that's random and unpredictable. This means we have good reason to think we could "fall off the cliff" any day and be back in the Ice Age.

In sum, the years from the 1980s forward saw the increasing unification of the realms of data production and data analysis, or field and mathematical models. It was a major step forward for climate science. The same period also saw a growing consensus among scientists that short- or long-term warming due to greenhouse gas emissions was our greatest fear and a growing commitment on the part of scientists to bring that message to the public square. Many parts of climate science were coming together, and some of the leaders of the field sounded the alarm about global warming and urged that more funding should be directed toward climate research.

At this point we can briefly reflect on how different modern climate science is from traditional geology as practiced in the days of Louis Agassiz, the discoverer of the Ice Age. Today climate scientists generally work in teams. They rely—of necessity—on government funding agencies for their support, for who else would put $25 million into a project such as GISP2 in Greenland? These differences are not just organizational; they can have direct, intellectual consequences. In Agassiz's day an academic geologist needed to support himself—usually by teaching—but beyond that he was as free as a summer breeze to look at glacial striations and boulders while on holiday and infer what he could from them. He wasn't influenced by the need to obtain the next research grant. One could say that the young Agassiz and the rocks of Switzerland had a much purer relationship than that.

Even some scientists feel unease about the "big group" research being practiced today, with projects funded by governments, scientists reviewing each other's grant proposals—and thus needing to get along over time— and professional conferences where scientists cheer politicians, like Al Gore, who symbolize major government funding. Some speak quietly of too much personal interdependency and too much dependence on big money. But at the same time it's true that what we learned from GISP2 and mud coring on the seafloor forms the backbone of what we understand about the details of climate change—and all such work is made possible by the multimillion-dollar grants that are most likely to come from only a few governmental sources.

One thing is certain: the tension between those who remember "the old days" of science as purer and those who have thrown themselves into the new mode is, in itself, nothing new. Although climate scientists who have been worried about global warming have made more and more calls for increased funding and a closer relationship with government, earlier than that some major players in climate science were lobbying the federal government due to genuine concern about the potential for global cooling. In 1972 a study group of glacial experts wrote to President Richard Nixon raising the alarm about the end of the Holocene and a return to Pleistocene levels of cold. Naturally, they wanted more funding for research. So, whether the concerns have been global warming or global cooling, for big science the baseline response has been to plead for more funding.

All of which brings us to the umbrella organization for modern climate science reports, the Intergovernmental Panel on Climate Change (IPCC). The IPCC is not a strictly scientific organization. It's a hybrid of scientists and representatives from governments around the world, working under the auspices of the United Nations. Saudi Arabia, a major fossil-fuel producer, is represented on the IPCC, as are nations with many souls living quite near sea level. The IPCC has had to deal with all the complexities of international diplomacy and politics that come into play whenever the global community considers its common needs and wants. Thus, from 1988, when the IPCC was established, to the present, the main scientific findings about global warming and climate change have been announced in the pubic square by an organization with at least some political as well as scientific sensibilities. About every five years, the IPCC reports what most climate scientists are predicting for climate in the coming decades—the subject that grabs headlines around the world. The IPCC's reports, therefore, lie at the heart of the public's understanding of global warming and climate change.

The first IPCC report was issued in 1990, and later ones have followed. We won't go into the details of the early reports because the documents were, for our purposes, quite similar, each helping the public to understand that greenhouse gases were increasing in the atmosphere, that they were likely to be a factor leading to a warmer climate, and that the dynamic of climate change might well accelerate. In the world of media "sound bites," however, the richer scientific framework was often lost; few reporters bothered to explain to their audiences that scientists had unearthed increasing evidence of climate "flips," not just warming trends. The message that got through to the public, from this perspective, was good only as far as it went—the naturally fragile nature of climate was lost in the shuffle and the *chaotic* nature of some natural climate change was not mentioned.

In the world around us we see many processes at work that are quite predictable—not chaotic at all. A swinging pendulum is an example of what a scientist would call a "system" that can be analyzed, understood, and predicted well into the future. If we disturb such a system a little (for example, by pushing the pendulum just a tiny bit as it swings away from us), the system will respond with just a small amount of altered behavior—by speeding up on the downswing, swinging farther out into the air, or so forth. The tools of high-school physics are exceedingly good at analyzing this kind of system and the regularized behavior it displays.

But there are other kinds of systems in the natural world that are quite unlike the swinging pendulum. Imagine you take seven basketballs to the top of a mountain. As precisely as humanly possible—including with all the tools of modern engineering—imagine you roll the first ball down a small chute at the top of the peak. The ball will roll inside the chute in a manner we can predict (like the pendulum). But once it hits the rough and complex natural surfaces of the mountainside, the boulders and the grains of sand, something else will happen. The first bounce will carry it to the left or right a bit, or make it spin as well as jump. The next bounce will be more unpredictable than the first. And so on and so forth, down the mountain it will go. Now imagine you release the second basketball into the launching device. It, too, will behave predictably and regularly in the chute—just like the first ball. But due to tiny differences in the way it hits the rocks and boulders, it will end up taking quite a different path down the mountain. In fact, about all we can say with confidence is that none of the seven basketballs you launch will take the same path. The natural process of rolling basketballs down mountains introduces an element of unpredictability that is simply not part of a regular system.

Weather and climate have chaotic elements embedded within them. Tiny differences in initial states can make for very large differences in outcome. That's interesting—or terrifying—from a human point of view, but it means that climate cannot be fully predicted the way the motion of a pendulum can. The surprising and impressive thing is that climate modelers have made as much progress as they have in isolating and understanding patterns in the climate upheavals of Earth's past. But explaining all that's happened—or predicting the future—when part of the system has chaotic elements will forever elude us. That, from my perspective, is the inconvenient truth we must simply accept. Still, given human nature, it's natural that climate scientists try to predict the climate trends of the twenty-first century, and that's one of the things that each recent IPCC report has done.

In 2001 the IPCC published a major finding on global warming called the Third Assessment Report. The report, often abbreviated as "TAR," was released to worldwide news coverage in all forms of media. The media attention surrounding the release and the initial pages of the TAR illustrate to many observers that climate science has become noticeably politicized. We'll therefore take a look at the way TAR introduces the subject of climate change, not because it is a very recent publication, but because arguments about it and its authors still reverberate on the Internet and in the public square.

First, just as a simple point of fact, the only part of the TAR that most nonscientists read is the Summary for Policymakers. That was the part of TAR used by the legions of reporters who covered the well-publicized release of the report. The content of the brief summary was condensed and distributed as sound bites and banner headlines all around the world, and many observers see 2001 as the turning point in American debates about climate change. The summary made a strong and clear case that the Earth was rapidly warming and that people were to blame for the change, a two-part claim most educated Americans have accepted from 2001 forward.

Near the beginning of the report, a headline states: "An increasing body of observations gives a collective picture of a warming world and other changes in the climate system."[3] Smaller print explains, "New analyses of proxy data for the Northern Hemisphere indicate that the increase in temperature in the 20th century is likely to have been the largest of any century during the past 1,000 years."[4]

Reporters who went deeper into the summary found a colorful graph that is reproduced here as figure 11.4. The figure shows past temperatures deduced from evidence like tree rings and glacial ice cores. The "younger" parts of the temperature line rely on records based on human-made thermometers in more recent years. The light-gray area indicates the range that a true value for average global temperature might reside within, the so-called error bar of the graph.

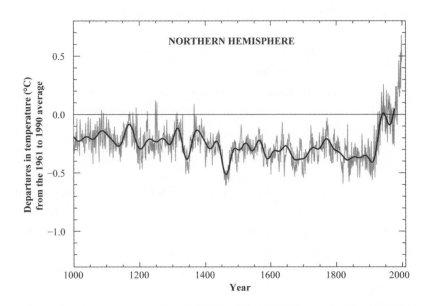

Figure 11.4. The controversial "hockey stick" figure shown prominently in the Third Assessment Report of the IPCC. The figure is available at a host of websites simply by searching for "hockey stick" using your web browser. It was originally published by M. E. Mann, Raymond S. Bradley, and Malcolm K. Hughes in their article "Northern Hemisphere Temperatures during the Past Millennium: Inferences, Uncertainties, and Limitations," *Geophysical Research Letters* 26, no. 6 (March 15, 1999): 759–62. Reproduced by permission of American Geological Union. Copyright 1999 American Geological Union.

We'll examine the assumptions behind the figure in a moment, but just taking it at face value, as you likely would have done if you had been a reporter or a lay reader of the TAR summary, you'd think that the end of the twentieth century—the far right of the graph—is hotter than any period in the preceding millennium. It's an alarming picture. In the TAR, the graph looked more alarming because it was printed in color, including the use of red for the "spiking upward" part of the graph.

The figure you see here and the verbal summary of it were reprinted and broadcast around the world. Millions of people saw it or heard about it. Not surprisingly, millions came to believe that scientists were sure the world was warmer now than in any time for at least one thousand years. It was time, many ordinary people felt, to wake up and smell the coffee.

Another important point about figure 11.4 is that the most significant changes shown occur just at the point in human history when industrialization was growing briskly and spreading rapidly in the early and middle 1800s. Many people were therefore ready to believe that the graph demonstrated not just that global warming was significant and growing, but that humankind was the main cause of recent warming. In the words of the report, "There is new and stronger evidence that most of the warming observed over the last 50 years is attributable to human activities."[5]

The famous figure we've been examining is known as the "hockey stick" graph. The name comes from the idea that the period from 1000 to 1850 CE is like the relatively straight shaft of a hockey stick lying on its side. The sharp upward movement of temperature starting at 1860 is like the blade of the hockey stick.

The hockey stick caught the eye of a Canadian geologist named Stephen McIntyre the first time he saw it. McIntyre is the first to admit he isn't a climate scientist. Rather, like many Canadians with interests in the Earth sciences, he is a practical, nuts-and-bolts mining geologist. Because of his background in the real world of mining claims and the business of promoting mining company stock, McIntyre thought he smelled a rat when he first saw the hockey stick. It looked, essentially, just like something a clever entrepreneur would use to mislead potential investors into sinking their money into a distant gold mine.

A bit of real-world background may help you understand McIntyre's point of view. In the long history of this sad and sorry world, some entrepreneurs and promoters have been known to paint too rosy a picture of certain investment prospects, such as the anticipated yields of mining operations. The tactics used by these clever promoters are often not based on simple lies, but rather on the *selection or manipulation of measurements* in some fashion to make the investment look better than it is.

McIntyre is a longtime mining geologist. So, just at a gut level, he suspected that the hockey stick had been created in some manner that was less than fully aboveboard. It was a manipulation, he suspected, not to sell shares in a mine, but to increase the importance of climate scientists as they made the claim that global warming was severe, worsening, and caused by human activities.

McIntyre could see from the TAR publications that the hockey stick was based on a figure in a full-fledged scientific journal. The lead author of that article was scientist Michael Mann. Mann was also one of the many climate scientists credited with authoring the TAR. McIntyre contacted Mann in 2002 after he saw the TAR's version of the hockey stick. McIntyre asked for the data on which the hockey stick was based as well as the statistical method used to evaluate various pieces of evidence and form them into the single line in the figure.

To follow the story any further, we'll have to work our way though just a few words about statistics. Climate science *should* go hand in hand with statistics. As you know from looking at weather maps, the temperature at noon yesterday varied a lot from place to place in your state. Climate, we can say, is generalized, or average, weather. To understand climate change, we've got to have some way to try to categorize what average weather was like long ago. The term *average* is itself, of course, a concept of statistics, so you see we've already got a painless start on statistical topics.

Let's say you want to determine average temperature for the whole Earth in the year 1066. Where might you start? There were, of course, no weather stations at the time, so we have no thermometer records. We do have some church records and occasional written comments about crops in places like Europe, which is why we know a little about births and deaths in parts of Europe and whether or not wheat or wine grapes did particularly well during that era. But "precise" and "complete" are not terms we could assign to such records, interesting though they are.

On the upside, we have a few physical samples that speak to temperatures for that year. For example, we have the 1066 CE layer of glacial ice in Greenland. Alas, that gives us a pretty clear temperature reading for the year only in one place in central Greenland.

Climate scientists try to add to information from ice cores by using other sorts of temperature-dependent samples of 1066 from elsewhere on Earth. As we've discussed earlier, the pollen in a bog in Denmark may suggest what plants lived there in the period roughly from 1050 to 1075. That community of plants suggests the temperature range of the time. That's not precise, obviously, but it's something.

But there may be no pollen record on hand for that same time period from much of Labrador, Arizona, or British Columbia. So scientists must look to still other types of evidence for anything they can glean about conditions in 1066. As we have seen earlier in this book, one such alternative is the width and density of tree rings growing at the time. That's only partly satisfactory, as we have seen, because trees are biological organisms influenced by a variety of factors. Still, it's at least some data, and a thick tree ring likely means it wasn't bitterly cold in 1066 where the tree was living. And on it goes, through a long list of potential bits of evidence that suggest temperature values or ranges for a specific year or the general time period.

You won't be surprised to hear that assigning temperature ranges to pollen in mud layers or to tree-ring measurements requires judicious interpretation. But scientists do the best they can in their labors, and researchers can indeed make meaningful sense of much of the raw information the Earth provides. But even putting the evidence from ice cores, bog pollen, and tree rings all together, there still are many, many sites for which there is no temperature evidence for 1066. If you were to look at a map of the world on the wall and insert a thumbtack for each place where we are confident about temperatures when William the Conqueror and his forces invaded Britain, you won't have to use lots of tacks—much of the world is blank.

For that matter, even temperature data from eight hundred years later—in 1866—is not all you would hope. Written weather and thermometer records, of course, exist from all over the world for 1866, but they are much more abundant around Canterbury, say, than across the tundra of Canada. And direct weather records on the vast oceans that cover most of our planet are extremely fragmentary at best for that year, one not so very long ago.

In short, knowing temperature on Earth is a problem because measurements are sometimes few and far between and often not spread out uniformly. Or, as we technical folks say, "the data are sparse and uneven."

Enter statistics to help us make the best sense of what we have.

With that background, we'll go back to McIntyre and the famous hockey stick graph. All scientists can agree that the line that makes up the hockey stick is based on a few bits of evidence of several different types, including evidence that must be interpreted, and all sides can agree that the resulting pool of numbers must be fed into a statistical calculation of considerable complexity in order to generate a picture of the Earth's temperature on a global basis.

So, in 2002 McIntyre asked Mann to send him both the temperature-related data and the statistical methods used to produce the figure shown in the hockey stick. Part of the ethic and culture of science depends on people being able to ask for—and receive—information from others. It's a bit like doctors in the medical community asking to see the results of a test that they may not have personally ordered but would like to have on hand for their own work to help address a patient's problem. Normally, doctors honor such requests for information as a matter of routine, just as do scientists.

In fairness to Mann, it's probably worth noting the obvious point that McIntyre wasn't a *climate* scientist. McIntyre was a mining geologist— someone who likely seemed to Mann like a proverbial hick chewing on a toothpick. Mann, in contrast, was an up-and-coming climate scientist, and his hockey stick work was being used as a central piece in the public argument about whether the world faced a grave crisis due to global warming. Mann and McIntyre tell different stories about what, exactly, happened between them in 2002. But it's fair to say that McIntyre did not see his request fulfilled until he had dogged Mann for the hockey stick data and methods.

McIntyre was soon joined in his policing work by a second Canadian, Ross McKitrick, an economist at the University of Guelph. Together, McIntyre and McKitrick dove into the materials they were eventually given by Mann. And the pair of Canadians quite quickly came to think the statistical method Mann and his colleagues had used was fundamentally flawed. The Canadians published a "corrected" version of Mann's graph, using basically the same measurements that Mann had but not treating them in the same statistical manner. The correction, McIntyre and

McKitrick argued, showed that there should be no blade going upward on the hockey stick plot, only temperature going up and down and up and down throughout many centuries.

It was a David-versus-Goliath story in some respects. A mining geologist and an economist were arguing, based on the use of different statistical methods, that the hockey stick of the TAR was misleading. The enormous and well-funded IPCC, the upstart pair argued, got it wrong on a basic level. Mann and his colleagues had set up a statistical formula that "mined" the data for any hint of an upward trend at the end. And the Mann method produced the hockey stick shape for all sorts of data. Even feeding random noise into Mann's method usually resulted in a hockey stick shape.

For his part, Mann issued a counterattack, criticizing McIntyre and McKitrick and their methods. The Canadians obliged with a reply. And, in some ways at least, the main parties in the dispute are still arguing about elements of this contentious saga on the web. You can read about it there any time insomnia plagues you.

Although the details of the dispute are numerous and complex, we should not become confused about the central point of the matter: either the hockey stick is valid and Earth temperatures are warmer than they've been in the past thousand years—perhaps meaning we humans are responsible for abundant and rapid warming—or that's simply not the case and the best scientific authorities have misspoken to the public about the matter.

Naturally, all sorts of people who can't follow statistics or climate science wanted to know whether or not the hockey stick was the best interpretation of temperature evidence. After all, national policies around the world are at stake, as is, potentially at least, the fate of our children. The US Congress therefore created a blue-ribbon panel of statisticians charged with studying the hockey stick dispute. The panel was instructed to bring back a report to Congress and the American public about who was right— Mann and his colleagues in climate science or their critics in mining geology and economics.

Edward Wegman enters the story at this point. Wegman is an eminent statistics expert, with credentials that make virtually any other statistician in the nation green with envy. He accepted the call of the House Committee on Energy and Commerce, assembled a panel of other experts in statistics, and started to study the whole hockey stick dispute from the ground up.

It wasn't a small project. The Wegman panel worked behind the scenes for a long time. They had to master a great deal of complexity in what lies behind the hockey stick, well beyond what we've discussed here. But in July 2006, the Wegman panel issued its report to our elected representatives.

Wegman's group sided with the "hayseed" geologist and his economist colleague. The hockey stick shape is primarily the result of poor statistical applications, Wegman and his coworkers wrote, and the criticisms issued by the Canadians are "valid and compelling." Further, Wegman pointed out that "it is important to note the isolation of the paleoclimate community; even though they rely heavily on statistical methods they do not seem to be interacting with the statistical community."[6] In short, Mann—who is a serious climate scientist by any measure—had made a crucial error in basic statistics. His colleagues, who had published with him, had also made that error, or had at least gone along with his mistake. Other climate scientists who reviewed the original paper before it was published also erred.

The main point of the whole sorry story about the hockey stick is this: it's pretty clear we cannot assume studies by major climate scientists are as sound as we would hope, nor can we assume they have been reviewed by others who have a strong enough background in statistics to ensure they are meaningful. This is just one specific example of the fact that all scientific studies—from routine ones to those broadcast around the world—are done by fallible humans and that even the peer-review process doesn't weed out all major errors. And, of course, it's simply not a good day for science when Congress has to get involved to correct scientific errors.

But why does all this matter? The bottom line is that the IPCC reports, especially their summaries for policymakers, and the media coverage of their releases, have a direct impact on what people around the world believe about global warming. And it's highly unfortunate that their public importance is not proportional to the care that goes into their synthesis. In the words of the Wegman committee report, "Especially when massive amounts of public monies and human lives are at stake, academic work should have a more intense level of scrutiny and review. It is especially the case that authors of policy-related documents like the IPCC report . . . should not be the same people as those that constructed the academic papers."[7]

Regrettably, it's safe to say that many ordinary Americans—who had seen the hockey stick when the TAR was released to worldwide publicity—didn't see Wegman deliver his report to the House Committee on Energy and Commerce. That's perhaps why many generally knowledgeable citizens believe quite firmly that we have recently endured warmth that's unprecedented in a thousand years or more.

But even the regrettable history of the TAR's introductory pages may well not speak to venal motivations. There are understandable reasons at the human level for climate scientists to feel the need to convince governments that global warming is rapid, is human-made, and will lead to problems soon. That kind of commitment—made clear at a personal level by some climate scientists when they write about their work—may lead to overreaching. (At the same time, of course, critics of climate scientists who are aligned with energy interests may also overreach in their statements and publicatons. That's why it is up to the public and policymakers to sort out, as best they can, who has overreached and why.)

But is there another reason climate scientists erred on the matter of the hockey stick? The question brings us back to the constant refrain of any branch of big science. Doing large research projects that depend on multimillion-dollar government grants always results at some point in pleas that more money be spent on research. That is a reasonable and understandable position, especially if researchers genuinely believe the world is reaching a tipping point and catastrophic changes are going to hit us due to greenhouse gas emissions. But it's also true that once scientists "connect the loop" in their own thinking and begin to see they can manipulate those with research funds (the public and Congress), the professionalism and objectivism of science can be lost. It's a simple truism that money can corrupt otherwise good people. And beyond even all the dollars at issue, climate scientists also face the seductive influence of real power. After all, those who had lived and worked in obscurity in the 1970s are now advising senators and prime ministers on major policy questions.

To sum up, some observers in the geologic community think the hockey stick saga undercuts our ability to place deep levels of trust in the IPCC. That's not to say that we "deny" the stark reality that climate changes. Nor do we dismiss the notion that our greenhouse gas emissions contribute to global warming. But citizens here and abroad can simply not afford worldwide publicity given to announcements that don't stand up to review from independent intellectuals.

Still, setting aside what may be some shortcomings of the IPCC, what most frightens reasonable observers of climate issues is that levels of major and minor greenhouse gases are rising in the air around us, and they are doing so at increasing rates. As you saw earlier in figure 11.3, our current carbon-dioxide levels are far above anything the Earth has seen in hundreds of thousands of years. And soon they will be much higher, as industrialization spreads around the world. Meanwhile, places like the arctic appear to already be showing significant increases in temperature.

Now is the time to loop back, as promised, to Berkeley physics professor Richard Muller. In the summer of 2012 he released an account of how and why his thinking about climate change has been turned around.[8] He and his research group have carefully studied the records of temperature on land and find that over the past two hundred and fifty years temperatures have risen by 2.5 degrees Fahrenheit. In the past fifty years, such temperatures have risen an impressive 1.5 degrees. The pattern of temperature increase does not fit well with solar activity, with global population growth, or with other factors Muller's group considered. The best fit for explaining this temperature change is increasing amounts of carbon dioxide in the air.

Muller is the first to admit that his work doesn't prove causality. But he argues that greenhouse gas concentrations are the single best explanation we now have for recently rising temperatures. His conversion from global-warming skeptic to accepting the basic idea of human-made increases in temperature has given many a skeptic pause, as well it should.

It seems probable we are indeed changing climate. It would be surprising if the enormous volumes of greenhouse gases spawned by agriculture and industrialization had no effect on global temperatures. The notion that the changes forced on the Earth may come at an accelerating pace is another feature of the issue that fully sobers most scientists. Indeed, it's because scientists understand such matters so clearly that many of us see it as doubly important that IPCC reports be grounded in excellent and impartially reviewed research. It's also doubly important, of course, that as much as possible the *science* of global warming should be separated from the *policy debate* about how we choose to respond to what the best science indicates.

Because climate on Earth is so very complex, there are going to be aspects of climate-science research about which reasonable people can disagree. Still, there's one point everyone should be able to accept. The growth in the amount of greenhouses gases in the air in the past two centuries makes it clear we are launching the planet into an experiment that the Pleistocene and Holocene Epochs have not seen before. Even those of us who like a dramatic experiment in the laboratory don't want to see one performed on the entire Earth and all its inhabitants. That's the fundamental reason that world leaders have tried to reach agreement on how greenhouse gases might be curbed. From 1992, when leaders met in Rio de Janeiro, to 1997, when they met in Kyoto, to 2009, when they met in Copenhagen, national representatives have tried again and again to find consensus on how to approach the problem. Essentially, nothing has yet worked—for a variety of reasons. A number of different proposals have been discussed, including nonbinding goals, carbon caps made mandatory by some sort of international agreement, and direct aid to developing nations so that they can expand their economies without simply using more and more fossil fuels. While opinions may differ about why the impact of this series of meetings has proven so small, everyone can agree that greenhouse gases pose a massively complex problem for any global agreement to successfully address.

One simple and positive note can perhaps be struck in this complex realm. There is a low-cost way to actually start to *reduce* the production of greenhouse gases without decreasing economic growth, agricultural production, or even the amount of energy we are accustomed to using in our homes and industries. It rests on a matter known well enough to geologists, but one that hasn't entered the realm of public discussion. The next chapter will explain what's at issue, as well as recap where we have been so we can look forward to the rest of the twenty-first century.

12

LEAVING THE GARDEN

We Americans have been living in the Garden of Eden. Our nation has been fortunate with respect to climate, having avoided the worst of the Little Ice Age that hit the Norse so hard in the early 1300s and brought repeated waves of suffering to Europe in the following centuries. We've not experienced anything like the climate change that slammed Egyptian civilization in the Bronze Age, let alone anything stronger, like the onset of the Younger Dryas, which swept across the Earth more than ten thousand years ago.

But our luck is guaranteed to run out. We will be thrown out of the garden and into the harsh reality of rapid climate change—it's only a question of time. And this will be the case whether the change is natural, human-made, or created by some combination of those two forces.

This book has explained how geologists and other scientists learned that climate has varied enormously in the past and is going to change still more. Whether from mapping mounds of glacial gravels, counting varve layers in ancient lake-bed mud, seeing the evidence of major ecosystem change in the turnovers of buried pollen, measuring the varied widths of tree rings, or analyzing the amazingly rich and detailed ice-core record, we know the changes to come will be enormous. The ice-core evidence, in particular, shows us that climate can "flip" like a light switch and be radically different over the timescale of just a few years, well within what a reader of this book could live through. The icy layers of Greenland's great glacier indicate that climate—at least on the regional level—also undergoes many quick blips within the times that lie between major flips. In short, the ice makes it clear that Earth's climate could become either substantially warmer or colder than it is right now—and if we are honest with ourselves about our precarious situation we have to acknowledge that the most threatening changes are likely to be breathtakingly rapid.

To get a sense of perspective on the basic challenge we face, let's look again at the football-field analogy of time with which we started this book. As you may recall, the gridiron has a referee standing in one end zone, marking the present day for us. At the far end of the field, some 1.8 million years ago in time, is the start of the Pleistocene Epoch. Roughly each hundred thousand years on the field—or 5.5 yards—is dominated by frigid temperatures worthy of every book about the Ice Age you ever read in childhood. So, if you started at the distant end zone of the field and counted out a little more than five yards toward the referee, those yards would correspond to a period of Ice Age cold.

Then there are briefer periods, most of which are about eight thousand to ten thousand years long, that are much warmer. They amount to half a yard on the football field. You could take one step toward the referee, measuring a foot and a half, to signify this warmer time. The exact details of the periods on the football field do vary a bit, but the pattern is always the same: a long period of crushing cold followed by a short period of balmier warmth that resembles the present epoch, and then a return to the long, bitter times.

Let's assume you walked the whole length of the field, from the distant past to where you were approaching the referee and the present day. The next-to-last warm period is one we have discussed in this book, the interval called the Eemian. It starts about 6.5 yards from today's end zone. The Eemian was actually *warmer* than the present. Glaciers melted back to nothing at all during this natural global warming, and sea levels stood very high indeed. The Eemian accounts for about half a yard, as usual, after which the Earth returned to bitter cold for several more yards. Then, about ten thousand years ago, the climate warmed once again. Our own balmy time, the Holocene Epoch, started abruptly, and warmth became the theme of Earth's global climate.

It's certainly disquieting to meditate on the fact that the Holocene has already run for ten thousand years, longer than many of the warm periods that have occurred in the past two million years. When I first took freshman geology, in the very early 1980s, I sat in the lecture hall listening to my professor explain the history of climate we've just described. After class, I summoned the nerve to go up to my instructor and ask him about what was troubling me. Clearly, from the pattern just sketched, it looks like we should soon be headed back into bitter temperatures, conditions that would guarantee disaster in the Earth's temperate zones, where so many of us live. Civilization looked doomed to me, with a return of the Ice Age imminent.

My professor, geologist Sheldon Judson of Princeton University, commended me for my observation about the significance of the length of the Holocene but said I need not lose sleep about the end of civilization. He assured me that the transition back to a bitter climate regime worthy of the Pleistocene Epoch would likely be fairly gradual, taking centuries or millennia to unfold. Climate change toward Ice Age conditions would affect only people alive five hundred or even fifteen hundred years in the future. We could hope that by then they would have acquired the wealth and technical sophistication to adjust to the change toward gradually colder temperatures.

But as the readers of this book know, science advanced substantially from where it was when Professor Judson and I spoke in the early 1980s. The evidence of the ice cores of Greenland and Antarctica showed that climate change is often rapid. Temperatures can lurch toward warmer regimes or plunge into bitter ones in just five, ten, or fifteen years, more like a switch being thrown than like the gradual process of change geologists had earlier envisioned. Standing as we do in the twenty-first century, with modern climate science to consider, one thing we can legitimately fear is the possibility that those reading this book will live through a time when global temperatures drop precipitously into conditions that have not been seen since the woolly mammoth and the saber-toothed tiger roamed the land.

As it happens, Professor Judson and I spoke about all of this again in the mid-1990s, when the modern understanding of rapid climate change had come to light. We laughed at our earlier notion that temperature change would be gradual. My beloved professor, who was nearly eighty years old at the time, said there were a few good things about being quite old. One was that it was unlikely he himself would live through the next period when Earth's climate flips, going suddenly toward colder, or for that matter, warmer conditions. But because I was a good bit younger than my teacher, I had no such comfort. Perhaps most disquieting of all for modern civilization is the fact that scientists are still far away from being able to predict the onset of the next rapid climate change event. *We just don't know when it will start.* That's a lot to chew on—and it's high time that we as a society masticate on it.

The basic idea we must take away from the different types of evidence we've seen in this book is simply that climate has always changed and always will do so. Often enough, the changes are fast. Those facts—noncontroversial though they are in the realm of science—are all too often left out of the public discussions of climate concerns. I would argue that it's impossible to have a rational conversation about climate and greenhouse gas issues until we first acknowledge how variable climate really is. We like to think the Earth is "rock solid." But in fact global climate—an essential part of the Earth as we know it—is more like a torn flag fluttering in a gale than it is like an outcrop of inert granite. We simply must acknowledge what natural climate change could mean to our civilization, even as we also consider what steps we might want to take to potentially reduce anthropogenic global warming.

In this book the reader has taken a tour of many different types of evidence that show natural climate variability. The basic facts of climate change are clear and not difficult to understand. The question of *why* it is that natural and devastating climate change doesn't come up for public discussion is perhaps a matter for psychologists or sociologists to explore. But I am sure that until we overcome our reluctance to look at the basic facts of natural climate change in the face, we won't be able to engage in the most meaningful dialogue about our collective future.

Geologists are also puzzled about why another climate-related matter has not come up for public discussion. For one of the few pieces of clear good news is that it's very much within our power to help the world significantly with respect to greenhouse gases in a way you have not heard about, and to do so at relatively modest cost. The matter will take a few pages to properly explain, but it's simple to grasp and would be easier for our society to address than any other approach to limiting carbon-dioxide production, especially in the near term.

While many people assume we left King Coal behind in the 1800s, it is in fact still a significant fuel that powers much of our economy. Aside from providing our cheapest and most abundant form of heat, coal is crucial to industrial purposes, like running the steam turbines that generate much of the electricity for the power grid, creating the ingredients for concrete, or refining and forging metals. Our varied uses for coal obviously all involve intentionally burning the fuel. But what nongeologists don't generally know is that we have a major problem on our planet with coal fires that are *unwanted* and burning out of control. In sum, these unintentional fires create a meaningful fraction of total global greenhouse gas production. That may be difficult for a layperson to believe, but let me assure you that, just like other geologists, I've stood on warm ground next to the expansive smoldering blazes of an underground coal fire—and choked on smoke, soot, toxins, and hot greenhouse gases, all spewing into the atmosphere from the blaze. And in some parts of the world, particularly India, unwanted coal fires are at the surface of the Earth, with massive flames actually towering into the sky. If more citizens became aware of all these blazes, we could choose to take action against them. The technical knowledge is in place to put many of them out; the main thing lacking is commitment.

Let me quickly explain the magnitude of the problem presented by these coal fires, starting by way of two brief examples. Then we'll turn to how we can address the issue, both in the United States and abroad, and what that would do to help us address our concerns about greenhouse gases.

In 1962 it wasn't remarkable to think of "cleaning up" a town landfill in America by setting fire to it. After all, fire destroys a great deal of trash and garbage and helps cleanse what metals remain. So when the members of the community of Centralia, a hamlet in east-central Pennsylvania, wanted to clean up a town landfill, they used the accustomed agent of fire.

Specific details are in dispute at this remove in time, but whatever the combination of factors of that particular trash-burning event, there is no doubt that the well-known Buck coal seam near the trash pit caught fire during the trash burn.

The Centralia coal fire is *still* blazing, roughly fifty years later. It's burning underground as coal fires do, very hot in places where oxygen is abundant, more slowly in places where oxygen is more limited. The fire is doubly pernicious because it's exploiting the honeycomb structure of the old mine workings under the town. It doesn't help that the coal in the Buck seam is anthracite—hard coal—which packs the most heat as it blazes into carbon dioxide, smoke, soot, carbon monoxide, and a host of other hellish gases that percolate up through small fissures and holes scattered around the town.

The carbon monoxide, in particular, was the first sign to local residents that the coal fire was going to threaten the existence of Centralia as a location of human habitation. People actually passed out from carbon monoxide effects in their own homes. Another problem was that underground voids were created over time as the fire caused the collapse of some of the underground mine workings. The empty spaces, in turn, created new sources of air that kept the fire supplied with oxygen. The collapses, for their part, have led Route 61—the main highway through Centralia—to drop eight feet in places, with resulting fissures and crevasses in the pavement. While it might be possible to live with smoke and soot emanating from fissures, it's not possible to manage with everything in the town descending at random times toward a hellish coal-stove below the surface. In short, Centralia has come to an end as a community due to a fire under its feet, a fire set inadvertently by its own residents.

Because the people of Centralia knew a great deal about coal mining, it's natural to ask why they didn't put out the fire right away. But they did try to do so, as did experts from outside the town. Altogether, eight attempts were made to put out the conflagration, using various firefighting tactics then available. All the work failed, and today the Centralia fire is massive, accounting for about four hundred acres in area on the surface of the ground, but burning at sharply different depths under the land.

Massive underground coal fires can be costly to combat. Because the dollar cost of fighting the fire at Centralia was ultimately estimated to be greater than the dollar cost of buying out all the residents of the town, a difficult decision was reached. In the 1980s, the federal government offered the residents of the town a multimillion-dollar bailout. The buyout of property allowed residents to hand over their keys to the government, receive a payment equal to the value of their house, and resettle elsewhere. Legally speaking, no one lives in Centralia anymore, although just a very few residents remain in their homes if they judge them to be unlikely to disappear into a fire hole soon.

But Centralia is a long way from being Pennsylvania's oldest coal fire. A fire started in a mine in the state's northeast corner has continued to burn underground since 1915. The Laurel Run fire, believed to have begun due to a miner's carbide lamp, creates toxic gases, hot underground temperatures, and the collapse or subsidence of ground. The towns around the Laurel Run fire have adapted better, perhaps, than Centralia, but the human suffering in both locations has been great, just as the amount of coal consumed by the unintended flames has been staggering.

Centralia and Laurel Run are hardly alone. In Pennsylvania there are over two hundred coal fires, and others burn elsewhere in the Appalachians. More fires burn in the western states and Alaska. The eastern fires are mostly underground, while most of the western ones are in low-grade coal at or near the surface of the Earth. Large coal fires, or dense clusters of them, blaze in Australia, India, South Africa, Indonesia, China, and France. Geologists regularly publish accounts of uncontrolled fires in global coal districts. In total, global coal fires number in the thousands. Some burn at ground level so that their smoke, soot, and fumes pour directly into the air, while others smolder underground, no less significant for the fact the flames themselves cannot be seen except perhaps as glimpses of cherry red through crevasses and cracks.

But it's not all our fault. As geologists know, there are some coal fires burning today that started naturally. Just as forest fires can start due to lightening strikes, coal fires can begin near the surface of the Earth for the same reason. And a wildfire that crosses a coal seam exposed at the surface will ignite the coal. Soft coal, known as bituminous coal, is also able to undergo spontaneous combustion and literally catch itself on fire at temperatures not much above 100 degrees Fahrenheit. The process is aided by the natural combination of pyrite (fool's gold) with oxygen. Pyrite is commonly found embedded in coal, and when it oxidizes, it generates heat. Just as on a hot summer's day dry weeds in a highway ditch can ignite spontaneously, so soft coal can combust of its own accord. And once coal has started to burn, it can continue to smolder, or blaze fiercely, for ages.

But it's still true that many modern coal fires start due to human activities. Mining itself creates some fires, as in the Laurel Run blaze in Pennsylvania. Sparks and fires created near a coal seam for reasons unrelated to mining can trigger a fire, as with Centralia. Because humans have mined coal for centuries in Europe and for much longer in eastern Asia, it's no surprise that unwanted coal fires have been around for a long time. Indeed, written accounts of unintentional coal fires go back to Alexander the Great. Just as in historical times, today's coal fires disproportionately affect the world's poor, with by-products like carbon monoxide, benzene, toluene, arsenic, and mercury sickening and occasionally killing people who have no option but to live near the fires.

In China and India today more people suffer directly from blazing coal fires than anywhere else on the planet. Geologists estimate up to 200 million tons of coal burn each year in China in these unwanted blazes, accounting for up to 10 percent of national coal production. Those figures are an upper limit, not a clearly established fact. But there's good reason for the estimates, and they clearly show the magnitude of the problem.

The Chinese, to be sure, are far from passive in the face of the fires. Though they almost always battle them, coal fires are fierce opponents. Chinese coal seams are honeycombed with the activity of mining, some with hand-dug tunnels and small pits that have been around for many centuries. That history means no one knows how and where air may flow through the coal—a fact very much to the fire's advantage. In the end, many Chinese coal fires are only put out when they are physically dug up. But excavation is a task that heavy equipment is best suited for—and until recently China has had virtually no heavy equipment for combating coal fires simply because it had not accumulated the wealth to invest in such capital.

But—and this is the important point—a great deal hinges on changing what's acceptable about unwanted coal fires. Some geologists estimate that if all unwanted coal fires in China were extinguished, a 2–3 percent decrease in worldwide carbon-dioxide emissions from fossil fuels would result.[1] Others describe it this way: putting out the coal fires in China would nearly offset the carbon dioxide created annually by all the cars in America each year.[2] Surely the fact that we could meaningfully decrease global carbon-dioxide production by putting out Chinese fires should have garnered widespread public attention before now. And the facts are similar for other greenhouse gases in the coal smoke, since the Chinese fires don't burn purely to carbon dioxide by a long shot.

To make matters worse, the coal-fire problem in China is growing, a by-product of the privatization of the coalfields. But the *good news* is that it's never too late to change our attitudes and practices and help the Chinese combat their coal fires. Doing so could easily be our first step in actually reducing total global greenhouse gas emissions, and it would be a more economical approach to accomplishing such a reduction than others being discussed in the international community.

Taking action on the issue of coal fires in China would be a good first step, but the situation is in some ways worse in India, the world's third largest coal-mining nation. Coal fires burning at the surface of the subcontinent's seams are dense and thick in many places—for example in the Jharia coalfield. Geologists have routinely documented individual flames over twenty feet high. Some towering flames up to three times that height have been reported. Technical estimates of seventy fires in that region show that about 1.4 billion tons of coal are involved to some extent in the fire zones with about ten million tons burned each year. Only the poor live near the fires, and the homes of the poor are eventually undermined as the ground moves downward into voids formed after a coal bed has been burned out. Images of the poorest of the poor—and their children—living in these hellish conditions are enough to affect even the hard-hearted. And there's no doubt that the toxins that are emitted by unwanted coal fires have made people ill—occasionally, fatally so. Yet on their own, and with only spades and buckets of water, impoverished people simply cannot put out a major fire rooted in the Earth itself. Only with technology and the invest- ment of significant resources can people successfully extinguish coal fires. Thus, the Indian blazes continue to burn unaddressed to the detriment of the local residents and the atmosphere of the planet as a whole.

With industrialization in India and China growing rapidly, the problem of coal fires in those countries will likely expand in coming years. Until India and China truly become first-world economies, their resources won't go into fighting coal fires anymore than ours did in the 1800s. And we Americans still have our own active coal fires! We need to address our own fires, as well as help with those in India and China. The next step should then be to branch out as more coal blazes start elsewhere. In Indonesia, for example, there's a significant and growing problem. Large proportions of the country were until recently covered by rain forests growing on soils that have coal seams near the surface. Those forests are now being cleared, commonly by fire. It's estimated that three thousand coal fires have been started since 1982 due to this practice. Thick smoke from ongoing fires covers the land and is a likely to cause of an epidemic of asthma among nearby residents. In short, the unintentional coal-fire problem is growing throughout the developing world, and as slash-and- burn agriculture and industrialization proceed, we can expect the problem to grow even greater.

This, then, is the plea of a geologist to her fellow citizens: it is past time to put out unwanted coal fires burning around the world. Extinguishing such fires is a much cheaper way of decreasing greenhouse gas emissions than many of the ideas on the table for discussion at present, and it also directly aids the world's poor because it cleans up their local environ- ments. It seems as close to a no-brainer as we have with respect to climate concerns, yet it has not been widely discussed in the public square. Perhaps a sociologist can understand why the coal-fire problem isn't the focus of intense media attention and why it's not a central concern of environmen- talists, but I cannot fathom why only geologists discuss the problem of out-of-control coal fires. If we fear anthropogenic climate change due to greenhouse gases, and I think we rightly do, it's past time we take action about coal blazes at home and abroad.

While the plague of coal fires receives almost no press, the Intergovernmental Panel on Climate Change (IPCC) has repeatedly grabbed headlines by making predictions about what the remainder of the twenty-first century will be like. The work of the international team of researchers has great strengths, but climate scientists cannot really foresee specifics about the future. After all, if scientists don't know when the next natural climate switch will be thrown, we simply cannot foretell what conditions will be like in 2050, let alone in 2100. That's not to say that it's not worth considering what we estimate greenhouse gases may do to global climate, only that our predictions could be entirely shattered by the reality of events. So practical considerations boil down to this: How can citizens and governments make any useful plans when we don't know when we will be thrust out of the Garden of Eden in which we have been so happily living? To put the matter in its starkest terms, if it's possible that global climate could lurch toward either warmer or colder regimes, that we could see either wetter or drier times in important agricultural regions, and that we don't know when the major changes will come, is there *anything* about future climate worth trying to anticipate or head off?

Let's start to explore that question with what we most clearly know. First, climate will change—that's the crucial idea we must always bear in mind. It's the basic fact we have seen from the evidence explained in this book. Beyond the simple but brutal fact of natural change, it may well be that we humans have been altering climate, bit by bit, for thousands of years through agriculture. It's also growing increasingly certain we have been contributing to temperature changes due to industrialization and the greenhouse gases we are emitting in increasing amounts. We humans are altering the global atmosphere in ways that really matter, and we are doing so at an accelerating rate. The changes in the air around us could have any of several effects. They could

- retard the Earth's return to Ice Age levels of cold, at least for a while
- launch us into steadily warmer times, as the IPCC projects

- shake up complex climate relationships in ways we can't anticipate but that would make a "flipping of the climate switch" more likely

That array of three possible effects is, regrettably, quite a wide one. It's exactly because the possibilities are so dissimilar that it's difficult to know how one might feel about the increases in greenhouse gases we have created—or what sacrifices one is willing to endure to curtail their production through the rest of this century. Let's examine the possible effects in turn, exploring what they could mean.

The first possibility—that greenhouse gases will retard the Earth's return to the bitter temperatures of the Pleistocene—is clearly a positive outcome for humanity. Returning to an Ice Age would drastically reduce human populations because so much of Earth's most productive farmland lies at temperate latitudes. A return to Pleistocene conditions would also, for that matter, stress all sorts of ecosystems besides those most vital to people.

We need not fully fall back to Pleistocene temperatures to see negative consequences for civilizations around the world. If climate were to stay within general Holocene ranges but became significantly cooler than it is now, the change would severely stress the American agricultural base. That would be a great hardship for our country, obviously, as a major domestic industry would suffer from coast to coast. But it also would be a disaster for the many millions of people around the world whom American farmers feed. In short, any significant cooling could cost many lives.

The second possible outcome, that anthropogenic greenhouse gases will lead to a warmer world throughout the twenty-first century, is the prediction of the climate science experts of the IPCC. It's a fearsome and authoritative prediction, worthy of respect, whether your politics are "red," "blue," or somewhere in between, in the zone of purple. We need to consider the IPCC reports in some detail at this point, for although many people have heard sound bites about IPCC predictions, few have read the thick volumes the panel has produced. Some of the information we will explore is disturbing and familiar. But other parts of the IPCC forecasts may well be material you have not heard about at all—and many of those parts have a definite upside for some of us living in the temperate part of the world.

The global climate changes the IPCC envisions will bring about different results in different places. One way to start cutting through all the complexity at issue is to note that the projected temperature changes will generally mean *more warming* where temperatures are *currently low* than where temperatures are already relatively high. Specifically this will mean greater warming for polar latitudes and only slight additional warmth for the tropics, greater warming for winters than for summers, and greater warming for nights than for days.

The most significant changes associated with global warming are expected to occur at and near the poles, on the tundra and taiga. Those changes will melt snow and ice in substantial quantity. While it simply isn't true that the IPCC predicts the glaciers of Antarctica will melt away to nothing in our lifetime—it will take much longer to melt such large masses of ice, even if there are sharp temperature increases—it is true that polar regions will feel much more of the effect of global temperature change than the Mediterranean or China. In the United States, of course, this means that Alaska will feel the effects of warming much more strongly than Hawaii. If the IPCC predictions fully pan out, temperature change will be rapid by historical standards. In that case, Alaskan arctic species used to the current climate regime will doubtless be strongly stressed. Many such species may see a decline in their numbers, and it is certainly possible that some species may not survive. If we as a society decide to take moral responsibility for all the global warming from 1850 to the present—as well as that which the IPCC projects to 2100—we must assume responsibility for species change, as well as for climate change. That's surely a weighty matter to consider.

Yet it's also true that global warming has occurred before in the polar latitudes. The Eemian was *warmer* than our own Holocene Epoch, and the change from the previous bitter time to the much balmier Eemian was not a gradual transition. This just highlights that the total temperature change the IPCC is predicting for our century looks rather limited compared to what the Earth's climate has *sometimes* gone through under natural conditions. That's not to say we needn't be concerned about our role in climate change. But it may suggest that species can be rather hardy—and that, in any event, they naturally face massive climate upheavals time and time again.

But the conditions of the arctic are quite different from where most of us live. Therefore, let's look at the pattern of changes the IPCC projects for much of the temperate world, where most Americans reside. Here the same rule of thumb we've already discussed applies: warming due to climate change will be greatest where colder conditions prevail, and it will be relatively modest where conditions are already relatively warm. This means that the IPCC predicts milder winters and fewer frost-filled nights rather than principally hotter summer days. One could surely argue that, for those of us living at mid-latitudes, what the IPCC projects is not all bad. Weather statisticians and agricultural scientists agree that if summer drought can be avoided, milder winters are mostly good for American farmers—it's unusually cold and long winters that often harm crops planted in the fall or delay planting in the spring. And from a broader economic perspective, mild winters would result in lower heating costs for American consumers and businesses. Fewer snowfalls also mean lower bills for local and state government because there is less snow to clear from streets and highways. If your recreational tastes run to skiing and ice skating, mild winters are not a good thing. But then again, if you are a year-round dog walker, mild winters are mostly positive.

For people living in temperate latitudes, the matter of milder winters is even more directly personal. That's because many fewer people die of heat in the summer than cold in the winter. The famous Danish statistician and environmentalist Bjorn Lomborg points this out, arguing that if the IPCC's predictions for a warmer world come true, there will be fewer deaths due to temperature in places like Europe than there will be if current climate patterns continue. Despite the tendency of the media to report deaths during heat waves in bold headlines—and link all such deaths to global warming—those statisticians who study death rates have no doubt that more people die during periods of significant cold relative to normal regional conditions than of significant heat.

There is actually a large host of costs *and* benefits due to global warming, as sketched by the IPCC, for people living in temperate latitudes. We won't try to discuss more of them. But although the IPCC reports make it clear that people in the United States will benefit in a number of ways from the warming the panel projects for the remainder of this century, it's also a fact that the media neglect to mention the matter to the public. To put the matter in charitable terms, the press has not been adept at dealing with the complexities of what scientists know about climate, or even at explaining what the IPCC really projects for the world. Our cultural move toward tiny scraps of news repeated *ad nauseum* until the media lurches to an entirely new story has not helped the matter, leading educated Americans to feel they know a lot about global warming while, in fact, they mostly have heard one or two sound bites over and over again. Surely people of goodwill across the political spectrum can agree that far too few people know about the possibility that agriculture has moderated climate for millennia, the certainty that unwanted coal fires around the world create meaningful amounts of greenhouse gases, or the statistical expectation that fewer Americans die from the effects of heat waves than from the effects of cold snaps.

But while the IPCC projections have a complex but real upside for some of us, global warming through 2100 can be expected to have negative consequences for other people around the world. The poor who live at or near sea level may well be impacted. In places like Bangladesh, where people live on delta sediments just barely above the elevation of the ocean, even a modest rise in sea level means more suffering and death from each significant marine storm. Another effect of sea-level change is that some Pacific Islanders may lose their homelands altogether due to rising seas. And the IPCC also predicts changes in regional patterns of drought over the twenty-first century. Particularly in places like Africa, where lack of rain is a constant threat to millions, geographic shifts in rainfall would be terribly problematic for those already hard-pressed to feed themselves. In addition, global warming may contribute to changing patterns of crop disease, an eventuality also more likely to affect the world's poor than those of us with some flexibility in our resources. To be sure, global warming such as the IPCC expects will have steep costs as well as some benefits, and unfortunately many of the costs appear as if they will be more heavily borne by the world's poor. Whether the same people would also suffer greatly from limiting the use of fossil fuels through caps or taxes is a crucial question, but one best addressed by economists rather than scientists.

Now it's time to turn away from global warming as the IPCC projects it. After all, the climate change the panel anticipates is actually relatively modest and not—by Mother Nature's standards—terribly fast. To go back to our list of three possible futures we could envision for the twenty-first century, let's address the idea that greenhouse gases may make a rapid "flipping of the switch" more likely in our lifetimes. This possibility is the most terrifying for us as individuals, and it's what disturbs this author's sleep the most at night. It's breathtaking to think that in just a few short years—perhaps eight or ten—the climate could go through a massive jolt like those recorded clearly in ice cores. Imagine, if you will, the chaos that such an accelerated interval of climate change would mean for even our diversified economy in the United States. If the rapid climate change event pushed us into bitter times, then agriculture would take a direct hit. Such a change would mean that while wealthy people the world around might still be able to buy enough to eat, ordinary people would not. Extensive famine in different regions could destabilize governments, leading to violent protests and perhaps even war. In short, the fast pace of devastating change in a climate flip would make real St. John's vision of the apocalypse. And if we do go through such a massive upheaval, we will have to admit that our contribution of greenhouse gases to the atmosphere may have been one factor involved in triggering the change. To go back to an analogy with which we started this book, a drunk man staggering down a sidewalk is likely to fall at some point. But we can contribute to his falling down sooner rather than later by giving him a shove. Our addition of greenhouse gases to the atmosphere is sometimes referred to as "pushing the drunk" of the staggering climate system, helping it to fall into a period of rapid change.

From my point of view, the main reason greenhouse gases matter most is not the IPCC's vision of global warming, but the fact that our emissions may destabilize complex climate relationships and promote a flipping of the climate switch. But at the same time, I also know that we could naturally fall into such a flip regardless of the extent of our production of carbon dioxide and methane. Further, as a student of human history, I know that fossil fuels stood at the base of the amazing revolution that started in the 1700s with the invention of the piston-driven steam engine and swept us through all the gains we made in living conditions into the twenty-first century. It's easy to romanticize the past as a simpler and more beautiful time, but I simply cannot wish we lived as we did in 1720. Before we used fossil fuels to our advantage, the death of children from disease was commonplace everywhere around the world, famine was a chronic threat for all societies, and education was a privilege few people—and virtually no women—ever enjoyed. And for me it's important to remember that even if we had stayed at the level of existence known in the 1700s—including the hunger and suffering that was woven into life the world around at that time—we would still be vulnerable to being swept into fully natural and rapid climate change.

There are many valid concerns about anthropogenic changes to the Earth's atmosphere. But I admit I often grow weary of news reports about melting glaciers, material that routinely leaves out the context of natural change as well as the multiple sources of greenhouse gases emitted today. The media have, perhaps by their very nature, broadcast some of the most alarmist of the IPCC predictions—and nothing more. It's understandable, therefore, that the American public thinks that the only climate change worth being concerned about is global warming, that all climate change is due to humans, and that the whole planet may be uninhabitable by 2100. But, of course, all of that is far from the truth.

It is indeed good to think about the problems we may face in a warmer world, and the changes such a shift would bring to ecosystems, particularly at extreme latitudes, but it's equally important to consider the clear evidence that climate is always in flux, that sharply colder temperatures would be a great threat to both Americans and those whom American farmers feed around the world, and that agriculture may have a long history as a contributor to climate evolution. Again and again, there is the recurring and important question of why so much of significance is routinely left out of the public discussion of climate.

Perhaps Bjorn Lomberg's ideas can help us with a tentative hypothesis that addresses why many vital facts about climate change have been neglected in the public arena for too long. Lomberg notes that climate scientists, like those who author the IPCC reports, are part of an interlocking network of researchers. They must constantly relate to one another, doing so because their work hinges on major grants. Government agencies are the source for the funds modern climate research requires. Many climate research projects take several years, often spanning multiple universities and institutes. The work could be termed big science, as opposed to the individual research projects costing vastly less that used to be the norm for laboratory and fieldwork projects. Let us be clear: *the researchers in big science are good people, and they are the most serious scientists we have working to learn more about climate change.* There is no question about that. But they are also part of a large, interlocking, and expensive undertaking that must be continually supplied with literally millions of public dollars.

When President Dwight Eisenhower left office he warned us of the "military-industrial complex" that he said was increasingly shaping national policy. In many ways, with respect to several branches of science, including climate research, there is now a similar "complex" that determines who in the scientific community is funded with millions of dollars and what type of research results. No longer does a lone geologist, like Louis Agassiz, deduce climate patterns by looking at glaciers during his summer holiday, a project funded by his own pocket money. To cite another example, no creative astronomer like A. E. Douglass is likely to support himself as a justice of the peace while he invents a field like dendochronology that helps propel research forward. In short, that earlier, individualized approach to science, one that lasted for many researchers well into the 1950s, gave us maximally free investigators, people who were much more at liberty to go where their ideas took them.

Today virtually all researchers in climate science and related areas of geology must start their work by asking themselves how best to secure major grants for teams of investigators doing costly and complex analyses. The successful among them often ask themselves how they can join established research teams, creating careers in which getting along with their fellow researchers may be as important as the specific results of a particular project. Scientists involved in big science testify before Congress, in large measure because what we know about climate research should indeed inform public policy. But it's also true that politicians use certain scientific findings for political ends. And it's even possible that, on occasion, scientists emphasize particular results to encourage Congress and the directors of major federal research agencies to devote more funding to certain types of work. Some would point to the sharply increasing *number* of climate scientists in the United States in the past two decades as a direct indication of how senior members of the field have been successfully commanding the attention of our government. Dollars have been flowing into climate science at rapidly increasing rates and, reasonably enough, young researchers have followed the money. I am not arguing that the new generation of climate scientists wants to mislead us. But I do think it could well be that the politicization of big science and the centralized funding of large research projects are not conducive to an open and honest discussion with the public about climate questions, any more than public discussions of defense funding are encouraged by the military-industrial complex. Big science, by its very nature, imposes some limits on our democracy.

But it's also true—as no reader of this book will forget—that big science has allowed us to understand a great deal about climate change. For it was big science that made possible all the ice-core projects. In other words, it's not an accident that we now know how lucky we've been as a nation to live in what has been a stable Garden of Eden with respect to climate. For myself, if global climate changes tomorrow and we are plunged into the chaos of a "flipped switch," I will be comforted in some way in *knowing* what's happening to us—and that knowledge flows largely from the ice-core research done at the end of the last century as one part of the realm of big science.

A few matters are so clear that they cannot be denied, no matter where you stand on the political spectrum or what you think should be done about climate and energy policy. The fundamental theme about the Earth that runs from the work of Louis Agassiz to the results of the ice-core research is that our world is fragile. It is much more prone to shattering than we like to think, including breaking apart for many fully natural reasons. That fact, I believe, is crucial. It is a fact we need to come to grips with. Here in the United States we have built a complex society, one that provides the basics of life to most of its citizens. We have built an amazing edifice, indeed, but all we have accomplished is built on shifting sands.

Because we know that climate is bound to evolve, it surely is past time to start new conversations not predicated on the delusional framework of somehow holding climate static through the sacrifices that would be imposed by carbon taxes or caps. We can adopt whatever carbon policies we choose, but we also surely had better invest in tools for climate adaptation and mitigation. It's high time we begin to think about how we will cope with sharp changes in weather patterns, those that could be in the direction of either warmer or colder conditions and wetter or drier years. For the important point is and always will remain that *if we think of climate change as our enemy, we will always be defeated.* Change is coming, and it will reshape our world. Our goal cannot be to hold climate static. We must understand its menacing and manic moods—and adapt as nimbly as we can to changes in whatever directions and at whatever rates they arrive.

ACKNOWLEDGMENTS

It's a pleasure to acknowledge the scientists who have helped shape my understanding of Earth's recent climates and the scholars who have guided my path as I learned how geologists originally advanced our understanding of climate. It's also a pleasure to thank those remarkably patient friends and family members who supported me on a personal level as I labored for far too long over the manuscript of this book.

Long ago the late professor Sheldon Judson of Princeton University's Geology Department taught me the basic outline of how radically different were parts of the Pleistocene Epoch from what we experience on Earth today. He explained the geologic evidence for the episodic cold-warm-cold-warm pattern of Earth's recent climates presented in the first chapter of this book. He made it clear to me that we are actually simply in one of the warm times of the misleadingly named Ice Age. After I returned from an East Coast education to my native Pacific Northwest, I started to study the field evidence for Ice Age glacial-outburst flooding near my home. Sheldon became a firm supporter of my work, corresponding to me faithfully about it in detail, even in the days before e-mail. When he visited me one summer, we toured part of the Channeled Scablands, a region scarred by climate effects discussed in chapter 3. I took him to the finest gravel quarry in the whole west, where we stealthily trespassed on a Sunday to see the natural record of the back flooding from Glacial Lake Missoula as well as earlier flooding from Glacial Lake Bonneville. Sheldon doffed his hat at the beauty of what lay before us, clear evidence of the truly violent effects of geologically recent variations in climate.

After Sheldon's death, his widow Pamela Judson-Rhodes helped me in my fieldwork one summer, navigating our journeys on a profusion of topographic maps and helping me collect sediment samples shaped by fluctuations in climate. It's a pleasure to publicly thank Pamela for her direct help that summer and for earlier lending me a considerable part of Sheldon's time during his retirement.

Lincoln and Sarah Hollister, also of Princeton, have supported me as an author for many years now, sending warm words across three thousand miles as I sat through various snowy and bitter Northwest winters at the desk of my basement study. They also read an early draft of this book and sent me valuable comments about it.

Washington State University has given me several colleagues whom it's a pleasure to publicly thank with respect to this book. Kent Keller, a geohydrologist, helped me when I was on WSU's teaching faculty, and he has shared with me some of his ideas and concerns about climate and greenhouse gases in more recent years. Talking with Kent about natural and anthropogenic climate change and related questions of energy policy has always been a pleasure, and I've learned a lot from our discussions. Gary Webster, David Gaylord, and Mike Pope, all of WSU's Geology Department, visited me in the field when I studied the late Pleistocene and Holocene sediments of northeastern Washington State while on sabbatical. That interval was the period of my life I was able to devote simply to exploring natural evidence of stupendous, natural climate change and the side effects entailed by such changes. Later, when I was teaching an interdisciplinary science course with Lisa Carloye, I reviewed my earlier field experiences to use them in freshmen-level lectures. Working with Lisa was itself a pleasure, and it was out of our common efforts to talk to nonscience majors about climate change that the idea for this book was formed. After the writing was well underway, George Mount helped me by critically reading the manuscript of what became chapter 11 of this book; I deeply appreciate both his technical corrections and how quickly he read what I gave him.

A colleague from outside technical life at WSU has also been of great assistance to me. At some point in the 1990s I was fortunate to fall into a series of conversation with Jerry Gough of WSU's History Department. Those talks led me to sit in on the classes Jerry taught for years on the history of science. The history of geology had been an interest of mine since my days as a teaching assistant for Stephen J. Gould at Harvard University.

Jerry quickly took up my education where I had left it in New England, and over many years now he has been an excellent teacher. With respect to this book, Jerry outdid himself, reading and editing both an early draft organized in one framework and a later and quite different draft. I don't think I would have persevered to the end of this project without Jerry's constant and cheerful encouragement.

The librarians at WSU's Owen Science and Engineering Library were essential to the preparation of this volume. The circulation librarians fetched obscure volumes for me via interlibrary loan. They also calmly coped with my ability to misplace the books I check out. Then there are the true heroines of the story, the reference librarians of Owen. Time and time again, they rescued me when I was about to give up hope of learning a bit more about a nineteenth-century geologist or tracking down something that was alleged to be in the *Congressional Record* but failed to appear there. My joy at finding pieces of good material for this book was shared by a revolving set of reference librarians who manned the help desk at Owen, and I appreciate their assistance more than I can say. When I am finally called home by the Lord, I firmly believe it will be to an enormous library, one staffed by dedicated librarians like we have here on Earth.

The last chapter of this book, which discusses in part the worldwide plague of unwanted coal fires around the world, was enriched by my correspondence with geologist Glenn B. Stracher of East Georgia College. Glenn is an authority on such fires, which burn out of control like forest fires but are scarcely reported in the news. My concern about the fires and their effects is surpassed only by my gratitude to those specialists who have done the careful work of showing just how detrimental such fires are to both local environments and the global atmosphere.

Turning to my more personal debts, it's a pleasure to note that several friends conspired to help me with this project. Dean Ritchie read and responded to the outline I first put together to organize my thinking. Karl and Mary Anne Boehmke generously read the entire first draft of the manuscript, as did Sharon Rogers. My loyal friends Mary Elisabeth Rivetti, Julia Pomerenk, and Susan Bentjen put up with my tedious reports about how the project was proceeding over the several years it unfolded. My friends, I suspect, may have suffered even more than I did during some of the difficult chapters, but they remained steadfast to the belief that one day we would all be released from this effort.

My colleagues at Prometheus Books have been helpful, prompt, and always professional. Brian McMahon deserves special mention for patiently copyediting the manuscript, finding many ways to improve the text.

Finally, but perhaps most importantly, Russell Galen in New York took me on as an author and pushed me to improve what I produced. We had to turn several corners together to reach a manuscript we hope might be useful to the reader. I sincerely thank Russ for his time, his criticisms, and above all his implicit encouragement.

Writing anything at all about climate is complex, and it is almost bound to be controversial in some quarters. It's therefore worth explicitly noting that although many colleagues and friends have helped shape my thinking about Earth's climate, I alone am responsible for the shortcomings of this volume.

ABOUT THE AUTHOR

D r. E. Kirsten Peters majored in geology at Princeton University and earned her doctorate in geology from Harvard. She has published technical abstracts and articles in her field of expertise as well as essays about science, religion, and the challenges of teaching college students to write. She has taught geology and interdisciplinary science classes at Washington State University, where she is a faculty member. She is the author of two textbooks in geological science and has been a freelance editor for college-level materials in oceanography, environmental science, and geology. In recent years she has created a nationally syndicated newspaper column called "The Rock Doc" that explains topics in science and technology to a general audience. *The Whole Story of Climate* is her eighth book.

NOTES

1. FACING OUR CLIMATE ADVERSARY SQUARELY

1. The name that comes from the Greek words meaning *most* plus *new* or *recent*. You can think of the Greek as suggesting that "this is most of the period of recent Earth history."

2. The name comes from the Greek words meaning *whole* or *entirely* plus *new* or *recent*. You can think of the Greek as suggesting that "this is the time that's the whole, most recent piece of Earth history."

2. THE ICE TIME

1. Edward Lurie, *Louis Agassiz: A Life in Science* (Chicago: University of Chicago Press, 1960), p. 100.

2. Elizabeth Cary Agassiz, *Louis Agassiz: His Life and Correspondence* (Cambridge, MA: Houghton Mifflin, 1893), pp. 445–46.

3. STAGGERING COMPLEXITIES AND SURPRISING SIDE EFFECTS

1. The forest bed is our American analog of Europe's Eemian time, the next-to-last warm period we met in chapter 1 during our discussion of the football-field analogy of climate history.

2. Stephen J. Pyne, *Grove Karl Gilbert: A Great Engine of Research* (Iowa City: University of Iowa Press, 2007). The title makes the case that Gilbert was first and foremost a researcher.

4. FROM WOOLLY MAMMOTHS TO SABER-TOOTHED TIGERS

1. Those who heartily scoff at such a view are welcome to come to some parts of the author's native Pacific Northwest today, buy a few beers for the locals in a bar, and then discuss their doubts about the existence of Bigfoot.

2. Donald K. Grayson, "Nineteenth-Century Explanations of Pleistocene Extinctions: A Review and Analysis," in *Quaternary Extinctions: A Prehistoric Revolution*, ed. Paul S. Martin and Richard Klein (Tucson: University of Arizona Press, 1984), p. 6.

3. Meriwether Lewis and William Clark led the Corps of Discovery expedition of 1804–1806, the first expedition sponsored by the US government to reach the Pacific Ocean. Lewis and Clark took notes on the flora and fauna they encountered and described the landscape of the parts of the West they traversed.

4. In the period in question, the French had the habit of measuring the brains of great men after they had died, with the idea that a massive brain contributed to tremendous intellectual power. Cuvier had one of the largest brains ever recorded in this long-term measurement effort that spanned decades, seeming to confirm the (false) view that size really does matter in the realm of the intellect.

5. William Coleman, *Georges Cuvier, Zoologist: A Study in the History of Evolution Theory* (Cambridge, MA: Harvard University Press, 1964), pp. 109–10.

6. Ibid., pp. 13–14.

7. Cuvier's work looks impressive from a modern perspective, from which we note dramatic changes from the Pleistocene to the Holocene about ten thousand years ago, with isolated bands of woolly mammoths on remote islands lasting to just about the very time Cuvier estimated!

8. Stephen J. Pyne, *Grove Karl Gilbert: A Great Engine of Research* (Iowa City: University of Iowa Press, 2007), p. 18.

5. MIRACULOUS MUD

1. John D. Cox, *Climate Crash: Abrupt Climate Change and What It Means for Our Future* (Washington, DC: Joseph Henry Press, 2005), p. 164.

6. WOOD REVEALS CLIMATE CLUES

1. Barometers measure atmospheric pressure. As you may know, barometric measurements are part of the meat and potatoes of short-term weather forecasting, since barometric

pressure falls as storm systems move into a region. But it's also true that during periods of stable barometric pressure, such as a series of sunny days, you can walk around with a sensitive barometer and have a good indication of your elevation; as you climb higher, barometric pressure drops. The author (and many other field scientists) used to use exactly this method of determining elevation, sometimes with an accuracy within ten feet, before the era of GPS devices.

2. George Ernest Webb, *Tree Rings and Telescopes: The Scientific Career of A. E. Douglass* (Tucson: University of Arizona Press), p. 48.

3. Ibid., p. 49.

4. A word to assuage the fears of the reader might be useful at this point. Modern researchers do not cut down living sequoia to study their rings. Instead, scientists sample the wood in a tree trunk with a small drill that has a long, hollow bit. The drill bit is made of tough steel, and it can be turned by hand. Easy to use, the hand drill digs into all softwoods easily enough that the author of this book—no Amazon, she—has performed the operation. It allows a core to be extracted from the living wood of a tree trunk without any significant damage to the tree.

5. Kendrick Frazier, *People of Chaco: Its Canyon and Its Culture* (New York: W. W. Norton, 1999), p. 75.

6. Ibid., p. 76.

7. A. E. Douglass, *Climatic Cycles and Tree-Growth* (Washington DC: Carnegie Institution of Washington, 1928), 2:133.

8. EVEN MORE FREQUENT BOOM-BUST CYCLES

1 Brian Fagan, *The Great Warming: Climate Change and the Rise and Fall of Civilizations* (New York: Bloomsbury Press, 2006), p. 12.

2. Ibid. Sometimes, it seems, Europe was awash in good wine in those days. During the 1100s and 1200s, the English actually exported wine from England to France. Wine was even produced in southern Norway. In Germany, Fagan tells us, vineyards grew at up to 2,560 feet in elevation, compared to a maximum elevation of only about 1,800 feet today. In short, the record of wine making speaks in a number of ways to the fact that Europe in the Middle Ages was warm, indeed.

3. Brian Fagan, *The Little Ice Age: How Climate Made History, 1300–1850* (New York: Basic Books, 2002), p. 29.

4. Jared Diamond, *Collapse: How Societies Choose to Fail or Succeed* (New York: Penguin, 2005), p. 250.

9. HAVE HUMANS SHAPED CLIMATE FOR MILLENNIA?

1. William F. Ruddiman, *Plows, Plagues, and Petroleum: How Humans Took Control of Climate* (Princeton, NJ: Princeton University Press, 2005), p. 12.

2. Ibid., p. 76.

3. It's interesting to note in passing that much of the methane today that's wafting into the air around us relates to intensive rice farming throughout Asia—and also rice farming in places like Louisiana and California.

4. Today, more than a third of the Earth's land surface is devoted to agriculture. The fraction would be higher except that enormous areas, like Canada's Northwest Territories, are simply unsuitable for farming due to their frigid climate, the Gobi and Sahara Deserts are too dry, and so forth. And despite modern population growth, the combined land areas devoted to cities, by comparison to farming regions, are trivial.

10. FROM EFFORTS TO MODIFY CLIMATE TO FEARS OF GLOBAL COOLING

1. United States Committee for the Global Atmospheric Research Program, National Research Council, *Understanding Climatic Change: A Program for Action* (Washington, DC: National Academy of Sciences, 1975).

2. Lowell Ponte, *The Cooling: Has the Next Ice Age Already Begun? Can We Survive It?* (Englewood Cliffs, NJ: Prentice Hall, 1976), p. 108.

3. Roger G. Barry, John T. Andrews, and Mary A. Mahaffy, "Continental Ice Sheets: Conditions for Growth," *Science* 190, no. 4128 (1975): 979–81.

4. George J. Kukla and Helena J. Kukla, "Increased Surface Albedo in the Northern Hemisphere," *Science* 183, no. 4126 (1974): 709–14.

11. GLOBAL WARMING DISCOVERED

1. Sadly, the news media seem forever stuck in the "warmer versus cooler" mode, as if that framework of thinking is the only one important to the issues under discussion in climate science today.

2. Richard A. Muller, *Physics for Future Presidents: The Science behind the Headlines* (New York: Norton, 2008), pp. 296–99.

3. J. T. Houghton et al., *Climate Change 2001: The Scientific Basis* (New York: Cambridge University Press, 2001), online at http://www.acrim.com/%5C/Reference%20 Files/CLIMATECHANGE%202001%20-%20The%20Scientific%20Basis.pdf (accessed August 31, 2012), p. 2.

4. Ibid.

5. Ibid., p. ix.

6. Edward Wegman, David Scott, and Yasmin Said, "Ad Hoc Committee Report on the 'Hockey Stick' Global Climate Reconstruction," July 14, 2006, http://heartland.org/ sites/default/files/wegmanreport.pdf (accessed September 1, 2012), p. 51.

7. Ibid.

8. Richard A. Muller, "The Conversion of a Climate-Change Skeptic," *New York Times*, July 28, 2012, http://www.nytimes.com/2012/07/30/opinion/the-conversion-of-a-climate-change-skeptic.html?pagewanted=all (accessed September 5, 2012).

12. LEAVING THE GARDEN

1. Ann G. Kim, "Greenhouse Gases Generated in Underground Coal-Mine Fires," in *Reviews in Engineering Geology* 18 (2007): 1.

2. G. B. Stracher and T. P. Taylor, "Coal Fires Burning out of Control around the World: Thermodynamic Recipe for Environmental Catastrophe," *International Journal of Coal Geology* 59 (2004): 10; "China's on Fire," *Discover Magazine*, October 1, 1999, http://discovermagazine.com/1999/oct/chinasonfire1697 (accessed September 1, 2012).

REFERENCES

1. FACING OUR CLIMATE ADVERSARY SQUARELY

Cox, John D. *Climate Crash: Abrupt Climate Change and What It Means for Our Future.* Washington, DC: Joseph Henry Press, 2005. This excellent and recent overview tells the tale of climate in a readable way. The story of the disastrous precipitation change in Egypt during the Bronze Age, for example, is told in this book.

Dawson, Alastair G. *Ice Age Earth: Late Quaternary Geology and Climate.* London: Routledge, 1992. This textbook covers the geology of the Pleistocene and Holocene Epochs. It's less than half the heft of the Richard Foster Flint volume mentioned below, and it's more recent.

Flint, Richard Foster. *Glacial and Quaternary Geology.* New York: John Wiley and Sons, 1971. One of the "bibles" of glacial geology textbooks, this volume was published by an expert we will meet in a later chapter. It is close to nine hundred pages long, and even geologists don't generally sit down and read it cover to cover. However, one can learn a lot from dipping into relevant subjects via the index.

Guyton, Bill. *Glaciers of California.* Berkeley: California Natural History Guides, 1998. This book covers glaciation in such majestic places as California's Yosemite National Park. It's a small yet well-illustrated book. Even if California is not of particular interest, the book is an example of the sort of natural field guides that discuss many glaciated parts of the country, though seldom are books of this type so well executed as what Guyton has done here.

Gwin, Peter. "Lost Tribes of the Green Sahara," *National Geographic Magazine*, September 2008. http://ngm.nationalgeographic.com/2008/09/green-sahara/gwin-text.html (accessed August 16, 2012). This article shows how the Sahara's climate has changed over the past few thousand years, going from a verdant and wet region full of people to the arid desert we know today.

Mithen, Steven. *After the Ice: A Global Human History*. Cambridge, MA: Harvard University Press, 2003. This archeologically based book tells the tale of humanity from twenty thousand years ago to five thousand years ago.

Pielou, E. C. *After the Ice Age: The Return of Life to Glaciated North America*. Chicago: University of Chicago Press, 1992. The Canadian author recounts how the northern half of North America was gradually transformed from a landscape dominated by thick ice to what we know today.

Roberts, Neil. *The Holocene: An Environmental History*. 2nd ed. Oxford: Blackwell Publishers, 1998. This is a textbook that takes a student of the subject through the late Pleistocene Epoch and the Holocene Epoch with special reference to human history.

Schultz, Gwen. *Glaciers and the Ice Age: Earth and Its Inhabitants during the Pleistocene*. New York: Holt, Rinehart, and Winston, 1963. This is a small but dense book that was in public libraries across the land for a generation or more. It helped shaped the lay public's basic understanding of the Ice Age. Although some details are out of date, the gist of the book is useful and the storytelling good.

2. THE ICE TIME

Bailey, Edward. *Charles Lyell*. Garden City, NY: Doubleday, 1963. Lyell's thoughts on glaciation overlapped to some degree with Agassiz's.

Bolles, Edmund Blair. *The Ice Finders*. Washington, DC: Counterpoint, 1999. This book discusses Agassiz, Lyell, and arctic explorer Elisha Kent Kane, weaving together the tales of the three men who helped establish the Ice Age as a worthy hypothesis in science and a fixture in the public mind.

Fenton, Carroll Lane, and Mildred Adams Fenton. *Giants of Geology*. Garden City, NY: Doubleday, 1952. This is not a deep book, but chapter 10 is about Agassiz, and it's easily read.

Hallam, A. *Great Geological Controversies*. 2nd ed. New York: Oxford University Press, 1989. As the title implies, the book covers many geological arguments, and the glacial theory of the Ice Age is one.

Holder, Charles Frederick. *Louis Agassiz: His Life and Work*. New York: G. P. Putnam's Sons, 1893. Although more than a century old, this book is perfectly readable and gives a good overview of Agassiz's work.

Imbrie, John, and Katherine Palmer Imbrie. *Ice Ages: Solving the Mystery.* Cambridge, MA: Harvard University Press, 1979. Covering not just Agassiz and his interests but also the Reverend William Buckland and others not discussed in this chapter, this book makes for fascinating reading.

Lurie, Edward. *Louis Agassiz: A Life in Science.* Abr. ed. Chicago: University of Chicago Press, 1960. This book is a readable account of Agassiz's life and work.

Lyell, Charles. *Principles of Geology.* New York: Penguin, 1997. Lyell's books were originally published between 1830 and 1833, but Penguin Books brought out this volume rather recently. Lyell—known as the father of geology— speaks in this volume for the Earth itself. Several chapters of the book directly address his thoughts on past climates.

3. STAGGERING COMPLEXITIES AND SURPRISING SIDE EFFECTS

Allen, John Eliot, and Marjorie Burns. *Cataclysms on the Columbia.* With Sam C. Sargent. Portland, OR: Timber Press, 1986. This is a readable and well-illustrated account of the Bretz story.

Alt, David. *Glacial Lake Missoula and Its Humongous Floods.* Missoula, MT: Mountain Press Publishing, 2001. This is a relatively recent popular account of the catastrophic floods unleashed by Glacial Lake Missoula.

Drake, Ellen, and William M. Jordan, eds. *Geologists and Ideas: A History of North American Geology.* Boulder, CO: Geological Society of America, 1985. This heavy—one could even say massive—tome contains some material covered in this chapter, although it's likely a volume you'll want to get from a library rather than buy.

Fenton, Carroll Lane, and Mildred Adams Fenton. *Giants of Geology.* Garden City, NY: Doubleday, 1952. This book was mentioned in the references for chapter 2. It's included in this section because it has material on Chamberlin and Gilbert.

Krajick, Kevin. *Barren Lands: An Epic Search for Diamonds in the North American Arctic.* New York: W. H. Freeman, 2001. This thoroughly readable book explains the manic intensity and dedication a handful of independent geologists displayed while finding the source of diamonds in the Canadian arctic that had spilled south on ice during the Pleistocene Epoch.

Peters, E. Kirsten. *No Stone Unturned: Reasoning about Rocks and Fossils*. New York: W. H. Freeman, 1997. This book (by the same author as the present volume) has a chapter on the great flood discovered by Bretz. It more fully explains why Bretz's hypothesis was resisted so strongly by so many for so long. It also briefly discusses the flooding from Glacial Lake Bonneville.

Pyne, Stephen J. *Grove Karl Gilbert: A Great Engine of Research*. Iowa City: University of Iowa Press, 1980. This is the best modern source I know on Gilbert.

4. FROM WOOLLY MAMMOTHS TO SABER-TOOTHED TIGERS

Coleman, William. *Georges Cuvier, Zoologist: A Study in the History of Evolution Theory*. Cambridge, MA: Harvard University Press, 1964. This book's main emphasis is on Cuvier's contribution to evolutionary theory, but it has a chapter devoted to his work on fossils and the rocks around the Paris basin.

Martin, Paul S., and Richard G. Klein, eds. *Quaternary Extinctions: A Prehistoric Revolution*. Tucson: University of Arizona Press, 1984. This book is serious going for the outside reader, but it offers a summary of much good information on extinctions in the Pleistocene and Holocene Epochs.

Rudwick, Martin J. S. *Georges Cuvier, Fossil Bones, and Geologic Catastrophes*. Chicago: University of Chicago Press, 1997. This is a blend of commentary by the author, which should be readable and informative, and the work of Cuvier in translation.

―――. *The Meaning of Fossils: Episodes in the History of Palaeontology*. 2nd ed. Chicago: University of Chicago Press, 1976. This excellent book is not light reading, but it should be manageable, and it gives a full picture of the subject of how paleontologists worked to learn not just the history of life, but also how their own research must be constructed.

5. MIRACULOUS MUD

De Geer, Gerald. *Geochronologia Suecica Principles*. 2 vols. Uppsala, Sweden: Almqvist and Wiksells Boktryckeri A. B., 1940. This is De Geer's massive explanation of his lifelong work on varves. It can be borrowed on interlibrary loan through a university library. The work runs to two volumes. The first contains De Geer's prose and beautiful photos of varves and other Ice Age geological features. The second contains highly detailed maps, also beautiful (at least to geologists).

Flint, Richard Foster. *Glacial and Quaternary Geology*. New York: John Wiley and Sons, 1971. This "Bible" of Pleistocene studies explains the work of both De Geer and Von Post. More importantly, the science explained rests on the work of De Geer, Von Post, and those who worked alongside them near the start of the twentieth century.

Gillispie, Charles Coulston, ed. *Dictionary of Scientific Biography*. 16 vols. New York: Charles Scribner's Sons, 1970–1980. This multivolume work can be found in university libraries. It contains entries for influential scientists in all fields. It looks imposing but is easy to use. For De Geer you simply look alphabetically for his last name, which you'll find in volume 5.

Manten, A. A. "Lennart Von Post and the Foundation of Modern Palynology." *Review of Palaeobotany and Palynology* 1 (1967): 11–22. This technical article contains a brief sketch of Von Post's life and a longer description of his work.

Williams, Trevor I., ed. *A Biographical Dictionary of Scientists*. New York: John Wiley and Sons, 1982. This is a single-volume compilation of brief entries about major scientists in all fields. You can find an entry about De Geer starting on page 210. Where a conflict between this volume and the *Dictionary of Scientific Biography* arises, I defer to the authority of the second work.

6. WOOD REVEALS CLIMATE CLUES

Briffa, K. R., et al. "A 1,400-Year Tree-Ring Record of Summer Temperatures in Fennoscandia." *Nature* 346 (1990): 434–39. This paper is just one example showing that dendochronology was a mature science with considerable depth by the late-twentieth century. As scientists around the world did more work, the picture of past climate became richer and more complex. In this publication, the authors argue that the density of tree-ring wood they studied correlates with average temperatures in the region from April to August. July is particularly important, meaning that a cool spring but a warm July could result in a tree ring similar to tree rings that would result from a warm spring but a cooler July. Interestingly, the authors find little trace of the Medieval Warm Period in their samples of wood from Fennoscandia, and the Little Ice Age period appears to be brief. But like all other dendochronological studies, the results show substantially different weather over time, including broad trends interrupted by sharp reversals. The implications for peoples of the past, who were trying to cope with what is a rather severe climate in the Scandinavian region, are clear.

Frazier, Kendrick. *People of Chaco: A Canyon and Its Culture*. New York: W. W. Norton, 1999. All armchair archeologists will enjoy this wide-ranging and helpful book about the culture that created Pueblo Bonito. The volume includes more details from the story of how A. E. Douglass and his colleagues were able to bridge gaps in tree-ring records using archeological samples, ultimately eliminating floating chronologies and replacing them with those linked to specific dates. Finally, the book explains what's known about local rainfall variations and the collapse of the civilization centered around Pueblo Bonito and Chaco Canyon. It explains that the natives of the area did not actually "disappear," but rather went through cultural evolutions to become the Pueblo Indians of the region today.

Roig, F. A., et al. "Climate Variability 50,000 Years Ago in Mid-Latitude Chile as Reconstructed from Tree Rings." *Nature* 410 (2010): 567–70. This study, discussed in the chapter, involved the type of work that uses radiocarbon dating to tie floating dendochronology records to an approximate but specific date. The work is significant because it gives us a year-by-year record from a natural sample that grew in the Ice Age or Pleistocene Epoch.

Stahle, D. W., M. K. Cleaveland, and J. G. Hehr. "North Carolina Climate Changes Reconstructed from Tree Rings: A.D. 372 to 1985." *Science* 240 (1988): 1517–19. Hardwoods in the eastern United States proved mostly unsuitable for dendochronologic research because their growth rings are largely uniform. But bald cypress trees in the lowlands of the Southeast have proven to be sensitive indicators of climate, and the region boasts millennium-old living trees along the Black River of North Carolina. Using wood from the bald cypress, this study pieced together a history spanning 1,614 years. Generally speaking, the researchers found evidence of wet-versus-dry climate regimes that persist for about thirty years. The Medieval Warm Period was a time during which the alternating precipitation pattern is particularly clear in the cypress record. Throughout the long cypress history of growth rings, the variability of weather is most impressive.

Stokes, Marvin A., and Terah L. Smiley. *An Introduction to Tree Ring Dating.* Tucson: University of Arizona Press, 1996. This slender volume is not necessarily intended for a general audience, but it's written so clearly and illustrated so usefully that a serious reader is sure to get a great deal from it. If you ever want to try your hand at cross-dating trees on a piece of property you may own, this is the guide to get you started.

Webb, George Ernest. *Tree Rings and Telescopes: The Scientific Career of A. E. Douglass.* Tucson: University of Arizona Press, 1983. This biography of Andrew Ellicott Douglass, the founder of dendochronology, is direct and readable. We owe Douglass a lot in the realm of both archeology and climatology, and his professional life story makes fine reading.

Zhang, Qi-Bin, et al. "A 2,326-Year Tree-Ring Record of Climate Variability on the Northeastern Qinghai-Tibetan Plateau." *Geophysical Research Letters* 30, no. 14 (2003): 1739. Discussed in the chapter, this is an example of the work that Chinese scientists have recently begun in order to assemble tree-ring data from central Asia. Evidence was gathered from both living trees and those used in ancient tombs. As the authors put it, "Our results show that climate on the [Tibetan] plateau has undergone oscillations and, sometimes, very rapid swings during the last two millennia." The picture of unstable climate in central Asia, like that of the American Southwest, is far from comforting.

7. THE EVIDENCE OF THE ICE

Alley, Richard B. "Ice-Core Evidence of Abrupt Climate Changes." *Proceedings of the National Academy of the Sciences of the United States* 97 (2000): 1331–94.

———. *The Two-Mile Time Machine.* Princeton, NJ: Princeton University Press, 2000. Alley is a dean of climate science and worked on one of the drilling projects in Greenland. This book is written at a higher level than *The Ice Chronicles*, but it should still be readable for many.

Cox, John D. *Climate Crash: Abrupt Climate Change and What It Means for Our Future.* Washington, DC: Joseph Henry Press, 2005. This is a punchy overview of how rapid climate change has dealt blows to humans over the millennia. It's a direct and approachable book.

Imbrie, John, and Katherine Palmer Imbrie. *Ice Ages.* Cambridge, MA: Harvard University Press, 1979. This book is a bit out of date when it comes to details, but the basic picture it paints about Earth's recent bitter times is still highly worth reading.

Mayewski, Paul A., and Frank White. *The Ice Chronicles*. Lebanon, NH: University Press of New England, 2002. Mayewski is a climate scientist who worked on ice-core projects, one of the most fruitful lines of research modern science has come up with for understanding past climate change.

Petit, J. R., et al. "Climate and Atmospheric History of the Past 420,000 Years from the Vostok Ice Core, Antarctica." *Nature* 399 (1999): 429–435. This article summarizes the hard-core science that came out of ice-core studies from both Greenland and Antarctica.

Sorge, Ernst. "The Scientific Results of the Wegener Expedition to Greenland." *Geographical Journal* 81 (1933), http://www.jstor.org/stable/1785439 (accessed August 17, 2012). This paper, read on December 12, 1932, to the Royal Geographical Society, is Sorge's own account of the major results he discovered while trapped in the snow cave during the life-threatening winter he endured in Greenland.

Steffensen, Jorgen Peder, et al. "High-Resolution Greenland Ice Core Data Show Abrupt Climate Change Happens in Few Years." *Science* 321 (2008): 680–83. This is just another example of the many scores of such technical articles that have been published in recent years about the ice-core data from both of the Earth's poles as well as intermediate areas, such as parts of the Himalayas, that contain major glaciers.

Weart, Spencer R. *The Discovery of Global Warming*. Cambridge, MA: Harvard University Press, 2003. This is a good history of climate science, especially in the latter half of the twentieth century. It is not easy reading, but it's worthwhile.

8. EVEN MORE FREQUENT BOOM–BUST CYCLES

Diamond, Jared. *Collapse: How Societies Choose to Fail or Succeed*. New York: Penguin, 2005. Diamond is good at discussing how societal choices can help trigger collapse. In short, weather need not be the only factor in the collapse of societies. Chapters 6 through 8 of this book discuss the Norse expansion and collapse in Iceland and Greenland.

Fagan, Brian. *The Great Warming: Climate Change and the Rise and Fall of*

Civilizations. New York: Bloomsbury Press, 2006. Historian Brian Fagan explains the blessings of the warm times of the Middle Ages, and what they meant for European civilization, as well as the more complex histories the interval ushered in for other parts of the globe.

————. *The Little Ice Age: How Climate Made History, 1300–1850*. New York: Basic Books, 2000. In this volume historian Fagan tells of the impact—and suffering—the Little Ice Age brought to Europe.

Hoyt, Douglas V., and Kenneth H. Schatten. *The Role of the Sun in Climate Change*. New York: Oxford University Press, 1997. Most people should find this paperback approachable, although it does have its technical moments. It's good at making the case that the sun is variable, and that its variations contribute to climate cycles on Earth.

Singer, S. Fred, and Dennis T. Avery. *Unstoppable Global Warming: Every 1,500 Years*. Lanham, MD: Rowman & Littlefield, 2007. This book is focused on making the case that current global warming is largely the effect not of human-made greenhouse gases but of the recurring Dansgaard-Oeschger cycle, which Singer and Avery call the fifteen-hundred-year cycle. Although Singer had a long, respected career in climate science, this book is well outside the norm today because climate scientists emphasize our own contribution to greenhouse gases as the cause for current warming. Still, Singer's is a perspective worth at least our consideration, since natural cycles are undoubtedly continuing on Earth today just as they have in the past. To put it another way, there's no reason to think that human-made climate change requires that natural climate change would stop, and Singer is good at emphasizing the significance of natural Dansgaard-Oeschger cycles.

9. HAVE HUMANS SHAPED CLIMATE FOR MILLENNIA?

Roberts, Neil. *The Holocene: An Environmental History*. Oxford: Blackwell, 1998. This is one of several recent textbooks on human and environmental history of the Holocene Epoch. This volume takes the reader through material that most directly relates to this chapter in the form of information on early farming and the spread of agriculture.

Ruddiman, William F. "GSA Position Statement on Climate Change." *GSA Today* 20 (2010): 40–43. Although Ruddiman believes we may well have influenced climate for millennia, he doesn't dismiss recent concerns about industrialization and the production of greenhouse gases. He is one of many who participated recently in forming the Geological Society of America's position statement on these these matters.

————. "How Did Humans First Alter Global Climate?" *Scientific American*, March 2005, pp. 46–53. This piece gives another view of the basic ideas presented in this chapter.

————. *Plows, Plagues, and Petroleum: How Humans Took Control of Climate.* Princeton, NJ: Princeton University Press, 2005. This book is Professor Ruddiman's effort to make his argument available to the nonspecialist. It's fascinating reading.

10. FROM EFFORTS TO MODIFY CLIMATE TO FEARS OF GLOBAL COOLING

Barry, Roger G., John T. Andrews, and Mary A. Mahaffy. "Continental Ice Sheets: Conditions for Growth." *Science* 190, no. 4128 (1975): 979–81. This is an example of a research publication looking at the conditions necessary for creating the next ice age—and finding we have been close to seeing a new glaciation. Specifically, this is the paper that found that the weather conditions in the Little Ice Age were similar to what is needed to produce a major ice sheet in northeastern Canada.

Kukla, George J., and Helena J. Kukla. "Increased Surface Albedo in the Northern Hemisphere." *Science* 183, no. 4126 (1974): 709–14. This is an example of a technical article reflecting concern that a new ice age might be on its way. The paper summarized findings that there had been more snow on the ground and a greater extent of pack ice in the preceding three years. Such changes affect the Earth's heat balance, as snow and ice act to reflect more energy from the sun back into space. If such changes were to continue, the authors argued, significant climate change could result.

Ponte, Lowell. *The Cooling: Has the Next Ice Age Already Begun? Can We Survive It?* Englewood Cliffs, NJ: Prentice Hall, 1976. This is a popular-level book written in a journalistic style. It's long out of print but is available through libraries or secondhand book purchases over the Internet.

United States Committee for the Global Atmospheric Research Program, National

Research Council. *Understanding Climatic Change: A Program for Action.* Washington, DC: National Academy of Sciences, 1975. This is not easy reading, but it summarizes the thinking of some of the best scientists of the time.

11. GLOBAL WARMING DISCOVERED

Caillon, Nicolas, et al., "Timing of Atmospheric CO_2 and Antarctic Temperature Changes Across Termination III." *Science* 299 (March 14, 2003): 1728–31. This technical piece shows that in at least one case in the past, temperature as recorded by an ice core changed well *before* carbon dioxide changed. It implies that temperature controls carbon-dioxide levels, not the reverse, as public spokesmen for global warming concerns often suppose.

Houghton, J. T., et al. *Climate Change 2001: The Scientific Basis.* New York: Cambridge University Press, 2001. This heavy volume is the IPCC report of 2001, the third assessment report, also known as the "TAR." The first few pages are a summary for policymakers. The "hockey stick" graph discussed in this chapter can be found in this summary.

Mayewski, Paul Andrew, and Frank White. *The Ice Chronicles.* Hanover, NH: University Press of New England, 2002. This book has been mentioned before, but it's a gem worth picking up if you are interested in more nuts-and-bolts information about what it was really like to be an ice-core researcher during the time the research in that area was exploding in significance.

McIntyre, Stephen, and Ross McKitrick. "Hockey Sticks, Principal Components, and Spurious Significance." *Geophysical Research Letters* 32 (2005): L03710–L03715. This is the technical piece in which McIntyre and McKitrick lay out their argument that the statistical methods behind the "hockey stick" graph are erroneous.

Muller, Richard A. *Physics for Future Presidents.* New York: W. W. Norton, 2008. Professor Muller is a member of the Physics Department of the University of California at Berkeley. The book, which is highly readable and entertaining, is based on his course for nonscience students. As discussed in this chapter, Muller takes the reader through the argument that Al Gore's presentation of the ice-core data regarding temperature and greenhouse gas concentrations does *not* show what the former vice president would have the audience believe.

Solomon, Lawrence. *The Deniers*. Minneapolis, MN: Richard Vigilante Books, 2008. The author is a columnist for the *National Post* (Toronto) and a self-described environmentalist who is the author of several books. This volume discusses scientists who, quietly and sometimes quite unwillingly, have brought to light some aspect of information that challenges the public orthodoxy about global warming. The book has a chapter devoted to the "hockey stick" controversy and the ensuing report to the US Congress.

Spencer R. Weart. *The Discovery of Global Warming*. Cambridge, MA: Harvard University Press, 2003. Weart is an authority on the history of the recent progress in climate science research and, in particular, how we learned in detail of global warming ideas.

Wegman, Edward, David Scott, and Yasmin Said. "Ad Hoc Committee Report on the 'Hockey Stick' Global Climate Reconstruction." July 14, 2006, http://republicans.energycommerce.house.gov/108/home/07142006_Wegman_Report.pdf (accessed August 18, 2012). This document was given to the House Committee on Energy and Commerce by the ad hoc Wegman committee.

12. LEAVING THE GARDEN

Kim, Ann G. "Greenhouse Gases Generated in Underground Coal-Mine Fires." *Reviews in Engineering Geology* 18 (2007): 1–13. This is a roundup at a technical level of unwanted coal fires the world around and what they mean for greenhouse gas production.

Krajick, Kevin. "Fire in the Hole." *Smithsonian Magazine*, 2005, http://www.smithsonianmag.com/travel/firehole/html (accessed August 18, 2012). This highly readable article by a skilled science writer is a place to start reading more about unwanted coal fires and what they mean, especially to the people who live near them.

Lomborg, Bjorn. *Cool It: The Skeptical Environmentalist's Guide to Global Warming*. New York: Alfred A. Knopf, 2007. This small book takes on a big topic, namely what the author sees as misguided hype about global warming. If you want an alternative view to what you commonly hear on the news or in the media, this book is for you.

Reilly, Michael. "Pollution from Underground Coal Fires Tallied." *Discovery News*, 2009, http://www.news.discovery.com/earth/coal-fire-pollution-global

.html (accessed August 18, 2012). We need more of this is the type of general-audience news piece about coal fires. Coal fires are truly a major problem about which the public is largely unaware.

Stracher, Glenn B. "Coal Fires Burning around the World: Opportunity for Innovative and Interdisciplinary Research." *GSA Today* 17 (2007): 36–37. Published in the magazine of the Geological Society of America, this short, fact-filled piece gives a clear overview of the magnitude and nature of the problem of coal fires burning around the world. The author is one of the world's leading authorities on unwanted coal blazes.

———, ed. *Geology of Coal Fires: Case Studies from around the World*. Boulder, CO: Geological Society of America, 2007. This volume is the bible of offerings on the subject of unintended coal fires. It's a compilation of technical articles covering a wide range of research and issues related to the problem of global coal fires.

Stracher, Glenn B., and Tammy P. Taylor. "Coal Fires Burning out of Control around the World: Thermodynamic Recipe for Environmental Catastrophe." *International Journal of Coal Geology* 59 (2004): 7–17. This article is a roundup of coal-fire issues that includes facts and figures. While it's not intended for a general audience, much of it should be completely readable to the interested lay reader.

INDEX